295   133

33015 000185560

KT-556-133

Coaching Children in Sport

Easton College

18 DEC 2007

Learning Resource Centre

Other titles from E & FN Spon

Children and Exercise XIX
Edited by N. Armstrong, B. Kirby and J. Welsman
Hb 0–419–22100–X 584pp.

Risk and Safety in Play
D. Potter
Pb 0–419–22370–3 264pp.

Drugs in Sport
Second edition
D. R. Mottram
Pb 0–419–18890–8 304pp.

Foods, Nutrition and Sports Performance
An International Scientific Consensus organized by Mars
C. Williams and J. T. Devlin
Pb 0–419–17890–2 194pp.

Introduction to Sports Biomechanics
Roger Bartlett
Pb 0–419–20840–2 304pp.

Kinanthropometry and Exercise Physiology Laboratory Manual
R. G. Eston and T. Reilly
Hb 0–419–17880–5 360pp.

Notational Analysis of Sport
M. Hughes and I. Franks
Pb 0–419–18010–9 232pp.

Sports Biomechanics
R. Bartlett
Pb 0–419–18440–6 304pp.

Visual Perception and Action in Sport
M. William, K. Davids and J. Williams
Pb 0–419–18290–X 304pp.

Journals

Journal of Sports Sciences

Leisure Studies

Managing Leisure

For more information about these and other titles, please contact: The Marketing Department, E & FN Spon, 11 New Fetter Lane, London EC4P 4EE; tel. 0171-583 9855; fax 0171-842 2303; or visit our website at www.efnspon.com

Coaching Children in Sport

Principles and practice

Edited by

Martin Lee
Institute for the Study of Children in Sport
Bedford College of Higher Education

London and New York

First published 1993 by Taylor & Francis
Reprinted 1995, 1996, 1997, 1999

Reprinted 2002 by Routledge
2 Park Square, Milton Park, Abingdon, Oxon, OX14 4RN
270 Madison Ave, New York NY 10016

Transferred to Digital Printing 2006

Routledge is an imprint of the Taylor & Francis Group

© 1993 Taylor & Francis

Typeset in 10/12pt Palatino by Best-set Typesetter Ltd, Hong Kong

All rights reserved. No part of this book may be reprinted or
reproduced or utilized in any form or by any electronic, mechanical,
or other means, now known or hereafter invented, including
photocopying and recording, or in any information storage or
retrieval system, without permission in writing from the publishers.

The publisher makes no representation, express or implied, with
regard to the accuracy of the information contained in this book and
cannot accept any legal responsibility or liability for any errors or
omissions that may be made.

British Library Cataloguing in Publication Data
A catalogue record for this book is available from the British Library

Library of Congress Cataloguing in Publication Data
A catalogue record for this book is available from the Library of Congress

ISBN 0–419–18250–0

Publisher's Note
The publisher has gone to great lengths to ensure the quality of this reprint
but points out that some imperfections in the original may be apparent

Printed and bound by CPI Antony Rowe, Eastbourne

Contents

Contributors

Martin Lee, Institute for the Study of Children in Sport, Bedford College of Higher Education, Bedford

Glyn Roberts and **Darren Treasure**, Department of Kinesiology, University of Illinois, Champaign-Urbana

Sarah Gilroy, West Sussex Institute of Higher Education, Chichester

Tony Byrne, National Coaching Foundation, Leeds

John Aldridge, Orthopaedic Adviser, British Amateur Gymnastic Association

Neil Armstrong and **Joanne Welsman**, Physical Education Association Research Centre, University of Exeter

Rosemary Connell, Trinity and All Saints College, Leeds

Jean Whitehead, Bedford College of Higher Education, Bedford

Stuart Biddle, University of Exeter

Stephen Rowley, Sporting Bodymind, London

Rod Thorpe, Department of Physical Education, Sports Science and Recreation Management, Loughborough University.

Lew Hardy, Sport, Health and PE Department, University College of North Wales, Bangor

Dennis Wright, Physiotherapist, Wigan Rugby League Club

Juliet Wiseman, Massey University, New Zealand

Ross Smith, Australian Institute for Sport, Canberra

Valerie Collins, Nottingham Trent University

Harry Towers, Managing Director, Perkins Slade Ltd, Birmingham

Preface

During the last 25 years or so there has been an enormous increase in the provision of sport for children. It appears to be part of the more affluent society in which we live, the growth in television and televised sport, and a decline in the informal active play of children in the fields and streets. More formal sport for children has resulted in a growth in structured competitions with leagues, cups, medals, and selection for representative honours at district, county, regional, and international levels for even quite young children. Indeed, the age of full international athletes continues to fall and it has been estimated that about 30% of athletes participating in the Los Angeles Olympic Games were under the age of 20. Now, as I write, a 13 year old Chinese diver has just won a gold medal at the Barcelona Olympics and a 14 year old has won a gold medal for swimming. However, these are, by definition, exceptional cases. Most coaches work with children who aspire to nothing more than doing sport at club and perhaps county level; this is the vast majority of children.

Increasingly formalized sports structures which culminate in international competition have led to a greater commitment by adults in the care and preparation of young athletes. It is thought that there are now over 100 000 coaches contributing to the development of children in sport in Britain. They bear a great responsibility because they are dealing with young people at a time in their lives when they are very easily influenced and are subject both to the traumas associated with growing up, and to changing interests and demands upon their time. Many coaches have the advantage of being parents themselves or have trained as teachers. Parents learn about how children develop and cope with the world through experience, while teachers may have similar understanding through studying child development. Understanding adults are aware that '. . . the child is not a mini-adult . . .' though they may not be able fully to explain why this is so.

However, some coaches are neither parents nor teachers and are involved in children's sport because they have had a lot of fun and satisfaction through their own participation and want to remain active in some capacity. Coaching allows them to do so and to help others gain similar satisfaction in something they love. But they may not have the advantage of knowing about children and how they differ from adults in their ability to meet the demands which sport places upon them. Whatever their background and motives coaches can only benefit, and so help their charges better, from understanding more completely the nature of children, their capabilities and limitations, their needs and desires, and the ways they change so rapidly.

Of course, the national governing bodies of sport provide coach education through a graduated series of coaching awards. These are designed to give coaches a fuller understanding of the technical and physical requirements of their sport and how to teach them; only rarely do they include elements which help coaches understand the people they are going to deal with. This situation has recently been addressed in England by the coach education programme provided by the National Coaching Foundation (NCF), which includes short courses about the particular nature and needs of children. Similar programmes are available in other parts of the world, for example the American Coach Effectiveness Programme (ACEP) which has provided a model for much of the NCF programme. However, some people are not able, or do not feel inclined, to attend formal courses but still want to improve their coaching. It is hoped that this book will both support the NCF courses and provide useful information for those who cannot attend.

The book has been written to provide information about children, and particularly young athletes, to practising or aspiring coaches in order that they may better understand the children's physical and psychological characteristics. It is intended as a source book that will enable coaches to know the child and not just the sport. A wide range of important topics is covered and care has been taken to present material which is scientifically sound in a way which can be readily understood by people who are not experts in the field. However, some of it requires specific scientific language; in cases where this is necessary a glossary is provided to help the reader. This book should also interest undergraduates in physical education and sports studies or sports science, hence the material presented is fully referenced.

The contributors to this book are all experts in their field and experienced in dealing with children, either as teachers, researchers or coaches, and in many cases as parents. They are distinguished by a common philosophy and approach to the material they have contributed. While most are, or have been, athletes in their own right and have devoted considerable effort to the pursuit of excellence and the promotion of their sport, they are concerned primarily with the welfare of the children who follow them. Hence the principle of 'Children first, coaches second' underlies all the contributions.

The book is in five parts which represent types of valuable information to help coaches provide both a great deal of enjoyment and also a sense of achievement for their athletes. Part One introduces the reader to the topic by drawing attention to the child in the essentially adult world of sport. Part Two describes how children develop, physically, physiologically, and psychologically. Part Three is essentially psychological and is concerned with how children actually experience sport. Part Four deals more directly with coaching skills such as communication, setting goals and developing good training programmes. These are the bread and butter of good coaching. The main part of the text finishes in Part Five by drawing on the earlier material to suggest and give examples of putting theory into practice. Finally there are two important appendices which outline the legal responsibilities of coaches and the value of good insurance.

MJL

Acknowledgements

I consider it a privilege to have been able to assemble a list of distinguished academics and practitioners to produce a book that will inform coaches and teachers of sport. I wish, therefore, to take this opportunity to express my sincere appreciation to all the contributors who have made it possible, and to thank them for their patience over what became an extended period of gestation. They are all recognized experts in their fields (several have international reputations) who have all given generously of their time and expertise and I am most grateful. In particular I would like to thank Glyn Roberts for providing the link between Britain and North America, Ross Smith for keeping me informed of developments in Australia that have been incorporated into Chapter 19, Rod Thorpe who undertook to translate a variety of theoretical material into practical advice, and Neil Armstrong for his expertise and friendship. I would also like to give special mention to my colleague Jean Whitehead for her unfailing integrity and support throughout this and other endeavours.

I am grateful for permission to report results from *Ethical Issues in Sport III: Emergent values among youth football and tennis players,* research commissioned by the Sports Council Research Unit and carried out as part of a Council of Europe programme.

Thanks are also due to my wife, Rosemary, for producing the anatomical drawings in Chapters 5 and 16, to Sue Perkins for assisting with word processing and secretarial tasks, to Brian and Lynn Rees for their hospitality, and finally, to Amanda Killingback of E. & F.N. Spon for seeing value in the project and promoting it in a period of economic stringency.

PART ONE
Children and Sport:
An Introduction

The first part of the book has been compiled to inform and challenge the reader. The information is contained in discussions of the importance of understanding children and the ways in which they fit into a world of sport which is essentially constructed by, and some might say for, adults. The reader is invited to see sport in a broad social context and examine his or her own role in introducing children to sport. The challenge is to be found in the questions that are posed by the authors, either implicitly or explicitly.

Glyn Roberts is a very experienced researcher who has worked primarily in children's sport for nearly two decades. He presents an overview of why it is necessary to study children in sport situations in order to provide better experiences for them. In reviewing the field he introduces the reader to some of the issues in paediatric sports psychology which have attracted attention in recent years. In particular he describes why sport is important to children and how it contributes to their psychological and social development, how they assess their ability and set goals, and finally deals with the importance of the motivational climate which coaches and teachers control and which has a significant effect on the enjoyment and participation of children in sport. Most of the research to which Dr Roberts refers is from North America. We recognize that it is not always directly applicable to British children, but as yet we are still in the process of building our own research base. Until we have it we can learn considerably from the work of others.

Sarah Gilroy is a sociologist who raises important questions about the role of sport in society and how sport is provided for children within the overall structure. She shows how sport can be differentiated into that in which the public takes part, a social model, and that which is public entertainment, a competitive model. Since the competitive, or professional, model receives considerable exposure children with sporting interests become influenced by prominent role models. Ms Gilroy goes on to describe the debate about the purpose and conduct of children's sport which has arisen as a result of the conflict of the two rather different value systems which underpin the two models and summarizes recent debates in physical education which have an impact upon the provision of sport for children. She points out the effects on the family and how parents inevitably become involved in structuring the child's progress. In this analysis children are caught up in a structure in which they may be the means to the achievement of other people's ends. The welfare of the child may become secondary to the desires of both the immediate family and society as a whole. Finally, Ms Gilroy draws attention to the changes in the conduct of children's sport which could be extended to the benefit of more young players.

In the next chapter, Martin Lee asks you directly about why you are coaching. The examination of motives which follows is based upon an explanation of the values which underpin our actions. Readers are invited to look at their own values both in life as a whole and in sport in particular. There is then a description of the reasons coaches commonly give for why they coach before another challenge is posed in the question 'Who is sport for, anyway?' in light of the values that young people express in relation to sport.

Coaching children differs fundamentally from coaching adults in that the whole family is necessarily involved in the process. Indeed it is extremely difficult for children to take part and develop in sport without the close support of their parents. Tony Byrne draws attention to the very important pattern of relationships between children, coaches and parents; what he calls the coaching triangle. Talking to coaches indicates that many consider parents to be the single biggest problem they have to face. Dr Byrne recognizes the different attitudes towards parents among coaches; those who welcome and use parents to help, and those who prefer parents to keep their distance. He then goes on to propose a continuum of parental involvement and describes ways in which different types of parents can be encouraged by coaches to help their children most effectively. He makes suggestions for the development of parental meetings in which the responsibilities and roles of parents and coaches are made clear. In this way both parties can work together more efficiently to help young athletes.

increasing aggression, retarding moral development and fostering an undesirable social climate for children.

The supportive evidence for either position is largely anecdotal, however. There are studies that give some insight into these issues, but systematic research which specifically focuses upon the impact of competitive sport on children's psychosocial development needs to be undertaken

1.2   THE IMPORTANCE OF SPORT PARTICIPATION TO CHILDREN

There are many reasons why we need to be concerned with con-ducting research on children who are engaged in competitive sport. First, organized sport for children has expanded dramatically in many countries and in many sports in the last few decades. In the United States, there is even organized competitive sport for three year old boys (Martens, 1986). Second, no reason is more compelling than the simple fact that children would often rather engage in competitive sports than any other endeavour of their experience. There is evidence to support this. Joan Duda (1981) assessed the preferred achievement domain of high school (14–18 years of age) males and females in North America. She found that males preferred to succeed on the sport field rather than in the classroom. This confirms other research which has shown that sport is an important achievement context for males (Coleman, 1961). Interestingly, females also preferred to succeed in sport contexts than classroom contexts! The only context females wished to avoid in sports was individual head-to-head competition with other females. This finding is consistent with other research (e.g. Kleiber and Hemmer, 1981) which has found that females prefer not to compete directly with other females. However, it is revealing that females con-sider sport contexts, especially team sports, as appropriate contexts in which to succeed against others.

Failure preferences were revealing also. Males indicated that failing in sports was the *most* aversive context in which to experience failure. Given the choice, males would rather do poorly in the classroom than in sports. Females were different to males in their failure preferences as they preferred to fail in sport than in the classroom. This interesting gender difference in failure preference underscores the differing social expectations males and females have, and how we socialize males and females toward different achievement goals.

Third, sport is very important for psychosocial development and is an important context in which peer status and peer acceptance is established and developed. Indeed, Veroff (1969) argues that games

The importance of the study of children in sport: an overview

1

Glyn Roberts and Darren Treasure

SUMMARY

In this chapter, we focus on why the study of children in sport is important. We contend that sport is highly valued by children and plays a key role in their psychosocial development. We argue that a child's perception of ability is one of the most important elements to study in order to understand children within the competitive sport experience. We conclude by suggesting ways in which adults can structure the sports context to make the competitive sport experience more enjoyable and beneficial for *all* children.

1.1 INTRODUCTION

It is generally believed that children's games and sport play an important role in socializing children to the values and beliefs of society. This is because children are brought into contact with rules, social values and other children, and need to develop the skills to survive and enjoy the competitive sport experience. Thus, games and sport are considered to be anticipatory models of society in which children learn important lessons which benefit them later in life.

That involvement in sport can lead to such valuable lessons and contribute to positive personality development has long been a coveted ideal for the supporters of competitive sport for children. Beyond question, sport can provide a forum for teaching responsibility, conformity, subordination of self to the greater good, and the shaping of desirable achievement and social behaviours. But the notion that sport builds character does not sit well with critics of the current structure of competitive sports for children who view the consequences of sport participation as mostly negative. The critics accuse participation of and sport are the domain in which young boys compare themselves in order to demonstrate their standing relative to their peers. In terms of peer acceptance, it has been suggested that many characteristics, e.g. early onset of pubescence, normalcy of a given name, birth position, gender, ethnicity, social class, physical attractiveness and academic achievement (Evans and Roberts, 1987), contribute. However, one way a child can gain acceptance is to be good at activities valued by other children. Because the sport experience is highly valued by children, being good at sports is consequently a strong social asset for children (Evans and Roberts, 1987; Kupersmidt *et al.*, 1990; Weiss and Duncan, 1992).

When one looks at children interacting in free play settings the importance of being physically able in the eyes of other children is clear. Evans (1985) examined children aged eight to 12 and found that team captains, group leaders, were almost always the most competent players and the selection of teams followed a strict hierarchical structure based upon ability. Not only were the better boys the captains, but they also assumed dominant roles in the game and decided who could and could not play. For those boys with poor physical skills, life on the playground was beset with a number of social problems (Evans and Roberts, 1987). They were chosen last, or not at all. When chosen, they were relegated to minor roles, and often prevented from entering games in progress.

The inferior status of such children was most evident when they attempted to enter games already in progress. Children made concerted efforts to accommodate skilled performers, but low ability players were frequently 'locked' out of games (Evans and Roberts, 1987). Research also indicates that popular children are better able to determine the social norms of situations and act upon them (Putallaz and Wasserman, 1990). Thus, it appears that high ability children are better able to act according to the prevailing behavioural norms which, in turn, affords them more opportunity to interact with other children and develop their social skills. Children with low physical skills are particularly at risk.

It is clear that children with above average physical skills are accepted more, and have more status than do under-achieving youngsters. Children with better motor skills are likely to have positive peer relations, while children with low motor skills are disadvantaged when trying to establish friendships with peers (Evans and Roberts, 1987).

As is obvious from the above, the sport experience is important for children. It can affect their peer relationships, their self-esteem and their self-worth (Roberts, 1984). It is no wonder that sport is a domain in which children can experience stress and anxiety.

1.3   PERCEPTION OF STRESS IN SPORT

Learning more about competitive stress and helping children cope with stress have been top priorities for researchers interested in children's sport. Today, with children's sport participation at an all-time high, interest in competitive stress and enhancing the general emotional quality of the sport experience is strong (e.g. Martens *et al.*, 1990; Passer, 1988; Smoll and Smith, 1988).

The most basic demands of sport focus on the demonstration, comparison and evaluation of ability. Children actively seek out competitive situations in order to gain information about their physical ability. Not to demonstrate ability in such a highly valued activity is therefore likely to be extremely stressful for less able children. Demonstration of ability, however, is not the only aspect of children's sport that participants perceive as important. For example, children concerned with learning new skills and improving their performance may find the sport experience stressful if the environment involves excessive amounts of interpersonal competition and evaluation based on normative standards (Roberts, 1986). Conflict, low popularity and the inability to be with friends may cause stress, even to the point that a child may choose to drop out of sport altogether (e.g. Gould *et al.*, 1982).

Recent research has highlighted fear of failure and concerns about adequacy of performance as the main sources of anxiety. Studies of 13–19 year old elite wrestlers (Gould *et al.*, 1983a and b) and 9–15 year old elite runners (Feltz and Albrecht, 1986) found that out of about 30 potential sources of anxiety, participants' concerns about fear of failure and adequacy of performance dominated.

Social evaluation from others is a significant but more minor source of anxiety to most young athletes (Feltz and Albrecht, 1986; Gould *et al.*, 1983a and b; Passer, 1982). Studies of male junior wrestlers (Scanlan and Lewthwaite, 1984) and male and female youth soccer players (Scanlan and Passer, 1979) indicate that before competition, children with low expectations for success had higher state anxiety than children with more positive performance expectations.

It is clear that stress and anxiety are important elements in the experience of children in competitive sport. Anxiety scores increase over the age span and are at their highest in adolescence (Brustad, 1993). This increase in anxiety occurs as children increase their use of social comparison processes (Horn and Hasbrook, 1986, 1987) and increase their focus upon relative ability (Nicholls, 1978). It is the contention of Roberts (1986) that as the impact of the competitive experience increases, in terms of assessing relative ability, some children increasingly perceive stress.

Evident in all of the above is the realization that one factor above all

assumes importance in the understanding of children within the competitive sport experience – the child's perception of ability. As we have documented, perceived ability is important in peer relationships, anxiety and self-esteem of children. While other factors obviously play a role, the self-perception of ability is one of the most important elements to study in order to understand children within the competitive sport experience.

1.3.1 PERCEPTION OF ABILITY

Most of the research on children's perceived ability has assumed a unidimensional perspective of the concept of ability (e.g. Harter, 1978, 1981, 1985). This research has, in the most part, assumed that the self-perception of ability refers to how much ability an individual has relative to others. The fact that individuals, when given ample information, can figure out where they stand relative to others is not necessarily all that interesting or informative. However, recent work in academic and sport contexts has revealed that ability, and thereby the behaviour of children, is better understood if we assume a multi-dimensional understanding of ability and concentrate our efforts on understanding what individuals think ability is (e.g. Nicholls, 1989; Roberts, 1992). This research has emerged out of the achievement goal approach.

1.3.2 THE ACHIEVEMENT GOAL APPROACH

Nicholls (1984, 1989, 1992) contends that two conceptions of ability manifest themselves in achievement contexts, namely a task involved conception of ability and an ego involved conception of ability. Nicholls contends that the two conceptions of ability are embedded within two independent achievement goal orientations. Within sport contexts, these goals are termed mastery and competitiveness (Roberts and Balague, 1989, 1991).

When a child has a mastery goal perspective, that child is concerned with demonstrating mastery of the task (Ames, 1984, Dweck, 1986; Maehr and Braskamp, 1986; Nicholls, 1984). This goal drives achievement behaviour when mastery is determined to be important. The child employs a task involved conception of ability (Nicholls, 1984, 1989) where perceptions of ability are self-referenced and dependent upon learning or improvement at the task.

When a child has a competitive goal perspective, that child is concerned with demonstrating ability compared to others (Ames, 1984; Dweck, 1986; Maehr and Braskamp, 1986; Nicholls, 1984). This goal drives achievement behaviour in circumstances where social comparison is extant. The child employs an ego involved conception of ability (Nicholls, 1984, 1989) where perceptions of ability are other referenced and dependent upon subjective comparison of one's ability with that of others.

There is considerable data to show that the goals exist and are relevant to the ongoing stream of behaviour of the child. If one has the goal of mastery, then the individual is likely to engage in adaptive patterns of behaviour such as choosing moderately challenging tasks, focusing upon effort within the context, trying hard in the face of difficulty or failure, being interested in the task, and persisting in the task over time. The same pattern of adaptive achievement behaviour is also assumed to hold for competitive goal oriented people when their perception of ability is high. That is, when a child is competitive oriented and has the perception that his or her ability is high, then he or she focuses upon effort, tries hard in the face of failure and persists in the task over time. Dweck (1986) has argued, however, that adaptive behaviours of individuals who are competitive oriented are very fragile in the face of failure or difficulty. The perception of ability may weaken and in such instances maladaptive patterns of behaviour manifest themselves. Maladaptive behaviours are choosing easy or hard tasks in order to avoid challenge, not exerting effort in the achievement context, having deteriorating performance over time and lacking persistence (Ames, 1984, 1992; Dweck, 1986; Duda, 1989, 1992; Nicholls, 1984, 1989; Roberts, 1984, 1992, 1993).

Within the academic context, evidence in support of behaviours consistent with the achievement goal held is now considerable. Children manifest adaptive achievement striving when mastery oriented and manifest maladaptive achievement striving when competitive oriented (Dweck, 1986; Ames, 1987, 1992; Nicholls, 1992).

1.4 ACHIEVEMENT GOALS IN SPORT

There is now ample evidence to illustrate that achievement goals function in the context of sport (see Chapter 9). Measures to assess the goals have been developed (Duda, 1989, 1992; Roberts and Balague, 1989, 1991) and ongoing research is assessing the relationship of the goals to achievement behaviours in sport. For example, when holding a mastery goal perspective individuals have self-referenced performance attributions consistent with adaptive achievement behaviours, whereas when holding a competitive goal perspective individuals who are low in perceived relative ability make attributions more consistent with maladaptive achievement striving (Duda, 1992; Jackson and Roberts, 1992; Hall, 1990; Roberts, 1992). For example, Jackson and Roberts found that competitive goal oriented individuals are less likely to experi-

ence positive performance states, such as experience of peak performance, than mastery goal individuals.

Roberts *et al* (1991) looked at achievement behaviours of adolescent
athletes in practice and competition in sport. They found that competitive
goals were related to being bored in practice, to focusing upon winning
in competition, and to believing that sport should enhance one's status. A
mastery goal, on the other hand, was found to be related to satisfaction
in sport, to learning and obtaining social approval in practice, and
believing that sport should enhance social responsibility. Thus, with
adolescents, the achievement goal perspective to understanding achievement behaviours of individuals within sport has had strong support.
When we consider younger persons within sport, however, the issue
does become a little more complex.

1.4.1 ACHIEVEMENT GOALS OF CHILDREN

It was Ewing (1981) who provided the first evidence that goal perspectives are important motivational correlates to behaviour. In her research
with 12 to 15 year old children, Ewing found that the younger children
in her study demonstrated goal perspectives of mastery and competitiveness (along with a social approval goal perspective). Ewing also
found that individuals who are high in competitiveness were the ones
most likely to drop out of sport; that is, competitive goal oriented
children were most likely to exhibit the maladaptive behaviour of
giving up.

In a follow-up study, Ewing *et al.* (1985) used factor analytic procedures
to investigate the development of the goals in nine to 14 year old
children and found developmental differences. Young children (9–11
years of age) had somewhat mixed goals; mastery and social approval
elements were very clear but the competitive goal perspective was not
fully developed. Children were approximately 11 to 12 years of age
before the competitive goal perspective emerged.

More recently, Buchan and Roberts (1991) assessed the perception of
success of children at two different ages (9–10 years of age and 13–14
years of age) and confirmed this hypothesis. Buchan and Roberts were
interested in determining the achievement goals held by the children.
They found that the older age children were clearly more competitive
goal oriented than the younger age group. The younger age group
had mixed interpretations pertaining to goal perspectives, but predominantly focused upon a mastery goal. In addition, Buchan and Roberts
found gender differences. Boys were more competitive goal oriented
than girls.

This increase in competitive orientation may have significant negative
consequences for children around the age of 12, particularly for those

who begin to have reservations about their relative ability. It is at this age that Nicholls and Miller (1984) found that children were able to differentiate skill, luck and effort from ability. After the age of 12, therefore, it should not be surprising that when children expect to look incompetent, greater impairment of performance will occur when competitive goals are salient (Miller, 1985). As Roberts (1984) argues, the culmination of this developmental process of differentiation, combined with increased emphasis on competitive goals, may be the reason why drop-out from competitive sport becomes such a large problem at age 12.

It is not inevitable, however, that children will develop a competitive goal orientation in the sport context. The cues and feedback given by significant adults is critical in determining the achievement goal children will hold (Ames, 1987), particularly for children under the age of 12 for whom social approval is very important (Ewing, 1981; Buchan and Roberts, 1991). Specifically, do the situational constraints have an impact upon the development of one goal versus the other? It is to that aspect we now turn; what is the impact of the perception of the sports context?

1.5   THE IMPACT OF THE MOTIVATIONAL CLIMATE

In an education setting, Carol Ames has looked at how achievement situations influence the adoption of competitive or mastery goal orientations. Ames' research suggests that the achievement context, whether the classroom or the sports field, can be considered more or less competitive or mastery involving depending on the demands of the situation. This research has indicated that in situations that are characterized by interpersonal competition, public evaluation and normative feedback, competitive involved goals are more likely to emerge. In situations which place an emphasis on the learning process and participation, mastery goals are more likely to emerge.

By giving certain cues and rewards, and making explicit expectations, significant adults structure the sport context so that task or ego involved conceptions of ability are the criteria by which performance is evaluated. The adults' goal preferences become manifest and children perceive the goal structure and act accordingly. In this way, the goal structure created by the adult establishes a *motivational climate* that makes one conception of ability or the other manifest. Children are exposed to the explicit criteria that impinge upon their own assessment within the context. The motivational climate created by parents, teachers and coaches therefore has the effect of developing one goal perspective over the other (Nicholls, 1989; Roberts, 1992).

Roberts *et al.* (1992) found evidence consistent with this hypothesis in a study that demonstrated that parents view the competitive sport experience for their children differently depending on their goal orientation. Parents endorsing a high competitive goal orientation emphasized normative standards when defining success, focusing on winning and being better than other children in assessing the success of their child in sport. In contrast, parents endorsing less competitive orientated goals placed greater emphasis on their child's success in developing positive peer relations through the sport experience, focusing on getting on with others and being accepted as part of the team. It would appear that by valuing how well their child gets on with others and is accepted as part of the team, less competitive oriented parents are providing a far better framework for the development of successful peer relationships.

1.5.1   CREATING A MASTERY CLIMATE

Research has demonstrated that students who perceive the motivational climate of the classroom to be mastery oriented are more likely to display adaptive behaviour than those students who perceive the climate to be competitive oriented (Ames and Archer, 1988; Ames and Maehr, 1988; Powell, 1990). Mastery related cues are conveyed by many aspects of the learning environment, from how tasks are defined to how children are grouped, to how they are recognized and evaluated by others. The premise of Ames' research is that the nature of children's experiences can influence the degree to which a mastery goal orientation is salient. Consequently, a child will develop adaptive patterns of behaviour in mastery climates.

Although research in sport is only just beginning to address the issue of motivational climate (e.g. Roberts *et al.*, 1992; Walling and Duda, 1992), many characteristics of the classroom are clearly shared by organized sport – where the authority structure is adult-defined and the reward structure is adult-imposed (Ames, 1992). Classroom and organized sport settings, for example, involve children in achievement related ventures where the outcomes are seen as important and valued, and formal evaluation is externally imposed. Individual performance is public, and children are often stratified or grouped by ability. In these settings, achievement behaviour can be evaluated in terms of improvement and progress toward individual goals, or in relation to normative standards. Children, therefore, can either focus on developing their abilities and learning new skills or on demonstrating or protecting their abilities. Extrinsic rewards, recognition and adult coercion can become the reasons for engaging in the activity, or personal satisfaction can come from participation, a sense of social activity or a belief that one's effort brings improvement. In these ways, sport and academic settings share similar structural features (Ames, 1992).

Ames is currently conducting a comprehensive classroom based intervention that is directed at changing the teacher's role and the teacher's behaviour so that a mastery orientation characterizes the totality of the classroom experience (Ames, 1992). Preliminary findings indicate that the psychological climate in the intervention classrooms is significantly impacted by changes in the teachers' strategies. Within the classroom, Ames and her colleagues have been able to identify those strategies that make a mastery orientation salient to individual students. They have found that the teachers who created the mastery climate enhanced children's involvement in learning as well as their quality of learning. In short, mastery climates enhanced adaptive strategies of children.

There is currently no work in sport involving children in which adults have specifically changed the motivational climate to the sport context. However, it would appear that the role of the parent, teacher and/or coach in the active construction of an individual's perception of the motivational climate is vital. How do they design practice sessions? How do they group players? How do they give recognition? How do they evaluate performance? What behaviour do they consider desirable? Do they congratulate players on ability or good effort? How do they react when the team loses? Persuasive evidence exists to suggest that by making certain cues, rewards and expectations salient a coach can encourage a particular goal orientation and in so doing significantly affect the way a child perceives the sport experience.

Practitioners should therefore work hard to establish a mastery climate by emphasizing short term goals and learning and skill development. To enhance motivation, children need to be evaluated for their improvement and effort, not their performance and ability (Ames, 1987, 1992; Roberts, 1984, 1992).

1.6 CONCLUSION

In this chapter, we have tried to illustrate the importance of the study of children in sport, and how practitioners, researchers and parents need to assess the way they behave when dealing with children in the competitive sport experience. The uppermost thought in our minds should be that we are trying to make the competitive sport experience more enjoyable and beneficial for *all* children. We must be cognizant of the fact that when success in sport is defined as winning in competition, children are given few opportunities to define their experiences positively. If children perceive they have little opportunity of developing the necessary skills or feeling they are valued, then they adopt maladaptive behaviours and are inclined to leave such unpleasant environments. But sport does not have to be like this for children. By adopting mastery concepts in competitive environments, children are more satisfied, enjoy the experience, and adopt adaptive achievement strategies.

We are not suggesting removing competition from sport. Competition is one of the most enjoyed aspects of sport; ask any child! Rather, we want to encourage coaches and parents to focus on criteria that emphasize a mastery goal orientation and de-emphasize a competitive goal orientation for children while competing (Roberts and Treasure, in press).

REFERENCES

Ames, C. (1984) Competitive, cooperative, and individualistic goal structures: a cognitive-motivational analysis, in *Research on Motivation in Education Vol. 1: Student Motivation*, (eds R. Ames and C. Ames), Academic Press, New York, pp. 177–208.

Ames, C. (1987) The enhancement of student motivation, in *Advances in Motivation and Achievement*, (eds D.A. Kleiber and M. Maehr), JAI Press, Greenwich, CT, pp. 123–48.

Ames, C. (1992) The relationship of achievement goals to student motivation in classroom settings, in *Motivation in Sport and Exercise*, (ed G.C. Roberts), Human Kinetics, Champaign, IL, pp. 161–76.

Ames, C. and Archer, J. (1988) Achievement goals in the classroom: students' learning strategies and motivation processes. *Journal of Educational Psychology*, **80**, 260–7.

Ames, C. and Maehr, M. (1988) *Home and School Cooperation in Social and Motivational Development*. Department of Education, OSER Grant No. De-H023T80023.

Brustad, R.J. (1993) Youth in sport: psychological considerations, in *The Handbook on Research in Sport Psychology*, (eds R.N. Singer, L.K. Tennant and M. Murphey), Macmillan, New York, pp. 695–717.

Buchan, F. and Roberts, G.C. (1991) *Perceptions of Success of Children in Sport*, Unpublished manuscript, University of Illinois.

Coleman, J.S. (1961) *The Adolescent Society*, Free Press, New York.

Duda, J.L. (1981) *A Cross-cultural Analysis of Achievement Motivation in Sport and the Classroom*, Unpublished doctoral dissertation, University of Illinois.

Duda, J.L. (1989) Relationship between task and ego orientation and the perceived purpose of sport among high school athletes. *Journal of Sport and Exercise Psychology*, **11**, 318–35.

Duda, J.L. (1992) Motivation in sport settings: a goal perspective approach, in *Motivation in Sport and Exercise*, (ed G.C. Roberts), Human Kinetics, Champaign, IL, pp. 57–92.

Dweck, C.S. (1986) Motivational processes affecting learning. *American Psychologist*, **41**, 1040–8.

Evans, J. (1985) *The Process of Team Selection in Children's Self-directed and Adult-directed Games*. Unpublished doctoral dissertation, University of Illinois.

Evans, J. and Roberts, G.C. (1987) Physical competence and the development of children's peer relations. *Quest*, **39**, 23–35.

Ewing, M.E. (1981) *Achievement Orientations and Sports Behavior in Males and Females*. Unpublished doctoral dissertation, University of Illinois.

Ewing, M.E., Roberts, G.C. and Pemberton, C.L. (1985) *A Developmental Look at Children's Goals for Participation in Sport*. Unpublished manuscript, University of Illinois.

Feltz, D. and Albrecht, R.R. (1986) Psychological implications of competitive running, in *Sport for Children and Youths*, (eds M.R. Weiss and D. Gould), Human Kinetics, Champaign, IL, pp. 225–30.

Gould, D., Feltz, D., Horn, T. and Weiss, M. (1982) Reasons for discontinuing involvement in competitive youth swimming. *Journal of Sport Behavior*, **5**, 155–65.

Gould, D., Horn, T. and Spreeman, J. (1983a) Competitive anxiety in junior elite wrestlers. *Journal of Sport Psychology*, **5**, 58–71.

Gould, D., Horn, T. and Spreeman, J. (1983b) Sources of stress in junior elite wrestlers. *Journal of Sport Psychology*, **5**, 159–71.

Hall, H. (1990) *A Social-cognitive Approach to Goal Setting: The Mediating Effects of Achievement Goals and Perceived Ability*. Unpublished doctoral dissertation, University of Illinois.

Harter, S. (1978) Effectance motivation reconsidered: toward a developmental model. *Human Development*, **21**, 34–64.

Harter, S. (1981) The development of competence motivation in the mastery of cognitive and physical skills: Is there still a place for joy?, in *Psychology of Motor Behavior and Sport – 1980*, (eds G.C. Roberts and D.M. Landers), Human Kinetics, Champaign, IL, pp. 3–29.

Harter, S. (1985) Competence as a dimension of self-evaluation: toward a comprehensive model of self-worth, in *The Development of the Self*, (ed R. Leahy), Fawcett, New York, pp. 51–121.

Horn, T. and Hasbrook, C.A. (1986) Informational components underlying children's perceptions of their physical competence, in *Sport for Children and Youths*, (eds M.R. Weiss and D. Gould), Human Kinetics, Champaign, IL, pp. 81–8.

Horn, T. and Hasbrook, C.A. (1987) Psychological characteristics and the criteria children use for self-evaluation. *Journal of Sport Psychology*, **9**, 208–21.

Jackson, S.A. and Roberts, G.C. (1992) Positive performance states of athletes: toward a conceptual understanding of peak performance. *The Sport Psychologist*, **2**, 156–71.

Kleiber, D.A. and Hemmer, J. (1981) Sex differences in the relationship of locus of control and recreational sport participation. *Sex Roles*, **7**, 801–10.

Kupersmidt, J.B., Coie, J.D. and Dodge, K.A. (1990) The role of poor peer relationships in the development of disorder, in *Peer Rejection in Childhood*, (eds S.R. Asher and J.D. Coie), Cambridge University Press, New York, pp. 60–90.

Maehr, M. and Braskamp, L.A. (1986) *The Motivational Factor. A Theory of Personal Investment*, Lexington Books, Lexington, MA.

Martens, R. (1986) Youth sport in the USA, in *Sport for Children and Youths*, (eds M.R. Weiss and D. Gould), Human Kinetics, Champaign, IL, pp. 27–35.

Martens, R., Vealey, R.S. and Burton, D. (1990) *Competitive Anxiety in Sport*, Human Kinetics, Champaign, IL.

Miller, A.T. (1985) A developmental study of the cognitive basis of performance impairment after failure. *Journal of Personality and Social Psychology*, **49**, 529–38.

Nicholls, J. (1978) The development of the concepts of effort and ability, perception of attainment, and the understanding that difficult tasks require more ability. *Child Development*, **49**, 800–14.

Nicholls, J. (1984) Conceptions of ability and achievement motivation, in *Research on Motivation in Education Vol. 1: Student Motivation*, (eds K. Ames and C. Ames), Academic Press, New York, pp. 39–73.

Nicholls, J. (1989) *The Competitive Ethos and Democratic Education*, Harvard University Press, Cambridge, MA.

Nicholls, J. (1992) The general and the specific in the development and expression of achievement motivation, in *Motivation in Sport and Exercise*, (ed G.C. Roberts), Human Kinetics, Champaign, IL, pp. 31–56.

Nicholls, J. and Miller, A.T. (1984) Development and its discontents: the differentiation of the conceptions of ability, in *Advances in Motivation and Achievement Vol. 3: The Development of Achievement Motivation*, (ed J. Nicholls), JAI Press, Greenwich, CT, pp. 185–218.

Passer, M.W. (1982) Children in sport: participation motives and psychological stress. *Quest*, **33**, 231–44.

Passer, M.W. (1988) Determinants and consequences of children's competitive stress, in *Children in Sport*, (eds F.L. Smoll, R.A. Magill and M.J. Ash), Human Kinetics, Champaign, IL, pp. 203–29.

Powell, B. (1990) *Children's Perceptions of Classroom Goal Orientation: Relationship to Learning Strategies and Intrinsic Motivation*. Unpublished master's thesis, University of Illinois.

Putallaz, M. and Wasserman, A. (1990) Children's entry behavior, in *Peer Rejection in Childhood*, (eds S.R. Asher and J.D. Coie), Cambridge University Press, New York.

Roberts, G.C. (1984) Achievement motivation in children's sport, in *The Development of Achievement Motivation*, (ed J. Nicholls), JAI Press, Greenwich, CT, pp. 251–81.

Roberts, G.C. (1986) The perception of stress: a potential source and its development, in *Sport for Children and Youths*, (eds M.R. Weiss and D. Gould), Human Kinetics, Champaign, IL, pp. 119–27.

Roberts, G.C. (1992) Motivation in sport and exercise: conceptual constraints and conceptual convergence, in *Motivation in Sport and Exercise*, (ed G.C. Roberts), Human Kinetics, Champaign, IL, pp. 3–30.

Roberts, G.C. (1993) Motivation in sport: understanding and enhancing the motivation and achievement of children, in *Handbook of Sport Psychology*, (eds R.N. Singer, L.K. Tennant and M. Murphey), Macmillan, New York, pp. 405–420.

Roberts, G.C. and Balague, G. (1989) *The Development of a Social-cognitive Scale of Motivation*, paper presented at the Seventh World Congress of Sport Psychology, Singapore.

Roberts, G.C. and Balague, G. (1991) *The Development and Validation of the Perception of Success Questionnaire*, paper presented at the FEPSAC Congress, Cologne, Germany.

Roberts, G.C., Hall, H., Jackson, S.A., Kimiecik, J. and Tonyman, P. (1991) *Personal Theories of Ability and The Sport Experience: Goal Perspective and Achievement Strategies*. Unpublished manuscript, University of Illinois.

Roberts, G.C. and Treasure, D.C. (in press) Achievement goals, motivational climate, and achievement strategies and behaviors in sport. *International Journal of Sport Psychology*.

Roberts, G.C., Treasure, D.C. and Hall, H. (1992) *Parental Goal Orientations and Beliefs about the Competitive Sport Experience of their Child*. Unpublished manuscript, University of Illinois.

Scanlan, T.K. and Lewthwaite, R. (1984) Social psychological aspects of competition for male youth sport participants. I. Predictors of competitive stress. *Journal of Sport Psychology*, **6**, 208–26.

Scanlan, T.K. and Passer, M.W. (1979) Sources of competitive stress in young female athletes. *Journal of Sport Psychology*, **1**, 151–9.

Smoll, F.L. and Smith, R.E. (1988) Reducing stress in youth sport: theory and application, in *Children in Sport*, (eds F.L. Smoll, R.A. Magill and M.J. Ash), Human Kinetics, Champaign, IL, pp. 229–51.

Veroff, J. (1969) Social comparison and the development of achievement motivation, in *Achievement Related Motives in Children*, (ed C.P. Smith), Russell Sage Foundation, New York, pp. 46–101.

Walling, M.D. and Duda, J.L. (1992) *The Psychometric Properties of the Perceived Motivational Climate in Sport Questionnaire: Further Investigation*. Paper presented at the annual meeting of the North American Society for the Psychology of Sport and Physical Activity, Pittsburgh, PA.

Weiss, M. and Duncan, S. (1992) The relationship between physical competence and peer acceptance in the context of children's sports participation. *Journal of Sport and Exercise Psychology*, **14**(2), 177–92.

Whose sport is it anyway? Adults and children's sport

2

Sarah Gilroy

SUMMARY

This chapter focuses on the social context of children's sport and identifies some problem areas that coaches, adults and parents need to address if they are to help children get the most out of sport.

It is tempting when you are a coach or a parent, dedicated to developing your child's sporting talent, to be concerned with the very real problems that either you or the child might encounter, e.g. those of over-arousal, types of training and injury. It must be remembered, though, that there are broader concerns which are just as important, if not more so. These are to do with the way in which children's sport is organized, who organizes it, and who benefits from it. Just as adults' sport has changed in recent years, for example in equipment, facilities and sponsorship, so has children's sport, and to understand what is happening to children we must first look more closely at what sport in general looks like. It is only by doing this that we can have a better understanding of why children's sport has developed in the way it has and why some of the negative aspects of adult sport have crept into it. Too often there is the tendency to assume that sport is somehow set apart from the rest of society and as such it will not be infected by the ills of society. If we want to ensure that our children find their involvement in sport fulfilling and rewarding then we need to retain a critical stance, and keep a 'weather eye' on sport in general and children's sport in particular.

2.1 THE NATURE OF SPORT IN THE 1990s

So what does sport in general look like? This may seem to be a redundant question, but if we are to take the process of reassessing sport seriously, particularly when it has undergone so much change, we must start with the basics. The general picture of sporting involvement, that is participating rather than watching, in this country is pretty bleak since only an estimated 37% of women (aged 16 and over) and 57% of men (aged 16 and over) are taking part in at least one outdoor or indoor sport (Sports Council, 1991). It is bleak because the breakdown shows that the highest participation in outdoor sports is in walking, with figures of 18% for women and 21% for men. For indoor sports the most popular activity for men is snooker (17%) and for women swimming (10%).

There is, of course, a problem in getting accurate figures for participation mainly because definitions of sport vary and also much of sport is 'informal' and therefore is impossible to quantify due to its often casual nature. So we are left with figures produced by the General Household Survey and the National Countryside Recreation Survey which ask people what they have done in a particular period prior to the survey. At best these figures give us a broad outline of participation patterns, and at worst they misrepresent actual participation.

The general picture is one of men participating more than women, and of participation by both dropping rapidly as they get older. The involvement of ethnic minority groups in sport is hard to gauge although there is evidence to suggest that minority groups are under-represented and are often subject to racial discrimination when they do participate (Jarvie, 1991). Ethnic minority women can suffer from the constraints of ethnicity and gender which limit their involvement, particularly when participation goes against cultural values and religious beliefs. A visit to any sports ground at a weekend provides further evidence that these are common trends.

2.1.1   THE TWO MODELS OF SPORT

It is clear that 'sport' means different things to different people. For a professional it means work; for an elite amateur it can be worklike and very competitive; for someone else it could just be a good way to meet people and get out. Despite these meanings we can still identify two dominant models. The first is predominantly a competitive form of sport. The word 'predominantly' is important here, because all forms of sport have some element of competition in them. Although for some people competition is the very essence of sport, for others it is the social element that is crucial. The second model of sport is therefore one where the social aspects of participation are more important than the competitive aspects. The difference between the models becomes clear when we look at the way sports are organized, the participants and their experiences.

2.1.2 THE SOCIAL MODEL OF SPORT

The social model is more concerned with sport which is done primarily for social reasons, i.e. it is enjoyable and has little pressure attached to it, it is a good way to meet people, it makes you feel good. The competitive element, although present, is only of secondary importance. Examples of this would be having a game of squash or badminton with friends or playing in a local soccer team. The second place given to competition would be supported by the fact that serious training would be unlikely and rewards for wining would be few, beyond the intrinsic satisfaction of doing well. It would just be playing for playing's sake. Just as in the wider scheme of things, men are more involved, in actual performance terms, than women (see Deem, 1986 and Green *et al.*, 1990 for reasons as to why this is the case). This is particularly true when comparing outdoor to indoor sports, with more men than women being involved in outdoor sports (Sports Council, 1991).

2.1.3 THE COMPETITIVE MODEL OF SPORT

The competitive model echoes the same social divisions seen in the social model, i.e. with women and ethnic minorities being under-represented. The major differences between the models concern the organization and the role that sport plays in an individual's life. Unlike the previous model competitive sport is highly structured and ultra-competitive. The stakes are high, and large sums of money can be earned by those who have turned professional. For the top class amateurs prestige and status and, increasingly, money to put into a trust fund are the main rewards. The intensive training that top class sports people undergo sets them apart from lesser mortals. They are, or become, highly motivated, disciplined and determined people and this enables them to spend hours training when others might be socializing. For many people our only knowledge of this kind of sport is what we gain from watching television or reading the papers and magazines. Sports people are fast becoming television personalities, who are presented as leading exciting, healthy and rewarding lives. In effect they are not only promoting a particular product but also a way of life. The cost of sustaining this kind of sport is high and much of it now comes from corporate sponsorship. As sport has begun to assume such importance it puts pressure on the participants, who need to continue performing at their best to retain their bargaining power. Frequently we see news reports of sports people competing despite serious injuries and at risk of causing permanent damage to themselves. We are also increasingly being presented with evidence that athletes are using illegal performance enhancing drugs. The cases of Ben Johnson and Katrin Krabbe are those that we are most familiar with, but as evidence presented to a Canadian inquiry into steroids in amateur sports suggested, steroid use is the rule not the exception in amateur sport.

What is it, then, that drives people to these lengths despite the damage it can do to their bodies? Some perhaps have come to rely on the 'star' status they have gained and are afraid to lose it, and others are driven by a desire to be the best, regardless of the means or personal cost.

Sport in this model is therefore often experienced as being highly structured and controlled, and very rewarding, both emotionally and financially. There are drawbacks, though, for sport of this kind can bring with it many pressures, it can be socially isolating and, even for amateurs, it can become like work.

2.2 PHYSICAL EDUCATION AND SPORT

With such models of adult sport it is hardly surprising that children begin to emulate the adults around them. Are there any other models that present an alternative type of sports involvement for children? The social model is the one to which children are introduced primarily through their families and school. It is in these environments that children move along the path from play to sport. The emphasis, particularly in schools, is on creating the 'right' kind of learning environment. Of course, who determines what is 'right' has been at the centre of the debates about competition in schools and the National Curriculum. It is perhaps worth spending some time looking at the issue of competition, because in many ways it encapsulates some of the problems currently being faced in the two adult sport models already described.

Recently opinion has been growing, in some schools and teacher training institutions, that much of what had been regarded as unquestionably good about physical education (and inter-school competition in particular) was, in fact, problematic. The common belief that competition within the physical education environment was inevitably wholesome, character building and a form of preparation for life has been questioned. How many children actually found it wholesome and character building? Even with hindsight adults were beginning to ask whether physical education should be offering something more. The continued drop-off in participation in the post-school years did not, and does not, give much evidence that physical education was succeeding in educating people to stay fit for life.

For some, physical education was about teachers gaining prestige and status through producing good school teams. In some schools the pursuit of success in the extracurricular activities led to a 'neglect' of the curricular activities. Also, within inter-school competition there was increasing evidence of children adopting the competitive adult model. As a result a 'do or die', 'win at all costs' attitude was creeping in. Doctors warned that children could not be expected to appreciate that such attitudes are inappropriate and that schools should recognize this and take action to prevent it. The response from physical educators was to reconsider who benefited from competition (particularly inter-school competition). If it was to be of benefit to the few at the expense of the many then clearly it was not suitable. Many schools, particularly in the former ILEA, restricted or 'banned' competition. The reaction that this brought from some members of the public and the media often revealed a misunderstanding of what was happening in schools. It was assumed that all competition was thought to be bad, and that the 'new' Physical Education (PE) contained no element of competition.

Politicians came forward in defence of the status quo:

I think the whole thing was very un-British. We all enjoy the competitive element of sport; indeed in all things. Life is competitive and as long as these sports are fun I think they should be encouraged.

(N. Lyell, MP for Mid Beds., *Bedfordshire Times* 23.10.86)

What is being forgotten here, of course, is the fact that competition comes in a variety of forms, e.g. competition versus yourself, versus the elements, versus another, and competition where one group competes against another. The comments also revealed a rather traditional and old fashioned view of physical education, that is one which saw the role of PE as that of producing test cricketers:

There is a massive void to be filled before we can dream once again of succeeding generations of super kids on their way to reinforce the Test cricket team.

(*Sunday Times*, 1986)

These 'new' ideas, however, were perceived as threatening. Some sections of the media sought to strike a chord with traditionally conservative sports enthusiasts by aligning the 'new' ideas to the political left and thereby trying to discredit and dismiss the ideas:

And from the left wing has come the demand that the competitive element should be phased out in school sport and again cricket suffers. You can even get a booklet from something called the National Coaching Foundation and Play Board which entreats us to chuck out words like winners and losers in favour of 'free expression' and 'self worth'.

(*Sunday Times*, 17.8.86)

The words used in the above quotation are calculated to ridicule the aims of the National Coaching Foundation (NCF) and Playboard, e.g. 'something called' and 'to chuck out words', but perhaps more serious is that in doing so the author misrepresents the aims of the NCF and Playboard (Playboard, 1986).

Times have changed. Gone are the days when there were just a handful of activities for people to do; leisure and sport have changed dramatically. Sport itself now competes for participants with a plethora of exciting computerized entertainment. Games which need fewer people have become much more popular than the large team games of cricket, hockey, rugby and soccer. In fact most of these games have developed smaller, sometimes indoor versions to widen the appeal, e.g. indoor cricket has become particularly popular, with specialist facilities now well established.

2.3   THE EFFECTS ON CHILDREN'S SPORT

The question that we must now ask is how far have the models of adult sport permeated into children's sport? The other consideration is the effect that the debates over the 'new' ideas are having on adults, for, after all, children's sport is largely organized by them either as parents and/or coaches. Children's experience of sport varies from going to relatively low key activities such as swimming classes, gym club or soccer practices on a Sunday morning to the more highly pressured activities such as going to the pool every morning before school for swimming training. The variety of activities open to children today is extensive, but only if the parents are able to support them with transport, equipment, and entry fees.

2.4   THE ROLE OF THE FAMILY

The family is undoubtedly one of the key elements in the child's involvement in sport (Rowley, 1986). Often family arrangements will have to be made around the child's commitments. Few children participate in sport without the financial and emotional support of their families. The more involved the child becomes and the better she/he gets, the more pressure grows, not only on them but also on their parents. This nebulous thing called 'pressure' has a lot to answer for. It can lead to parents and coaches becoming obsessive about the child succeeding; it can lead to the child seeing winning as being the 'be all and end all'; it can lead to unfair means being employed to ensure success; it can lead to physical injury as the child competes when she/he should not, just because winning is so important (Hellstedt, 1990; Lindner et al., 1991). Pressure can lead to stress, which can often, although not always, be harmful and although sport psychologists are able to help us with techniques to reduce stress the problem still remains. It remains because the pressure comes largely from outside the individual, from the way in which sport and competition are valued in society. Competitive sport as we know it in Britain is not inherent; anthropologists have shown that not all societies are based on competition as we are in the industrialized West. Accepting this fact can take us some way in appreciating that it is theoretically possible for us to modify the way in which sport is structured and, therefore, experienced.

2.5 *IN LOCO PARENTIS*

The concern over the nature of children's sport and whether it is harmful or beneficial to them is a very real one. The excesses of children's sport are being revealed as just that, excesses; but they are also revealed as being the excesses of adults expressed through children. The question this comes back to is that of our responsibility as adults to raise children in the 'correct' way and to realize that what might be for the apparent good of the child in the short term might be detrimental to him/her in the long term. Also on a broader scale what some might regard as being good for the country and our society might not always be what is best for each child. Recent moves to make education more vocationally orientated and therefore more instrumental have concerned some educationalists who fear that the general education of the child is being sacrificed on the altar of technological and industrial growth. Who is to decide what is best for the child?

2.6 THE REGULATION OF CHILDREN IN SPORT

Unlike education and employment, children's sport is as yet relatively untouched by direct legislation. There has been legislation which has the potential to have a major impact on children and sport, but it is unclear as yet just how much effect it has had. For example, health and safety regulations have been implemented to improve the standards of child care in terms of facilities, equipment and staff training at nurseries, but it is unclear how this will impact on voluntary work with children.

The Children Act 1989 is concerned with getting the best for children, by promoting and safeguarding their welfare (Brayne and Martin, 1991). Whilst no specific mention is made of sport, those of us working with children in sport need to make ourselves aware of what the Act seeks to do. The Act puts the child first and considers what is in the best interests of the child. If a child is likely to, or is, suffering from significant harm then action can be taken. This could mean that when the health or development of a child is put at risk this could be defined as 'significant harm'. 'Development' is not just physical but also intellectual, emotional, social and behavioural.

It is clear, then, that the excesses in children's sport that the NCF (Lloyd and Campbell, 1990) and the Sports Council have documented may fall within the scope of the Act if young sports people are suffering 'significant harm'.

Rowley's (1986) early study points to potential problems concerning the drive for excellence and international success which pushes people (coaches, parents and children) into believing that routine and specialized training needs to start even earlier. Such action could lead to significant harm to the child's development. The problem is that because children are thought to be taking part because they want to, their participation is not seen as being problematic, despite the harm it may cause later. Also, sport is not regarded as being a danger area as child abuse or children working in dangerous environments might be.

In reality, training, for some children, is worklike and potentially could lead to significant harm by adversely affecting the child's development. For example, one girl took up swimming when she was five and quit when she was 14 having done an estimated 10 000 hours of training in the pool. Such a commitment of time and energy would not have been tolerated had the child been at work in a shop, but because sport is seen to be 'play' it escapes our critical eye. Children are particularly vulnerable to a variety of injuries, some caused by overuse, e.g. epiphyseal injuries, and others caused by specific training, e.g. back injuries in young gymnasts due to training to develop spinal mobility. The problem is not only that the children do not know when to say no to what their coach or parent wants them to do, but also that many of us do not know enough about the dangers they can be exposed to.

The NCF echoes the Children Act by putting children's needs first. Children's sport is for the children, not for coaches to gain glory or make a name for themselves, and not for parents to relive their lost sporting past through the lives of their children.

2.7 AN ALTERNATIVE MODEL FOR CHILDREN

There is a problem, then, with children's sport following the adult models. Firstly, the children themselves are not mature enough (physically, socially or mentally) to cope with the stress that is associated with the competitive model, nor are they able to make decisions which necessitate long term as opposed to short term plans. Secondly, the adults who help organize children's sport often try to fulfil their own sporting ambitions through the children; thus it often becomes too serious and worklike. This has been cited by researchers in both Britain and North America as being one of the reasons that children give for opting out of sport in search of something which is more enjoyable. The problem comes in trying to strike a balance between the social and competitive approaches to sport. If it is too social the children may become frustrated at the lack of challenge, and also may want to emulate their sporting models. If it is too competitive the drop-out rate and dissatisfaction rate may be higher.

Almost in response to this problem has been the development of the modified game approach, which tries to retain the basic nature of the game whilst modifying the equipment, the playing area and the rules to match the physical and mental development of the children. Sports such as rugby and tennis have led the way in this area by developing mini-rugby and short tennis. Although some of the problems children once encountered while playing the full version of the game have been addressed, many of the developments, far from creating a more wholesome environment for children, have done little except reproduce, on a smaller scale, the same problems of a highly structured, competitive and adult-dominated sport. There is a tension here between what the children seem to enjoy, what the sports and clubs, i.e. adults, think is best for the sport and club, and finally what adults think is best for the children in the long term. For example, adults might think that mini-rugby is good for children because there is less physical contact allowed, and the sport and clubs might see it as being a very useful way of recruiting members and identifying talent early, but others might see it as reproducing an adult, ultra-competitive approach to sport too early.

2.8 CONCLUSION

On its own the modified game approach does not guarantee an answer to our problems; what is needed is greater sensitivity towards children's experiences in sport. To develop this we need to understand how sport is changed by, and can have an impact on, the rest of society. As adults, we need to reflect on whether any of our actions are directly or indirectly leading to children not getting the best out of sport for themselves. We need to reflect on what kind of model of sport we are promoting, consciously or unconsciously, and what kind of example we set when playing or coaching or indeed just watching sport. We need therefore to look critically at what is happening in children's sport. Sport can be harmful; we need to guard children's sport from the excesses so often seen in adult sport. Children need our support, and we need to make sure that we strive to give them the best that we can. We need to give children a sporting chance.

REFERENCES

Brayne, H. and Martin, G. (1991) *Law for Social Workers*, Blackstone Press, London.

Deem, R. (1986) *All Work and No Play*, Open University Press, Milton Keynes.

Green, E., Hebron, S. and Woodward, D. (1990) *Women's Leisure? A Feminist Perspective*, Macmillan, London.

Hellstedt, J.C. (1990) Early adolescent perceptions of parental pressure in the sport environment. *Journal of Sport Behavior*, **13**(3), 135–44.

Jarvie, G. (1991) *Sport, Racism and Ethnicity*, The Falmer Press, London.

Lindner, K.J., Johns, D.P. and Butcher, J. (1991) Factors in withdrawal from youth sport: a proposed model. *Journal of Sport Behavior*, **14**(1), 3–18.

Lloyd, W. and Campbell, S. (1990) *The Playsport Guide*, National Coaching Foundation, London.

Playboard and NCF. (1986) *Play the Game*, Playboard and NCF, Leeds.

Rowley, S. (1986) *The Effect of Intensive Training on Young Athletes. A Review of the Research Literature*, Sports Council, London.

Sports Council (1991) *People and Sport Fact Sheet*, Sports Council, London.

Why are you coaching children?

3

Martin Lee

SUMMARY

In this chapter I argue that people who coach children have a responsibility to educate them which cannot be avoided and has effects which may extend beyond the playing field. The basis of why people coach lies in their value system and hence it is important to understand your values. I will describe a model for looking at values and invite you to examine your own value system. Then I will discuss some commonly expressed reasons for coaching and pose questions about who coaches are really doing it for, the children, themselves or others. Finally I will describe values which children express in sport and suggest that coaches should try to match them to their own values.

3.1 INTRODUCTION

When people do anything their reasons for doing it affect both what they do and the ways in which they do it; they influence their targets and their actions. When their activities involve others it is clear that their motives will be important in relationships established between those involved and the experiences they have. Glyn Roberts and Darren Treasure (Chapter 1) and Jean Whitehead (Chapter 9) explain the motivations of children in some detail. In this chapter I want to discuss motives which coaches have for coaching and, more importantly, the values which they bring to the sport situation.

Coaching children differs from coaching adults in that the athletes are more easily influenced and constantly faced with new situations and experiences. At the time when they are most involved in sport, say between the ages of six and 16, children undergo rapid changes in which they are greatly affected by what happens to them and around them. So coaches have the added responsibility of taking on an educational function which has an effect beyond the sport itself. That means that they must be aware of the impact that their priorities and actions have on the children they coach.

Against this background it is important for coaches to establish those priorities and be clear about their philosophy of coaching. This is a process which is often neglected or ignored when coaches meet to further their own education or simply talk about coaching their sport. Yet without it their efforts may be misunderstood or even lack direction altogether. Commenting upon youth sport coaches in America, Dr Rainer Martens, founder of the American Coaching Effectiveness Program (ACEP), has pointed out that without a clear philosophy coaches '. . . tend to adopt the most prevalent philosophy . . . , the professional or elite sports model which emphasises winning' (Martens, 1988, p. 103). It is this attachment to winning which frequently places young athletes at the centre of the hopes and aspirations of others so that their own wants and needs may be forgotten.

Clearly, then, it is most important that coaches clarify their values and motives and understand the part they play in the lives of the children they coach. It is essential to recognize that, like it or not, coaching children is an educational activity, not just concerned with encouraging competitive success but, inevitably, with the effect of developing values in the athletes. Perhaps, above all, coaches must come to grips with who they are doing it for: themselves, the club, the sport itself, the country, the parents or the children.

3.2   VALUES

3.2.1   THE IMPORTANCE OF VALUES

Let us look at the influence of human values on coaching. The ideas presented here are drawn from the work of an eminent American psychologist, Milton Rokeach, who has spent much of his life studying the ways in which people organize their beliefs about what they think is important in life – their values (Rokeach, 1973).

The ways in which we coach, or do anything else for that matter, reflect our values. Briefly, values are those things which we believe to be important in our lives; they express what we believe to be preferable between competing goals and actions. Values may be either things which we strive to achieve (terminal values) or ways in which we behave (instrumental values), both of which can be limited to those things which are (a) essentially personal and do not involve other people, or (b) social and, hence, have interpersonal effects. We tend to organize our values into systems; that is to say that different values take on an order of priority in our thinking which guides the choices we make in our behaviour.

In an extensive discussion of values in physical education, Jim Parry from Leeds University points out that 'Games are laboratories for value experiments' (Parry, 1985). We might extend that and say that sport is an arena for values testing. For example, coaches may often be faced with the choice of insisting that children play fairly, even when they are likely to lose a contest, or showing them how to cheat in order to win it. This is a conflict between personal values of success at whatever cost and social values of moral responsibility. Each coach's value system affects the way he or she decides; and those decisions tend to be consistent.

3.2.2   THE NATURE OF VALUES

Values can be said to have certain characteristics. Firstly a value is a form of belief, something that exists in our minds rather than in the objective world. Like other beliefs it has three aspects to it: (a) what we know, or believe to be true, (b) how we feel about it – good or bad, and (c) how we behave as a consequence. So, for example, if we believe that learning new skills contributes to self-knowledge then we will probably think that it is good, value skill teaching and try to emphasize it in our coaching. Or if we believe that children learn about themselves and grow from being challenged we will always try to set difficult, but attainable, targets for them.

Secondly values appear to be rather enduring; when we believe that something is worth pursuing or a particular way of behaving is important it is not easy for us to be persuaded otherwise. This may be because we tend to learn values in childhood in a rather isolated, all or none fashion. As we mature we encounter more complex situations where we are forced to choose between competing values and, eventually, we develop a mature value system which is difficult to change. Thirdly, they are thought to operate consistently across different situations. Therefore we would expect that people would hold the same values in sport as they do in other walks of life; the system would not change in different settings.

Because value systems can be thought of as a combination of both terminal and instrumental values which are either personal or interpersonal it is possible to put them into a simple framework (Table 3.1).

Attainment values

Attainment values are thought of as those goals that we have for ourselves and are not concerned with the welfare of other people or society at large. So we might think in terms of accomplishment, of

Table 3.1 Classification of human values according to dimension and focus

Focus	Value dimension	
	Terminal	Instrumental
Intrapersonal	Attainment	Competence
Interpersonal	Social	Moral

gaining social recognition or of self-respect. Thus striving to win a particularly important event or achieve a level of performance in sport represents the behavioural manifestation of values associated with attainment.

Social values

Social values are goals that we have for society as a whole, or the small part of it with which we are concerned, like the club or team. They will include such things as providing justice (being fair), freedom (allowing people to have control), and equality of opportunity (treating everybody the same). Social values may be demonstrated in, for example, club policies which facilitate access to minority groups, or ensure that all members have equal playing time in a basketball team.

Competence values

Competence values represent the extent to which we consider it important to show how good we are at whatever we are doing. They are personal and concerned with how we behave and with demonstrating our abilities. So we might think about being ambitious, disciplined or capable. In sporting terms they might be represented by setting high goals, being dedicated and skilful. Failure to achieve these standards results in feelings of disappointment or even shame. Coaches who emphasize competence values will concentrate on maintaining high levels of performance at all times; this may contribute to the experience of anxiety among young competitors (as explained by Stephen Rowley in Chapter 11).

Moral values

Moral values are interpersonal and instrumental. That is, they are concerned with how we behave in situations which involve others. They might include such things as being honest, accepting and forgiving.

In the field of sport moral values form the basis of that which we call sportsmanship. Failure to adhere to them results in feelings of guilt since we violate a set of guidelines for behaviour towards others which we feel is important. A good example of the impact of moral values occurred in the Winter Olympics of 1956 when the Italian bobsleigh pairs team lent a critical piece of equipment to the British pair who went on to win the gold medal (BBC TV, 1992). The Italians were the only threat to the British at the time. For them the values of fairness and altruism were more important than the attainment value of winning the championship.

Perhaps what is important about this breakdown is to recognize that while values guide our actions, they do not all refer to moral or social values and that personal values to do with attainment and competence are perfectly valid and desirable. Indeed, no judgements are made about the relative desirability of any values, they are all 'good' and the priorities are the province of each coach. However, they are important in our understanding of not only why we coach children but also how we go about it.

3.2.3   EXAMINING YOUR VALUES

In recent years I have asked coaches and students about their values in sport and in life. Using the same technique as Milton Rokeach (1973) and adapting his value labels for sport, I have produced a short questionnaire (Table 3.2) to help coaches explore their value systems. You may like to try it yourself.

Instructions

Rank each of the values listed in order of importance to you both in column (a) and in column (b). In (a) rank them on how important they are in your life in general; in (b) rank them on how important they are to you in sport. Identify which values in each list you think are intrapersonal and interpersonal.

Now ask yourself three questions:

(a)   Are you consistent in sport and life in general?
(b)   How do your values affect your coaching?
(c)   Which values are strongest in your system:
    (i)   Attainment or social?
    (ii) Competence or moral?

You may find, as have many of my students, that there are differences between what they value, and consequently how they behave, in life generally and in sports. As a result many of them have begun to look

Table 3.2 Sports Value Survey (adapted from Rokeach, 1973)

Terminal values			Instrumental values		
	(a)	(b)		(a)	(b)
Accomplishment	–	–	Accepting	–	–
Equality	–	–	Ambitious	–	–
Freedom	–	–	Capable	–	–
Friendship	–	–	Considerate	–	–
Justice	–	–	Disciplined	–	–
Pleasure	–	–	Forgiving	–	–
Self-respect	–	–	Honest	–	–
Social recognition	–	–	Independent	–	–

again at what they believe to be most important. However, among coaches I have found that there is more agreement between their instrumental values in life and sport; they set their priorities about conduct in much the same way in both situations. But their goals, terminal values, in sport tend to be personal while in life they valued social goals more strongly.

3.2.4 COACHING VALUES

The values that coaches hold are reflected in their motives for coaching; hence the importance of the question 'Why are you coaching?'. They are also readily transmitted to the children who frequently look upon their coaches in awe and take them as significant role models: they think as the coaches think, their attitudes are the coaches' attitudes, their values are the coaches' values. It is important, therefore, not to underestimate the impact you have on your young athletes.

3.3 REASONS FOR COACHING CHILDREN

Let us turn to the reasons which people give for coaching children. Not only do those reasons determine in many ways, both explicitly and implicitly, what coaches do and how they do it but they are also important in shaping their success in coaching different children. This is because they should, ideally, fit the reasons the children have for being there.

3.3.1 COACHING CHAMPIONS

Some coaches are very keen to coach champion performers, elite athletes; they get great satisfaction from helping them to reach both the pinnacle of their performance and public competitive success. This means focusing on children who have unusual ability, emphasizing skill and fitness, and training them in a limited range of activities, often from a very early age. This approach may be good, even necessary, for those children who have a similar commitment and the ability to achieve; but, of course, others may be passed over and, perhaps, miss the opportunity to develop in the sport. The values involved here are personal and competence; the focus is on accomplishment, and on being ambitious and disciplined. Above all else it is important to succeed and success is frequently seen primarily as winning. While winning is an integral part of sport Frank Smoll and Ron Smith, two American researchers, have shown that it can sometimes become more important to coaches than to the children (Smoll and Smith, 1979). They have pointed out that children can learn both from winning and from losing. As a result of their research they emphasize that firstly *winning is not everything, nor is it the only thing,* and secondly *failure is not the same as losing* (Smoll and Smith, 1979, p. 4). This last comment draws attention to the personal definition of success and failure which has a significant influence upon children's interpretation of their experiences in sport. This is explored in more detail by Stuart Biddle in Chapter 10.

3.3.2   KEEPING IN THE SPORT

Many coaches become involved with coaching children as a way of keeping contact with their sport and making a contribution to it. Indeed, in a small study of coaches which I have carried out this is given as the most common motive. While this finding may be influenced by the self-selection of those who returned the questionnaire it is clearly a very widespread motive and was considered by them to be more important than coaching champions. The terminal values reflected here may again be personal, focusing on pleasure and friendship.

3.3.3   INTEREST IN CHILDREN

Some coaches like to coach children rather than adults because they are interested in the welfare of children, either in general or, in particular, of their own children. Many coaches may be teachers and so already be aware of the educational impact of what they do. But this motive suggests a general concern for interpersonal values and the benefits of the sport for others.

Coaches whose main interest is in children's welfare may consider sport to be a means to either personal development or social development. The former will mean developing ability at all levels for its own sake and the ability to cope with success and failure is as important as the outcomes themselves. The latter will result in placing a priority on such things as co-operation with others, the development of sportsmanship, accepting rules, and creating opportunities for leadership.

3.3.4 ENJOYMENT

Some coaches simply enjoy the contact with children and like to help them to enjoy sport. Research has shown consistently that coaches and parents are very important in determining how much enjoyment children get in their sport. However, it is often very difficult for people to say what it is that they enjoy about an activity and, of course, different people will enjoy different things in the same event. Frank Smoll and Ron Smith (1979) have found, in America, that coaches for whom players most enjoyed playing were those who made them feel good. I have found that a most important feature of what children like in their coaches is a sense of humour so that they can relax and have fun (Lee and Austin, 1988). This may be a reflection of the enjoyment that coaches get from being involved with children; the greater the enjoyment the more fun the children can have.

3.4 WHO IS SPORT FOR?

Throughout our lives we are all subject to the needs and wishes of other people. This may be specially true for children, who have less control over their own lives than adults. Children who get involved in sport often find that there are pressures on them from many different sources. This happens particularly to very able children who find that many different groups want their services and they often have to make difficult choices. They may have to meet the needs of a school team; they may be a coach's pathway to higher things; they may represent their parents' hopes for achievement; or they may be considered as future international stars to represent their country. With these demands being made upon them it is not surprising if their own wishes sometimes get lost, and if they sometimes wonder who they are doing it for.

So, to conclude this short discussion let us ask: Who is children's sport for? People who conduct children's sport have a variety of reasons for doing so. The outcomes of good sports provision for children may enhance the prospects of the clubs, the national teams, the reputation of the coach, or the pride of the parents. While these may all be valuable outcomes they should not become the primary reasons for doing it. If they do the welfare of the children becomes secondary.

3.4.1   COACHES' NEEDS AND CHILDREN'S NEEDS

Naturally people who devote their time to coaching children must satisfy their own needs or they will cease to do it. At the same time there should be a recognition of the children's needs and a desire to meet them. Jean Whitehead, whose work is fully explained in Chapter 9, has found that children like sport for a number of different reasons. They fall into three main categories: being able to do something well, being involved with or recognized by others, and demonstrating superiority. Coaches who recognize these benefits will also see that they affect the way in which children approach sport. Most importantly, a balance between coaches' needs and children's needs will help to ensure that coaches work with children whose goals are the same.

3.5   CHILDREN'S VALUES IN SPORT

So far I have been considering values from a coach's point of view. This is because it is not unreasonable to suggest that coaches can and do transmit their values to young athletes. Let us now turn briefly to values which are expressed by young athletes themselves.

I have recently carried out research commissioned by the Sports Council to identify values which are important to young football and tennis players (Lee and Cockman, 1991). We interviewed players between 12 and 16 years old and discussed how they would respond in critical situations in their sport which presented a moral dilemma. Table 3.3 presents the values which were identified from an analysis of the transcripts of the interviews. We also recorded the frequency with which each value was expressed; this revealed information about children's awareness of different aspects of the sport experience.

There are some interesting aspects of the findings. Firstly, we found that young athletes appeared to express values which are specific to sport, or at least particularly important in sport settings. This is in contrast to the assumptions made by Rokeach and other researchers in the field of values who conclude that values are universal, that is, they apply in all areas of life. However, it vindicates the view of others who recommend identifying values specific to the groups in which the researcher is interested.

Secondly, an analysis of the frequency of occurrence showed differences between sexes and players in different sports. Enjoyment was more commonly mentioned among tennis players than footballers; footballers were more concerned with collective values such as conformity, obedience and team spirit. This suggests that there is a value culture which is associated with different sports which may be transmitted by coaches.

Table 3.3 Spontaneously expressed values identified from football and tennis players aged 12–16 years

Value	Descriptor
Accepting	Being able to get along with others despite apparent differences
Achievement	Being personally or collectively successful in a contest
Caring	Showing concern for other people
Conformity	Conforming to the expectations of others
Companionship	Being with friends who have a similar interest in the sport
Conscientious	Doing one's best at all times and not letting others down
Contract maintenance	Supporting an implicit agreement to play the game; playing in the spirit of the game
Enjoyment	Experiencing feelings of satisfaction and pleasure
Fairness	Not allowing or taking any unfair advantage
Good game	Enjoying the contest regardless of the outcome, usually embodying a balance between contestants
Health and fitness	Becoming healthy as a result of participation and becoming fit to compete
Obedience	Carrying out instructions to avoid punishment
Public image	Gaining the approval of others
Sportsmanship	Being of good disposition, accepting bad luck with good humour, showing positive behaviour towards opponents, and accepting defeat with grace
Self-actualization	Simply getting a thrill from the activity
Showing skill	Being able to perform the skills of the activity well
Team spirit	Doing something for somebody else and the team
Winning	Demonstrating superiority in the contest

Thirdly, the most frequently mentioned values were winning, enjoyment and sportsmanship. However, it is not possible to describe the relative importance of these values at this time. It is sufficient to say that it is consistent with the bulk of available research that young people are primarily concerned with enjoyment and satisfaction in their sport. The problem is that children enjoy different things about sport and cannot always articulate their feelings very well (see Wankel and Kreisel, 1985).

It is interesting that all the values presented were found during the analysis of the first 20 interviews; thereafter nothing new was added. In support of these findings the study was replicated in Spain using junior football players only and gave very similar results. This indicates that the values identified may be common to sports in different national cultures. Again the values were all identified within 20 interviews (Cruz *et al.*, 1992).

This research highlights the importance of coaches understanding children's values, both about their goals and their modes of behaviour in sport, and the influence they themselves have upon those values.

Motives and values are closely related though not identical. Motives may be considered to be reasons why we do things; values, however, may refer to a variety of outcomes which may or may not constitute primary motives. A coach's motives may be explicit and clearly understood but coaches are not always aware of the values which underpin their behaviour and may be transmitted to children. A greater understanding of their own and their children's values will enable coaches to meet the needs of the children they work with more closely.

3.6 WHY CHILDREN FIRST?

The ACEP programme in America has the motto 'Children first; winning second'. It could, as with Jim Parry's comment (see above), be restated as 'Children first; coaches second'! You may ask how this can always be justified and the answer lies in a principle stated by the philosopher Immanuel Kant. He suggested that certain actions were necessary regardless of the outcomes. So coaching children should be thought of as a worthwhile thing to do regardless of the result. It has also been interpreted to mean that nobody should be the means to another's ambitions. If the coach and athlete agree about their goals then the relationship is equal, but if coaches have goals which can only be realized through children, whose real needs are not met, then it is unbalanced and wrong.

3.7 CONCLUSION

In this chapter I have tried to present some food for thought about why you are coaching children. I have argued that coaching children is inevitably an educational process, the effects of which reach beyond the confines of the playing field, gymnasium or swimming pool. Because of this it is important to understand your own values and that these values are transmitted to the children in your care in ways that may affect them throughout their lives. The goals we hold reflect our values but coaches should recognize the motives and needs of children, putting their welfare above all else. Let us recognize that good coaching increases the performance potential of children, gives enjoyment, and contributes to their development as people. It is not always easy to do all three and demands a great deal of understanding and commitment.

In order to be most effective it is important to:

(a)   be clear about why you are coaching;
(b)   examine your own value system, both terminal and instrumental;
(c)   examine the relationship between your motives, values and behaviour;
(d)   be aware of the values you transmit to the athletes in your care;
(e)   understand the athlete's motives and values.

REFERENCES

BBC TV (1992) *More than a Game*, May 27th.

Cruz, J., Boixados, M., Valiente, L., *et al.* (1992) *Identification of Salient Values among Junior Football Players*. Research report to Cosejo Superior de Desportes (Spanish Sports Council) and the Real Federacion Española de Futbol (Spanish Soccer Federation).

Lee, M.J. and Austin, H. (1988) *Dimensions of Coaching Behaviour in Children's Sport*. Report to the Research Committee of the National Coaching Foundation, Leeds, England.

Lee, M.J. and Cockman, M.J. (1991) *Ethical Issues in Sport III: Emergent Values among Youth Football and Tennis Players*. Report to the Sports Council Research Unit, Tavistock Place, London WC1H 9RA, England.

Martens, R. (1988) Helping children to become independent, responsible adults through sport, in *The Growing Child in Competitive Sport*. Proceedings of the Second International Congress of the British Association of National Coaches, Cardiff, December 1987.

Parry, J. (1985) Values in physical education, in *Values Across the Curriculum*, (eds P. Tomlinson and M. Quinton), Falmer, Eastbourne.

Rokeach, M. (1973) *The Nature of Human Values*, The Free Press, Glencoe, IL.

Smoll, F.L. and Smith, R. (1979) Coach effectiveness training: a cognitive behavioral approach to enhancing relationship skills in youth sport coaches. *Journal of Sport Psychology*, **1**, 59–74.

Wankel, L. and Kreisel, P.S.J. (1985) Factors underlying the enjoyment of youth sports: sport and age group comparisons. *Journal of Sport Psychology*, **7**, 51–64.

See also:

Lee, M.J. (1987) *Values and Responsibilities in Children's Sports*. Invited paper to the International Conference of the International Council for Health, Physical Education, and Recreation, University of British Columbia, Vancouver, B.C., June 9th–13th.

Sport: it's a family affair

4

Tony Byrne

SUMMARY

When children engage in sport it is inevitable that their families are drawn in to providing support. For children who aspire to excellence as much as ten years of the family's life can be organized around the demands of training and competing. This chapter explores the relationships between athletes, coaches and parents. A 'circle of influence' model identifies the variety of people who have an effect upon children's participation in sport, but particular attention is paid to the triangular pattern of interaction between children, coaches and parents which is critical to the children's experience. It is important to promote harmony and minimize conflict if children are to benefit fully and the advantages of open communication between parents and coaches are discussed. A model of parental involvement proposed by Jon Hellstadt (1987) forms the basis of a description of different types of parental involvement. Those who are under-involved may simply lack interest or may lack information, and those who are over-involved may be merely excitable or quite fanatical in their commitment. Finally, I (a) suggest a strategy for resolving conflicts that requires that coaches to keep parents informed, listen to their concerns and invite them to participate fully in supporting their children, and (b) provide guidance to parents on how best to support their children.

4.1 INTRODUCTION

In recent years children's sport has become a very controversial area. Proponents and opponents continually voice their opinions and beliefs about the benefits to be reaped or costs to be incurred from sports

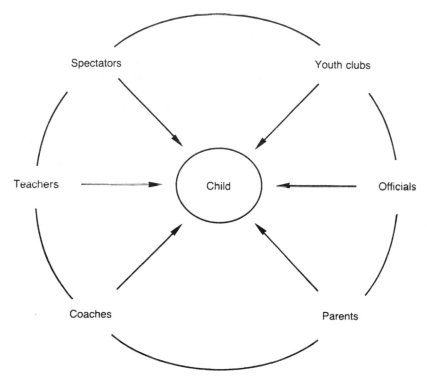

Fig. 4.1 Circle of influence

participation. Those in favour of children's sport see it as a land of promise where participants develop future skills, sportsmanship, self-esteem, independence, loyalty and a commitment to excellence. Those against view sport as a den of iniquity arguing that the 'win at all cost' attitude fosters violence, cheating, drug abuse and dissent.

It is evident that both those for and those against sports participation for children assume that these positive and negative effects are automatic. This clearly is not the case. Sport is inherently neither good nor bad. The positive and negative effects associated with sport do not result from participation per se but from the nature of the sport's experience. It has frequently been shown that an important feature in determining the nature of the experience is the quality of adult leadership. In fact it has been suggested that sport should be thought of as a two-edged sword, capable of cutting in opposite directions, the direction the sword cuts being dependent upon those who swing it, not on the sword itself.

There are a number of different adult groups actively involved in sport who can have an influence upon the athlete (Figure 4.1).

Teachers, officials, spectators, coaches and parents all affect the nature of the sports experience and to a large extent determine whether this experience is a positive one. However, of all the adults involved in this 'circle of influence', the coach and the parents are perhaps the most important. It is their attitudes, beliefs and behaviour which undoubtedly affect the child's experiences in sport.

Although much has been written and said about the roles and responsibilities of the coach there is little to be found with regard to parents. The purpose of this chapter is to redress the balance and tackle the important but often ignored question of parental involvement. I will argue that, in order to meet the objectives of youth sport (physical, social and psychological development, fun and family unity) and thereby reap the benefits of sports participation, the coach must develop excellent working relations with the parents of his or her athletes. Suggestions for involving and dealing with parents will be made and behavioural guidelines offered. I believe these guidelines, if adopted, will help swing the sword in the right direction.

4.2 THE SPORTING TRIANGLE

The sporting triangle (Figure 4.2) is an inherent part of children's sport. The inter-relationships between the coach and the child, the coach and the parent and the parent and the child are inevitable. Few could disagree that coaches, in order to be effective, must have excellent working relationships with their athletes. However, when discussing parental involvement in youth sport views differ greatly and emotions run high. 'The kids are great, it's parents that cause the problems. If I had my way I'd ban 'em all.' Such comments are commonly expressed and reflect the views of many sport coaches. Discussions with numerous coaches from a wide variety of sports indicate that three distinct points of view exist when it comes to parents and their involvement in sport.

First, there are those who welcome and encourage parental involvement. Parents are accepted as a vital element in the coaching process.

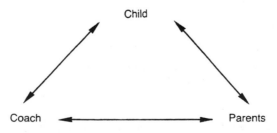

Fig. 4.2 Sporting triangle

They are seen as an important human resource capable of reinforcing the views of the coach. Second, there are those who view parental involvement as an inevitable yet at times unnecessary aspect of working with children. Parents are at best an inconvenience, something to be tolerated but certainly not encouraged. Finally, and by no means a minority, there are those coaches who believe parents should be excluded from the sporting arena altogether. For these coaches, parents are more trouble than they are worth.

Horrific stories of parental behaviour recalled by some coaches lead one to appreciate their opinions. The pressure parents exert on their children, and the abuse they give coaches, officials and other parents allow one to share coaches' concerns. However, the solutions offered by many coaches are not acceptable. Neglecting or, worse still, rejecting parental involvement is tantamount to burying one's head in the sand. Like the ostrich you might not see the problems coming but you will certainly feel them when they arrive.

It is clear that if misunderstanding or conflict occurs between any two of the members in the sporting triangle, relationships with the third will be affected. Careful cultivation of the relationships between the coach, the child and the parent is essential if the sports experience is to be enjoyable and successful. Parents need to be made aware of their roles and responsibilities within sport. This awareness can only be achieved through effective two-way communication.

Those coaches who communicate with parents can avoid conflict within the confines of the sporting triangle. Talking and listening to the parents of their athletes will enable coaches to achieve greater understanding, establish respect and increase the chances of meeting their objectives. Coaches who choose to ignore parents do so at their peril. They will without doubt be faced with numerous problems. At the very least these problems will result in the child receiving inconsistent messages from two very important people, causing them confusion and uncertainty. At worst these problems could result in conflict between all three parties making the sporting experience a thoroughly unhappy one for *all* concerned.

The remainder of this chapter will address some of the problems that commonly occur in the sporting triangle and offer guidance to help the coach avoid and overcome them.

4.3   THE PARENTAL INVOLVEMENT CONTINUUM

Jon Hellstad (1987) has suggested that the involvement of parents in their children's sporting career falls on a continuum ranging from underinvolvement through moderate involvement to overinvolvement. This continuum offers a convenient means of considering parents and

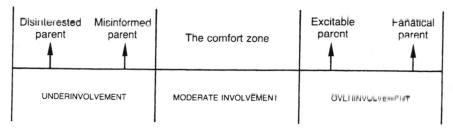

Fig. 4.3 The parental involvement continuum

the problems that sometimes arise (Figure 4.3). To help in the discussion of the relevant issues four types of parents will be described. Names and places have been changed to protect the innocent. However, any resemblance to parents past or present is *not* coincidental.

4.3.1 UNDERINVOLVEMENT

Disinterested parents

Some parents are heavily involved in the social activities of the local community. They frequently attend civic events, cocktail parties, gala evenings and the like. In such situations children may be members of every sport club in town. The child's sporting involvement is clearly beneficial for the parents as they don't require a babysitter. They just drop the children off at the leisure centre/sport club and leave the rest to the coaches. While the idea of leaving everything to the 'coach' may appeal to many, it is all too obvious that children placed in such a situation will not reap the full benefits of sport participation.

A recent study revealed that of the children interviewed, 32% participated because their parents wanted them to. If children are forced to take part in sport there is a very good chance that the experience will be both unenjoyable and stressful. Children should take part because they want to, not because they have to. We will return to this point again when we discuss overinvolved parents.

Misinformed parents

There are those parents who allow their children to join local clubs, having firt spoken to them about involvement, yet who decide not to attend practice or competitions. In such cases the reason seems to be a lack of understanding with regard to parental roles rather than disinterest. The media and to a certain degree coaches often quote examples of parents who spoil their children's involvement in sport by placing too much stress upon them. In an attempt to ensure they don't detract from their children's enjoyment of sport, some parents decide not to get involved.

Children want to please their parents and show them what they can do. Sport offers a wonderful environment for this. It allows the children to display the new skills they have learnt, to demonstrate effort and show commitment. The smiling face of a parent to share in the successes and a hug to console in defeat go a long way toward making sport an enjoyable experience. It also brings the family closer together in an area which the child values.

Coaches must therefore get parents involved but they need to be careful. First, it is important that the coach ensures parents are aware of their roles and responsibilities with regard to children's sport. Second, financial constraints or family pressures, such as shift work and other children, may make attendance difficult. Tactful discussions with the athletes will provide all the information a coach needs to approach and encourage parents to take up their roles in the sporting triangle.

4.3.2   OVERINVOLVEMENT

Although underinvolvement may present coaches with some difficulties it is overinvolvement which causes the most headaches. The most noticeable problem with regard to parental overinvolvement is misbehaviour during competitive events. The reasons for this problem differ and to highlight this it is helpful to classify overinvolved parents into two categories: excitable and fanatical.

Excitable parents

Initially parents who fall into the excitable category seem to be a coach's dream. They tend to be very supportive of the coach and attend practices and games without interfering in the coaching process. Unfortunately, they often get caught up in the heat of the moment. The sheer excitement of a goalmouth scramble or a game point rally turns them into screaming spectators who hurl abuse at all and sundry. Those most likely to incur the wrath of such parents are the officials. 'Are you blind?', 'Get your eyes tested' and other such comments stream from their ever-open mouths. Excitable parents are often as tired as their children, having lived every moment of the game. Parents in this category are not bad people, they just do not realize what they are doing. They don't recognize that their behaviour is embarrassing their children and setting a very poor example. They have forgotten, or never knew, that as far as children are concerned actions speak louder than words.

In situations like this where parents get caught up in the exciting world of children's sport the coach must be able to communicate on a personal level with parents. It will be necessary to take parents to one side and reinforce the idea that they must set a good example if they want their children to benefit and enjoy sport. Parents should be seen but seldom heard and when they do speak it must be positive.

Fanatical parents

Without doubt the most problematic parent a coach has to deal with is the fanatic. This type of parent comes in all shapes and sizes. He or she may have been either extremely successful or unsuccessful in sport. The one thing all fanatical parents have in common, however, is the desire for their child to be a sporting hero or heroine. A successful performance on the part of the child leads to celebrations for the parents. These celebrations are accompanied by minute analysis and suggestions for improvement. Fanatical parents are never quite satisfied.

Poor performances or, worse still, a loss result in a long flow of criticism aimed at everyone but especially the child whose performance is a clear reflection of his or her parent's worth. The coach also receives advice/criticism irrespective of whether he or she wants it. Coach–parent conflict often occurs over the position or amount of time a child is allowed to play. The intense pressure placed on the children shows up on their faces and in their performance. They often argue with the officials because they know their parents expect it. They work hard in practice but don't enjoy it. Quite often children whose parents fall into this category have trouble sleeping and eating prior to competition.

Clearly, when attempts are made to experience success which is missing in their adult lives or that eluded them during their own sporting careers, parents are imposing on their child's participation in sport. When parents push their children to achieve the same, or greater, success in sport as they did, they are imposing their motives on them. Children are not mini-adults and they should not participate for the entertainment and gratification of adults.

External pressure from adults for children to take part in sport, to win at all costs, to be number one, will undermine their motivation and turn play into work. The stress of having to perform to adult expectations and achieve adult set goals will take a heavy toll on a child. Undoubtedly, the fear will lead to dissatisfaction and ultimately attrition.

Identification with one's child is natural. It is overidentification, the taking control and manipulation of the child that lead to problems in sport. Youth sports participation can provide parents and their children with common interests. It can also lead to tension between them. A coach can explain that excessive emphasis upon outcome and consistent criticism cause stress. By encouraging the more officious parents to praise children and to focus their attention on performance rather than outcome, many of the problems can be overcome.

4.4   CURING THE CONFLICT AND PREVENTING THE PROBLEMS

As with medicine, prevention is better than cure. Martens *et al.* (1981) have suggested that many of the problems that arise between parents and coaches can be avoided if a parent orientation meeting is held before the season begins. Martens and his colleagues outline seven objectives for such a meeting, the most important of which are:

1. to inform the parents about the coach's philosophy and objectives;
2. to inform the parents what is expected of their child and of them;
3. to listen to the parents' concerns and objectives;
4. to establish clear lines of communication between the parents and the coach.

By holding a parent orientation meeting prior to the start of the season, coaches will avoid many of the problems discussed in this chapter and get parental involvement into the comfort zone (Figure 4.3). They will also have the ability to refer back to the discussions at that meeting should any problems arise.

The parental guidelines in Table 4.1 are given to enable you, the coach, to state clearly your expectations of parents. They will allow you to talk through some of the thorny issues such as parental pressures and misbehaviour. Effective communication will develop the links you

Table 4.1 Parental guidelines

Should	Should not
Attend games	Force children to participate
Encourage their child to play by the rules	Question officials
Set an example by being friendly to the parents of the opponents	Shout derogatory comments at players, other parents or officials
Emphasize fun and enjoyment	Interfere with their child's coach
Praise and reinforce effort and improvement	Criticize their child's performance
Applaud all good play irrespective of who it's from	

want and need with parents. Remember, when it comes to children's sport, we must all be on the same side if the experience is to be a positive one.

REFERENCES

Hellstadt, J.C. (1987) The coach/parent/athlete relationships. *Sports Psychologist*, 1(2), 151–60.
Martens, R., Christian, R.W., Harvey, J.S. and Sharkey, B.J. (1981) *Coaching Young Athletes*, Human Kinetics, Champaign, IL.

FURTHER READING

McGuire Jr, R.T. and Cook, D.L. (1983) The influence of others and the decision to participate in youth sport. *Journal of Sport Behaviour*, 6(1), 9–16.

PART TWO

Developmental Changes in Children: Why the Child is not a Mini-adult

It is almost becoming a cliché to say that the child is not a miniature adult. This part of the book explains some of the ways in which they differ from adults and describes how they change physically, physiologically and psychologically during their development from young children into young adults. The changes which are described here are most important for an understanding of the limitations of what coaches can expect children to be able to do in sports.

John Aldridge is an orthopaedic surgeon and medical officer to the British Amateur Gymnastic Association. Consequently he is very well qualified to write about growth and development in relation to athletic performance. His chapter describes the development of the skeleton and how it is affected by hormonal changes, diet and sex differences. He also discusses the effect of training on skeletal growth and on menstrual patterns in girls.

A particularly important part of the duties of coaching is to organize suitable training programmes for children. While the topic is addressed specifically later in the book, the next chapter, by Neil Armstrong and Joanne Welsman, lays the foundations by describing the ways in which energy is generated within the body. Most importantly, they draw the reader's attention specifically to differences between children and adults in the ways in which they generate energy and hence differ in their capacity to undertake different forms of training and competition. This has very strong implications for the structure of both training and competitive programmes for boys and girls as opposed to adolescents.

Understanding how children learn skills in sport is of fundamental value to teachers and coaches. Part of the developmental process is that of the ability to learn motor, cognitive and social skills. This ability is partly limited by the maturational state of the nervous system and the capacity of children to process information. Rosemary Connell explains the psychological mechanisms of learning and controlling movements and the difficulties which face children as they attempt the complex skills required in sports.

The final chapter in Part Two deals with how children develop personally and socially in a sporting environment. A major element in the progression from childhood to adulthood is the gradual recognition of a sense of self. Martin Lee shows how children develop a sense of self and how, for some, the experience of sport is an essential part of the process. He then describes the importance of the group in social development and explains how children change in the ways they are able to work with others in teams. This leads to advice to coaches about what they can expect children in teams, or other groups, to achieve and how they can help children by structuring their sport to make it easier for children to understand their own roles and the rules.

Skeletal growth and development

5

John Aldridge

SUMMARY

This chapter describes the patterns, mechanisms and processes of skeletal growth and development. The changes in size and shape from childhood to adolescence are outlined, and the anatomical mechanisms are described in more detail. Bone length is governed by the activity of growth plates and the maturation of bone is a result of ossification in primary and secondary centres within the bone. The effect of factors which affect bone growth, such as nutrition, hormones and mechanical stress, are described prior to a discussion of the effect of training on skeletal growth, body build and composition, and sexual maturity.

5.1 INTRODUCTION

A basic knowledge of skeletal growth and development is important in understanding many aspects of performance and ability in sporting activities at different ages. It is also the key to appreciating many types of injuries that occur in children (see Chapter 16).

Children grow at different rates at different ages and different children also develop at different rates, so there are early and late developers. Not only do children grow at different rates but there are also changes in body proportions that can put limitations on their ability to perform. During foetal life the head is relatively large and at birth accounts for 25% of body length. From birth to one year the trunk is the fastest growing part, whereas from then until puberty the lower limbs account for 66% of the total increase in height (Figure 5.1).

We are all aware of long-legged gangling youngsters at puberty who are rather clumsy and apparently lack co-ordination because of the

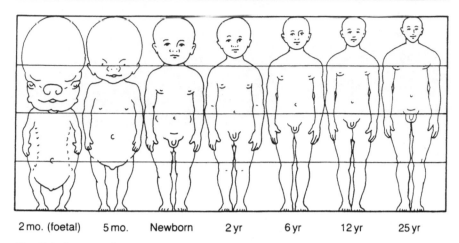

2 mo. (foetal)   5 mo.   Newborn   2 yr   6 yr   12 yr   25 yr

Fig. 5.1 Growth of head, trunk, arms and legs at various ages (from Lowry, G.H. (1973) *Growth and Devleopment of Children*, Year Book Medical Publishers, Chicago; by kind permission of the publishers)

disproportionate trunk and limb length. After puberty increase in trunk length accounts for 60% of further growth. Figure 5.2 illustrates this change in proportion.

At puberty, differences in body shape and proportions become apparent between the sexes and these changes can create difficulties in certain activities. In females total body fat increases, the pelvis widens and breasts develop; these are all very awkward changes to accommodate and make some sports extremely difficult.

As the pelvis broadens the hips move further apart and away from the midline. This is associated with increased angulation of the thigh and necessitates greater muscle strength to stabilize the pelvis in walking. The hip abductor muscles are used to fix the pelvis to the weightbearing leg when the other is raised from the ground.

In women the increased width of the pelvis requires greater muscle action during locomotion. Hence there is a tendency for them to tilt from side to side when they walk (Figure 5.3).

5.2   ANATOMY OF SKELETAL DEVELOPMENT

The body grows by the formation of new cells. As cells divide, they then differentiate into specific types of cell and tissue. Cellular division, differentiation and the migration of cells in the foetus lead to the skeleton being laid down mostly as a scaffolding of a substance called cartilage. Cartilage consists of cells called chondrocytes in a bed of formless tissue. It is the substance we see in the end of a chicken

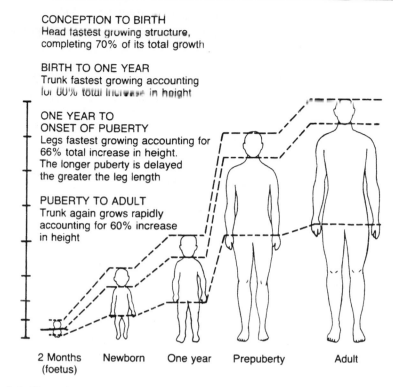

CONCEPTION TO BIRTH
Head fastest growing structure,
completing 70% of its total growth

BIRTH TO ONE YEAR
Trunk fastest growing accounting
for 60% total increase in height

ONE YEAR TO
ONSET OF PUBERTY
Legs fastest growing accounting for
66% total increase in height.
The longer puberty is delayed
the greater the leg length

PUBERTY TO ADULT
Trunk again grows rapidly
accounting for 60% increase
in height

2 Months   Newborn   One year   Prepuberty   Adult
(foetus)

Fig. 5.2 Changing body proportions from conception to adulthood (from Whipple, D. (1966) *Dynamics of Development: Euthenic Paediatrics*, McGraw-Hill, New York; by kind permission of the publishers)

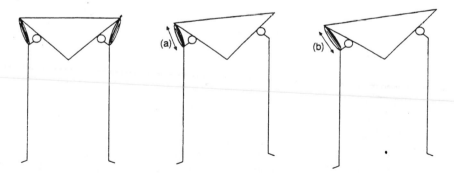

Fig. 5.3 Contraction of the abductor muscle requires less power (a) when the pelvis is narrower than (b) when it is wider

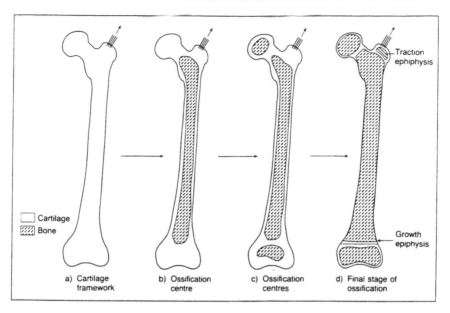

Cartilage
Bone

Traction
ephiphysis

Growth
epiphysis

a) Cartilage
framework

b) Ossification
centre

c) Ossification
centres

d) Final stage of
ossification

Fig. 5.4 Conversion of the cartilaginous scaffold into bone (adapted from Aldridge, J. (1987) in Lee, M.J. *et al.*, *Coaching Children: A Level 2 Course*, National Coaching Foundation, Leeds)

drumstick that is rather hard and gristly. In a few places in the skeleton, the clavicles and parts of the skull for example, bone develops without this cartilaginous stage.

The cartilaginous framework is converted into bone by a process called endochondral ossification. Different areas of the scaffold called ossification centres develop and progressively replace the cartilage with bone. Using the long bone of the thigh, the femur, as an example, a single primary area of ossification develops within the shaft. Subsequently separate secondary areas of ossification develop at either end of the bone (Figure 5.4). Additionally other centres can arise at the site of attachment of major tendons and are called traction epiphyses.

Eventually the whole of the cartilaginous framework is converted into bone. The secondary centres of ossification at both ends increase in size but remain separated from the primary ossification centres of the shaft by a plate of cartilaginous cells. These cells are capable of division and are known as epiphyseal growth plates (Figure 5.4). The cells in these plates divide continually during growth and result in the bone increasing in length. Bone growth also occurs outwardly so the bones become thicker. Because bone is a living tissue it is continually being removed and replaced. Remodelling can therefore take place during growth and this is important when fractures occur. More will be said about this in Chapter 16.

5.2.1   COMPONENTS OF SKELETAL GROWTH

There are two important components of skeletal growth: longitudinal linear growth and skeletal maturation.

Linear growth

Increase in bone length occurs by the division of cells in the growth plates at either end of the long bones. Similar growth in the vertebral bodies in the back occurs at both the upper and lower surfaces. Usually the growth epiphysis at one end will grow more than the epiphysis at the other so that most growth in the lower limb, for example, occurs about the knee, because the lower femoral and the upper tibial epiphyses grow more than the growth plates at the upper and lower ends of the limb. In the upper limb, however, most linear growth occurs at the wrist and at the shoulders.

From birth the rate of growth in length slows with age and is represented in Figure 5.5 as an exponential fall. This fall is interrupted between the ages of five and seven by the so called mid-growth spurt and more importantly later by the adolescent growth spurt.

Boys grow slightly faster than girls in the first year of life, but between the ages of one and nine they grow at the same rate. This is known as the asexual phase of growth. Girls begin their adolescent spurt on average two years earlier than boys. Boys grow more in the first year of life and have a longer adolescent growth spurt than girls and so tend to be taller.

Skeletal maturation

Maturation of the skeleton depends on the rate of ossification, which can be determined by X-ray examination. Different parts of the skeleton begin to ossify at different ages and the growth plates in different bones also stop growing and ossify at different ages.

In the hand and wrist the ossification centres of the carpal bones appear at different times and their size and shape change at a regular rate. An X-ray of a hand and wrist can be used to estimate the bone age of an individual by comparing it with an atlas of wrist X-rays taken at different ages. In most people the bone age will correspond with their chronological age.

The balance between linear growth and skeletal maturation governs final stature. Skeletal maturity is reached when all the growth plate

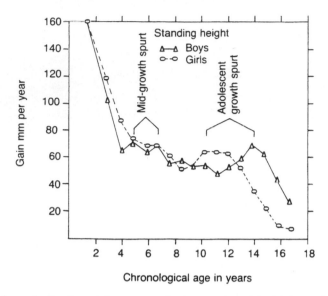

Fig. 5.5 Longitudinal growth curves of a boy and a girl which are halted at the 'mid-growth' and 'adolescent' growth spurt periods (from Duthie, R.B. (1959) The significance of growth in orthopaedic surgery. *Clinical Orthopaedics*, **14**, 7–18)

epiphyses have fused the shafts and ends of the bones (Figure 5.6). Once this has happened then no further linear growth can occur.

5.2.3   FACTORS AFFECTING SKELETAL GROWTH

Patterns of growth are closely linked to genetic make-up and environmental factors. Genetic potential, known as the genotype, determines the limits of growth. Whether this potential is realized in final physical appearance, known as the phenotype, depends upon environmental influences. In general linear growth is affected by the environment whilst skeletal maturation is much more closely controlled genetically.

Environmental factors can affect growth both prenatally and postnatally. Those factors which will be considered here are nutrition, disease, hormones and mechanical stress.

Nutrition

Nutrition is important in physical growth and development. Diets which are deficient in minerals and vitamins adversely affect both. Prolonged periods of poor nutrition limit both linear growth and bone maturation, and result in a reduction in expected bone length. So where there is a shortage of food children tend to be rather short.

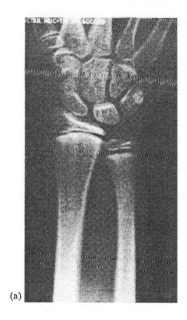 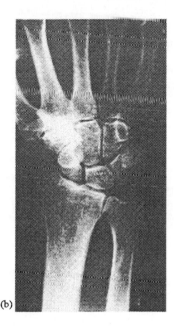

(a)   (b)

Fig. 5.6 X-ray photographs of growth epiphyses showing growth plates (a) open and (b) fused

Similarly an adequate intake of protein is essential for growth and if affected by diseases which cause protein deficiency, children will also be shorter. It is very important to recognize that dietary requirements differ at different ages but high metabolic rates, which result from physical activity, must be satisfied, particularly during periods of increased growth.

Debilitating disease

Any serious illness can retard bone growth. X-ray examinations of children who have been ill often show some evidence of arrested growth by a series of dense lines across the shaft of the bone (Figure 5.7). When children recover, catch-up or compensatory growth occurs so that they still attain normal stature.

Hormones

Hormones are closely involved with the control of normal skeletal development. The correct balance between the growth hormones, insulin and thyroxine is important in influencing the asexual phase of growth. During the sexual phase sex hormones have a more important effect.

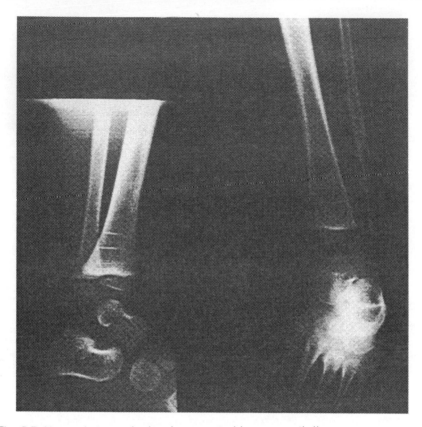

Fig. 5.7 X-ray photograph showing arrested bone growth lines

Growth hormone

Growth hormone is produced by the pituitary gland and acts on growing epiphyses by stimulating cellular division and the production of the intercellular matrix. A lack of growth hormone results in dwarfism whilst overproduction leads to gigantism. In the latter condition the length and thickness of bone are increased, the jaw becomes protuberant and mental retardation can occur. After the growth epiphyses have fused an excess of growth hormone causes thickening of bone so that the chin, the cheeks and the forehead become very prominent.

Thyroxine

The thyroid hormone, thyroxine, maintains the metabolic rate necessary for normal growth. Increased production accelerates skeletal maturation and premature closure of growth epiphyses, deficiency in childhood leads to failure of expected linear growth, retardation of maturation and dwarfism.

Insulin

Insulin, produced by the pancreas, controls normal blood sugar levels and is essential for normal growth hormone activity.

Steroid hormones

Adrenal steroids

The adrenal gland produces two groups of hormones both related to cortisone. One group, the mineralocorticoids, regulate fluid and mineral balances in the body. The other group, the glucocorticoids, are concerned with metabolism in general.

Sex hormones

Sex hormones, androgens in males and oestrogen in females, are concerned with the development of secondary sexual characteristics and with fertility. They stimulate longitudinal bone growth but also cause growth to cease by causing fusion of the epiphyseal plates. In excess they cause retardation of growth and short stature. They have an anabolic effect and stimulate growth in most cases.

Administered hormones

Hormones are administered as drugs in the treatment of conditions caused by their deficiency in the body. For example, in diabetes insulin administration is used to control blood sugar levels.

Steroids, which are related to the male sex hormone testosterone and have anabolic properties, have been misused in sport in an attempt to increase muscle bulk and strength. If they are administered artificially before maturity then adolescents may suffer from premature ossification and fusion of the growth plates and not reach their full stature. They can also have adverse psychological effects, cause liver damage, and upset the cardiovascular system. In males they can reduce sperm production and cause infertility. In females their use causes masculinization, acne, clitoral hypertrophy and suppression of ovarian function and menstruation.

It is not surprising, therefore, that this group of substances is banned in sport as an aid to performance, not only for the unfair advantages they give to the users but also for the serious side effects that may result from using them.

Mechanical stress

Normal bone growth requires a certain amount of stimulation by mechanical strain being applied to it by normal muscle action. The limbs of children who have paralysed muscles, as a result of poliomyelitis for example, do not develop normally and remain small.

Prolonged periods of non-weightbearing on a limb, as may happen when children have a limb splinted in plaster for any length of time, will cause its growth to be retarded. This can cause an inequality of limb length until catch-up growth occurs. However, it should also be recognized that excessive strain applied across an epiphyseal plate can cause retarded growth.

5.3 THE EFFECT OF TRAINING AND EXERCISE ON GROWTH AND DEVELOPMENT

I shall consider the effects of training on three aspects of development: (a) skeletal growth and maturation, (b) body build and composition, (c) sexual maturation.

5.3.1 SKELETAL DEVELOPMENT

A great deal has been written on this subject but the findings are rather inconclusive. The results of research are confusing because of the difficulties of standardizing the methods, samples and variables selected for observation. Some studies have shown a slowing of the normal growth curve whilst others have shown no effect of exercise on growth rate.

Since it is very easy to measure, many studies have concentrated on whether the skeletal age is advanced or retarded in athletes when compared with their chronological age. However, it is difficult to draw conclusions about the causal effects of exercise on growth because of the simultaneous effects of normal growth.

However, the relationship between sports activity and growth does appear to differ at different stages in the growth pattern and with different sports. A very large growth study in Medford, Oregon undertaken by Harrison Clarke and graduate students at the University of Oregon during the 1960s (Clarke, 1971) showed that outstanding football players were advanced in skeletal maturity between the ages of ten and 15 years when compared with non-participants. However, between the ages of 15 and 18 years there appeared to be no differences. Among track and field athletes this pattern was noticeable between 12 and 15 years. Similar results have been found in Little League baseball and among young basketball players. Compensatory growth would therefore apparently have occurred in the late developers so that they had caught up.

Different patterns have been found among swimmers and gymnasts. A study of young swimmers indicated no differences between skeletal and chronological age but showed that in the 8–10 age group those who produced the best performances were skeletally advanced. The effect was most noticeable among breast-strokers. Among gymnasts, however, the tendency is to have delayed skeletal maturity. Studies at various major championships have confirmed this finding. Clearly late development and short stature give a considerable advantage in this sport (see Malina, 1982, for review).

While it is difficult to separate maturation and training effects on performance there is one facet of skeletal growth which clearly can be affected by training. Bone density increases with activity and decreases with inactivity. The effects can be seen, for example, in tennis players where the bone of the dominant arm is of higher density than that of the non-dominant arm.

In summary there appears to be a sports specific relationship between skeletal development and maturation, and success. This relationship is probably not produced by the different training required for different sports but is more probably an inherited characteristic in the individual. Thus naturally late developers are most suited to sports such as gymnastics whilst the more skeletally advanced are more suited, say, to rugby football. Of particular interest are the observations that children with advanced skeletal development are at an advantage during the early teens but the advantage is lost as others mature. This makes it difficult to predict ultimate attainment in sports where strength and speed are advantageous.

5.3.2 BODY COMPOSITION AND SHAPE

The body is composed of three different tissues: fat, muscle and bone. In this section we shall consider lean body mass, the muscular part, and total body fat which consists of subcutaneous fat, depot fat and essential fat.

Physical activity is important in maintaining body weight; it increases lean body mass and reduces total body fat. It is, however, very difficult, especially in children, to separate training effects from normal growth and other effects such as diet.

Differences in body composition can be seen in different sports.

Swimmers are much heavier and have more body fat than athletes in most sports. In other sports lower total body fat measurements range from more than 20% as in tennis and basketball players to about 15% in long distance runners and gymnasts.

There is little doubt that diet plays a large part in this. However, training is also an important factor and in one series of studies it was shown clearly that adolescent boys who trained longest had more muscle and less fat than boys who trained less. Nevertheless, although training can modify the shape of the body by increasing muscle bulk and reducing fat, in general body build is much more genetically controlled.

5.3.3   MENSTRUAL DYSFUNCTION

Studies on twins and family units have shown that the onset of menstruation is primarily genetically controlled. However, environmental factors such as nutritional status, socio-economic class and family size can all affect it. For athletes intensive training has become an accepted cause of a delayed menarche among adolescent girls or the arrest of a normal menstrual cycle in older athletes (Malina, 1983; see Wells and Plowman, 1988, for review).

Swimmers are perhaps the only sporting group where early menarche is common. Since the age of onset of menstruation is significantly related to the skeletal maturity, this fits well with the observation that swimmers tend to have advanced skeletal age. In sports when skeletal maturation is delayed then so is the onset of menstruation.

There also appears to be a relationship between the age of the menarche and body composition. It is suggested that a minimum level of 17% total body fat is necessary for the onset and maintenance of a normal menstrual cycle (Frisch and McArthur, 1974). So it can be argued that training affects menstruation by reducing body fat.

We have noted earlier that physical activity can increase bone density. Bone density is also affected by female sex hormones, principally oestrogens. Post-menopausal osteoporosis, or thinning of the bone, is well known to occur as oestrogen levels fall at the time of the menopause. There is therefore a risk that non-menstruating athletes, whose oestrogen levels will be low, are also at risk of developing a reduced bone density and so may be more likely to develop stress fractures. Certainly Drinkwater et al. (1984), who compared 14 normally menstruating women with 14 amenorrhoeic women in training, showed that bone mineral content of the spine was reduced in the latter group. This indicates that amenorrhoeic athletes in intensive training did not increase their bone density as normal but rather suffered a reduction in it.

5.4 CONCLUSION

Physical development is a complex process that is affected by many factors. Although it is essentially genetically controlled it is also affected by environmental conditions. The effect of training on this process is not clear and more investigation has to be done before firm conclusions can be drawn. However, a knowledge of the processes of growth and development will enable coaches to make more informed decisions about training procedures and programmes for children which may be more beneficial to them.

REFERENCES

Clarke, H.H. (1971) *Physical and Motor Tests in the Medford Growth Study*, Prentice-Hall, Englewood Cliffs, New Jersey.

Drinkwater, B., Nilson, K., Chesnut, G.H., Bremner, W.J., Shainholts, S. and Southworth, M.B. (1984) Bone mineral content of amenorrheic and eumenorrheic athletes. *New England Journal of Medicine*, **311**, 277–81.

Frisch, R.E. and McArthur, J.W. (1974) Menstrual cycles: fatness as a determinant of minimum weight for height necessary for their maintenance or onset. *Science*, **185**, 949–51.

Malina, R.M. (1982) Physical growth and maturity characteristics in young athletes, in *Children in Sport*, (eds R.A. Magill, M.J. Ash and F.L. Smoll), Human Kinetics, Champaign, IL.

Malina, R.M. (1983) Menarche in athletes: a synthesis and hypothesis. *Annals of Human Biology*, **10**, 1–24.

Wells, C.L. and Plowman, S.A. (1988) The relationship between training, menarche, and amenorrhea, in *Competitive Sports for Children and Youth*, (eds E.W. Brown and C.F. Branta), Human Kinetics, Champaign, IL.

Children's physiological responses to exercise   6

Neil Armstrong and Joanne Welsman

SUMMARY

This chapter is concerned with the physiological responses of the child to physical activity. Changes with growth and maturation are central to the discussion and differences between children and adults are highlighted. The chapter opens with an explanation of the three processes by which energy for muscular contraction is generated: the ATP-CP and lactacid anaerobic systems and the aerobic system. The relationship between energy systems and muscle fibre type is discussed. The aerobic and anaerobic energy systems are then described in greater detail with consideration of the means by which these may be measured. Changes in maximal oxygen uptake during development are discussed before a more detailed consideration of the cardiovascular and pulmonary components of the oxygen transport system which serves to illustrate more clearly child–adult differences. The measurement of blood lactate responses to exercise provides an important additional assessment of aerobic capabilities. The necessity for child-specific reference values when interpreting children's blood lactate responses is emphasized, as is the need to consider carefully the impact of methodological factors upon the blood lactate measures obtained. The measurement and interpretation of children's anaerobic power and capacity are then examined. Children's clear inferior ability to perform intense anaerobic exercise compared with adults is described but as highlighted, the methodology used to attempt to explain and quantify these differences has serious limitations.

An understanding of the physiology of the exercising child is vital if coaches hope to optimize the performance of young athletes. This chapter should be read in advance of Chapter 15 where the physiological principles are applied in the development of training programmes for children.

6.1 THE ENERGY SYSTEMS

Exercise requires energy and the energy to support muscular contraction is produced during the breakdown of adenosine triphosphate (ATP) to adenosine disphosphate (ADP) and phosphate (P) (Figure 6.1). ATP is a complex chemical compound formed during the breakdown of food and the quantity of ATP stored in the muscles is very small, perhaps sufficient to sustain a sprinter for about one second of maximal running. ATP must therefore be regenerated very quickly if activity is to continue beyond this time. Initially it is resynthesized from the breakdown of another high energy phosphate, creatine phosphate (CP) (Figure 6.2).

Unfortunately, maximal exercise can only be supported in this manner for a further 4–5 seconds because muscular stores of creatine phosphate are also limited. However, well before the high energy phosphate stores (phosphagens) are used up, more ATP is provided from the breakdown of carbohydrate to pyruvic acid (Figure 6.3). Carbohydrate (glucose) is stored in both the muscles and the liver in the form of glycogen. Liver glycogen is primarily used to maintain blood glucose concentration. Muscle glycogen is used to provide energy (ATP) for muscular exercise, a process called glycogenolysis. Blood glucose can also be used as an energy source, although to a lesser extent than muscle glycogen, and the breakdown of glucose to pyruvic acid is known as glycolysis.

The generation of energy through the breakdown of glycogen or glucose is often called the lactacid energy system and it is most important at the beginning of exercise, when oxygen consumption is low, and during very intensive exercise when pyruvic acid production exceeds the capacity of the aerobic system to oxidize it. A build-up of pyruvic acid results in the formation of lactic acid which accumulates in the muscle and eventually brings muscular contraction to a halt. Both the phosphagen system and the lactacid system can operate in the absence of oxygen and they are therefore known as anaerobic energy systems. On pages 71–74 we will explain the production of lactic acid in the muscle and its subsequent accumulation in the muscle and the blood.

The oxygen transport system is relatively slow to adapt to the demands of exercise and the rate at which ATP can be generated anaerobically greatly exceeds that of the aerobic system (Figure 6.4). The aerobic system is, however, the most efficient in terms of ATP production and because of its ability to use fat, in the form of fatty

$$ATP \quad \rightarrow ADP + P + \text{energy for muscular contraction}$$

Fig. 6.1 The generation of energy from adenosine triphosphate

$$CP + ADP \quad \rightarrow ATP + \text{creatine}$$

Fig. 6.2 The resynthesis of ATP from creatine phosphate

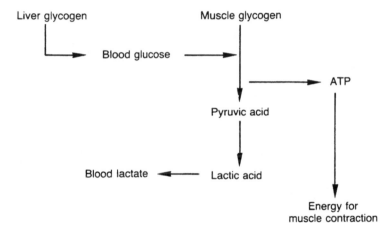

Fig. 6.3 The lactacid energy system

acids, as an energy source it has a much greater capacity for energy generation than the anaerobic systems. During prolonged exercise the child's performance capacity therefore depends largely upon his or her ability to deliver oxygen to the working muscles.

Genetically determined muscle fibres possessing different properties have been identified and it seems that preferential recruitment of specific fibre types is dependent upon the precise demands of the exercise. Sprinters tend to have a predominance of type II (anaerobic) fibres whereas marathon runners may have as many as 80–90% of their muscle fibres in the type I (aerobic) form. The distribution of muscle fibre type in children and adolescents is the same as in adults and is not fundamentally altered even by prolonged training. Consequently, children and adolescents who are capable of high anaerobic performance may not have a similar aerobic potential. Young children may well have less specialized energy responses during exercise than adolescents and adults, but if we are interested in improving children's

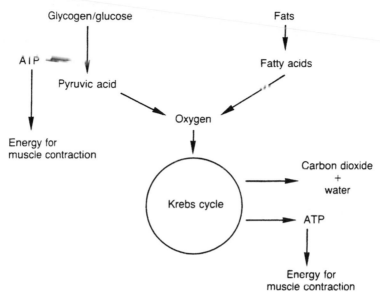

Fig. 6.4 The aerobic energy system

performance we need to consider each of the energy generating systems in relation to growth and development.

6.1.1   THE AEROBIC ENERGY SYSTEM

Maximal oxygen uptake

The maximum energy output of the aerobic system is best described by measuring the maximal oxygen uptake (VO_2 max). For reasons discussed elsewhere (Armstrong et al., 1991) the correct term to use with children is peak oxygen uptake but for ease of exposition we will use the more common term VO_2 max in this chapter. VO_2 max is widely recognized as the best single measure of cardiopulmonary fitness.

Some investigators have been reluctant to carry out direct measurements of VO_2 max with children and have predicted the parameter from submaximal laboratory tests (e.g. Astrand nomogram) or field tests (e.g. multi-shuttle run). We have demonstrated that the standard error of prediction is 10–12% with young boys which indicates that there is no substitute for a direct determination of VO_2 max. Maximal (or peak) oxygen uptake can be successfully achieved on a treadmill with children of five years and older. When determining the VO_2 max of child athletes, however, it is important to simulate their competitive performance as closely as possible. Very little valid feedback can be given to a coach if his swimmers are tested on a cycle ergometer or a treadmill. Testing must be specific to be of value.

When expressed in litres per minute (1/min), VO_2 max increases with age in both boys and girls. There is little difference between boys and girls until puberty, although there is some evidence to suggest that boys attain higher values from the age of five years. At puberty, boys exhibit a spurt in VO_2 max which often occurs just after the time of the greatest increase in height and corresponds with the increase in male hormone secretion. The steep rise in the VO_2 max of boys continues until about 16 years after which there is a slower rise which may continue until about 18 years. In girls VO_2 max reaches its maximum at about 14 years and from 16 years it may fall with increasing age.

At first glance it seems that maximal aerobic power is less well developed in children who are therefore placed at a disadvantage in comparison with older subjects. However, for tasks that involve moving the body, the child, whose body mass is much smaller, may not require as high a VO_2 max as the heavier adult and when VO_2 max is related to body mass a different picture emerges. In boys, values are remarkably consistent throughout childhood and adolescence since the gains in VO_2 max are closely matched by parallel increases in body mass. Girls reach their maximum between ten and 12 years and thereafter a progressive decline sets in with increasing age. The deterioration of the girls' mass related VO_2 max is partially due to an increase in body fat and levelling off of haemoglobin concentration but a substantial component of the sexual discrepancy may well be sociocultural.

Although the mass related VO_2 max of children is at least as good as that of adults, their movements are less efficient, they have lower reserves of power and smaller stores of muscle glycogen. During prolonged activity (e.g. long distance running) children are therefore at a disadvantage when compared to adults. A further consideration when contemplating entering children for long distance events is the environmental conditions. Young children have immature temperature regulatory systems which limit their ability to sweat. They also have large body surface areas compared to their muscle mass which makes them particularly vulnerable at extremes of temperature. When these observations are coupled with the possible skeletal damage and psychological trauma, one can understand the recommendation of the American Academy of Pediatrics that under no circumstances should a full marathon be attempted by immature children.

The cardiopulmonary system

In order to obtain a more complete picture of child–adult differences it is necessary to consider the components of the oxygen transport system, in particular the pulmonary and cardiovascular responses to exercise.

The pulmonary response to exercise

Minute volume is a function of respiratory frequency and tidal volume (Figure 6.5).

Children respond to exercise with shallower respirations and higher respiratory frequencies than adolescents and adults. During maximal exercise children may reach over 75 breaths/min compared with a normal adult response of about 45 breaths/min.

Maximal minute volume increases with age and body size. A five year old child may be able to breathe up to 35 l/min, whereas a young adult may reach values in excess of 150 l/min. Nevertheless, when ventilation is expressed in relation to body size, maximal values are much the same in children, adolescents and adults. Similarly, the lung volumes of children and adults are as expected on the basis of body dimensions. During exercise the pulmonary ventilation is initially matched to the oxygen consumption, but both children and adults experience a ventilatory threshold beyond which ventilation rises in a more accelerated manner.

Some physiologists relate the ventilatory threshold to the so-called 'anaerobic threshold' but the issue is controversial and only limited data are available for children (see the section on blood lactate responses to exercise).

In terms of oxygen uptake, children have a less efficient ventilation system and during both submaximal and maximal exercise, the younger the child the higher the pulmonary ventilation per unit of oxygen consumption. On the other hand it is the alveolar ventilation rather than the pulmonary ventilation that determines gas exchange, and alveolar ventilation accounts for a larger proportion of the total ventilation in children than in adults. The alveolar ventilation is the portion of air that reaches the tiny terminal air sacs in the lungs where gaseous exchange with the blood in the pulmonary capillaries occurs. The pulmonary capillary blood volume and the diffusing capacity of the lung increase in parallel with growth and the maximum diffusing capacity of the child's lung is at least as great as in the adult, whether related to body mass or oxygen consumption.

The cardiovascular response to exercise

The principal factors limiting oxygen uptake are the maximum cardiac output and the maximum arteriovenous oxygen difference (Figure 6.6).

Minute volume = Respiratory frequency × Tidal volume

Fig. 6.5 Pulmonary ventilation

Maximal oxygen = Maximal cardiac × Maximal arteriovenous
uptake   output   oxygen difference

Fig. 6.6 The determinants of maximal aerobic power

The cardiac output of children is significantly less than adults at any given level of oxygen consumption. This indicates that children have a more favourable peripheral distribution of blood during exercise which facilitates the transport of oxygen to the working muscles. The cardiac output of children may be as much as 1–2 l/min lower at the same oxygen uptake compared to adults so the child must rely on a higher peripheral oxygen extraction (i.e. a greater arteriovenous oxygen difference). As long as the child works at a submaximal level the increased oxygen extraction from the blood can compensate for the low cardiac output, but maximal arteriovenous oxygen difference is limited by the haemoglobin content of the blood.

Young children have a low blood haemoglobin concentration and therefore a limited ability to transport oxygen in the blood. There are no gender differences during the first few years of life but boys demonstrate a steady increase in blood haemoglobin concentration up to puberty with a subsequent spurt in their late teens. Haemoglobin concentration in girls is similar to that of boys until the time of menarche but their haemoglobin concentration remains relatively constant from that point. Despite their lower haemoglobin concentration and red blood cell count, the maximal arteriovenous oxygen difference of children is comparable to that of adults. Children seem to be able to extract almost all of the oxygen circulating through the working muscles. Blood haemoglobin concentration is very useful to measure, particularly with girls, as it may help to account for fluctuations in performance and it therefore should be included in any monitoring programme.

The components of cardiac output are heart rate and stroke volume (Figure 6.7). The maximal heart rate of children is higher than that of adults, and the younger the child, the higher the heart rate at any given level of oxygen consumption. This partially compensates for the child's small stroke volume compared with adults during both maximal and submaximal work. When taking differences in body size into

> Cardiac output = Heart rate × Stroke volume

Fig. 6.7 The components of cardiac output

account, however, the child's stroke volume is comparable to that of adults.

Stroke volume, cardiac output and arteriovenous oxygen difference are very difficult to measure in the exercising child and as a result heart rate has become the most commonly used measure. The heart rate response to exercise (and to a lesser extent during recovery) has proved to be very valuable in the analysis of exercise response and its sensitivity to changes in conditioning has provided a useful means of monitoring training programmes. The maximal heart rate of children and adolescents ranges, on average, between 195 and 215 beats/min, although it is not unusual to observe rates in excess of 220 during maximal exercise. After maturity maximal heart rate declines with age and with adults the formula 220−age provides a useful indication of maximal rates. Submaximal heart rates recorded at any given exercise level decline with age and although girls follow the same trend their heart rates are significantly higher than similarly aged boys at any intensity of exercise. The reasons for the sex differences are unknown. Although a lower haemoglobin concentration, a smaller stroke volume and lower levels of habitual physical activity may account for adult differences, they cannot explain the differences which have been demonstrated between boys and girls as young as six years. It may be that there are sex related differences in the regulation of the heart which may help to explain why boys also have faster recovery rates following exercise.

The blood lactate response to exercise

In addition to the determination of VO_2 max, the measurement of the blood lactate response to a series of submaximal exercise bouts of increasing intensity provides a reliable assessment of aerobic fitness.

As illustrated in Figure 6.3, lactic acid is formed when pyruvic acid is broken down anaerobically (without oxygen) to provide ATP for muscular contraction. At low exercise intensities energy requirements can be met almost entirely from aerobic metabolism. With increases in intensity the aerobic system is unable to meet the energy needs and the contribution from anaerobic sources progressively increases, lactic acid is produced in the muscle and blood lactate levels rise accordingly. Figure 6.8 illustrates the typical pattern of blood lactate increase which is observed during an incremental treadmill test. It is clear from this

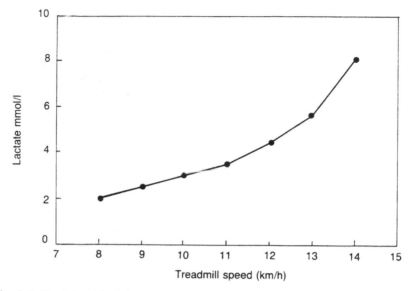

Fig. 6.8 The blood lactate response to incremental exercise

diagram that, unlike oxygen uptake and heart rate, blood lactate does not increase linearly with exercise intensity. The explanation for this is that the lactate level measured in blood does not simply reflect increased lactate production but represents the balance between the processes which both add lactate to and remove lactate from the blood. These include the rate of lactate production in the muscles, muscle fibre type, the rate of lactate release from the muscles and the rate of lactate use as an energy source by the muscles, the liver and the heart. Therefore at moderate exercise intensities, lactate production may be increased but as this is matched by a corresponding increase in the removal of lactate from the blood the result is that blood lactate levels remain low or only slightly elevated.

The point at which the rapid increase in blood lactate occurs (the lactate threshold) has been termed the 'anaerobic threshold'. This has been considered to represent the onset of anaerobic metabolism due to insufficient oxygen supply to the muscle. This assumption has been extensively challenged and in the light of the above discussion it is clear that the lactate threshold reflects the point at which production of lactic acid and its release into the blood outstrips its removal, with the net result of an increase in blood lactate.

Under normal circumstances ventilation increases in a similar fashion to changes in blood lactate during incremental exercise, i.e. an initial slow rate of increase followed by a rapid increase. Because of this the blood lactate 'anaerobic threshold' has frequently been estimated from changes in ventilation. In children, whose breathing patterns during exercing tend to be erratic, the identification of a threshold is particularly difficult. Furthermore, the precise identification of clear 'thresholds' from either blood lactate or ventilatory data is fraught with difficulties and the underlying physiological significance of the 'anaerobic threshold' remains an area of contention.

For coaches with access to a method of blood analysis, submaximal aerobic fitness is best determined through the measurement of performance (e.g. % VO_2 max or heart rate) at a fixed level of blood lactate. For the assessment of adults a level of 4.0 mmol of lactate per litre of blood (4.0 mmol/l) has been recommended as a reference value. Originally this level was chosen because it was assumed to represent the maximal lactate steady state. It is now recognized that lactate metabolism during exercise and consequently the maximal lactate steady state does, in fact, vary widely between individuals. Nevertheless performance at the 4 mmol/l level is highly related to aerobic endurance ability and is sensitive to improvements in submaximal aerobic capacity following training. This concept is developed further in Chapter 15.

Clear differences in lactate responses to exercise exist between children and adults. Both the muscle lactate and blood lactate concentrations of children are lower than adults at all submaximal exercise intensities. The maximal post-exercise blood lactate levels of children rise with age and the maximal muscle lactate concentration is much lower in the child than the adult.

The reasons behind these child–adult differences have still not been fully explained. It has been suggested that the ability to derive energy from anaerobic sources is related to hormonal changes during sexual maturation. However, there is clear evidence that even mid to late adolescents who are sexually mature respond to exercise with lower blood lactate levels than adults. Some evidence from studies which have examined children's muscle tissue (using muscle biopsies) suggests that children have lower concentrations of the enzyme phosphofructokinase (PFK) than adults. As this enzyme regulates the rate at which glycogen is broken down this would explain children's lower blood lactate levels during exercise. Other studies have not, however, confirmed this although there is consistent evidence to suggest that the enzyme profile of children's muscle is geared towards providing energy from oxidative (aerobic) rather than glycolytic (anaerobic) sources.

Because of children's lower blood lactate response to exercise many children will not reach a 4.0 mmol/l lactate level during an exercise test to determine VO_2 max. Therefore this adult reference level for submaximal aerobic performance assessment is not appropriate. A blood lactate level of 2.5 mmol/l represents approximately 80% VO_2 max in adolescents and so is more suitable for use in this age range. The use of this lower level is supported by the finding that, although lactate metabolism during exercise in children varies considerably between individuals (as in adults), their maximal lactate steady state occurs close to a value of 2.5 mmol/l.

The pattern of blood lactate increase with exercise will be influenced by the testing conditions and the methods used to analyse the blood. Interpretation of test results must therefore consider the following points:

1. Blood lactate responses are specific to the test protocol used, for example, the duration of each exercise stage, and whether the test is continuous or includes rest periods between stages. The type of exercise (i.e. running or cycling) will also have an influence on the blood lactate levels obtained so results from a treadmill test cannot be used to monitor swimming performance.
2. Various sites are available for blood sampling including artery, vein or capillary. Capillary sampling from the fingertip is most likely to be used (and is recommended) with children. It is important to realize that the blood lactate levels obtained may vary according to the site of sampling. For example, during cycle ergometry, blood lactate levels in venous blood are lower than in arterial or capillary blood. The difference increases as exercise intensity increases. These differences also exist during treadmill running but are less pronounced.
3. The actual lactate value obtained will depend upon the preparation of the blood prior to assay. For example, lactate levels differ between whole blood, lysed blood, plasma or serum due to the presence or absence of red blood cells in the assay sample. Most of the semi-automatic and portable analysers favoured by coaches for field use are whole blood assays.

Because of these factors it is not possible to compare test results from different laboratories unless the testing conditions are identical. This is an important consideration for coaches using lactate testing to monitor training. In Chapter 15 the practical applications of blood lactate measures to training are discussed in more detail.

6.1.2 THE ANAEROBIC ENERGY SYSTEMS

The phosphagen energy system

Much less attention has been paid to the measurement and interpretation of children's anaerobic power and capacity than to their aerobic characteristics despite the predominance of anaerobic metabolism in activities involving supramaximal efforts of short duration (e.g. sprinting).

The muscular concentration of high energy phosphates (ATP and CP) is very similar in adults and children and they are used at much the same rate during intensive exercise. Children should therefore be as well equipped as adults to compete in events of very short duration. The Margaria Step Test is an established test of anaerobic power. The speed at which the child can run up a staircase of known height is measured, and from this information power output is calculated. The short duration of the test means that the high energy phosphate stores are maximally stressed with minimal involvement of the glycolytic process. The phosphagen system can also be assessed from the Wingate Anaerobic Test. Here the subject pedals a cycle ergometer at maximum effort against a known, constant resistance for 30 seconds. The peak power obtained in any five-second period (usually within the first five seconds) reflects energy provision from the ATP–CP system. However, this test has its limitations when used with children. Cycling engages a smaller muscle mass than running, with a high proportion of the total power output produced by the quadriceps muscle. Prepubertal children and older girls often lack sufficient strength in these muscles to pedal against a heavy resistance and so their performance on the test is compromised.

Laboratory estimates of peak anaerobic power using the Margaria Step Test and the Wingate Anaerobic Test have consistently demonstrated that the peak power output of males increases with age, whether the results are expressed in absolute power units (watts), or normalized for body mass (w/kg). The peak power output of females attains a maximal value during the teen years and then stabilizes with a few minor variations.

It seems that the results of laboratory tests are in conflict with the known underlying biochemical characteristics of children. The reasons for this lack of agreement are probably a function of the performance nature of the laboratory tests and the reluctance of investigators to use invasive techniques (e.g. muscle biopsies) on children. Perhaps the recently developed technique of nuclear magnetic resonance spectroscopy which is completely non-invasive may clarify the situation in the near future. Coaches need to be aware of the limitations of currently available laboratory tests of anaerobic performance.

The lactacid energy system (glycolysis/glycogenolysis)

Although the question of whether or not children have an inferior phosphagen system may be debatable, the evidence concerning the generation of energy via the lactacid system is conclusive, regardless of the method of analysis. Although, as previously described, blood lactate is a reflection of many factors it is usually assumed to be an indication of the rate of glycogenolysis and therefore the rate of anaerobic energy generation.

The most popular tests of the lactacid energy system are the Wingate Test (described above) and the Cunningham Speed Test. This latter test involves running on a treadmill at a speed of 3.56 m/s at a gradient of 20%. The subject's time to exhaustion and post-exercise blood lactate level are recorded. Obviously this test relies heavily on the child's motivation to do well and performance will alter with growth, particularly with improvements in running efficiency and co-ordination. For these reasons and as exercise intensity is not standardized according to body mass it is difficult to compare children or monitor individual changes year by year.

The Wingate Test provides perhaps the most reliable estimation of anaerobic capacity although interpretation of the results must take into consideration the limitations described above. The mean power output over the 30 second period and the fatigue index (the difference between the peak power and the minimum power as a percentage of the peak power) reflect the capacity of the lactacid system especially when supported by post-exercise blood lactate measures.

The results of laboratory tests have consistently demonstrated that the lactacid anaerobic performance of males increases with age from childhood to adulthood. Several studies have indicated that females attain their maximal performance during their teens. This hypothesis has yet to be proven but it is consistent with the observation that male and female differences in anaerobic performance are minimal during the pre-adolescent period, yet during adolescence boys become significantly better anaerobic performers and retain this advantage in adult life.

6.2   CONCLUSION

Some of the important differences between children and adults in their responses to physical activity have been noted and it has been shown that children are not mature working machines. In the vast majority of sports, lack of maturity is a severe handicap and children cannot hope to compete on an equal basis with adolescents or young adults. Age and maturational differences are more pronounced in activities demanding the generation of energy anaerobically and children are at a severe functional disadvantage compared with adults when performing strenuous (supramaximal) activities of between 10s and 60s duration. Boys and girls are fairly evenly matched before maturation, but during adolescence boys develop major functional advantages which generally facilitate superior sporting performance.

If laboratory tests of children's performance are repeated at regular intervals the results may enhance the information available to the coach and facilitate the development of optimum training programmes (see Chapter 15). Coaches must, however, be aware of the limitations of laboratory testing of children.

REFERENCES

Armstrong, N., Williams, J., Balding, J., Gentle, P. and Kirby, B. (1991) Peak oxygen uptake of British children with reference to chronological age, sex and sexual maturity. *European Journal of Applied Physiology*, **62**, 369–75.

FURTHER READING

Armstrong, N. and Davies, B. (1984) The metabolic and physiological responses of children to exercise and training. *Physical Education Review*, 7, 90–105.
Armstrong, N. and Welsman, J. Laboratory testing in young athletes, in *A Colour Atlas of Sports Medicine in Childhood and Adolescence*, (ed N. Maffuli), Wolfe Medical, London (in press).
Bar-Or, O. (1983) *Paediatric Sports Medicine for the Practitioner*, New York, Springer-Verlag.
Bar-Or, O. (1989) *Advances in Paediatric Sports Sciences Vol 3*, Human Kinetics, Champaign, IL.
Boileau, R. (1983) *Advances in Paediatric Sports Sciences Vol 1*, Human Kinetics, Champaign, IL.
Borms, J. (1986) The child and exercise: an overview. *Journal of Sports Science*, **4**, 3–20.
Krahenbuhl, G.S., Skinner, J.S. and Kohrt, W.M. (1985) Developmental aspects of maximal aerobic power in children. *Exercise and Sports Science Reviews*, **13**, 503–38.
Malina, R.M. and Bouchard, C. (1991) *Growth, Maturation and Physical Activity*, Human Kinetics, Champaign, IL.
Rowland, T.W. (1990) *Exercise and Children's Health*, Human Kinetics, Champaign, IL.
Sharp, C. (1991) The exercise physiology of children, in *Children and Sport*, (ed Vivian Grisogono), Murray, London, pp. 32–71.
Williams, J. and Armstrong, N. (1991) The influence of age and sexual maturation on children's blood lactate responses to exercise. *Pediatric Exercise Science*, **3**, 111–20.
Williams, J., Armstrong, N. and Kirby, B. (1990) The 4 mM blood lactate level as an index of exercise performance in 11–13 year old children. *Journal of Sports Sciences*, **8**, 139–47.
Williams, J., Armstrong, N. and Kirby, B. (1992) The influence of site of sampling and assay medium upon the measurement and interpretation of blood lactate responses to exercise. *Journal of Sports Science*, **10**, 95–107.

Understanding the learner: guidelines for the coach

7

Rosemary Connell

SUMMARY

Coaching is no easy task. Not only must coaches have expert knowledge of their sport, they must understand the individuals they are coaching. This means more than knowing how confident they are or what motivates them. It requires knowing how children think and learn, how they attend, perceive, remember, and make decisions. This knowledge can then be used by the coach to determine which learning tasks are set, the way they are set, the style(s) of practice to adopt, the way feedback is used. In this way the coach matches the coaching style to the child.

A recurring theme has been that the coach should engage learners to a greater extent in their own learning. This is not only effective in terms of performance outcomes but also in learning outcomes. The coach has done more than teach a sport, but has developed children's learning strategies so that, whatever sport they engage in, they will be able to tackle it with confidence. They know how to learn.

7.1 INTRODUCTION

Understanding how children think and learn is critical for the coach. While the physical characteristics of children are relatively easy to judge from observation and measurement, their thinking or cognitive abilities are less obvious. If coaches are to maximize children's learning, they will need to ask themselves such questions as, 'Will the child understand what I say?', 'How many coaching points will he be able to take in?' and 'How well will she cope with difficult decisions?'. Clearly, knowing the answer to such questions will help coaches in planning practice sessions, and thus optimize learning.

This chapter briefly outlines a historical approach to motor learning and then presents a model known as the information processing model which is helpful in understanding the learning of skills. Each component of the model, attention, perception, memory, decision making and motor control, is described and guidelines for coaches working with children of varying ages are suggested.

7.2 HISTORY

In the 1950s and 1960s most motor skills research did not focus on the learner, but rather on the method or structure of practice. For example, it was found that spacing coaching sessions (distributed practice) was more beneficial than fewer larger sessions (massed practice), especially for physically and mentally demanding skills. Another finding was that breaking the skill into parts rather than teaching the whole skill was best if the skill was complex and could easily be broken down without destroying the continuity of performance, e.g. swimming the front crawl. On the other hand, teaching the whole skill was better for simple or tightly integrated skills, e.g. a tennis forehand drive. While these research studies told the coach something about the relative effectiveness of various practice methods they did not explain the processes underlying learning, or whether these changed with age. The last 20 years have produced information which helps the coach to understand how an individual performs and learns skills. Researchers such as Connell (1984) and Keogh and Sugden (1985) have taken a process rather than a product approach in their examination of children's motor performance and learning, i.e. they have focused on *what happens during learning* rather than on what is learned.

7.3 INFORMATION PROCESSING

Borrowing terminology from the computer world, a number of models of skill performance and learning have explained how people process information. Figure 7.1 is a simplified information processing model.

Just as a computer receives information, codes, stores and performs various operations on it before producing a response, so the human central nervous system receives information via its senses, interprets it, and then produces some sort of motor response. For example, the child sees the ball travelling towards him, feels where his body is and recognizes that if he is to catch the ball he must move in a particular way. He has to decide when, where and how quickly to move, and how to place his hands to trap the ball. Throughout the action he continues to receive information about his body and the ball via feedback, and if there is time, adjusts his initial plan. The results of his

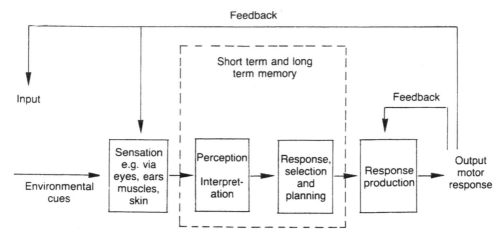

Fig. 7.1 A simple information processing model applied to motor performance

efforts are checked and stored in memory and can be used the next time a catching action is planned. Although the model gives the appearance of sequential processing of information, more than one mechanism may operate at the same time; for example, a child can organize the jumping movements of skipping while watching and listening to the turning rope. The model is particularly helpful to the coach in his analysis of task demands, and in his search for sources of performance error.

Humans, like computers, have finite limits to the amount of information they can process, and the speed with which they can deal with information. This is known as information processing capacity. It is helpful to think of processing capacity as a pool of attention which can be allocated at will by the individual (Kahneman, 1973). If more attention is needed than is available the person becomes overloaded. As children develop, they learn more sophisticated ways of dealing with information so that they can cope with more information at once, and more quickly. It is important for coaches to make sure that they do not overload children, for example by giving only one coaching point at a time. They should also help children to develop more mature processing strategies. Examples of such strategies will be detailed in the following sections.

7.3.1 ATTENTIONAL CHARACTERISTICS OF CHILDREN

Learning sports skills does not simply involve learning movement patterns, it also involves learning which cues to pay attention to. For example, in swimming and gymnastics, attention to the feel of the movement is important, while in games playing, cues in the environment are far more critical. When there are large numbers of cues competing for attention some selection must be made. Imagine children in a team game where there are numerous cues competing for their attention: team-mates, opponents, pitch markings, audience, coach, their own thoughts and feelings. To play effectively they must selectively attend to those cues which are relevant and block out those which are not. Because the cues in the display change frequently, attention needs to be directed to the most important ones quickly.

Research has shown that children scan their environment in an exploratory, disorganized way, in which both relevant and irrelevant cues are sampled. Adults on the other hand show organized search strategies in which they focus on relevant cues only. This developmental change in attentional allocation may involve a progression from over-exclusive attention at up to age six, to over-inclusive attention between six and 11, before becoming selective at age 12 onwards. This could explain the young child's narrow focus on the ball followed by his distractibility in the face of other players, audience, coach, etc., and then finally his ability to focus on relevant cues only. While these types of behaviour appear to be age-related, with careful structuring of the practice situation and with guidance, even young children can be taught to attend selectively. One way to do this would be to reduce the information to relevant cues only, for example by restricting such things as number and space, and then gradually to introduce the irrelevant cues.

Most sports demand that more than one thing is done at once, e.g. dribble the ball and look for a team-mate. It must be recognized that the child will experience difficulty doing both tasks together until the performance of one of them demands less attention. To cater for this coaches should allow their pupils time to practise dribbling alone, then past static players or cones before introducing moving players. This allows the dribbling action to become automated, i.e. less attention demanding, and frees attention for perception or decision making.

7.3.2 PERCEPTUAL CHARACTERISTICS OF CHILDREN

Perception means interpretation or recognition of the information detected by the sense organs. It involves the interplay of information from the senses and from memory. Because young children have fewer past experiences they will be naive perceivers. It *is* possible to recognize something which has not been experienced before if other similar perceptions have been stored in memory, for example, young children's perceptions of a ball travelling towards them will be directly influenced by past experiences of all objects moving towards them. This suggests that a wide range of perceptual experiences will best equip the child to make accurate judgements. Recognizing spaces, judging direction and speed of movement of other players and balls needs practice, and with that practice will come faster, more precise judgements which demand less attention.

Many sporting situations involve picking out items of interest from a background. This is known as figure-ground differentiation and individuals differ in how easily they can do this. Herman Witkin (1954) described people who find difficulty with this as field dependent, while people who deal with such a problem quickly are field independent. Children progressively become more field independent until approximately 18 years of age. Coaches, therefore, should help children to pick out objects from their backgrounds by making the object distinctive, such as using multicoloured balls and/or by making the background as plain as possible and of a contrasting colour.

Teaching children to look for patterns is another way of reducing attentional effort. For example, when dribbling down the basketball court the player looks for a pattern of defensive players rather than focusing on each individual player in turn. Similarly, teaching children to anticipate the rest of an action from early cues, for example, the type of tennis serve from body position, helps them respond more quickly.

Accurate perception of fast moving objects, such as balls or shuttlecocks, is common in sport. The child must learn to judge the significance of the object, predict its future position and plan and initiate a counter move. The sharpness with which moving objects can be perceived is known as dynamic visual acuity. As this ability improves between ages five to 12 (Cratty et al., 1973), coaches should ensure that young children have plenty of time to make accurate perceptions.

Children also show an increasing ability to integrate information from several senses. Connolly and Jones (1970) conducted an interesting experiment in which they presented wooden rods of varying lengths to adults and children of five, eight and 11 years of age. They were allowed either to see the rod or feel it when blindfolded, and then were asked to identify the same length but using the other sense, for example, feel a six inch rod and then judge the same length visually. Accuracy in such judgements was found to increase with age. This would suggest that a child who may see a demonstration, perhaps a gymnastics vault, and then attempt to copy it will not find it easy to match the feel of the performance against the visual image stored in memory. It may be helpful if the coach encourages the child to try to feel the movement while watching the demonstration.

Sometimes, if children experience difficulty in getting the idea of the movement coaches use a method known as manual guidance when they guide the child through the correct movement pattern. Research suggests that this is not an especially useful type of practice because movements which are planned and actively made by the child are remembered such more clearly than movements which are passive and are constrained by the coach.

7.3.3   MEMORY CHARACTERISTICS OF CHILDREN

Without memory it would be impossible to learn anything. A popular view of memory holds that there are three separate forms of memory: a short term sensory store (STSS), a short term store (STS) and a long term store (LTS). Each sense is thought to have its own STSS although research work has been limited to the visual system. Some research has indicated that all information is initially registered for up to approximately one second and that a small fraction passes into STS whilst the rest is lost. This shows how important it is for children to be taught to anticipate likely cues as these may be the ones more likely to be passed on for further processing. The good coach will tell children what to look for in a demonstration, for example.

It is thought that the short term store can only hold between five and nine items for a period of about 30 seconds. These items will be displaced by incoming ones unless they are maintained in STS by repetition (rehearsal). Sugden (1980) has found that young children do not spontaneously use rehearsal strategies, so simply encouraging pupils to repeat the coach's instructions before going off to practise will help ensure that they do not forget what to do.

In order to increase the storage space in STS, information can be organized so as to take up less room; for example, remembering the details of a tennis serving action as 'scratching the back' and 'throwing the racket'. This strategy is known as chunking. Strategies are also important for transferring items from STS to LTS. While the number of items or experiences and the length of time that they can be kept in LTS are thought to be unlimited it is often difficult to recall them. Retrieval can be improved if new experiences can be linked to those already in store, e.g. relating a badminton overhead clear to throwing a ball. Another useful strategy is to store the new memory in an especially meaningful code, e.g. using a rhyme to remember shot put technique:

Chin knee toe
Make a bow
See it go

or using a familiar visual image like the clock to remember hand entry position as 'five to one' in backstroke.

The way in which actions are stored in LTS is not really known. One view is that each action has its own detailed representation in memory, while another suggests that classes of actions are stored, for example, the overarm throwing class of actions. For this to work two rules or schema are also stored which control the use of each specific class of actions, rather like a recipe must be present as well as the ingredients. The latter theory was proposed by Richard Schmidt in 1976 and is known as the schema theory of motor learning. The attractiveness of his view is two-fold. Firstly, it reduces the amount of storage space needed, and secondly, it allows for the production of novel actions, i.e. actions never made before. Since virtually all our actions are to some extent novel, especially those which take place in changing environments, for example team games, a theory which allows for actions to be performed in slightly different ways is critical. The development of the rules or schema for each class of actions can be fostered by variable practice.

At first, the value of variable practice was tested by comparing practice of a single instance of a skill like shooting basketballs from the free throw line against several variations, i.e. from different positions around the basket. Surprisingly, varied practice proved to be equally effective and sometimes superior, even if the test was to shoot from the free throw line from which the varied group had not practised at all. This effect has been especially strong with children (Kerr and Booth, 1978; Shapiro and Schmidt, 1982).

Schmidt has explained the results by suggesting that varied practice enables a stronger schema to be developed, and this schema can be used to accurately plan movements never experienced before. Of course, another explanation might be that varied practice is simply more interesting.

Having recognized the value of variable practice, motor learning researchers have recently turned their attention to the structure of the practice. Let us imagine that four variations of a football pass are to be practised. The coach could organize four blocks of practice in which one type of pass is concentrated on in turn, or he could randomly organize the practice so that all four passes are worked on throughout the session.

A coach may feel that it is better to 'block' practice in order to 'groove' the skill, and while there is some research which does suggest that complete beginners may benefit from a small amount of blocked practice (Shea *et al.*, 1990), research has found that in general, giving learners a range of experiences in a random order is more effective (Lee, 1988).

Another rather surprising research finding about practice is that learning can be optimized if several quite different skills are practised in each session. For example, Goode and Magill (1986) have shown that three different badminton serves, a high serve, a short serve and a flick serve, are remembered best if they have been practised in a random order in the same session rather than blocked in separate sessions. During the practice sessions themselves improvement was greater if single skills were experienced; however, when tested some time after practice, those who learnt the three skills together performed best. What can explain these unexpected findings? The most obvious answer would be that varying practice is more motivating. Yet if this were the case, performance during practice should also be better with random practice. Two other explanations have been suggested, each based on the premise that the learner will remember and thus learn more if he is forced to process information more deeply.

One suggestion is that when learners change from one skill to another they forget the solution to the first skill and thus have to regenerate the solution when they return to it. Thus a considerable amount of problem solving is involved during practice.

A second explanation is that changing the task on every trial enables the learner to distinguish between the skills more clearly so that they will be stored in memory in a more meaningful way.

These findings suggest that coaches might need to reconsider some of their habitual practice methods. It would call into question such practices as taking successive netball or basketball shots from the same spot, or serving a bucket of balls to a target, or performing a single cricket stroke against a ball machine. During the practice session the learner is likely to be seen to improve, which will give both learner and coach satisfaction. However, once in a performance situation the performer seems to have lost the new-found skill. If we consider what is needed in many sports it quickly becomes clear that repetition of the same skill or even the same variation of a skill is rarely needed. Rather, the particular skill may be used only once and thus an important task for the learner is to select the appropriate response. The most effective coach will be the one who can find ways of involving the learner in response selection rather than mindless repetition of skill execution.

Of course, there are some sports which require only the perfect execution of a movement pattern such as a gymnastic vault or a high-board dive, and such highly specific programmes could be effectively learnt with repetitious practice.

7.3.4 DECISION MAKING CHARACTERISTICS OF CHILDREN

A variety of decisions must be made during the performance and learning of skills. Children have been shown to be slower than adults in making simple decisions like which button to press when one of several lights is illuminated (Fairweather and Hutt, 1978) or which playing card to put into which pile (Connolly and Jones, 1970).

The decisions which are required in sporting situations are usually much more complex, for example, which pass shall I use, with how much force, in which direction, when shall I start it?

Furthermore, in many sports, decisions have to be made quickly, so it is important for coaches to help learners to recognize which response is best in each situation. For example, squash players learn that a boast shot (stimulus) should be met with a drop shot (response). If these stimulus–response pairs are stored in LTS, decision making time can be cut and attention can be focused on the execution of the response, which will be especially necessary for the beginner. Of course, the coach needs to help the learner to link a narrow range of appropriate responses with each stimulus to prevent their performance becoming too predictable. Children also need to be taught to plan ahead. McPherson (1989) studied young tennis players and found that a significant difference between the better and weaker players was the ability to plan ahead between points.

A criticism which is often levelled at coaches of games is an over-emphasis on technique and practice of isolated skills at the expense of tactical awareness. If a coaching session consists of isolated skills practice for 50 minutes with a game for ten minutes at the end, not only is children's enthusiasm likely to wane but their awareness of 'what to do when' will not develop. Starting the practice session with a game and then working on a skill which is causing the game to break down will show children the value of practising and provide a specific game context to the practice. They are learning to link certain responses with particular situations.

The importance of the game has been behind the Teaching for Understanding approach, an initiative which fosters discovery and comprehension of the principles of games playing rather than the development of isolated skills. An example of this approach with racket games would be to set children the task of playing a game which uses short and deep shots. The intention is that they should develop an awareness of the tactical value of such shots. As they play they will experiment with methods of achieving a drop shot and a length ball. The coach can then work on the execution of these skills in a more closed or predictable practice situation before returning to the open, less predictable situation of the game.

7.3.5 RESPONSE CHARACTERISTICS OF CHILDREN

Once a response has been selected it must be organized and carried out. The extent to which individuals use feedback to control ongoing movements depends on the speed of the movements and the capability and choice of the performer. Feedback is information fed back from the eyes, ears, muscles, joints and skin, which tells the performer about the movements which have just occurred. Feedback can only be used during the action if the action itself is slow. In 1979 Hay, a psychologist, studied the way movements were controlled by children between five and seven years old when reaching to point at a target when they could not see their arms. Five year old children tended to use a ballistic movement, i.e. a fast movement with very sudden braking near the end of the movement. Seven year olds started a braking movement very early on, or began the movement quickly and then used a smoother two-stage braking strategy. The older children predominantly used the latter strategy. This shows that feedback was used more efficiently by the older children. At first feedback was hardly used at all, and then it was used too much for a smooth performance, with finally the older children showing the ability to integrate kinesthetic feedback from the muscles and joints of the arm with visual information of the target position.

Children need help in paying attention to the relevant feedback. They tend to rely heavily on visual information and are often far more interested in the end result, for example, how far the javelin goes rather than what the angle of release was like. Some research by Jerry and Kathy Thomas in 1988 has shown that children are much less accurate than adults at detecting errors in their movements. In learning the correct technique, it is valuable for the learner to note what the action feels like as this can become the basis for detecting errors in performance later on. An example of a performer going through the error detection and correction process can be seen when a racket player makes a poorly executed stroke, loses the point, and then immediately shadows or rehearses the correct movement pattern.

As far as possible coaches should encourage learners to evaluate their own performances with the coach adding necessary refinements only. This encourages learners not to become too reliant on their coaches, who often will not be present during competition. Knowledge of results (KR) can also motivate learners to continue to strive for goals although special care must be taken with the child whose performance is poor. After successful attempts KR can act as reinforcement, i.e. it will encourage repetition of good performance. If KR is to be effective in terms of error correction it must be given sufficiently often for the child to continue to modify his developing response, but not so often that he cannot work on previously received feedback. In the same vein it has been found that KR which is too precise can overload the child. Coaches should be careful as they may be tempted to give too much detail if they use video playback. They must be prepared to use the video interspersed with practice, concentrating on one point at a time only.

It was previously noted that children are slower in making decisions. This applies equally to making decisions about KR. If the child is slow at processing information, more time will be needed after the presentation of KR and before the next attempt. Teaching young children how to deal with KR is particularly important as there is evidence that given freedom of choice, the younger the child, the less time he gives to processing KR. This is probably because he does not know how to use it. Therefore, coaches may need to help children to think about what the KR after each attempt means. They need to ask themselves such questions as, 'Did I do what I intended?', 'Did I succeed?', and 'Shall I change my next response and if so how?'.

7.4 SELECTING A COACHING STYLE

The style which the coach adopts must take into account children's thinking and learning abilities. As outlined in this chapter, the ways in which children attend, perceive, remember, make decisions and control movements are very different. Jack Keogh and David Sugden have summarized this very well in their book *Movement Skill Development*:

> As they grow older, children develop more proficient processing abilities. This proficiency encompasses skills in memory, attention, and general processing abilities together with better performance when speed is required. Children also develop strategies that aid in attaining, retaining or transferring information. These strategies and their appropriate use become part of children's knowledge base and allow them to approach tasks differently and to process more quickly and efficiently.
>
> (1985, p. 344)

Coaches develop preferred ways of coaching their sport and there is a danger that they may focus on the activity and forget that they are coaching children who need to learn how to learn, as well as to learn the particular activity.

The aim of the coach should really be to make herself redundant; in other words, as a result of coaching, children should learn how to learn so that they can become increasingly self-reliant.

One way in which a coach can fulfil this aim is to engage learners to a greater extent in their own learning. For guidance on how to do this the coach might consider Muska Mosston's spectrum of teaching styles. Mosston and Ashworth (1986) describe a range of coaching styles which differ according to the role played by the learner and the coach in decision making.

At one extreme the coach is autocratic and makes the decisions, for example, decides what the goals of the session are, plans the practice, evaluates the performance and provides the feedback to the learner. At the opposite extreme, the learner self-programmes, that is, she makes decisions about her goals, her method of practice and her performance independent of the coach. In between are a range of coaching styles where the learner and coach share and often negotiate over what, when and how to practise.

Let us compare two teaching styles, one which is frequently used by coaches, the practice style, and one which is less often used but has much to offer, the reciprocal style.

The practice style involves the coach determining the aims, selecting the method of practice and, having set the task to the group, moving around providing individual and group feedback. This can be a highly effective method of coaching. The reciprocal style involves the coach determining the aims, planning a series of practice work cards and organizing the children into pairs. Each pair then works at the practice, one member using a coach-prepared checklist to evaluate their partner's performance, and then reversing roles. The coach's job is not to provide feedback directly to the performers but to help the observers in their evaluation and provision of feedback. In this way the children are learning to analyse critically and to decide on methods of improving performance. This style will not work with all children and may be most profitably employed with those who are at intermediate stages of learning. As all coaches know, observation is a skill which takes time to develop and even carefully detailed observation and feedback cards will not guarantee that optimal feedback is given. However, a reciprocal style does demand more attention and effort on behalf of the learners and it has the potential to increase the amount of feedback each child receives.

For a number of reasons, coaches are often more comfortable with styles where they are in control. They see it as their job to make the decisions, and fear that time and effort will be wasted as well as a greater likelihood of discipline problems resulting if children are given more power. Whilst these are valid concerns, giving children a greater role could actually increase their learning. There are several reasons for this. Firstly, youngsters have a chance to learn what they see as important, resulting in high motivation. Secondly, they can set goals which are congruent with their confidence levels, and thirdly, they will engage in their practice with more thought and learn to evaluate and correct errors in their performance. Through taking a more active role in learning they have the opportunity to become self learners. Since the coach will not always be present during practice or competition this is a highly desirable outcome.

Of course coaches need to help learners to take more responsibility for themselves and each other in a gradual way and their selection of coaching styles will depend upon the physical and intellectual ability of the individuals, their levels of motivation and confidence, the aim of the session and the time available.

REFERENCES

Connell, R.A. (1984) *Cognitive Explanations of Children's Motor Behaviour*, Unpublished doctoral dissertation, University of Leeds.

Connolly, K. and Jones, B. (1970) A developmental study of afferent-reafferent integration, *British Journal of Psychology*, **61**, 259–66.

Cratty, B.J., Apitzsch, E. and Bergel, R. (1973) *Dynamic Visual Actuity: A Developmental Study*. Unpublished paper, University of California, Los Angeles.

Fairweather, H. and Hutt, S.J. (1970) The development of information processing and reaction times in normal schocol children. *Bulletin of the British Psychological Society*, **23**, 61.

Goode, S. and Magill, R.A. (1986) The contextual interference effects in learning three badminton serves. *Research Quarterly for Exercise and Sport*, **57**, 308–14.

Hay, L. (1979) Spatial–temporal analysis of movements in children: motor programs versus feedback in the development of reaching. *Journal of Motor Behaviour*, **11**, 189–200.

Kahneman, D. (1973) *Attention and Effort*, Prentice Hall, New Jersey.

Keogh, J. and Sugden, D.A. (1985) *Movement Skill Development*, Macmillan, New York.

Kerr, R. and Booth, B. (1978) Specific and varied practice of motor skill. *Perceptual and Motor Skills*, **46**, 395–401.

Lee, T.D. (1988) Testing for motor learning: a focus on transfer-appropriate processing, in *Complex Motor Behaviour: The Motor-Action Controversy*, (eds O.G. Meijer and K. Roth), Elsevier Science, Amsterdam, pp. 201–15.

McPherson, S.L. (1989) *Development of Children's Expertise in Tennis: Knowledge Structure of Sport Performance*. Unpublished doctoral dissertation, Louisiana State University, Baton Rouge.

Mosston, M. and Ashworth, S. (1986) *Teaching Physical Education*, 3rd edn, Merrill Publishing Company, Columbus.

Schmidt, R.A. (1976) A schema theory of discrete motor learning. *Psychological Review*, **82**, 225–60.

Shapiro, D.C. and Schmidt, R.A. (1982) The schema theory: recent evidence and developmental implications, in *The Development of Movement Control and Coordination*, (eds J.A.S. Kelso and J.E. Clark), Wiley, New York, pp. 113–50.

Shea, C.H., Kohl, R. and Indermill, C. (1990) Contextual interference: contributions of practice. *Acta Psychologica*, **73**, 145–57.

Sugden, D.A. (1980) Developmental strategies in motor and visual motor STM, *Perceptual and Motor Skills*, **51**, 146.

Thomas, J.R. and Thomas, K.T. (1988) Development of gender differences in physical activity, *Quest*, **40**; 3, 219–29.

Witkin, H.A., Lewis, H., Hertzman, M., Machover, K., Messner P. and Warner, S. (1954) Personality through perception, Harper Collins, New York.

Growing up in sport   8

Martin Lee

SUMMARY

This chapter deals with psychosocial development of children and how it affects their perceptions of and participation in sport. Personal and social development are identified as two important elements of the process of children's progress to adulthood. The idea of how people see themselves, self-concept, is the central focus of the chapter and the way in which children use different sorts of information to describe and evaluate themselves in a sport situation is explained. The development of mature social behaviour is a critical part of being able to take part in many sports, especially games, and the way in which children learn the rules and roles of groups is explained in order to help coaches understand the difficulties faced by children when they first begin to play games. Finally I make a few suggestions for how coaches can reduce the demands on children in group situtations.

8.1 INTRODUCTION

Earlier chapters in this section have dealt with ways in which children change in their physical characteristics, their response to exercise, and learn to control movements. This chapter will show how they come to understand themselves and relate to others in social situations. This is known as psychosocial development.

An understanding of psychosocial development is important for a number of reasons. Firstly, it provides the basis for understanding how and why children are likely to react in different situations. Secondly, it helps the understanding of the psychological demands that sport places on participants, adults or children, and its powerful psychological effects on them. Thirdly, it helps coaches to become more aware of the effects of their own behaviour on the children they coach.

Sport plays a big part in the lives of many children, particularly between about ten and 15 years of age in Britain, and a study in Australia indicates that 64% of young people between 13 and 18 take part in sport (Australian Sports Commission, 1991). It is also prominent in society and for individuals it is made more or less important by the interest shown by their families. To the extent that it is important to them it provides children with personal challenges and opportunities to assess their capabilities; their success affects their self-esteem, and a variety of attitudes, values and beliefs. For those children for whom sport plays a significant role, it can have a profound effect on how they view themselves. Conversely, the way in which children perceive themselves may have a significant effect upon their participation in sport (Australian Sports Commission, 1991; Weiss et al., 1990). The Australian study revealed clearly that low perceived ability, or physical self-esteem, is a major contributor to non-participation. This was frequently brought about by the comments and judgements of coaches, which caused children to drop out. Children's sports experiences are affected very much by the expectations and reactions of those around them: parents, teachers, coaches and other children. What coaches do and say has powerful effects upon children's self-perceptions and their psychological responses (Horn, 1987; Smith et al., 1979).

8.2 PSYCHOSOCIAL DEVELOPMENT

The course of development from childhood to adulthood is long and arduous, particularly so for parents perhaps! The process is of primary interest to psychologists and is known as psychosocial development. It involves learning to integrate in a social world in which individuals are able to establish productive relationships with others. The eminent child psychologist Jean Piaget considered that a crucial phase of the process occurs in middle childhood, a time when children are likely to be introduced to sport (Smith and Cowie, 1988).

There are two elements of psychosocial development to consider: that concerned with individuals learning to understand themselves and that concerned with interpersonal relationships, though this separation is probably more a matter of convenience than anything else. The first describes how children come to see themselves, their self-concept, and, perhaps more importantly, to evaluate themselves, their self-esteem. The second shows how children learn to respond appropriately to the demands of others, deal with increasingly complex social situations, and become independent while being able to co-operate effectively.

8.2.1 PERSONAL DEVELOPMENT

One of the special attributes of being human is the ability to reflect upon ourselves as we would think about another person; we are able to become the objects of our own thoughts. In effect there is an 'I' which thinks about a 'me' which can be referred to as the self-concept. Essentially the self-concept is a set of attitudes towards a particular object, oneself. Therefore it has the usual components of attitudes. First, there is a cognitive component, what we know or believe about ourselves; second, there is an affective component, how we evaluate and feel about that knowledge, usually referred to as self-esteem; and finally a behavioural component, how we are likely to act as a consequence. The peculiar quality of the self attitude (self-concept) is that it is about an object which only one person knows. While others know and can have feelings about us as another person, only we can know and have feelings about our own selves. An important process in psychosocial development may be the progressive differentiation of self, in which sports experiences may play an important role.

The development of the self-concept is important because it provides a framework by which children interpret their experiences, structure their behaviour, and create expectations about what they expect to happen to them. The way in which people look at the world depends upon their background and their past experience (Berger and Luckmann, 1963). This means that we all live in different worlds which we construct for ourselves. Although the events we see may be common, the way in which we interpret them differs. For example, the way in which we see decisions made by officials may depend upon how the contest is going at the time; sometimes we feel very hard done by, at others the same decision might be considered quite just. Moreover, our perceptions will be affected by the relationship we have to the players or teams. Identification with sports teams can result in biased interpretation of events on the field in favour of one's own team (e.g. Hastorf and Cantril, 1954).

The self-concept also acts as an inner filter which lets through certain sorts of information and shuts out, or rationalizes, others. We frequently accept the good things about ourselves and ignore the bad things and consequently maintain a desirable self-image. This is known as a self-serving bias. As children gradually create a more clearly defined picture of themselves they may filter out information which doesn't fit it. If they have a good self-image they may ignore or deny negative comments about themselves and, just as important, the reverse may be true. This can have profound effects on their experiences and expectations of success and failure; they may see themselves habitually as 'winners' or 'losers' (see Chapter 10 for further discussion).

Structure of self-concept

That part of the self which we call 'I' is the subject, or doer, which thinks about the object, the 'me' (William James's discriminated aspects). Children begin to learn from birth the distinction between themselves and the world around them and then they become aware of their own peculiar qualities; the 'I' gradually comes to know more about 'me'. The relationships between the different parts of the self are shown in Figure 8.1.

The model shows that 'me' can be thought to have two parts: each person has a picture of themselves, a self-image, to which he or she attributes more or less value, self-esteem. Of course, pictures have different parts, some of which may be good, others less so. The self-image is the same. So children can think well of themselves in some things they do and not so well in others. Research has shown that children assess their competence both in general and in physical, social and cognitive skills in particular (Harter, 1978, 1981). Hence, they might feel very good in sport but inadequate in school or with other children. Further, the model also draws attention to the distinction between what we think we are, what we would like to be, and what we think other people think we are. Differences between these perspectives can result in changes in behaviour or perceptions which bring them closer together. For example, a child whose ideal is to be a national champion but who sees himself as merely competent may be motivated to practise and train hard to bring the two aspects of self together. Conversely, if he makes little progress or finds that the competition is greater than he thought it would be, he may change the ideal and drop out of the sport.

Recent research in motivation and self-concept has focused on competence. Hence children's self-evaluations could be expected to vary according to fluctuations in performance. What is not well known is the degree to which adequacy in sport generalizes to other areas of children's experience. In contrast to the focus of self-esteem another aspect of self, self-acceptance, is considered to be independent of competence. Hence it is less susceptible to the inevitable fluctuations of sports performance and may provide the basis for a more stable self-concept (Waite et al., 1990). It may be important for coaches and others to encourage children to realize their potential but also to accept themselves as they are rather than as they would like to be. Making realistic assessments of ability is an important skill for coaches and one which is frequently set aside!

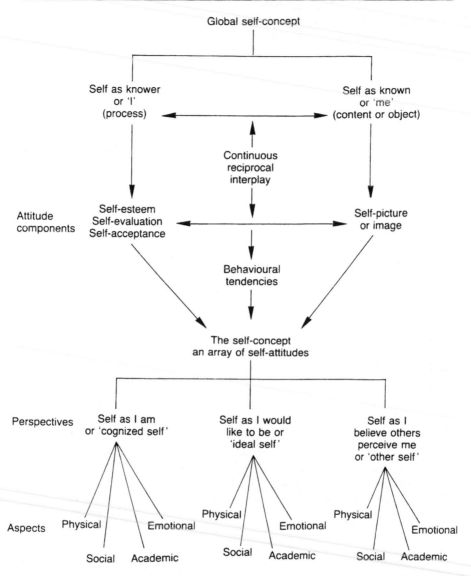

Fig. 8.1 The structure of self-concept (reproduced from Burns (1982) by kind permission of the publishers)

Development of self-concept

Children develop a self-image initially through their physical characteristics, then through what they can do and what other people say about them. When they become aware of themselves as distinct from others they tend to describe themselves by simple external features and physical characteristics but as they get older they use their achievements and more sophisticated non-objective features such as psychological characteristics, personal attributes and relationships (Burns, 1982).

Body image

The picture children have of their bodies and evaluations of them is their body image. Unfortunately these are often equated to stereotypical body builds and the personality associated with them. Children who are muscular may be thought of as active, aggressive, outgoing and being leaders; tall, thin children as quiet, nervous and shy; fat children as lazy, jovial, non-athletic. Naturally, such ideas are often inaccurate and cause both embarrassment and frustration, but they still influence children's feelings about themselves.

Performance

When children learn skills they are able to describe themselves in terms of their competence. Initially they are concerned with simply being able to do certain things; kick a ball, do a cartwheel and so on. During the primary school years, say six to ten, abilities in particular activities become more important elements of self-description. Children begin to learn sports-related skills, they become more aware of other children and they start to evaluate their ability by comparison with them. In our society being 'good at games' is highly valued and may provide children with status and influence among peers. It has been shown that among children aged eight to 13 who took part a summer sports camp those who perceived themselves as being good at sport were more successful in social relations and better accepted by others (Weiss and Duncan, 1992). Perhaps more importantly, success in sport has been shown to be an important determinant of status in adolescent subcultures in general (Coleman, 1961; Eitzen, 1979).

Significant others

Quite clearly information from other people is important in fashioning the way in which children see themselves. The comments of those who are most important in their lives, significant others, have most effect on children's feelings about themselves and even casual remarks can have a great impact. Significant others include the family, teachers, coaches, and other children.

(a) *The family*   The family is initially the most important influence on children. Parents, brothers and sisters are all closely concerned with each other and continually give messages about the competence and worth of growing children. The more accepting, warm and interested parents are towards their children the more confident and positive they will become.

(b) *Coaches* Coaches and teachers become influential as children move away from home and develop outside interests. If children are interested in sport then coaches assume a very important role and at times they can become just as important in children's lives as parents.

Remember that coaches are both instructors and judges and hence affect both self-image and self-esteem. It is sometimes difficult to distinguish between teaching and evaluating and it is important to give information, or instruction, in a non-judgemental way. Yet children respond better to being taught in a way which does not 'put them down' or suggest that they are fools because they have made a mistake.

(c) *Peers* The role of other children in influencing self-perceptions comes about through comparison and through direct evaluation. In addition to comparing the outcomes of what they do children also listen to the comments made about them by other children. These comments can have great impact and observant adults know that children can be very cruel.

Comparing self with others

The comparison of one's own performance with that of others is a major process in the assessment of self-worth. Research indicates that children begin spontaneously to compare themselves to others by about six or seven and that the tendency to do so grows to a peak at about 11 or 12 (Toda *et al.*, 1978; Weiss, 1987). The comparison process gives rise to a pecking order of competence which becomes more clearly differentiated into distinct areas of achievement as the children grow older.

Quite clearly the selection of appropriate people to compare oneself with affects the outcomes of the comparison. Children who compare themselves with others who are less able may get an inflated sense of ability; those who compare themselves too soon with others who are much better may become so deflated that they may feel like giving up their sport. Helping children to select the most appropriate reference group is an important coaching function which enables children to assess themselves realistically while maintaining motivation.

How children use different sources of information

Adults can assess their competence at a task not only by comparing themselves with others but also by using other criteria and sorts of

Table 8.1 Sources of evaluation used in assessing competence

Internal	External
Effort exerted	Match outcome
Skill improvement	Feedback from others
Ease of learning	(a) Adults
	(b) Peers
	Peer comparison

Derived from Horn and Hasbrook, 1987

information. Children are limited in their ability to do this and, consequently, may become unduly depressed or elated about their performance. The sources of information which children use to assess their own competence are presented in Table 8.1.

In essence the sort of information that children use changes according to their age and how independent they are. The information can come from within themselves (effort exerted, improving skill, and ease of learning new skills) or from external sources such as the outcome of the contest and feedback from others. Pre-school children mostly use achievement and parental approval. When they go to school they like to maximize the differences between themselves and others and do this by trying to get more rewards, an external criterion. As they progress they use information from a wider variety of sources, tending to depend mostly on external results and approval, though these may be applied inconsistently. It is not until late childhood at about 11 or 12 that they see that they have more control over their own destiny and shift to standards that they set for themselves. This becomes more normal during adolescence, but it is not until late adolescence that they are able to balance external and internal sources to evaluate themselves realistically (Horn and Hasbrook, 1987).

At Bedford we have begun to look at the sorts of information used by children to evaluate themselves in relation to self-esteem. In a preliminary study one of my students measured the perceived competence of a group of club swimmers between eight and 15 years of age. Swimmers who scored high or low were asked to complete a questionnaire which elicited information about what information they used to assess themselves. The major finding was that all the swimmers used more internal sources than external, but those with high levels of self-esteem were significantly less reliant on external sources than those of low self-esteem (Christensen, 1991). This suggests that less confident children rely on coaches to give feedback about their competence, while those who are more confident are more able to make their own assessment. However, all the swimmers involved could be described as high flyers, yet they still use all the information available. It may be that children who perceive themselves as less competent by virtue of experience and attainment may be more reliant on information given by the results of a contest and comments from coaches, parents and peers than was the case with these swimmers.

So what should coaches do? They can help young athletes to develop a more realistic view of their progress and abilities. Some children may over- or under-rate their efforts because they concentrate on results and do not look at their performance. If they over-rate their ability they may suffer a later setback because they have used limited sources of evaluation, e.g. comparing with less able children, and have not listened to the comments of experienced observers. They are not necessarily being obtuse, they may simply be at that particular stage. They need patient help to get to a more mature assessment of their own competence. This means learning to accept and integrate information from different sources; to keep results in perspective; to focus on performance; and to use the comments of others constructively.

8.2.2   SOCIAL DEVELOPMENT

The development of social behaviour, the way in which children relate to others around them, is a long and complex process which can become particularly difficult during adolescence. It is important to coaches because they work with groups of children. Although some concern has been expressed that the demands of intensive training may cause young athletes to become rather isolated (Rowley, 1988), a study of elite young athletes in England showed that most of those involved described themselves as having good friends and being popular (The Sports Council, 1992). However, it may be that friendships are restricted to those who share the sport involvement.

Problems of working in groups

Most sports, whether team sports or not, demand the co-operation of individuals in groups. This means that they must be capable of mutual assistance and support and coaches are faced with three tasks. First, they must keep the group moving towards a common goal. Second, they must use the abilities and personalities of the individual members most productively. Third, they must look after the welfare and progress of individuals. Sometimes these requirements conflict and cause strains within the group. For example, team members may have different goals and want to go their own way; they may have to work, or play, with others they don't like, or have to play out of position; and helping individuals may mean encouraging them to leave the club and go to another, thereby weakening the team. We know that children have different motives for doing sport (see Chapter 9); some do like to compete and win, others participate for the companionship that sports provides. In order for children to realize their different motives it may be necessary to accommodate the needs of other children. Thus a rugby player who is committed to excellence may need to accommodate the needs and attitudes of others in the team who have different ambitions; it is hard to play rugby alone. Different goals such as those among group members inevitably demand a degree of negotiation and accommodation if the group is to be successful in meeting both individual and communal goals.

Self-concept and group affiliation

I have already described how children's self-concept grows from their interaction with other people and, not unnaturally, the groups and teams to which they belong are part of that process. Groups become a part of our identity and when the group's activities are important to us then it becomes a more important part of that identity (Hogg and Abrams, 1988). So if children are very interested in, say, football then being a member of the local football team is likely to be an important ambition and they will be proud to describe themselves as members of the team or club. A good example of social identity is the habit that many children have of expressing their loyalty to particular sports teams by wearing their colours. As children enter adolescence they may enter a gang culture which has a strong influence on their identity. Membership of sports teams may perform a similar function, particularly if the sport is important to them. This is not necessarily restricted to competent performers. You may know cases of children for whom the sport is important but who are not very good yet they still come to practice and, perhaps, play a role in helping run the club. They are establishing a social identity as club members and can be very helpful, and encouraging their input can be valuable both to them and to the club.

Pattern of social development

During early childhood, until about five years old, children are self-centred; they do not readily distinguish self and others and they expect other people to adapt to their needs. It is not easy for them to play co-operatively and, typically, they play alongside rather than with each other. Because of this it is very difficult for them to enter into team activities because they do not understand co-operative behaviour.

Between six and nine, children form small friendship groups which gradually become more enduring. They may play in a world of make-believe and act out different parts, taking a role. Thus they learn what is expected of those roles without having to create them. Peers also become more influential and they make more comparisons with each other; in short, they compete. It is a period of 'Let's see who is best'. The competition is immediate in that it happens in a particular event and time; it takes the form of pursuing rewards at the expense of others, a sort of 'one-upmanship' in which it is important to have more than other children. At this time you may find it difficult, and inappropriate, to channel children toward the more long term goals normally associated with sport.

During late childhood, between ten and 12 or 13, friends play a bigger part in children's lives and they may do sport because their friends do. They are better able to understand the demands of teamwork and become a part of the team, rather than merely acting out a role. They are more sophisticated in their reasoning but are only able to assimilate fully the causes of competitive results towards the end of this period (Passer, 1986).

As children move into adolescence they form strong ties with peer groups which have a strong influence on their values, attitudes and behaviour which may conflict with adult expectations. They also provide a major source of information by which adolescents evaluate themselves. On the positive side adolescents can learn to work together very effectively, creating roles for themselves, and real teamwork is possible. They are now mature enough to make more realistic assessments of performance and results and more able to enter fully into the adult competitive world.

Sports teams as working groups

Members of sports teams have to work together in the same ways as members of other groups, such as working groups and families! They need to agree about what they are trying to achieve, how to best use the resources (e.g. abilities) available to them, to understand their place in the team, and to understand the social patterns within the team. It is also important that their contribution to the team is recognized by the coach and other members.

Understanding the ways in which people in the team interact means that the players must know both the rules of the game and the job that everyone else is required to do. This puts quite sophisticated demands on children as they learn to play games and their ability to meet them depends upon their cognitive and social development. Various observers of child development (e.g. Erikson, Piaget, Smilansky) have concluded that children move gradually towards games with established, public rules which are accommodated by about the age of seven (Smith and Cowie, 1988). This observation means that those who organize sport for children should understand the psychological demands of sport, as opposed to games, on those children and not expect them to play as adults. This applies particularly to understanding the demands of the rules of the sports and the roles which different participants are required to play in them.

Rules

The rules of a sport are important because they not only prescribe the framework within which the game is played, they also determine the skills of the sport. In most cases the rules are laid down to accommodate adults and depend upon mature levels of cognitive development. The more complex the rules the less likely it is that children will be able to follow them. Take for example the game of rugby. Here the object is to get the ball forward while being allowed only to throw it backward. Children who have started playing informal invasion games not unnaturally assume that to move a ball forward it is OK to throw or kick it in that direction. Yet in rugby this is not allowed, it can only go backward and, what is more, while you are in front of the ball you cannot take any further part in the game! Small wonder that some children become a little confused as to what to do and don't always stay behind the ball! Fortunately recent changes in the way rugby is introduced to children have helped overcome this problem (see Chapter 19).

Roles

When children do sports, particularly team games, they have to take different roles in those teams, each of which contributes to the team effort. These roles are determined by the accepted structure of the team and tactical demands of the game, not necessarily by the formal rules. For example, there is a variety of formations used in football and the evolution of positions in rugby has occurred over a long time and can still change. The formation of the team means that players in each position have specific jobs to do. While this may seem obvious it may not be so readily recognized that in order to carry out their own job properly every player must have a good understanding of the job associated with every other position and what everyone else is likely to do in a given situation; they must be able to take the role of the others

(Mead, 1934). The more involved the demands of the sport and the more players there are, the more difficult this is. It is not surprising that early efforts at team sports result in children clustering around the ball, like a beehive. To reduce the psychological demands of the game the number of players should be reduced to the extent that children can understand the roles required and the likely outcomes of their, and others', actions. It also helps if children play in a variety of positions in a team so that they have to develop an understanding of different roles. Many sports have already produced mini versions of the adult game, but coaches should be personally aware of the difficulties faced by children, through no fault of their own, and be able to modify their practices accordingly.

Making team play easier

To overcome the problems that beginners face it helps to adapt the activity to the level of cognitive and social development of the children. Here are some simple guidelines:

1. Modify the rules to make the game easier and so that they are easily understood and applied.
2. Keep the numbers as small as possible; it is easier for children to see what they and everybody else should do.
3. Children learn best by doing, so put them in different positions, giving different roles, to help them to understand their job in relation to others.
4. Start by using simple small-sided situations which only give one or two options, then gradually increase the demands on players by giving opportunities for more complicated decision making and integration as they become more able to cope.

8.3   CONCLUSION

This account of psychosocial development may have given some insights as to why young children can excel in individual sports such as gymnastics, iceskating, swimming and why success in team games comes later. Team games demand a degree of social maturity that is not required for individual sports. Furthermore, children are only ready for competitive sport when they are able to cope with the demands of the situation. Before placing children in formal competitions coaches and parents should recognize the pressures on psychological as well as physical capacities. While there can be no hard or fast rules the results of extensive experience in examining children's sport have led Jay Coakley, of the University of Colorado, to conclude that formal sport competition is not appropriate for children before they are eight years old because of their limited ability to assume different roles and understand what competition is really about. Until this age the emphasis should be on skill development and until about 12 it should be balanced with the *gradual* introduction of rules, more complicated roles, and strategies. When children reach their teens it is more realistic to introduce formal competition because they are more fully able to absorb the complex relationships involved (Coakley, 1986). Of course there are, increasingly, examples of precocious child athletes but there are also notable examples of those who have suffered because of it, and most coaches deal with those children for whom membership of the sporting elite is not a possibility and for whom youthful sporting experiences are meaningful in themselves, not as a passport to a career.

The psychological development of children has many facets. The ability to reason, the ability to control movements, the dawning of self-knowledge, the ability to establish and maintain relationships, and learning to control emotions are all part of growing up. They also contribute to children's achievement and satisfaction in sports. Hence an understanding of them, however brief, can only increase coaches' capacity for providing satisfying sports experiences for those in their care. This chapter provides the basis for coaches to get to know the personal and social characteristics of their athletes and not to restrict themselves to assessing their physical features and skill when advising them either in the short term or the long term.

REFERENCES

Australian Sports Commission (1991) *Sport for Young Australians: A Summary of Market Research Findings*, Australian Sports Commission, Canberra.

Berger, P.T. and Luckmann, T. (1963) *The Social Construction of Reality*, Archer, Garden City, NY.

Burns, R.B. (1982) *Self-concept Development and Education*, Holt, Rhinehart & Winston, Eastbourne.

Christensen, N. (1991) *Effects of Age, Gender, and Self-esteem on Children's Achievement in Sport*. Unpublished bachelor's dissertation, Department of Human Performance, Bedford College of Higher Education, Bedford, England.

Coakley, J. (1986) When should children begin competing? A sociological perspective, in *Sport for Children and Youths, Proceedings of the 1984 Olympic Congress*, (eds M.R. Weiss and D. Gould), Human Kinetics, Champaign, IL.

Coleman, J.S. (1961) *The Adolescent Society*, Collier-Macmillan, London.

Eitzen, D.S. (1979) Athletics in the status system of male adolescents: a replication of Coleman's *The Adolescent Society*, in *Sport Sociology: Contemporary Themes*, 2nd edn, (eds A. Yiannakis, T. McIntyre, M. Melnick and D. Hart), Kendall/Hunt, Dubuque, IA.

Harter, S. (1978) Effectance motivation reconsidered. *Human Development*, **21**, 34–64.

Harter, S. (1981) A model of intrinsic mastery motivation in children: individual differences and developmental change, in *Minnesota Symposium on Child Psychology: Vol. 14*, (ed W.A. Collins), Erlbaum, Hillsdale, NJ, pp. 215–55.

Hastorf, A.H. and Cantril, H. (1954) They saw a game: a case study. *Journal of Abnormal and Social Psychology*, 19, 129–34.

Hogg, M. and Abrams, D. (1988) *Social Identification: A Social Psychology of Intergroup Relations*, Routledge, London.

Horn, T.S. (1987) The influence of teacher-coach behaviour on the psychological development of children, in *Advances in Paediatric Sports Sciences: Vol. 2 Behavioral Issues*, (eds D. Gould and M.R. Weiss), Human Kinetics, Champaign, IL.

Horn, T.S. and Hasbrook, C. (1987) Psychological characteristics and the criteria children use for self-evaluation. *Journal of Sport Psychology*, 9(3), 200–21.

Mead, G.H. (1934) *Mind, Self, and Society*, University of Chicago Press, Chicago.

Passer, M. (1986) When should children begin competing? A psychological perspective, in *Sport for Children and Youths: Proceedings of the 1984 Olympic Congress*, (eds M.R. Weiss and D. Gould), Human Kinetics, Champaign, IL.

Rowley, S. (1988) *Preliminary Findings of the Training of Young Athletes (TOYA) Project*. Keynote paper presented at the Student Conference of the British Association of Sports Sciences, Bedford, England.

Smith, P.K. and Cowie, H. (1988) *Understanding Children's Development*, Blackwell, Oxford.

Smith, R.E., Smoll, F.L. and Curtis, B. (1979) Coach effectiveness training: a cognitive behavioral approach to enhancing relationship skills in youth sport coaches. *Journal of Sport Psychology*, 1(1), 59–74.

Sports Council (1992) *Training of Young Athletes Study: TOYA and Lifestyle*, The Sports Council, London.

Toda, M., Shinotsuka, H., McClintock, C.G. and Stech, F.J. (1978) Development of competitive behaviour as a function of culture, age, and social comparison. *Journal of Personality and Social Psychology*, 36, 825–39.

Waite, B.T., Gansneder, B. and Rotella, R. (1990) A sport specific measure of self-acceptance. *Journal of Sport and Exercise Psychology*, 12(3), 264–79.

Weiss, M.R. (1987) Self-esteem and achievement in children's sport and physical activity, in *Advances in Paediatric Sports Sciences: Vol. 2 Behavioral issues*, (eds D. Gould and M.R. Weiss), Human Kinetics, Champaign, IL.

Weiss, M.R. and Duncan, S.C. (1992) The relationship between physical competence and peer acceptance in the context of children's sport. *Journal of Sport and Exercise Psychology*, 14(2), 177–91.

Weiss, M.R., McAuley, E., Ebbeck, V. and Wiese, D.M. (1990) Self-esteem and causal attributions for children's physical and social competence in sport. *Journal of Sport and Exercise Psychology*, 12(1), 21–36.

FURTHER READING

Lee, M.J. (1987) *Psychological Readiness of Children for Competitive Sport*. Invited paper presented at the Second International Congress of the British Association of National Coaches: The Growing Child in Competitive Sport. Cardiff, December 4th–8th.

PART THREE
Important Psychological Aspects of Children's Participation in Sport

In Part Three some important topics in the psychology of sports participation for children are discussed. These topics have been selected to give coaches a more complete picture of the ways in which children actually experience taking part. They are concerned with the motives which children have for taking part in the first place, perceptions of the processes of success and failure, causes and manifestations of anxiety, and with helping children set suitable goals for themselves. The reason for selecting these topics is to alert coaches to individual differences in children's experience of sport which may provide insights into how to promote, maintain and deal with problems of interest and motivation which may arise.

One of the major difficulties faced by coaches, and one which may not be immediately evident, is that their motives and goals may be very different from those of the children they coach. Jean Whitehead has made an extensive study of what children in Britain want to achieve in sport. In Chapter 9 she discusses what success means to different children and outlines the main types of goals that they set for themselves. In distinguishing between different types of goals Dr Whitehead shows how coaches and parents can affect children's perceptions of their success by the ways in which they direct their judgements. The importance of coaches in guiding children to set appropriate goals is made very clear. Finally Dr Whitehead shows the relationship between why children drop out and the goals they set for themselves.

Stuart Biddle has made a special study of the reasons people give for the success or failure of their attempts to achieve their targets. In his chapter he applies his expertise to explaining children's reaction to winning and losing. After an event, particularly after losing, it is common to ask 'Why did I win/lose?'. Dr Biddle explains how children change in their ability to assess the causes and goes on to discuss the important idea that they may actually learn to become 'helpless' when they find that whatever they do doesn't appear to affect their success. Finally he offers advice to coaches on helping children to become realistic in their assessments and so make it easier for them to accept both their successes and failures.

Probably the most frequently discussed issue in children's sport is the distress which children may experience in sport. While this concern should not get out of proportion (it may well be no worse than in other areas of children's lives such as music or doing examinations), it does demand the attention of coaches and parents. Stephen Rowley, of the Sports Council's Training of Young Athletes project, first explains the different types of anxiety which children may suffer and how children differ in their susceptibility to anxiety provoking situations. He goes on to outline causes of performance anxiety and then suggests how coaches can help children cope with anxiety caused by the pressures of competition.

In Chapter 9 Jean Whitehead draws attention to the different explanations of children's sense of achievement in sport and includes reference to the importance of goal setting. Rod Thorpe develops this and gives both a rational basis and practical advice on how to help children set realistic and challenging targets for themselves. He explains the principles of goal setting as a motivational strategy and shows how coaches can incorporate it into a teaching and training strategy in a way which recognizes the individual characteristics of different children.

Why children choose to do sport – or stop

9

Jean Whitehead

SUMMARY

This chapter is about children's motivation in sport. It summarizes their reasons for participating or stopping, then focuses on their achievement goals. The first part is about what children think success is. It outlines the great variety in their views, then examines the most common goals in more detail and considers how they can be met. It shows how some kinds of goals make it easier to feel successful than others, and it explains how goals change with age, and how boys and girls tend to choose different kinds of goals. The second part is about why children leave sport. It describes how dropping out is linked with different types of goal, then explains how children's judgements about their ability change, how goals have different time scales, and how sport becomes less attractive than other activities. A general recommendation is that coaches encourage children to set task mastery or process goals, to improve their feelings of success.

9.1 INTRODUCTION

Research generally shows that children participate in sport in order to have fun, improve skills, belong to a group, be successful and gain recognition, get fitter, and find excitement. Reasons for withdrawing from sport include having other things to do, boredom, lack of success, too much pressure, loss of interest, friends leaving, expense, injury, work, and problems with facilities or support.

These results suggest that it isn't a simple matter to understand children's motivation in sport. Children have many different reasons for the things they do, and some of their reasons change from day to day. Most importantly, children don't think like adults. For example, their capacity to judge their own ability develops very slowly, so they cannot have clear expectations about how successful they may be in competition. Sometimes children drop out of sport because they do not feel successful in just the way they would like to, and they do not see any way to change the situation. If we are to help, we must first know what success means to them.

9.2 WHAT SUCCESS MEANS TO CHILDREN

9.2.1 A GREAT VARIETY OF VIEWS

I have asked over 3000 children aged nine to 16 years to describe a time when they felt successful in sport. Here are some replies from primary school children.

> I did my first back dive ever in front of my brother and my dad.
> We were practising and I was the only one who could do it.
> I raised £59 for the British Heart Foundation and swam 50 lengths.
> I passed my gymnastics badge.
> When I scored my first goal for cubs because it was a good goal.
> I moved out of the little pool into the big pool.
> I scored 2 goals for my team and we won things for my school.
> I swam a length with nobody helping me.
> I practised and practised then one day I did it.
> I swam underwater for nearly a width and I was happy because the
> instructor said 'You went miles!'

These answers show that children don't see winning as the only kind of success. Indeed, they can even be unhappy winners if they don't think they played well, or happy losers if they know their opponent was very strong. One girl described a successful moment like this: 'It was a competition and I came second and the girl who won was brilliant'.

I found that children had about 16 major views of success that didn't overlap with each other. These views varied somewhat in different age groups, but the 13 most general ones are shown in Table 9.1. This table shows that children have a diversity of reasons for taking part in sport. If coaches understand the wide variety in children's motives and have time to get to know their athletes, it can help them to select a suitable approach for coaching a particular child in a one-to-one situation. For example, a child who is keen to improve can be set some specific goals and asked to keep a training diary to record progress towards each one.

When a coach is working with large groups for short periods it is not possible to adapt to what each child needs. It is then more useful to

Table 9.1 Children's major reasons for feeling successful

Showing superior ability
Feeling pride in performance
Pleasing other people
Surpassing own limits
Being needed by others
Defeating others
Achieving something independently
Having fun
A feeling of adventure
Improving
Understanding something important
Being noticed
Competing fairly

know which goals are most common, so that programmes can be planned to suit the majority of children.

9.2.2   SIX COMMON GOALS

I shall focus on six main goals found in my research (Whitehead, 1990a): demonstrating ability, task mastery, social approval, victory, breakthrough, and teamwork. The first three goals apply to all situations in life when it is important to perform well, for example in examinations and auditions as well as in sport. They were suggested in 1980 by two psychologists in the United States, Martin Maehr and John Nicholls, who had studied the contrasting views of success held by people in different countries and who thought that these three goals might be common worldwide. Glyn Roberts has written about two of these goals in Chapter 1. Martha Ewing (1981), one of his students, was the first to find these goals in school sport.

Demonstrating ability

The aim here is to demonstrate high ability and avoid exposing low ability. Children who have this goal may take part in events when they expect to do well, but try to avoid events in which they expect to do poorly, and drop out when things begin to go wrong. They judge their ability by comparison with other children but not necessarily by direct competition with them.

Task mastery

Children with this goal do not think about other people. Success for them is in mastering the skills for their own sake. They may become so involved in what they are doing that they lose track of time. They don't avoid tough competition because they have no worry about comparison with others. This goal is particularly important in young children who are learning to master their environment.

Social approval

With this goal, children will try to do whatever they think will please people. They usually put out great effort because they think praise is earned simply by trying hard. Strictly speaking, social approval is not an achievement goal because it may not be given for good performance. For example, children can earn praise by helping with kit. However, it is common in competitive conditions. Children who work to win because they think winning is what pleases their coach or parents have different motives from those who want to win to show their ability.

The second three goals are linked in some ways to the first three, but are more specific to sport or children. They came out clearly in the reasons that children gave me for feeling successful in sport.

Victory

The focus here is on doing better than others in direct competition with them, either by winning or by defeating an important rival or capable opponent. It differs from simply showing ability and is generally stronger in boys than girls.

Breakthrough

Success here is the feeling of breaking frontiers to do something that seemed impossible or is quite new in itself, or finding unexpected inner qualities. It is like task mastery because no one else is involved, but the experience is quite different in quality from anything that has gone before. It is important in children and can link with a feeling of adventure.

Teamwork

Children with this goal emphasize working well in a team, in contrast to achieving something alone. There is a link with the approval motive but the focus is on helping others, not simply impressing them. The teamwork goal fits sport achievement more than school examinations, and it is more important in team sports than individual sports.

9.2.3 HELPING TO MEET THE GOALS

Coaches who understand these goals can help children in at least two ways. First they can include different activities in their programmes to meet the contrasting goals. Here are some examples:

Ability   Ask children to demonstrate their skills to others.
Mastery   Give attention to improving specific skills.
Approval   Praise different aspects of performance and attitude.
Victory   Provide graded or handicapped competition to enable all to win.
Breakthrough   Introduce exciting new activities, and encourage children not to give up.
Teamwork   Help players to co-operate both on and off the field.

A second way for coaches to help is to recognize how the type of goal can restrict children's experience of success, and to help them change to a different type in order to be more successful. This is explained below.

9.2.4 HOW GOAL TYPES LIMIT CHILDREN'S SUCCESS

Table 9.2 shows how the six goals fall into three pairs with contrasting characteristics. These three types of goal actually control how easily children can feel successful.

Outcome goals focus on the results of a competition (e.g. winning) so success depends partly on the opponents. With these goals a child might give maximum effort, exceed previous performances and still fail – because the opposition is better. In contrast, *process goals* focus on what children actually do when performing their own activities (e.g. becoming more consistent in one aspect of their technique) so success is largely under their own control. If process goals are well set by coaches, children can feel some success even when they lose. For

Table 9.2 Types of goals

Individual goals	Common features	Type of goal
Demonstrating ability Victory	Superiority over others	OUTCOME GOAL
Task mastery Breakthrough	Personal progress	PROCESS GOAL
Social approval Teamwork	Pleasing others	APPROVAL GOAL

example, hockey defenders can improve their ability to reposition quickly when possession of the ball is lost. Lastly, *approval goals* are like outcome goals because they place success partly in the hands of other people. For example, even if a child wins, he or she may feel no success if a coach or parent has unrealistically high goals and wanted a better result.

In effect, when children try to beat others or please others, success is out of their control. This makes it important for coaches to include some process goals in their sessions so that everyone can feel some success if they try hard. Process goals are targets for improving the way in which an activity is performed. They can be achieved by individual effort and don't depend on the performance of anyone else. In interactive team sports, however, process goals can also be set to improve team co-operation.

Most children have elements of all these goals, although their importance varies on different occasions. A sensitive coach can use this knowledge, not only to provide realistic praise to meet children's social approval goals, but to choose which behaviour he or she praises or rewards in order to help children set the most appropriate goals. For example, a coach who praises children for trying hard or improving the quality of their performance, not only for good results, will encourage them to set process goals rather than outcome goals.

9.2.5   HOW GOALS CHANGE WITH AGE

In a study of the most common achievement goals, I found that task mastery was most important in primary schools, but the demonstration of ability became most important in secondary schools. This is consistent with the studies that Glyn Roberts and Darren Treasure report in Chapter 1. Young children are more concerned with mastering their own environment and developing their own skills than with beating others – at least until someone tells them that it is important to win!

When I looked at some of the additional goals, I found that fun and breakthrough were important in primary school children, and motives for independence and perfection developed later. Teamwork was important by adolescence. Teenagers had clearer ideas than younger children about which actions would earn approval, and were more concerned with the views of their friends than with the views of adults.

Young children need realistic praise from others, not only to satisfy their social approval goals but also to indicate how well they are doing in meeting their other goals. For example, children are not good at judging their own ability so they rely on other people to tell them how well they are doing in mastering skills, and how they compare with other children. This places a great responsibility on coaches and parents not to set standards which are too high for a child's ability and will lead to disappointment if they cannot be met.

9.2.6   HOW GOALS DIFFER IN BOYS AND GIRLS

Some research shows that boys and girls tend to prefer different kinds of achievement goals, but the differences are not consistent in all conditions. More frequently boys are concerned with the outcomes of their performance, and girls with its quality. Martha Ewing (1981) found that teenage boys tended to expect that success would lead to external rewards, like fame and popularity, but girls viewed it more in terms of bringing self-satisfaction. Boys were generally more depressed than girls by failure. I found that victory was clearly more important to boys, and social approval to girls.

In a nutshell, this indicates that boys will generally be more attracted by competition than girls will. It suggests that some girls will even avoid sports programmes that are very competitive, although they may like the sporting activities themselves. Coaches of competitive teams will naturally have met the many girls who are exceptions to this overall tendency, but if more of the average adolescent girls are to remain in sport and experience its benefits, coaches may need to give opportunities for them to enjoy the sporting activities for their own sake without competitive pressure.

Although motives for recreational and leisure sport participation are somewhat outside the scope of this chapter, it is worth noting here that Leo Hendry (1992) at the University of Aberdeen has shown a consistent trend for adolescents to move away from organized sporting activities to casual and commercial leisure activities.

9.3   WHY CHILDREN MAY GIVE UP SPORT

In general, sport participation increases in primary and middle school years and decreases in upper school years, and boys do more sport than girls (Whitehead, 1988). This may be partly because more teams are run for boys than girls, so they have more opportunities. The lack of suitable opportunities and support to develop their talents may sometimes cause children to withdraw from sport, but their achievement goals generally have more to do with it.

9.3.1   HOW SPORT GOALS INFLUENCE SPORT PERSISTENCE

The type of goal that children have affects the length of time they may stay in sport. Martha Ewing's (1981) pioneering work showed that the continuing competitors in an American high school were more oriented towards gaining social approval than the drop-outs who were more oriented to demonstrate their ability. Other researchers, for example Joan Duda (1992), report that ability-oriented motivation is generally linked with dropping out rather than continuing in sport, although it depends also on the situation and on children's views of their ability. It is initially surprising that children who most want to do better than others would drop out of sport, but it is understandable when one recalls that most participants cannot be winners. Hence if the *only* goal that children have is to show superiority and they aren't able to do this, they may drop out. The same thing would probably happen if children had any other single goal that was not being met in sport, and this indicates the desirability of helping children to develop multiple goals.

Of course, other factors could also influence Dr Ewing's finding. In some sports it may be quicker and easier to gain approval than to show ability. In many American sports, for example, a boy who sits on the bench hoping to play can more easily gain approval for loyalty than he can show his ability! So children who seek praise may stay in sport while those who want to show ability drop out if they get little chance to play.

This suggests that dropping out is partly influenced by perceived *opportunities* to meet different kinds of goals, and that sometimes there may appear to be more opportunities in sport to meet social approval or task mastery goals than to demonstrate ability. If ability-oriented children are to stay in sport, coaches must therefore give them many opportunities to show their ability. Also children like to be part of the action, so they prefer to play and lose rather than sit out while their team wins.

However, different goals can influence withdrawal in different situations. I followed up some young sports club competitors for two years (Whitehead, 1990b) and found that the drop-outs from athletics had higher motivation to show superiority than did those who persisted, but the drop-outs from rugby had lower motivation for teamwork.

This suggests that coaches need to think what opportunities there are for different goals to be satisfied in their particular sport. Stella Wilson (1989) compared the achievement goals of international synchronized swimmers and squash players and found the teamwork goal to be relatively higher in synchronized swimmers and the victory goal to be higher in the squash players. It further suggests that the motivational climate, which Glyn Roberts wrote about in Chapter 1, varies with the sport. It also varies with the context. I found differences in the goals that led children to leave school sport and club sport – and in the middle school age group and the upper school age group. One reason for this is because children's judgement of their ability changes with age.

9.3.2   HOW CHILDREN CHANGE IN JUDGING THEIR ABILITY

John Nicholls (1989) has reported a comprehensive series of studies in which he and others have shown how children go through four stages in learning to distinguish between effort and ability as causes of their performance. In primary schools, they generally think that success comes simply from trying hard, but by secondary school they can see that effort by itself is not enough, because their ability puts a limit on their possible performance.

When they see the great importance of ability, several things may happen. If they like to show ability but don't think they have enough of it, they may drop out because they don't want others to know this or to see them fail. On the other hand, if they are keen for social approval but think that ability is the only thing that is approved of by their coaches, I suspect they may also drop out. Certainly teenagers think that coaches value ability very highly. One group who answered questionnaires for me thought that their coaches valued (1) winning or showing ability, (2) effort or trying hard, and (3) having fun. They ranked these things in the opposite order for themselves!

This withdrawal from sport because of a perceived lack of ability can restrict the potential development of an individual child, and is particularly likely to affect late developers who temporarily lack speed, power or other physical attributes when compared to their peers, but who could eventually become very good. It is therefore particularly important for coaches and parents to show that they value things other than ability.

9.3.3   HOW GOALS HAVE DIFFERENT TIME SCALES

All goals can lead to children dropping out if they are not met, but children also leave sport when their goals *are* met and some goals have shorter time scales than others. For example, if a child participates in a new sport because of curiosity about what it is like, this goal will be quickly met. If curiosity goals bring youngsters into sport they will rapidly take them out again as they seek novelty elsewhere. However, a good coach can keep curious children coming by 'keeping them guessing' about what is coming next, and including amusing new activities. In this way the children may remain long enough to develop other goals which will be more enduring.

Children's approval goals are met as long as people seem pleased with what they are doing, particularly if these people are important to them. Such goals could keep young people in sport for a life time because praise can be given by so many people for so many things – even when skills are no longer approving or if ability is low. However, children who aim to please may leave sport when important people want them to.

Mastery goals can keep youngsters in sport for years because skill learning takes time and there are always more complex skills to learn. However, mastery-oriented youngsters may lose interest if everything is too easy for them. Because they enjoy challenge they may not be happy with a very easy win, whereas a child who is oriented to demonstrate superior ability may revel in an easy win.

Outcome goals may be effective only as long as youngsters get good results, and the same thing may apply to extrinsic rewards, like prizes or badges. Deci's (1975) theory of intrinsic motivation explains that, depending on how they are used, rewards can actually reduce teenagers' own intrinsic motivation. Then when the rewards are no longer available, the activity is no longer attractive. In contrast, children who take part for the physical thrill of the activity itself may be the most persistent participants because they can't be turned off by the sport, only frustrated by deprivation of it! Mastery goals, which are associated with the process of performance, are linked with longer participation in sport than competitive outcome goals (Duda, 1985).

9.3.4 HOW SPORT BECOMES LESS ATTRACTIVE THAN OTHER ACTIVITIES

So far it may have seemed that children enter or leave sport because of what they think about success in sport. But they are more likely to leave because other things in their lives are becoming more important. The commonest reason given for leaving is simply having other things to do (Gould, 1988). Sometimes this may cover up a more sensitive reason such as worry about a lack of ability, but children's priorities do change in adolescence.

Glyn Roberts in Chapter 1 reports Joan Duda's (1981) finding that success in sport was more important to North American teenagers than success in schoolwork. This is not the case in Britain, where the examination system, school leaving age and routes to success in sport and higher education differ from the USA. I found that success in schoolwork was consistently more important than success in sport in teenagers aged 13 to 16, particularly in girls (Whitehead, 1987). Moreover, with increasing age the relative importance of both of these activities declined in comparison with other things in the youngsters' lives, like music, going out with friends, TV, reading and computers. Interviews with the competitors who had withdrawn from the rugby or athletics teams suggested that long term objectives, perhaps to do with a future career or family, were becoming important. Anita White and Jay Coakley (1986, p. 21) found that young people reached a participation turning point when they thought their skills were at a peak in a particular activity and that further improvement would demand more time and energy than they were willing to commit, given their expanding interests.

One theory of behaviour explains this by arguing that people participate in an activity when its 'benefits' or attractions exceed its 'costs' or disadvantages. When children have been in sport for some time they will have experienced most of its benefits. Its relative costs then increase because more time, money or effort may be needed, and schoolwork or friendships may suffer. These rising costs are accepted only by those who hope for increasing benefits such as selection for higher level competition. Withdrawal may also occur because activities with lower costs and more benefits are available. For example, two boys may see equal benefits in sport but one may stop before the other because he has more attractive alternatives such as a part-time job or a girl friend.

Lastly, some young people may develop a dislike for sport because of bad experiences, such as injury, exhaustion, embarrassment, ridicule, or rejection by coach, team-mates or others. Physical and emotional stress, whether within the sport or related in some way to it, can cause withdrawal. However, if coaches understand children's needs and do not make unreasonable demands on them, nor allow others to do so, such experiences should be relatively rare. Coaches can also actively show a sense of humour and encourage fun, because children experience less stress when they have more fun.

In summary, children may *choose* to leave sport because they have reached their original goals or decided they cannot reach them, or because they have developed a liking for other activities or a dislike for sport. Alternatively they may be *forced* to leave because they become injured, move house, have problems with money or transport, are dropped from a team, or their club closes. Some of these reasons are outside the coaches' control, but others are not. A better understanding of children's motives can help coaches to adapt practices to improve the satisfaction that children gain from their experience in sport. Most importantly it should not be assumed that there is a fault in the child or the sport programme if a child withdraws. There could be much benefit in replacing the term 'drop out', which implies some kind of deficiency, with the notion of 'drop in'. Then it may be realized that children drop in to sport for a period of their lives, in order to further their personal development, then 'drop in' to other activities to continue this process on a firmer foundation.

9.4 CONCLUSION

This chapter has emphasized that children have contrasting views of what success is, and that these views differ with age, gender and type of sport. Children's interpretations of success will influence their enjoyment and behaviour, how hard they try in different situations and how long they continue in sport. In particular, if children are keen to do better than others, but don't think they have enough ability or opportunity to do this, they may drop out.

Coaches can improve children's feelings of satisfaction by recognizing the differences in their views, including activities to satisfy different goals, encouraging children to set process or mastery goals, giving them plenty of opportunities to play, and showing that winning is not the only important thing in sport. Then when children leave sport for other activities in life, they will carry with them the fruits of a positive experience.

REFERENCES

Deci, E.L. (1975) *Intrinsic Motivation*, Plenum, New York.

Duda, J.L. (1981) *A Cross-cultural Study of Achievement Motivation in Sport and the Classroom*. PhD dissertation, University of Illinois.

Duda, J.L. (1985) *Goal Perspectives, Participation and Persistence in Sport: A Test of Nicholls' Theory of Achievement Motivation*. Paper presented to the Canadian Society for Psychomotor Learning and Sport Psychology.

Duda, J.L. (1992) Motivation in sport settings: a goal perspectives approach, in *Motivation in Sport and Exercise*, (ed G.C. Roberts), Human Kinetics, Champaign, IL, pp. 57–91.

Ewing, M.E. (1981) *Achievement Orientations and Sport Behavior of Males and Females*. PhD dissertation, University of Illinois.

Gould, D. (1988) Attrition in children's sport, in *Advances in Paediatric Sports Sciences: Vol. 2*, (eds D. Gould and M.R. Weiss), Human Kinetics, Champaign, IL.

Hendry, L.B. (1992) *Sport, Leisure and the Development of Adolescent Lifestyles*. Paper presented at the Olympic Scientific Congress, Malaga, Spain.

Maehr, M. and Nicholls, J.G. (1980) Culture and achievement motivation: a second look, in *Studies in Cross-cultural Psychology: Vol. 3*, (ed N. Warren), Academic Press, New York.

Nicholls, J.G. (1989) *The Competitive Ethos and Democratic Education*, Harvard University Press, Cambridge, MA.

White, A. and Coakley, J. (1986) *Making Decisions: The Response of Young People in the Medway Towns to the 'Ever Thought of Sport?' Campaign*, Sports Council, London.

Whitehead, J. (1987) To succeed in sport or schoolwork? Children's priorities. *Journal of Sports Sciences*, 5(1), 64–5.

Whitehead, J. (1988) Why children take part. *The ISCiS Journal*, 1, 23–31.

Whitehead, J. (1990a) *Motivation and Sport Persistence*. Report to the National Coaching Foundation, Leeds.

Whitehead, J. (1990b) Achievement orientations and sport persistence. *Journal of Sports Sciences*, **8**(1), 87–8.

Wilson, S. (1989) A Study of Women's Achievement Orientation in Two Types of Sport. MA dissertation, University of Warwick.

How children see success and failure

10

Stuart Biddle

SUMMARY

It is important to understand how children view the reasons associated with success and failure in sport. This chapter summarizes reasons often given by children and what consequences these may have for the way they feel and act in sport. Practical applications centre on the best ways of using this information for making sport a positive experience for all children.

10.1 INTRODUCTION

A friend of mine told me with great pride that he had recently completed a marathon. However, in response to my somewhat insensitive question of 'What was your time?' he simply threw up his arms in frustration and said 'Oh, don't ask me that! I just wanted to finish!'

I appeared to have fallen victim to the obsession that we have in sport of relying almost exclusively on the result rather than the process of participation. We often forget that simply taking part is what spurs many people on. My friend had the goal of completing a marathon. He succeeded, yet my definition of success appeared to centre only on the time it took. Nevertheless, sport must involve some recognition of competition and consequently the result cannot be ignored. Indeed, to many people the result is all-important, while to others the process of competition is just one way of taking exercise, meeting a personal challenge or enjoying the company of friends.

For many children who play sport, success and failure, and winning and losing are likely to be important considerations. Sport is an environment where one's competence is on display, and for certain age groups (e.g. adolescents), it is very important to demonstrate competence in front of friends.

This chapter, therefore, will address the issue of how children view success and failure in sport. The kinds of reactions to success and failure will be discussed first, then the consequences of these reactions will be considered from the viewpoint of the child and the coach–child relationship. Practical considerations and recommendations will given throughout.

10.2 ASKING THE 'WHY?' QUESTION AFTER SUCCESS AND FAILURE

In the 1960s and 1970s, psychologists working in education were interested in how children and college students evaluated the results of examinations. After numerous studies a pattern emerged. First, people gave reasons associated with themselves if they passed the exam, so they would make replies such as 'I passed because I studied hard', or 'I passed because I'm good at this subject'. Second, those who failed the exam often made statements referring to outside influences or things outside of their control, such as 'I failed because the teacher set the exam at the wrong level', or 'I failed because I was unlucky with the choice of questions on the paper'. What these researchers found, therefore, were four main reasons people gave for their exam result. These reasons – referred to as 'attributions' – were labelled effort, ability, difficulty of the task and luck. Other factors were also thought to be important, of course, but these were identified as the main attributions for examination success or failure (see Weiner, 1986).

During the 1970s, sport psychologists started to ask similar questions about winning and losing in sport. For example, competitors were requested to rate the extent to which winning or losing a game was the result of effort, ability, task difficulty or luck. Similar results to those in the classroom also emerged in sport with winners reporting factors associated with their own ability and effort more than losers. This came to be known as the 'self-serving bias' whereby successful participants tended to attribute success to themselves but failure to a mixture of factors, some of which were unrelated to themselves. This bias is thought to be a conscious effort by the participant to 'feel good' after success and not so bad after failure. Similarly, in team sports it has often been reported that players take credit for team successes and do not take the blame for team failures. This was once referred to as the 'I'm OK but the team's so-so' phenomenon! [See Biddle, 1993].

10.2.1 LITTLE BOXES: CLASSIFYING ATTRIBUTIONS

In order to make better sense of these reasons, one of the main researchers studying this field, Dr Bernard Weiner, drew up a model to

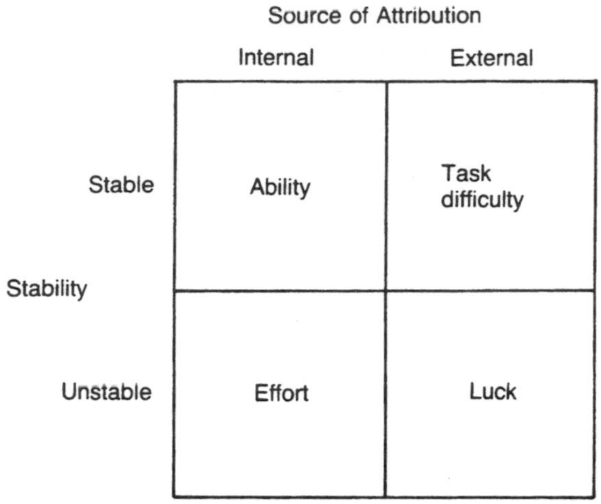

Source of Attribution

		Internal	External
	Stable	Ability	Task difficulty
Stability			
	Unstable	Effort	Luck

Fig. 10.1 An early classification model of attributions in the classroom

classify attributions (see Weiner, 1986, 1992). He suggested that attributions could be placed along two continua or dimensions: locus of causality and stability. The locus dimension referred to attributions that were associated with the person ('internal') or not associated with the person ('external'). For example, effort and ability were considered internal whereas luck and the task were considered to be external attributions.

The stability dimension classified attributions according to whether they were stable and unchanging over time, such as ability or the task, or whether they were unstable and variable over time, such as luck and effort. This classification allowed for a simple model to be drawn up, as shown in Figure 10.1. More complex models have also been developed, but this one should be sufficient to understand the main points.

The same model was also suggested for sport situations, although the number of attributions made in sport was thought to be higher than in examination situations and the placement of the task attribution was moved. A sport-related model, therefore, is shown in Figure 10.2 (Roberts and Pascuzzi, 1979). The consequences of making attributions along these dimensions will be discussed later.

10.2.2   DO CHILDREN REALLY MAKE ATTRIBUTIONS, EXCEPT WHEN ASKED?

Although children will make attributions, young children (i.e. below about 10–11 years of age) probably find it difficult to distinguish between some factors. For example, children aged 5–7 years appear not to be

Source of attribution

	Internal	External

Stability

Stable	Stable ability	Coaching
Unstable	Unstable ability (form) Practice Effort	Luck Task ease

Fig. 10.2 A model of sport-related attributions (adapted from Roberts, G.C. and Pascuzzi, D. (1979) Causal attributions in children's sport; some theoretical implications. *Journal of Sport Psychology*, 1(3), 203–11)

able to differentiate too easily between effort, ability and outcome. They tend to report that those who try hard are successful and if you are successful you must have tried hard. Children at five or six years tend to think of success and failure from a personal, rather than comparative, orientation. Finishing the race is a success, regardless of place. Slightly older children – at about 6–7 years – start to adopt a more normative comparative perspective. Now they start to think whether others can do the task or not. Tasks that are 'hard' are those few others can do. Children at 7–9 years are strongly focused on effort as the cause of outcomes, whereas from 9–10 years, ability and effort become differentiated as ability is seen as 'capacity' and that this will limit the effect of effort on the outcome (Duda, 1987).

Researchers into attributions have often questioned whether people actually do make attributions, except when asked by an attribution researcher! A review of studies that looked at 'spontaneous' attributions (those made without prompting) concluded that attributions are made during everyday life, and particularly when a goal has not been achieved or when the outcome is unexpected (Weiner, 1985). This suggests that losers, or those thinking they have failed, will engage in more attributional thinking than winners or those seeing themselves as successful.

Just to show that attributions really are made, a report on a recent American football game said that 'the coach has eliminated bad luck, biorhythms, and sun-spots as the reasons why his football team has lost 9 of its last 10 games. Now he's considering the unthinkable possibilities of (a) he has lousy players or (b) they aren't really trying'. One of the most famous sports quotes of all time is based on attributions. Gary Player, the South African golfer, on hearing that his successful putt was labelled 'lucky', retorted, 'Yes, the more I practise, the luckier I get!'. Of course, his somewhat ironic remark was aimed at highlighting the link between practice (effort, not luck) and outcome. This reminds me of the comment made by a 14 year old after I had asked a group of children to see if they could touch their fingers behind their back with one hand going up the back and the other down. On concluding that he had 'failed', the boy, in response to my question 'What does this test tell us about flexibility?', replied 'I've got really short fingers'! Misattribution at its best!

Another example of 'real life' attributions was given by Mike Gatting, captain of the England cricket team at the time, when he said after his dismissal at the hands of Allan Border in a World Cup match, 'Perhaps as it was Allan's first ball, I must accept limited responsibility'. By attributing a 'failure' like this to himself it is likely to affect the way he feels and acts. This will now be considered.

10.2.3   MAKING ATTRIBUTIONS: DOES IT REALLY MATTER?

The attributions given by children can have important consequences for the way they feel about the sport in question and their future motivation towards it. Using the models illustrated in Figures 10.1 and 10.2, it is possible to trace the likely consequences of making attributions.

Self-confidence

One of the predictions from the early research on classroom attributions was that expectations about future successes and failures could be made from knowing the stability of the attribution (Weiner, 1986). For example, attributing success to a stable factor, such as personal ability, predicts future success. Similarly, stable attributions for failure will predict future failure. Unstable attributions, however, do not allow clear predictions since, by definition, the attribution is changeable. For example, attributing success to your own effort does not predict success since next time you may decide not to try so hard. Hopefully, success can be attributed to stable factors as this sets up a positive confidence cycle, as shown in Figure 10.3.

Children's feelings

The attributions we give for sport performance can help determine how we feel about the performance. For example, children who attribute

Fig. 10.3 A confidence cycle associated with stable attributions for success

a win in a race to having tried hard are likely to feel more pleasure and pride than if they thought it was due to luck or weak opposition. The type and intensity of emotional feeling, therefore, is thought to be related to the attributions given.

My own research has focused on this issue and found support for three main propositions:

(i)   emotions are more likely to be related to internal rather than external attributions;
(ii)   emotions associated with self-esteem, such as pride, are more likely to be felt after internal attributions given for success in *important* events;
(iii) in addition to attributions, emotions felt after sport are strongly associated with how we think we played, rather than the result of the game (Biddle and Hill, 1988, 1992a, 1992b).

Feeling helpless

There has been a great deal of research on how children react to failure in the classroom (Dweck, 1989). Why is it that some children are spurred on to greater effort, while others slide down the spiral to despondency and apathy?

A series of experiments by Dr Carol Dweck at the Universities of Illinois and Harvard showed that the reactions of children to failure were related to the attributions the children gave for such failures. In particular, children who felt that their failure was due to their own lack of ability were most likely to give up. Such apathy was termed 'learned helplessness' since these children believed that no matter how hard they tried, they would not succeed. Such children tended to dwell on negative thoughts whereas other children who did not display such reactions to failure tended to think more positively after failure, rarely doubted their own ability, and sought out solutions to problems. Dweck called these children 'mastery-oriented' (Dweck, 1980).

If their attributions predicted a helpless or positive response to failure, Dweck summised, then changing children's attributions for failure should change their reaction to failure. This led to Dr Dweck conducting a study on the 'retraining' of attributions (Diener and Dweck, 1978). She caused two group of young children to fail at a task and then gave one group periodic success while the other were taught to think that their failure was due to their own lack of effort. This was the attribution retraining group. After future failure, the attribution retraining group showed a positive response and improved their performance. However, the 'success' group did not improve as their attributions remained the same. By allowing the attribution retraining group to think that failure was due to lack of effort, they were shown that there was an escape from failure – more effort. A possible attribution retraining sequence is illustrated in Figure 10.4.

Although attribution retraining has been shown to be successful (Forsterling, 1988), a word of caution is called for. Effort has been referred to as the 'double-edged sword' of achievement because if children fail after thinking that they tried hard, it is likely that they will make attributions to low ability. This is to be avoided as it could lead to learned helplessness. For this reason, while the principles demonstrated by Dr Dweck are probably correct, it may be better to reattribute failure to something like 'wrong playing strategy' rather than low effort. Whatever the new attribution is, it should be a factor open to personal control and influence.

10.3 THE MEANING OF SUCCESS TO CHILDREN

In addition to understanding the attributions children make in sport, parents and coaches might also find it interesting to consider the question 'What is the meaning of success to children?'. This is more than just an academic question. To understand how children define success in sport should help us promote motivation and enjoyment.

It has been suggested that children have at least two ways of defining success in sport:

1. Ability or ego orientation: children supporting this orientation have as their main goal the demonstration of superior ability relative to others. This is called an *ego goal* as it is 'other person' referenced. Such children will tend to focus on ability, believe that sports success is related to ability, and hence make ability attributions.
2. Mastery or task orientation: children supporting this orientation have as their main goal the successful completion or mastery of a

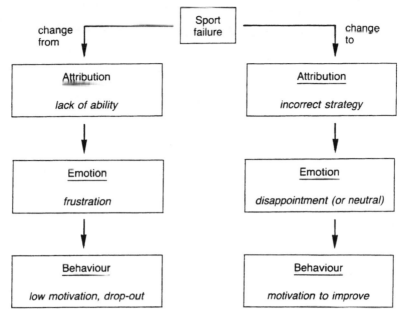

Fig. 10.4 A possible attribution retraining sequence

task, or self-improvement. This is called a *task goal* as it is self-referenced. A task goal has been associated with effort attributions since these children believe that high effort brings success (Duda, 1987; Duda, Fox, Biddle and Armstrong, 1992).

As suggested, the type of goal adopted by the child will affect the type of attribution used. We have already said that attributing failure to lack of ability may have particularly negative consequences. As a result, one might cast some doubt on the wisdom of encouraging an ego goal. It is likely to force children into defining success as winning rather than self-improvement. Not all children can win regularly whereas many children, if not all, can improve on their own performance. The ego goal is likely to be most damaging when the individual lacks self-confidence. This is shown in Figure 10.5.

A recent study of ours at Exeter (Duda *et al.*, 1992) has shown that higher levels of enjoyment in sport reported by 11–12 year olds are associated with having a task goal rather than an ego goal. In fact, boredom was more associated with the ego goal. In short, it appears that the promotion of a task orientation is to be recommended for enjoyment and motivation in children's sport.

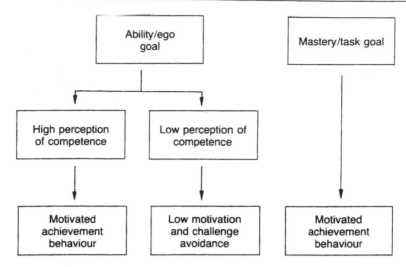

Fig. 10.5 Possible consequences of different goal orientations in sport

10.4   HOW OTHERS SEE CHILDREN'S SUCCESS AND FAILURE

While concentrating on how children see success and failure, this chapter would be incomplete without considering how other people, such as parents and coaches, see this process too. It is common for other people to make their own judgements about why they think the child succeeds or fails. For example, let us consider the girl who has just finished a tennis match in a local tournament. She has lost the match and has the following thoughts:

'I tried hard, but. . . .'

'I tried to keep her on the baseline, but she was too strong with her ground strokes.'

'I guess I did all I could, but she was a good player . . . I should be OK with more work on my second serve.'

Now along comes her coach. The first thing she says is 'Come on Steffi, you were really lazy today!' Immediately an attributional conflict has been created. The child believes she tried hard, but the coach says she didn't. Fortunately, the child believes that she can make progress in the future, with practice. However, if the coach gives an attribution that future success is unlikely ('you've got a tremendous amount of work to do if you're going to make it!'), then self-doubt can creep in.

Coaches, and others working with children, should allow children to make their own attributions first. They should then give their own thoughts in a constructive manner without causing unnecessary conflict.

After 'failure' or defeat, try to look towards positive factors which can be controlled in the future.

10.5 CONCLUSIONS AND RECOMMENDATIONS

By studying attributions made by children in sport, as well as understanding the goals adopted by children, we move closer to the situation of seeing sport from the point of view of the child. Dr Charles Corbin, a leading American physical educator, in his book on primary school physical education (Corbin, 1976), recalls an article published in 1952. In this article the author speaks of the 'Principle of priority of man' ('man' here is used to refer to all humans – it was 1952!). This principle states that the interests and needs of people must take priority over activity; and the worth of every activity is measured in terms of its contribution to the advancement of people. Dr Corbin then applied this principle to children in sport. He said:

> Too often we ask 'What's wrong with sport for children?' This is the wrong question! The child's involvement in sport is for the benefit of the child. The question should be 'what does the sport do for the child'?

He goes on to question the motives of those who put the activity first and the child second and violate the principle of priority of man. Dr Corbin gives four examples of ways in which sport is done for sport's sake:

1. not adapting sport to meet the needs of all children;
2. using full-size courts and equipment instead of adaptations more suitable for children;
3. excluding girls;
4. copying 'big time' sports.

He says

> if we *really* were designing play experiences for *children*, I suspect that the activities we provided would be much different than what we currently offer . . . Sport, including winning in sport, should never be more important than the benefits of the sport for sportspeople.

These general comments are made so that we can put sport into its proper perspective for children. This should include an understanding of the way children think about sport and the attributions they make.

In conclusion, therefore, the following points are made from the information presented in the chapter.

1. Children will make attributions in sport, particularly after failing or losing.
2. Self-confidence could be related to the attributions made, particularly whether the attributions are stable or unstable.
3. Children are likely to experience emotion that is a consequence of the way they thought they played. However, in addition, emotions will be related to their attributions.
4. The nature and extent of negative feelings after failure will be a function of the attributions made and the importance attached to winning. Coaches can reduce the importance of winning by highlighting personal performance instead.
5. Avoid children feeling helpless by helping them reattribute failure to controllable factors rather than just providing 'instant' and 'easy' success.
6. Avoid attributional conflict by asking for the child's attributions first.
7. Try to understand the meaning of success to the individual child. An ego goal may be dysfunctional for some children, particularly if they lack self-confidence. A task goal may be more appropriate.
8. Children are not miniature adults. They will not always think and act in the same way as adults and they should not be expected to handle success and failure in the same way. Children learn the process of competition from the people around them. Let's help them learn in the best possible way by providing an environment rich in personal challenge. Let's put into practice the 'principle of priority of *children* in sport'!

REFERENCES

Biddle, S.J.H. (1993) Attribution research and sport psychology, in *Handbook of research on sport psychology*. (eds) R.N. Singer, M. Murphey, and L.K. Tennant, Macmillan, New York.

Biddle, S.J.H. and Hill, A.B. (1988) Causal attributions and emotional reactions to outcome in a sporting contest. *Personality and Individual Differences*, **9**, 213–23.

Biddle, S.J.H. and Hill, A.B. (1992a) Relationships between attributions and emotions in a laboratory-based sporting contest. *Journal of Sports Sciences*, **10**, 65–75.

Biddle, S.J.H. and Hill, A.B. (1992b) Attributions for objective outcome and subjective appraisal of performance: Their relationship with emotional reactions in sport. *British Journal of Social Psychology*, **31**, 215–26.

Corbin, C.B. (1976) *Becoming physically educated in the elementary school*. Lea and Febiger, Philadelphia.

Diener, C.I. and Dweck, C.S. (1978) An analysis of learned helplessness: Continuous changes in performance strategy, and achievement cognitions following failure. *Journal of Personality and Social Psychology*, **36**, 451–62.

Duda, J.L. (1987) Toward a developmental theory of children's motivation in sport. *Journal of Sport Psychology*, **9**, 130–45.

Duda, J.L., Fox, K.R., Biddle, S.J.H. and Armstrong, N. (1992) Children's achievement goals and beliefs about success in sport. *British Journal of Educational Psychology*, **62**, 313–20.

Dweck, C.S. (1980) Learned helplessness in sport. In *Psychology of motor behavior and sport 1979*, (eds) C. Nadeau, W.R. Halliwell, K.M. Newell and G.C Roberts. Human Kinetics, Champaign, IL.

Dweck, C.S. (1989) Motivation. In *Foundations for a psychology of education*, (eds A. Lesgold and R. Glaser), Erlbaum, Hillsdale, NJ.

Forsterling, F. (1988) *Attribution theory in clinical psychology*. Wiley, Chichester.

Roberts, G.C. and Pascuzzi, D.L. (1979) Causal attributions in sport: Some theoretical implications. *Journal of Sport Psychology*, **1**, 203–11.

Weiner, B. (1985) 'Spontaneous' causal thinking. *Psychological Bulletin*, **97**, 74–84.

Weiner, B. (1986) *An attributional theory of motivation and emotion*. Springer-Verlag, New York.

Weiner, B. (1992) *Human motivation: Metaphors, theories and research*. Sage, Newbury Park, CA.

FURTHER READING

Carron, A.V. (1984) *Motivation: Implications for coaching and teaching*. Sports Dynamics, London, Ontario.

Fox, K.R. and Biddle, S.J.H. (1988–1989) The child's perspective in physical education. *British Journal of Physical Education*. 6-part series.

Martens, R. (1978) *Joy and sadness in children's sports*. Human Kinetics, Champaign, IL.

Advanced

Dweck, C.S. and Leggett, E.L. (1988) A social-cognitive approach to motivation and personality. *Psychological Review*, **95**, 256–273.

Roberts, G.C. (ed) (1992) *Motivation in sport and exercise*. Human Kinetics, Champaign, IL.

Causes of children's anxiety in sport

11

Stephen Rowley

SUMMARY

Over the past few years concern has been expressed about the cumulative effect which repeated stress and anxiety, caused by taking part in youth sport, may have upon the emotional development of the child. However, research has so far failed to provide any data to establish the number of young athletes suffering from sports related anxiety, or to indicate why some appear more resilient and cope with the anxieties caused by sports participation better then others.

The aim of this chapter is twofold. Firstly to provide a general guide to the different causes of anxiety in childhood and adolescence with specific reference to sport; and secondly to describe ways in which the coach and parent can identify and help the anxious child.

11.1 INTRODUCTION

Perhaps the most universal and potentially most disruptive emotion found amongst children and adolescents taking part in competitive youth sport is anxiety. The effect it has upon a child's behaviour and performance varies considerably, as do the things which make children anxious; much depends upon the youngster's ability to cope with the threat and uncertainty posed by particular situations within sport. Yet despite numerous attempts by researchers to describe reasons for individual differences in its cause and effect, for the coach, parent or athlete involved with the practicalities of coping with anxiety, the emotion remains ill-defined and poorly understood.

Until recently, most coaches were mainly interested in understanding how anxiety affects performance: the experience of anxiety is often associated with poor performance. Lately, however, concern has been expressed by coaches, parents and educationalists about the cumulative effect which repeated stress and anxiety, caused by taking part in youth spuil, may have upon the emotional development and well-being of the child. Such has been the worry that some are now questioning whether young children should be involved in organized training and competition at all. The reason given is that children are not old enough to cope with the anxieties generated by the sports environment. Yet although potential sources of stress have been identified by sports psychologists, they have failed to provide any data to establish the numbers of young athletes suffering from anxiety or why some cope with the anxieties caused by sports participation better than others. Little attention has been given to evaluate ways in which youngsters can learn to cope with the effects of sports related anxiety. Moreover, it is wrong to assume that there is a tidy relationship between a stressful event, anxiety, age and coping. Studies monitoring the effect on children of such stressful life events as divorce or death of a parent do not suggest that vulnerability to emotional problems such as anxiety increases or decreases at any particular age. Furthermore, it has been suggested by Albert Bandura (1977), an American social psychologist, that avoidance of stressful or anxiety provoking situations will hinder the development of coping skills. Preventing children from taking part in sport will not therefore stop anxiety but may only delay the age at which it might occur.

Part of the problem lies in the fact that anxiety, like stress, is a concept understood by all, as long as it is used in a sufficiently vague and general way. A more comprehensive understanding of the cause and also the role of anxiety in youth sports has proved elusive mainly because of the failure of many researchers to take account of the child's emotional development – in children the cause of anxiety changes as the child progresses from infancy through childhood to adolescence. But also too much emphasis has been placed upon the competitive situation itself as the main cause of anxiety rather than the personality and motivation of the performers, their families and coaches.

11.2 ANXIETY IN CHILDREN AND ADOLESCENTS

Normal anxiety is usually described as an unpleasant state of psychological tension, often accompanied by physical symptoms, caused by anticipation of a threatening event or situation. The onset, severity and duration of anxiety vary. It may come on gradually over a period of minutes or hours, or it may strike without warning. It may last for only a few seconds or for hours or even days. In children the number of situations or events which cause anxiety increase as they grow older. Typically, anxiety in childhood and adolescence takes five main forms:

generalized anxiety, separation anxiety, social anxiety, performance anxiety and fears and phobias. The main features of each type of anxiety are described below.

Generalized anxiety describes worries or fears which are not isolated to any one situation or event but which are generalized by the youngster to cover a wide range of future events.

Separation anxiety is caused by worries about real or imagined separation from a parent because of illness, injury or death.

Social anxiety is caused by fears or worries about loss of friends, attractiveness or meeting new people.

Performance anxiety can occur when the child is called upon to take a test, speak in front of others in the classroom, or compete against someone in sport.

Fears and phobias are extreme states of anxiety linked to particular objects, persons or situations. For example, visiting the dentist or having an injection are common childhood fears. In some cases, though, extreme fear can result in the child avoiding certain situations (phobias).

Each of these different types of anxiety has a part to play in the normal child's emotional development although their importance alters as the child grows older. Dangerous or unfamiliar situations or separation anxiety from parents are characteristic anxieties of the very young child. The older child is more threatened by social anxieties such as loss of friendship, whereas the adolescent is more concerned with fear of failure, ridicule or any situation which involves evaluation by peers or significant other people such as a parent, coach or friend. These sorts of worries are the ones most often expressed by youngsters taking part in sport, and are good examples of performance anxiety. However, it is important that coaches who deal with very young children should not discount the effect which separation anxiety, caused by real or threatened separation from parents, may have upon performance.

Characteristically the sensations of anxiety include psychological, physiological and behavioural components such as loss of concentration, worry, rapid heart rate, nausea, stomach ache, fidgeting, restlessness and fatigue. There are some effects, however, which deserve particular mention because of their importance for young performers.

11.2.1 PHYSIOLOGICAL EFFECTS OF ANXIETY

The physiological effects of anxiety are many and varied. They include, for example, increased heart rate and blood pressure, sweating and stimulation of metabolism. One important effect involves a change in muscle tension. Anxiety increases muscular tension in the body which may reduce the effectiveness of certain muscle groups, particularly in sports which involve repeated or dynamic muscular effort such as soccer, swimming or athletics. Sustained muscular tension also leads to an accumulation of lactic acid which causes pain, stiffness and fatigue.

11.2.2 PSYCHOLOGICAL EFFECTS OF ANXIETY

The psychological effects of anxiety include an inability to make decisions, forgetfulness and impaired concentration. A wide variety of research is available which suggests that the ability to concentrate or focus on the task in hand is advantageous in performance settings. In contrast the tendency to self-preoccupations or self-focusing has generally been associated with poor performance. Michael Mahoney (1979, 1983), an American psychologist who has worked with Olympic gymnasts, has suggested that the ability to concentrate or focus on the task at hand is what makes the difference between highly successful and less successful athletes. Better performers are able to control their attention, remain task oriented and block out distractions. Athletes who focus on themselves and how they are doing, and view themselves from an external perspective tend to perform less well because they focus on their own negative characteristics which may increase feelings of anxiety.

The intensity of the psychological and physiological reaction caused by performance anxiety depends upon the significance of the situation – whether it is perceived by the young athlete as irrelevant, benign, stressful or challenging – and his or her ability to cope with a perceived danger or threat. Research in child psychology suggests there are several different factors which influence children's ability to cope with stressful situations. These include the sex of the child, the presence or absence of support from the parent or coach, the child's intelligence and other problem solving skills.

Sex differences

Unlike the pattern which emerges during adolescence and which continues into adulthood, before puberty boys are more vulnerable to emotional problems like anxiety than girls. The reasons for this difference remain unclear although it has been suggested that parents are less supportive of boys in their attempts to cope, or the perceived importance of stressful events like sport may sometimes be greater for boys.

Social support

The presence of close, supportive relationships with family, friends or the coach plays an important part in protecting the child from stress. If children feel they can talk about their worries and anxieties to someone it significantly decreases the symptoms of physical and psychological stress.

Intelligence

There is some evidence from research in psychology that good intelligence and school achievement may also act as a protective buffer from stress and anxiety. Little is known about why this should be so, although it may be that these children have high self-esteem or better problem solving skills than their peers.

11.2.3 INDIVIDUAL DIFFERENCES IN PERFORMANCE ANXIETY

Anxiety can range from mild arousal, characterized by 'butterflies in the stomach' and anticipation of the tournament, match or competition, to extreme fearfulness, panic and, occasionally, avoidance of the performance situation. This avoidance need not necessarily mean retirement or giving up sport – an athlete may pretend to be ill or injured in order to cope with the threat of a particular competition. Injury proneness may provide an acceptable form of retreat from sport seen by the child as socially, psychologically or physically threatening. However although this defence against anxiety may be useful in the short term, it could result in the athlete developing a mental barrier about training or competing if used persistently.

These types of extreme anxiety states can develop in all children. However, often they arise because of a pre-existing tendency within the child to react with increased anxiety to a wide range of ordinary stresses seen by other children as non-threatening or challenging. The term 'trait anxiety' has been developed to describe these individual differences in anxiety proneness. Children high in trait anxiety tend to view the world as more threatening than children with low trait anxiety: and they tend to respond to their perceptions of threat with more frequent increases in state or real anxiety. In sport, research consistently indicates that children who are high in trait anxiety show greater state anxiety before and during a competition than their contemporaries with low trait anxiety. The tendency to respond with high levels of anxiety is characteristic of children with poor self-confidence and low self-worth, who feel they have little control over events or situations. These thoughts and feelings often become self-perpetuating. Children like this regard effort and persistence in the task as self-defeating and so reduce their exertion ensuring a mediocre performance.

11.3 PERFORMANCE ANXIETY IN YOUTH SPORT

There are three major causes of performance anxiety in children's sport – the attitudes and motivations of parents and coaches, the attitude of the athlete him or herself, and overtraining or staleness.

11.3.1 SIGNIFICANT OTHERS: PARENTS AND COACHES

For many parents and coaches the young athlete can be a source of vicarious enjoyment and success. Parents report feeling 'great pride' and 'living out (their) own fantasy' through their child's sporting endeavours. Alternatively, observers of youth sport have proposed that when adults become involved in children's sport they have a tendency to place unreasonable demands on the young athlete, following ambitions of their own and placing an excessive emphasis upon winning. Under these circumstances children learn to fear evaluation from their parents who 'watch them like a hawk', or video the whole performance for later analysis. This can result in some young athletes developing unrealistic hopes and commitment to training as feelings of personal worth become equated with success in sport; a fear of failure or rejection may result if parental love is perceived to be contingent upon winning.

Kate, an 11 year old swimmer, is a typical example of this group. Her training load had increased and she had recently begun to feel anxious before training. Her main worry was that she would not be able to keep up with the other swimmers and that the coach would ignore or reject her. This meant that a lot of the time she didn't want to go training but felt she must, as 'If I missed one training session I would get unfit and wouldn't be able to win'. Her mother reinforced this notion by saying that she had to go training as 'You don't want to be unfit the next day'. Apart from the extreme anxiety which Kate experienced as a result of this situation, she also developed an unrealistic belief as to the meaning of training. Her attitude towards training became almost obsessional such that if she missed just one training session it would be calamitous – becoming unfit, being left behind in training and rejected by her coach.

A less well documented but equally effective cause of performance anxiety is for the athlete to 'catch' it from a parent or coach. A parent or coach who becomes overly anxious before competition can often transfer their apprehension and worry to the athlete. Children may be affected as much by the attitudes and mental state of their parents as by any pressures caused by the sports environment.

Examples such as these are often used by critics of youth sport to support their case that young children should be prevented from taking part in competition. Yet although it is clear that emotional problems do occur in children's sport it is more likely that sport *highlights* problems that already existed in the family; it does not *cause* them. Children's beliefs about competition are shaped largely by parents, as are attitudes towards failure, persistence and commitment. It is likely that many of the emotional problems which occur during performance are simply mirror images of those which occur in the home.

11.3.2   THE ATHLETE

There are three specific areas of vulnerability which may put the young athlete at risk of developing an anxious reaction to competition: (a) frustration of achievement; (b) the conflict between schoolwork and training; and (c) peer relationships.

Frustration of achievement

Many children report feeling worried or anxious if expected to win. Frustrated achievement or the setting of unrealistic objectives can cause problems particularly if supported by a coach or parent, although the high achieving child may also develop emotional difficulties. Bryan Lask (1986), a psychiatrist working at a children's hospital, has described a group of children who 'somatize' their anxiety. They manifest their anxious feelings in terms of physical symptoms. Based upon clinical observations he describes children, usually girls aged between ten and 14, permanently disabled by mild illness or injury. These children are 'good at everything', particularly sports. Lask suggests that as the pressures build up so the child becomes anxious but feels unable to show or share it. Illness or injury provides a respite from the threat of continued participation.

Conflict between schoolwork and training

Although it is possible that many young athletes perceive educational attainment as another area of high achievement and are highly motivated to succeed in this as well as sport, the demands of school and sport can cause considerable stress for the child. Young swimmers and gymnasts taking part in intensive training routines have described difficulty concentrating at school due to tiredness, and homework being completed late at night or early in the morning. This conflict seems to be most stressful during mid-adolescence when national examinations occur. Recent findings of the Training of Young Athletes (TOYA) study (Rowley, 1992), a population based survey looking at the effects of intensive training in young children, found that 25% of athletes who retired from sport did so because of pressure of schoolwork.

Peer relationships

Concern has been expressed that the long hours spent training and competing may prevent the child from making or retaining lasting friendships, as she or he is unable to share in the common activities of the peer group, a factor which could influence the popularity and status of the young athlete.

A recent report based on findings from the TOYA study (Rowley, 1993) indicates that for many young athletes the problem may not be one of peer relationships but bullying and teasing. A significant number of children reported being teased and bullied because of their involvement in sport. In primary education young athletes appear more likely to experience severe bullying than a comparable group of children. Over a third attributed being teased to their involvement in sport. Gymnasts and footballers in particular reported being teased significantly more than other children their age. One young female gymnast said that the headmaster announced her sporting success to the school and this led to problems with peers. 'Other girls are jealous, they are horrible to me, I sometimes don't want to go to school.' Another complained of name calling 'and being pushed around' by other girls. Both boy and girl gymnasts described being bullied because of their size. 'I'm teased because I'm small', or 'Boys pick on me because I'm smaller than other girls'.

11.3.3 OVERTRAINING AND STALENESS

For some endurance sports, such as middle or long distance running and swimming, overtraining appears to be a prerequisite for peak performance in the elite athlete. Research on elite swimmers suggests that in certain cases overtraining can cause changes in mood suggestive of anxiety and depression. Sports psychologist Bill Morgan and his colleagues (Morgan et al., 1987) discovered that as the training load increased many swimmers became irritable, had poor concentration, felt tired and depressed. These symptoms disappeared when training was tapered down or a swimmer was rested. Young children may be particularly susceptible to this problem as they are still growing and are therefore subject to the physical stress of growth and maturation as well as training effects.

11.4 COPING WITH PERFORMANCE ANXIETY

The final part of this chapter will suggest how coaches and parents can help to alleviate performance anxiety in young children. Coaches and parents often seem more willing to attribute failure to a lack of effort or fitness rather than psychological preparedness, yet many athletes would benefit from an improvement of their understanding and skills in the productive use of performance anxiety.

11.4.1   IDENTIFYING THE ANXIOUS CHILD

The first stage in learning how to work with rather than against performance anxiety is for the coach to be able to identify those youngsters who are most at risk of experiencing high levels of anxiety. Unfortunately there is little research available to show how effective coaches are at identifying overly anxious athletes, although results suggest that many are poor judges. It is often difficult to establish children's emotional state. They may be unwilling to talk about their feelings because of embarrassment or the fear of being ridiculed, although their behaviour may show that they are anxious. There are, however, some common signs and symptoms associated with childhood anxiety. The following list contains several which coaches and parents need to monitor in order to help identify anxious children.

1.   Loss of sleep, early waking or any change in sleep pattern;
2.   Nightmares or bad dreams;
3.   Any change in dietary habits such as loss of appetite;
4.   Mood changes such as irritability or uncharacteristic displays of aggression either at home or during competition;
5.   Manipulativeness – the child may become very controlling of situations;
6.   Restlessness or fidgeting;
7.   Hypochondriasis – the child may complain of physical symptoms on the days preceding a particular event in training or a competition;
8.   Frequent urination or diarrhoea.

11.4.2   EDUCATION

Anxiety can be legitimized by explaining to the child that he or she is not unique in worrying about training or performance. Athletes at every level experience anxiety. Understanding this principle is the first and probably most important stage in teaching the athlete how to control and use anxiety. This explanation can be incorporated into a general educational package where the athlete is taught how to identify anxiety and about its cause and effect.

11.4.3   FEEDBACK

Girls differ from boys in the way in which they respond to feedback from adults that they are failing. Carol Dweck, a psychologist who specializes in children's development, and her colleagues (1982) have shown that whereas boys tend to respond with greater efforts when they receive feedback from adults that they are failing, girls tend to give up and attribute their failure to their own lack of ability. It is important therefore that a coach does not adopt a stereotyped or fixed response to coping with failure, as in some cases this may actually increase the chance of anxiety occurring in the future.

11.4.4 GRADED EXPOSURE TO COMPETITION

Rainer Martens (1981), one of the foremost experts on children's sport, suggests that competitive stress may be likened to a virus. A heavy dose all at once can make a child ill. A small dose carefully regulated permits the child to learn how to channel anxiety so that it aids rather than inhibits performance. Carefully selected competitions together with realistic objectives and expectations will enable the child to learn that sport is fun and can be enjoyed whatever the result.

11.5 CONCLUSION

The two main causes of performance anxiety are uncertainty and threat. Yet these need not result in an impairment or avoidance of sport. Uncertainty should concern the result, not the child's emotional security, and any threat can be transformed into a healthy challenge by reviewing goals and objectives. The coach and parent must recognize their responsibility in making the experience of sport enjoyable and productive for the child. Most important is that winning does not have to mean coming first. A personal best, playing a certain stroke or shot, or successfully marking an opponent can be goals every child can strive for; all encourage the child to try to give his or her best. Every child can be a winner – if only the adults let them.

REFERENCES

Bandura, A. (1977) Self-efficacy: towards a unifying theory of behavioural change. *Psychological Review*, **84**, 191–215.

Dweck, C.S. and Wortman, C.B. (1982) Learned helplessness, anxiety and achievement motivation, in *Achievement, Stress and Coping*, (eds H. Krohne and L. Laux), Hemisphere Publishers, New York, pp. 93–124.

Lask, B. (1986) The high achieving child. *Postgraduate Medical Journal*, **6**, 143–5.

Mahoney, M.J. (1979) Cognitive skills and athletic performance, in *Cognitive-Behavioural Intervention: Theory, Research and Procedures*, (eds P.C. Kendall and S.D. Hollon), Academic Press, New York, 423–43.

Mahoney, M.J., Avener, J. and Avener, M. (1983) Psychological aspects of competitive athletic performance, in *The Mental Aspects of Gymnastics*, (ed L. Unestahl), Orebro, Sweden.

Martens, R. (1981) *Stress or distress?* Paper presented at the Guinness Conference of Sport, Towards Sporting Excellence.

Morgan, W., Brown, D. and Raglin, J. (1987) Psychological monitoring of overtraining and staleness. *British Journal of Sports Medicine*, 107–14.

Rowley, S.R.W. (1992) *TOYA and Retirement*, Sports Council Publications Unit, London.

Rowley, S.R.W. (1993) *TOYA and Education: The Effect of Intensive Training on Educational Attainment*, Sports Council Publications Unit, London.

Selecting the right targets

12

Rod Thorpe

SUMMARY

This chapter identifies some of the key evidence and opinion about goal setting. It is not intended to be a review of the topic, which has been done elsewhere (Beggs, 1990). Rather the intention is to provide a background of knowledge against which the coach can assess the value of goal setting with young people. Wherever possible sport examples are related to a central idea, rather than a specific piece of research, to enable the coach to transfer the 'principle', rather than the specific finding, to his or her coaching act.

12.1 WHAT IS GOAL SETTING?

> Goal Setting is simply identifying what you are trying to do or to accomplish; basically it is the aim of an action or series of actions.
>
> Harris and Harris, 1984

The critical word in the quotation above is 'identifying'. It is possible to take part in an activity with only a vague idea of what the intention is but for most people this is insufficient to maintain motivation. Identifying a goal gives purpose. This process of identification is even more important when a coach and athlete are working together. The coaching world abounds with anecdotal evidence of how the goals of the performer do not match that of the coach, often because they have failed to discuss them together. Perhaps by the end of this chapter you may feel that the word 'identify' is insufficient to reflect the care and attention that should go into the act of goal setting.

The procedures which sports psychologists suggest for goal setting are derived from studies from a variety of sources, not least the area of business management, but also more structured academic studies in psychology and more recently in sport. An extensive review by Locke *et al.* (1981) based on the previous ten years of work in both laboratory and field situations (not sport specific) led to a number of conclusions, most importantly for us, that goal setting was a particularly powerful aid to motivation. The following two quotations reflect the importance placed on goal setting by sports psychologists.

> The accomplishment of individual goals is the key to each person's success and to the development of their self concept. To know who you are and what you wish to accomplish is critical to each person's happiness.

> Bunker, 1985

Expressed in performance achievement terms:

> Success is about goal achievement; the more goals achieved, the more success the performer experiences, and the greater his self confidence becomes. The relevance of all this to the coach should be fairly clear. The setting of appropriate goals is critical for all performers in all sports.

> Hardy, 1985

12.1.1 WHY DOES GOAL SETTING WORK?

Sports psychologists who advocate the use of goal setting (Bunker, 1985; Carron, 1984; Harris and Harris, 1984) agree that it is a powerful technique because it:

- directs and focuses attention;
- helps the individual mobilize energy and effort;
- encourages persistence and practice over time.

Bunker *et al.* add that it:

- forces the individual to take responsibility for his/her actions and attributions;
- influences expectancies;

and Harris and Harris suggest that it:

- generates the motivation to develop relevant and alternative strategies for reaching goals.

12.1.2 EFFECTIVE GOAL SETTING

Having accepted that goal setting is an important element of coaching there are some general findings which appear to apply to the sport situation. (It is important to note that there is some debate about just how universal these findings are (Weinberg *et al.*, 1988).)

Coaches who set difficult or challenging goals do better than those who set 'do your best' goals.

Goals seem to motivate best when stated in specific quantitative terms or actions rather than 'trying harder', 'giving 100%', 'concentrating better' – more judgemental/qualitative terms.

Harris and Harris, 1984

Because many of the major goals in sport may be several months or even years away, it is often necessary to develop short and long term goals. Bunker (1985) sees goals as 'stepping stones to success'.

Such an approach necessitates careful planning, firstly to identify the long term goal, and secondly, to see how a series of steps (short term goals) can lead to the long term end. Recognizing progress requires consideration of the ways in which achievement of the goal can be evaluated.

Embracing many of these ideas, Harris and Harris developed a list of guidelines for coaches in setting goals.

1. Goals are established by performer or performer and coach.
2. Goals should be put in writing.
3. Goals must be challenging but attainable, measurable, realistic and manageable.
4. When two or three goals are established they must be compatible.
5. Goals should be flexible enough to allow for revision and change.
6. Goals should have structured time frames or target dates.
7. Priorities should be structured for goals.
8. All factors related to goal attainment should be taken into account.
9. Goals must be stated to allow for evaluation of effort as well as performance.
10. Goals should be related to the overall aim of performance.

Harris and Harris, 1984

12.2 GOAL SETTING AND CHILDREN

Whilst there is evidence that school aged children are affected in much the same way as adults by goal setting, it is important to remember that there are some key differences which must be considered when dealing with children in the coaching situation.

The coach should be aware of some of the broad principles of child development and individual differences and thus develop a framework within which to work.

12.2.1 PLANNING THE FUTURE WITH YOUNG CHILDREN

With the realization that the experience children receive in their early years can influence their attitudes to, and abilities at, sport for years to come, governing bodies and coaches see a value in working with the very young. In many cases the sports are adapted to encourage this to happen. For example, the Lawn Tennis Association and the Rugby Union have developed short tennis and mini rugby to give children the opportunity to play, practise and compete in games in a way commensurate with their age and ability.

It is not the intention of this chapter to discuss the merits and demerits, or the dangers and benefits of such developments, but it is important to note the major changes that affect the relevance of goal setting that can occur in the years before age 12. To do so it is perhaps necessary to look at the conclusions drawn by psychologists about child development as it might affect goal setting.

Whilst there is always some disagreement amongst psychologists about the precise nature of children's development there are some broad areas of agreement.

Awareness of time

In the 1950s and 1960s, a famous educational psychologist, Piaget, carried out a whole series of tests on children based on the understanding of time (Piaget, 1969). One simple conclusion from these tests is that many children, up to primary age, will have a quite poor understanding of time and would certainly not be capable of understanding the idea of a 'long term goal'. As the children pass through the primary school the time relationship develops, but even so, understanding goals requires an understanding of intention, etc.

This sort of information suggests that there is value in the exploratory form of play that young children often take part in, i.e. 'Let's try this – I'll have another go – Yes, that's O.K. – I like this – O.K. I've had enough for now'. Perhaps all we need do at this stage is provide equipment that allows this sort of 'play'.

This notion of immediacy and non-adult values might be made clearer by the following example. While on holiday I once watched a young boy, 2–3 years old, pick up a 'large' pebble and throw it. His pleasure seemed to be in the fact that it had gone – when he found it again he repeated the throw. This occurred several times and then he went to paddle. The satisfaction was very much in the movement, one could identify a curiosity satisfied in some way by the act itself, there was no concern as to where the pebble went and the whole throwing experience lasted only a few minutes. A child a little older may throw the pebble at something or someone but may still have no thought beyond the immediate throw.

It concerns me somewhat when young children are subjected to heavily directed practice which the coach says is necessary for some future goal. The best teachers and coaches of the young seem to be those who can provide varied 'play' experiences that are enjoyable in their own right but which form the basis for the achievement of more long term goals. These goals are frequently recognized by the coach but not stated to the child.

The parent or coach who throws and catches a ball with a child may well hope the child will become a good games player but might do better to show the pleasure in throwing and catching than express the goal for the future.

Time, intention and consequence

It is misleading to believe that, as youngsters begin to develop the idea of time and the future, they will necessarily link this accurately with consequence. Again it may be worth recounting a classic experiment, 'the well intended act' from the field of psychology.

A group of children between five and 12 years of age were told a number of stories. The basic story would consist of a well intentioned act which went wrong – e.g. 'A young boy helps a shortsighted old lady across the road at a zebra crossing but a speeding car rounds a corner and the lady is knocked down' – followed by an appropriate question, e.g. 'Is the boy naughty?'.

This sort of story elicits a 'Yes, the boy was naughty' from the younger children and 'No, it was not his fault' from the older children.

Whilst all the children can follow some sequencing of events young children have not as yet learnt to place intention and consequence within a moral framework. Events are usually judged simplistically.

At first sight the coach might ask what this has to do with coaching. Great care is necessary with young children to ensure that short term events 'satisfy' the child. A coach working with adults might well explain that on first developing a new skill they will perform 'badly' but by the end of the lesson the performance will be much improved. A similar strategy may not work with the very young. A coach who identifies a fault in an action with an adult will usually be accepted because the adult can place the fault identification into the larger context of improving the skill. This is not necessarily so with the child.

Similarly, whilst we might wish to develop the idea that 'It is the pursuit of victory that yields the joy, the fun, in sport' (Martens, 1985) we must recognize that the relationships involved in working for victory are complex and that, for the children, intention and effort may be less easily associated with consequence than for adults. It is not surprising, therefore, that children find it difficult to separate effort and ability, as described by Glyn Roberts in Chapter 1.

What seems to be needed is a development from a purely 'experiential play' situation, through a more guided period in which situations are designed to present quite immediate and achievable goals, e.g. 'I wonder if you can run all the way to the tree?', 'Can you throw the ball high?' and then with care toward goals which may last a few minutes and be a little more 'risky', e.g. 'Can you get five out of 10 in the bucket?'. Eventually longer term goals can be set, but there is evidence that the children are still not ready to move into adult goal setting strategies. When young children can set long term goals, they may still be unable to subdivide that goal into the stepping stones of short term goals (Bandura and Schunk, 1981). Clearly those working with the primary aged child, or indeed an elder performer with learning difficulties, must assess just how well these concepts like time, division and consequence are developed.

The 'well intentioned act' experiments discussed earlier are often further developed to show the importance of respected models when arriving at decisions. Very simply, the way a child reacts to the question 'Is the boy naughty?' is noted and similar stories are told, but this time before the child answers another person answers in a converse way to that expected of the child being observed. Very often the youngster conforms with the model, i.e. answers in a way differently to the way s/he would have answered alone. Although the results are a little more complex, suffice it to say that the young people changed their answers to conform. (Readers interested in the development of time, morality, etc. in children may wish to follow up the work of Wimmer or Kohlberg in the general psychology literature.)

Once again this has important implications for the coach in that setting 'having fun' and 'helping young people develop' objectives is doomed to failure while practising 'winning at all costs'. If performers are surrounded by 'win at all costs' models – in the coach or perhaps senior performers – the evidence seems to suggest that this will certainly override what the coach says and will probably override the performers' personal goals. Equally, it must be remembered what pressure the young performer is under when attendance at practice breaks the demands for conformity from a peer group.

At the specific level, the commitment to a goal may be affected by the way other performers accept similar goals (Hollenbeck and Klein,

1987). In other words, the goals set must match the social environment in which they are to operate.

Coaches and sports psychologists have recognized the importance of ensuring that, in team activities, individual goals fit with team goals. The coach of younger children must consider whether the youngsters have developed the social skills necessary to understand how their behaviour affects others. How well do the youngsters grasp the inter-dependence of individual and team goals?

12.3   SPORT – AN ACHIEVEMENT SITUATION

McClelland (1961) and Atkinson (1964) in the now famous books *The Achieving Society* and *An Introduction to Motivation* began to formulate an approach to motivation called Achievement Motivation. The case is presented that to be an achievement situation, three conditions are necessary:

1.   The performer is more or less in control of his/her behaviour.
2.   There is some risk (of success or failure).
3.   The performer knows whether s/he has succeeded or failed.

It has been argued that competitive sport is a particularly good example of this form of situation in that it often meets all three criteria in a very clear way. This is particularly so in 'head to head' competition in sports as different as boxing, tennis, ice skating, high jump, swimming, etc.

Researchers in the area went on to investigate how variations in the chances of success and failure might influence the enthusiasm with which different individuals approached the task. They thought that as the probability approached 50:50 then the more attraction the task held for individuals who had a high need to succeed (sometimes called high achievers) but the less attractive it became for individuals who had a high fear of failure (often expressed as a low need to achieve). The situation was reversed when tasks were perceived as very easy or very hard, (i.e. the individuals who feared failure were more attracted to these tasks than the 50:50). Since much of competitive sport, e.g. leagues, ladders, knockout competitions, qualifying times, is structured to bring people of very similar abilities together in competition it follows that the 50:50 situations occur regularly in competitive sport. It is not surprising, therefore, that Carron (1980), in reviewing the evidence, noted 'that higher levels of nAch (need to achieve) are associated with superior performance'.

As will be seen later the theoretical base of attraction to the task has since been modified and the 50:50 goal is not always the appropriate goal, even for the higher achiever. Even so, the underlying theory draws the attention of the sporting world to the nature of competition and the need to recognize that there are many people who might benefit from a sport experience but who fear failure to the extent that they do not welcome some of the challenges that sport poses. Carron (1984) further noted that 'research which has been carried out with motor skills has generally found that high nAch (need to achieve) individuals demonstrate superior performance to low nAch individuals but only in the early stages of development'. Clearly, first contacts with sport are most important in determining future participation, but a particular sport setting may present challenges unsuitable for some children.

12.3.1 LEVEL OF GOAL SETTING AND THE INDIVIDUAL

It is important to realize that everyone has motives to achieve success and to avoid failure which are independent of each other. That is, we would all like to enter a situation where we could succeed but we may be worried about failing. The key issue is how the balance of these two motives occurs. Other psychologists, notably Maehr (1974), question whether an individual's balance of motives are the same for every situation. Suffice it to say that children in sporting situations will wish to succeed, may fear failure, and will persist despite failure to different degrees. Much will depend on what they consider to be success or failure.

As an oversimplification, many coaches and most top performers can be expected to be high achievers; that is, they enjoy the risk that sport offers because they like to put themselves on the line and rise to the challenge. The danger is that many coaches believe that everyone who comes to sport thinks as they do. This is a commonly accepted phenomenon known as the 'assumed similarity of others' syndrome and is not restricted to coaches.

Let us suppose that the children are shooting basketballs. The danger is that the coach assumes the best place to shoot from is far enough away to provide a good challenge, i.e. where we might get 4 or 5 out of 10. Having achieved 5 the first time, the coach might then think it reasonable to suggest the shooter now tries to get 6. This may make the task attractive for some, but not all of the children. It may be that some children would prefer, certainly at first, to shoot from much nearer to get 8 or 9 out of 10; having got 8 a few children may welcome a goal of 7 from 10, something they are certain they can achieve.

Clearly, if we hope to keep all children playing basketball we will need to set individually determined goals. As this is not always easy to do with quite large groups, two strategies might be considered;

(a) Careful note should be taken of those who relish the challenge, and those who do not, so that some option to continue practising or enter the challenge can be given;

or

(b) A movement toward child determined goal setting should be initiated.

Not surprisingly, different youngsters have different forms of goals, and Glyn Roberts (1984, 1986) has suggested that stress, competence and drop-out in adolescent sport are strongly related to the sorts of goals the youngsters focus on when competing. Certainly those young performers who strive to demonstrate ability and avoid demonstrating lack of ability (ability oriented) are the youngsters who only see winning and losing as important. Consequently they see competitive sport as stressful, in comparison to youngsters who focus more on mastery of the task for its own sake (task oriented). It is also important to note that the early teenage years are years of social comparison and therefore there seems some sense in recognizing:

> The need to decrease the threatening nature of competitive sport for adolescents by emphasizing intrinsic enjoyment and the pursuit of personal performance goals . . .
>
> Vealey and Campbell, 1988

Are performance goals always necessary?

A far more common indication of children's unwillingness to put themselves on the line is a lack of enthusiasm to keep score. How many times have coaches set a task or game which involves a fairly tight scoring system only to find that whilst some children (and perhaps adults) keep score with relish, others avoid scoring at all costs. Instead of admonishing the children for not keeping score the coach might make a note of the fact and consider the implications. The first step is to identify why they are in the sporting situation in the first place if they do not want to score. The incentives identified by Alderman and Wood (1976) have provided a framework for considerable research. This research suggests that being with friends and interacting with people (affiliation), doing something well and feeling competent (success), being active and stressed in a controlled way (stress), were the most powerful incentives even with young people in serious competitive situations. Jean Whitehead's extensive work with children in Britain (Chapter 9) indicates that whilst these incentives can be used as a broad framework, a slightly different approach to children's goals might be more appropriate.

Often the children who avoid scoring get considerable pleasure from playing, perhaps taking satisfaction from playing with a friend or the pleasure of doing something well by their own standards. They may simply enjoy 'running about'. It is not that they do not have goals, it is that they do not wish to accept those of the coach, i.e. they may not see the value of the goal and/or may reject the level set by the coach. They may see it as a good goal, but may not be interested in attempting to achieve it.

12.3.2 THE LEVEL OF GOAL SETTING AND THE SITUATION

It should now be apparent that goal setting should be related to the individual and a major influence on the goals is the confidence of the performer. Confidence in oneself is linked with personality dimensions like self-concept but confidence is also affected by the situation (self-efficacy).

Sport abounds with stories of individuals who can perform well in practice but cannot do the same in competition. Recognizing this, Hardy (1985) makes the link between an anxiety caused by competition, underperformance, acceptance of goals and therefore resultant goal setting. Simply put, the recognition that competition causes competitive anxiety leads Hardy to suggest that the goal difficulty likely to be accepted for competition should be less than that for training. What is perhaps worth remembering is that when children first attend a session with a new coach, etc., anxiety will be high. What might seem to be quite a reasonable goal for a confident youngster in a familiar situation will almost certainly be too hard for an anxious newcomer. It follows that the youngster may not accept the hard goal and one way to do this is to go away and not come back!

12.4 HOW IMPORTANT IS THE GOAL?

12.4.1 DREAMS AND GOALS

There will be little doubt that as young performers mature and associate with heroes they will have dreams of winning an Olympic gold, the Wimbledon Tournament or scoring the winning goal at Wembley, etc. This long term goal Orlick (1986) appropriately calls a dream goal. More realistically, the youngster might be aiming to win the regional championships. One has to question the need for the coach to set such absolute goals when the youngster has them anyway; more importantly, these forms of goal are largely outside the control of the performer and it may be inappropriate for the coach to stress them, e.g. failure to achieve these goals may be due to the inclusion of an 'international star' in the draw or an injury to the performer. Equally a win may be because other good players are at another tournament. Hardy (1985) presents the case that

> ... specific goals within the control of the performer should:
> (i)   set a target for the next competition;
> and
> (ii) reduce the influence of other performers upon that target to a minimum.
> Consideration of these two factors leads to the view that effective goals must be phrased in terms of scores, or times, rather than positions.
>
> Hardy, 1985

The necessity for such an approach is of course magnified when one deals with young people. The young performers mature and develop skills at different rates. The youngster who is winning the Under 12 may not be winning the Under 14, despite ideal coaching and practice opportunities, perhaps because his or her peers have matured later and caught up, as John Aldridge has explained in Chapter 5.

12.4.2   WHEN THE SPORTING GOAL BECOMES TOO IMPORTANT

There has been considerable concern that in those sports which take large amounts of the athlete's time, if coach and parent are not careful, then the sport assumes such a central role in the child's life that achievement or failure to achieve major goals set in the sport become associated with feelings of self-worth in life. This has been documented in games like tennis in which precocious youngsters who have been successful as juniors begin to judge themselves and see others as judging them in terms of sport success to the extent that they dare not lose or they fail as a person.

> Three years ago Lori said 'Tennis is everything; I wouldn't want to live without tennis'. A year later she walked away from the game.
>
> McDermott, 1982

Whilst it is difficult to amass more than anecdotal evidence about this concern it is real enough to suggest that coaches must consider sport in the context of the total development of the young performer. Martens (1985) identifies three major objectives: 1) winning, 2) having fun, and 3) helping young people develop physically, psychologically and socially. Whilst it is possible that some coaches work for all three, others tend to favour one or another. This might be acceptable with adults but it could be that all coaches who work with children should place objective 3 as the major coaching goal.

12.4.3 WHAT SORT OF GOALS?

It has already been argued that performance goals, e.g. scores or times, are more appropriate than outcome goals, e.g. positions, because they are within the control of the performer. It can, of course, be argued that many performers set themselves this sort of goal anyway (Weinberg et al., 1985), e.g. at this time the child is jumping 1.20m, she thinks she can manage 1.25m in two weeks and maybe 1.30m by the end of the season. With a little encouragement and sound reasoning she begins to see this as preferable to wanting to beat 'X' in two months time, which may happen anyway.

Even so, this approach has dangers in that, with rapidly maturing youngsters, these goals may become quite inappropriate. For example, as the child becomes sexually mature, physiological changes may combine to cause rapid increase in explosive power. This is not to say the coach should not use performance goals but there are other forms of goals which are within the performer's grasp, particularly (process) goals about training, attitude and behaviour. At a time when predicted performance can be difficult to assess it seems sensible to use these forms of goal as well.

An example might illustrate the point. A young cricketer loses concentration after a relatively short spell of bowling. Merely to say 'Concentrate more' is unlikely to help. If, however, the young bowler is asked to record his/her ability to concentrate on a given target during the bowling spell by giving the concentration a score out of ten, then the coach has caused attention to be given to the task. Of course, this assumes that the player is receptive to this sort of work, but many are. As matches are played, a row of concentration scores appears and it becomes a simple matter to set a goal for the next match or end of season, etc. This identification of present status and a future goal is at the root of an approach which encompasses much of the underlying theory of such goal setting (see Achievement Management Plans below).

12.4.4 WHO SETS THE GOALS?

Whilst you may well be able to set the most appropriate goals and should certainly have in mind short, intermediate and long term goals, you should take care when presenting them. Part of the education of young athletes might be to help them to develop responsibility for their own goal setting. This has a number of advantages:

1. If performers set their own goals, and particularly when they begin to enjoy the whole process involved in setting and working towards goals, motivation remains high.

2. Goals will only be valuable if accepted and it goes without saying that this is more likely if the performers are involved in developing their own goals.
3. When goals are set by the coach, failure to reach them may not be accepted as the responsibility of the performer
4. Coaches cannot be present for all of the training time, and may be unavailable for relatively long periods. If youngsters get used to designing purposeful activity, this may not be a problem.
5. It is perhaps worth remembering that there are times (e.g. the early teens) when youngsters view adult intrusion with suspicion; striving to meet adult goals may cease to be relevant; striving to meet personal or peer group goals may remain attractive.
6. Older children will set, independently, goals of various types (Weinberg et al., 1988); it seems sensible to encourage this 'natural' process to occur.

Of course, coaches play a major role in helping young performers arrive at sensible goals. Let us suppose that a coach and player are trying to set appropriate training time goals. The athlete might decide to practise two hours a day for five days each week. Notice that the goal is one of the sort described earlier and within the control of the performer. In this situation, it may be that the coach adds a touch of realism by pointing out that the athlete has homework or an alternative social commitment. The coach becomes a mentor and coaches should plan a little more carefully how to move the athlete to independent goal setting by the early teens. Understanding the social development of youngsters is as vital as understanding the physiological development.

12.5 ACHIEVEMENT MANAGEMENT PLANS

An approach which helps goal setting within the context of a training programme, and encompasses many of the points identified above, is the Achievement Management Programme described by Singer (1984, 1986). Examples from tennis are included in the explanation to help clarify the approach.

Singer outlines the stages in the process. First, coach and/or performer must identify what aspects are to be worked on (Skills and Processes). These might include performance skills, e.g. forehand; performance strategies, e.g. when to approach the net; physical conditioning, e.g. mobility; and psychological factors, e.g. coping with frustration. Secondly, if progress is to be assessed, the methods of measuring the skills and processes must be determined (Assessment Techniques). Singer recognizes that this assessment will, in some cases, be objective, but in others, e.g. coping with frustration, assessment will rely on the coach or performer's subjective assessment. Even so, a numerical score must be attributed. The third step is to identify the nature and amount of training to be allocated to any given aspect of the work (Training Procedures). With a clear measure of the performer's present ability (Status) and recognizing the practice time available, goals can be set. Recognizing the need for steps along the road to the long term goal, Singer recommends regular checks on progress (New Status) and reassessment of the next short term goal. It is quite apparent from this how the goals and the feedback provided by the assessment function are embraced in a progressive learning experience. The approach outlined by Singer illustrates how goal setting is best seen as a central part in the design of the total development programme. Because the whole process is recorded both coach and performer are clear about the objectives and are making a commitment to them.

12.5.1 AND AFTER THE PERFORMANCE

It would be quite wrong to forget that once the performance has occurred the goals may or may not have been attained. What does the coach say? Stuart Biddle in Chapter 10 indicates just how important this can be.

12.6 SUMMARY OF THE KEY POINTS

1. Goal setting is a particularly powerful technique to aid motivation.
2. Goal setting should be adapted to suit not only physical maturity but also cognitive development. Coaches should be aware that young children have incomplete understanding of time and the relationship between intention and consequence.
3. Remember that what coaches often perceive as an appropriate challenge (harder than a 50:50 chance of success) motivates some children but may have the reverse affect on others.
4. Some children take part in sport for reasons other than winning competitive situations.
5. The logic that led Hardy (1985) to propose that goals should be reduced when the performer is in the stress of competition can be extended to the youngster (particularly those lacking confidence) in a strange environment, with a new coach, learning a new skill, etc.
6. Most young athletes will be dreaming of winning prestigious events. That goal is already there so the coach should concentrate on setting goals within the control of the individual, i.e. personal performance goals.

7. There are goals associated with training, concentration, emotional control, attitude, etc. completely within the control of the young performer and yet of perhaps longer term value than the more obvious goals of event success. (Remember these must be quantified to be most effective.)

8. Never let the attainment of sporting goals become so significant that the whole self-esteem of the youngster is affected by success and failure in the particular sport.

9. Long term motivation is best enhanced when intrinsic incentives are operating and work is self-directed. Goal setting is just one of the many things which can be moved from coach to performer.

10. In sport, goal setting usually occurs in a social context. Younger children may not have learnt the interdependence of social behaviour. For older youngsters the social situation can be a major factor in goal focused behaviour.

11. Remember goal setting is only effective if well planned and designed to suit the individual youngster.

REFERENCES

Alderman , R.B. and Wood, N.L. (1976) An analysis of incentive motivation in young Canadian athletes. *Canadian Journal of Applied Sport Science*, 1, 169–76.

Atkinson, J.W. (1964) *An Introduction to Motivation*, Van Nostrand Rheinhold, New York.

Bandura, A. and Schunk, D.H. (1981) Cultivating competence, self-efficacy and intrinsic interest. *Journal of Personality and Social Psychology*, 41, 586–98.

Beggs, W.D.A. (1990) Goal setting in sport, in *Stress and Performance*, (eds G.L. Jones and L. Hardy), Wiley and Sons Ltd, USA.

Bunker, L.K. (1985) Goal setting; the key to success, in *Sports Psychology*, (eds L.K. Bunker, R.J. Rotella and A.S. Reilly), Mouvement Publications, Ithaca, New York.

Carron, A.V. (1980) *Social Psychology of Sport*, Mouvement Publications, Ithaca, New York.

Carron, A.V. (1984) *Motivation: Implications for Coaching and Teaching*, Sports Dynamics, London, Ontario.

Hardy, L. (1985) *Factors Affecting Performance*. National Coaching Foundation Level 2 Resource Pack (recently revised as *Mental Preparation*), Springfield Books Ltd, Denby Dale.

Harris, D.V. and Harris, B.L. (1984) *The Athlete's Guide to Sports Psychology*, Leisure Publications.

Hollenbeck, J.R. and Klein, H.J. (1987) Goal commitment and goal setting process: problems, prospects, and proposals for future research. *Journal of Applied Psychology*, 72(2), 212–20.

Locke, E.A., Shaw, K.N., Saari, L.M. and Latham, G.P. (1981) Goal setting and task performance; 1969–1980. *Psychological Bulletin*, 90, 125–52.

McClelland, D.C. (1961) *The Achieving Society*, Van Nostrand Rheinhold, New York.

McDermott, B. (1982) All the glitter has gone. *Sports Illustrated*, **12**, 83–96.

Maehr, M. (1974) Toward a framework for the cross-cultural study of achievement motivation: McClelland reconsidered and redirected, in *Psychology of Motor Behaviour and Sport*, (eds M.G. Wade and R. Martens), Proceedings of North American Society for the Psychology of Sport and Physical Activity, Human Kinetics, Champaign, IL.

Martens, R. (1985) Coaching Philosophy – Winning and Success. In Competitive Sport and Young Children. Coaching Focus, **2** Autumn; National Coaching Foundation.

Orlick, T. (1986) *Psyching for Sport: Mental Training for Athletes*, Human Kinetics, Champaign, IL.

Piaget, J. (1969) *The Child's Conception of Time*, Routledge and Kegan Paul, London.

Singer, R.N. (1984) *Sustaining Motivation in Sport*, Sport Consultants International, Florida.

Singer, R.N. (1986) *Peak Performance and More*, Mouvement Publications, Ithaca, New York.

Vealey, R.S. and Campbell, J.L. (1988) Achievement goals of adolescent figure skaters; impact on self-confidence, anxiety and performance. *Journal of Adolescent Research*, **3**(2), 227–43.

Weinberg, R.S., Bruya, L.D. and Jackson, A. (1985) The effects of goal proximity and goal specificity on endurance performance. *Journal of Sports Psychology*, **7**, 296–305.

Weinberg, R.S., Bruya, L.D., Longino, J. and Jackson, A. (1988) Effect of goal proximity and specificity on endurance performance of primary grade children. *Journal of Sport and Exercise Psychology*, **10**(1), 81–91.

PART FOUR
Applications to the Coaching Process

Up to this point the contributions in the book have provided, first, reasons why coaching children merits serious consideration beyond simply teaching skills and trying to win contests; second, descriptions of different aspects of development, why children '. . . are not mini-adults.'; and third, a review of some particularly important aspects of children's psychological experiences in doing sport. In Part Four the authors give specific advice on specific skills which will help coaches to meet better the needs of their athletes. The material deals with the psychology of the relationship between coaches and children and helping children to deal with disappointments. It then goes on to give guidance on setting up appropriate training schedules, prevention and treatment of injuries, and encouraging children to eat healthily both in training and in competition.

The topics addressed are all to do with skills which coaches must call upon in order to do their job most effectively. They are also skills which are all too often left to chance. Coaches who attend the courses run by their governing bodies are, quite naturally, given considerable advice on how to teach specific sports skills, They will probably also receive instruction on developing fitness to meet the requirements of their sport, usually in adults. Less frequently do such courses include the design of programmes specifically to meet the special case of children. Even less frequently is advice given on how to communicate most effectively or how to deal with the individual problems which athletes experience as a result of the difficulties they face.

Martin Lee and Lew Hardy are psychologists who have considerable experience of working with young athletes. They use their experience to show how best to develop good coaching relationships. Martin Lee shows how coaches can learn to communicate most effectively with young players. He draws attention to the need for clarity and using language suitable for young people based on a social skills training and shows the value of recognizing children's behaviour using a technique derived from counselling psychology.

It is inevitable that coaches find themselves in the position of dealing with children under stress and often in states of some distress. Lew Hardy explains how coaches can help children deal with problems caused by the stresses of competition. He gives good advice on the importance of being able to ask good questions and to listen carefully to the answers before suggesting ways of dealing with some of the different problems which commonly occur.

Neil Armstrong and Joanne Welsman build on their earlier explanation of how children respond to exercise by showing how to set up suitable training programmes specifically for children and young athletes. They outline the principles upon which training programmes should be based and introduce the acronym FIT (frequency, intensity, time) which is applied to aerobic, anaerobic, muscular fitness, and flexibility training.

Coaches are usually the first people on the spot when children suffer injuries and to whom children and parents turn for advice on dealing with them. While you should have a knowledge of first aid you cannot and should not be expected to undertake the role of a doctor or physiotherapist. However, it is important that you know something about the nature and treatment of different types of injury to which children are susceptible. Skeletal injuries are more common among children yet receive little attention in most texts. John Aldridge tells us about the ways in which injuries to the skeleton can occur as a result of training and the effects they can have upon development. Dennis Wright describes the processes involved in the repair of both hard and soft tissue injuries. He gives guidance on first aid but draws attention to the importance of seeking professional advice as soon as possible, in many cases immediately.

Lastly in this section is some very good advice on helping children to eat properly in a society where convenience foods are increasingly common. Food is the fuel for the body's engine and 'You can't run a Formula One car on 2-star petrol'. Juliet Wiseman explains the value of different types of food material and where they may be obtained before giving clear guidelines and examples of the types of diet children should be encouraged to follow. She finishes by suggesting meals for active children and the sort of food to take to competitions.

Communicating effectively with children

13

Martin Lee

SUMMARY

Good coaches are usually good communicators. In this chapter we will be exploring the skill of communication. Communication is examined as a social skill using an information processing approach similar to that used to analyse physical skills. The importance of understanding and using different forms of communication, words, tone of voice, and posture and gesture, is explained. In order to help coaches become sensitive to the nature of interaction between coach and athlete the principles of a counselling technique, transactional analysis, are explained. The chapter is concluded with some suggestions about how to use these techniques in the coaching situation.

13.1 INTRODUCTION

13.1.1 THE NEED FOR COMMUNICATION SKILLS

The need to exercise good communication skills is commonly held to be an important quality of people in authority. We all like to be 'kept in the know' by our superiors, especially when decisions which affect our lives are being made. As part of the communication process we also like to be listened to, consulted, as well as being given information and instructions. Not only are these things important but the way in which they are done is also very important. If instructions are not clear we often make mistakes; if information is incomplete we cannot make informed decisions; if nobody listens to us we feel unimportant; and if we are not consulted we may become apathetic.

Like others in positions of influence, good coaches are good communicators. Indeed, in a survey of young athletes opinions about the qualities of ideal coaches one experienced junior commented that being able to communicate well was essential because '. . . it's no good (him) having knowledge if he can't tell me; it might as well be locked up' (Lee and Austin, 1988). But communication is not only concerned with imparting knowledge, it is also a major ingredient of promoting and maintaining relationships. The way coaches manage relationships with their athletes has an important influence on the enjoyment of the sport by the athletes, their continued participation, and the ways in which they perceive themselves (Horn, 1985; Smith *et al.*, 1979; Smith *et al.*, 1983).

13.1.2   COACHING AS SOCIAL INTERACTION

Sport is an example of a social situation in that it involves the action of individuals in association with others. Therefore the patterns of interpersonal behaviour that apply are the same as those which apply in other settings. One person's actions are usually influenced by the behaviour of those around him or her. Therefore some form of agreement on the conventions involved and the understanding of signals from each other is necessary. There are rules of communication just as there are rules of sport to which people agree to play.

The purpose of this chapter, therefore, is to examine the processes which underlie communication in coaching. This will be done by introducing communication as a social skill and by describing a counselling approach to help understand the conflicts that sometimes occur between coach and athlete.

13.2   SOCIAL SKILLS

I want now to describe briefly a social skills approach to communication. It is akin to theories of skill acquisition. As with throwing a discus, performing a back somersault or shooting an arrow, social interaction may be described as skilled behaviour and assessed in terms of the attainment of certain goals. Any difference between the goal and the outcome can be used as feedback to the performer and result in a modification of the action next time.

Communication skills are an integral part of all social skills; it might be argued that the two are synonymous, and clearly the same processes of goal directed behaviour accompanied by feedback and subsequent modification apply. A most important element in the sequence is the feedback which demands that coaches are not only competent senders of messages but must also be expert at 'listening' to them. Listening here is taken to include not only perceiving verbal messages but also to interpreting non-verbal messages.

13.2.1   COMPONENTS OF SOCIAL SKILLS

Good communication is conducted through a series of sequential processes and may use one or more different channels. This is much the same as the broadcasting process which involves programme making, transmission and reception, and then the programmes may go out on the radio or television.

Processes

Successful communication with others depends upon integrating a number of different processes. These include selecting material (selection), putting it into an amenable form (coding), sending it (transmission), another person receiving it (reception), recognition (decoding), and interpretation. How this is done may be different for different children and mistakes will result in unintended messages being received.

Selection is the process of choosing the most appropriate information to give in a particular situation. The type and amount will often differ according to the level of ability of the performer.

The form in which we present information is called the code. Verbal instruction is an oral code, demonstrations are visual, physical guidance may be a kinesthetic code. To be effective the code should be clearly understood by the learner. We have to use a language that children understand.

Transmission is the process of actually giving the information. Rather like a radio signal it should be loud and clear, and free from interference in the form of distractors.

Receiving the message can only be done if the receiver is attending. So it is important to gain attention, get the group to 'tune in' to your signal as it were, before giving information.

Once received, a message must be decoded and interpreted. That is to say, the information must be recognized by the athlete in a way that is meaningful to him or her. Clearly, if the coach uses a code that the child readily understands then it will be more easily understood. This may mean using particularly meaningful images with which they associate.

This is a complicated series of stages at any one of which mistakes can occur which may destroy the effectiveness of the coaching. For example, improving performance of a basic skill in a beginner will probably demand a different set of instructions from those for an experienced performer. Similarly it may be more helpful to use more than one code, for example demonstrating a movement (a visual code) after explaining it (a verbal code). Even within the choice of a verbal code we often find that we use language which children do not understand. Research has shown that people from different social groups use different forms of language which results in some messages not being properly understood, so it is important to use a form of language or imagery which the child is happy with.

Communication channels

An understanding of good communication is not possible without a clear awareness of the channels we use. The most obvious is the spoken word, verbal communication. Nevertheless, the content of the spoken word is modified, most importantly by the patterns of speech – pauses, pace, intonation, and hesitations, for example – which are known as paraverbal, and also by non-verbal forms which include, for example, gaze, posture and gesture. Such is the importance of these other channels that it has been estimated that as much as 90% of the information in a message may be transmitted by non-verbal and paraverbal (body language and speech patterns) means (Mehrabian, cited in Turner, 1983) and Professor Michael Argyle of Oxford University has estimated that non-verbal messages are 16 times more powerful than verbal ones (Argyle, 1988).

Verbal

Speech takes several forms and provides the explicit content of the messages. Three forms are most commonly used in normal situations: giving information, giving instructions, and asking questions (Argyle, 1988). Good coaching requires the effective use of all three. Information is important for explaining to children what they are trying to do and how to do it. Instructions tell them what they must do; they may form a large percentage of coaching communications and can be persuasive or authoritarian. Questions extract information; good coaches can use questioning effectively to check children's understanding of what they are doing and their instructions.

Paraverbal

The way in which we speak gives a great deal of information to listeners. Hesitancy signals lack of confidence; slow speech may signal control and seriousness; the tone of voice gives clues to emotional states. Effective communicators command attention by change of tone and judicious use of pauses, and the voice is a prime tool for showing enthusiasm and urgency. Practising and varying the use of the voice is particularly valuable when dealing with young children who may not recognize the intended messages in paraverbal signals because they are different to those used at home. I have come across one child who dropped out of a sport because he didn't like the voices of the coaches! They spoke rather harshly and he wasn't used to it. The inference here is to get to know the children individually and address them in a language and manner to which they can relate easily.

Non-verbal communication

It is not possible within the space available to explore comprehensively the forms and impact of non-verbal behaviour. However, such is its importance that we must refer to it, especially since it betrays our attitudes so clearly (Argyle, 1981). No matter what our words say, the gaze, facial expressions, gesture and posture we adopt give the game away.

Gaze Where we look and for how long is a very powerful non-verbal signal. On average people in neutral conversation look at the other for 60% of the time, but more when talking (75%) than listening (40%) and look only for about 3 seconds at a time. Eye contact occurs about 30% of the time and for 1.5 seconds on each occasion (Argyle, 1988). Changes from these rates might then be interpreted as unusual and associated with special qualities. For example, high rates of gaze generally indicate attention, high rates of gaze while talking indicate power over others, and high status people gaze more while talking and less while listening. There is also evidence that high rates of gaze indicate confidence, friendliness and maturity, while low rates of gaze indicate nervousness, coldness, caution and indifference (Argyle, 1988). Finally, people tend to look away from a speaker if they don't understand what is being said (Turner, 1983).

Facial expressions are particularly important for showing emotions and attitudes. Six major categories of emotion have been consistently identified and can be recognized by children by the age of two. They are: happiness, surprise, fear, anger, sadness and disgust (Argyle, 1988). Since facial expressions give so much away, lack of expression can result in lack of security in the observer. However, when we try to show emotions which we don't feel older children are able to detect it because they can take account of the context as well as the behaviour (Argyle, 1988).

Gestures can be used to support and emphasize words, to give feedback, and to simulate movements in coaching. Perhaps most important are the gestures of the head, arms and hands. Nodding while a child is talking, for example, signifies approval and encourages more talking. Looking away can signify boredom or disinterest and cause some anxiety.

Postural messages are given by the whole body and it has been suggested that they indicate the intensity of an emotion. For example, if you are happy with the performance of an athlete you may stand and become very animated, gesturing with your hands and arms. Clearly if you do not behave in this way children may interpret it as indifference. Urgency is conveyed by leaning forwards, looking directly at the other person, standing close, touching. Folded arms are perceived as rejecting and unyielding while standing with hands on hips expresses a negative attitude (Argyle, 1988). In a study of children's preferences for an ideal coach one swimmer told us that she hated to come out of the pool after a poor swim and see her coach at the other end of the pool with her hands on her hips. When that happened she kept away from the coach for at least an hour!

Both gestural and postural messages reveal our attitudes, however unconsciously. Nevertheless we can use them to convey important messages to children quite deliberately, although it requires becoming a bit of an actor. Not only should we be conscious of our body language but we must also be able to read the body language of the children we coach. This may not be as easy as it seems, specially in a multicultural society where cultural norms of behaviour may differ from our own. For example, some Asian children are brought up not to look adults in the eye. This may be interpreted as indifference or even insolence when it is intended to be respectful.

13.3 TRANSACTIONAL ANALYSIS

I would now like to turn to the perceptual side of good communication; the ability to observe and listen to what children are saying and feeling. It is rather like listening to a song; the words convey some meaning but the music can convey so much more!

A key feature of listening to the 'music' is the ability to develop empathy with the other person, the 'singer'. Empathy means being able to see others as they see themselves, to understand their view of the world, and to be able to help them to develop more fully (Nelson-Jones, 1982). When dealing with children, adults can be at a disadvantage because they haven't been that age for some time! We may not readily understand the difficulties that children face when learning or practising skills. Using the world of play and fantasy, for example, may be a better way of giving information than formal explanation in adult terms.

Transactional analysis (TA) is an approach to counselling which emphasizes the development of rational behaviour. It is based upon a particular view of personality and focuses on the behaviours shown in a relationship which was developed by psychotherapist Eric Berne

(Berne, 1968). TA uses a simple, colloquial language and ideas which are based on common sense experience. It is both a method of analysing communications and a theory of psychological development (Turner, 1983).

13.3.1 EGO STATES

The view of personality proposed in TA is encapsulated in the idea of 'ego states'. When we watch people, adults or children, we can describe their behaviour as if they were in one of three different roles or ego states: Parent, Adult or Child (Figure 13.1). The clues may be verbal or non-verbal but the behaviour represents a position which the individual is adopting at that time.

Parent

When people are in the Parent ego state they are concerned with care, control, and with goals that 'should' be pursued. Their views represent an internalization of the influence of their parents and teachers – and

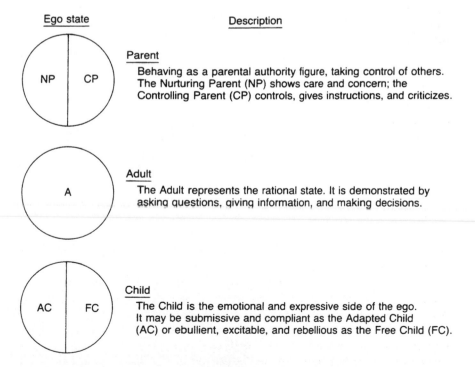

Ego state   Description

Parent
Behaving as a parental authority figure, taking control of others. The Nurturing Parent (NP) shows care and concern; the Controlling Parent (CP) controls, gives instructions, and criticizes.

Adult
The Adult represents the rational state. It is demonstrated by asking questions, giving information, and making decisions.

Child
The Child is the emotional and expressive side of the ego. It may be submissive and compliant as the Adapted Child (AC) or ebullient, excitable, and rebellious as the Free Child (FC).

Fig. 13.1 Characteristics of ego states

maybe coaches, of course. Parent behaviour has two sides: (a) Controlling Parent which is judgemental and sets rules, and (b) Nurturing Parent which is concerned with caring for the well-being of others.

Adult

The Adult is often likened to a computer and is characterized by information processing. So we see the Adult in operation when the person is asking questions, giving answers, making assessments, and selecting between alternatives. It is objective and not concerned with emotions. The Adult develops very rapidly between the ages of six and 12 (Turner, 1983).

Child

The Child is characterized by the expression of feelings, responding to demands made by others, positively or negatively, and being creative, perhaps in playing. As with the Parent, the Child can take two forms. The Free Child is the first to appear and gives vent to powerful feelings, of pleasure and anger for example. The Adapted Child develops as the child learns to adapt his or her behaviour to meet the demands of parents and other adults. So he may learn politeness, submissiveness, and feelings of guilt and anxiety (Turner, 1983).

Table 13.1 summarizes the behaviours, attitudes and communications which identify different ego states. If you think of some youngsters in your care you can probably identify the ego states they are in at different times. You will also notice that different children spend more time in one ego state than another. There is always one who is mucking about when you want him to listen (Free Child); another who is serious and frequently asking questions (Adult); a third who likes to boss the others about (Controlling Parent).

13.3.2 TRANSACTIONS

A transaction occurs when two people communicate. It may be verbal or non-verbal. Clearly, if we can operate from any of five ego states, what we say or do is an expression of one of them. Further, it is directed at a particular ego state in the other person and may draw a reply from that ego state. This is called a complementary transaction (Figure 13.2). For example, a tennis coach may approach teaching a stroke differently for children at different ages. For a youngster who is habitually Adapted Child, the Controlling Parent may speak quite effectively like this:

Table 13.1 Behavioural indications of ego states (From Turner, 1983 by kind permission of the publishers)

	Controlling parent	Nurturing parent	Adult	Free child	Adapted child
Behaviour	Criticizes Commands Dictates	Protects Comforts Helps	Enquires Tests Reasons Gives and receives information	Cries Laughs Rages	Submits Accepts Rebels Reacts
Attitude	Judgemental Moralistic Authoritarian	Understanding Caring Giving Smothering	Interested Observant Rational Evaluating	Curious Fun-loving Changeable	Compliant Ashamed Apologetic Demanding
Key words	Must, Ought Always, Should, Wrong	Love, Good, Splendid, Well done, Help	How, What, Why, Consider, Probable	Super, Wow, Want, Fun, Ouch	Can't Try Sorry Thank you
Voice tone	Critical Condescending Sarcastic Firm Dominating	Loving Comforting Helpful Sugary	Calm, clear Enquiring Precise Monotone	Free, Loud, Sexy, Energetic, Happy, Angry	Whiny Defiant Placating Moaning Demanding
Gestures, postures	Pointing finger Hands on hips Foot tapping Looking down on	Arm round shoulder Leaning forward	Erect Pointing (to demonstrate)	Active energy Cuddles	Slumped Pouting Cringing Foot stamping
Expression	Frowning Set jaw	Smiling Sympathetic Accepting	Alert Interested Pre-occupied	Uninhibited Laughter Excited	Dejected Apprehensive Pleading

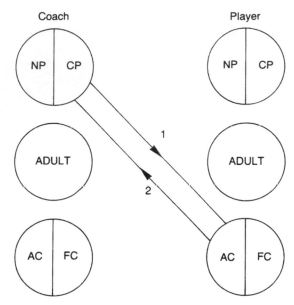

Fig. 13.2 Complementary transaction: Parent to Child

Coach: You *must* always get sideways on when you play the forehand.

Player: OK.

For a player who resists instructions and prefers to make his own judgements (Adult) the coach may find the relationship benefits by teaching from within the Adult as well (Figure 13.3).

Coach: If you get sideways on with your front foot to the ball you can get more weight into the shot.

Player: Oh, now I see what you mean. I'll try it.

In the second case the coach is supplying information which the player can evaluate and act upon if she wishes. Of course, the coach may not wish to give any choice in the matter. If that happens and the player responds from the Adult, the transaction may look like this:

Coach: You *must* always get sideways on when you play the forehand.

Player: But if I do that all the time I won't be able to get as much topspin. I can get more when I hit it front on.

This is known as a crossed transaction (Figure 13.4) and is a common source of conflict between people. When this happens the coach could carry on with Parental, controlling messages, trying to 'hook' the player's Adapted Child without trying to explain why the player

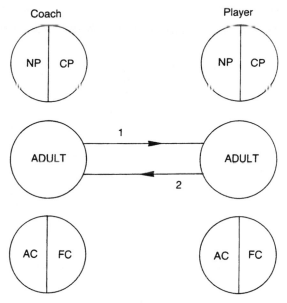

Fig. 13.3 Complementary transaction: Adult to Adult (exchanging information)

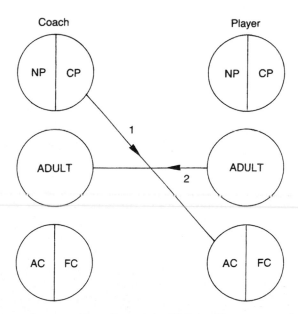

Fig. 13.4 Crossed transaction: Parent to Child with response from Adult to Adult

should take the advice. But this may just provoke conflict and she could change her approach and give information from her Adult to the player's Adult.

Child to Child transactions occur when both coach and player are relaxed and having fun, sharing a joke or enjoying a performance. It is very important for coaches to let their Child show through and have some fun. Many young athletes we have interviewed consider having a good sense of humour to be an essential coaching quality and echo this remark: 'I like the person (*coach*) to have a joke. I like it when they joke about it . . . it makes you try harder' (U16 female international badminton player).

A final form of common transaction is the ulterior transaction in which the spoken message is used to mask another clear message apparent by implication. This may be conveyed by tone, speech pattern or by body language, or be couched in the situational context; whichever, it is the more powerful message. Ironic or sarcastic comments may fall into this category and can be damaging to the relationship because they are not honest.

This is just a very brief introduction to TA. It provides useful insights into social relationships and covers a great deal of ground which is relevant to coaches, teachers and managers. Above all it provides guidance into developing listening skills, being able to distinguish words and music. Readers who wish to pursue the ideas presented here are referred to Eric Berne's *Games People Play*.

13.4   APPLICATIONS TO COACHING

So what does this mean in practical terms for coaches? First, let us consider the outcomes of coaches' efforts to use the principles outlined here. There is strong evidence that learning to use good interpersonal skills greatly benefits young athletes.

A series of extensive studies with children's baseball and basketball coaches in America showed that players whose coaches who had been trained in a programme of interpersonal skills expressed more satisfaction with the season, were more likely to return to play again, and, most importantly, the teams had playing records as good as those whose coaches were not trained (Smith *et al.*, 1979; Curtis *et al.*, 1979; Smith *et al.*, 1983). In other words good communication skills are effective in enhancing children's sports experiences without detracting from success.

In a more recent study Thelma Horn, another American sport psychologist, looked more closely at the effects of coaches' feedback on girls' perceptions of their own competence in softball. She concluded that coaches' practice behaviour was related to children's perceptions of their ability and to changes in those perceptions; to be effective, feedback, praise and criticism must be related to a specific performance, i.e. contingent upon behaviour. Further, children perceived criticism after failure as indicating that the performer had high ability and was expected to do better; overpraining of less successful girls indicated lack of ability (Horn, 1985). This study also showed that young athletes are, not unnaturally, less able to assess their ability than older athletes and rely on their coaches to tell them how good they are. Furthermore, they are not easily fooled!

On the basis of the account of communication given above, it is possible to make some suggestions about how best to communicate most effectively. I'll do this by making suggestions to facilitate different purposes. But first keep firmly in mind that children like to be coached by people who are happy and friendly with a good sense of humour and are consistently patient and understanding (Lee and Austin, 1988).

13.4.1   GAINING CONTROL

1. Be well prepared and have a programme ready to go. This shows that you are organized, are not there to waste time and have expectations of the group.
2. Cut down distractions: remove loose equipment, close doors to cut extraneous noise if you are inside, have the class face away from other groups moving about, and face the sun yourself. With children it is helpful to sit the group down; they can see you more easily and it reduces restlessness.
3. Be positive with your body language: give yourself some distance from the class, say 1.5 to two metres for small groups and up to four metres for larger groups, stand erect, establish eye contact, and wait until you have everybody's attention. To encourage informality and friendliness, specially with little children, sit down to be on their level.
4. Use your voice as an instrument, change the tone, pitch and volume. Sometimes it is best to talk very quietly so that children have to attend carefully to hear, but only if they are already interested.
5. Be prepared for a joke. Children like coaches who are human and can have a laugh with them.

13.4.2   GIVING INSTRUCTIONS

1. Choose material appropriate to the age, ability and experience of the children. They need to have their attention drawn to different aspects of the skill at different times. Detailed instructions that are important to a U15 county champion pole-vaulter are very different

to those required by a child who is just starting – it is actually a different activity!

2. Don't give too much information. As they get better they need to know more, and younger athletes cannot deal with as much information at once as older more experienced athletes.
3. Build on what has gone before, and check that it has been learned.
4. Keep the number of choices a child has to make small to start with. Don't expect children to make all the decisions that you can without thinking. Recall how children with a ball in their hands do not pass it because they are overwhelmed with choices which change continually – they freeze!
5. Use a language that the children understand easily. Find words that are meaningful to them and use visual images that capture their imagination.
6. Be clear and concise; don't ramble on too much, you may lose their interest because they want to do things. Watch and listen to the 'music'; if they get fidgety it is a sign they are ready to do something else, and looking away may mean that they don't understand.
7. *Always* check to see that instructions are clearly understood before starting a practice.

13.4.3 GIVING FEEDBACK

1. Start by asking questions about a performance. Children will learn more if they have to recall and think it through themselves.
2. Find something to comment positively about; mention the 'good news' first, then the 'bad news' (the things that need correcting next time) and finish with some more 'good news'. Criticism *must* be constructive; tell them how to correct a fault. As an U16 footballer said to us, '. . . they should tell you *how* you went wrong . . . and you can change it next time'.
3. Again, don't give children too much to think about; deal with one thing at a time.
4. Don't use 'we' when the athletes do well and 'you' when they do badly. These pronouns indicate identity and can imply credit and blame.
5. Give messages which are high on information and not overlaid with judgement unless that is specifically the purpose. For example, 'If . . . I have done something wrong I should be told . . . but (she should) not start complaining . . . because . . . it is finished, but (she should) tell you how to improve it' (U16 swimmer).
6. Choose your time carefully. 'I like to sit down and think about it myself, and then I go and see the coach and he tells me what I have done wrong' (U16 badminton player).

13.4.4   REINFORCEMENT

1. Always reward children when they have done something well and ensure that they know what they have done. In other words make your reinforcement contingent upon behaviour. Give praise when it is earned and make sure your body language matches your words. It might be, '"Well played", and pats you on the head' (U10 rugby player).
2. Do not overpraise as you will lose credibility. Save the superlatives for superlative performance. 'It doesn't mean much when they go over the top' (U12 swimmer).
3. Be consistent, don't have favourites and be fair.
4. Don't let misbehaviours pass; use some sort of sanction immediately, but do not punish poor performance.

13.4.5   ASKING QUESTIONS

1. Use questions to check comprehension and give yourself the opportunity to listen to your athletes.
2. Encourage children to talk by asking open-ended questions. Closed questions which require 'yes' or 'no' answers cut off conversation.
3. Listen attentively to the answers; don't interrupt, look at the speaker, use nods and phrases like 'Yes, I see', 'Mmm', 'Uh-huh' so that he knows you are listening.
4. Paraphrase the answers to check that you understand correctly.
5. Listen with your eyes as well as your ears. Try to see where the athlete's response to you is coming from, Parent, Adult or Child, and address him or her accordingly. When you get a crossed transaction change your own messages.

13.4.6   A WORD ABOUT PARENTS

This chapter has focused on communication with the children you coach. This is because most of your interaction will be with them. However, children cannot take part in sport these days without the support of parents and to maximize the benefits of the experience to the children, coaches have to deal with them in some form (see Tony Byrne's review and advice in Chapter 4). Although the most common complaint of coaches, in my experience, is about parents, coaches do not always initiate good relationships and some even promote antagonism by excluding them completely. The relationships between athletes, coaches and parents are of paramount importance to successful outcomes and coaches can use their skills to involve the parents in the coaching process by keeping them informed fully about what is going on and what is expected of the child. Remember, the child is part of their family, not yours! Hence the skills which have been outlined here should be used to promote good relationships between all those involved.

REFERENCES

Argyle, M. (1981) Social behaviour, in *Psychology for Teachers*, (ed D. Fontana), Macmillan/BPS, London.
Argyle, M. (1988) *Bodily Communication*, Methuen, London.
Berne, E. (1968) *Games People Play*, Penguin, Harmondsworth.
Curtis, B., Smith, R.E. and Smoll, F.L. (1979) Scrutinizing the skipper: a study of leadership behaviours in the dugout. *Journal of Applied Psychology*, **64**(4), 391–400.
Horn, T.S. (1985) Coaches' feedback and changes in children's perceptions of their physical competence. *Journal of Educational Psychology*, **77**(2), 174–86.
Lee, M.J. and Austin, H. (1988) *'My Ideal Coach'. Children's Preferences for Coaching Behaviour*. Report to the Research Committee of the National Coaching Foundation, Leeds, England.
Nelson-Jones, R. (1982) *The Theory and Practice of Counselling Psychology*, Holt, Rinehart and Winston, Eastbourne.
Smith, R.E., Smoll, F.L. and Curtis, B. (1979) Coach effectiveness training: a cognitive-behavioural approach to enhancing relationship skills in youth sport coaches. *Journal of Sport Psychology*, **1**, 59–74.
Smith, R.E., Nolan, W.S., Smoll, F.L. and Coppel, D.B. (1983) Behavioural assessment in youth sports: coaching behaviors and children's attitudes. *Medicine and Science in Sports and Exercise*, **15**(3), 206–14.
Turner, C. (1983) *Developing Interpersonal Skills*, The Staff College, Bristol.

FURTHER READING

Amison, P., Armstrong, M., Crisfield, P., Shedden, J., Watts, D. and Whittaker, D. (1989) *Delivering the Goods*, The National Coaching Foundation, Leeds.
Crisfield, P. (1990) *Improving Coach/Athlete Communication*. Proceedings of the British Institute of Sports Coaches (BISC) 1989 International Congress Proceedings: The Growing Child in Competitive Sport. BISC, Leeds.
Lee, M.J. (1987) Establishing good relationships. *Coaching Focus*, **2**, 6–7.
Martens, R., Christina, R.W., Harvey, J.S. and Sharkey, B.J. (1981) *Coaching Young Athletes*, Human Kinetics, Champaign, IL.

Counselling young athletes and how to avoid it

14

Lew Hardy

SUMMARY

This chapter discusses some of the more commonly occurring problems: problems of interpersonal relationships, difficulties in coping with failure, recurring negative self-talk, performance anxiety, coping with injuries, and fear of physical harm. It suggests ways in which coaches and parents can reduce the probability of these problems occurring and how they might be dealt with if they do. The strategies discussed include development of communication skills, reward patterns, helping children to develop and maintain self-confidence, sustaining positive training environments, reframing thoughts, and a structured programme of competition training as part of a preparation strategy.

14.1 INTRODUCTION

Essentially, the need for counselling athletes arises because the complex interaction between athlete and environment which constitutes performance goes wrong. Figure 14.1 shows some of the factors which influence this interaction, and hence determine its outcome.

It is perhaps worth noting how loosely the term environment is used here, since many of the major determinants of a performer's environment are in fact other people. Indeed, many of the psychological problems which lead to young performers requiring counselling involve the very people who love the performer most dearly; for example, parents, coaches and friends. It is with relationships with those others that I wish to begin since they can have a profound influence on the athlete's progress.

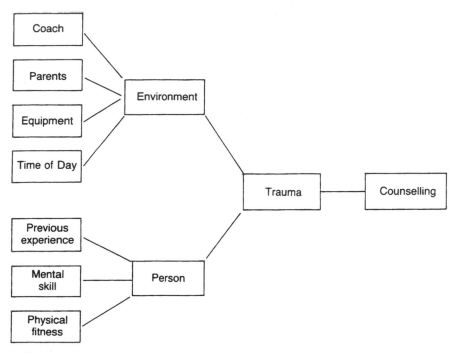

Fig. 14.1 Interaction of personal and situational factors contributing to trauma and a need for counselling

14.2   COACH–PERFORMER AND PARENT–PERFORMER RELATIONSHIPS

In order to perform or train at their optimal level, any performer must have a positive, supportive environment. For example, two Swedish psychologists have shown that one of the most important factors which determined whether good young tennis players became genuinely world class or not was how supportive and democratic (even permissive) their relationship was with their parents and coach. Another important finding was the lack of expectancy which the parents of successful players had regarding their children's involvement in tennis; that is not to say that the parents were disinterested in their children's progress, it is just that they did not put their children under pressure to achieve (Carlson and Engstrom, 1987). The line between being supportive and expressing expectancy about a child's involvement in sport is clearly a very thin one which needs treading carefully. However, actively involving children in decision making processes, and respecting and supporting their decisions and objectives will go a long way towards establishing the sort of relationship which is required. The reason why this sort of relationship is so important is probably because it helps to develop the child's (non-critical) awareness and independence – crucial commodities if the performer is going to cope with the pressures of serious sport. Remember, it is the performer who has to get up and perform, not the coach or the performer's parents!

Other ways of enhancing awareness and independence include asking questions, listening to answers, allowing mistakes to happen, providing informational rather than extrinsic rewards, and developing good goal setting skills.

14.2.1   ASKING QUESTIONS

For example, when one of my gymnasts has a technical problem with a move which they cannot identify, I often tell them that after their next attempt I am going to ask them a question about whatever part of the movement I think is causing the problem. Often, just drawing their attention to a problem area in this non-judgemental way is all that is required for them to be able to put the problem right. The important thing about asking questions like this is that the question should not imply that something is 'wrong', and should not *lead* the person to a 'solution'. The question should simply guide the performer's attention to where it is required. In this way, the performer develops his or her own awareness of the relationship which exists between certain actions and the environment, rather than being dependent upon the coach for instruction all the time. The most important thing to realize is that some questions imply considerably more criticism of the performer than others. As a rough guideline, questions which ask 'What?', 'Where?', 'When?' or 'How?' are fairly safe, whilst questions which ask 'Why?' seem to contain some threat.

14.2.2   LISTENING

I am sure that we all believe that we listen to our performers. Yet coaches are busy people whose time is in great demand, and I cannot help wondering how many of us can honestly put our hands on our hearts and say that we never cut our performers off in mid-sentence even though it is only to agree with them. It is not that long before 'Yes, that's right, well done!' comes to be interpreted as 'There's not much point saying anything to him because he will already know about it anyway'. I wonder when was the last time you heard a coach say 'That's a good idea, I would never have thought of that. How did you work it out?' after the performer had finished speaking. Listening is a skill, and a very powerful one at that. Cultivate it!

14.2.3   ALLOWING MISTAKES TO HAPPEN

Knowing when to allow mistakes to happen and how far to let them develop is another skill which good coaches possess. Unfortunately, there are few easy guidelines, although encouraging children objectively to evaluate the consequences of their actions and decisions will help to resolve the problem. The decision of whether or not to let someone make a mistake should be largely determined by a consideration of the relative value of letting the mistake occur, in terms of experience and lessons learned, versus the psychological or physical damage which could occur as a result of the mistake. Of course, allowing mistakes to happen takes time; but this is well spent, for in the long run it will save far more time than it costs.

14.2.4   INFORMATIONAL REWARDS

Another area where counselling is frequently required is when the athlete has motivational problems. Whilst all performers will need emotional support when they are having a 'hard time of it', children who regularly need motivational help are probably engaged in the sport for inappropriate reasons; for example, because they think their parents want them to do it, or because they get badges and trophies when they do well. Such performers would probably be well advised to seek out other activities which they find more inherently enjoyable. The likelihood of this sort of situation occurring can be reduced by providing children with 'informational rewards' which tell them that they are competent, rather than 'controlling rewards' which lead the child to believe that the reason for being involved in the sport is to obtain the reward.

14.2.5   GOAL SETTING

Many of the worst pressures which children have to overcome can be traced to inappropriate or unrealistic goals. This only serves to emphasize how difficult parents' and coaches' roles are. On the one hand, they must allow performers the scope to make their own decisions and develop their independence whilst, on the other, they must somehow try to protect them from decisions which they know will cause damage or disappointment at some future time. Goal setting is therefore a most important skill for performers, coaches and parents to develop. It is discussed in more detail by Rod Thorpe in Chapter 12.

14.3   COPING WITH FAILURE

14.3.1   DEVELOPING SELF-CONFIDENCE

It could be argued that if appropriate goals are set, then failure should rarely occur. However, when setbacks do occur self-confidence plays an important part in coping with them. Although it takes quite a lot of planning and structured hard work to increase self-confidence, it does not seem to take quite as much planning and hard work to change it in the other direction! A theory by an American psychologist called Albert Bandura helps to explain how self-confidence is developed.

Bandura showed that self-confidence is influenced by four main factors:

1.   previous success;
2.   observing others succeed;
3.   verbal persuasion;
4.   interpretation of your physiological state.

All these factors are important determinants of self-confidence, but one of the crucial things about Bandura's work is that it implies that performance accomplishment is by far the most important of them. It really doesn't matter what your performers say to themselves on the day; if they have only ever experienced failure in the past, then they are unlikely to feel confident in the present! Now, to complete the circle, performance accomplishment is about success, and success is about goal achievement; the more goals your performers achieve, the more success they experience, and the greater their self-confidence becomes (Figure 14.2). The ability to set goals in an appropriate way is therefore once again a most important skill.

14.4   DEALING WITH NEGATIVE SELF-TALK

Whilst negative self-talk disrupts performance by distracting attention and lowering self-confidence, positive self-talk can form a very important part of peak performance by focusing attention, raising self-confidence and enhancing motivation.

14.4.1   POSITIVE TRAINING ENVIRONMENTS

Perhaps the simplest thing you can do to encourage young performers to think positively is to create a very positive training environment. For example, every failure provides at least two opportunities. One is to practise goal-setting, and the other is to achieve a whole set of new goals, thereby enhancing self-confidence. Of course, it is hopeless

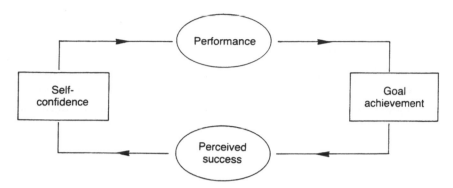

Fig. 14.2 Positive feedback cycle of success and confidence

expecting young performers to think positively if they work in an environment where they are bombarded with negative criticism. Consequently, it is important to try and phrase your coaching in terms of positive statements telling your performers what you would like them to do, rather than negative statements telling them what you would like them not to do.

14.4.2   REFRAMING

Reframing is a means of changing the way you think about situations so that instead of describing them in negative terms you describe them in positive terms. For example, instead of thinking 'I hate bumpy pitches, we never play well on them', the performer could think 'Nobody likes playing on bumpy pitches. I bet they get really fed up with playing on it every week. We've only got to play on it this once, so I am just going to go out there and keep everything very simple'. The key to reframing is that the athlete must recognize what it is that he dislikes about the situation, and why he is worried about it. He should then change the negative self-statement to a positive one. A useful exercise to help develop reframing skills is to have performers keep a log of all their negative self-statements, then sit down with them and identify what is involved in each statement and why they feel negatively about that situation. They should then write down next to each negative statement a positive substitute statement (Table 14.1). In doing this, they should use the present tense, and try to avoid using perfectionist statements like 'I always...' or 'I never....', as these can end up putting them under considerable pressure at a later time.

14.4.3   SUPPORT 'ON THE DAY'

Sooner or later you will probably have the misfortune to find yourself at a major competitive event faced by a performer who has 'gone

Table 14.1 Reframing negative thoughts as positive ones

Negative Thoughts	Positive Thoughts
There's no point trying. I'm useless.	I've seen some really good players who had to work hard to succeed. If I can just stick at it I'm bound to make progress after a couple of sessions.
Oh no, she's here. She always beats me.	She isn't relevant to how I perform. I am going to concentrate on my game regardless of what she does.
If I can just win this point I'll win the match.	This point is just like any other point. Let's just concentrate on playing it the same way as the last one.
I don't really feel like training today. I think I'll have a play with Jack today.	Jack's always ready for a play. I must take care not to be distracted today. I think I will pair up with someone else.
The coach never takes any notice of me. He's always too busy with Steven.	The coach has a lot of people to look after. I must go up to him and ask him what he thinks I should do next.
Why can't I do this? I could do it yesterday, and even Amanda can do it today.	I know I can do this because I did it yesterday. I must be doing something not quite right. I wonder if Amanda can help me to sort it out.

negative'. You might reasonably expect that this chapter should enable you (and the performer) to cope with that event. Unfortunately, I would be doing you both a great disservice if I led you to believe that you could easily talk the performer round into thinking positively. Once things like attitude or motivation have gone wrong on the day, it is very rare that anyone can get the performer into a good performing state. However, if you manage to catch things early enough, you can sometimes get performers back on an 'even keel', by:

1. being generally supportive without smothering them;
2. reassuring them that other people do not have unreasonable expectations of them; and
3. reassuring them that their worth as human beings does not depend upon their performance in the competition. This is difficult to do without diminishing their self-confidence if you only ever reward 'performance' in training. On the other hand, it will be much easier to do if you reward things like effort, persistence and determination in training.

14.5 PERFORMANCE ANXIETY

Most performers experience some anxiety when they are about to perform and there may even be some beneficial effects to be obtained from a mild concern about the importance of an event, since this will presumably lead the performer to invest an appropriate amount of effort in the event. Furthermore, learning to cope with such stressors is an important aspect of the sport experience. However, there can be no place in children's sport for the high levels of performance anxiety which are occasionally observed in young performers. Excessive anxiety is also thought to disrupt performance by tampering with the body's physiological readiness to perform, and by distracting the performer's attention away from the task in hand towards task irrelevant thoughts, which are usually associated with the consequences of failure.

14.5.1 COMPETITION TRAINING

The most effective way for coaches to combat performance anxiety is by careful preparation and planning for events in terms of structured goal setting to build self-confidence. For, as well as being an important factor in coping with failure, self-confidence is probably the best insurance there is against failure occurring. Part of this preparation should include a programme of competition training. This is a programme of training situations structured to reduce the impact of the competitive environment by desensitizing the performer to it. Usually, this is done by constructing a mock competitive environment which gradually includes more and more aspects of real competition.

The idea of slow and steady progress, so that the performer never experiences failure, is central to all forms of competition training for two reasons. First, competition training is almost always done during the 'run-in' to competitions, so that every effort should be made to build self-confidence; and secondly, if failure is experienced then the anxiety which accompanies it can easily become conditioned to the competition training, and even the competition itself.

The detailed format for competition training programmes will, of course, vary from sport to sport, and even sometimes from person to person within a sport. However, Table 14.2 gives an example of a competition training programme for a group of young male gymnasts preparing for an important competition.

Competition training can, of course, be made as general or as specific as you like. For example, the technique can be used to help performers develop strategies for coping with poor refereeing decisions, evaluative audiences, failure feedback, verbal abuse, niggling fouls, etc. All that is required is an appropriate response to the troublesome stimulus. As an

Table 14.2 A programme of general competition training for a group of young gymnasts

Step	Goal	Achievement
1.	Perform routines in two halves after a prolonged warm-up.	
2.	Full routines after a prolonged warm-up.	
3.	Judged routines after a prolonged warm-up.	
4.	Judged routines after a 5 minute warm-up.	
5.	Judged routines after a 2 minute warm-up.	
6.	Judged routines after a formally structured warm-up (30 seconds work followed by 10 minutes sat waiting). No feedback on how mark is arrived at until the end of the session.	
7.	Introduce co-performers.	
8.	Introduce more judges, and 'bad' scores.	
9.	Invite people to come and spectate.	
10.	Play tape recorded distractions from a real competition.	

example, suppose that you wanted to help a young footballer who was easily distracted by refereeing decisions which he considered to be poor or unfair. This sort of distraction usually manifests itself in two ways. Firstly, the player is likely to criticize other decisions made by the referee; and secondly, he is likely to make silly mistakes during the period immediately following the decision (e.g. commit unnecessary fouls, miss shots, fail to identify team-mates in space, etc.). The solution is to structure training sessions so that bad refereeing decisions are deliberately given against the player during certain practice games. Of course, the player must understand the purpose of the practice, and must agree to take part in it of his own free will; otherwise, he will simply get frustrated (or, worse, still, upset) and give up. The practices must also always be structured so that the player succeeds.

To start with, you might only give one or two bad decisions against him, but gradually you must build up the number so that he is able to handle however many may occur during a game. Sometimes the player will cope quite easily with the distraction, but at others he will start to get upset and you will have to take him quietly on one side to patiently remind him that the practice is structured to help him with his problem, and that every distraction which he copes with represents an improvement to his game.

Eventually, when he has learned to cope with the distractions in these games, you can introduce them into practice games without prior warning, so that he gradually learns to cope with them in 'real' games. Remember, however you structure competition training, success is absolutely essential.

Finally, it is worth noting that general competition training desensitizes the performer to both the good and the bad aspects of competition stress. Consequently, some performers are likely to lose 'that little extra spark' which competition can give. In some non-technical/high effort sports (for example, middle distance running, distance swimming) this might be disastrous. However, in my experience, young athletes who consistently perform better in big competitions are a rare breed, so that young performers in most sports are much more likely to benefit than lose out from some form of competition training.

14.5.2   RELAXATION

It will probably be very obvious to most readers that I have so far studiously avoided mentioning relaxation strategies in this discussion. Most psychologists agree that, in all things except name, deep relaxation is the same thing as hypnosis. Furthermore, whilst deep relaxation and self-hypnosis are enormously powerful and useful skills to learn, they can also release very powerful emotions from deep in the subconscious. Children are particularly suggestible in terms of hypnosis, so that the teaching of relaxation skills is beyond the scope of most coaches. They are best left for qualified and experienced sport psychologists to teach.

14.6   INJURY

The frustration and negative moods which often accompany injury are probably brought about by two factors: anxiety about the amount of hard-earned ground which will be lost as a result of the enforced inactivity; and hormonal imbalance due to a suddenly changed lifestyle. The best thing you can do is reassure the performer that they will quickly recover their previous form, and may even lose some 'bad habits' as a result of the rest, then encourage them to reframe their negative worries and feelings into statements about things which they can do whilst they are injured. For example, they could work on mental training techniques, catch up on school work, or engage in other activities which they do not normally have time to do.

14.7   FEAR OF PHYSICAL HARM

Because of the adventurous nature of young people's lives, fear of physical harm is not usually a serious problem except in situations of very obvious potential danger or when someone has just had a 'narrow escape', for example, almost hurt themselves in a tackle or fallen from a piece of equipment. Helping young performers who are afraid of hurting themselves because they perceive the situation to be potentially dangerous is really just another application of Bandura's theory of self-confidence. Verbal persuasion needs to be handled carefully. Trying to deny that there is a problem by convincing the performer that 'they can do it' can have disastrous effects upon the coach–performer relationship if either you or the performer fail! The real solution lies in acknowledging the fact that the situation is threatening, and helping the performer to structure a set of realistic goals which they are committed to and which will overcome the problem.

14.7.1   NARROW ESCAPES

The 'narrow escape' syndrome is analogous to falling off a horse, and there is an important part of this analogy which coaches often seem to forget. When someone falls off a horse, they usually do so because they have done something wrong. It is therefore important that they identify what this something is, and change it before they get back on the horse to have another go. The performer is also highly likely to be understandably worried about the outcome of his next attempt anyway, and this anxiety will probably further disrupt an already faulty performance. Consequently, it is inappropriate to say to someone in this position, 'Now, get back up and have another go straight away, otherwise you will lose your nerve'. Something must be done about the problem which led to the fall before the rider can reasonably be asked to have another go! This statement is particularly true for young performers, as they are very vulnerable, and you command great respect.

The best thing to do in this situation is to analyse the problem and make whatever technical changes are necessary, then encourage the performer to go back a stage if he is in any doubt, or leave the practice until the next training session. Children often forget all about such problems between sessions, and in any case, you can always go back a few steps at the start of the next session 'to warm up for it'.

14.7.2   MENTAL REHEARSAL

A good way of deciding whether or not someone is ready to have another go at something like this is to ask them to mentally rehearse, or 'see' themselves, doing the activity, but not let them actually try it until they report that they can successfully mentally rehearse it. Mental rehearsal is in fact a very powerful technique, which can be used for many things from mentally warming up to improving self-confidence. It is also a very easy skill for young children to acquire.

14.8   CONCLUSION AND RECOMMENDATIONS

This chapter has discussed ways of avoiding and dealing with six different types of emotional problem which arise with young performers.

These problems were associated with personal relationships, coping with failure, negative self-talk, performance anxiety, injury, and fear of physical harm. In order to avoid these problems as far as possible, and to deal with them should they arise, coaches can:

(a)   help their performers to develop good goal setting skills;
(b)   encourage their performers to use mental rehearsal;
(c)   help the performers to develop positive self-talk;
(d)   develop their own listening skills;
(e)   prepare structured competition training programmes;
(f) learn how to use mistakes when they do occur.

REFERENCES

Carlson, R. and Engstrom, L.-M. (1987) *The Swedish tennis Wonder of the 80's: An Analysis of The Players' Background and Development*. Proceedings of the British Association of National Coaches 2nd International Congress. National Coaching Foundation, Leeds.

FURTHER READING

Beggs, W.D.A. (1986) Developing independence and responsibility in performers. *Coaching Focus*, **4**, 5–6.

Byrne, T. (1987) *The Coach and the Athlete: Working as a Team*, National Coaching Foundation Resource Pack No. 9. The National Coaching Foundation, Leeds.

Hardy, L. and Fazey, J.A. (1987) *Mental Preparation for Performance*, National Coaching Foundation Resource Pack No. 10. The National Coaching Foundation, Leeds.

Kreigel, R. and Kreigel, M.H. (1987) *The 'C' Zone: Peak Performance Under Pressure*, Cedar, London.

Williams, J.M. (1986) *Applied Sport Psychology: Personal Growth to Peak Performance*, Mayfield, Palo Alto, California.

Training young athletes

15

Neil Armstrong and Joanne Welsman

SUMMARY

This chapter builds upon the information describing children's physiological responses to exercise in Chapter 6 and aims to provide guidelines for the safe and effective enhancement of children's aerobic and anaerobic performance based upon sound physiological principles. Central to all training programmes are the key principles of overload, progression, reversibility, adaptability, periodization and evaluation. These, along with the FIT taxonomy for recommending appropriate frequency, intensity and duration of exercise, provide the framework for training programmes and are discussed with particular reference to children and adolescents. Aerobic and anaerobic training programmes are considered separately with consideration given to the trainability of children, appropriate types of activity and the physiological changes which result from training. The ways in which these changes may be used for the evaluation of the progress of the training programme are key elements of the discussion. The appropriateness of muscular fitness training at different stages of maturity is considered and the importance of concurrent flexibility training to optimize fitness gains emphasized.

15.1 INTRODUCTION

Research concerned with the response of the growing child to physical training is accumulating but is still relatively rare when compared to the number of adult studies in the area. The main reason for this lack of documentation is the confounding problem that children grow at their own rate and it is very difficult to separate the relative contributions of growth and training to the observed changes.

With adults, training effects are dependent upon intensity, frequency, duration, specificity of training, and the subject's fitness at the onset of the programme. With children there have been few controlled studies which have systematically analysed the effects of training intensity, frequency, duration and specificity and even then the results available are often conflicting. Some workers have reported higher training thresholds for children than for adults while others have found the training threshold to be the same for both adults and children. The contrasting results probably reflect differences in the initial fitness of the subjects. Some investigators have used non-specific criteria to assess the effectiveness of their training programme. It is not uncommon for a swimming training programme to be assessed by the determination of maximal oxygen uptake (VO_2 max) on a cycle ergometer! Few studies have analysed the effects of specific training programmes and researchers are loathe to expose children to invasive techniques such as muscle biopsies in order to investigate subcellular changes.

For the above reasons knowledge of children's and adolescents' responses to training is still fragmentary and the optimum training programmes for children have yet to be designed. Nevertheless, in the following sections we will try to provide guidelines to be followed when developing training programmes for children.

15.1.1   SAFETY

Coaches working with children and adolescents must stress the importance of taking sensible precautions before, during and after exercise sessions. Safety precautions cannot be overemphasized and considerations should include appropriate footwear and dress in relation to the weather conditions – children are particularly vulnerable at extremes of temperature – and current health status. As a general principle children should be feeling well when they train. It is probable that all viral illnesses, including the common cold, will respond negatively to exercise and attempts to 'sweat out' colds are not to be recommended. It is quite possible that the heart can be affected during or after a non-specific respiratory infection and following a high temperature illness, exercise should be avoided for several days. Children and adolescents should be taught how to warm up correctly before exercising and how to cool down progressively following the exercise session. The benefits of a warm-up in terms of both improved performance and avoidance of injury are well known but the cool-down phase is often ignored despite the abrupt changes in blood pressure resulting from a sudden termination of exercise. The optimum warm-up should include some general whole body activities, some flexibility (stretching) exercises and some specific activities related to the following sessions. The warm-up prior to a training session should last about 10 to 15 minutes and the cool-down perhaps 5 to 10 minutes. Children should gradually assume responsibility for their own warm-up and cool-down.

Coaches who use external resistance such as weights in their programme have additional responsibility when working with children. The safety precautions necessary when using weights should be emphasized and time spent educating children in the correct procedures will be a sound investment for the future.

15.2 TRAINING PRINCIPLES

The principles upon which training programmes should be based are described in Figure 15.1 and are applicable to both adults and children.

The fundamental principles of training are said to have been discovered by Milo of Crotona who developed his muscles by lifting a young calf each day until it grew to be a full-sized bull. Milo progressively increased the load as the calf gradually grew heavier and as he was forced to lift more and more weight he consistently *overloaded* his muscles. Gradual *progression* is particularly important with young athletes but it is necessary to habitually overload a system to cause it to respond and adapt. Training for sport must also adhere to the principle of *specificity* to derive optimum benefits. A particular activity may induce a change in one tissue or organ but not in another; therefore training programmes should reflect the specific requirements of the sport or particular needs of the athlete. For example, although swimming and running are both excellent activities for improving

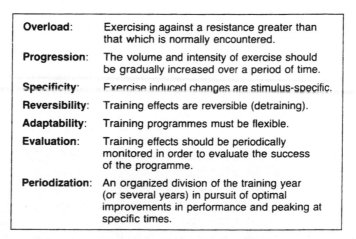

Overload:	Exercising against a resistance greater than that which is normally encountered.
Progression:	The volume and intensity of exercise should be gradually increased over a period of time.
Specificity:	Exercise induced changes are stimulus-specific.
Reversibility:	Training effects are reversible (detraining).
Adaptability:	Training programmes must be flexible.
Evaluation:	Training effects should be periodically monitored in order to evaluate the success of the programme.
Periodization:	An organized division of the training year (or several years) in pursuit of optimal improvements in performance and peaking at specific times.

Fig. 15.1 The principles of training

cardiopulmonary fitness there is no doubt that swimmers will improve their performance more by exercising in a pool than by running around a track. If training is infrequent or not sufficiently intensive the effects of a previous training programme will be *reversed* (see our section on detraining).

All training programmes must be *adaptable* with allowances being made for illness and injury. With adolescent athletes individual growth and development rates must also be considered in relation to training demands, particularly in fixing appropriate overloads. Because of different and largely unpredictable rates of growth and development it is extremely difficult to *periodize* programmes for young athletes to peak at specific times. Periodization techniques are therefore probably of limited value with young children. It is, however, important to periodically *evaluate* training programmes so that appropriate modifications can be made if necessary. Evaluation using simple tests is problematic with growing children and adolescents (we have discussed this in detail elsewhere (Armstrong and Biddle, 1992)). Coaches working with children and adolescents should contact laboratories accredited by the British Association of Sports Sciences if they require an accurate physiological assessment[1].

Training prescriptions based on these principles can be easily described in terms children can understand using the FIT taxonomy.

```
F   Frequency – How often?
I   Intensity  – How hard?
T   Time       – How long?
```

Fig. 15.2 The FIT principle

Because of the interaction between frequency, intensity and duration there is no single optimal frequency that is suitable for all purposes. However, from a physiological viewpoint the frequency of training sessions with children and adolescents should not be more than five per week with the possible exception of flexibility exercises which may be performed on a daily basis. Increases in the intensity of training must be progressive and optimum intensity is best described in terms of a percentage of the child's maximum. There is an intensity threshold below which little or no training effect will result and in some situations (e.g. aerobic training) there is also an upper limit above which no significant further benefits will accrue although there may be disadvantages (e.g. excess lactate formation). When deciding upon the

[1] A list of accredited laboratories can be obtained from the National Coaching Foundation, 4 College Close, LEEDS LS6 3QH.

duration of a training session the coach must consider the child's attention span and seek to maintain interest during the whole session. A well structured session may consist of 10 minutes warming up, 20 to 40 minutes during which the intensity threshold is exceeded, and 5 to 10 minutes cooling down.

15.3   AEROBIC TRAINING (CARDIOPULMONARY FITNESS)

Any activity which is rhythmical, uses large muscle groups and can be maintained continuously for a reasonable length of time can be used to improve cardiopulmonary fitness. Typical activities include running, swimming, cycling, skipping, skating, some types of dancing and cross-country skiing but remember the principle of specificity. Activities which involve the predominant use of small muscle groups and/or static contractions are not recommended because of the enhanced blood pressure response.

The aerobic fitness of children and adolescents seems to respond to training in a similar manner to that of adults but some evidence suggests that a maturational threshold exists below which pre-pubertal children do not respond. The evidence is conflicting and several investigators have demonstrated that the pre-pubertal child will respond to appropriate aerobic training. The explanation for these contrasting findings probably lies in the interaction between the intensity, duration and frequency of training, mode of exercise, initial fitness and habitual activity of the subjects. Children's systems may respond in a different manner to various training protocols. For example, logging miles by continuous running has been shown to be more effective than interval training in one study and others have shown swimming to be a more effective stimulus than other sports in improving aerobic processes. It may be that the 'sacred cow' of VO_2 max is not the most sensitive indicator of changes in children's aerobic fitness.

The decrease in heart rate in response to standardized submaximal exercise is a very sensitive indicator of improved aerobic function and

Frequency:	3–5 times per week
Intensity:	80–90% of maximal heart rate*
Time:	20–40 minutes at the above intensity

* Although there are individual variations in maximal heart rate a value of 200 beats/min can be assumed for the design of training programmes with children and adolescents

Fig. 15.3 Aerobic training prescription

coaches can use this parameter as an easily determined method of monitoring improvement as long as they realize its limitations. Growth and maturation may also reduce submaximal heart rate regardless of training!

15.3.1 THE USE OF BLOOD LACTATE TO MONITOR TRAINING PROGRAMMES

Once an individual's ceiling for VO$_2$ max has been reached further training can result in improvements in aerobic endurance performance through adaptations within the muscle which improve the muscle's capacity for aerobic metabolism. These include an improved capillary supply to the muscle and increased activity of oxidative enzymes. These improvements will not be reflected in a laboratory measure of VO$_2$ max but can be accurately and sensitively detected through monitoring changes in the blood lactate response patterns during graded exercise. With training the blood lactate curve shifts to the right (Figure 15.4) and the athlete is able to exercise closer to VO$_2$ max before a given level (2.5 or 4.0 mmol/l) of blood lactate is reached, i.e. for a given intensity of exercise post-training blood lactate levels are lower than those demonstrated pre-training.

Few training studies with children have included blood lactate

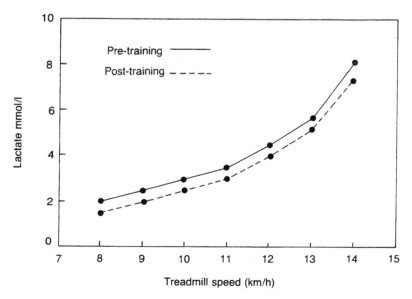

Fig. 15.4 Pre- and post-training blood lactate responses to a graded exercise test

measures but the data available do indicate that trained and untrained children can be differentiated by their blood lactate responses to laboratory tests. Decreases in blood lactate at the same relative exercise intensities have been demonstrated after short term training programmes in children. Monitoring blood lactate responses over longer periods of training must be interpreted carefully and with regard to growth. Although blood lactate responses in children and adolescents are clearly lower than adults, the exact age or stage of biological development at which these responses become adult has not been firmly established. Some evidence has indicated that changes occur with sexual maturation but more recent work suggests that responses are consistent between the ages of 11 to 16. However, as responses at age 16 and full sexual maturity may still differ from adults at some point regular monitoring will detect changes which will reflect growth rather than training. As this change is likely to be in the opposite direction to those expected with training, interpretation of blood lactate indices of aerobic performance may be difficult during late adolescence and should be considered in conjunction with growth, particularly muscle development.

There is some evidence – at least in adults – that superior training benefits can be accrued by maintaining a given blood lactate level during exercise rather than adjusting intensity according to VO_2 max or heart rate responses. Usually the recommended training intensity has been set at a blood lactate of 4.0 mmol/l as this has been assumed to correspond to the maximal lactate steady state. However, this assumption has been questioned as the level of blood lactate at the steady state varies considerably between athletes. Indeed there is evidence to suggest that training is associated with a maximal lactate steady state which is lower than 4.0 mmol/l. If this type of training is required then the maximal lactate steady state must be determined individually by monitoring blood lactate during a series of steady state exercise bouts of increasing intensity. The anaerobic threshold has also been suggested to represent an optimal training intensity but, once again, there is very little conclusive evidence which supports this premise.

Scientific evidence to support the value of lactate training with children and adolescent athletes is insufficient for unequivocal recommendations to be made. Some swimming coaches have employed lactate training with children, often based upon the 4.0 mmol/l level. This is likely to be misguided in the light of children's lower blood lactate levels during exercise. Training set at this level may be too intense for aerobic conditioning and therefore may result in increased susceptibility to injury and overtraining. During treadmill running children's maximal lactate steady state tends to occur close to 2.5 mmol/l when a whole blood assay is used. However when the concept of specificity is considered it is unlikely that this value can be extrapolated for practical use in, for example, swim training.

One further problem with the use of the 4 mmol/l level is that it was developed on the basis of laboratory data which often derived the lactate measures from plasma. Most poolside lactate analysers are whole blood assays and so will give lactate values which are approximately 30% lower than plasma values (see Williams *et al.*, 1992).

15.4 ANAEROBIC TRAINING

The effects of training on children's and adolescents' anaerobic energy systems are not well documented and the available information is fragmentary. Only a limited number of studies have employed the necessary invasive techniques with children but these have demonstrated similar improvements to those expected in adults. Pre-pubescent children are known to have a low anaerobic capacity and power but little or nothing is known about their trainability in this dimension. The available evidence suggests that lactacid training with children is probably of little value until late adolescence.

Training prescriptions are difficult to ascertain but adherence to the principles and examples outlined in Figures 15.5 and 15.6 will allow effective programmes to be developed.

Lactacid anaerobic training is very strenuous and coaches should carefully plan when they wish to include it in their training cycles. Heavy anaerobic training may require some dietary modifications including an increase in the carbohydrate content of the child's diet.

15.5 MUSCULAR FITNESS TRAINING

Muscular strength and endurance programmes may be structured around each type of muscular contraction (Figure 15.7). However, because of the disadvantages of isometric (enhanced blood pressure response), eccentric (increased muscle soreness) and isokinetic (expensive apparatus required) contractions, isotonic exercises are usually acknowledged as the most appropriate for children although successful programmes may be designed using other methods.

Pre-pubescent children have low levels of male sex hormones (androgens) and immature nervous systems. These biological facts, combined with the results of early studies which failed to show significant increases in muscular strength following training programmes, led to the belief that training could not improve the strength of pre-pubescent children. However, more recent research has demonstrated that pre-pubescent children are quite capable of increasing

Frequency: 3 times per week
Intensity: Maximal
Time: 5–10 seconds work period with a 'rest':
work ratio of 5:1. 5 repetitions per set,
3 sets with a recovery of 5–10 minutes
between sets*

e.g.	Exercise	Repetitions	Sets	Intensity	Rest recovery
	50 metre run	5	3	Maximal	40 seconds walk between repetitions. 5 minute jog between sets

*The rest recovery period is extremely important if the
quality of work is to be maintained

Fig. 15.5 Prescription for training the phosphagen system

Frequency: Not more than 3 times per week
Intensity: Not less than 90% of maximum
Time: 20–30 seconds work period with a 'rest':
work ratio of 3:1 (which may be eventually
reduced to 2:1 as training progresses).
5 repetitions per set, 2 sets with up to
10 minutes jogging between sets

e.g.	Exercise	Repetitions	Sets	Intensity	Rest recovery
	150–200 metre run	5	2	90% max	90 seconds jog between repetitions 10 minutes jog between sets

Fig. 15.6 Prescription for training the lactacid system

muscular strength in response to resistance training although they
experience more difficulty in increasing muscle mass.

Due to the possible damage which could occur to the growth zones
of the skeleton (epiphyses) it is, however, probably best to be cautious
about maximal resistance training until the growth spurt is virtually
over. On the other hand the capillary blood supply to the muscles
appears to be highly responsive during the growth period and therefore
local muscular endurance exercises may be particularly suitable at this
age. Pre-pubescent children should be encouraged to use submaximal
resistances perhaps using their own body weight (e.g. sit-ups,

Isotonic (dynamic or concentric):	The muscle shortens with varying tension while lifting a constant load
Isometric (static):	Tension develops but there is no change in the length of the muscle
Eccentric:	The muscle lengthens while developing tension
Isokinetic:	The tension developed by the muscle while shortening at constant speed is maximal over the full range of motion

Fig. 15.7 Types of muscular contraction

Frequency:	3 times per week
Intensity:	6–8 RM per set
Time:	3 sets

Fig. 15.8 Strength training prescription

Frequency:	3 times per week
Intensity:	10–25 RM per set
Time:	3 sets

Fig. 15.9 Local muscular endurance training prescription

press-ups, pull-ups), but heavier weight training is advantageous during late adolescence.

In addition to the principles of training previously described, it is necessary to understand the concept of a repetition maximum (RM) in order to design isotonic muscular fitness programmes. RM is the maximal load that a muscle group can lift over a given number of repetitions before fatiguing. Training prescriptions for muscular fitness are outlined in Figure 15.8 and Figure 15.9 but for balanced development each muscle group should be exercised and it is advisable to start with large muscle groups and work down to smaller muscle groups. Upper legs and hips, chest and upper arms, back and posterior aspects of legs, lower legs and ankles, shoulders and posterior aspect of upper arms, abdomen and then anterior aspect of upper arms would be a suitable rotation of exercise. The resistances used should be

Frequency:	3–7 times per week
Intensity:	muscle stretched beyond normal length
Time:	3 times

Fig. 15.10 Flexibility training prescription

periodically checked and when, say, the 8 RM becomes a 12 RM the resistance should be increased to the new 8 RM.

15.6 FLEXIBILITY TRAINING

Poor flexibility can be a cause of overuse injuries and imbalance between muscle strength and flexibility may result in muscle or joint injury. There appear to have been no investigations showing on a scientific basis how training of flexibility affects children. It does seem, however, that training for increased joint mobility should start before puberty as long as it is carried out with a concern to avoid damage to the joints and vertebral column.

Two basic kinds of stretching exercises can be used to develop flexibility: ballistic stretching and static stretching. Ballistic stretching uses momentum to produce the stretch. The momentum is generated by a bouncing, bobbing or jerking movement and because this produces a sudden and sometimes excessive stretch on the muscle there is a potential for injury through overstretching the muscle. Static stretching involves slowly stretching a muscle longer than its normal length and holding the stretch for 6–10s. There is much less chance of tearing the soft tissue and less likelihood of causing muscular soreness. Static stretching is therefore recommended for the development of flexibility and an appropriate training prescription is described in Figure 15.10. More advanced flexibility training techniques (e.g. assisted passive stretching and the use of proprioceptive neuromuscular facilitation) are available but they must be carried out cautiously and further explanation is beyond the scope of this chapter (see Alter, 1988, or McNaught-Davis, 1991, for details).

15.7 DETRAINING

Elucidating the effects of detraining (reversibility) on children is confounded by the child's continued growth and development during the detraining period. As in adults it seems that adaptations to training are transient and will steadily decay once training has stopped. Long term benefits depend upon the continuance of training sessions into adult life.

A classic study of young female swimmers (12–16 years) who trained from six to 26 hours a week demonstrated that both functional and dimensional measures of cardiopulmonary fitness may be improved by long term, strenuous swim training. The girls were followed up ten years later and by this time all of them had stopped swimming and most did not engage in any physical activity in their spare time. All the girls showed a decrease in VO_2 max which was 29% on average and took them to a level some 15% below the mean for women of the same age. Despite the marked detraining effects the most striking impression left by this study is the way that the girl swimmers were 'turned off' activity as adults. In spite of the physiological advantages they had developed through training they were functioning at levels below average for women of the same age. It seems likely that chronic, intensive training from a young age had turned them off exercise during adulthood.

15.8   CONCLUSION

Children are adequately equipped to handle activities which require short but intensive exertion (phosphagen system) or more prolonged periods of moderate exertion (aerobic system). They are not well equipped to cope with training which demands a significant contribution from the lactacid system. Training of the lactacid system should therefore generally be left until after the peak of the growth spurt has been reached. Similarly children are responsive to muscular endurance training but work with heavy weights should probably be avoided until puberty is complete.

Training regimes introduced at the appropriate time in the child's development will induce favourable changes in the child's physiology of a similar magnitude to those expected in adults. A period of detraining will cause many of these changes to decay gradually. There is no strong evidence to support the suggestion that training must be started early in order to experience success as an adult and early specialization is often counter-productive. Coaches need to be sensitive to the fact that childhood success in sport is often linked to rate of maturation – early maturing boys have a distinct advantage in most sports but with girls it is often the late maturers who are successful (e.g. gymnasts). Children should be encouraged to internalize the motivation to exercise so that when the extrinsic motivation of the coach is removed they are not 'turned off' like the girl swimmers described earlier. Youngsters must be helped to understand the principles underlying fitness and health and taught how to develop their own training programmes which can be periodically re-appraised and modified as they grow older and their aspirations change.

REFERENCES

Alter, M.J. (1988) *Science of Stretching*, Human Kinetics, Champaign, IL.
Armstrong, N. and Biddle, S. (1982) Health-related physical activity in the national curriculum, in *New Directions In Physical Education Vol. 2 – Towards a National Curriculum*, (ed N. Armstrong), Human Kinetics, Champaign, IL, pp. 71–110.
McNaught-Davis, P. (1991) *Flexibility*, Partridge Press, London.
Williams, J., Armstrong, N. and Kirby, B. (1992) The influence of site of sampling and assay medium upon the measurement and interpretation of blood lactate responses to exercise. *Journal of Sports Science*, **10**, 95–107.

FURTHER READING

Armstrong, N. and Davies, B. (1984) The metabolic and physiological responses of children to exercise and training. *Physical Education Review*, **7**, 90–105.
Rowland, T.W. (1990) *Exercise and Children's Health*. Human Kinetics, Champaign, IL.
Sady, S.P. (1986) Cardiorespiratory exercise training in children. *Clinics in Sports Medicine*, **5**, 493–514.
Sale, D.G. (1989) Strength training in children, in *Perspectives in Exercise Science and Sports Medicine Vol. 2 – Youth, Exercise and Sport*, (eds C.V. Gisolfi and D.R. Lamb), Benchmark Press, Indianapolis, pp. 165–222.
Shephard, R.J. (1992) Effectiveness of training programmes for prepubescent children. *Sports Medicine*, **13**, 194–213.
Vaccaro, P. and Mahon, A. (1987) Cardiorespiratory responses to endurance training in children. *Sports Medicine*, **4**, 352–63.
Williams, J. and Armstrong, N. (1991) The maximal lactate steady state and its relationship to performance at fixed blood lactate reference values in children. *Pediatric Exercise Science*, **3**, 333–41.
Zauner, C.W., Maksud, M.G. and Melichna, J. (1989) Physiological considerations in training young athletes. *Sports Medicine*, **8**, 15–31.

The effect of injuries on growth   16

John Aldridge

SUMMARY

Injuries in children more commonly involve damage to bone than injuries in adults. This chapter presents a description of both traumatic and stress injuries to the skeleton that can occur in children. Descriptions of injuries to long bones, growth plates, the spine, joints, and tendon–bone attachments are accompanied by a brief statement of the causes (aetiology) of the common sites of occurrence, and likely outcomes. Particular attention is paid to injuries to the growth plates of the long bones and vertebrae in view of the effect they can have on future development.

16.1 INTRODUCTION

Children run the same risk of being injured during sport as adults but the results can be more serious. The skeleton is at considerably more risk in children than in adults although soft tissue injuries do still occur. This chapter will deal with the effects of trauma on the immature skeleton and identify problems which can interfere with normal growth. Some injuries can lead to asymetrical growth and long term disability. Most children, of course, go through their developing years without suffering any long term consequences as a result of their sporting activities. Injuries that cause disability are generally rare but nonetheless are important and coaches should know about them.

16.2 ACUTE INJURIES TO THE SKELETON

16.2.1 SHAFT FRACTURES

Types

An acute injury to the skeleton is known as a fracture. In children fractures differ from those in adults because of the peculiarities of growing bone. Because it is more resilient and springy growing bone can accept a greater degree of deformity before it breaks. As a result there are three types of fracture commonly found in children which are described below. They are greenstick fractures, complete fractures and buckle fractures.

Greenstick fractures

These are the most common type of break in children. They are so called because what happens to the bone is similar to what happens when you try to break a young tree shoot. There is an incomplete break which tears the bone on the convex side and compresses it on the concave side of the fracture (Figure 16.1a).

Complete fractures

These occur when the bone is completely broken and are caused, as are greenstick fractures, by excessive angular or rotational forces (Figure 16.1b).

Buckle fractures

When forces are transmitted through the long axis of the bone, such as in a heavy landing, there is a compression of the bone tissue. In adults it results in an impacted fracture. In children it causes a buckle fracture characterized by a bulge on the surface ring which encircles the shaft (Figure 16.1c). Injuries like this are very minor and can often be missed because they do not cause recognizable deformity and often only very little swelling.

Outcomes

Angular deformity

Those fractures which result in angular deformity usually heal very well. If the deformity is marked the bone can usually be manipulated into an acceptable position and the damaged parts will unite very

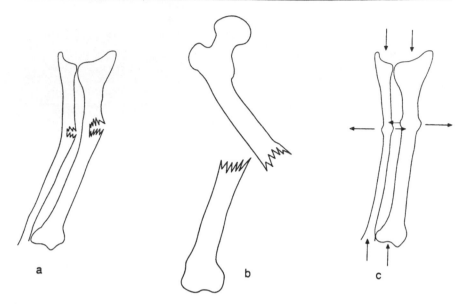

Fig. 16.1 Three common types of fracture: (a) greenstick, (b) complete, (c) buckle

quickly due to the active nature of growing bone. Indeed, the bone is so active that remodelling can occur and a certain degree of angular deformity can be corrected naturally. Figure 16.2 shows how bones will grow straight by deposition of new bone on the concave side of the fracture and reabsorption on the convex side. Hence these fractures need not cause great concern to parents or coaches.

Rotational deformity

The ability to repair and remodel bone is very important in children and makes the treatment of acute injuries very successful. However, whereas angular deformity can to some extent be overcome, rotational deformities do not correct naturally and, if untreated, will persist permanently. For example, if a tibial fracture is left in a rotated position it will unite but the deformity will not grow out and the child will walk with the toes permanently pointing in or out (Figure 16.3).

Overgrowth

Fractures of long bones can stimulate the epiphyseal growth plates to increased activity. Hence the bone grows longer more quickly. So, while a fractured femur will unite perfectly well, for a while the overall

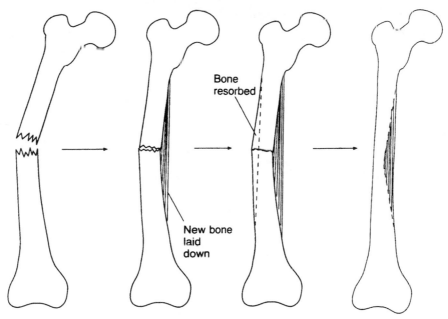

Fig. 16.2 Correction of deformity in fractured long bone during healing

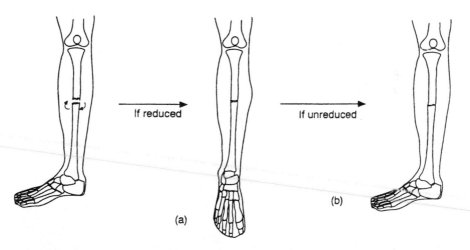

Fig. 16.3 Repair of rotational fracture in lower leg if (a) reduced, and (b) unreduced

length will be greater than in the opposite leg. Catch-up growth usually takes place in the other limb. However, occasionally, a fracture of a long bone can lead to unequal limb length at maturity. It is important therefore to recognize which deformities are acceptable, which have to be reduced, and which can be left for nature to take its course.

16.2.2 JOINT INJURIES

Unlike shaft fractures injuries to joints can often cause permanent problems in spite of adequate treatment. Three types of injury will be described before explaining their outcomes. The injuries are dislocations, articular surface injuries, and meniscal injuries.

Types

Dislocations

Almost any joint can be dislocated by trauma. In children the elbow, patella and shoulder are perhaps the most common sites.

Articular fractures

Articular surfaces are those surfaces of bones that move on each other in a joint. They can be damaged by shearing and compression forces. The fracture then extends through the cartilaginous layer of the joint into its underlying bone. Figure 16.4a shows the appearance of such a fracture. Sometimes pieces of the articular surface separate and become loose in the joint capsule (Figure 16.4b). The fracture causes bleeding into the joint which results in intense swelling and great pain.

Meniscal injury

Menisci are the cartilages in the knee joint and are commonly damaged in adults. However cartilage injuries are becoming increasingly common in young athletes. The damage occurs when a part of the meniscus becomes trapped by the articular surfaces of the knee joint and a rotational stress causes it to tear. The torn portion can then flip in and out of the joint.

Outcomes

Dislocations

Dislocation of the shoulder and patella can commonly cause weakening of the joint capsule so that recurrent dislocation occurs and surgical intervention has to be undertaken. Dislocations, and indeed fractures,

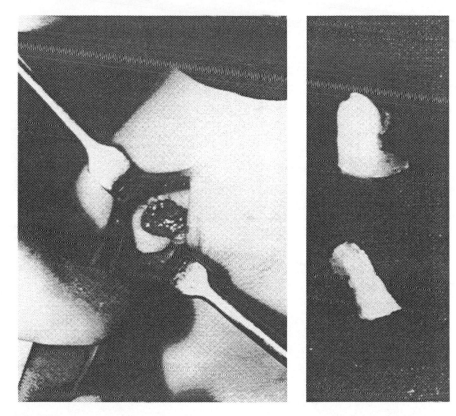

Fig. 16.4 (a) Example of ankle joint injury; (b) loose pieces removed from the joint surface

around the elbow joint can be complicated by myositis ossificans. This is a condition in which new bone forms within the damaged soft tissues. This then interferes with joint movement and causes permanent stiffness, although growth is not impeded. A late complication of dislocation is arthritis.

Articular fractures

Articular fractures leave the joint surface damaged and scarred. Consequently the joint can wear more rapidly and degenerate arthrosis can occur. The rate at which this wear occurs depends on the degree of scarring and the stresses placed upon the joint. Intense activity is, therefore, not advisable especially if it involves a weightbearing surface.

Meniscal injury

The function of the meniscus in the knee is to distribute the weight evenly throughout the joint. If one of the menisci is damaged this function is lost, the loading of the joint becomes uneven and can lead to early arthritis. Unforunately there is little which can be done to avoid this happenining though surgery tries to preserve as much meniscal tissue as possible to reduce the risk.

16.2.3 EPIPHYSEAL INJURIES

Fractures that involve the epiphyseal growth plates (Figure 16.5) form a special group of injuries that have no counterpart in adults. They are common fractures because the cartilaginous plate is weaker than bone and may be caused by shearing, avulsion and compression forces. These fractures are of particular concern because damage to the dividing epiphyseal cells or interruption of their blood supply can interfere with the growth of the bone.

Types

Epiphyseal fractures have been classified into five types (Salter and Harris, 1963) so that a more accurate prognosis in terms of growth interference can be made. The different types of injury in the classification are shown in Figure 16.6.

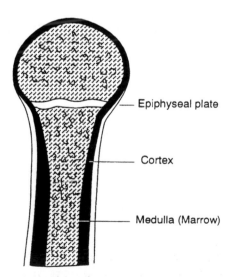

Fig. 16.5 Growth area of long bone

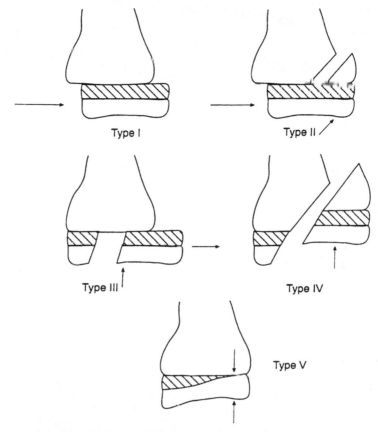

Fig. 16.6 Classification of epiphyseal fractures (adapted from Salter and Harris (1963) by kind permission of the publishers)

Outcomes

Type I and Type II fractures are common but, since the growth plate is intact, they have a good prognosis and no long term deformity is likely. Even some deformity and displacement can be accepted at the time of the injury since growth will progress normally and deformities can be corrected as part of the growth process.

Type III and Type IV fractures are more serious and can, even with good management, lead to deformity. In these cases the plate has been divided and displaced. Unless the fracture can be reduced anatomically normal growth can be disturbed (Figure 16.7).

Figure 16.8 shows what can happen when a displaced Type IV fracture is not properly reduced. Bone at B will unite with bone at B1 so that the epiphysis at C will be fixed and further growth will not

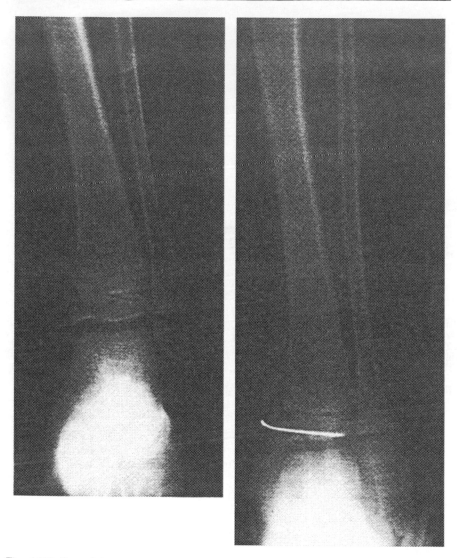

Fig. 16.7 Type IV fracture (a) before treatment, and (b) after treatment

occur. The result is an asymetrical growth of the bone and a deformity. The results of this can be seen in the example given in Figure 16.9. These angular deformities are often unsightly and occasionally disabling, in which case corrective surgery may be necessary. Whether such deformities will affect athletic performance depends upon the degree of displacement.

In Type V fractures the epiphysis is compressed and the resulting

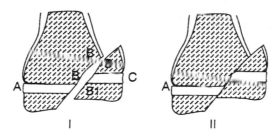

Fig. 16.8 Progress of unreduced Type IV fracture on bone growth

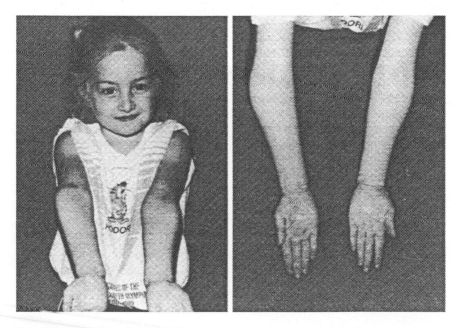

Fig. 16.9 Outcome of unreduced type IV fracture (note the deformity of the right elbow

damage can stop further growth or cause unequal growth and lead to deformity or shortening of the bone. Unfortunately this can be a difficult injury to recognize because the X-ray appearance may be normal and the extent of the damage may only become apparent over a period of time.

16.3   STRESS INJURIES TO THE SKELETON

Acute skeletal injuries should not be difficult to recognize although minor buckle fractures may be missed. Acute injuries occur at a specific moment as a result of a sudden force on the bone. Stress or overuse injuries, on the other hand, result from repeated stress over a period of time and may be slow to show themselves. They initially present as a minor pain for no particular reason which gradually gets worse. Therefore they can easily be ignored and progress to a point when treatment may be difficult and prolonged.

Stress fractures occur in both children and adults. In youngsters they can be seen as early as seven years of age and their frequency increases through adolescence. They may result from a frequently repeated movement under normal load, as in long distance running, or by less frequent movement with a higher load, as in weight lifting. A combination of high frequency and high load is most dangerous. Fractures of this sort are similar to metal fatigue, which can be demonstrated by repeatedly bending and straightening a paper clip until it breaks. As with the metal, microscopic changes in the bone structure get worse until the bone breaks.

It is important to recognize the symptoms of a stress fracture as early as possible. Typically there are 'crescendo pains' in which the pain experienced in the activity comes on sooner and more severely in each training session. It also lasts longer after each session and eventually becomes continuous.

16.3.1 LONG BONE FRACTURES

In principle, fractures can occur in any bone but they are most common in the lower limbs. They occur in the metatarsals, the navicular, the fibula above the ankle, the tibia, less commonly the femur, but certainly the pelvis. Typically these injuries are associated with local tenderness on examination.

Initially X-rays can be normal and it can be some time before the fracture can be seen (Figure 16.10). Sometimes it is necessary to confirm the diagnosis by a technique known as isotope scanning (Figure 16.11). If a fracture is suspected on clinical grounds, even if not on the evidence of X-rays, the athlete must be made to rest.

Once the stressful stimulus has been removed then the fracture will heal but the process of healing can sometimes be very protracted. It is unlikely, however, that there will be any long term consequences.

16.3.2 SPINAL FRACTURES

Stress fractures in the vertebrae occur in the part of the vertebral arch known as the lamina between the upper and lower articular processes (Figure 16.12). The defect in the bone is known as spondylolysis. A

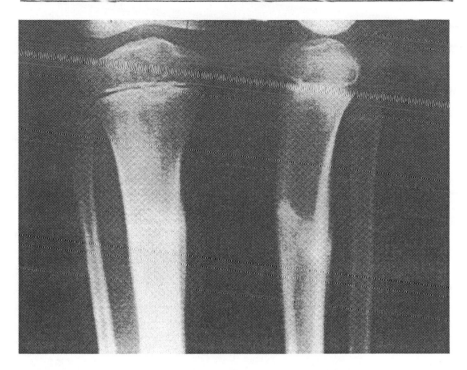

Fig. 16.10 X-ray photographs of stress fractures in the tibia

similar defect can sometimes be seen as a congenital anomaly. These fractures can affect normal growth and development. They rarely heal and occur in a position in the vertebra which can lead to instability in the spine. It allows one vertebra to slip forward on the one below; when this happens the condition is known as spondylolisthesis (Figure 16.13).

The younger the age at which this stress defect occurs, the greater the risk of suffering the slippage. After skeletal maturity has been reached it is unusual for it to occur. Not all spondylolyses develop into spondylolistheses. Slipping occurs when shearing forces are large and is most commonly seen in gymnastics, diving, javelin throwing, wrestling, and weight lifting.

This injury is typical of adolescents. It is not necessarily a reason to give up activity, provided that limits imposed by pain are observed. If a vertebral slip occurs, and if there is evidence of nerve roots being involved, then it is more serious and surgery to stabilize the spine must be considered. Sometimes pain alone indicates the need for surgery.

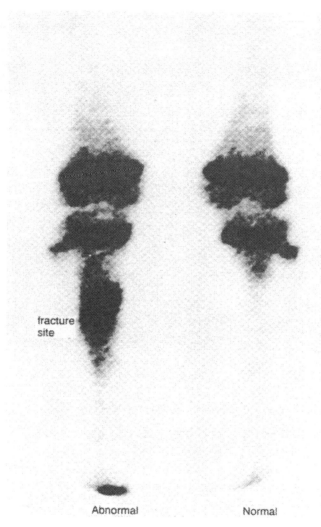

Fig. 16.11 Bone scan of stress fracture of the tibia

16.4   TENDON–BONE ATTACHMENT INJURY

16.4.1   DESCRIPTION

Growth can be modified by injury mainly in those areas where there is actively growing bone. Points of major tendon to bone attachments, the traction epiphyses, are at great risk and it is not uncommon to find problems there. In adults the stress at these points is almost always taken by the muscles and tendons themselves, so causing soft tissue

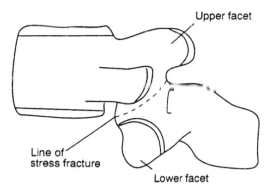

Fig. 16.12 Stress fracture of vertebral lamina

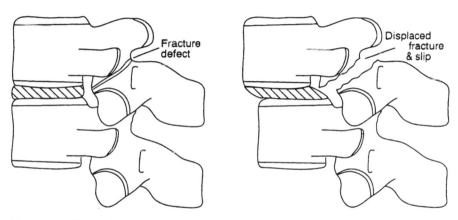

Fig. 16.13 Spondylolysis developing into spondylolisthesis

injury. In children, however, the normal process of ossification is more likely to be disturbed and the bone can fragment (Figure 16.14). This is a condition known as osteochondritis.

16.4.2   AETIOLOGY

Because physical training increases the strength of muscles and tendons more quickly than a comparable change in bone, the attachment is at risk. To be safe it is best if children only use their own body weight as a load. However, the limit at which osteochondritis occurs differs from child to child; some can take bigger stresses than others. Certainly the condition can occur in children who are not particularly active; others appear to be able to undergo heavy training without developing any symptoms.

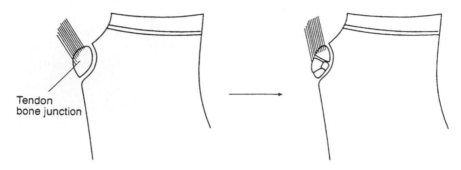

Tendon
bone junction

Fig. 16.14 Osteochondritis of a traction epiphysis

During the adolescent growth spurt the increases in bone length outstrip increases in muscle length. The muscles are relatively shorter and exert a greater pull on the bony attachments which increases the risk of osteochondritis of the bone. The greatest risk occurs during adolescence and periods of intense activity.

16.4.3 SITES

The most common site for osteochondritis is the attachment of the patellar tendon to the tibial tuberosity just below the knee. The condition is known as Osgood-Schlatter's disease. The child experiences local pain, tenderness and swelling. The condition is very common among young football players but may also occur in other sports. Other common sites for osteochondritis are the lower end of the patella itself and the insertion of the Achilles tendon at the heel. In the upper limb the insertion of the triceps tendon into the olecranon process, the point of the elbow, is another area at risk.

16.4.4 OUTCOME

If it is untreated osteochondritis can take a long time to heal. Apart from some residual bony swelling in the case of Osgood-Schlatter's disease, there are rarely any permanent complications. Healing can be encouraged by a period of relative rest by restricting activity or by complete rest in a plaster cast.

16.5 JOINT SURFACE INJURIES

16.5.1 DESCRIPTION

The surface of a joint consists of cartilage laid on a base of bone. Segments of cartilage and subchondral bone can die and separate from the underlying bone. This is known as osteochondritis dessicans (Figure 16.15).

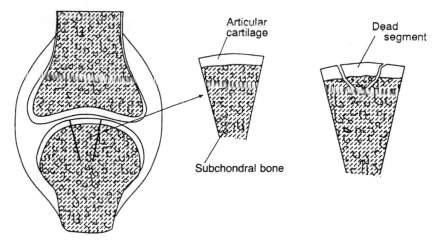

Fig. 16.15 Osteochondritis dessicans

16.5.2 AETIOLOGY

This injury is usually caused by repetitive jarring of the joint. The blood supply to an area of articular surface is damaged and a segment dies. The condition can occur within families and it is possible that it can be genetically determined.

16.5.3 SITES

This injury occurs most commonly in the knee but can also be seen at the ankle and the hip. In throwers and gymnasts the elbow can be affected. The child suffers a painful joint which is often swollen. If a loose fragment develops the joint can give way and lock. Any child with a swollen joint must seek medical advice.

16.5.4 OUTCOME

The blood supply to a dead fragment may slowly be re-established and permit healing to take place. Otherwise the fragment may separate and float within the joint (Figure 16.16a). If it heals perfectly the articular surface will be normal but usually there is some remaining irregularity (Figure 16.16b).

The long term consequences are not good. Since the joint surface is damaged it will wear more quickly and early arthritis may develop. In some cases it may be necessary to give up sport altogether. Treatment is by rest which includes non-weightbearing and occasionally

(a)

(b)

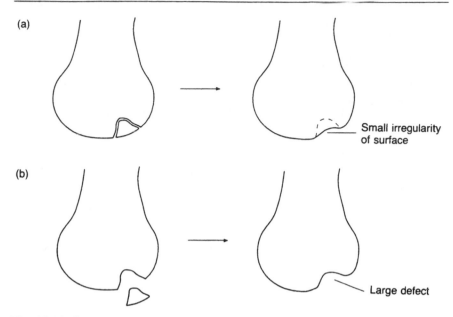

Small irregularity
of surface

Large defect

Fig. 16.16 Common outcome of osteochondritis dessicans

immobilization. If the fragment is loose or separated then an operation
to replace or remove it is necessary.

16.6   EPIPHYSEAL GROWTH PLATE INJURIES

16.6.1   DESCRIPTION

The epiphyseal plates at the ends of the bones can also be damaged by
overstress. When this happens the normal process of ossification can
be interrupted, growth is affected and deformity can follow.

16.6.2   SITES

The spine

One of the most common sites for epiphyseal damage is in the growth
plates at either end of the vertebral bodies in the spine (Figure 16.17), a
condition known as Scheurmann's disease. The region most affected is
the thoracic spine but it is also found in the lumbar region.

Repeated flexion causes stress which can damage the anterior part of
the growth plate and prevent further growth. The vertebrae then
become wedge-shaped instead of rectangular (Figure 16.18). The

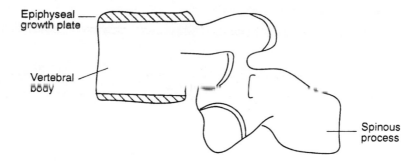

Epiphyseal growth plate

Vertebral body

Spinous process

Fig. 16.17 Growth plates in a typical vertebra

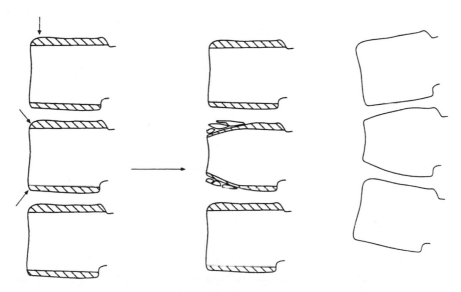

Fig. 16.18 Results of repetitive flexion stress on vertebral growth

condition can occur in non-active children and is often associated with tight hamstrings. This muscle group limits flexion at the hip so bending forward puts extra stress on the back. Typically adolescents are most affected. They report back pain which can be associated with some tenderness, muscle spasm and limited movement.

Long bones

A common site for this condition in gymnasts is the lower end of the arm, the distal radial epiphysis. When it is damaged through stress

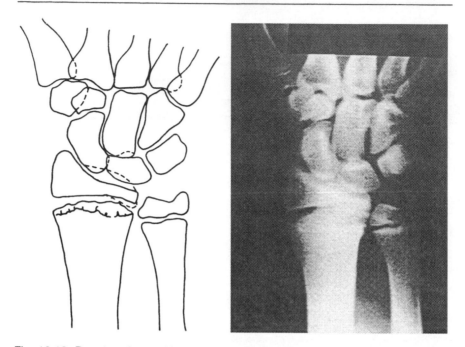

Fig. 16.19 Results of repetitive stress on long bone growth: (a) diagrammatic representation of distal radial epiphysis; (b) equivalent X-ray showing widened growth plate

growth temporarily stops. There is usually pain and swelling in the area and X-rays show a widened plate (Figure 16.19b). In other athletes, notably throwers and others who do activities which place great demands on the arms, the olecranon epiphysis at the back of the elbow can be damaged.

16.6.3 OUTCOME

Spine

The treatment for Scheurmann's disease is rest when the pain is severe during the acute stage. It may include a period of splintage in a spinal support. The condition heals as bony maturity is reached. More than one segment of the spine may be affected and if several vertebrae are involved there is a marked forward curve and the person becomes very round-shouldered. There may be no ongoing pain but any resulting severe deformity may cause degenerate change later in life.

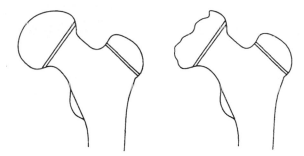

Fig. 16.20 Epiphyseal collapse in femur (Perthes disease)

Long bones

Again rest is the treatment until the appearance of X-ray photographs returns to normal. However, it is possible that growth in length may be depressed; the radius may finish up shorter than the ulna causing a permanent deformity at the wrist.

16.7   EPIPHYSEAL COLLAPSE

16.7.1   DESCRIPTION

The final group of growth injuries is one in which the whole epiphysis undergoes an avascular necrosis; the epiphysis dies, softens and collapses.

16.7.2   AETIOLOGY

A similar condition called Perthes disease can occur in any child when the head of the femur dies and collapses (Figure 16.20). Children who develop this problem often have a bone age which lags behind chronological age. Repetitive impact appears to be the reason this condition develops in other bones. However it may be that delayed skeletal maturity puts some children at greater risk.

16.7.3   SITES

Many epiphyses can suffer from this condition. It can occur in the wrist and the foot, and in the elbow the epiphysis of the capitellum can collapse (Figure 16.21).

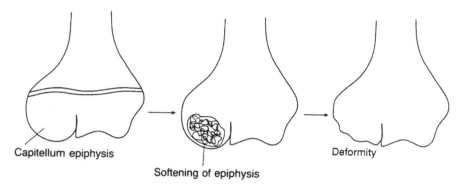

Fig. 16.21 Epiphyseal collapse of capitellum in the elbow

16.7.4   OUTCOME

As with all osteochondroses disturbance to the normal process of ossification eventually heals. However, since the bone has softened and become deformed it may heal misshapen. Because the epiphyses are associated with joints, deformity can lead to early arthritis with its pain and disability. They are therefore serious conditions and necessitate giving up active sport.

16.8   CONCLUSION

Growing bone is vulnerable to damage as a result of accidents or overuse in sport and long term harm may occur from participation. But there are other influences which affect the outcomes. Heredity, skeletal maturation and growth spurts are all important. The common factor, however, is trauma. Fortunately the great majority of children can, and do, withstand the stresses inherent in sport but in some their biological limits are exceeded and injury occurs. Occasionally there are long term effects and it is essential that accurate diagnoses are made at the outset and the prognosis made clear.

REFERENCES

Salter, R.B. and Harris, W.R. (1963) Injuries involving the epiphyseal plate. *Journal of Bone and Joint Surgery,* **45-A**(3), 587–622.

Treating and managing injuries in children

17

Dennis Wright

SUMMARY

In this chapter the immediate response to injury is explained and different degrees of severity are described in order to assist coaches to recognize the symptoms, relieve pain and minimize the initial reaction. Different forms of injury to soft tissues, bones and joints, head and spine are briefly described and, where appropriate, guidance is given on the steps that coaches can take to assist control of damage and aid recovery. The importance of suitable training is emphasized and coaches are urged to seek expert help immediately where there may be a suspicion of serious injury.

17.1 INTRODUCTION

Coaching children carries considerable responsibilities, not least of which are the care and management of injuries. The possibility of injury is present in all physical activities but coaches who are able to deal with injuries can reduce both the short term and long term effects on children and their participation. This chapter will explain and clarify the problems encountered and provide guidelines for a sensible approach to treatment and management. It is not intended that it should substitute for proper first aid training which is recommended to all coaches.

17.2 THE BODY'S REACTION TO INJURY

The body reacts to all injuries in a standard sequence of events known as the inflammatory reaction. It may be localized or widespread, according to the nature of the injury, but always includes redness, swelling, heat, pain and restricted function.

Redness is caused by increased blood flow to the damaged area and its surroundings, bringing cells and substances which help to remove debris and promote the healing process. The depth of the structure involved determines the extent to which the redness is visible. For example, an infected cut may be readily visible where a pulled deep muscle may not be.

Swelling is an accumulation of excess tissue fluid which provides the nutritional link between the capillaries and the cells. It is facilitated by the permeability of the capillary walls and may be increased by bleeding from ruptured blood vessels.

Heat or, more accurately, the rise in temperature of an inflamed area is caused by the activity of cells involved in the healing process and the increase in blood supply.

Pain is an important symptom of injury and inflammation without which athletes would not be aware of the occurrence or status of an injury. The pain may result from damage to nerves, chemical irritation or pressure from the swelling at the site.

Restricted movement associated with injuries is due to the pain, swelling and stiffness.

17.2.1 SEVERITY OF THE INFLAMMATORY REACTION

Inflammation occurs with different degrees of intensity which are classified as acute, subacute and chronic. Not all injuries provoke acute reactions; the severity depends on the circumstances of the particular injury.

Acute reaction is produced by a considerable degree of sudden physical damage. Within hours the symptoms will be at their most severe and remain so for between two and three days.

Subacute reaction may result from a less severe trauma or be the natural sequence of improvement from the acute state. There are no rigid time schedules but an additional seven to ten days of symptoms can be expected.

Chronic reaction is important because it may easily be dismissed. It may result from relatively minor physical damage or again be part of the continuing progression from the subacute stage. In either case there are minor grumbling symptoms of minimal pain, negligible and localized swelling, undetectable heat, and only slightly impaired function. However, coaches should not ignore them because lack of care and discipline can lead to deterioration and recurrence.

17.2.2 TREATMENT OF THE INFLAMMATORY REACTION

While treatments are designed to be anti-inflammatory, there will always be some reaction. It is important to stop further activity immediately and prompt attention, first aid, will minimize the reaction. This is a natural response which reduces the effect of the injury and protects the injured part after which the repair process can begin.

Acute stage

The main objectives are to relieve pain and stop swelling. Pain can be reduced by rest, support and the application of cold to the affected part. The degree of rest and support needed depend on the extent of the injury; complete bedrest at one extreme and a bandage support at the other. The severity of the injury also determines the period of rest and support needed but 72 hours is recognized as the minimum period before real improvement will be seen.

Applying cold reduces the metabolic rate in the area and slows the conductivity in the nerves which signal the pain. It can be done by applying an ice pack followed by cold water compresses. Compresses should be replaced regularly because the heat produced by inflammation dries them out. Do not put ice or ice packs directly onto the skin since they will burn. Put them in a plastic bag or smear a film of oil on the skin first.

Because first aid is so important young athletes should be told what to do in case of an accident. The basic rules are:

- Stop the activity;
- Move only within the limits of pain;
- Keep the part cool, do not apply heat;
- Do not rub it;
- Do not try to 'run it off'.

Sub acute stage

It is still important to relieve pain but further treatment can now be given. Gentle radiant heat, perhaps from a hot water bottle or a lamp, whilst not directly influencing deep circulation, will relieve pain by soothing nerve endings and relaxing protective muscle spasms. The blood supply is increased and provides the nutrition necessary for the healing process.

Despite precautions, some swelling will accumulate and must be removed or minimized. The increased tissue fluid contains a clotting factor which can create adhesions between adjacent structures. These are inelastic strands, both across joints and within and between muscles, which can prevent a return to full mobility.

The most effective method of removing inflammatory swelling by physical measures is a combination of massage, simple active exercises and elevation of the part. Massage helps drainage through mechanical pressure on the veins and lymphatic vessels and promotes mobility between adjacent structures. Exercise enhances the 'muscle pump' action on surrounding vessels and helps to retain the mobility and tone in muscle. It should be restricted to the limits of discomfort. In the case of injury to joints static tensing of muscle may be sufficient. Keeping the part elevated helps drainage of tissue fluid.

Chronic stage

More vigorous physical measures can be implemented here whether or not the stage is a progression from the acute or provoked by a minor longstanding irritant. Progression from the acute stage still requires attention to the factors creating discomfort such as residual swelling, adhesions or shortening of structures. Relief of pain from deep structures requires treatment by professionals. Residual swelling and thickening can only be dispersed with deep and specific massage procedures. The restoration of joint mobility is achieved by movements in a greater range and in sport specific patterns. Rest results in loss of strength and endurance. Carefully controlled resisted movements within the limits of discomfort and selected with particular sporting skills in mind can be used to offset these losses during the chronic stage.

Chronic inflammation is often produced by overuse. Injuries are typically brought about by inappropriate training, overspecific activities and neglect of warning signs. It is always best to take advice until the discomfort has gone. Chronic 'overuse' injuries often gradually limit mobility and function. Mobility can be restored by careful use of specific exercises which conform to neuromuscular and biomechanical principles.

17.3 REPAIR PROCESSES FOLLOWING INJURY

The inflammatory response is the start of the repair process. The final outcome depends on how the injury is managed subsequently.

The repair process consists of a series of overlapping changes in the blood vessels and tissues surrounding the damaged area. A fibrous tissue is produced both to repair damaged tissue and replace that which has been destroyed. It is tough and pliable but insensitive and inelastic and needs efficient treatment to limit its production. Initially, the tissue contains capillaries but later the shrinkage of collagen fibres strangles them. The healed area then becomes avascular and is known as scar tissue. This process may take as long as nine months.

If injuries are neglected inflammation is prolonged and the repair process is delayed with the result that more fibrous tissue forms which may lead to reduced mobility and joint instability. Insensitivity and a lack of elasticity in tissues can impair function and the risk of injury recurrence increases.

17.4   TREATMENT OF SPECIFIC INJURIES

While all injuries provoke the inflammation reaction, different injuries require particular treatments.

17.4.1   SOFT TISSUE INJURIES

Soft tissue injuries can be conveniently divided into four categories: contusions, strains, sprains, and lacerations and abrasions. Each has specific characteristics and requires specific treatment.

Contusions

Contusions are caused by direct blows which both squeeze and stretch the tissues. Blood vessels are ruptured and the escaping blood creates pressure which causes pain. External bleeding, though unpleasant, releases the pressure and often results in less pain and discomfort. Where there is extensive damage a whole limb may become distended and remain extremely painful until the contained blood is absorbed. The discolouration known as bruising is due to the dead red cells lying in the superficial tissues.

Immediate swelling indicates bleeding and, in the case of a joint, suggests serious injury. If this happens you must call a doctor immediately because there may be a fracture or serious ligament damage.

The management of contusions is straightforward and is concerned with stopping the bleeding, relieving pain and promoting drainage.

First aid

(a)   Stop activity in order to reduce blood flow and lower local blood pressure.
(b)   Apply ice packs or cold compresses to discourage bleeding and to relieve pain.
(c)   Elevate the part to reduce pressure and aid drainage.

Early treatment

(a)   Stroking massage towards the heart to assist drainage further.
(b)   Gentle active exercise or static muscle tensing within the limits of pain to maintain mobility.

Later treatment

This is designed to improve the general circulation of the part and remove the clot of blood. It should consist of (a) gentle heat, (b) more specific, localized massage, and (c) a gradual resumption of activity.

Comment

When treating bruises, never use forced stretching. It may restart bleeding or damage deeper structures and start calcification of deep blood clots. When this does occur there is a loss of mobility, pain when stretching, and a gradual loss of function in that limb. The only cure is complete rest for a long time or surgery.

Strains

Strains of muscles or joints result from prolonged irritation by minor trauma such as overuse or postural problems. Common examples of strain from sporting activities in children are tendon strains around the ankle in athletes and low back strain in swimmers. Strain typically produces chronic inflammation.

Treatment

A period of complete rest is essential until there is no pain on normal function and when the part is pressed with the fingers. The ligaments or muscles should be pain free both when stretched and when resisting movement. Recurrence is inevitable if the cause has not been isolated and eliminated.

Sprains

Sprains are due to sudden traumatic events. Muscle sprains usually involve those which act on two or more joints and perform several functions, e.g. hamstrings. Joint sprains result from forced excessive movements, e.g. sprained ankle, which stretch the tissues and cause inflammation and accumulation of fluid within the joint. This produces a swelling and the pressure causes severe pain.

Treatment

Immediate first aid measures, as described above, are particularly successful and a full recovery in three to six weeks can be anticipated.

Lacerations and abrasions

No matter how small the break in the skin there is a risk of infection. Because bleeding often washes out dirt and infection it is a good idea to avoid stopping the bleeding too quickly unless a major blood vessel is cut. If this is suspected (bright blood which flows freely) then the blood flow must be stopped.

Lacerations (cuts) create the problem of deciding when stitching is needed. In full thickness cuts the edges fall apart and bleeding is profuse; they should be stitched within 12 hours. In partial thickness cuts the blood tends to seep out and the edges can be pulled together satisfactorily by adhesive strips.

Abrasions are caused by friction and most frequently involve skin overlying bone, e.g. kneecap, hip and elbow. There may be extensive superficial open wounds with initial bleeding followed by seepage of straw-coloured serous fluid.

First aid

Clean the wound with antiseptic solution followed by dusting with antibiotic powder to dry it. Later, to allow further activity, a raised ring of adhesive felt can be used to prevent direct pressure on the affected area. Do not seal in infected material by spraying with a plastic skin dressing before cleansing.

17.4.2 BONE AND JOINT CONDITIONS

Growing bones are particularly vulnerable to the extra demands of sport. If there is any reason to suspect damage to bones always arrange for an X-ray examination. Inform the family doctor and make sure that any paramedics who help are qualified. There are several injuries associated with bones which coaches may spot. They are described below.

Apophysitis

Apophysitis is the condition in which inflammation occurs at the attachment of tendons to bones as a reaction to the pulling action of the muscles. It may be noticed as an ache following activity or after resting in a fixed position and occurs frequently during the adolescent growth spurt. Apophysitis is an excellent example of a chronic inflammatory condition. Although it is possible to get short episodes of an acute flare-up where the area is tender, even to a light touch, it is more generally a low level persistent discomfort.

Treatment

The first step is to ensure complete rest from activity, possibly for several weeks. Physical therapy is designed to (a) relieve pain by ice, cold compresses or heat, depending on the inflammatory state, and (b) subsequently offset the effects of rest by static muscle tensing. As the immature bone ossifies and matures the effect of muscle pull becomes less.

Stress fractures

Stress fractures result from prolonged high intensity training and are frequently indicated by persistent activity-related pain in the limbs. The feet and lower legs are commonly affected but stress fractures also occur frequently in the spine. Diagnosis may require the magnification of an ordinary X-ray, repeated X-rays, or even a bone scan. Clearly, when there is reason to suspect a stress fracture medical opinion should be sought immediately.

Treatment

Immediately stop weight-bearing stress for a period of 4–6 weeks. To retain some fitness, alternative activity may be considered, e.g. swimming in the case of limbs.

Osteochondritis

Osteochondritis refers to inflammation of an area of bone and overlying cartilage the causes of which are not clearly understood. It tends to occur most commonly in the hip, knee and spine. Because the condition is so common in non-active children, sporting activity is not the cause. However, activity makes it more evident and it will eventually seriously limit participation. The condition is, again, indicated by persistent discomfort and should be investigated through correct medical channels.

Treatment

Effective management of osteochondritis is based on its self-limiting nature. Rest is relative to the degree of discomfort experienced. Physical activity need not be stopped but excessive strain as in strong muscle work or excessive weight-bearing, e.g. weight-lifting, running on hard surfaces or jumping on unyielding floors, should be avoided.

Chondromalacia

The softening of articular cartilage covering bone at a joint is known as chondromalacia. It is almost exclusively confined to the under-surface of the patella (kneecap) and is most noticeable when the quadriceps muscles contract strongly. When the kneecap is pulled firmly against the underlying bone the contact with the ulcerated cartilage is painful.

The degree of damage does not always correspond with the amount of discomfort experienced and it is frequently incorrectly diagnosed. Therefore it is important to seek advice from doctors or paramedicals who have a particular interest in biomechanical analysis and can examine lower limb posture, joint mobility and muscle strength. Incorrect footwear can be an important contributory factor.

Treatment

Adopt the procedures previously described in line with the stage of inflammation.

Postural defects

The relative position of our joints determines the posture of our body as a whole or the position of a single limb. Within broad limits coaches can recognize acceptable general and local postures during performance of skills, e.g. a forehand stroke in tennis. Such deviations from normal posture may often arise from poor technique which later results in a condition requiring medical treatment. The lower limbs and the trunk are the areas most frequently affected.

Asymmetric development may occur in young athletes as a result of overspecificity of training and indicates a lack of balance in the programme. Imbalance of muscle strength and asymmetric joint mobility always threaten efficient postures which allow maximum effect with minimal effort. Since exercise increases muscle tone, overdevelopment can cause an imbalance of opposing groups and create malposture of joints. This may result in reduced joint mobility.

Treatment

Discomfort or pain from postural problems can usually be temporarily relieved by rest but the underlying cause must be overcome if physical measures are to be successful. The problem can be treated by gradually stretching the tightened structures, strengthening opposing groups, teaching relaxation and practising posture correction. If children complain of persistent aching in muscles, medical advice should be sought, particularly if the ache is accompanied by increasing weakness.

17.4.3 HEAD INJURIES

These injuries are the dread of all involved in sport. They can occur in most sports but are obviously more prevalent in the contact sports. Because head injuries can have serious consequences they should never be ignored or neglected. The manifestations of head injury are too complex for this short text but the length of time for which the memory fails is often an indication of severity. There are several rules of thumb which should be firmly applied in guiding decisions about continued participation.

(a)   Loss of consciousness, no matter how brief, should result in immediate withdrawal from participation and medical advice should be sought.
(b)   The athlete should not compete or train for six weeks.
(c)   After three occurrences the athlete should give up the sport.
(d)   Sickness and vomiting associated with head injury is an adverse sign and medical aid is necessary at once.

Treatment

First aid measures are designed to revive the patient by applying strong sensory stimuli such as cold water douche, shouting, smelling salts, etc. A period of observation in a quiet environment until medical assistance arrives is necessary. Do not give painkilling drugs, such as codeine or alcohol, because they will cloud the clinical picture.

17.4.4 SPINAL INJURIES

The proportion of young athletes who suffer spinal injuries is, fortunately, extremely small. Nevertheless the lack of knowledge and equipment necessary to deal with this possibility at sporting events is very worrying. Safe handling of suspected spinal injuries is essential for minimizing the damage and coaches and officials should attend an approved course, e.g. St. John's Ambulance First Aid Course, to at least acquaint themselves with the problems which can occur. **In the absence of detailed knowledge the athlete should not be moved and must be kept still and warm until trained ambulance personnel arrive.**

17.5   CONCLUSION

The so-called pressure to succeed in sport, when applied to children, is a figment of the imagination; no sporting award is important enough to risk damaging future health. Furthermore there is little virtue in trying to understand every possible injury which could affect children involved in sporting activities. It is better to appreciate the basic facts which apply to all and to realize that there is a simple plan in dealing with them. If at all possible, coaches should attend a recognized course in first aid and/or sports injuries.

FURTHER READING

Grisogono, V. (1991) *Children and Sport: Fitness, Injuries and Diet*, John Murray, London.

Healthy eating for sport

18

Juliet Wiseman

SUMMARY

Good nutrition is necessary to support growth and activity, and young athletes need a balanced diet to provide all the necessary nutrients which the combination of growth and very high levels of activity demand.

The first section of this chapter describes the nutrients needed in any diet; those which provide energy (carbohydrates, fats and proteins) followed by other elements such as fibre, fluids, vitamins and minerals. The contribution towards health of the present United Kingdom diet is discussed and recommendations are given which would improve the balance of the diet. The way in which food provides energy for the body is also described.

The second section is specific to the needs of children and child athletes. This section includes a review of what children eat, what shapes their eating habits, the nutrient needs of active children, and practical guidelines relating to food provision for children in sport.

18.1 THE ENERGY PROVIDING NUTRIENTS

Energy from food is used by the body to fuel muscular activity and for normal metabolism at rest. Obviously, people who are active for a greater proportion of the time use more energy and need to eat more energy providing foods. Fats, carbohydrates, proteins and alcohol are all able to supply energy in the diet. Each provides a different amount of energy per gram, which may be measured either in calories or joules (1 kcal = 4184 kJ). Fat and alcohol are the most concentrated sources of energy, providing nearly twice as much energy as either carbohydrate or protein. This is clearly shown in Table 18.1 which gives the energy

Table 18.1 Energy value of nutrients

Nutrient	Kcal/g	kJ
Fats	9.00	37.6
Carbohydrate	4.00	16.7
Protein	4.00	16.7
Alcohol	7.00	29.3

Table 18.2 Recommended daily energy intake for children by age and sex

Age	Boys		Girls	
	Kcal	MJ	Kcal	MJ
1	1200	5.00	1100	4.5
2	1400	5.75	1300	5.5
3–4	1560	6.50	1500	6.25
5–6	1740	7.25	1680	7.00
7–8	1740	8.25	1900	8.00
9–11	2280	9.50	2025	8.50
12–14	2640	11.00	2150	9.00
15–17	2880	12.00	2150	9.00

(1 MJ = 1000 kJ = 239 Kcals; DHSS, 1979)
(Adapted from Department of Health and Social Security, 1979)

available in different nutrients in both kilogram calories per gram and in kilojoules.

In a typical British diet 40–45% energy is provided by fat, 47% by carbohydrate and the rest from protein and alcohol (MAFF, 1985).

The DHSS has produced guidelines giving recommended daily amounts of energy for children and adults. The recommended amounts for children aged 1–17 are given in Table 18.2. The following foods would provide 100 kcals each: one large slice of bread (50g), one small portion of boiled spaghetti (100g), a medium sized bowl of cornflakes (30g).

Recommended amounts of energy for children (unlike those for adults) do not vary according to activity; it is assumed that children are all similar in their activity levels. Recent research indicates that in fact children consume less than the recommended amounts of energy foods, due to reduced levels of physical activity.

However, while most children are becoming less active a minority who train or play sport regularly have energy needs as high as and in some cases higher than the recommended amounts. For example, a cross country run lasting half an hour would use about 300 kcals, a game of tennis for one hour about 400 kcals, so a child who trains and competes daily will be adding considerably to her or his basic energy needs.

18.1.1 BODY STORES OF ENERGY

The body is not dependent on a continuous supply of food for activity, because considerable amounts of energy are stored. The main energy store is fat which can provide enough energy to last 40–50 days, whereas glycogen in muscles and liver can provide only enough energy for 6–8 hours. Glycogen stores can only be maintained by a supply of carbohydrate in the diet; fat cannot be converted to glycogen. The brain and central nervous system depend on a constant supply of glucose from the liver. Muscle glycogen can only be broken down to supply glucose locally, it is not transported to other tissues.

Eating excess protein will not result in more and more muscle being synthesized. The glucose from amino acids may be used as an energy source or may be converted to fat. High protein diets containing little carbohydrate and fat are sometimes used by body-builders, but these diets will not result in any greater gain in muscle than could be achieved on a normal balanced diet. Also they will not prevent body fat from being synthesized and stored, if immediate energy requirements are exceeded.

18.1.2 FUEL FOR EXERCISE

The major fuels used by active muscles are glucose (from glycogen) and fatty acids (from fat stores). A mixture of these is usually used, in proportions which depend on the intensity and duration of exercise and the availability of glycogen. Each muscle cell contains a substance called adenosine triphosphate (ATP) which releases energy when it is broken down to adenosine diphosphate (ADP). This is a constant process. The energy is used to power the contraction of the muscle cell. Energy is needed to re-synthesize ATP, and this is supplied by the breakdown of glucose or fatty acids.

Metabolism and energy sources

Although most of the energy releasing reactions require oxygen, break-down of glycogen can also occur to some extent without oxygen, providing a very limited immediate energy release. The advantage of this process, anaerobic metabolism, is that it can provide some energy when exercise is so intense that oxygen supply cannot meet demands.

At lower intensities, with adequate supply of oxygen most glycogen and all fatty acids are broken down by aerobic metabolism (oxygen dependent) although both types of metabolism occur at once. A complete description of these processes is given in Chapter 6.

Muscle activity is normally fuelled by a mixture of fat and carbohydrate. Some muscle cells are better adapted to oxidizing fats and some to using carbohydrate as the main fuel. There is no sudden switch from one energy source to another, but as glycogen stores become more and more depleted a greater proportion of energy is derived from fats. At the start of exercise, or when exercise is very intense, glycogen provides the majority of the fuel needed. Some energy is obtained from glycogen even when oxygen cannot be supplied rapidly enough; in this case glycogen is partially broken down to pyruvate and then to lactic acid. Only a small amount of energy is generated in this way, so high intensity exercise cannot be maintained for very long.

Fat used for energy is first released from fat stores as fatty acids which are transported in the bloodstream to the muscle where they are needed. Fatty acids are then oxidized within the muscle cells to produce ATP. The energy yield from fat is far higher than that from carbohydrate, but fat cannot be used anaerobically so it cannot provide the rapid energy needed for high intensity exercise.

Because glycogen supplies in the muscle are limited any condition which increases the capacity to use fat or maximize glycogen stores will be an advantage in ensuring fuel supplies for prolonged or regular activity. Three conditions which help are training, diet and rest. Training improves the muscle's capacity to use fat as a fuel source. A diet which is high in carbohydrate, that is in which 50–70% of the total energy is supplied by carbohydrate, will ensure maximum glycogen storage. Carbohydrate foods eaten straight after exercise, when glycogen stores are depleted, will ensure highest rates of replacement of glycogen. Finally, adequate rest periods between training or events will ensure that glycogen stores are fully replaced. Training continually on depleted stores results in fatigue.

Energy density

Most foods contain a mixture of the energy providing nutrients; for example, biscuits contain fat and carbohydrate, cheese contains fat and protein. A food which contains a high level of energy per unit weight is termed *energy dense*. Such foods are high in fats and/or sugars. Foods which are high in complex carbohydrates, fibre and water are less energy dense; examples are foods such as bread, potatoes, cereals, fruit and vegetables. A diet based on these will tend to be higher in volume and lower in total energy and they are therefore advised for weight reducing. Highly energy dense foods are not necessarily the best sources of energy for health. Foods which are high in energy and low in bulk are too easily overeaten and may contain a high proportion of fat.

18.1.3 COMPARISON OF SOURCES OF ENERGY

Dietary energy should, and does, come from a mixture of sources: carbohydrate, fat and protein. It is important to achieve the correct balance of energy giving nutrients.

Carbohydrate

Carbohydrate is the preferred 'main' energy source, both for general health and for sports activity although, per gram, it provides less energy than fat. This is because (a) it can readily replace the body stores of glycogen in muscles and the liver, and (b) it does not increase the risk of conditions such as coronary heart disease, obesity and diabetes. A diet in which too much of the energy comes from fat and too little from carbohydrates inhibits the replacement of glycogen and may increase the risk of certain diseases and conditions (NACNE, 1983).

There are two main groups of carbohydrates: (a) simple carbohydrates (sugars) which in turn may be disaccharides (sucrose, maltose, lactose) or monosaccharides (glucose, fructose and galactose), and (b) complex carbohydrates (starch and glycogen). Starch, a polysaccharide consisting of many linked sugars, is by far the commonest dietary complex carbohydrate. It is broken down to simple sugars by the process of digestion.

Simple carbohydrates

Sugars occur in table sugar, honey, jam and confectionery, and are often associated with fats in manufactured foods such as biscuits, chocolate and cakes. Sugar is a pure carbohydrate which provides nothing but energy. For example, a 1 lb bag of sugar provides roughly the amount of energy needed for a woman each day. However, as sugar provides no other nutrients it could not support life for any length of time.

Complex carbohydrates

The main sources of starch are potatoes, cereals and cereal products such as bread. Starch is often associated with dietary fibre in foods for example in unrefined or 'whole' cereals such as wholemeal bread, oats and wholemeal flour products. Until quite recently starch and carbohydrate were often considered to be 'bad' for health. Foods were, and still are, promoted as 'starch reduced' or 'low in carbohydrates', and carbohydrate and starch were described as 'fattening'. Now it is recognized that starchy carbohydrate foods would form the main part of a healthy diet.

Dietary fats

Fat is the most concentrated source of energy and fat stores are the greatest energy reserves in the body. Excess energy in the diet which is not used will be stored as fat, whether it comes from protein, carbohydrate or dietary fat.

Fats contain fatty acids and different types of fatty acids occur in mixtures in foods. Fatty acids may be saturated, mono-unsaturated or polyunsaturated. The amounts and types of fatty acids determine the characteristics of the fat. Those which contain mostly saturated fats will tend to be solid at room temperature, like lard, hard cheese or butter; those which contain more polyunsaturated fat tend to be liquid, like sunflower oil.

Some polyunsaturated fatty acids are essential in the diet, because they cannot be manufactured in the body. They are found in vegetable, nut and seed oils and in oily fish. Most of our dietary fat is saturated, for example the fats of meat and dairy products. Saturated fats are not essential, but do provide energy and the fat soluble vitamins A, D and E.

Other energy providing nutrients

Protein provides about 10% of the total energy in the UK diet. However, it is not primarily an energy source and protein is only used for energy when excess protein is eaten or when there is a shortage of other energy sources. A wide variety of proteins occur in foods, made up of smaller units called amino acids. There are 20 different amino acids, eight of which are essential in the diet because they cannot be synthesized in the body. The main function of protein is to provide these amino acids for body protein manufacture. Alcohol also provides some energy in the diet but is not a necessary source of energy.

18.2   DIETARY NEEDS

It is now thought that the average British diet contains too much fat, too much saturated fat and too little starchy carbohydrate and fibre. In addition we eat more sugar and salt than is recommended for health. This type of diet is believed to contribute to the increasing incidence of obesity, coronary heart disease, diabetes and other diseases linked with carrying excess weight. Recommendations have been made in order to improve the average diet. These are primarily for older children and adults, but the diets of younger children should approach the recommended changes so that they become accustomed to eating healthy foods. Children's diets are often very high in fatty and sugary foods. Some parents may think this is acceptable for active children who show no signs of becoming overweight, but poor eating habits in childhood tend to be continued and may contribute to health problems later.

The amount of total fat and saturated fat in the diet should be reduced (NACNE, 1983). If the intake of fatty food is reduced more energy must be provided by carbohydrate containing foods. This would result in a less energy dense diet, which would be higher in fibre from the carbohydrate foods. In practical terms this means eating less fatty meats, dairy products, biscuits and confectionery, spreading fats, high fat cheeses and fried foods, and eating more bread (wholemeal and white), potatoes, fruit and cereals, pasta and rice.

While these dietary measures seem quite simple, they are often not compatible with the current trend of relying on convenience foods. It is quite difficult to achieve a lower fat, higher fibre diet in these circumstances and motivation is needed to eat healthily when it is easier to eat whatever is most readily available and takes least preparation.

18.2.1 HOW FOOD PROVIDES THE BODY WITH ENERGY

Carbohydrates, fats and proteins are digested in the stomach and small intestine to give glucose (and other sugars), fatty acids and amino acids. These are absorbed and provide the fuels needed by the tissues. The time taken for digestion and absorption to occur is dependent on the types of food eaten. Fats and certain types of fibre delay the process, while sugars are absorbed more quickly. Nutrients are taken to the liver and processed in various ways which depend on the current needs of the body.

Carbohydrates

Glucose, from starch and sugars, may be taken directly to tissues where it is needed and used for energy, or it may be taken to muscles and converted to glycogen for future use, or it may be converted to fat and stored.

Fats

Fatty acids when absorbed will be transported to the liver and may be used as fuel, rebuilt into fats and exported for storage, or they may bypass the liver and pass straight into the circulation to be distributed to tissues for storage or use as an energy source.

Protein

Protein is broken down into amino acids and transported to the liver. Some may be converted to other amino acids, depending on the body's needs. Most are rebuilt into proteins such as muscle protein, hormones and enzymes, but once this need is met excess dietary amino acids are used as an energy source. The nitrogen containing part of the amino acid is removed and used to form urea which is excreted, and the remaining part of the amino acid can be converted into glucose in the liver. Fluid is lost as urea is excreted (in urine or in sweat) so a diet very high in protein, in which a lot of the energy is provided in this way, will increase fluid losses and might result in dehydration. (The effects of dehydration are described more fully below.)

18.2.2 FOOD FOR GROWTH

Growing children require far more protein per unit of body weight than adults. The main function of dietary protein is to provide the amino acids needed to synthesize body proteins. These are needed to replace worn out proteins or for synthesis of muscle tissue and growth. The recommended daily allowances for protein are given in Table 18.3.

Table 18.3 Recommended daily allowance of protein for children by age and sex

Age (yrs)	Boys (gms)	Girls (gms)
1	30	27
2	35	32
3–4	39	37
5–6	43	42
7–8	49	47
9–11	57	51
12–14	66	53
15–17	72	53

(Adapted from Department of Health and Social Security, 1979)

One pint of milk contains about 18g protein, an egg 5g protein, an ounce of beef (28g) provides 6g protein and 100g baked beans contain 5g protein. The total daily requirement for a ten year old girl, for example, could be met from:

One pint of milk	18g
Two slices of bread	9g
A portion of baked beans	5g
An egg	5g
A bowl of cornflakes	3g
An ounce of cheese	8g
A pot of yogurt	5g

Dietary proteins contain a mixture of amino acids so they are not equally good at providing the essential amino acids which cannot be made in the body. Bread and cereal products do provide considerable amounts of protein in the diet, but as they have a poorer balance of essential amino acids it is important to include some better amino acid sources such as pulses, cheese, milk, meat, fish and nuts in the diet as well.

Protein is constantly being made and broken down, particularly in the liver and muscles. The breakdown product of protein is urea, excreted in urine and in sweat. A daily supply of amino acids in the diet is needed for protein manufacture to continue.

Because muscle is made of protein, the importance of protein in the sports person's diet may have been exaggerated in the past. Diets containing large quantities of meat, eggs, milk and cheese have often been advocated as 'muscle building'. In fact, above a given level there is no advantage in eating excess protein; it is simply broken down, partly used as energy or stored as fat, and partly excreted as urea. A disadvantage of a high protein diet is that it is often high in fat and low in carbohydrate, the opposite of the diet currently recommended for health.

In practice, the foods which supply protein in the diet are meat, eggs, dairy products, fish, cereals, pulses, nuts. The lower fat sources of protein are fish, lean meat and poultry, low fat dairy products, e.g. skimmed milk, pulses and cereal.

18.2.3 MAINTENANCE OF HEALTH

In addition to providing energy and the materials for growth, an adequate diet also ensures the continuing health of the body. The primary materials for this are vitamins and mineral salts which must be taken in small quantities and are present in most normal diets.

Vitamins

Vitamins are essential to health. All are needed in relatively small quantities and do not provide energy. They are usually referred to as 'fat soluble' and 'water soluble' groups. The fat soluble vitamins A, D, E and K can be stored in the body and so deficiencies are slow to appear; symptoms will not show until body stores are used. The water soluble vitamins, C and B groups, are needed on a daily basis; they cannot be stored so any excess is excreted. Vitamin deficiencies are rare in this country and are not liable to occur in a good mixed diet of sufficient energy content.

The only circumstances in which shortages might occur are when the diet is restricted in any way, for example, vegan diets (those which exclude all animal products), food preferences which limit the diet to a small range of foods (quite common in young children), or in those who are attempting to lose weight by restricting their total energy intake.

Sources of vitamins

Vitamin A comes from two sources in the diet, a fat soluble form (retinol) from liver and dairy products, and a water soluble form (carotenes) from carrots, tomatoes and dark green vegetables. A very low fat diet might be deficient in vitamin A unless a good range of vegetables is included to provide carotenes.

B group vitamins are widely distributed in foods including meat, milk, cereals, pulses and nuts. A varied diet is needed to provide all of these vitamins. The diets most likely to be deficient in the B vitamins are very low energy diets such as weight reducing diets. This group includes thiamin (B1), riboflavin (B2), pyridoxin (B6), pantothenic acid, niacin, folic acid and cyanocobalamin (B12). Folic acid is mainly found in liver, pulses and leafy vegetables, so diets which are low in vegetables might be lacking in this vitamin. B12 is only found in animal products (meat and dairy), so strict vegetarians might need a supplement. However, there is some B12 in yeast extracts such as Marmite.

Vitamin C (ascorbic acid) is provided by fruit, vegetables, fruit juice and potatoes. A daily supply of fresh (or frozen) vegetables and fruit will ensure an adequate vitamin C intake. Fruit juice is a useful and convenient source.

Vitamin D is contained in the fat part of dairy produce and in oily fish. Low fat diets may lack vitamin D, but our main source of this vitamin is from the action of sunlight on skin so deficiency is unlikely to occur except in housebound people.

Vitamin E is present in vegetable oils, liver and dairy products and grains. It is unlikely to be lacking in a varied diet.

Many of our foods are now fortified with extra vitamins and minerals; for example, breakfast cereals are mostly fortified with extra B group vitamins, and some low fat dairy products (milk and yogurt) have added vitamins A and D. These may be useful sources of these vitamins if the diet is restricted in any way. It is worthwhile reading the small print on food packets to see what has been added to processed foods.

There should be no need to take extra vitamins in the form of supplements if the diet is sufficient in quantity (i.e. energy intake is high enough) and is varied. There is also little evidence that exercise increases the need for any vitamin. Increased use of vitamins associated with energy metabolism (e.g. thiamin) will occur but if the required amount of energy is eaten the extra vitamins should also be provided.

Minerals

Several minerals are essential in the diet, some form part of the structure of the body (e.g. calcium and phosphorus in bones) and some are needed to take part in reactions which occur constantly in the body. They are widely distributed in foods. One group is needed in relatively large amounts – calcium, magnesium, sodium, potassium and chloride – and another group is essential but only needed in tiny amounts – iron, copper, zinc, manganese, iodine sulphur, cobalt, chromium and selenium.

Mineral deficiency

Mineral deficiencies are unlikely to occur if a varied diet is eaten; however, iron and calcium supply may be low in certain restricted diets. Since the best sources of both iron and calcium are restricted to a single group of foods, a diet might be deficient when these are avoided.

Calcium is widely found in dairy products and may hence be deficient in the diet if dairy products are avoided, due to allergy or strict vegetarianism. It is important then to eat enough non-dairy sources of calcium, e.g. nuts, tahini (a paste made from sesame seeds, now sold in most health food shops), fortified soya milk or to consider supplementing the diet. Calcium is particularly important during periods of bone growth.

Iron is found in red meat and is likely to be lacking in the diet where this is avoided. There are vegetarian sources of iron, but iron from them is less available. Vitamin C aids iron absorption, so drinking fruit juice with meals will assist the iron absorption from foods such as cereals and pulses.

Other minerals, including sodium, potassium, copper, fluoride, manganese, chromium and selenium, are available in a variety of foods and from water. They are unlikely to be lacking in the diet, and we may eat more sodium (salt) than is ideal for health as salt is present in so many processed foods. Zinc, which is present mainly in protein containing foods, may be low in a low protein diet.

18.2.4   NUTRIENT DENSITY

Any diet may be made less adequate in terms of vitamin and mineral content by diluting the 'nutrient density' with foods which supply large amounts of energy but no nutrients. The more dietary energy that is supplied by sugar, alcohol and confectionery, the less chance there is of meeting vitamin requirements, unless a very high energy diet is consumed. This is increasingly relevant in children's diets as many now depend on large amounts of sugar and sweets and sweet drinks for energy.

Any or all vitamins and minerals will be low in the diet if total energy is overrestricted, and supplementation is necessary on very low energy diets. However, a healthy active child or teenager eating a varied diet is unlikely to be lacking in any vitamin or mineral.

In general, it is not necessary to rely on supplements to supply minerals and vitamins, but these might be useful if:

1.   a child is extremely fussy and eats only a small number of foods. However, he or she should still be constantly encouraged to try a greater range of foods;
2.   the diet is very low in energy (not recommended for growing children for any reason);
3.   the diet is restricted for other reasons: allergies, religion, strict vegetarianism.

18.2.5   FLUIDS

A high percentage of the body is water. It is the means by which waste products are removed and the body is kept cool. Fluid losses in urine and sweat have to be replaced or dehydration will occur. In hot weather during exercise large amounts of fluid can be lost, and loss of fluid may impair performance.

A normal diet provides adequate fluid from water, milk, sweet drinks, watery foods, tea and coffee. We drink as a habit, as well as to satisfy thirst. Although thirst is used to indicate the need for fluid, it only operates when fluids are already depleted and it is better if fluids are replaced before thirst occurs. The body is able to absorb fluid from water and dilute solutions while exercising, and it is important to take some fluid during prolonged exercise. Children may need to be reminded to do this as they may become so involved in the activity that they forget to drink.

The best drinks to take generally are those which do not provide sugar (water, tea) or drinks which may provide some sugar but also provide some useful nutrients (milk, low fat milks, fruit juice).

The drinks often preferred by children, e.g. squash, fizzy drinks and milk shakes, also provide large amounts of sugar. On a warm day, an active child who relies on lemonade or Coke to quench thirst might also consume up to 250g of sugar. Very concentrated sugary solutions such as these are more slowly absorbed, so are not ideal for rapid replacement of lost fluid. Water and very dilute squash would be far more effective.

18.3 WHAT CHILDREN EAT

It is pointless to consider what children should eat for health without looking at what they like to eat, and what influences their choice of foods. Any advice given must take into account the current patterns of eating among young people. Changes in eating habits have occurred in recent years; fewer formal meals are eaten and frequent snacks are taken instead. The content of school meals is no longer specified by law and cafeteria style meals are now more common, allowing children complete choice over most of their own daily food intake.

A recent report on the diets of British school children (DHSS, 1986) indicates that chips, crisps, fried foods and sweets and biscuits provide an increasing proportion of the energy content of children's and teenagers' diets. Most children are now less active than in the past and energy intakes are lower than the levels recommended to match reduced energy output. This combination of falling energy intakes, plus sugary foods and drinks playing an increasing part in the diet, may mean that diets are low in useful nutrients. Influences such as food advertising, friends' eating habits, the contents of the snack machine at school, the proximity of a chip shop to school, all have an effect on children's diets now, perhaps more so than family eating patterns. These trends in eating habits result in diets with a high proportion of energy from fat and sugar, and children and parents with little knowledge of planning or preparing balanced meals.

Because snack foods (sweets and fizzy drinks) often do form an important part of the diet they cannot be cut out without finding an alternative. In fact, there is nothing wrong with 'snacking' if the foods eaten are providing useful nutrients. This means replacing chips, burgers, sweets and crisps (or most of them) with lower fat, higher carbohydrate foods such as bread, toast, teacakes, sandwiches, fruit and yogurts, which are still portable or available instantly as required. Sugary drinks must be replaced with lower sugar drinks to maintain the same fluid intake.

18.4 NUTRITION EDUCATION

With so many influences encouraging poor eating habits, it is important for children to learn about good nutrition. Children are notoriously difficult to influence towards measures which might protect future health; by and large they are healthy and have difficulty considering the future effects of their actions. However, children who are actively involved in sports and keen to optimize their performance do have an immediate reason for health to be an important consideration. For this reason they may be more readily influenced towards good eating habits. For this to occur the adults around them must themselves consider nutrition to be important. They must understand the influence of diet on health and must be prepared to explain it. Even very young children can understand that (a) when they have used energy they need to replace it with food, (b) certain foods are good sources of energy, and (c) fluids are necessary before and after exercise, particularly on hot days.

If this type of advice is given from a very early age and linked to training and performance, more complex ideas of nutrition can be introduced as appropriate and poor eating habits are less likely to develop. Coaches as well as families and teachers are in an excellent position to provide a positive influence by offering healthy and palatable foods and by setting an example of good eating habits.

18.5 FOOD FOR YOUNG ATHLETES

For any child, a diet of fast food and sweets is undesirable. For the child athlete, with added constraints of limited time and extra nutrient needs, this is also true. A balanced diet is important for all children, but there are a few points to emphasize for very active children.

18.5.1 NUTRIENT NEEDS

Energy

While most children are eating less than the recommended amounts of energy, very active children may need as much as or more than is recommended to support activity and growth. A high proportion of this energy should come from carbohydrate foods, which includes mainly starchy foods and some sugars. Energy is provided by the carbohydrate containing foods, e.g. bread, potatoes, cereals, pasta and rice.

Growth and development

Most people receive sufficient protein from a normal mixed diet. There is no reason to take any form of protein or amino acid supplement. Good dietary sources include meat, fish, cheese, milk, pulses. At least three portions of protein containing foods should be eaten each day. Lower fat sources such as fish, poultry and pulses should be eaten frequently.

Fluids

Children are less well able to control their body temperature than adults, so dehydration during or after exercise, particularly in hot weather, is a common problem. Children should be encouraged to take drinks with them to training sessions and events. Suitable drinks are fruit juice, diluted fruit juice, water, tea.

Vitamins and minerals

Very active children may actually have an advantage in respect of vitamin and mineral intake. Those most likely to be deficient in nutrients are on the lowest energy intakes. Active children on the highest energy diets should easily be able to meet their needs for vitamins and minerals through diet alone. There is no evidence that extra vitamins are helpful in improving sports performance, although such claims are sometimes made by supplement manufacturers.

Only those children whose diet is very restricted for any of the reasons mentioned earlier might benefit from a good mixed multivitamin and multi-mineral. In such a case, a dietitian should be consulted first as many of the supplements on sale are unsuitable and could be dangerous if taken in the wrong combinations.

18.5.2 PRACTICAL GUIDANCE FOR TRAINING AND COMPETITION

Young athletes with high energy and nutrient needs require a good balanced diet to support training. Meals in preparation for particular events are important, but far more important is the basic day to day eating which establishes good habits and provides the energy needed for constant training and growth.

The following guidelines may help in designing a good daily diet.

Food content

Carbohydrates

A complex carbohydrate source (without added fat) should be the basis of each meal, e.g. *breakfast* – cereals (less sweet ones are better), bread (preferably wholemeal but white is OK if brown is not acceptable); *lunch* – pasta, rice, bread or potatoes, cooked without added fat; *evening meal* – as lunch. Make sure this carbohydrate source is varied, i.e. not always bread or always potato. Variety will help to provide necessary vitamins and minerals.

Protein

Make sure that three portions of protein containing foods are eaten daily: meat, milk, cheese, pulses, nuts and fish. Ensure that the majority of this is low fat protein foods; meat should be lean, and fish, poultry, lower fat milks and cheeses could be used.

Fruit and vegetables

Include some fresh fruit and vegetables in the diet daily. Try to vary these to include as many different varieties as possible, to ensure vitamin and mineral supplies.

Availability of suitable food

(a) Provide regular meals including breakfast, midday meal and evening meal with between meal snacks. If training times prolong the school day always provide suitable snacks and drinks for before and after. Do not allow young children to choose their own food.

(b) Do not rely on cafes (e.g. at leisure centres) or snack and drink machines to provide food and drink. They usually sell only sweets and sugary drinks.

(c) Investigate food provision at school and at sports clubs or centres. Complain if food provision is poor, and provide alternatives when necessary.

(d) Make sure that suitable drinks are always available before, during and after training.

Explaining the importance of diet

(a) Explain the importance of diet for sports performance and health to children from the youngest possible age. With all the other influences to eat badly, they will need to have good reasons to eat well. Children who are highly motivated to succeed at their sport may be receptive to advice on good eating.

(b)   Don't overdo it. Children will always eat some sweets and crisps, and the occasional snack food does no harm if the basic diet is good.

18.5.3   FOOD FOR EVENTS AND COMPETITIONS

It is not advisable to try out any new meals, diets or drinks just before a major event. At this time familiar foods should be eaten; a reasonable amount of carbohydrate foods and plenty of fluids.

The pre-event meal should be taken at least two hours before competing and should consist of easily digested carbohydrates, e.g. toast, cereal, sandwich, with plenty of fluids, e.g. water, tea, orange juice. Sugary foods and chocolate bars are not an ideal source of instant energy. The sugar will increase the levels of sugar in the blood rapidly, but then levels will fall again quickly. More slowly absorbed carbohydrate foods are better in this respect.

Fluids can be taken up to ten minutes before competing and drinks should be taken at intervals in events, if possible. Drinks should also be given straight after an event.

It is important to always take food and drink to an event, particularly for long or all day events, and those distant from home. A child who has competed and is not given food or drink before a long journey home will arrive home exhausted and dehydrated. Recovery from the event will be delayed and car sickness is more likely to occur. If such feelings of discomfort become associated with competitions or matches they may reduce the child's interest in taking part in such events.

If there is a long gap between training and evening meal (more than an hour) it is useful to have an after-training snack, e.g. bowl of cereal, muesli bar, toast or sandwich. An after-training drink is also essential, particularly in hot weather; diluted fruit juice is ideal.

Quantities of food should depend on the child's appetite and individuals will vary considerably. However, the main part of each meal should be the carbohydrate foods, bread, potato, rice, pasta, etc. If the child is continually hungry (e.g. after the midday meal) give extra bread, sandwiches or rolls rather than including sweets in the meal or providing extra biscuits.

Foods to take to events and competitions

You can't rely on the organizers of events to provide suitable food and drink. It is important to be adequately fed prior to competition, and to replace energy and fluid as soon as possible after competing. When a child must compete several times at intervals during the day it is vital that food and fluid are available between events, for example in an all-day athletics or swimming match when a child may take part in several races.

The following are useful:

(a) Sandwiches (e.g. cheese, jam, honey, peanut butter, Marmite), scones, fruit, dried fruit (e.g. dates, raisins, sultanas), muesli bars, fruit yogurt, malt loaf, fruit cake.
(b) Drinks: diluted fruit juice or water enough to ensure a supply throughout the day; flasks of tea, soup and hot milk are useful for cold days, and for swimming when the child may become very cold between races. Always drink after an event and at intervals throughout the day. Food should be taken as soon after an event as possible.

Example of appropriate meals for active children

Breakfast

Cereals; corn or branflakes, Weetabix, muesli, etc.
Milk
Bread or toast, honey or jam
Fruit juice
Tea

Mid morning snack

Fruit juice
Banana or apple
Digestive biscuits

Lunch (packed)

Sandwiches or rolls with lean meat, cheese, fish
Tomato
Fruit
Yogurt
Milk or fruit juice to drink

School lunch

Potatoes (not always chips) or pasta or rice
Meat or vegetarian alternative

Vegetables
Pudding or fruit (fruit based or milk puddings are preferable to pastries)

Mid afternoon (pre-training)

Muesli bar or digestive biscuits or scone
Fruit
Fruit juice or milk (extra water pre-training in hot weather)

Evening meal

Potatoes, rice, pasta or bread
Lean meat, poultry, fish or vegetarian alternative
Vegetables
Fruit, yogurt or pudding

18.6   CONCLUSION

Clearly a healthy diet is essential to the health of all children and adults. It is important to encourage children to eat a balanced diet, and coaches can be influential in supporting parental efforts to ensure that children eat properly. However, young athletes have particular nutritional requirements to support high levels of energy output and the demands of muscular development associated with exercise. Yet frequently children are under pressure to fit the demands of school, travel and training into very short time periods. Under these circumstances they may easily neglect their food and exist on snacks and convenience foods. The problem may be worse where both parents work and there is no-one at home after school. But it remains the case that 'You can't run a high performance car on two star petrol!' and coaches can have a valuable influence on the eating habits of their athletes. Encourage them to eat a healthy diet, to eat sensibly to support their training and performance, and to take suitable food to events.

REFERENCES

Department of Health and Social Security (1979) *Report by the Committee on Medical Aspects of Health Policy: Recommended Amounts of Food, Energy and Nutrients for Groups of People in the United Kingdom*, Reports on Health and Social Subjects 15, HMSO, London.
Department of Health and Social Security (1986) *The Diets of British School-children*, HMSO, London.

Ministry of Agriculture, Food and Fisheries (1985) *Manual of Nutrition*, HMSO, London.
National Advisory Committee on Nutrition Education (1983) *Proposals for Nutrition Guidelines for Health Education in Britain*, Health Education Council, London.

FURTHER READING

Department of Health and Social Security (1984) *Report by the Committee on Medical Aspects of Food Policy*, Reports on Health and Social Subjects 28, HMSO, London.
Griffin, J. (1991) Diet for children, in *Children in Sport: Fitness, Injuries, and diet*, (ed V. Grisogono), John Murray, London.
Lobstein, T. (1988) *Children's Food*, The Food Commission, London.
Peterson, M. and Peterson, K. (1988) *Eat to Compete: A Guide to Sports Nutrition*, Year Book Medical Publishers, London.
Shrimpton, D. and Berry, P (1985) *Proceedings of the National Symposium on Nutrition in Sport*, Ottaway, London.
Wooton, S. (1989) *Nutrition for Sport*, Simon & Schuster, London.

PART FIVE
Good Practice in Coaching

Part five of this book is directed towards providing examples of how the principles put forward earlier can be put into practice. The idea that children are substantially different from adults in the structure and proportions of their bodies, their physiological responses, their ability to deal with information, and their perceptions of the world has been put forward to give coaches a more complete basis from which to make decisions which may profoundly affect the experiences of the athletes. As a result they may engage in the activities more safely, with less frustration and more satisfaction, and be more likely to carry on. However, whatever the future holds for them, coaching which is based upon an understanding of the material presented here will ensure that what they do in sport is more likely to be fun and will contribute to their growing up.

We have seen that children differ from adults in the proportions of their bodies and the ways in which they respond to exercise. This means that the rules, sorts of implements and size of playing areas which are laid down for adults are often totally unsuitable for children. Martin Lee and Ross Smith suggest ways in which coaches can modify sports so that children can more easily learn the skills and sustain the activity. In recent years this has become rather easier thanks to the introduction, by sports goods manufacturers, of modified equipment. However, many sports are not yet catered for. Dr Lee and Dr Smith lay down a challenge to coaches to look at their own methods and ask how they can modify the structure of the activities for children to learn and perform more easily.

Rod Thorpe is an experienced university lecturer and tennis coach who is well known for his work with children and in teacher education. Because of this he has undertaken to pull together the information in earlier chapters and explain how coaches can have an effect on the children they teach and shows how the principles introduced can be incorporated in the coaching process. In Chapter 20 he is directly concerned with putting theory into practice and shows how coaching children implies responsibilities which extend far beyond teaching skills. He discusses the responsibilities of various adult agencies involved with the provision of sport for children and outlines the implications of recent initiatives which relate to the accreditation of coaches. Using illustrations from tennis, which is his specialist activity, he then discusses the specific responsibilities of coaches for the safety of the children not only in the sense of protection from injury but also in the sense of avoiding upsetting normal growth patterns. He shows why it is important to work within a framework which includes parents and schools to provide the best possible support for children when they may come under the pressure caused by conflicting demands. In particular it is important to work alongside parents and encourage them to understand how they can contribute to the child's experience by reducing pressures on them.

Making sport fit the children

19

Martin Lee and Ross Smith

SUMMARY

Earlier chapters presented strong arguments to support the modification of sports activities to allow children to develop competence, confidence and enjoyment. In this chapter we review the implications of the theoretical and research information for the modification of sports so that children can more easily master the skills required. We acknowledge that in many cases governing bodies of sport in England have instituted modified sports which fit children better than the adult form and we provide examples from Australia. However, we also provide a rationale to encourage coaches to make changes to their sport at a local level to assist children to enjoy and benefit more. We suggest that changes can be made to playing areas, equipment, rules and organization. For each we provide a rationale based on physical, physiological or psychological knowledge and examples of how different sports have been, or may be, modified.

19.1 INTRODUCTION

Research has shown that children do sport because they want to have fun, learn new skills and be with their friends (see Chapter 9). They should be given the greatest possible opportunity to experience the joy and satisfaction they seek. It is better for them to see the cricket ball going to the boundary of a small field rather than only reaching halfway on an adult field, or a netball scoreline of 20–18 and not 2–1 because they can't get the ball up to the ring and the result is more a matter of luck than skill. It is possible and fruitful to structure coaching situations and competitions to work within the capacities of the competitors so that they have a greater number of successful experiences before having to meet the more rigorous demands of adult oriented playing conditions. The rules and conditions imposed on children in the early stages of learning a sport can be crucial not only to immediate enjoyment and satisfaction but also to long term involvement. Effective coaching means making the sport fit the child as much as possible.

To help achieve this there has been a gradual change in the conduct of many games in recent years. Adaptations have been made with the purpose of making it easier for children to experience the nature of the sport, to understand the basic structure of games, and to develop skills in a simplified setting. This has resulted in changes to the size of equipment and playing area, the duration of play, the rules of games, and the ways in which they are organized. Where such modifications have been introduced it has been important that the integrity of the game should not be altered and the participants see and experience the game as very similar to the adult model (e.g. rugby union).

The purposes of this chapter are to give an understanding of why such changes are helpful, to describe some of those that have been developed, and to encourage coaches to examine critically and creatively the ways in which they present their sport to children.

19.1.1   NATIONAL INITIATIVES

A very extensive application of the principle of adapting sports to meet the needs of children has been instigated by the state government of South Australia. It has produced a policy for the provision of sport for children and young people between five and 17 based upon six fundamental principles:

1. A focus on enjoyment, participation, success, and developing self-esteem.
2. An assumption that sports help develop team skills and co-operation.
3. Progress is developmental from fundamental movement skills to sport specific skills.
4. Children develop at different rates.
5. Games should be modified to take account of children's physiological and psychomotor limitations.
6. The nature of competitions should differ from that of adults by emphasizing participation, performance, enjoyment and satisfaction rather than outcomes.

Education Department of South Australia, 1990

As a result of this statement the state governing bodies of sport have prepared extensive guidelines for the conduct of junior sport. Each set is designed within a format designated by the South Australian Junior Sports Development Unit (see example in Table 19.1). Notice that recommendations are made on skill development, competition, the development of talented performers, and minimal coaching qualifications for five age groups. The detail within the categories may deal with length and content of practice sessions, modifications to equipment, the organization and nature of competition, and the responsible agencies.

As we have seen, in comparison with adults children have limited capacities, not only in their growth and development and physiological capabilities, but also in their perceptual-motor and psychosocial development. Programmes like those outlined above take account of those differences and, in Chapter 20, Rod Thorpe develops in detail ways in which the information in earlier chapters can be translated into practice. While physical differences are easily recognizable only informed coaches are aware of, and make allowances for, the less obvious differences children display in physiological, decision making, motor control and psychosocial capacities. In Britain there is not yet an equivalent policy to that developed in South Australia. However, there is a thriving programme of coach education operated by the National Coaching Foundation, a significant element of which is designed specifically to assist coaches who work with children.

19.2   AREAS TO CONSIDER FOR MODIFICATION

There are a number of ways in which coaches can alter the characteristics of a sport so that children are more easily able to participate with enjoyment. In some instances these may be promoted by governing bodies with the intention of advantaging all participants; but your own situation may pose specific problems which could be solved by applying your understanding of children to creating new conditions of practice and even competition. The areas which we will consider here are playing areas, equipment, rules, and organization.

19.2.1   PLAYING AREAS

Rationale

We have seen that children go through a series of stages in their physical growth and that the timing of the stages varies across the sexes and between individuals. The differences in size which are not only inherent between individuals but which are frequently exaggerated during the growth spurts can make a great difference to the demands placed on performers. It is no accident that the most successful high jumpers and basketball players are very tall! The effects of difference in size can be seen in the number of steps that a player

Table 19.1 Example of a policy of adaption of sport for children and youths (by kind permission of the Education Department of South Australia)

	Rugby league					
Age & year level	Skill development		Competition			
	Frequency and duration of sessions	Organization	School responsibilities			
			Intra school	Zone district	Metro & country knock out comps	State competition
Age 5–7 yrs year levels R-2	Introduction to the basic general movement and coordination skills. Development of group cooperation and participation.	No regular organized structured competition offered to boys or to girls at this level. The equipment used and the activities conducted are modified. Maximum participation is encouraged which may include appropriate small-sided, modified games. Children of either sex and/or with disabilities are encouraged to participate.	Regular, organized, structured competition not appropriate at this level			
Coaching level	Level 0 Desirable qualification	Level 0 Desirable qualification				
Age 8, 9, & 10 yrs year levels 3, 4, & 5	1 or 2 Sessions per week. Modified game – Mini Footy. Size 4 ball. Duration 45–60 minutes maximum. Development and awareness of the principles of good sporting behaviour.	Modified. Modified game. 1 Game per week. Modified ball, laws and rules. 8 players per side. Rotation of players optional. No premiership points. No finds. Maximum participation encouraged. Offered to boys and to girls as a single sex competition. Lightning carnivals offered as required. Children with disabilities encouraged to participate.	Aussie sports 'Mini Footy' offered and conducted in schools as a class activity only.	NIL	NIL	NIL
Coaching level	Level 1 Mandatory qualification	Level 1 Mandatory qualification	Level 0 Desirable			
Age 11, 12 yrs year levels 6 & 7	1–2 Sessions per week – 'Mod League'. Modified game. Modified ball. Duration 45–60 minutes maximum. Development and awareness of the principles of good sporting behaviour.	Modified. Modified game – 'Mod League'. 1 Game per week. Modified ball, laws and rules. 11 players per side. Controlled, organized and supervised environment. Maximum participation encouraged. Offered to boys and to girls as a single sex competition. Lightning carnivals offered as required. Children with disabilities encouraged to participate.	Aussie sports 'Mod League' offered and conducted in schools.	NIL	NIL	NIL
Coaching level	Level 1 Mandatory qualification	Level 1 Mandatory qualification	Level 0 Desirable			
Age 13, 14 yrs year levels 8 & 9	1–2 Sessions per week. Adult game. Modified ball. Modified game. Duration 45–60 minutes maximum. Development and awareness of the principles of good sporting behaviour.	Adult game – Modified game when necessary. 1 Game per week. 11 players per side. Maximum participation encouraged. Offered to boys and to girls as a single sex competition. Players with disabilities encouraged to participate.	Adult Rugby League offered and conducted in schools as a class activity only.	NIL	NIL	NIL
Coaching level	Level 1 Mandatory qualification	Level 1 Mandatory qualification	Level 0 Desirable			

Table 19.1 *Continued*

Rugby league						
Competition			Talent development			Responsible agencies
Level responsibilities		National competition	Talent squads	Talent camps		
Country	Local/district					
Regular, organized, structured competition not appropriate at this level		NIL	NIL	NIL		South Australian Rugby League inc. education authorities & junior sports development unit
NIL	NIL	NIL	NIL	NIL		South Australian Rugby League inc. education authorities & junior sports development unit
NIL	NIL	NIL	Talent squads Identified and conducted by Australian Rugby League Mod League authorities.	Talent camps Identified and conducted by Australian Rugby League Mod League authorities.		South Australian Rugby League inc. education authorities & junior sports development unit
			Level 1 Mandatory	Level 1 Mandatory		
NIL	NIL	NIL	NIL	Talent camps Selection by South Australian Rugby League Criteria.		South Australian Rugby League inc. education authorities & junior sports development unit
				Level 1 Preferred		

Table 19.1 *Continued*

	Rugby league				
Competition		Talent development			Responsible agencies
Club responsibilities		National competition	Talent squads	Talent camps	
Country	Local/district				
Age 15, 16, & 17 yrs year levels 10, 11 & 12	1–2 Sessions per week. Modified game when necessary. Development and awareness of the principles of good sporting behaviour. Physical fitness programme under the supervision of qualified coach.	Adult game – Modified game when necessary. 1–2 Games per week. Modified game when necessary. 7 players per side with up to 3 substitutes. Maximum participation encouraged. Offered to boys and to girls as a single sex competition. Players with disabilities encouraged to participate.	Adult Rugby League offered and conducted in schools as a class or interclass activity only.	Adult Rugby League offered and conducted between schools by the Education Authorities & SARL.	NIL	Under 15 and Open School Age Competition offered and conducted by SARL Authorities & Education Authorities.
Coaching level	Level 1 Mandatory qualification	Level 1 Mandatory qualification	Level 1 Preferred			Level 1 Preferred

must take to move about a tennis or badminton court, the time taken to run between the wickets in cricket and the length of the field in rugby, or in the distance a child can hit, throw or kick a ball.

Not only does physical size of the participant influence the dimensions of ideal playing areas but so do the limitations of physiological development. Young children do not have the strength, speed or endurance of fit adults. They cannot, therefore, run similar distances so easily, cover the ground in the same time, or throw, hit, kick a ball as far as adults. To play on a full sized pitch changes the nature of the game for children. If you have taught football on a full-sized, muddy field to a group of ten years olds playing eleven-a-side, you will be familiar with either 'beehive' soccer, where everyone chases the ball around the field, or with half of the kids standing around at one end of the field hoping that one of those at the other end is strong enough to kick over the halfway line! This suggests that it is wise to adapt the size of playing areas to the physical size of the players. After all, this is the case for adult sports.

Examples

Smaller playing fields have long been the norm in junior football (soccer) and are becoming formally promoted in junior versions of rugby league and rugby union in Britain. But even in these sports formal pitches may still be too large for certain age groups and levels of skill and coaches could adapt their own organization to make adjustments specifically for children of different age and size. The

Table 19.1 *Continued*

			Rugby league			
Competition				Talent development		Responsible agencies
Club responsibilities		National competition	Talent squads	Talent setting		
Country	Local/district					
NIL	Club competition offered and conducted by South Australian Rugby League.	Under 16 or open age competition selected & conducted by South Australian Rugby League Authorities.	Talent squads selected and conducted by South Australian Rugby League Authorities.	NIL		South Australian Rugby League, education authorities, Australian Rugby Association & junior sports development unit.

relationship between the size of the pitch and the ability of the player to kick a ball over a distance or run the length of the field may change dramatically during childhood and again change the nature of the experience of the sport.

The introduction of short tennis, in which the size of the court is reduced and the net is lower, has allowed many more children to enjoy the game in ways which were not possible on adult sized courts. They are also able to learn more sophisticated techniques of play. The advantages of such adaptation have been possibly even more salient in badminton. By adapting the court dimensions short badminton allows children to approximate more closely the movement patterns of adult players and hence the techniques of the game, which can be taught and can more readily transfer to adult form later.

In cricket the use of short pitches allows bowlers to be more accurate which itself benefits batsmen because the ball will arrive more often in the striking area. However, faster bowling will pose a further problem to batsmen because they will have less time to see the ball and respond so it is important to create a balance between the demands of batting and bowling.

19.2.2 EQUIPMENT

Rationale

Changes in the size of equipment for children's sports is made necessary not only by the physical size limitations but also by the relative lack of skill of children. For example, boys of ten and 11 have difficulty in performing a lay-up in basketball because the ball is too large and heavy to handle with the ease required for the adult skill; not to mention that a ten foot high ring poses entirely different problems for them! Some years ago one of the authors attended a conference on encouraging children to take part in sport. In one presentation a leading basketball coach showed a film used as a motivational aid in which top players were seen making slam dunks, a technique available to only a few. A member of the audience commented that he would find the film demotivating because very few youngsters could aspire to such techniques. This story highlights the point that the relative size of the players to the equipment changes the nature of the skill to be learned. Perhaps this is best demonstrated by the changing demands of pole-vaulting as the bar is raised. Vaulting at 1.50 metres or 2.00 metres is very different from vaulting at 4.50 metres or 5.00 metres.

Portable equipment

Fortunately small sizes in balls, bats, racquets, and so on are now commonly available though in some cases this has taken some time to be accepted and there may still be further miniaturization possible and desirable in certain sports. Little research is available which examines the effects of relative size of implements on the mechanics of skill performance and any gains may need to be set against the psychological disadvantages that children have in manipulating smaller objects.

Because children have small hands with which to hold and control a ball or grasp a bat or racquet, the use of lighter implements is particularly important in facilitating handling skills. Young beginners do not have the accuracy of movement of adults and it helps if they can use equipment with an increase in the relative size of striking surfaces and target areas. This facilitates contact in striking games and goal scoring potential respectively. For example, junior cricket bats and tennis racquets may be reduced overall but retain a large hitting surface to increase the likelihood of contacting the ball which makes it easier to succeed without imposing excessive demands on accuracy.

Fixed equipment

The same rationale of estimating the ratio between size of participant and size of equipment also applies to such fixed equipment as nets, goals and so on. Junior sized equipment is available in many sports but some coaches continue to use adult sized fixed equipment for children when smaller versions could be provided.

Examples

The advent of new materials used in the manufacture of sports equipment has advantaged not only professional players but also children. If the material is light children can manipulate the implements more easily than when it is heavy which can result in developing incorrect movements or techniques to compensate for lack of strength. The ratio of length to striking surface has also benefited in tennis from the evolution of mid-size racquet heads as the norm. In cricket, however, smaller bats tend to be proportionately smaller and hence there is a reduced contact area, making hitting the ball a little harder than it need be. Coaches could overcome this by cutting down larger bats to fit children.

A striking example of adapting equipment from that used by experts to meet the needs of beginners, whether children or adults, has been the development of the *ski evolutif* method of teaching skiing. A major difficulty faced by beginner skiers lies in turning the ski. The longer the ski the more difficult it is. *Ski evolutif* meets this problem by starting beginners with very short skis, little longer than a boot, and progressing through a series of skis of graduated length until the full length is reached. The method enables learners to experience the skills of skiing more easily and to achieve success and confidence more quickly. In other sports, such as sailing, equipment has also been designed specifically to allow children to enjoy the fun of the sport without having to meet excessive demands.

One area which does not perhaps receive the consideration it deserves is the nature of the balls which are used in certain sports. For example, a common problem that junior tennis players have, particularly when they start, is in dealing with high bouncing balls. Yet because they are shorter than the adults for whom the balls were originally designed, many more balls come to them at or above shoulder height. Tennis balls are now available which bounce less and are particularly suitable for children.

Adaptations to fixed equipment are exemplified by tennis, badminton and basketball. In the first two, the net is lower than normal. This is particularly advantageous in badminton because it enables children to get the racquet head above the net and hit the shuttle downwards. Thus the smash can become an integral part of the game from an early age which would not be possible for small children using a standard net. In both these sports the combination of smaller court and lower net enables children to enjoy the game and develop more sophisticated techniques and patterns than was possible previously. The use of a slower and lower bouncing ball in tennis and slower shuttle in badminton also allow beginners to play more easily. The object can be seen for longer before it must be played and therefore allows a longer time for decisions affecting shot selection, positioning and completion of the shot.

In mini basketball, court size, basket height, ball size and length of playing time are all modified to fit children. In this sport, for which there is an international organization, the basket height is specified to enable children not only from different clubs but also from different countries to play together. The demands for a formal requirement which are brought about by the needs of competition conceal the possibility of further adaptations at a club level for teaching and coaching purposes. Hence the use of adjustable height baskets has much to recommend it.

19.2.3 RULES

Rationale

Just as playing areas and equipment can be adjusted to meet the needs of children, so too rules can be changed to allow them to learn and enjoy the game better. Some governing bodies have already introduced laws of play specifically for the junior game which can apply in competitive matches and there is now a wide range of activities which have well established 'mini' versions of the parent game. Mini rugby, mini basketball and short tennis are widely played. The latter has national championships and we have already referred to the international organization of mini basketball which is played worldwide.

However, the guidance given by institutionalized rule changes which different groups may use as the basis for competition may only be the beginning of adaptation for modifications which can help children to get more enjoyment from their sport. There is no reason why local rules need not be applied for teaching purposes and even be agreed between teams for competition. The key is to determine the essence of the activity and devise ways of allowing children to experience it within the limits of their ability and skill level. For example, allowing the ball to bounce once when starting children playing volleyball allows children to experience the pattern of the game without the frustration of the ball falling to the floor after each shot.

Examples

Good examples of rule adaptations can be found in rugby union and basketball. Each case has special rules (laws in the case of rugby!) which encourage children to play and have fun, which may not be possible under the conditions of the full game.

The governing body of rugby in England, the Rugby Football Union (RFU), has developed a game known as 'new image rugby' in which children from both sexes and of differing ages can take part together. This is achieved by removing the rougher aspects of contact from the game. Children often find that tackling and contact in scrums and in loose play put them off the game, at least at first. By substituting a two-handed touch for tackle, introducing scrums in which there is no pushing, and removing contact in loose play by having a pass after a 'tackle', this fear is removed. Moreover, the dominance of big children is eliminated and the emphasis is on running and handling skills. In doing this the game retains the structure of the full game. The purpose is to carry a ball over the opponents' goal line by running, carrying and passing among the players. Players assume the roles of ball winners (forwards) and runners (backs), and the game can accommodate groups of three to 12 players. Consistent with the advice in Chapter 8, coaches are advised to start children in small groups to enable them to understand better the structure of the game. However, this might be extended by requiring children to play in different positions from an early stage in order that they can experience the different demands of those positions.

Adaptations to equipment in mini basketball have been referred to previously. In addition the game, which is designed for children up to 12 years old, incorporates some changes in rules. The game is divided into four periods of ten minutes and if scores are equal at the end of that time then the game is drawn; there is no extra time to get a winner. In order to encourage maximum participation teams may consist of ten players of whom five may be on court at any given time. Each member of the team must play in at least one period and substitutions may only be made at the intervals, except for once in the last period of play. This sort of organization encourages participation and enjoyment as we know that children prefer to take part than sit on the bench. A further modification could be introduced in relation to the three second rule. Relaxation of this requirement to four seconds in the mini game would allow for the longer period of time it usually takes for children of this age to make decisions.

The notion of substitution for young players can readily be extended to other sports. As a teacher, one of the authors recalls frequently arranging rugby and soccer matches for 11 year old boys with other schools in which substitution was agreed in order to allow more children to play. In one case we would also mix the teams to create more balance if it was necessary, so essentially the match became a learning experience rather than merely a contest. Of course, not all teachers supported the idea!

19.2.4 ORGANIZATION

Finally let us turn to the question of how sport for children is organized. The provision of sporting activities for children is not the same as the provision of sport. The latter has a ring of institutionalization in which the activity is owned by adults. Sports activities, or games, on the other hand may be thought of as being owned by the children, as an extension of their play. While we acknowledge that as children get older, as athletes, they become more accomplished, a transition from playing to achieving must be assisted to make that change in a way that retains enthusiasm and keeps as many children in sport as possible.

The importance of acknowledging the constraints introduced by adults into children's sport are perhaps best demonstrated by the sadness expressed by Ray Williams of the Welsh RFU who was instrumental in developing the game of mini rugby as a means of allowing young players to develop the skills of the game without the pressures of competition. Within a relatively short time, competitions had been established in which the prime object was victory, not learning, and the game was owned by the adult coaches (Williams, 1986).

Rationale

So what can be done? The first thing is to return to the ideas in Chapter 3 and examine the goals of a programme and ask to what extent are children's needs being made a priority. Secondly, ask to what extent those needs are being met by the way in which the programme is organized. Thirdly, examine the competitive structure of the programme in the light of the demands on the children. When competitive demands exceed children's perceptions of their ability to meet them then they will be under stress and not enjoy the game.

The timing and way in which competition is introduced and developed is an important issue in children's sport, so much so that the Olympic Scientific Congress of 1984 in Eugene, Oregon, devoted a session to considering children's readiness for competitive sport. Robert Malina, an expert in growth and development from the University of Texas, has argued persuasively that readiness for competitive sport is determined by the individual characteristics of children, that is growth, maturation and development, and the nature of the sport. He has also commented that the focus of youth (children's) sport should be children but that focus is often distorted (Malina, 1986). Other speakers drew attention to the need to develop 'competitive' environments which emphasize skill development prior to adolescence so as not to disadvantage those who are small or late developers; to the need to allow for the relative immaturity of children in being able to assess productively the competitive experience itself; the need to promote success experiences as an aid to enhancing self-esteem in younger children; and the need to ensure that coaches are adequately prepared for the specialist task of coaching children (Coakley, 1986; Halbert, 1986; Passer, 1986; Sharkey, 1986).

Examples

So what can be done to organize sports more beneficially for children? The key here seems to be to develop a competitive structure which maximizes enjoyment for the children participating, while at the same time acknowledging that different children enjoy different aspects of the sport. There is good reason to make changes to the competitive structure with changes in age, as has been done in the South Australian system mentioned previously.

Coakley (1986) suggests that pre-teen children need a less demanding structure than those who have reached teenage. During the 1980s a study commissioned by the International Tennis Federation recommended restrictions on the liberty of children to play at the top level which included the abolition of international tournaments for children under 12. This prompted the withdrawal of Swedish and German federations from such tournaments and a requirement in Germany that young tennis players also did other sports (Ryan, 1988).

Tournament organizers can further examine the extent to which events should follow senior patterns. When tournaments run from early morning to midnight in order to find 'winners' and those who survive can think not of winning but only of getting home, one is left wondering about the value of the event. In mini basketball, which caters for children under 12, one strategy is to organize 'rallies' and 'jamborees'. In both cases mixed sex teams are encouraged and in rallies, while teams play against each other, the organizers do not make a final ranking of the teams, hence there is no formal winner or loser! In jamborees children come from different clubs, areas or countries to play together and teams are composed of members from all the different groups which attend. Both of these strategies have the effect of focusing on playing performance rather than outcome. How different from the organizers of a mini rugby tournament in which winners of each match were given a soft drink for which the losers had to pay (Tennick, 1987).

19.3 RECOMMENDATIONS

There are compelling arguments to support the modification of sports activities to allow children to develop competence, confidence and enjoyment. In recent years the governing bodies of many sports have initiated appropriate modifications but for the purposes of promoting participation, learning and enthusiasm coaches should consider making local adaptations for teaching and possibly for competition which should be incorporated wherever children demonstrate difficulty in carrying out the task. Many adaptations already adopted in specific sports can provide models for similar changes in others. These changes should make the task easier for the players, promote success, encourage continuation in the sport, and maintain the integrity or essence of the activity.

REFERENCES

Coakley, J. (1986) When should children begin competing? A sociological perspective, in *Sport for Children and Youths, The 1984 Olympic Scientific Congress Proceedings*, (eds M.R. Weiss and D. Gould), Human Kinetics, Champaign, IL.

Education Department of South Australia (1990) *Junior Sports: A Policy Statement*, Education Department of South Australia, Adelaide.

Halbert, J.A. (1986) When should children begin competing? A coachs perspective, in *Sport for Children and Youths, The 1984 Olympic Scientific Congress Proceedings*, (eds M.R. Weiss and D. Gould), Human Kinetics, Champaign, IL.

Malina, R. M. (1986) When should children begin competing? Readiness for competitive sport, in *Sport for Children and Youths, The 1984 Olympic Scientific Congress Proceedings*, (eds M.R. Weiss and D. Gould), Human Kinetics, Champaign, IL.

Passer, M. (1986) When should children begin competing? A psychological perspective, in *Sport for Children and Youths, The 1984 Olympic Scientific Congress Proceedings*, (eds M.R. Weiss and D. Gould), Human Kinetics, Champaign, IL.

Ryan, A.J. (1988) Perspectives on children's sports with suggestions for future directions, in *Competitive Sport for Children and Youths*, (eds E.W. Brown and C.F. Branta), Human Kinetics Champaign, IL.

Sharkey, B.J. (1986) When should children begin competing? A physiological perspective, in *Sport for Children and Youths, The 1984 Olympic Scientific Congress Proceedings*, (eds M.R. Weiss and D. Gould), Human Kinetics, Champaign, IL.

Tennick, R. (1987) Personal communication.

Williams, R. (1986) Mini-rugby, in *The Growing Child in Competive Sport*, (ed G. Gleeson), Hodder and Stoughton, Sevenoaks, pp. 80–84.

FURTHER READING

Haywood, K.M. (1986) Modification in youth sport: A rationale and some examples in basketball, in *Sport for Children and Youths, The 1984 Olympic Scientific Congress Proceedings*, (eds M.R. Weiss and D. Gould), Human Kinetics, Champaign, IL.

Pooley, J.C. (1986) A level above competition: an inclusive model for youth sport, in *Sport for Children and Youths, The 1984 Olympic Scientific Congress Proceedings*, (eds M.R. Weiss and D. Gould), Human Kinetics, Champaign, IL.

Rugby Football Union (1990) *New Image Rugby* (video), RFU, Twickenham.

Putting theory into practice – a sport example

20

Rod Thorpe

SUMMARY

Throughout the previous chapters one statement – 'children are not miniature adults' – frequently appears. The occurrence of this statement is equalled only by the statement that 'our knowledge of children in sport is incomplete'. Unfortunately the coach has to work with this incomplete knowledge.

It is not the intention here to review each chapter or even to relate each topic area to coaching practice; rather it is the intention to develop selected examples in a practical way to indicate how the coach of children, and those others responsible for promoting the coaching environment, might have to review more carefully the way in which they think about organization and content. It is hoped to clarify some of the issues raised by focusing on one sport, tennis, which has at various times been highlighted because;

(a) of the pressure it places on youngsters;
(b) it can provide an enjoyable pastime for many;
(c) it can be perceived as a lucrative profession for some.

Whenever appropriate, examples will be given from other sports.

20.1 IMPLICATIONS FOR THOSE ORGANIZING AND/OR PRESENTING SPORT FOR YOUNG PEOPLE

Two things have become apparent. Firstly, coaches who have not been alerted to the issues that are important when coaching young people might be at best inefficient and at worst a danger to the young people in their care. Secondly, sport can be a powerful influence in the physical, psychological and sociological development of young people.

It follows, therefore, that coaches working with young children should have the necessary training to do so, safely and efficiently. In a country that has traditionally accepted that much of the sport experience has been provided by volunteers, it is difficult to see how such training can reach the many people involved in young people's sport. There are, however, some points of influence that might, if prompted, be able to help spread 'good' practice.

20.1.1   THE EMPLOYERS

It may be that the local authority, sports club, youth centre, play scheme, etc., who 'employ' a coach to work with children should look first for the qualification that indicates an ability to work with young people, and only second for the qualification that indicates sport specific knowledge. In the short term, it would seem sensible to encourage employers to build into their conditions of employment the completion of the National Coaching Foundation (NCF) course 'Coaching Children'. The development of Scottish/National Vocational Qualifications (S/NVQs, see later) pertinent to both coaching and working with children may in the near future provide a mechanism for ensuring that all coaches employed to work with children are appropriately qualified.

20.1.2   GOVERNING BODIES

The basic coaching award in many sports is seen as the qualification that prepares the coach to introduce the activity. Of course, a large number of the people being 'introduced' to many sports are children. The National Coaching Foundation course 'Coaching Children' presents, in four hours, the information considered essential to the coach of children. Entry to the Lawn Tennis Association Intermediate Coaching Award is now dependent, in part, on completion of this course. Other governing bodies recommend or require coaches to attend this course. In some cases this may not be enough. In tennis, the Intermediate coaches often find themselves operating with county and regional level youngsters, who give considerable time and effort to their sport. These children can be said to be truly competitive, and it would seem desirable that the more extensive knowledge provided by the NCF Advanced Level course 'Children and Competitive Sport' be embraced.

As mentioned earlier, so many of the sporting opportunities provided for young people, even at the competitive level, are run and organized by amateurs who have given their time and money to take coaching awards. Many may feel that the additional time for specialist courses, like those of the NCF, requires a commitment they cannot give. It is vital, therefore, that in a desire to produce the 'ideal' provider of sport opportunity for children, we do not exclude the many people who, with an appropriate short training, can make a valuable contribution. Thus a major task for those who design coaching awards is to determine just how much information about children they can include within the programme without excluding prospective coaches because the time or expense becomes too great.

It may be that the obligation to attend the more advanced course on children should not be governed by the coaching award, but rather by the role the coaches occupy. Thus all intermediate coaches may not be obliged to take the course, but all county and regional development officers would.

The evidence from earlier chapters suggests that more time spent on considering the adaptations necessary to meet the needs of particular groups, even if this means a little less on the technical and/or tactical elements, might be advisable. Even so one must question how much time can be allocated to children, how much to players with disabilities, etc. Those in the sport must assess the relative values of each element of the course; for example, I would expect as much information about some aspects of child development in a one-day 'Tennis Leaders' course as in a 36-hour 'Elementary Coaches' course, because of the anticipated markets in which these leaders and coaches will operate. The tennis leaders will work predominantly with the younger child, the coach will be expected to develop technique and tactics with a wide range of ages and abilities.

Clearly each governing body must make this sort of decision. In sports like tennis, swimming and gymnastics in which the young dominate the competitive scene, a considerable input about children would seem to be advisable. In other sports where coach/leader awards are designed for the young, for example mini basketball, mini rugby, etc., these particular awards could well include considerable information on children, whereas the normal coaching award may not (see NVQ).

Ultimately, the idea of incorporating material about child development into coach training programmes would seem to be the most suitable way forward. Certain aspects of child development may be important in one sport but only peripheral in another. Clearly the emphasis given to the different aspects of child development will, and should, vary from sport to sport. An attempt to integrate child development issues into sport specific coaching was central to the philosophy of the training of coaches for the Champion Coaching Programmes run in 1991 (NCF, 1992). Incorporating child development into national governing body coach education might at first sight appear to put pressure on the 'tutors of the coaches'. In 1989, the LTA asked all their panel tutors to include the information from the NCF Introductory

Study Packs in their courses for the Elementary Coaching Award (LTA, 1989). It appears that, after a little difficulty, most tutors feel comfortable with the material and a thorough integration of theory and practice can now take place. At the time of writing a number of NGBs are wrestling with the problems of ensuring that the coach training syllabus can be interpreted as competencies measurable in the coaching situation, in order to satisfy NVQ requirements. Because many tennis coaches work with children, and because the need to match the coaching behaviour to the needs of the group is central to good coaching, it follows that any assessment should ensure the coach has knowledge of, and competencies in, coaching tennis to children.

20.1.3 SPORTS COUNCIL AND GOVERNMENT

A number of important events have occurred, and are continuing to occur, at the national level which will affect the coach of children. It is beyond the brief of this chapter to do more than highlight the main implications; indeed, any attempt to discuss finer points would be futile because, at the detailed level, change is so rapid that the information presented would be outdated before publication.

During the 1980s it would seem that the Sports Council retained a focus towards Sport for All and targeted a variety of groups such as the over-50s and women, with an underlying thrust towards 'participation'. In the 1990s, the balance has shifted somewhat, with more attention being given to 'performance and excellence', i.e. to those who wish to improve and those destined to reach the top levels. In addition, the Sports Council made a strong commitment to the support of young people (5–18) in sport, in the belief that if you 'catch them young', they will wish to continue in sport. These re-orientations of Sports Council objectives, coupled with the development of the national curriculum for physical education which clearly highlighted the need for partnerships between schools and other sports providers, has thrown the need for 'good' coaches of children into the spotlight. Certain other legislative changes, like local management of schools and the Children Act, have changed the 'climate' in which sport provision for children may be offered. These issues are beyond the scope of this chapter, but suffice it to say that the need for a more informed, better qualified coach of children is apparent.

The Industry Lead Body for Sport and Recreation, a group of people chaired by a representative of the Sports Council, has been charged with bringing some order to the multitude of sport (and recreation) qualifications and determining the knowledge and competencies required for given levels of sport workers. Work is ongoing, through the NCF, to help sport governing bodies to review their coach training programmes against this framework. It may take some time before we see all coaching awards embrace the common framework, and there will always be sport specific differences, but as an employer of coaches or as a parent whose child is being coached I am sure I would welcome a clearer idea of what I can expect the coach to know and be able to do. It is comforting to note that the needs of children are well represented within the NVQ awards and these issues will reach the coach trainers and assessors.

20.1.4 BRITISH INSTITUTE OF SPORTS COACHES (BISC) AND THE NATIONAL COACHING FOUNDATION (NCF)

In 1991, the four Sports Councils in the United Kingdom produced *Coaching Matters – A Review of Coaching and Coach Education in the United Kingdom* (Sports Council, 1991). In addition to representatives from the Sports Councils, the other officers contributing were the Director of the NCF and Chief Executive of BISC. In some senses this reflects the fact that it is these two agencies, working together, who will be charged with moving coaching forward. *Coaching Matters* provides a framework and embraces many of the 'person awareness' issues which become so important when coaching children. Coaches have ready helplines in these two organizations.

20.1.5 IMPORTANT OTHERS

It is important to recognize that much of the sport provision for children has been developed, and is presented by, individuals and organizations not mentioned so far. The list is immense and varies from the helper at Brownies or Cubs evening to the lecturer in Higher Education who has given a lifetime to producing materials suitable for children's sport experiences. It is beyond the scope of this chapter to discuss the roles of all of these, but it is important for the coach to be sensitive to the fact that there are many different perspectives of sport, and there is a need to enter some situations with tact and diplomacy. There are people who spend a considerable time working with children who are yet to be convinced that sport is a positive experience. Coaches would do well to listen to the reasons these people give for this negative response as often it is based on their own experiences of sport as children.

20.2 IMPLICATIONS FOR THE COACHES

20.2.1 THE PHYSICAL SAFETY OF THE CHILD

Coaching responsibility (short term)

Most parents entrust their children to a person called a 'coach' in the expectation that that person would, at the very least, provide a safe environment in which to learn. It seems reasonable to anticipate that the law would expect that a coach of children would take extra care of the child, because children cannot be expected to foresee danger or understand the concept of responsibility.

Before and after the session

This added responsibility requires thought even at the simplest of levels; for example, the coach may well have to assess the point at which responsibility is taken from and passed back to the parent. It is not uncommon to see young children waiting for parents unaccompanied because the coach has left or is taking the next class. The coach of children may have to build into the session planning the 'handover' procedure – once this is defined, the coaching session can then be planned with safety in mind.

A particular problem with tennis is that coaching sessions often occur outside and children leaving the court thus easily leave the confines of the coach's perception. Coaches can of course overcome the problem of safe transfer by devising a rota which nominates one parent to take on the role of ensuring all children are safely collected.

Within the session

In Chapter 7, Rosemary Connell makes the point that 'Recognizing spaces, judging direction and speed of movement of other players and balls needs practice . . .'. These skills are not well developed in children. Place this alongside the fact that children tend not to walk onto court and await instruction, particularly if the sessions are 'fun', and it becomes quite apparent that the safety procedures which operate for adults, e.g. checking space to swing the racket, ensuring balls are not underfoot and that there is a clear space to hit into, have to be extended. The fact that many coaches use modified courts to ensure more appropriate activity can mean that the children may operate in areas less well defined than adults playing on a full court. There are clearly laid down guidelines for spaces between and at the back of regulation tennis courts, but the good coach modified the court to suit ability and as a result markings may be less clear, distances between courts more arbitrary, etc. Modification may occur at an age when space, consequence of actions, etc., are not fully understood so it follows that safety has to be a priority. A gentle introduction of the rules we apply to play safely need not be oppressive and can be a first step from free play toward the organized world of competitive sport. It can also be the first step toward understanding that all competitive sport is played within agreed rules and that most sport is played with friends.

Often, in those sports in which the environment risk is obvious, for example the gymnasium, climbing wall or diving pool, safety is often built into the coaching programmes. It is often those activities like badminton, soccer, basketball, which people play unsupervised and with no formal tuition, in which the safety is overlooked. The argument that children 'play' these activities unsupervised may not satisfy the parents of a child who has an accident when care was entrusted to the coach.

The reader might accept that showing 'care to those you are coaching' and identifying 'foreseeable risks and taking positive action to prevent them' (see Appendix 2) can, whilst protecting the coach, be an integral part of the education of the children.

Coaching responsibility (long term)

Whilst accepting that sport is often associated with a healthy lifestyle, it is immoral to ignore the fact that youngsters may be seriously injured by sport. We have to be concerned at the number of young players who play in strapping, who complete games only to rush for the 'ice', who spend hours with the 'physio', etc. Some injuries occur through accidents, but some overuse and stress injuries can be avoided if the coach takes the time to consider the risks. Many of the risks are obvious once the coach considers them. For example, many British youngsters play tennis on 'hard' porous concrete courts, therefore the moment a commitment is made to the game it is vital that the coach educates the performer and parent about the need for appropriate footwear. Children often attend their first session with a racquet borrowed from a friend or parent. Few know what to buy, but it should be obvious that an inappropriate racquet could cause injury. The coach can remedy these factors quite quickly, but there are often less obvious influences on the child's safe development.

Tennis is one of the sports which can cause asymmetric development. It is not surprising that tennis players have relatively more muscular development of the hitting arm but it is perhaps less well known that the bone density is also greater in the hitting arm. These developments may not be directly linked to injury in themselves, but it would seem logical to suggest that extreme asymmetry will put disproportionate stresses on the body. Far more concern has been expressed about the stresses produced by extreme asymmetric body rotation, particularly with certain double-handed techniques. The tennis coach must, when dealing with young children, consider the need for a balanced physical development; if tennis does not provide it, then it seems desirable to encourage compensatory exercise. In the older, committed children this might well take the form of a prescribed exercise regime. In the younger children, the encouragement of other forms of activity, e.g. swimming, team passing games or gymnastics, might be appropriate.

One further observation about tennis is necessary. Neil Armstrong points out why the American Academy of Pediatrics recommend 'that, under no circumstances, should a full marathon be attempted by immature children'. Whilst tennis tournaments are not the same, it is worth considering that many junior matches last over an hour and the youngsters are often called upon to play more than one match in a day, particularly if entered into singles, doubles and handicap competitions. Often these matches take place on porous concrete and can occur in very warm weather. Most tournaments last several days. The implications for diet, fluid intake, rest, overuse injury, etc., may be as important, but are far less obvious than those anticipated for marathon running.

Clearly each sport places particular physical demands on players. The example of tennis is used to illustrate how what at first sight appears a 'safe' activity can, under certain circumstances, put the child at risk. It is necessary to look beyond the obvious, like the possible head injuries in boxing and neck injuries in rugby, and include the more cumulative effects of training and competition.

At times, governing bodies may be competing for youngsters, particularly the talented. It is not uncommon to find youngsters who are talented in more than one sport. One can understand why a coach may be reluctant to encourage the player to take part in the other activities (s/he might fear that the youngster will begin to prefer another sport), but coaches have to realize that they are important people in the child's overall physical education and a single sport may not best provide a healthy physical development.

20.2.2 PSYCHOLOGICAL WELL-BEING OF THE CHILD

Whilst it would be difficult to make the case that the 'over-zealous' or 'careless' coach had damaged the child emotionally, there is sufficient evidence, in tennis at least, that the intensely competitive junior circuit can dramatically affect the well-being of the child (see Chapter 12).

'Fortunately' many children drop out before this becomes a major problem. Several chapters deal with the way factors as varied as the coach's values, goal setting, anxiety control and so on, can influence the way children associate sport performance with self-worth. Once again there would appear to be certain principles that might alert the coach to possible dangers in their sport. Does the activity demand a large time commitment? Can the child be easily judged by others? Can conflicts arise between school and sport? Is success likely to be affected by physical maturation? Are parents involved in the sport? Are children individually ranked? Of course, the answer to these questions for tennis is 'Yes'. It follows therefore that tennis coaches must be sensitized to these dangers. It would seem desirable that all governing bodies examine the likely sources of psychological pressure in their sport and ensure that coaches are made aware of them. It is not surprising that gymnastics and swimming are coupled with tennis as examples of sports with mid-teen drop-outs. All contain the elements that make them prone to rejection during adolescence.

20.4 ACCESS TO SPORT

20.4.1 THE PARENT/GUARDIAN–CHILD–COACH INTERDEPENDENCE

Tennis typifies the need for the coach and parents to act as a co-ordinated team. The sport itself recognizes the value of family interaction at top level with father/son, mother/daughter events, and at the lower club levels with handicap tournaments, which are often peppered with family doubles. The game is difficult to play (although short tennis overcomes this somewhat) and parents can be quite important as practice partners. Those parents who cannot become the practice partner often act as transporters to meet a prearranged practice partner. As the child reaches the higher levels, it becomes apparent that appropriate practice partners, coaches, squad sessions and competitions become more widespread. The time and the cost become prohibitive for some, and inconvenient for most. Whilst the Indoor Tennis Initiative is designed to bring appropriate facilities nearer to the player, the problem will never be totally eradicated; the coach might do well to consider how s/he can reduce this pressure. John Atkinson, Director of Coaching for the British Amateur Gymnastics Association, made the comment that a mini-bus might be one of the best pieces of equipment for a gymnastics club, in order to overcome the major problem of 'getting the children to the venue'.

If we consider that social interaction is a most valuable part of the sport experience and that travelling together allows time for 'gossip', etc., and if we add to this the fact that children around age 12 sometimes make moves away from parental control toward their peers, it follows that coaches should consider the methods of 'getting the children to the event' as an important educational tool and an important motivational factor. It might need only a word to arrange that two players call round for a third, to ensure that child, who would not be allowed to go alone, can attend. The advantages may go far beyond the obvious safety factors, in that affiliation incentives may be satisfied.

20.4.2 THE SCHOOL

The dependence of children on their parents to play sport is unfortunate for those whose parents lack the time, means and/or inclination to support their children. One site of access to sport has always been the school. Contrary to media myth, even the much maligned Inner London Education Authority (ILEA) saw the value of competitive sport (ILEA, 1988), and the sport input to the 'new' PE is perhaps better reflected by an attempt to provide more balanced sporting opportunities for more children. One sure fact is that the extra-curricular opportunities to fulfil this aim cannot be met by the PE staff. The Report from the School Sport Forum (Sports Council, 1988) and the ILEA Report, *My Favourite Subject* (ILEA, 1988) anticipate an increased relationship between coaches and PE teachers.

The coaching world has to accept that teachers must be cautious when opening the doors to a coach who in all probability has had no specific training to work with children. Additionally, the coach may have to recognize the way in which the extracurricular activity is being offered. If the teacher provides a tennis-like activity, for example a short tennis type of game, presented in a way that attempts to overcome the problems of different physical abilities (see Thorpe *et al.*, 1986) and thereby interests many of the youngsters, there may be a great demand for extracurricular sessions. If the tennis coach who helps with the extracurricular activity immediately focuses on the technical aspects, thus excluding many less able children, the teacher will immediately see the extracurricular activity undoing a major aim of the PE programme.

This situation need not occur, but it is important that coaches become aware of the different ways in which sport is used by agencies dealing with young people. The recent School Sport Forum indicates a climate in which this form of co-operation can work, but Chapters 2 (Whose sport is it anyway?) and 3 (Why are we coaching children?) raise some of the issues the coach must face before s/he is welcomed into the school. It is the opinion of this author that the curriculum PE has to be an integrated whole and as such should be the domain of the PE teacher, but a child should not have to take the giant steps from school to club, from teacher to coach, and from an approach which recognizes relative ability to one based on performance criteria, all at the same time. By welcoming the coach into the school facilities, but ensuring the coach understands both the developing child and the aims of the PE department, the opportunities open to children can be much increased. These working relationships have been expanded elsewhere (Thorpe, 1990).

Attention has been drawn earlier to the fact that children receive a sport experience in many other situations (playschemes, voluntary organizations, etc.). In all situations the coach must try to be sensitive to the ethos of the particular group with which s/he is working.

20.5 EDUCATING THE PARENT

Tony Byrne in Chapter 4 has dealt fully with the performer–parent–coach triangle, but to understand the problems, the coach may have to look more carefully at his or her particular sport. In tennis, a major problem is that the performance is so easy to judge. We can all see when a young player hits a ball, which ought to have produced a winner, well out into the back netting. We can sit 'calmly' on the side and recognize that if s/he had played a gentle drop shot instead of trying to 'blast' the ball, the point would have been won. We can see that the decision as to which shot to play was inappropriate, and the execution of the shot was poor. Whilst the young performer should not be 'overloaded' with the theory, a little time spent with the parent explaining why we cannot expect good decisions to be made when under stress in a game would be time well spent. Further, if we can explain why comments made at that point about bad decision making might increase the anxiety, which in turn makes good decision making even less, rather than more likely, most reasonable parents will try to react in a way which reduces rather than increases the pressure.

The fact that in tennis parents can easily evaluate both the intention and the result is even more apparent with technique than with decision making. One of the most commonly heard comments at the tennis court is 'How can you play such a bad backhand? You were working on that shot with the coach last week'. By definition, if the coach was working on an aspect of the game, it was probably because s/he wished the performer to learn something. Experienced coaches and sports scientists interested in skill learning would anticipate that whilst the backhand works perfectly well in practice, even under a little pressure, it will not work every time in the game. It needs practice. The parent needs to understand this so that, if the child attempts the shot and it goes wrong, the reaction is not blame, but may even be praise for putting it into the rally at the correct time.

Tennis is somewhat unique in that, whilst many children have lessons from coaches, only a few have a coach watch their matches; most, particularly the younger ones, have parents watching the matches.

Coaches of other sports might take time to consider the areas in which the shortcomings of performers are most obvious and most embarrassing; the missed tackle in rugby, the shot 'off-goal' in hockey, soccer or basketball, the slip on the beam in gymnastics, and so on. These provide the basis of parental criticism because they are obvious but, because they are also the sources of embarrassment, the last thing the child needs is parental criticism. The coach should be aware of these sources of conflict and ensure that the parent does not magnify them.

Because many parents become involved in the sport through their children, coaches might do well to recognize that there are many areas of the sport experience where parents can help; for example, keeping an eye on play, running the games that occur in most coaching sessions and so on, freeing time for the coach to coach. Indeed tennis coaches now have the chance to encourage parents to take 'leader's courses'.

20.6 THE ADULT MODEL

Whilst accepting that children are not miniature adults, the coach has to recognize that imitation is a strong learning vehicle. In my experience, coaches rarely consider the environment in which the children operate. It might be that arranging to have good players, perhaps a little older, working hard on the next court but reacting to success and failure in ways which the coach would wish to instill will do far more than any degree of 'telling'. It might do much to overcome other undesirable models which the children may meet elsewhere.

20.7 WINNING AND LOSING

A number of authors make the point that winning is not synonymous with success and losing does not mean failure. Stuart Biddle (Chapter 10) describes how the coach can help the performer develop a sensible approach to 'attributing cause', whilst Jean Whitehead (Chapter 9) gives some insight into the variety of reasons that children give for playing sports. It is not the intention here to deal with the way the coach can exploit this knowledge (this has been done perfectly well in the respective chapters); rather it is the intention to suggest that governing bodies and sport organizations often make it difficult for the coach to operate in a way which facilitates long term development. Tennis is a particularly good example of this.

I welcomed the advent of short tennis in that it seemed to provide a medium in which children could show ability and task mastery, and gain social approval. In that a variety of new tactics and skills are possible (in direct contrast to tennis), breakthrough might seem to occur more often, games could be structured quickly, with simple scoring that satisfied the victory goal, and the pleasure of seeing lots of youngsters having fun together seemed to suggest that teamwork was a real possibility. Thus the modified game seems appropriate to meet the six main goals identified by Jean Whitehead. It was unfortunate, therefore, that a game designed for young children became structured in a way which exaggerated the 'showing ability', 'victory' or 'outcome' goals. One has to question (and indeed sensitive people in the LTA have) the wisdom of allowing club, county, regional and national short tennis competitions to dominate the sport if one accepts the rationale for drop-out suggested by Dr Whitehead. Of course, such a structure reflects the junior tennis game which is based on an 'outcome' pyramid; any child with ability is soon drawn into the selection procedure based predominantly on victories at tournaments that mirror senior play. But how does this match the statement made by Whitehead that 'When there seem to be no more new or exciting things to do, a curiosity goal that brought children into sport will naturally take them out again . . .'?

Some tennis coaches share this concern, in that they feel that many children who have their competitive tennis experience early may not stay through the teens. This becomes more critical if the children who gain success early cease to achieve later on. Other children who start late may not be able to break past the reputations of the early starters.

These concerns are real, but can be overcome if the sessions are structured to meet different needs; this may be easier if the coaches, parents and children are not led to believe that the central reason for the activity is to 'Search for a Champion'. It is unfortunate that in a game which so adequately brings tennis to a wide range of abilities, the desires of the sponsors force the 'search for a champion' onto much of the short/mini tennis literature and packaging. Of course, coaches can rapidly overcome the implication that if 'you are not going to be a champion, you can leave', but governing bodies might well consider the way they promote their mini game by recognizing that 'packaging' that embraces more of the children's likely incentives and goals will attract and, perhaps more importantly, keep them in the game.

It is often difficult for the coach of a mini basketball team, a junior sailing squad or a primary school soccer team to see the 'winning and losing' as part of a development of their performers, rather than an end in its own right. For the coach, the performer or team then move on.

The winning team or performer is often seen as the test of the coach's own competence. This need not be detrimental to the child's progression through sport, but the coach has to be able to assess his or her own involvement in the coaching process. It is often worth reminding ourselves that success at this age is often a function of early maturation, and that 'good' coaches are often merely the coaches who have access to good performers. It is also worth the coaching world considering how it can reward those coaches who can lay the foundations that allow youngsters to become committed senior performers, rather than short-lived junior champions.

20.8   CONCLUSION

Childhood is the time when most people are introduced to sport. The attitudes they develop at this stage will influence them for life. Pertinent knowledge, like that presented in this book, is becoming available, but how quickly this influences coaching behaviour will be dependent on the many organizations who provide the sport opportunities, particularly those that train the coaches. Coaches of the young, perhaps more than any others, need to reflect on the aims of their coaching.

REFERENCES

ILEA. (1988) *My Favourite Subject*, Report of the Working Party on Physical Education and School Sports, ILEA, London.
Lawn Tennis Association. (1989) *Instructions to Course Organisers*, LTA, London.
National Coaching Foundation. (1992) *After School Sport – 24 Recipes for Action. The Story of Champion Coaching*, National Coaching Foundation, Leeds.
Sports Council. (1988) *Sport and Young People – Partnership in Action*, Report from the School Sport Forum. Sports Council, London.
Sports Council. (1991) *Coaching Matters – A Review of Coaching and Coach Education in the United Kingdom*, Sports Council, London.
Thorpe, R.D. (1990) New directions in games teaching, in *New Directions in Physical Education*, (ed N. Armstrong), Human Kinetics, Champaign, IL.
Thorpe, R.D., Bunker, D.J. and Almond, L. (1986) *Rethinking Games Teaching*, Loughborough University, Loughborough.

FURTHER READING

Lee, M. National Coaching Foundation Resource Packs: Level 2 (Key Course) *Coaching Children*, and Level 3 (Advanced Course) *Children and Competitive Sport*, NCF, Leeds.
Murdoch, E. (1987) *Sport in Schools*, DES/DoE, London.

Appendices: Legal Matters

In recent years there has been a marked increase in the number of cases brought to court concerning behaviour in sports settings and the pursuit of claims for sports injury. Since the damages awarded can be quite substantial, coaches are well advised to be aware of their legal responsibilities and how they can insure against claims against them. The following two appendices are included in order to provide that information, albeit to a minimal degree, and not in order to be alarmist. Since accidents can easily happen and, in an atmosphere where pressure to win is on the increase at all levels of sport, the margins for error are smaller, coaches should be clear about their position.

Valerie Collins explains how the law applies to coaches. She makes it clear that people who are injured in sport can seek compensation if they can show that someone else has been negligent in a way which contributed to the injury. Most importantly, where children are concerned coaches have a greater responsibility since they are charged with the care of the athletes and that duty is greater according to, among other things, the age and experience of the athletes. Miss Collins explains the conditions of care and how negligence may be shown. She also describes the defences which may be used and how damages are awarded.

Finally, in Appendix B, Harry Towers follows the explanation of coaches' legal position with specific advice on the steps to take to protect yourself against claims which may arise. He outlines the practical problems of coaching from which claims may arise. These include the nature of the facilities and equipment, the organization of practices, the vexed question of when you may safely join in, and the problems caused by adventurous and ambitious children. Lest you may think it is not worth your while getting involved at all he then goes on to explain how to protect yourself against unfortunate events. As a coach you may find this the most important part of the book!

Appendix A
Coaching and the law

Valerie Collins

A.1 INTRODUCTION

All participants in sport run the risk of injury and the problem facing lawyers when a participant is injured is to decide which injuries must be accepted as 'occupational hazards' and which should be the subject of a claim for financial compensation from the person responsible. The person responsible may be either a fellow participant, the organizer of the activity, the occupier of the premises used or the coach. This section is dealing with the liability of coaches. Coaches should be aware of the tort of negligence which is particularly relevant to them. A tort is a civil 'wrong' and anyone committing a tort may be sued in the civil courts for compensation by anyone who has suffered personal injury or damage to property as a result.

A.2 NEGLIGENCE

A person who has been injured while taking part in sport may seek financial compensation at civil law if that person can show that somebody has been negligent and that it was that negligence which caused the injury.

To establish that there has been negligence, the following elements must exist:

1. A duty of care must be owed.
2. There must be a breach of that duty of care.
3. Actual damage must have resulted from breach of the duty of care.

To decide whether or not a duty of care exists in a particular situation one must apply the test established in the case of Donoghue *v*. Stevenson in 1932. This test is known as 'the neighbour test' and was formulated as follows:

You must take reasonable care to avoid acts or omissions which you can reasonably foresee would be likely to injure your neighbour. Who, then, in law is my neighbour? The answer seems to be – persons who are so closely and directly affected by my act that I ought reasonably to have them in contemplation as being so affected when I am directing my mind to the acts or omissions which are called in question.

(Donoghue v. Stevenson [1932] AC 562, p580)

Anyone involved in coaching must owe a duty of care to those being coached. However, difficulties may be experienced in deciding exactly what comprises the duty of care. The law is not and cannot be precise on this matter; it can only lay down principles to be applied in each particular situation. However, the following matters should be considered:

1.   The age of the persons being coached;
2.   Their experience/expertise;
3.   How dangerous the particular activity is;
4.   The degree of risk and the cost of prevention;
5.   'Foreseeability' of the accident occurring;
6.   Suitability of the environment/premises/equipment;
7.   Adequate instruction/supervision.

These matters will now be considered separately.

A.2.1   AGE

Where children are involved a stricter duty of care is imposed than would be the case with adults. This is particularly true where coaches and children are concerned because they will be considered by the law to be *in loco parentis* where the pupils are under 18. This means that a general duty of care is owed to the pupils to exercise reasonable care for their safety. This duty is to take the care that one would expect reasonably prudent parents to take. For example, a coach would be expected to supervise the activity properly and also to be aware of the strength and capabilities of the persons concerned. In Affuto Nartoy v. Clarke and ILEA (1984), a teacher forgot momentarily that he was playing rugby with young schoolboys who were smaller and weaker than himself and he injured a 15 year old boy when he tackled him. The teacher was found to be negligent.

A.2.2   EXPERIENCE/EXPERTISE

The experience, expertise or any other relevant characteristics of the people being coached should be taken into consideration. For example, more care should be exercised in taking a class of beginners for gymnastics than in supervising a training session for Olympic gymnasts.

A.2.3   DANGER

The more dangerous the activity the higher the degree of care that should be exercised. A further consideration would also be the potential danger of any equipment that was being used. For example, there would be a breach of the duty of care to leave a trampoline out in a sports hall which was unlocked and unattended.

A.2.4   THE RISK OF INJURY AND THE COST OF PRECAUTIONS

The court will consider the risk of a particular accident occurring and the cost of taking precautions and will usually conclude that there has been no breach of duty where the risk of the particular type of injury was small and the cost of guarding against it prohibitive.

A.2.5   FORESEEABILITY

A coach will be expected to take reasonable precautions to prevent accidents which are reasonably foreseeable. Foreseeability was discussed in the case of Clarke v. Bethnal Green Borough Council (1939). In this case a child was preparing to dive off a springboard when another child holding on to the under part of the board let go. The child on the board was thrown onto the edge of the pool and injured. The court decided that there had been no negligence as this type of accident had not occurred before and was not foreseeable. But note, once a particular type of accident has occurred it may be deemed to be foreseeable in the future.

A.2.6   SUITABILITY OF THE ENVIRONMENT, PREMISES OR EQUIPMENT

It is important before commencing any activity that the coach should ensure that the environment, premises or equipment are suitable for the particular activity. In Ralph v. London County Council (1947), Ralph was a pupil at one of the defendant's schools. He was taking part in a game of 'touch' supervised by a teacher in the assembly hall, one side of which consisted of a glass partition. During the game, which involved a lot of running about, Ralph put his hand through one of the glass partitions and was injured. The court decided that the teacher was negligent because he should have foreseen that such an accident might occur.

If faulty equipment is responsible for an accident the coach may be liable if the fault could have been found easily. The duty here includes regular safety checks of any equipment used. Complex or technical equipment should be regularly checked and serviced by the manufacturer to fulfil this duty. The checking of most equipment used for sport can be done easily although equipment such as trampolines would require regular servicing. Should a fault have occurred which could not be discovered by a simple safety check then the manufacturers may be liable to anyone injured while using that equipment, to whom they will owe a duty of care (see Donoghue v. Stevenson).

A.2.7 ADEQUATE INSTRUCTION/SUPERVISION

To fulfil the duty of care a coach must be both qualified to teach the particular activity and to coach to the standard he is coaching. Coaches should also ensure that the group is small enough to be properly supervised.

In any case that comes before the courts it will be up to the courts to decide whether or not there has been a breach of duty in each particular situation. The court will look at cases decided previously before reaching a decision.

However, the court could find that there has been no negligence because the activity had been conducted as safely as could reasonably be expected. In Jones v. London County Council (1932) Jones was doing a course of physical exercises which included the playing of certain games. An experienced instructor had been appointed to supervise the games. During one of these games Jones fell and was injured. The court decided there was no evidence of negligence. An experienced instructor had been in charge and there was no evidence the particular game was dangerous. The court said it would be unreasonable to consider an activity dangerous just because an accident might happen at some time.

If the court decides that there has been negligence the question then arises concerning who actually pays the damages. The person responsible will be liable to pay but through the operation of the principle of vicarious liability, that person's employer can be sued and be liable to pay any damages awarded. This is because an employer is more likely to be able to pay the full amount than the employee; they will also usually have to be insured against the public liability of their employees. Difficulties may arise concerning the position of coaches who may be either employees or independent contractors; in other words, self-employed. Self-employed coaches will be liable personally.

An employer will only be liable where the employee is negligent during the course of his employment, in other words, he must be doing what he was employed to do. Employers are also under a duty to ensure that a person employed to do a particular job is competent to do that job.

A.3   DEFENCES

One of the following defences may be pleaded to try and avoid liability:

1.   A claim that the particular accident was unforeseeable.

2.   Volenti. This defence, which is given the Latin tag *volenti non fit injuria* meaning 'no harm is done to he who consents', is available where the person injured has freely consented to the particular risk resulting in the injury. Volenti cannot be claimed if the injury is caused negligently or deliberately or is not a risk associated with the particular activity concerned, for example, injuries caused by faulty equipment.

To establish the defence of volenti it would have to be established that the 'victim' 'consented' to the act complained of with full knowledge of the risks involved and that he consented voluntarily. If a participant in sport is subjected to risk in the course of his employment or education, for example because participation in sport is compulsory, then he cannot be said to have consented freely. In Hall *v.* Brooklands Auto Racing Club (1933) a spectator at a motor race was injured when two cars collided in the race. The court decided that the owners of the race track were not liable in respect of the spectator's injuries. In such cases there is no liability for dangers inherent in a particular sport which could have been foreseen by a spectator who therefore accepted the risk of them occurring.

3.   Another defence, or partial defence, is that of contributory negligence. Should a participant suffer injury partly due to his fault and only partly due to the conduct of another then the amount of damages recoverable for his injuries will be reduced by an amount adjudged by the court to cover the participant's share of responsibility for the injuries. Anyone pleading this defence must prove that the participant was negligent and that this negligence contributed to the injuries suffered.

There are three qualifications relating to this defence. First, that the person concerned should take into account the possibility of others being careless in relation to his own actions. Second, that although a child may be negligent the age of that child will be taken into consideration and, in fact, this defence is rarely pleaded against children successfully. The third qualification is that the participant will not be considered to have been negligent where he has acted reasonably in the face of sudden danger even though his action contributed to his harm. When deciding how much responsibility should be attributed to each party the judge is under a duty to be fair and just according to the circumstances but he has no set rules to follow. Contributory negligence has been successfully pleaded in cases concerning accidents involving motor cyclists who have not been wearing crash helmets.

4.   Liability may also be avoided where another event occurs which breaks the chain of events started by the defendant's conduct. In such a case the defendant is only responsible for the loss occurring prior to the intervention, and not for the whole loss. A classic example of this type of situation is where a person is taken to hospital with a minor injury and due to an error at the hospital ends up having major surgery!

A.4   DAMAGES

A participant bringing an action for negligence will be claiming damages as compensation for injuries suffered. Although the aim of an award of damages is compensation some injuries that have been suffered may be felt by the court to be too 'remote' from the conduct complained of and that it would be unfair to make the defendant liable for all the injuries resulting from his conduct. There will always be total responsibility for all injuries arising from intentional conduct. Where unintentional injuries have been caused then the person responsible will only be liable for the injuries that were reasonably foreseeable as a result of his action (or inaction).

Once it has been established that the kind of injury that occurred was foreseeable, the person responsible will be liable for that injury even though it was more extensive than he could have anticipated. Anyone who is negligent must 'take his victim as he finds him' and will be liable if an injury is more serious than anticipated due to a weakness of the participant; for example, a person who suffers a fractured skull from a blow that would normally only cause a slight head wound because he has an unusually fragile skull.

Any attempt to avoid liability is now subject to the Unfair Contract Terms Act 1977 (something of a misnomer as it does not apply only to contractual situations). This Act provides that liability can no longer be excluded or restricted for negligence arising in a 'business' context resulting in death or personal injury.

Damages may be claimed for pain and suffering, the cost of medical treatment, loss of earnings, loss of potential earning capacity and loss of enjoyment of life as these are all deemed to be foreseeable losses by the court.

A.5 COMMUNITY LAW DIRECTIVE

In November 1990 a proposed European Directive was put forward that the supplier of a service should be liable for damage to health and physical integrity or the physical integrity of movable or immovable property, caused by a fault committed by him in the performance of the service. Such a Directive was felt to be necessary to take account of legal developments and case law in Member States which could create an atmosphere of uncertainty to consumers and to the forthcoming single market in services.

Discussions concerning this Directive have resulted in a lot of opposition as many Member States resent this interference with existing laws relating to civil liability. There has also been a lot of opposition to the inclusion of all services which means the Directive will extend to recreational activities.

The principal aim of the Service Liability Directive (COM (90) 482) is to reverse the burden of proof so that the onus is on the supplier to prove he was **not** negligent when a consumer suffers because of poor or defective service.

This proposed Directive was still the subject of debate at the time of writing but readers should be aware that the burden of proof concerning negligence may be reversed.

A.6 CONCLUSION

Anyone who undertakes the coaching or supervision of another person or persons puts themselves in a duty of care situation. This situation arises whether or not the person concerned is paid for their work. Such people should remember the following points:

1. Always take reasonable care.
2. Follow any codes of practice issued by and therefore accepted by the governing body of the sport concerned.
3. In any legal action the above recommendations will not guarantee success as the outcome will depend on what the judge considers to be reasonable in the circumstances.

FURTHER READING

Bischert, R., Taylor, J.R. and Fitzsimmons, D. (1992) *A Practical Approach to and Administration of Leisure and Recreation Services*, 4th edn, Croner, London.
Collins, V. (1993) *Recreation and the Law*, E. & F.N. Spon, London (2nd edn).
Llewelyn, R.L., Collins, V., Rustage, A.F. and Church, B. (1991) *Sport in Higher Education: Code of Practice; Physical Education, Recreation and Sport*, Polytechnic of Wales, Pontypridd.

Appendix B
Ensure you are insured

Harry Towers

B.1 INTRODUCTION

If one of your charges is injured while you are coaching or giving instruction you must assume that 'someone's going to pay'. Sensible and responsible people will recognize that in all areas of competitive sport accidents do occur and can result in injury. This appendix will seek to demonstrate where, in general terms, risks to the coach lie, how they might be minimized, and, most importantly, how the coaches might protect themselves against those risks which cannot be eliminated.

B.2 THE PROBLEMS

Simply by putting yourself forward as a coach, instructor or teacher in a sport or leisure environment you inevitably place yourself in a position of risk. Like it or not, you assume the following responsibilities

1. You owe a duty of care to those you are coaching.
2. You must identify foreseeable risks and take positive action to prevent them.
3. If you fail, you will place yourself in breach of duty and will be liable in negligence and for any injury or damage sustained.

All of this is perfectly reasonable, but it is aggravated by the fact that young athletes are juveniles and many are, in the eyes of the law, minors. Consequently you are standing in a position of parent or guardian, i.e. *in loco parentis*. For practical purposes you are absolutely responsible for those children under your control because, in the majority of cases, the law will not ascribe to them any responsibility for their own stupidity.

B.2.1   SOURCES OF RISK

After you have defined your position you need to recognize the sort of situations and incidents that may threaten you and, indeed, make you vulnerable to allegations of negligence, litigation and the award of damages against you. Let us consider some of the common sources of threat of which you should be aware.

Environment

Whether your activities are indoor or outdoor, land-based, water-based or, indeed, airborne, the following considerations are constant and relevant to all coaches and teachers. The environment in which you conduct your activities must be a safe and suitable place bearing in mind the nature of the activity. For example, you must take into account the amount of glass in the activity area, protruding radiators, the suitability of the floor space and surface, available lighting, the weather conditions, and so on. Standing in the place of the parent you must make a value judgement and satisfy yourself that it is reasonable and safe to proceed. If your judgement is in error and an accident occurs you will be in severe difficulty.

Equipment

Any equipment, from a table tennis bat to a javelin, from a judo mat to a canoe, must be in good repair and suitable for the practice of your activity. It is your responsibility to ensure that this is the case prior to using it.

Matching participants

Overcrowding, which in itself can lead to accidents, may well prove to be indefensible. Matching incompatible children has been, and will continue to be, frowned on by the courts. Children may be considered incompatible on grounds of differences in ability, or of disproportionate height and weight despite being of the same ability, age and experience.

Joining in the activity with young athletes

Involving yourself in competitive situations with children is fraught with danger. There is a catalogue of case law in which a coach has been successfully prosecuted in negligence for injuries sustained by children arising directly out of a coach's participation in an activity. Obviously the greatest risk occurs in contact sports, such as rugby football, but it may also be dangerous to join in other types of sport.

Facilities

Your responsibility is not restricted to the welfare of the children you coach; you are also responsible for the facilities you use. Wherever you conduct your sport you are likely to be using premises owned by someone else. Whether you have a lease, a verbal agreement or just a tacit understanding, you will, almost without exception, be obliged to hand back those premises or facilities in the condition in which you found them at the outset. It is likely to be your responsibility to repair any damage which occurs whilst you are in occupation. This may amount to a broken light fitting in a gymnasium, a broken hand basin in a changing room, or a broken window following a five-a-side session. These and similar problems are likely to find their way to your door sooner or later.

Ambitious athletes

Young athletes often wish to excel. Perhaps more importantly, and more seriously, their parents also wish to see them excel. From time to time, therefore, it will be necessary to be absolutely certain that your athletes are physically capable of undertaking the rigorous activities you propose for them. You should be particularly wary in relation to children returning to activity following a period of sickness or injury. Remember, you are *in loco parentis* and there is a grave danger that over-ambitious parents will react violently against you if they believe that you have in any way damaged their children or, more significantly, their children's potential!

B.3   THE SOLUTIONS

If you are still interested in coaching after reading about these responsibilities this section will show how you can minimize the risks involved and, where they cannot be removed, transfer a significant proportion of the responsibility to someone else.

B.3.1   AFFILIATION

The first and most important step is to recognize the risks involved in coaching; the second is to set about reducing them. In this regard the governing body of your sport or activity will, almost without exception, prove to be a valuable ally. It is most important that all coaches are affiliated to their appropriate governing bodies and, wherever possible, carry the endorsement of the governing body as an accredited coach. Contrary to the popular view, in matters like this the 'Lone Ranger' is seldom the victor.

Many governing bodies license or register their coaches and registration automatically affords a degree of protection. It is also probable that the governing body will issue a code of conduct, the observance of which will, to a very large degree, eliminate a great many potential claims against the coach.

B.3.2 INSURANCE POLICIES

Most governing bodies carry public liability insurance on their own behalf which can be extended to include both coaches and participants who are affiliated. All too frequently coaches are unaware of the nature and extent of the insurance programme provided by the governing body and it is vital that, in the absence of the fullest information, they take the initiative and establish their own position quite clearly. It is a good idea, if you have not already done so, to contact your own national governing body (NGB) to establish the protection that is available to you and what your responsibilities are.

Strengths and weaknesses

Governing body insurances, whilst always desirable, may not always be enough; of necessity they tend to reflect what is affordable rather than what is adequate. With some justification NGBs frequently assume that coaches have made their own arrangements.

Currently there are clearly moves to take sport out of the public sector and there is evidence that a substantial proportion of sport and leisure facilities, such as sports centres and swimming pools, are coming increasingly under private control. The effect of these developments on coaches is difficult to forecast but certainly it will become increasingly dangerous to rely on the protection of the operator of the facility you intend to use.

Once you have identified the risks involved, reduced them as much as possible by your own careful actions, and assessed the degree of protection you can be afforded by others, you are left with a final opportunity to protect yourself. The risk remains with you but it can be transferred to someone else simply by buying an insurance policy. For the payment of a premium an insurance company will take over your risks.

Personal insurance policies

Since there are well over 100 insurance companies and over 6000 registered insurance brokers in the United Kingdom, all aggressively seeking to sell insurance policies to all and sundry, you could be forgiven for resisting advice to buy further protection. Nevertheless, it is advice that you should seriously consider in order to protect yourself against potential claimants. If you wish to buy a policy make certain that you use only a registered insurance broker for advice. In order to be registered he, in turn, must carry his own form of insurance that protects him if he fails to do his job adequately.

So, what policy should you look for? Quite simply a policy known as a Public Liability or Third Party Policy that will provide you with insurance protection for claims made against you for injury or damage to others arising from your activities as a coach. Such policies are generally sold to provide cover in multiples of £250 000. In current terms, you should purchase one with a limit of not less than £1 000 000 and, if you can afford it, you should increase this amount to £2 000 000.

A word of warning

The pursuit of excellence continues to foster the development of coaching techniques in every sport. Consequently many coaches seek to sell their expertise and many more athletes are prepared to pay for it. Almost all Public Liability Policies provide cover for the provision of advice and tuition; equally, almost all then go on to exclude such cover where the coach charges any sort of fee. Unfortunately, the word 'fee' is not defined and there is no way of knowing whether it extends to include expenses or benefit in kind, such as free use of club facilities.

Historically the insurance industry has always regarded professionals as those members of the classical professions, e.g. lawyers, accountants, doctors, architects, etc., who sell their expertise for a fee. Only a limited number of insurers are prepared to offer cover for professionals, whilst the whole insurance industry is happy to provide cover for sports clubs. Unfortunately, there is a lack of recognition of currently changing conditions within sport and, regrettably, in too many areas coaches compound the problem themselves.

Many coaches are reluctant to admit that they enjoy fees of any kind, but there is no doubt that aggrieved parents in hot pursuit of a negligent coach will quickly bring to the attention of their solicitor the fact that they were actually paying for the coach's expertise. When this information reaches the insurer the insurance policy may prove to be a worthless piece of paper. There may be a reluctance to admit or acknowledge receipt of payment, but if that refusal is likely to invalidate your insurance protection it must be regarded as naive at best and, at worst, crass stupidity! The absence of insurance protection will not inhibit the court in awarding damages against negligent coaches, and if the family home must be sold to satisfy a judgement the court is unlikely to show any sympathy.

B.3.3 CHECKLIST OF THINGS TO DO

1. Affiliate to the governing body.
2. Observe the recommended code of conduct.
3. If no code exists, ensure that:
   (a) the environment is suitable;
   (b) the equipment is safe;
   (c) participants are suitably matched;
   (d) you limit your participation to supervision;
   (e) you always err on the side of caution.
4. Participate in the NGB insurance scheme.
5. Check the adequacy of the scheme.
6. Consult a registered insurance broker if you are in doubt.
7. If still in doubt, insure yourself.

B.4 CONCLUSION

If you are providing advice and tuition you put yourself at risk; it is highly unlikely that anyone will remove that risk for you. At the same time it is highly probable that accidents will happen and possible that allegations will be made to the effect that you were responsible. It is at that point that you should be in a position to hand over the whole problem to an insurance company which will, under the terms of the policy, defend you. Don't take a chance!

Glossary

Abduction	Movement of a limb away from the midline of the body.
Ability	A goal to show high ability and avoid showing low ability.
Achievement goal	A child's view of what success is.
Adrenal gland	A hormone producing gland situated on top of the kidney.
Aetiology	Causes of a condition.
Ammenoerhoeic	Indicates failure to menstruate.
Anabolic	Growth promoting.
Anaerobic threshold	Originally hypothesized to represent the onset of anaerobic metabolism in the muscle due to insufficient oxygen supply. Identified during incremental exercise as the point at which blood lactate levels begin to increase rapidly.
Approval goals	Goals which depend on satisfying other people.
Arterio–venous oxygen difference	The difference in oxygen content between the blood entering and leaving the pulmonary capillaries.
Attributions	Reasons or causes stated for outcomes, such as ability and effort. Attributions are thought to be related to expectations about future performance, and emotional feelings.
Bone density	A measure of the strength of bone.
Breakthrough	A goal to experience novelty and progres
Capitellum	That part of the lower humerus wh articulates with the radius.

Cardiac output	The volume of blood ejected into the main artery per minute.
Cardiopulmonary fitness	The ability of the circulatory and pulmonary systems to supply fuel and to eliminate waste products during physical activity.
Carpal	Bone of the wrist.
Chondrocytes	Cells that produce cartilage.
Clavicle	Collar bone.
Clitoral hypertrophy	Enlargement of the clitoris.
Diffusion	In the lungs, the process by which the exchange of respiratory gases between the lungs and the blood occurs.
Ego goal	When success is defined as demonstrating superior ability in comparison to others.
Endochondral ossification	Process of converting cartilage into bone.
Epiphyseal growth plates	Area where linear bone growth occurs.
Epiphysis	Area of bone growth.
Femur	The long bone of the thigh.
Fibula	The smaller of the two bones in the lower leg; it is found on the outside of the tibia.
Flexibility	The range of motion about a joint.
Glucocorticoids	Hormones produced by the adrenal gland.
Glycogen depletion	A decrease in the stores of glycogen in the muscle and liver.
Heart rate	The number of ventricular contractions per minute.
Hormones	Chemical produced by endocrine glands and carried in the blood. They exert a control on physiological processes in the body.
Hypertrophy	Becoming larger.
Lactate steady state	The highest level of blood lactate which can be sustained without a progressive increase during an extended bout of exercise.
Lactate threshold	Often used in preference to anaerobic threshold to describe the point at which blood lactate begins to increase rapidly during incremental exercise.
Lamina	The posterior part of a vertebra.
Learned helplessness	Apathetic response resulting from perceived lack of control over failure and recovery from failure. Thought to be related

	to the type of attributions given for failure.
Lysed blood	Blood which has been chemically treated to break open the red blood cells (cell lysis) thus releasing intracellular lactate.
Maturation	Increase in the ability to function, usually associated with growth.
Maximal oxygen uptake	The highest rate of oxygen consumed by the body in a given period of time during exercise involving a significant portion of the muscle mass.
Menarche	The age of the onset of menstruation.
Meniscus	The cartilaginous body in the knee that distributes the weight in the joint. It can be torn and become the subject of a 'cartilage operation'.
Metatarsals	The long bones in the foot that articulate with the toes.
Mineralocorticoids	Hormone produced by the adrenal glands.
Minute volume	The volume of air inspired per minute.
Muscle biopsy	The removal of a portion of muscle for examination.
Muscular endurance	The ability of a muscle group to perform repeated contractions against a light load for an extended period of time.
Muscular strength	The ability of a muscle group to exert force against a resistance in one maximal effort.
Navicular	A small bone in the foot.
Osteoporosis	Thinning of bone associated with loss of calcium and resulting in weakness.
Outcome goals	Goals which relate to the result of an event.
Peak oxygen uptake	The highest rate of oxygen consumed during an exercise test to exhaustion.
Plasma	The fluid portion of the blood. When blood is centrifuged before coagulation occurs the red blood cells are separated from the plasma.
Process goals	Goals which relate to the process of performing.
Puberty	Onset of sexual maturation associated with physical and psychological changes.
Radius	The outer of the two bones in the forearm.
Reduce	To put back into place.
Respiratory frequency	The number of breaths per minute.

Serum	The yellow coloured fluid which separates from the clot when blood is left to coagulate.
Skeletal maturation	Level of maturation of the skeleton. May be considered complete when ossification ceases.
Social approval	A goal to gain the approval of others.
Spondylolisthesis	A slip of one vertebral body on another.
Spondylosis	Osteoarthrosis of the spine.
Stroke volume	The volume of blood ejected by each ventricular contraction.
Task goal	When success is defined as task mastery or self-improvement.
Task mastery	A goal to master skills and learn more.
Teamwork	A goal to succeed by working with others, rather than independently.
Tibia	Major bone of the lower leg; the shin bone.
Tidal volume	The volume of air inspired per breath.
Ulna	The inner of the two bones in the forearm.
Ventilatory threshold	The point at which ventilation increases disproportionately to the increase in exercise intensity. Originally hypothesized to coincide with the anaerobic threshold.
Vertebral bodies	Major part of the vertebra which is responsible for weight bearing.
Victory	A goal to defeat others in direct competition.
Whole blood assay	Most modern semi-automatic and automatic lactate analysers measure lactate levels in blood as soon as it has been sampled and without any further treatment.

Index

Entries in **bold** type represent figures, those in *italics* represent tables.

Sheffield Hallam University
Learning and IT Services
Collegiate Learning Centre
Collegiate Crescent Campus
Sheffield   S10 2BP

102 075 283 1

Sheffield Hallam University
Learning and Information Services
Withdrawn From Stock

Withdrawn From Stock

Practical Child Law
for Social Workers

Practical Child Law
for Social Workers

A Guide to English Law and Policy

CLARE SEYMOUR
RICHARD SEYMOUR

Los Angeles | London | New Delhi
Singapore | Washington DC

Learning Matters
An imprint of SAGE Publications Ltd
1 Oliver's Yard
55 City Road
London EC1Y 1SP

SAGE Publications Inc.
2455 Teller Road
Thousand Oaks, California 91320

SAGE Publications India Pvt Ltd
B 1/I 1 Mohan Cooperative Industrial Area
Mathura Road
New Delhi 110 044

SAGE Publications Asia-Pacific Pte Ltd
3 Church Street
#10-04 Samsung Hub
Singapore 049483

Editor: Luke Block
Development editor: Lauren Simpson
Production controller: Chris Marke
Project management: Swales and Willis Ltd,
Exeter, Devon
Marketing manager: Tamara Navaratnam
Cover design: Wendy Scott
Typeset by: Swales and Willis Ltd, Exeter, Devon
Printed by: MPG Printgroup, UK

MIX
Paper from
responsible sources
FSC
www.fsc.org   FSC® C018575

© Clare Seymour and Richard Seymour 2013

First published 2013

Apart from any fair dealing for the purposes of
research or private study, or criticism or review, as
permitted under the Copyright, Design and Patents
Act, 1988, this publication may be reproduced, stored
or transmitted in any form, or by any means, only with
the prior permission in writing of the publishers, or in
the case of reprographic reproduction, in accordance
with the terms of licences issued by the Copyright
Licensing Agency. Enquiries concerning reproduction
outside these terms should be sent to the publishers.

Library of Congress Control Number: 2012955070

British Library Cataloguing in Publication Data

A catalogue record for this book is available from the
British Library

ISBN 978 1 44626 652 6
ISBN 978 1 44626 653 3 (pbk)

SHEFFIELD HALLAM UNIVERSITY
WL
344.0327
SE
COLLEGIATE LEARNING CENTRE

Contents

Table of cases

Table of international treaties

Table of statutes

Table of statutory instruments

About the authors

Clare Seymour is a registered social worker and qualified teacher at post-16 level. She has 16 years' experience of local authority children and families' social work and has taught social work degree students at undergraduate and master's level. She is currently working as a trainer and practice educator. She co-authored *Courtroom and Report Writing Skills for Social Workers*, second edition, published in 2011 by Learning Matters, and contributed to *Newly Qualified Social Workers: A Handbook for Practice*, published in 2009, also by Learning Matters.

Richard Seymour is a senior circuit judge assigned to the Queen's Bench Division of the High Court of Justice. He was in practice as a barrister for almost 30 years and has been a President of Mental Health Review Tribunals. He co-authored *Courtroom and Report Writing Skills for Social Workers*, second edition, published in 2011 by Learning Matters.

Acknowledgements

We express our grateful thanks to Dave Barron, Olive Irwin, Sue Kettlewell, Maire Maisch, Alison Maylor, Corné Van Staden and all the social workers we have met through our court skills training courses, for sharing their knowledge and experience of the practical application of law and policy in working with children and families.

Introduction

The application of social work law and policy is never far from media headlines and government policy initiatives. This is a time of significant, and primarily politically driven, change in social work, with the implementation of the Task Force and Munro report recommendations, the establishment of the College of Social Work and the introduction of probationary practice following qualification as a social worker. Severe economic pressures also mean that, like other professionals, social workers must be accountable for the nature and quality of their work, which requires them to communicate effectively with the media and general public. At the same time, an often unanticipated consequence of using the law to solve social problems is that the very process of creating new law or policy can result in the creation of new problems (Partington, 2010). It is salutary to note, for example, that around one quarter of parents who were living together when their children became subject to public law care applications were found to have separated during the course of those proceedings, in many cases as a direct consequence of them. In addition, 12 per cent of children had their paternity called into question during the course of the case (Masson et al., 2008).

This book takes a critically analytic approach to child care law and policy in social work practice. Our rationale is based on the premise that:

Law learning is more effective when closely aligned to the tasks, dilemmas and situations that social workers encounter in practice. It should have as its purpose a moral/ethical and rights-based framework to enable practitioners to bring critical enquiry and reflection to their roles and tasks.

(SCIE, 2005, summary)

Commentators and researchers (Preston-Shoot, 2000; Dickens, 2006; Beckett et al., 2007) suggest that social workers often find the law intimidating, confrontational and more likely to be obstructive than empowering, which matches our own experience. This can be compounded by the level of technical detail contained within some social work law texts which poses barriers in terms of the development of the confidence and assertiveness necessary to make and defend sound professional judgements involving legal powers and duties. Many of these texts are written by lawyers who are not accustomed to working with what Lord Laming (2003) described as the 'respectful uncertainty' of social work. Munro, for example (2011, p20), acknowledges that 'even defining what counts as unacceptable parenting and what is abusive or neglectful is problematic'. These are the kinds of dilemmas that you face every day in practice and for which answers are not found in a book. Our aim, therefore, is to support you in establishing effective links between social work with children and families, policy and the law, so that you have tools at your disposal with which to undertake robust assessment, analysis, debate and, if necessary, legitimate challenge.

Social work's research profile has undergone considerable development in recent years, which means that recommendations and decisions made within statutory frameworks must incorporate analysis of 'what works', and take account of the range of opinions and options that might be relevant to the case in question. Research that has been objectively assessed and fairly presented potentially is a strong element of the rationale that should underpin all social work decisions and recommendations made within a legal and policy context. Consequently, relevant research is an integral part of the text.

A significant finding of recent formal investigations into social work practice is that managerial demands and inspection processes are undermining, and occasionally obscuring altogether, the ability of social workers to exercise professional judgements whilst remaining focused on the best interests of service users. Munro (2011, p8) notes that 'compliance with regulations and rules often drives professional practice more than sound judgement drawn from the professional relationship', and further reports that some social workers consider that 'their professional judgement is not seen as a significant aspect of the social work task' (ibid., p29). Indeed, we have read social work reports that specifically exclude the exercise of professional judgement, even in apparently extreme situations, on the premise that it might be regarded as discriminatory or unfair. We therefore support Munro's call for a learning culture to replace prescription and compliance, with a distinction drawn between rules which are essential for effective working, and guidance or advice which should inform, but not be a substitute for, professional judgement (Munro, 2011). Alongside Munro's recommendations, the Family Justice Review (MoJ, 2011b) has affirmed social work's key role in family justice and highlighted the need for more confident, authoritative and reliable professional decision-making by social workers. However, this is not straightforward: in the course of researching this book we have been astonished by the quantity (and often the quality and inconsistency) of government guidance, advice and policy statements which has fallen on the weary shoulders of social workers and their managers within the past few years.

A further important factor in the context of providing statutory social care services to children and families is the increasing importance of partner agencies, where organisational and cultural differences influence how law and policy is interpreted and applied. Of particular significance is that social work with children and families has become closely allied with education in terms of policy development, inspection and regulation. Therefore, we aim to provide you with a framework within which to establish a personal culture of continuing professional development, so that you can communicate effectively with lawyers, educators and other professionals where there are areas of disagreement, misunderstanding, cultural difference or lack of knowledge or experience.

ACTIVITY O.1

Without thinking too deeply, rank the following scenarios according to their apparent seriousness in the context of child welfare (1 being least serious, and 7 the most serious). Do you think that any of them would reach the legal threshold of 'significant harm'?

1. Your neighbour's 14-year-old son walks to school alone along a busy road.

2. You observe a child of about 11 sitting alone in a parked car.

ACTIVITY O.1 (CONT.)

3. A boy in your son's class has missed more than 70 per cent of his schooling over the past term.

4. A work colleague tells you that her new partner has offered to look after her 5-year-old daughter while she attends a Christmas party.

5. An 8-year-old boy returns home from a weekend with his father and reports that he stayed out all night, and had some whisky and 'weed'.

6. A group of children are playing a skipping game in the stairwell of a block of flats.

7. Your daughter's 8-year-old friend asks to keep the light on when she stays overnight.

Now reconsider the scenarios with the additional information below. Would you change the ranking? Does any of your legal knowledge or experience help you? Do you think a non-social work professional would reach the same conclusions? If not, why?

1. Your neighbour's son has learning disabilities and a severe hearing impairment.

2. The outside temperature is 28°C.

3. He is undergoing treatment for leukaemia.

4. The partner has convictions for offences against children.

5. The father took him on a camping trip and bought him some whisky-flavoured fudge. The 'weed' was a blackberry they picked from the hedgerow.

6. The children are unsupervised, all under 7 and the stairwell is covered with broken glass and drug-taking paraphernalia.

7. She is regularly locked in a cupboard as a punishment at home.

This exercise shows that whatever the law may say about welfare, risk, harm or grounds for statutory intervention, it is no substitute for the complex combination of knowledge, skills, values and professional judgement that you must exercise in order to complete a competent assessment and decide what course of action to suggest. In order to keep the interests of the child central to your practice, you must be confident in your knowledge and understanding of legal and ethical frameworks, and you must be able to undertake the enquiry, assessment and problem-solving necessary to make judgements that are legally sound, based on clear evidence and supported by a rationale which stands up to scrutiny and challenge. However, we also acknowledge the fact, which lawyers and policy-makers sometimes fail to appreciate, that working with people often does not hold the potential for clear-cut decisions as in, say, a legal dispute about the quality of a second-hand car, and that finely balanced judgements, which usually can only be evaluated with the benefit of hindsight, frequently have to be made. If you have an understanding of decisions in previous similar cases, and an ability objectively to assess relevant research and to weigh up competing needs and rights within the relevant legal framework, it is more likely that the resultant decisions will be of good quality, having been fully argued and tested, if necessary in a multi-professional arena.

As a result of the process by which laws are enacted in this country, it is not uncommon for legal frameworks to appear illogical and outdated. A particular example at the time of writing is adult community care law, which incorporates a large number of statutes covering a wide range of issues, some of which date back more than 60 years to a time when society, and the language used, was very different from how it is today. Even the Children Act 1989, still regarded as representing a ground-breaking shift in the approach to family and child welfare, is now nearly 25 years old. Government policy and guidance, too, reflects the political and economic priorities of the time it is issued and frequently provides considerable scope for practical interpretation. We adopt a robust and critical approach to the law's contradictions, inconsistencies, confusions and dilemmas, and encourage you to regard yourself as an equal player in the legal arena. This is not to say that you do not need the advice of lawyers – we are hardly likely to suggest this in view of our own professional backgrounds – but, rather, that having confidence in the exercise of your legal powers and duties will support you in upholding the confidence of others in the social work profession and, most importantly, will help you to take advantage of the opportunities the law presents to shape professional decision-making in the interests of your service users.

Our analysis of current law and policy relating to social work with children and families is structured around a number of key themes, which link to social work's value base, and include constructive exploration of the challenges that they pose to social workers in practice. Relevant legal decisions are examined in the context of the reasoning that appears to support them since, although most of the cases with which you work will not reach court, family court judgements often identify practice dilemmas faced in the course of reaching a decision:

> *I am very conscious of the difficulties confronting social workers and others in obtaining hard evidence, which will stand up when challenged in court, of the maltreatment meted out to children behind closed doors. The task of social workers is usually anxious and often thankless. They are criticised for not having taken action in response to warning signs which are obvious enough when seen in the clear light of hindsight, or they are criticised for making applications based on serious allegations which, in the event, are not established in court.*
>
> (Extract from judgement in *Re H (minors) (sexual abuse: standard of proof)* [1996] AC 563)

These themes support the Health and Care Professions Council's standards of proficiency for social workers (SoPS) and the Professional Capabilities Framework (PCF) developed by the Social Work Reform Board (SWRB) to shape both initial social work education and continuing professional development, starting with the Assessed and Supported Year in Employment (ASYE). The themes are therefore allied with social work tasks and several also relate to established legal principles. They include:

- rights;
- responsibilities;
- relationships;
- participation;
- support;

- protection;

- substitute care;

- permanence;

- independence;

- cooperation.

We incorporate learning objectives, activities, case studies, practitioner reflections and research summaries, all of which are intended to support critical reflection and your continuing professional development. We have intentionally confined the amount of substantive law we include to that which provides a sufficient basis for analysis and discussion and a valid context for research findings. If more legal detail is required, it is readily available from the sources identified.

A note about terminology

The simplest model for understanding our legislative system is that of a pyramid, with statutes or primary legislation, such as the CA 1989, at the top, complemented by subordinate legislation and increasingly complex and numerous publications containing statutory guidance. At the base of the pyramid is advice issued by government to explain what the law requires and suggest how it may be complied with in practice. There is a developing tendency for social care legislation to incorporate a number of strands concerned with different fields of practice, which means that each strand is explained separately, often at considerable length, to the people likely to be affected by it.

Acts of Parliament are binding upon all those to whom they apply. They may also contain provision for the making of **statutory instruments** which is subordinate legislation authorised prospectively by Parliament by including a power for someone, usually a minister, to make them. Statutory instruments generally contain more detail than the statute under which they are made, such as requirements in relation to timescales and other practical matters. Statutory instruments are numbered, such as SI 2000 No. 415, which is statutory instrument 415 of the year 2000. Each has a name, followed by **order**, **regulations** or **rules**. The choice of order, regulations or rules is not important to those who have to comply with them. In the event of a dispute, it is for the courts to interpret Acts of Parliament or statutory instruments.

An Act of Parliament may also provide for **guidance** to be issued, in which case the Act will prescribe its significance. In the field of social services guidance is important because the Local Authority Social Services Act 1970 s7(1) provides that:

> Local authorities shall, in the exercise of their social services functions, including the exercise of any discretion conferred by any relevant enactment, act under the general guidance of the Secretary of State.

This means that, subject to complying with the duties expressly imposed by Acts of Parliament and statutory instruments, local authorities must have regard to the guidance given by the Secretary of State. An example of this type of guidance is the *Framework for the Assessment of Children in Need and Their Families* (DoH, 2000). Large quantities of guidance have been issued in recent years, much of it written in rather general terms by civil servants who do not necessarily have a full understanding of the subject matter. Indeed in the course of researching this book we have read a great deal of guidance which many social workers would regard as stating the obvious. Sometimes guidance permits a degree of discretion as to how it is applied in local circumstances, in which case the local authority would have to be able to justify any departure from it.

Apart from statutory guidance, advice is sometimes given, in the form of circulars, by government departments in relation to Acts of Parliament or statutory instruments. At its simplest this type of guidance is a statement of opinion as to what the Act or statutory instrument means and is intended to assist those who must comply with it. However, it is of no legal significance since those concerned must comply with the law as set out in Acts or statutory instruments, rather than the government's opinion of what it means, and the need for social workers to exercise professional judgement in relation to such guidance is acknowledged (HMG, 2010, p6).

A local authority may produce guidance on the policies, practices or procedures to be applied within its own organisation. This applies only to its own employees or, possibly, to those seeking its services, and is unlikely to be of much legal significance.

Decisions of courts

An important element of English law is precedent, which means decisions in other cases. Any case that results in a court hearing will generate a **judgement**. Decisions on new points of law need to be disseminated and so professional law reporters decide whether judgements are worth writing up for publication. Many judgements, particularly in family cases, are shaped by the particular facts of the case and do not seek to lay down any legal principles. Some judgements do set out legal principles and their legal significance depends on the level of the court that decided them. We have not referred to any judgement of a court lower than the High Court since they do not usually establish legal principles and are rarely reported. A statement of legal principles by a High Court judge may be adopted by other High Court judges, but they are not bound by them. County court judges and magistrates are bound to follow statements of legal principles made by a High Court judge. Court of Appeal decisions which lay down legal principles establish the law to be applied in all courts below the Supreme Court. Court of Appeal decisions can be overturned by the Supreme Court, so judgements of the Supreme Court, or the House of Lords which preceded it as the highest court in the United Kingdom, establish definitively what the law is on a particular point.

Case references

Since 2002, all legal cases in the High Court or above have been allocated a case reference, known as a neutral citation number, which enables them to be identified and referred to in subsequent cases if necessary. Neutral citation numbers are assigned administratively in a chronological sequence and identify the year in which the decision was made, the level of the court which made it, the number of the decision and, for decisions of judges of the High Court, the relevant Division of the court in which it was given. Thus, [2006] EWHC 1465 (Fam) is the neutral citation number of the decision in *Borough Council v A* given in the Family Division of the England and Wales High Court in 2006, the 1465th judgement assigned a number in that year, and [2009] EWCA Civ 59 refers to the Court of Appeal's decision in *Webster v Norfolk*

County Council given in 2009. *EWCA Civ* represents the Civil Division of the England and Wales Court of Appeal (there is also a Criminal Division). As the Supreme Court is the ultimate court of appeal for the whole of the UK its neutral citation numbers include the letters UK in place of EW. In [2009] UKSC 8, *UKSC* represents United Kingdom Supreme Court and [2008] UKHL 35 is the decision of the House of Lords in *Re B*, given in 2008 before the Supreme Court came into being.

Due to the importance of precedent in English law, court decisions have been published commercially in what are known as law reports since the sixteenth century. Any case decided before 2002 will be cited by reference to the name of the case, the year in which it was reported, the series of law reports in which it was reported, together with the volume of the series in that year and the page reference.

FURTHER READING

www.bailli.org. The full text of judgements with a neutral citation number is available free on the British and Irish Legal Information Institute website.

www.familylawweek.co.uk. The Family Law Week website offers summaries of family court judgements, together with articles by lawyers and a monthly newsletter on free e-mail subscription.

www.legislation.gov.uk. Contains all UK statutes and accompanying explanatory documents.

Chapter 1
Rights

CHAPTER OBJECTIVES

The aim of this chapter is to support the Professional Capabilities Framework (PCF) requirements by exploring how the principles of human rights and equality are protected within international conventions, English law and policy. We particularly consider how the concept of children's rights is reflected in practice and encourage you to engage with the intellectual debates, ethical dilemmas and apparent inconsistencies you encounter in the course of your work, so that your judgements and decision-making are firmly and confidently set within a rights-based framework, shaped by your legal powers and duties.

Introduction

The law continues to lurch unevenly between protecting children from harm and protecting family privacy.

(Fortin, 2009, p555)

The twin concepts of rights and justice underpin almost every social work activity, whether in formal settings such as courts or reviews, or in daily tasks such as interviews or home visits. Social work is committed to individual rights and to the philosophy that people who have experienced unfair or discriminatory treatment should be helped and enabled to reduce the nature and effects of the inequalities they have faced. In many circumstances, this does not require you to resort to the authority or provisions of the law; rather, it is a natural reflection of your commitment to the values and ethical framework of social work. However, in addition to circumstances in which rights might have been overlooked, or even on occasions deliberately denied, situations in which there appear to exist conflicting rights, or where the concepts of rights and justice do not seem to coincide, are becoming increasingly common. If it were simply a question of respecting a person's right to privacy if they refuse entry to their home, no particular dilemma arises. However, if you are responding to a referral which suggests that a child might not be receiving good enough care, you have a legal duty to ensure that you are admitted. But how far does that duty go? If you can detect nothing amiss in that first visit, but you consider that the referral came from a reliable source, how much further should you interfere with their right to privacy? If you were the parents (or even the child) concerned, at what point would you consider that your right to respect for your family life was being infringed? If you are subsequently invited to a meeting about the matter, how would you expect to see justice being done and what would persuade you that you had had the equivalent of a fair trial? No book can tell you the answers to such questions and our understanding of rights and justice is made more complex by the fact that they tend to be subjective, rather than objective, concepts, as the first activity will show.

ACTIVITY 1.1

What thoughts and feelings do you associate with the concept of 'rights'? First, identify your instinctive reactions to these news headlines.

- *Government to stop human rights law 'exploitation'.*
- *PM defies rights court over prisoner voting rights.*
- *Bombers ask human rights court to quash their convictions.*
- *Killers use human rights to stay in the UK.*
- *Satellite dish a 'human right'.*
- *Firefighter wins £80,000 for breach of human rights over complaint about chair.*
- *Christians 'have no right' to wear crucifix at work.*
- *Judge criticises CPS for putting stalker's rights before victim.*

*(Source: **www.thetimes.co.uk**)*

Now consider how you might express your views in a professional arena. Are there any differences, however subtle, between your private and public views? What effect might this have on your professional role and responsibilities or the experience of service users?

This activity should show that our understanding of, and attitudes towards, the concept of rights represent a complex mix of values, knowledge, experience and political ideology, and, as such, are difficult to present or exercise with the level of objectivity we normally seek to achieve as a professional. It also highlights the limitations, and potential contradictions, of the law's role in reflecting the views and values of the society it seeks to regulate.

What is a right?

Politicians sometimes like to contrast the concept of *rights* with that of *responsibilities* when considering how society should be organised and how citizens should conduct themselves. The legal concept of a right, however, needs to be distinguished from the rather imprecise references to rights that can arise in general conversation. No legal right can exist in a vacuum. The idea, for example, of a person living alone on a desert island having a right to respect for their family life is meaningless, for there is no family. The concept does not necessarily acquire any more substance if the desert island supports a traditional family unit of parents and children, for although each member can enjoy family life, no external factor is likely to interfere with that enjoyment. Consequently it is an important feature of a legal *right* that it has an impact on others.

Broadly, that impact on others can operate either at a personal level or in relation to society as a whole. At a personal level a *right* stems from values and ethical principles and can confer an entitlement on a person to do something or to be treated in a particular way, which might affect other people and with which those people might otherwise wish to interfere. Therefore, a right of freedom of speech allows you, subject to any legal constraints, to express opinions with which others might not agree. A right not to be discriminated against inhibits those inclined to discriminate from doing so. A right can be either positive or negative. For example, the right to be paid a state retirement pension is positive in that a person receives the benefit by virtue of their right to it. However, a right not to be imprisoned unlawfully is negative in that it inhibits the powers of the state to act arbitrarily. Without rights of this type those holding power could disregard the interests of those who do not.

A right might arise from a duty imposed by statute but Parliament also gives local authorities powers, which are essentially discretionary rather than compulsory and usually identified within legislation by use of the word *may*. No one can claim a right to a service which a public body has only a power to provide. However, public bodies must exercise their powers rationally, reasonably and fairly and it is possible to challenge a decision on the grounds of procedural unfairness, even though the only possible successful outcome would be that the public body is ordered to go through the decision-making process again, offering no guarantee that the requested service ultimately would be forthcoming. What public bodies cannot do is to decide never to use a particular power, or to decide only to use it in a specific way. If a public body holds a power, then each time the opportunity arises when it could be exercised, it must consider whether or not to do so. This clearly has implications in the context of referral and eligibility criteria, for example.

What are human rights?

Inherent in the whole of the Convention is a search for the fair balance between the demands of the general interest of the community and the requirements of the protection of the individual's human rights.

(*Soering v UK* [1989] 11 EHRR 439)

Other than in a philosophical sense, all so-called human rights are created by statutory enactment, which can be of a constitutional nature. For example, some provisions of the Constitution of the United States of America are expressed in terms of rights to which all those within its jurisdiction are entitled. A variation on a constitutional enactment is the making of an international treaty, such as the European Convention on Human Rights (ECHR), agreed by the Council of Europe in 1950 and ratified by the UK in 1951. However this was only binding on the government, not the courts. As the United Kingdom has no written constitution, one of the motivations for adopting the ECHR was a desire to incorporate and nurture within legal systems in which they had not been formally established, rights and freedoms considered essential for the maintenance of democracy in the aftermath of the Second World War. The ECHR was largely written by English lawyers and intended to embody what were considered to be the rights and freedoms actually enjoyed in England and Wales at that time. Consequently, as it was considered to represent the law as it already existed, it was not then incorporated into English law by statute. In 1965 the UK agreed to the citizen's right of direct petition to the European Court of Human Rights (ECtHR) in Strasbourg but although the ECHR has been interpreted by the ECtHR when hearing cases, its decisions were of limited significance in England until the enactment of the Human Rights Act 1998. Thereafter there was incorporated into English law not only the provisions of the ECHR, but also the ECtHR interpretations of those provisions by judges, most of whom came from legal backgrounds different from those of English lawyers, arising from political, economic and social circumstances different from those prevailing in England and Wales.

A consequence of the source of human rights having to be some enactment is that each so-called *right* has to be formulated in writing, often using uncontroversial and, consequently, rather imprecise language. However, legislative language must then be interpreted in order to produce effects, otherwise it is no more than the expression of pious hopes. For example, most people would declare themselves to be opposed to *sin*. However, what behaviour is included within this description? There are respectable Christian groups which contend that divorce, or homosexuality, amounts to *sin*, but many would disagree. It is at the point at which the language is interpreted that what initially appears uncontroversial can become controversial and subject to dispute. The interpretation of language critically depends on the values of those engaged in the interpretation. The less specific the language in the document being interpreted, the greater the scope for manipulating it in order to produce what is considered to be a desirable result, as we shall see in later chapters.

The purpose of the HRA is to require all public authorities to act in accordance with the ECHR's requirements, to permit alleged breaches to be tried in English courts and to ensure that English courts take account of previous decisions of the ECtHR. It gives rights to individuals to challenge decisions made by public bodies, such as local authorities, government departments and the National Health Service. Although courts may overrule secondary legislation if it is found to be incompatible with the HRA, they may not overrule an Act of Parliament: if a court cannot interpret or apply a particular Act of Parliament in a way that respects or fits ECHR rights, all it can do is make a *declaration of incompatibility*. The government and Parliament then have to decide if the law should be changed.

It is necessary to distinguish between rights that are *absolute*, those that are *limited* and those that are *qualified*, in which a balance may need to be struck between the competing interests of the individual and society. Understandably, the Articles which most often require interpretation are those that are not absolute. In such situations the key concept is that of *proportionality*, meaning that interference with the right in question may be justified if there is a legitimate aim and the interference is proportionate to the achievement of that aim. Thus, for example, the right to respect for private and family life potentially can be interfered with if it appears that forcibly removing a child from its family is the only way by which to ensure the child's safety and welfare.

The HRA has brought changes to the culture of policy-formation and decision-making in local authorities and other public bodies. In particular:

- it made discretionary policies and decisions challengeable on the basis of an alleged breach of human rights and provided a new ground for judicial review in addition to unreasonableness, illegality or procedural unfairness;

- in introducing a new test for judicial intervention, that of *proportionality*, public bodies must be able to justify decisions, policy changes or even adherence to existing policy on occasions;

- the HRA requires positive action from local authorities, and in certain circumstances their agents, in furtherance of people's human rights. It is not sufficient to sit back and await any possible challenge;

- its influence is recognisable in the language adopted in government policies and official guidance, although as we shall see this can pose more problems than it solves.

It also gives rise to a number of practice issues, the overarching one being that of procedural fairness and reasoned decision-making. This should form the foundation of good social work practice and be incorporated into all assessments and service decisions. In order to provide evidence of this, every stage of the social work decision-making process must be supported by timely, accurate and comprehensive records which show that in each case there has been recognition, and a considered balancing, of competing interests, supported by competent analysis and a rationale that can stand up to challenge. Therefore, an awareness of legal reasoning and a commitment to clarity of language is essential.

Articles of the ECHR

The Articles include:

- Article 2 – right to life (Absolute (A))
- Article 3 – freedom from torture and inhuman or degrading punishment (A)
- Article 4 – freedom from slavery (A) and forced labour (Limited (L))
- Article 5 – right to liberty and security (L)
- Article 6 – right to a fair trial (L)
- Article 7 – freedom from retrospective punishment (A)
- Article 8 – right to respect for private and family life (Qualified (Q))
- Article 9 – freedom of thought, conscience and religion (Q)
- Article 10 – freedom of expression (Q)
- Article 11 – freedom of assembly and association (Q)
- Article 12 – right to marry and found a family (L)
- Article 14 – freedom from discrimination
- Article 16 – restrictions on the political activity of aliens
- Article 18 – limitation on use of restrictions on rights

(Article 13 – the right to an effective remedy – is not incorporated into the HRA as it was thought to be covered elsewhere.)

The HRA also incorporates rights in the Conventions Protocol 1 which were added after ratification, namely:

- Article 1 – right to peaceful enjoyment of property
- Article 2 – right to education
- Article 3 – right to free elections

ACTIVITY **1.2**

In relation to each of the Articles listed above, identify circumstances within your professional role and responsibilities which may be relevant to the Article in question. Each Article is likely to relate to a number of different professional social work activities.

For example, Article 3 may be relevant to the right of a young person seeking asylum not to be returned to a country where there is evidence that they may be at risk of being tortured.

Children's rights

If I talk to a lot of grown-ups and say: 'What do you think your rights are?' they'll give me a list. If I say to them: 'What do you think children's rights are?' they'll say 'Oh'. And some will say: 'Well, I don't think children have rights really, they're just children.'

(Children's Rights Director, 2010, **www.eastendtalking.org.uk/ schoolcouncils/childrens-rights-day**)

I think that usually we take account of adults' rights in the course of making decisions, but often children's rights are secondary, if they are acknowledged at all.

(Child protection social worker)

There is too much contact done for parents' benefit that doesn't take sufficient account of a child's need for a secure attachment with the person looking after them.

(Munro and Ward, 2008, p232)

Children's wrongs in numbers 2010/11

- *Number of children who died as a result of deliberately inflicted injury, abuse or neglect and who were, or had been, subject to a child protection plan, England: **40**.*

- *Proportion of children in children's homes who have at least one sibling from whom they are separated: **94 per cent**.*

- *Proportion of children in foster care who have at least one sibling from whom they are separated: **71 per cent**.*

- *Proportion of looked-after children who had an advocate at their review meeting: **1 per cent**.*

- *Number of children aged 9–13 detained in police cells overnight: **13,000**.*

- *Proportion of youth offending workers who had made a home visit prior to submitting a home circumstances report to court: **18 per cent**.*

- *Number of children remanded in custody from the crown court: **1,041**.*

(CRAE, 2011, p1)

Despite various international and domestic declarations and commitments, the concept of children's rights, and in particular the means by which they should be promoted and enforced, remains problematic in our society, not only as a result of lack of legal commitment. Historical, cultural and religious attitudes to family life, prevailing theories of child development and political, philosophical and economic factors all influence how childhood is regarded and, consequently, the way in which the law seeks to influence and regulate it. Children are barely mentioned in the ECHR, which reflects society's attitudes towards them at the time it was written. Now it is more generally recognised that there are situations in which there are potential conflicts between the rights and interests of children and those of their parents and families, for example in the context of child protection, where separate policies and actions might be justified. A child's right to family life could, if ill-treatment is occurring within their family, be inconsistent with its right to be protected from inhuman or degrading treatment. However, in child protection there will always be a need to justify intervention in a human rights context, although Beckett (2001) highlights the risks inherent in the fact that delay is sometimes attractive as the line of least resistance and that trying to maintain individual rights can mean that the rights of parents, who are usually more vocal and assertive, take precedence over the rights and needs of children.

Until the Children Act 1975 introduced separate representation for children in public law proceedings, parents were permitted to represent their children in circumstances in which they themselves might be facing allegations of abuse or neglect. Henricson and Bainham (2005, p8) suggest that there has been a 'relentless internationalisation of family law' in recent decades and emphasise the need to seek balance both between the rights of individuals and between those of individuals and of collective entities, such as families or society as a whole. They suggest that incorporating within child care law and policy the single objective of giving prime importance to children's rights or welfare is 'unsatisfactory and unhelpful' (ibid., p21) in that it risks leading to violations of the ECHR by undervaluing of the rights of other family members.

ACTIVITY 1.3

D is 12 and has been looked after for over a year. The care plan envisages that she will return to her parents but this is not likely to happen in the short-term, as her father is in prison and her mother is being treated for severe depression. D is settled in her foster home and at school, where she has a good circle of friends and takes part in several after-school activities, and she maintains a relationship with her mother whom she understands is not able to care for her at present, although she can safely manage day visits. D's mother would like to see her daughter every Saturday and Sunday, and also twice a week after school. In the school holidays she would like to see her more often which she contends is necessary in order to maintain D's enjoyment of family life with her birth family. The foster carers, however, feel that this level of contact would interfere with D's enjoyment of family life within the foster home and also mean that she would miss out on social activities with her friends.

As D's social worker, how would you show that you had recognised and taken account of the rights of all concerned to respect for their private and family life and that your contribution towards decision-making is supported by clear analysis and balancing of the competing claims? If the final decision is challenged, what factors would evidence the concept of a legitimate aim and the principle of proportionality in this case?

The concept of children's rights, as distinct from those of adults, did not attract widespread recognition within society or in terms of social workers' powers and duties until the enactment of the CA 1989 in 1991, the same year in which the UK adopted the United Nations Convention on the Rights of the Child (UNCRC). Although the UNCRC has not been formally incorporated into domestic legislation as has the ECHR, the judgement in *Smith v Smith and another* [2006] UKHL 35 clarified the importance of adhering to its principles:

> *Even if an international treaty has not been incorporated into domestic law, our domestic legislation has to be construed so far as possible so as to comply with the international obligations which we have undertaken. When two interpretations of these regulations are possible, the interpretation chosen should be that which better complies with the commitment to the welfare of children which this country has made by ratifying the United Nations Convention on the Rights of the Child.*

Both the CA 1989 and the UNCRC promote the philosophy that children are neither the property of their parents nor objects of concern. Rather they are unique individuals, who are part of a family and a community, with rights and responsibilities to match their age and development. However, the UNCRC supports the premise that it is the primary role of parents to decide how to bring up their children.

The significance of the CA 1989 in the context of children's rights is reflected in the language adopted, which is notably different from that contained in preceding legislation (see Chapter 2). However, the principles reflected by the shift in language were not expressly articulated as children's rights, which many feel is regrettable. Indeed, during the Parliamentary debate which preceded the enactment of the CA 2004, the government rejected proposed amendments that would have included references to the UNCRC within the legislation (Williams, 2008). Surprisingly, *Every Child Matters* (DfES, 2003) makes little reference to human rights, either of parents or children, being primarily concerned with outcomes, which had become the preferred way of expressing aims within government guidance.

Nevertheless, the UNCRC provides a framework which articulates the basic human rights held by all children, including the rights to:

- survival;
- develop to the fullest;
- protection from harmful influences, abuse and exploitation; and
- participate fully in family, cultural and social life.

The obligations under the UNCRC in relation to child protection and achieving permanence for children who cannot live with their birth families pose considerable challenges to local authorities. They must ensure that resources are available to protect children at risk of significant harm, and they must also work with families to reunite them with children temporarily looked after by the state. For example, it is open to debate as to whether government-imposed targets for adoption are consistent with the expectation that local authorities should be doing everything possible to keep children in their birth family and to achieve reunification for those who become looked after, an issue which has attracted recent media interest.

Another area of controversy is that concerning the physical chastisement of children. After the United Kingdom was found to be in breach of Article 3 of the ECHR in failing to protect children from excessive physical punishment (*A v United Kingdom (Human Rights: Punishment of Child)* [1998] 2 FLR 959), a public consultation exercise was undertaken, shaped by the premise that physical punishment should not be outlawed altogether. As a consequence the CA 2004 s58 introduced the provision, which has since been the subject of sustained criticism by organisations concerned with children's rights, that the physical chastisement of children by parents is permitted as long as it does not result in actual bodily harm. Physical punishment in all other contexts, such as by teachers and childminders, is unlawful. The UK is considerably out of step with its European partners in this context in that 16 European countries have banned all forms of physical punishment of children (Keating, 2011), further illustrating the subjective nature of the concept of rights. The current state of legislation also lacks clarity in terms of what constitutes *actual bodily harm* and the fact that the vulnerability of a baby or a disabled child in terms of punishment is clearly different from that of a healthy and robust older teenager.

LEGAL CASE STUDY **1.1**

RK v BCC *[2011] EWCA Civ 1305*

Parents who signed a 'Looked After Care Plan', which included provision for their daughter to live in a specialist residential establishment, had agreed that their child's liberty be restricted by the local authority responsible for managing the establishment as she required supervision for her own safety. The restrictions were no more than what was reasonably required to protect her from harming herself or others.

LEGAL CASE STUDY **1.2**

Re CA (A Baby) *[2012] EWHC 2190 (Fam)*

As part of the final placement proceedings in this case described in Chapter 7, there was a claim by the mother under the HRA 1998 relating to the manner in which her agreement to her baby being accommodated under the CA 1989 s20 was obtained. The local authority agreed that an s20 agreement should not have been sought on the day of the child's birth and that removal of the child from the mother at that time was not proportionate, given the risks that existed in this case. The local authority accepted the breach of the mother's and child's Article 8 rights. The mother requested that the remedy to be applied was the cost of her receiving the therapy that had been advised in the course of the assessments undertaken for the court hearings.

In this case, the fact that the local authority accepted that the mother's and child's human rights had been breached did not affect the ultimate outcome, which was that final care and placement orders were made for the child, her welfare being paramount. Instead, the mother received compensation in the form of therapeutic help which it was hoped would enable her to manage her life more effectively in the future.

LEGAL CASE STUDY 1.3

Re J (a child) (care proceedings: fair trial) *[2006] EWCA Civ 545*

This concerned a baby with a 17-year-old mother. The local authority applied for a care order and, prior to the final hearing, arranged a meeting in order to tell the mother of its plan to place the baby for adoption. There were three stages: first, a meeting between social workers and the local authority's solicitor; second, a meeting between all of them and other interested professionals; and third, a meeting with the mother and her legal representatives. At the final hearing the mother, through her lawyers, criticised the local authority's conduct of the meeting and contended that its handling of her case was an infringement of her human rights under Articles 6 and 8. The trial judge recognised that there had been procedural defects in the meeting in that the mother and her solicitor had been excluded from discussions; however, he found that even if they had participated, the local authority's plan would not have been any different, and he made a care order in respect of the baby with the plan that she should be adopted. The mother's appeal against this was dismissed. The appeal judges stated that the departures from good practice had not been sufficiently substantial to affect the fairness of the proceedings and there was nothing that the mother could have said which would have persuaded the local authority to change its care plan. In the circumstances there had been no infringement of the mother's human rights.

This case shows that although human rights legislation potentially influences almost every action that you will take professionally, courts have to take account of all the circumstances in order to reach decisions which meet the tests of legitimate aim and proportionality. In this case the welfare of the baby was paramount, but you may also be able to understand the mother's sense of grievance in the circumstances.

LEGAL CASE STUDY 1.4

Re B (Care: Interference with Family Life) *[2003] EWCA Civ 786*

The judgement in this case stated that:

> Where the application is for a care order empowering the local authority to remove a child or children from the family, the Judge in modern times may not make such an order without considering the European Convention for the Protection of Human Rights and Fundamental Freedoms Art 8 rights of the adult members of the family and of the children of the family. Accordingly he must not sanction such an interference with family unless he is satisfied that that is both necessary and proportionate and that no other less radical form of order would achieve the essential end of promoting the welfare of the children.

LEGAL CASE STUDY 1.5

Re H (Care Plan: Human Rights) *[2011] EWCA Civ 1009*

This case determined that in public law family proceedings a judge can hear an application for an injunction under the HRA s8(1) preventing the local authority from removing a child from her mother, despite having made an interim care order in favour of the local authority.

Protecting children

The UNCRC states that a child's right to protection incorporates a duty on the part of the state not only to react to incidents of maltreatment but also to seek to reduce their incidence in the first place.

Article 19 sets out that:

1. *States Parties shall take all appropriate legislative, administrative, social and educational measures to protect the child from all forms of physical or mental violence, injury or abuse, neglect or negligent treatment, maltreatment or exploitation, including sexual abuse, while in the care of parent(s), legal guardian(s) or any other person who has the care of the child.*

2. *Such protective measures should, as appropriate, include effective procedures for the establishment of social programmes to provide necessary support for the child and for those who have the care of the child, as well as for other forms of prevention and for identification, reporting, referral, investigation, treatment and follow-up of instances of child maltreatment described heretofore, and, as appropriate, for judicial involvement.*

Working Together to Safeguard Children (DfE, 2010d) includes the statement that it reflects the principles contained within the UNCRC and takes into account the ECHR, in particular Articles 6 and 8.

Children within the justice system

The vulnerabilities of childhood are given relatively perfunctory recognition or accommodation by the justice system, which struggles to deal with children's reduced level of comprehension and emotional and behavioural development.

(Newbury, 2011, p94)

The way in which children are regarded and treated within our justice system illustrates the limitations of the law in relation to the promotion and maintenance of the rights of vulnerable people. Nevertheless, there exist many opportunities for individual practitioners to make a difference in terms of advancing the rights of children who have offended or are at risk of offending, with many of these concepts applicable to other aspects of work with children and families.

The age of criminal responsibility in England and Wales remains 10, the lowest in Europe, and there appear to be no plans to increase this, other than in Scotland. Consequently many more children in the UK than in the rest of Europe acquire a criminal record by the end of their childhood, and significant numbers experience being held in custody in one form or another. In addition, a curious anomaly dating back to the Children and Young Persons Act 1933 means that within the criminal justice system children are treated as adults when they become 17. This could be seen to reflect tensions in society between the understanding of adult responsibilities towards children and what rights they are considered to have. Henricson and Bainham (2005) suggest that the relationship between state and child appears to have gone somewhat awry in the criminal justice context in that the state's protective obligations to support children's welfare are not being met, with adult status being placed on children too early and a preoccupation with the act of punishment at the expense of the need to reduce crime in the interests of society. Even apparently welfare approaches to youth crime may incorporate elements of coercion, containment and restriction on the basis that such measures meet the child's needs which are usually determined by others. Recently the concept of restorative justice has gained recognition and support, although there is debate as to whether this approach is welfare driven, punitive, or a mixture of both and, more significantly in relation to children's rights, how it is regarded by the children who experience the process (Newbury, 2011). The case study below offers an interesting insight into the latter

---

CASE STUDY *1.1*

Q: How would you have felt if the victim had been at the panel meeting?
A: Not bothered.

Q: Would you have wanted to talk to him?
A: No.

Q: What if the panel asked you to apologise for kicking him?
A: I wouldn't.

Q: Why?
A: He kicked me first.

Q: What do you understand by reparation?
A: Nothing.

Q: Have you heard it called anything else?
A: No.

Q: What did you have to do in your anger management course?
A: She told me not to fight back but just walk away.

Q: And have you been in situations when you've done that?
A: No.

(12-year-old boy convicted of assault answering researcher's questions about his experience of restorative justice, quoted by ibid., p98)

Many children who commit offences are dealt with outside the court system but where a child is subject to criminal proceedings, a court must have regard to:

- the principal aim of the youth justice system (the prevention of offending or re-offending);

- the welfare of the offender;

- the purposes of sentencing (punishment, reform and rehabilitation; protection of the public; reparation).

However, it is not difficult to see that these provisions cannot always co-exist and raise the central dilemmas in the context of children's rights: should offending by children be punished or should it be seen as an indication of welfare or support needs? And is there sufficient recognition of the fact that some forms of penalty imposed by the criminal justice system have the potential to damage children still further?

Surprisingly, there is no provision in law for courts to take account of children's welfare when sentencing their parents. Some 160,000 children experienced the imprisonment of a parent in England and Wales in 2010 (CRAE, 2011).

Children in custody

At any one time, there are around 3,000 children held in custody, 90 per cent of them male and 60 per cent of whom have been in care (YJB, 2011). The case of *R (on the application of the Howard League for Penal Reform) v Secretary of State for the Home Department (No. 2)* [2002] EWHC 2497 (Admin) established that children in custody have the same rights and entitlements as any other child in need in the community and remain eligible for support under the CA 1989; by 2013 children in custody will automatically become looked-after children (see Chapter 7). A government circular (DfES, 2004) sets out the current responsibilities of local authorities towards looked-after children in Young Offender Institutions (YOI).

By the age of 10 looked-after children are more than twice as likely to have been cautioned or convicted of an offence as other children of the same age. In 2010/11, 4,177 children received custodial sentences in England, of whom 93 per cent were boys (YJB, 2011). Some 85 per cent were held in Young Offender Institutions, with the remainder in Secure Training Centres (STC) or Secure Children's Homes (SCH). Children in the care of the local authority are over-represented within the custodial population with over a quarter having spent some time in care (HMIP, 2011).

> *It makes you madder – you want to rip someone's head off. I felt like that for ages – pure adrenalin going round my body.*
>   (Young person in custody, interviewed by Smallridge and Williamson, 2008, p16)

The use of restraint in custodial establishments poses particular dilemmas in the context of children's rights. As a public authority a YOI is required to act in a manner that is compatible with the ECHR. Rights which may be engaged by the use of force are the right to life (Article 2), the right to protection from torture or inhuman or degrading treatment or punishment (Article 3) and the right to respect for private and family life (Article 8). Where excessive or disproportionate force is used, or where the application of force is maintained for longer than necessary, even if its use is intended to achieve a lawful aim, this may constitute a breach of

Convention rights. In the UK there is also an established common law principle that a person has the right to act in defence of themselves or others and so restraint may be justified provided its use is reasonable in the circumstances.

Under the Secure Training Rules 1998 the physical restraint of detainees is permitted in certain circumstances, but not solely for the promotion of good order and discipline. However, it became clear during inquiries and investigations following deaths that occurred in STCs that, in practice, restraint was widely used for this purpose. Smallridge and Williamson (2008), in an independent review of the use of restraint in secure settings, reported widespread acceptance among staff that it was sometimes necessary to use force to restrain children. They also found that (p16):

- young people accept that restraint may be justified on occasion but believe that it should be fair, proportionate and safe;

- restraint is chaotic, traumatic and stressful and can have significant impact on both young people and staff;

- for some young people, restraint can trigger complex responses that make them actively seek it.

They recommended that future policy should be developed in accordance with the following principles (ibid., p10):

- force should be used only as a last resort;

- force should be used only to prevent the *risk of harm*;

- the criteria for using force should be consistent across settings;

- the minimum force necessary should be used, proportionate to the identified risk;

- only approved restraint techniques should be used;

- force should only be used in the context of an overall approach to behaviour management, including de-escalation and de-briefing, in which children and young people are actively involved.

The Physical Control in Care Training Manual (NOMS, 2010), based on the principles of reasonableness, necessity and proportionality, has been developed as an interim curriculum pending the introduction of a new holistic behaviour management system to be used in STCs, known as Conflict Resolution Training (CRT). Meanwhile the Youth Justice Board's Code of Practice supplements the sector-specific rules applicable to YOIs, STCs and SCHs. *Managing the Behaviour of Children and Young People in the Secure Estate* (YJB, 2012) aims to be consistent with, and encourage recognition of, the rights of children and young people incorporated in both domestic and international law, specifically the UNCRC, HRA and CAs 1989 and 2004.

The Children's Rights Alliance for England continues to monitor the use of restraint on children in custody and press for an automatic, independent and public review of any unexpected death or serious injury involving children in care or in custody.

LEGAL CASE STUDY 1.6

CRAE v Secretary of State for Justice & (1) G4S Care & Justice Services (UK) Ltd, (2) Serco PLC (Interested Parties) *[2012] EWHC 8 (Admin)*

Against a background of 285 instances since 2006 of restraint of children in custody leading to serious injury and hospitalisation, the Children's Rights Alliance for England brought judicial review proceedings in respect of what it alleged was the government's failure to review the restraint records of four STCs and to notify former detainees who may have been subject to unlawful restraint that they could be entitled to redress. However, whilst accepting that it was likely that there had been widespread, unlawful use of restraint and that few, if any, of the children appreciated at the time that it was unlawful, the court decided that it could not be said that the refusal to disseminate information impeded the access to justice of those potentially affected. There was available information in the public domain about what happened within STCs during the relevant period and steps could be taken by those affected without the need to be told about it directly by the Secretary of State. Therefore, it was not appropriate to impose a positive obligation on the Secretary of State for Justice to provide details of children formerly detained in secure training centres who had been subjected to unlawful restraint procedures in order for them to seek redress if they chose.

This case illustrates that whatever may be regarded by the layman as the fairest or most just outcome, courts are concerned with interpreting and applying the law. In its judgement, the court in this case stated that to grant the order sought would 'represent the thin end of an ever-expanding wedge without a clear appreciation of where the expansion would lead'.

Children arriving from abroad

Of the 1,800 unaccompanied children who arrive in the UK each year (Matthews, 2012), some are seeking asylum with others having been trafficked for exploitation. Article 22 of the UNCRC requires member states to ensure that children seeking asylum receive appropriate protection and assistance. In addition, they are entitled to universal UNCRC rights, such as not to be discriminated against, to be treated with humanity and respect, to have their voices heard and for the 'best interests of the child' principle to apply to decisions made about them. The UK Border Agency is therefore required to safeguard and promote the welfare of children whilst exercising its immigration and customs functions (Border, Citizenship and Immigration Act, 2009, s55). However, a report by the Council of Europe (2012) expresses concern that significant numbers of potential and confirmed child victims of trafficking currently go missing from local authority care in the UK and urges that all unaccompanied children be assigned a legal guardian at the point of arrival in the UK.

RESEARCH SUMMARY 1.1

A report on behalf of the Office of the Children's Commissioner (Matthews, 2012) found that children arriving in the UK were being detained in contravention of UNCRC standards. Unaccompanied children were being held under detention powers on, and immediately after, their arrival despite government policy, arising from Article 37(b) of the UNCRC, that they should only be detained in the most exceptional circumstances while arrangements for their care are made. Instead of being held for the 'shortest appropriate period of time', children were being detained whilst facing significant interviews that affected their prospects of being granted permission to stay in the UK. The local authority was only informed of their arrival several hours after initial detention and well into the interviewing process. The report's key recommendation was that interviewing, beyond the gathering of basic identity data, should be postponed until a child has had time to recover from their journey and the opportunity to instruct a legal representative. An appropriate adult should also be present to safeguard their interests.

Children with disabilities

It should not be regarded as an exotic idea for disabled children and those close to them to aspire to a quality of life comparable to that enjoyed by others who do not live with disability . . . it should be seen as unacceptable in the twenty-first century for the lives and experiences of disabled children and their families to be bereft of those features that many others take for granted, features that make an essential contribution to an ordinary and reasonable quality of life.

(Read *et al.*, 2006, p17)

Some 7.3 per cent of children in the UK are disabled, using the Equality Act 2010 definition, the majority of whom live at home with their families (Broach *et al.*, 2010). The social model of disability which assumes that many of the oppressive and limiting aspects of disabled people's lives are caused by ameliorable social, environmental and political factors has shaped the way in which disability is understood and has been influential in relation to the formulation of government policy, international treaties and international classification systems of health, illness and disability.

The state has duties to promote the rights of disabled children and their families and to counter any discrimination they experience. The most relevant Article of the ECHR is Article 8, the right to respect for private and family life, which is a qualified right. The courts have applied a broad definition to the concept of *private life*, which encompasses not only the notion of respecting privacy, but also those of identity, ability to function socially, physical and psychological integrity and the right to develop a personality and relationships with other people without outside interference (Broach *et al.*, 2010). Thus, for example, Article 8 could potentially be engaged if it was found that there had been a failure on the part of a local authority to remove barriers preventing a disabled child from forming friendships or taking part in social and recreational activities.

Human Rights Articles of particular relevance to disabled children

Article 23 of the UNCRC relates specifically to disabled children and requires states to recognise that they should enjoy *full and decent* lives. It further recognises the right of disabled children to *special care*. The aim of such support should be to allow every child to *achieve the fullest possible social integration and individual development* which should be provided without charge if possible, subject to resources.

Other articles in the UNCRC of particular relevance to disabled children include:

- *Article 2 – non-discrimination*

- *Article 3 – the best interests of the child to be a primary consideration*

- *Article 4 – states to use the maximum extent of available resources to realise children's economic, social and cultural rights*

- *Article 12 – the right to participation*

- *Article 24 – the right to the highest attainable standard of health.*

In addition, the UN Convention on the Rights of Persons with Disabilities (Disability Convention), ratified by the UK in 2009, includes the following articles relevant to the needs of disabled children:

- *Article 3 – general principles, including respect for inherent dignity and full and effective participation in society*

- *Article 7 – to ensure the full enjoyment by children with disabilities of all human rights and fundamental freedoms on an equal basis with other children*

- *Article 9 – accessibility*

- *Article 19 – independent living and inclusion in the community*

- *Article 24 – the right to an inclusive education.*

The UK Government has entered a reservation to Article 24 in relation to education in the following terms:

> *The United Kingdom reserves the right for disabled children to be educated outside their local community where more appropriate education provision is available elsewhere. The United Kingdom Government is committed to continuing to develop an inclusive system where parents of disabled children have increasing access to mainstream schools and staff, which have the capacity to meet the needs of disabled children. The General Education System in the United Kingdom includes mainstream and special schools, which the UK Government understands is allowed under the Convention.*
>
> *(**www.disabilityaction.org/centre-on-human-rights-and-disability/ reservations-to-the-convention/**)*

ACTIVITY 1.4

The paragraphs above illustrate the influence of cultural values in relation to the concept of rights and provides considerable scope for interpretation of language.

If you were responsible for ensuring that your agency's policy and practice in relation to services for children with disabilities was compliant with the Articles set out above, how would you show that the 'highest attainable standard of health' had been achieved? Against what should it be measured? What account should be taken of genetic, environmental and social factors? At what points in a child's life should it be assessed and against what criteria? What constitutes a 'full and decent life and inclusion in the community'? What should follow if the expected standards are not achieved? How should service users be helped to understand and receive their entitlements?

Young carers

'I don't have anyone back and I don't go out – just say I can't be bothered, it's easier than explaining.'

'I was quite lonely; I didn't know how many people were like me.'

(Young carers, quoted in OFSTED, 2009, p17)

Article 31 of the UNCRC recognises the right of all children to rest and leisure and to engage in play and recreation activities, which has particular relevance to the needs of young carers. A child who is aged under 16 years and caring for someone else may request an assessment under the Carers (Recognition and Services) Act 1995, and this request must be granted whenever the person they care for is assessed or reassessed for community care. However this requires liaison between children's and adult services (see Chapter 10), and OFSTED (2009) found that local authorities were not doing enough to identify 'hidden' young carers; it was estimated that there were between 250,000 and 350,000 children of problem drug users in the UK who could potentially be considered as carers (Home Office, 2003). If this number, which is likely to have increased, is added to the number of children undertaking caring duties towards parents with mental health needs, it represents considerable challenges in terms of children's rights.

The rights of parents

When considering children's rights, we should not overlook the rights of parents. Although the CA 1989 heralded a shift from the concept of parental rights to that of parental responsibilities, the philosophy that informs much of the legal framework of children and families social work is that of the right of parents to determine how they bring up their children, with state intervention to be invoked only as a last resort. The UNCRC specifically refers to the family as the fundamental group in society and the natural environment in which to bring up children and member states are expected to respect parents' prime responsibility for providing care and guidance for their children and support parents in providing material assistance and support. However, in practice it is not always straightforward to balance parents' rights with those of children and, if there is a conflict, whose should prevail? For example, the *Every Child Matters* outcomes (DfES, 2003) take no account of the rights, aspirations or possible limitations of parents. Similarly the *Common Assessment Framework* (CWDC, 2009) contains little that relates to the needs or entitlements of parents. In addition, recent restrictions to the legal aid budget have resulted in a system in which parents of children involved in public law proceedings receive assistance by means of pre-determined tiered levels, which might not necessarily meet their specific needs at the time (Broadhurst and Holt, 2010).

The Laming Report (2003) highlighted the tension between the state's duty to protect and promote children's development and the human right to privacy and family life. This is particularly apparent in relation to private fostering, where a dilemma for policy-makers and practitioners is the extent to which it is right, or proportionate, to impose controls on private arrangements made by parents for the care of their children. The judgement in the case of *Gillick v West Norfolk & Wisbech Area Health Authority* [1986] AC 112 (see Chapter 9) also commented on parents' rights in relation to those of children:

> *Parental right yields to the child's right to make his own decisions when he reaches a sufficient understanding and intelligence to be capable of making up his own mind on the matter requiring decision.*

However, this leaves plenty of scope for individual judgement.

Mental capacity

An important aspect of the concept of rights is that of capacity, since there are some circumstances in which social workers have to make judgements in respect of the capacity of people to make decisions (for example, to consent to their child being accommodated under the CA 1989 s20 – see legal case study in Chapter 7) or address assumptions by others that silence indicates consent (for example, if a parent does not attend a decision-making meeting). The Mental Capacity Act 2005, which removes the medical connotations previously attached to the concept of capacity, applies to people over 16, resulting in a potential overlap with the CA 1989 for young people between 16 and 18.

Principles of Mental Capacity Act 2005

- A person is assumed to have capacity to make their own decisions, unless proved otherwise.

- Until all practicable steps have been taken to help and support someone to make a decision without success, they cannot be treated as lacking capacity.

- An unwise or eccentric decision is not to be taken as lack of capacity.

- Any act should aim to be the least restrictive option to the person in terms of their rights and freedom of action.

- Any act or decision taken on behalf of someone lacking capacity must be in the person's best interests, subject of course to the overriding interests of a child.

Defining capacity

A person lacks capacity in relation to a matter if at the *material time* he is unable to make a decision for himself *in relation to the matter* because of an *impairment of, or a disturbance in,* the functioning of the mind or brain (covers a range of conditions, including illness, learning disability, brain damage or toxic confusional state). It is not relevant whether the impairment or disturbance is permanent or temporary. Assessment of capacity is:

- **time specific** – it relates to a specific moment in time and may change;

- **decision specific** – it may vary depending on the decision;

- subject to a **diagnostic threshold** – evidence of impairment or disturbance is needed in order to engage legislation. A doctor is not required for this, despite use of word *diagnostic*;

- **not solely based** on appearance, age, behaviour or condition.

Test for capacity

The assessor must have a reasonable belief that a person can:

- *understand the information relevant to the decision (nature, purpose, consequences);*

- *retain the information for as long as it takes to make the decision (ability to retain information for only short periods does not in itself indicate lack of capacity);*

- *use or weigh the information as part of decision-making process;*

- *communicate the decision (in any recognisable way).*

At each stage, appropriate support must be provided in order to facilitate the process (language, environment, communication aids, time, consultation with family or others). The rest of the Act is not applicable if the test confirms capacity.

Anyone can make an assessment of capacity and there are no statutory forms.

Future developments

The government intends to introduce a new Children and Families Bill during 2013 which will include provision for strengthening children's rights, specifically in relation to the following:

- strengthening the Children's Commissioner's remit, with a new function to *promote and protect children's rights* as set out in the UNCRC;

- granting new powers to carry out assessments of the impact of new policies and legislation on children's rights;

- ensuring more independence from ministers by means of a requirement to report directly to Parliament, which will assume a stronger role in monitoring the Commissioner's performance.

FURTHER READING

www.childrenslegalcentre.com. The Coram Children's Legal Centre provides free legal advice, assistance and representation on children's rights in the UK.

www.crae.org.uk. The Children's Rights Alliance for England aims to protect the human rights of children by lobbying government and others who hold power and by bringing or supporting test cases.

www.equalityhumanrights.com. The Equality and Human Rights Commission is an independent statutory body that reports on legal developments, operates a helpline and produces a variety of training resources related to human rights.

www.rights4me.org. The Office of the Children's Rights Director for England produces regular reports on children's experiences and views.

Watson, J and Woolf, M (2008) *Human Rights Act Toolkit* (2nd edition). London: Legal Action Group.

Chapter 2
Responsibilities

CHAPTER OBJECTIVES

Within this chapter we consider how far the law seeks to determine your professional responsibilities as a social worker and show that in most situations it offers no more than a framework within which you need to exercise professional judgement in individual cases, and have an ability to defend it if necessary. We encourage you critically to reflect on the opportunities and constraints that this presents and consider how, and to what extent, the law defines responsibilities of others, with examples of its practical application, thus supporting the requirements of the Professionalism, Contexts and Organisations and Professional Leadership PCF domains in particular.

Introduction

We referred in Chapter 1 to the contrasting concepts of rights and responsibilities. In addition to legal responsibilities towards service users, you also have responsibilities to your employer or organisation within which you work, to other professionals and to your professional body, some of which might appear to be conflicting on occasions. As with the need to demonstrate the existence of a legitimate aim, proportionality, balance and procedural fairness in the context of rights, professional responsibilities require a proactive, transparent and reflective approach.

Confidentiality and information handling

Confidentiality represents a core social work value and is one of the key factors that distinguishes professional relationships from personal ones. However, this needs to be understood within increasing policy demands for inter-professional communication and collaboration. The Laming Report (2003) in particular noted that confusion over the concept of confidentiality and its interface with rights and multi-disciplinary working contributed to failures in the sphere of child protection.

Confidential information is:

- of a private nature;

- not already lawfully in the public domain; and

- given in circumstances in which the person providing it could reasonably expect that it would not be shared with others.

In addition to Article 8 of the European Convention on Human Rights, the primary constraints that exist in relation to the divulging of information are the common law duty of confidentiality and the Data Protection Act 1998. Breach of a common law duty could result in legal action with a view to seeking an injunction or damages as recompense, and could also give rise to disciplinary action by an employer. The main exceptions to the common law duty of confidentiality are where the public interest overrides the individual's right, or where disclosure is required by law, such as could arise in connection with the prevention, detection or prosecution of crime.

LEGAL CASE STUDY **2.1**

D. v National Society for the Prevention of Cruelty to Children [1978] AC 171

The NSPCC received a report that a child was being ill-treated. Following investigation, it was decided that the allegation was unfounded and the child's mother wanted to know who had made it, so that she could sue the person concerned. The NSPCC refused to say and the court decided that NSPCC records were covered by public interest immunity, because the NSPCC's work depended on people being confident that they could report cases without their identity being revealed.

The DPA, although widely misused to justify the withholding of information or refusal to communicate about particular matters, was intended to provide a framework for the management of personal information, to protect the individual's right to privacy and to ensure that people have access to, and the opportunity to correct, information held about them by others. The DPA does not allow information to be disclosed which would be regarded under common law as confidential. Its main provisions are:

- data subjects, meaning those about whom information is held, must be told the identity of data controllers, meaning those who hold the information, and the purpose for which data is to be processed. Information can be disclosed for many purposes without obtaining consent so long as it was fairly obtained and there is no breach of common law;

- personal data can be obtained only for one or more specified lawful purposes, and must not be further processed for purposes that are incompatible with the original purposes;

- information must be fairly and lawfully processed, and adequate, relevant and not excessive in relation to the purpose for which it is processed;

- information must be accurate, up-to-date and not kept longer than necessary;

- it must be processed in accordance with data subject's rights and kept secure against unauthorised use, accidental damage or destruction;

- it may not be transferred to countries that do not have adequate protection against unlawful disclosure.

Individuals can see information held about them in:

- electronic records;

- health, social work, housing and school paper records;

- all structured files held by organisations.

However, health or social work records can be withheld if disclosure is likely to cause serious harm to a person's physical or mental health, which includes that of the social worker. Requests must be made in writing, may be subject to a fee and should be complied with within 40 days.

Exempt information, meaning information that does not have to be provided, includes:

- personal information about someone else, unless it can be revealed without identifying the individual;

- information that would reveal who had supplied it (except in relation to a health professional, social worker or teacher);

- information required for law enforcement, national security or the prevention of crime;

- adoption reports and records.

Challenge to decisions about personal information held by others can be made to the Information Commissioner, an independent officer who reports directly to Parliament, or, in some circumstances, a court. As a general rule, unless a statutory requirement exists, a decision to disclose merits more rigorous analysis than maintaining confidentiality, even with the consent of the person concerned.

When deciding whether to share information, consider the questions below.

1. Are you legally authorised to hold the information?

2. What are the legal and policy constraints?

3. Are you permitted to share?

4. Are the provisions of Article 8 ECHR relevant?

5. Is it in pursuit of a legitimate aim?

6. Does DPA 1998 apply?

7. Do you have informed consent?

8. If not, do you have a statutory obligation or court order, or is it in the public interest to disclose?

9. If the decision is to disclose, are you sharing necessary and relevant information with the people or agencies who ought to have it?

10. Have you recorded your decision and the reasons for it?

An example of difficulty in maintaining confidentiality in practice arises from the *Public Law Proceedings Guide to Case Management* which states that a local authority should be 'required to demonstrate that it has considered family members when presenting the care plan' (MoJ, 2010, para. 3.8). However, often this cannot be undertaken without sharing confidential information with family members, which normally requires the consent of those concerned. Such dilemmas are particularly likely to arise in the 20 per cent of public law care cases that result in a kinship placement (Masson *et al.*, 2008). Even the concept of family group conferences (see Chapter 5) potentially poses challenges in the context of maintaining confidentiality between family members who may have different knowledge, understanding or interests in the case.

Children and confidentiality

Government guidance (DCSF, 2008, p18) includes criteria to be followed when assessing whether a child or young person has sufficient understanding to consent, or refuse consent, to sharing information about them.

- Can the child or young person understand the question being asked of them?

- Do they have a reasonable understanding of:

    o what information might be shared?;

    o the reasons for sharing it?; and

    o the implications of sharing and of not sharing it?

- Can they:

    o appreciate and consider alternative courses of action open to them?;

    o weigh up one aspect of the situation against another?;

    o express a clear personal view on the matter, as distinct from repeating what someone else thinks they should do?; and

    o be reasonably consistent in their view?

Guidance on the *Common Assessment Framework* (CWDC, 2009) states that a child or young person who has the capacity to understand and make their own decisions may give, or refuse, consent to sharing information. It advises that children aged 12 or over are generally expected to have sufficient understanding, although they may also have it at a younger age. However, this does not absolve you from exercising professional judgement in individual cases.

Consent should not be sought, or subjects informed that information will be divulged, if doing so would (DCSF, 2008, p21):

- place a person at increased risk of significant harm if a child, or serious harm if an adult;

- prejudice the prevention, detection or prosecution of serious crime; or

- lead to unjustified delay in making enquiries about allegations of significant harm to a child, or serious harm to an adult.

You should not seek consent when you are required by law to provide information through a statutory duty or court order, but you should normally follow legal advice in relation to informing the individual concerned that you are sharing the information, why you are doing so, and with whom.

ACTIVITY 2.1

Kate is 16 and you have been working with her for six months. Recently her behaviour has become erratic and she is associating with older men. She has told you that she has been experimenting with drugs and has made some money by selling some to her friends. She says she trusts you and knows you will not tell anyone because you would not want to get her into trouble.

Do you share this information with anyone? If so, how would you go about it? Does your knowledge of the legal and policy framework help you in your decision?

Comment

You should have made the limits to confidentiality clear to Kate at the start of your relationship. In this case, sharing confidential information without consent can be justified in the public interest in order to prevent significant harm to her and potentially serious harm to those to whom she sells drugs. Sharing the information could also contribute to the prevention, detection and prosecution of crime. However, you are in a trusted position and need to be open and honest with Kate to try to protect your working relationship. The reasons why the information has to be shared must be clearly explained so that support can continue to be given to her. They should also be carefully recorded.

Adoption

The Adoption and Children Act 2002 and associated regulations include provision for obtaining, recording and keeping confidential information about adopted children and their birth relatives, including the Adoption Contact Register (s98). Adoption records are exempt from the DPA and normally legal advice should be obtained before any disclosure from adoption records.

Looked-after children

Records relating to looked-after children must be kept until the 75th anniversary of their birth or 15 years from the date of death of a child who dies before the age of 18. DPA guidance (ICO, 2010) suggests that social work support be offered to adults seeking information about their time in care but local authority provision is variable (Kirton *et al.*, 2011). Some give it high priority as a social work task, while others regard it as an administrative responsibility. The 40-day time limit for response is met by less than a third of authorities, with some taking up to six months.

CASE STUDY 2.1

A local authority was issued with a penalty by the Information Commissioner's Office (ICO), following two breaches of the DPA involving the disclosure of confidential and sensitive personal data relating to vulnerable children. The first occurred when the core assessment of one child was sent to the child's sibling instead of to their mother, who lived at the same address. The second breach concerned the inclusion within a child's placement information record (PIR) of their foster carers' address which became known to the child's mother and resulted in the child having to be moved to another placement to ensure their safety. An investigation found that the relationship records on the children's information system were set up so that details of individuals were printed automatically on the assessment unless the user actively prevented it and there was no procedure for checking documents before they were posted. An investigation into the second breach found that the default setting included foster carers' details in the PIR, and there was no procedure for checking it after printing.

(Family Law Week, July 2012, p4)

CASE STUDY 2.2

A Sure Start Children's Centre (SSCC) manager was told that there were 42 children under five with disabilities in her centre's catchment area but the health authority in question would not divulge their names and addresses. As a member of the area's strategic steering group for SSCCs, the manager challenged this, as a result of which the health authority agreed to send an open letter informing the families concerned of the services offered by the SSCC.

(Pinney, 2011, p5)

Government guidance in relation to placement and care planning (HMG, 2010) states that social workers should discuss with parents, any previous carers and children (having regard to their age and understanding), information to be given to foster carers and why. Where there is a specific reason for withholding significant information, it should be recorded. Some of the information that carers need may be difficult to convey, and there could be a temptation to withhold potentially negative information about, for example, a child's past behaviour. However, carers must be informed of factors that might put their home or their family at risk and failure to do so could place the authority at risk of legal action (see *A v Essex County Council* [2003] EWCA Civ 1848 discussed in Chapter 8).

Case records

For some children, and particularly those who are placed permanently away from their family, the case record provides an important narrative of their childhood which is all too frequently lost.

(HMG, 2010, p118)

Local authorities have a responsibility to maintain case records which, in relation to looked-after children, must include (HMG, 2010):

- documents created as part of the assessment process (including health care and education documents);

- any court order relating to the child;

- the first care plan, any changes made to that plan and any subsequent plans (including the health, placement and education plans);

- any arrangements for the local authority's functions to be discharged by an independent provider of fostering or social work services;

- arrangements for contact;

- reports provided during court proceedings, such as guardian's reports and specialist assessments;

- information about educational progress;

- documents used to seek information, provide information or record views given to the authority in the course of planning and reviewing the child's case and review reports;

- records of visits;

- any contribution the child might wish to make; and

- other relevant correspondence.

Although assessment documents and the care plan are included, there is no reference to analysis, professional opinion, evaluation or the rationale for decision-making, all of which form an essential part of social workers' roles and responsibilities. For example, a case record that sets out arrangements for contact without any explanation as to how or why they have been made is of limited use in relation to continuity, accountability, monitoring or evaluation, and would certainly be considered inadequate in a legal context. Records of visits need to be much more than the diary suggested by the terminology used here. This illustrates the difficulties that arise in practice as a result of the proliferation of official guidance, often written by people who do not have full understanding of the context and complexities of social work practice, and which risk concealing the nature and extent of professional responsibilities under a surfeit of procedural requirements.

Although the nature of social work records is increasingly shaped by electronic systems and templates, this does not absolve you of the responsibility to ensure that your recording is clear, comprehensive, honest, fair and, if necessary, capable of standing up to challenge in formal settings.

RESEARCH SUMMARY 2.1

Problems that have been identified in relation to electronic recording systems (Shaw et al., 2009; Munro, 2011; Ince and Griffiths, 2011) include:

- *lack of narrative focus on the child;*

- *fragmentation of the assessment process;*

- *undermining of professional authority and autonomy;*

- *inflexible timescales;*

- *duplication of information where there is more than one family member;*

- *difficulties in translating electronic records into reports for formal contexts, such as courts;*

- *large amount of screen navigation required;*

- *technical problems and restrictions impeding the recording of relevant information;*

- *not obviously supporting reflective practice and professional development.*

A review of the Integrated Children's System (Shaw et al., 2009) reported that social workers found templates 'prescriptive, repetitive, bitty and inclined to divide the story into chunks which were difficult to follow'. Specific problems identified were inaccuracy, duplication and failure to return to gaps if information became known subsequently. Some given categories were thought insufficiently precise (for example, 'mental health difficulties'), standard headings lacked flexibility, certain terminology was considered offensive (such as 'parenting capacity') and it was difficult to share information with service users.

> You don't get a picture of the child and their needs. It is lost in all these questions and jargon.

> *(Social worker)*

A report by OFSTED (2012e) into managerial support for children and families social workers found that few case records did justice to the quality and impact of critical analysis that inspectors identified as taking place, and the extent to which written plans and reviews clearly identified aims and the changes that subsequently occurred was variable.

We consider case recording in the context of inter-professional communication and collaboration in Chapter 10.

Investigation and assessment

The significance of seeing and observing the child cannot be overstated. The child should be spoken and listened to, and their wishes and feelings ascertained, taken into account (having regard to their age and understanding) and recorded when making decisions about the provision of services. Some of the worst failures of the system have occurred when professionals have lost sight of the child and concentrated instead on their relationship with the adults.

(DfE, 2010b, para. 5.5)

You live by the form.

You can't see the wood for the trees, so what doesn't come out is the priority for the child.
(Social workers quoted in Horwath, 2011, p1077)

Under the Children Act 1989 s47 local authorities have a duty to make enquiries if it is suspected that a child is suffering, or is likely to suffer, significant harm. There were 439,800 initial assessments undertaken in the year ending 31 March 2011, 64 per cent of which were completed within seven working days and 77 per cent of which were completed within ten working days. 185,400 core assessments were undertaken, 75 per cent of which were completed within 35 working days (DfE, 2011g).

The initial assessment, which is deemed to be completed once it has been discussed with the child and family or carers and the team manager has authorised the assessment (DfE, 2010b), determines whether:

- the child is in need;

- there is reasonable cause to suspect the child is suffering, or is likely to suffer, significant harm;

- any services are required and of what types; and

- further, more detailed core assessment should be undertaken.

The initial assessment, which should be led by a qualified and experienced social worker, supervised by a highly experienced and qualified social work manager, should be completed within seven working days of the date of the referral. The problem with this is not only that there is no indication of what evidence would satisfy the description 'experienced' or 'highly experienced', but also use of the word 'should'. Does it mean 'must', 'this is what we want you to aim for', or something in between?

The *Framework for the Assessment of Children in Need and Their Families* (DoH, 2000) and *Working Together to Safeguard Children* (DfE, 2010b), state that assessments should include information and analysis to provide evidence on which to base professional judgement about whether, and how best, to intervene to safeguard the child's welfare. Core assessments involving families affected by parental learning disability should include specialist input concerning the impact of learning disability and it is good practice to identify a person or agency that can help the parent understand the process. Assessments should also address the possible vulnerability of the learning disabled parent and their need to be protected from harm (DoH and DfES, 2007).

The Assessment Framework does not state precisely when an initial assessment should progress to a core assessment, which may take up to a further 35 working days. The presumption seems to be that if a child has needs that are likely to require the involvement of more than one agency, then a core assessment should be undertaken. However, as even an initial assessment includes three 'domains' and 20 'dimensions' and should result in a care plan, in practice little difference exists between them, apart from the nature and extent of the involvement of other agencies.

LEGAL CASE STUDY **2.2**

R (AB and SB) v Nottinghamshire CC *[2001] 4 CCLR 295*

In this case the judge commented on the quality of a social work assessment:

> . . . it was essentially a descriptive document rather than an assessment, and in any event sufficient detail was still lacking both as regards the assessment itself and as regards the care plan and service provision. There was no clear identification of needs, or what was to be done about them, by whom and by when.

(para. 43)

The case also established that assessments must address foreseeable future needs as well as present needs.

LEGAL CASE STUDY **2.3**

K v Manchester CC *[2006] EWHC 3164 (Admin)*

This case concerned the adequacy of an assessment of a 15-year-old boy detained in a secure children's home. After K was refused parole when the Parole Board concluded that he would be vulnerable in the community and likely to revert to criminal behaviour, K requested an assessment of his needs by the local authority under the CA 1989 s17 to show the Parole Board that he would have the necessary support when he was released. The assessment concluded that there could be an increase in the risk factors affecting him, depending on the environment in which he found himself on his release but that as 'protective factors' remained in place during his continued placement in the secure home, K had no needs that required the local authority to provide services and his case was closed. The local authority's assessment was quashed on two grounds.

1. *It failed to look to the future.*
2. *It did not comply with the criteria contained within statutory guidance on assessment of children in need by failing to consider all the required domains.*

LEGAL CASE STUDY **2.4**

R (L) v Nottinghamshire CC *[2007] EWHC 2364 (Admin)*

The local authority arranged for a young person who had been turned out of her mother's home to stay for a few days in a local hotel, paid for on the team manager's credit card. Perhaps unsurprisingly, the local authority sought to classify this as 'help with accommodation' under the CA 1989 s17 rather than 'accommodation' under s20 (see Chapter 7). The court stated that it was not open to the local authority to classify her as having been provided with s17 assistance when it had not completed a proper assessment to inform such a decision.

RESEARCH SUMMARY 2.2

Masson et al. (2008) in a survey of court documents relating to public law proceedings found that:

- *initial assessments were referred to in only a quarter of the social work statements filed;*

- *core assessments were found in 43 per cent of the sample, some of which were undated;*

- *only 15 per cent of cases had a core assessment dated within three months of the start of the court proceedings.*

Requirements to carry out initial and core assessments to national timescales have formed the basis of assessment since 2000 and were intended to address deficiencies in assessment identified during the previous decade, including an overly narrow focus on protection at the expense of support and prevention, insufficient attention given to the capacity of parents to meet their children's needs, and inadequate account taken of the inter-relationship between socio-economic factors and the quality of care given to children. The original framework consisted of over 100 pages (subsequently expanded to nearer 300), support materials, practice guidance, questionnaires, scales and templates and was based on the principle that all agencies concerned with the welfare of children should contribute to the assessment and information-sharing process.

However, apart from the fact that inflexible timescales take no account of the individual circumstances of each case and are not a good basis for establishing trusting and constructive professional relationships, the 'question and answer' model of assessment which is encouraged by the use of templates risks being regarded by service users as more of an interrogation than a partnership (Horwath, 2011). Some of the language adopted is imprecise and inclined towards jargon, leading to subjectivity and variations in interpretation.

ACTIVITY 2.2

In the context of assessment frameworks, how would you define the following?

- *Social presentation*

- *Identity*

- *Self-care skills*

- *Seeing the child*

Now ask a colleague to do the same and compare the results. What implication does this have in terms of achieving objectivity in assessments?

Following the recommendations of the Munro report (2010, 2011) that prescriptive requirements discourage autonomy and the exercise of professional judgement, selected local authorities were exempted from statutory assessment timescales for a pilot study which

concluded that flexibility encouraged more thoughtful working practices and clearer consideration of priorities (Munro and Lushey, 2012). A less prescriptive format also:

- improved the narrative and flow of assessments;

- enabled social workers to arrange visits at times that were convenient for children and
families rather than imposing visits on them at short notice to meet organisational
timescales;

- allowed time to engage with children and explore their wishes and feelings;

- increased the scope for additional visits to the child, family or extended family network to
explain what is happening, build rapport and trust, collect and clarify information;

- allowed time to review and reflect on historical information and liaise with, or obtain input
from, other agencies.

PRACTITIONER REFLECTION 2.1

Team manager for looked-after children:

Hopefully we are moving towards a recording system which is driven by professional
requirements rather than vice versa. I hope I never again have social workers complaining
that 'the system won't let me'.

The government is proposing that local authorities conduct assessments to timescales agreed
by social workers and their managers, taking account of the nature of the case, with locally
determined frameworks to ensure that assessments are timely, transparent and proportionate
to need and that a review point is established in each case. *Managing Individual Cases: the
Framework for the Assessment of Children in Need and Their Families* (2012) is published as a
stand-alone document and includes a series of flowcharts setting out how professionals should
manage different types of case. Assessment is to be regarded as an ongoing process which, if
necessary, can provide a framework for care applications and care plans for looked-after
children. Social workers should take into account the child's needs, wishes and feelings, and
agree with fellow professionals when meetings need to be convened, although local authorities
can retain initial and core assessments if they choose. These proposals have not been met with
universal approval. A pressure group, Every Child in Need Campaign, comprised of charities,
campaigners and lawyers, considers that:

> *The legal framework is not 'red tape' – it is an essential safety net for children when they
> are failed by their local authority. Basic minimum national standards and requirements are
> essential. A hands off approach, allowing local authorities to do what they want, when they
> want, is dangerous.*

> (**www.communitycare.co.uk**, 26 July 2012)

CASE STUDY **2.3**

A local authority developed an assessment process to be used during court proceedings, independent of case line management. This was accepted by children's guardians, the judiciary and families as sufficiently independent to reduce the need for externally commissioned assessments in many cases. Two social workers from different teams carried out the assessment, with one taking the lead role and the other undertaking tasks such as direct work. Differences between assessors were carefully mapped so as to ensure that a range of perspectives was included. Initial evaluation suggested that court delays had reduced, permanency planning progressed more quickly, there was less parental hostility towards workers who had had no previous involvement and social workers' confidence and skills had improved.

(OFSTED, 2012e, p44)

Parental responsibility

Parents should be expected and enabled to retain their responsibilities and to remain as closely involved as is consistent with their child's welfare, even if that child cannot live at home either temporarily or permanently.

(HMG, 2010, p3)

The term parental responsibility, introduced by the CA 1989, describes the legal rights, duties, powers and responsibilities that parents have in relation to their child until the age of 18 years (16 years in Scotland). These include determining the child's religious and educational upbringing, where they live and deciding matters such as whether to consent to medical treatment, marriage under the age of majority or to the child travelling abroad.

Mothers and married fathers automatically have parental responsibility, as do unmarried fathers named on the birth certificates of children registered since 1 December 2003 in England and Wales. An unmarried father whose child's birth was registered before these dates, or afterwards if they are not named on the birth certificate, does not automatically have parental responsibility, although he can obtain it by the birth being re-registered, by entering into an agreement with the mother or by having parental responsibility granted by a court. Married step-parents and registered civil partners can gain parental responsibility in the same ways.

Parents do not lose parental responsibility if they divorce. If a child is subject to a care order, those with parental responsibility share it with the local authority, which can limit the extent to which it is exercised, as can a court. The local authority has no parental responsibility for children accommodated under the CA 1989 s20. Adoptive parents, special or testamentary guardians and those holding a residence order all have parental responsibility for the child concerned but only an adoption order has the effect of completely removing parental responsibility from those holding it prior to the order being made.

If a person with parental responsibility refuses to allow a child to be interviewed in the course of a police criminal investigation, and the child is not assessed as competent to give their own consent, the interview cannot take place. In such circumstances the police and the local authority should consider whether to make an application for an Emergency Protection Order under the CA 1989 s44 and to seek a direction from the court for an interview to be undertaken as part of an assessment of the child (MoJ, 2011a, p19).

Professional social work responsibilities in a legal context

In any case involving children, you hold statutory responsibilities to each individual child, their parents and others such as foster carers. In addition you may have responsibilities to society as a whole which override any responsibilities you may have towards service users, colleagues or other professionals. You have professional responsibilities as a result of your registration with the Health and Care Professions Council and you also have responsibilities towards your employer which, as we consider below, may on occasions conflict with your professional ones. Linked to these are the responsibilities that your employer has towards you. All social workers worry about what will happen if something goes wrong. There cannot be a social worker, or indeed any professional, who has not, with the benefit of hindsight, thought they should have done something differently. If you have acted with reasonable care, compiled your records promptly and accurately, followed the guidance and procedures relevant to the situation in question and are qualified to an acceptable level of competence, then there is a good chance that your practice will stand up to scrutiny. However, social work poses many challenges, not all of which can be addressed by consulting legal and policy guidance.

In Chapter 8 we refer to the case of *A v Essex County Council* [2004] 1 WLR 1881. Although this case was concerned with determining points of law arising from the circumstances surrounding a child's placement for adoption, it also emphasised social workers' responsibilities towards people who are affected by the decisions they make (Brayne and Carr, 2010). Doing your best might not always be good enough and you must take the initiative to seek out and understand the legal and policy guidance that is available to support you in working with particular types of case.

LEGAL CASE STUDY **2.5**

Kent County Council v A Mother *[2011] EWHC 402 (Fam)*

Care proceedings were brought in relation to the children of parents, both of whom had a learning disability, and the judge criticised the social workers and their managers for not being aware of, and therefore not having followed, the provisions contained within Good Practice Guidance on Working with Parents with Learning Disabilities (DoH and DfES, 2007).

Re G (Care: Challenge to Local Authority's Decision) *[2003] 2 FLR 42*

In this case the judge said that:

> [W]here for whatever reason – whether physical or mental disability, illiteracy or the fact that English is not their mother tongue – parents cannot readily understand the written word, the local authority must take whatever ameliorative steps are necessary to ensure that the parents are not for that reason prevented from playing a full and informed part in the decision-making process.

(para. 59)

A situation that could potentially pose ethical and professional dilemmas in practice is where decisions have been taken in a case which you as the case social worker feel unable to support on professional grounds. It might be that a child protection conference has made a collective judgement that you feel is unjustified or that a legal planning meeting has recommended a course of action that you do not believe is in the child's best interests or likely to achieve a successful outcome. If you are then expected to take forward actions arising from the decision with which you do not agree, what, if anything, can you do?

The case of *F v Suffolk County Council* [1981] 2 FLR 208 established that social workers are considered by courts as experts in child care issues, although they do not have expert status in relation to the diagnosis of sexual abuse, nor as to whether children's evidence can be accepted. Therefore, if the case is one that has reached the stage of presenting evidence to court, the position is clear: your primary duty is to the court, which requires you to give evidence of your own knowledge and professional opinions, not those of anyone else. You do not have to support the line of the party on whose behalf you are giving evidence if, on professional grounds, you do not, and if the court wishes to hear from your team or service manager or anyone else, they can be called to give evidence and, indeed, should be if their views and decisions are important to the case (Seymour and Seymour, 2011). You must comply with the statement of truth which is attached to any written evidence, and the oath or affirmation that witnesses must make before giving oral evidence in court. However, it is good practice to ensure that your managers and legal representatives are made aware of your views in good time, since it is open to them, if not necessarily wise, to reallocate the case to someone who holds a different view. You should take account of the fact that your evidence will also be assessed against factors such as your qualifications, experience, quality of analysis, consistency, grasp of detail and apparent willingness to assist the court, which is the most important aspect of your role.

In cases that do not involve court proceedings, the situation can be more difficult. As an employee, you must follow the instructions of your managers; if, for example, it is decided by a review that grandparents should be assessed as potential carers for a child and you are instructed to take this forward, then you must do this even if you have doubts as to whether it is likely to be the best way in which to meet the child's needs. It is also important to remain open to other points of view, if necessary with the support of professional supervision, since many social work decisions cannot fully be evaluated without the benefit of hindsight.

Working in situations of conflict

Guidance (DfE, 2010b) makes it clear that local authorities have a responsibility to ensure that children and adults understand what is likely to happen when there are concerns about the welfare or safety of a child, and that information should be provided in the family's preferred language. Additionally, children and families *may* (not *must*) be supported through their involvement in safeguarding processes by advice and advocacy services, and they should be informed of services that exist locally and nationally. However, in practice this can be difficult to achieve, particularly if there is resistance, disagreement or hostility existing between your services users and your agency in general, or you in particular.

RESEARCH SUMMARY 2.3

Lindley et al. (2001) found that pre-proceedings advocacy support for parents whose children were the subject of a child protection plan helped them work with the local authority and facilitated the building of bridges between them. The advocates had a key role in translating jargon, helping explain the nature of the welfare concerns, and providing support at meetings, a particular source of stress.

In studies reviewed by Hunt (2010) parents reported feeling isolated, unsupported, intimidated, alienated and confused by the formality and language of safeguarding procedures, and were overwhelmed by the number of people involved in their affairs. Where there were a number of court hearings, each one tended to reactivate their distress. Many parents, particularly those with learning or language difficulties had little understanding of how to identify a suitable solicitor and were rarely offered advice in how to go about it.

Brophy et al. (2005) found that among parents of children who were the subject of care proceedings, in addition to the fear that having their parenting called into question would become public knowledge, lengthy statements, use of jargon and long waiting times in public areas added to their stress. Parents often associated family courts with crime, particularly when they shared the same building as criminal courts, and many were unclear about the purpose of different types of hearing.

Research into the experiences of children who had been the subject of family court proceedings (OFSTED, 2010b) found that they disliked having strangers discussing their lives and problems and thought that people would assume they were involved in court because they had done something wrong. They would have welcomed prior information about what was likely to happen, who would be present and how long the hearing would last. Comments made to researchers included:

- *'The court made me feel like an ant against a human.'*

- *'It seemed as if my life was in the hands of a random group of strangers.'*

- *'I felt I had to say what they wanted to hear.'*

RESEARCH SUMMARY 2.3 *(CONT.)*

Research undertaken into parents' perceptions of professional practice in public law child care and adoption proceedings (Smeeton and Boxall, 2010) found evidence of deep distress and sense of abandonment: 'I got no support when the kids were taken off me. I got no support when they went up for adoption. I got no support from anywhere at all.'

Monitoring and evaluation

CASE STUDY 2.4

A local authority arranged regular 'audit of practice' days when a cross-section of front-line staff working with children and families met to audit case files and practice, with an emphasis on ownership of professional accountability. Audits focused on 'what difference does it make?' and took account of relevant research. Examination of files audited 18 months previously enabled progress to be assessed over time. Social workers and managers received written feedback on cases on which they had worked and reported feeling proud when their work was commended. Social workers took turns to assume the role of auditor and stated that this had improved their own practice.

(OFSTED, 2012e, p31)

Local authorities administer their own internal evaluation systems, but legal, financial and public accountability requires that their activities are also externally assessed and monitored. The Office for Standards in Education, Children's Services and Skills (OFSTED) reports directly to Parliament on its inspection of children's social care services, including children's homes, family centres, child protection, services for looked-after children, fostering and adoption. From 2013 it is intended that the inspection system will separate child protection services from those for children looked after, which incorporates adoption, fostering and looked-after children. OFSTED, HMI Probation, HMI Constabulary and the Care Quality Commission, with the involvement of HMI Prisons where appropriate, have agreed to develop a joint inspectorate framework for multi-agency inspection of services for the protection of children due to be implemented in 2014. However, you should keep up with developments on OFSTED's website (**www.ofsted.gov.uk**).

Inspection generally tests compliance with relevant regulations, guidance and any national minimum standards, with the focus on the measurement of 'outcomes' and the views of the parents, children and young people who are using the service.

There are four elements to OFSTED's functions:

- registration;

- inspection;

- compliance; and

- enforcement.

Following inspection, inspectors make judgements, including recommendations for improvement, and identify any action required to ensure that provisions fully meet the requirements. However, frequently the standards or requirements are insufficiently specific to be objectively measurable with any degree of precision, which means that it is difficult to know how well you are performing in practice.

ACTIVITY 2.3

As an example, the National Minimum Standards for Fostering Services includes the following 'outcomes' to be assessed during inspection:

> Children can take up issues in the most appropriate way with support, without fear that this will result in adverse consequences. Children receive prompt feedback on any concerns raised and are kept informed of progress.
>
> *(DfE, 2011f, outcome 1.6)*

- *What might constitute an 'issue'?*

- *How would you decide what was 'the most appropriate way?'*

- *Who should provide 'support' and what form should it take?*

- *What would come within the definition of 'adverse consequences'?*

- *How does 'feedback on concerns' and being 'kept informed of progress' relate to effective action being taken?*

- *What length of time would meet the description of 'prompt' in this context?*

This activity illustrates that general guidance and overarching standards are no substitute for the exercise of competent professional knowledge, skills and judgement. Many of the other outcomes contained within these standards pose similar difficulties, as do those of Every Child Matters (DfES, 2003).

The concept of targets is also problematic in terms of assessing the quality of professional practice. For example, a target formulated to indicate the effectiveness of child protection procedures related to the proportion of children who were made the subject of second or subsequent child protection plans after having a period without one, the implication being that the decision to remove the child from the register was unsound. However, such a target could prove counter-productive in that children might remain subject to child protection plans for longer than was necessary to avoid the risk of an adverse judgement if a further plan was later found to be required.

From an individual social worker's point of view, an important aspect of evaluation is timely, comprehensive and objective recording which enables the agency to monitor what is happening in each of the cases on which you are working. Equally important in the context of complex decision-making is effective use of supervision.

RESEARCH SUMMARY 2.4

A report by OFSTED (2012e) into the nature and quality of the management of children and families social workers identified the following key aspects of effective support:

- clearly defined standards and expectations were accompanied by systematic performance audits and evaluation of the quality of practice and supervision;

- regular and high-quality line management support and supervision were most effective when staff were helped to manage the emotional impact of the work and to critically reflect on practice;

- social workers considered that scrutiny and knowledgeable challenge were integral to them feeling confident in exercising professional judgement.

FURTHER READING

www.ofsted.gov.uk

OFSTED provides copies of inspection reports and reviews, both specific and thematic, and a large amount of information relevant to regulation and compliance.

Chapter 3
Relationships

CHAPTER OBJECTIVES

This chapter aims to demonstrate that the nature and quality of professional relationships, whilst increasingly influenced by law and policy, nevertheless continue primarily to depend on individual input and interpretation. We consider the extent to which the law shapes relationships within society and, in particular, the need to keep up with case law as it adapts to reflect changing values, attitudes and political priorities. The chapter supports the requirements of the PCF and, in particular, those of the Values and Ethics, Diversity, and Intervention and Skills domains.

Introduction

Continuity of relationships is important and attachments should be respected, sustained and developed. A change of home, carer, social worker or school almost always carries some risk to a child's development and welfare.

(HMG, 2010, p3)

Social work owes much to the fact that since its transition from the historical models of charitable relief it has been firmly rooted in the belief that professional therapeutic relationships, which are necessarily authoritative, controlled and time-limited, are effective vehicles for change. Theorists such as Florence Hollis (1981) laid the foundation for the psychosocial casework model which has strongly influenced social work training over the past 50 years, and the Barclay Report (1982), set up to define social workers' role and tasks, drew a distinction between the 'counselling' or 'casework' element of social work practice and what it described as the 'social care planning' component, whilst promoting the potential for 'neighbourhood social work' to support and develop local networks. However, although there has been interest in other theoretical perspectives, the community relationship model has not progressed to any significant extent, particularly outside the voluntary sector.

The international definition of social work still includes the key concept of 'problem-solving in human relationships . . . utilising theories of human behaviour and social systems' (**http://ifsw.org/policies/definition-of-social-work/**), professional codes of practice promote the principle of relationship-based social work, and service users consistently emphasise the value they place on the quality of their relationship with their social worker (Parr, 2009; DCSF, 2010c; and others).

Professional social work relationships incorporate (Wilson *et al.*, 2008):

- recognition of the uniqueness of each individual service user;
- understanding of the relationship between service users and their social circumstances;
- the nature of the social worker's relationship with individual service users; and
- the nature of the social worker's relationship with the organisational, social and political context in which they practise.

However, it is impossible to approach the concept of relationships in social work without also taking account of the increasing impact of statutory requirements, economic constraints, managerial controls, targets, procedures and bureaucracy, particularly in relation to the identification and management of risk.

ACTIVITY 3.1

In relation to the following circumstances, which you may encounter as a social worker, consider how, and to what extent, the nature of the relationship may be influenced or controlled by statutory provision:

- *A health visitor is unwilling to provide a written statement for a multi-agency meeting of the concerns about a family that she has expressed by telephone.*

- *A looked-after child who has been frightened by police involvement in the past tells you that he has stolen some alcohol from a shop.*

- *A mother with whom you have been working for some months refuses to allow you to see her children's bedrooms.*

- *A girl who has recently left care after being looked after for several years has been evicted from her accommodation as a result of holding frequent and noisy all-night parties and not paying her rent.*

- *Foster carers who have successfully looked after a large number of children in the past tell you that they do not want to have any more children from Bangladesh placed with them as it is too difficult to meet their dietary requirements.*

- *It is the deadline for you to complete an initial assessment and a looked-after child review. You will not have time to do both and your team manager is on leave.*

- *Your cross-examination in court will extend over lunchtime into the afternoon. A colleague wants to meet you for lunch so she can 'hear all about it' and give you some support.*

- *A worker from a drug and alcohol agency refuses to discuss the barring of your service user from the agency premises, due to confidentiality.*

ACTIVITY 3.1 (CONT.)

Comment

This exercise shows that many relationships in social work are subject to statutory influence, if not direct control. For example, whatever you might think about the need for the girl who has been evicted to accept some responsibility for her actions, your continuing duty towards her is defined by statutory provision. Similarly, however much you may welcome support, court rules prevent witnesses from discussing any aspect of a court hearing whilst they are in the course of giving evidence or being cross-examined.

Social workers understand that working with people incorporates uncertainty, ambiguity and the exercise of professional judgement, which often cannot be evaluated without the benefit of hindsight. For the most part, however, the law seeks to minimise or eradicate risk by identifying circumstances in which it may appear to exist and defining actions which may, may not or must be taken in response to it. Any of these actions potentially can influence the nature of the service provided and, consequently, the quality of the relationships established between social workers, service users, other professionals, stakeholders and colleagues. However, as we have seen and will continue to do so throughout the text, the law can be imprecise, unclear, inconsistent or confusing. It can never anticipate all the circumstances that you will face in situations which are uniquely shaped by the individual qualities of those involved. Courts spend much of their time trying to establish how the law applies to a unique set of individual circumstances, particularly in the family courts, and they do not always get it right, which you can see evidenced in many Appeal Court judgements. Often, the pace of legal change does not match that of social work practice and attitudes within society as a whole. For example, adoption legislation was slow to respond to the recognition in the 1980s that few children being placed for adoption were small babies and therefore the question of maintaining relationships with their birth families needed to be addressed.

Parent–child relationships

The Children Act 1989 substituted the concept of 'parental responsibility' for that of 'parental rights' to reflect the fact that children were no longer regarded as possessions of their parents but, rather, as having individual needs and entitlements which can only properly be discharged within a parental relationship stemming from the exercise of responsibility rather than rights. However, policy development and audit in the field of child and family social work has moved increasingly towards 'outcome' focused practice which has produced what Broadhurst and Holt (2010, p98) describe as 'an abstract and disembodied approach to parenting which has become increasingly constructed in terms of a set of techniques to be taught rather than understood in terms of relationships that operate across gender and generation'.

The provisions of the CA 1989 also stem from the principle that children are best brought up within their own families if possible, which reflects a belief that a child's relationship with their parent is generally superior in welfare terms to any that can be substituted by the state. If a local authority does assume parental responsibility for a child as a result of a care order (CA,

1989, s31), it is not removed from those who hold it and there is a presumption in favour of contact being maintained with the birth family unless the child is adopted. However, as we show in Chapter 9 in the case of *Gillick v West Norfolk & Wisbech Area Health Authority* [1986] AC 112, the law has defined the tapering nature of the parent–child relationship and acknowledged the difficulties inherent in making hard and fast rules in this context.

LEGAL CASE STUDY 3.1

The judgement in Re C (A Child) *[2011] EWCA Civ 521 set out the principles established in case law in the context of the relationship between parent and child when they are not living together:*

- Contact between parent and child is a fundamental element of family life and is almost always in the interests of the child;

- Contact between parent and child is to be terminated only in exceptional circumstances, where there are cogent reasons for doing so and when there is no alternative. Contact is to be terminated only if it will be detrimental to the child's welfare;

- There is a positive obligation on the state, and therefore on the court, to take measures to maintain and to reconstitute the relationship between parent and child, in short, to maintain or restore contact. The judge has a positive duty to attempt to promote contact. The judge must grapple with all the available alternatives before abandoning hope of achieving some contact. He must be careful not to come to a premature decision, for contact is to be stopped only as a last resort and only once it has become clear that the child will not benefit from continuing the attempt;

- The court should take a medium-term and long-term view and not accord excessive weight to what appear likely to be short-term or transient problems;

- All that said, at the end of the day the welfare of the child is paramount; the child's interest must have precedence over any other consideration.

(para. 47)

Nevertheless, in the case in question, direct contact between a three-year-old child and her mother was terminated, although indirect contact was to continue.

LEGAL CASE STUDY 3.2

However, in the case of Re A & D *[2010] EWHC 2503 (Fam) the judge said:*

The local authority is under a duty to allow reasonable contact between a child in care and his parents: CA 1989 section 34(1). In determining an application for contact under section 34(3), the court must apply the provisions of section 1. The child's welfare is the paramount consideration. The factors in section 1(3) must be given their due weight and the court under section 1(5) must not make the order unless it considers that doing so

LEGAL CASE STUDY 3.2 *(CONT.)*

would be better for the child than making no order at all. Guidance as to the exercise of its discretionary powers was given by Butler-Sloss LJ, as she then was, in *Re B (Minors) (Contact: Local Authority's Plans)* [1993] 1FLR 543. Although that authority is now nearly twenty years old, the guidelines remain important:

> *Contact applications generally fall into two main categories – those which ask for contact as such and those which are attempts to set aside the care order itself. In the first category there is no suggestion that the applicant wishes to take over the care of the child and the issue of contact often depends on whether the contact would frustrate the long term plans for the child in a substitute home such as adoption where continuing contact may not be for the long term welfare of the child. The presumption of contact which has to be for the benefit of the child has always to be balanced against the long term welfare of the child particularly where he will live in the future. Contact must not be allowed to de-stabilise or endanger the arrangements for the child and in many cases the plans for the child will be decisive on the contact application. There may also be cases where the parent is having satisfactory contact with the child and there are no long term plans or those plans do not appear to the court to preclude some future contact. The proposals of the local authority based on their appreciation of the best interests of the child must command the greatest respect and consideration from the court but Parliament has given to the court, and not the local authority, the duty to decide on contact between the child and those named in section 34(1).*
>
> *(paras 45–47)*

Family relationships

Prior to the enactment of the CA 1989, social workers generally adhered to a philosophical belief in the importance of the nuclear and extended family as the most effective way in which to provide for a child's needs throughout their childhood and, as we have seen, this is now incorporated within statute.

LEGAL CASE STUDY 3.3

The case of Re H [2010] EWCA Civ 1200 highlights two developing principles in family law. First, a child's right to know who is within their family and second, the significance of sibling relationships, both of which form part of a child's right to a private and family life. The right of a child to have key information in respect of their identity is also recognised as one of the factors to be considered in the context of a child's emotional needs.

The applicant, H, was the adult half sister of two children aged 10 and 9. They shared a mother but had different fathers. The younger children lived with their father and his new partner and had not seen their mother or half sister for several years. H applied to the court

LEGAL CASE STUDY **3.3** *(CONT.)*

for contact with her half siblings. CAFCASS prepared a report confirming that the children did not know that they had a half sister and had limited and incomplete knowledge of their maternal family and recommended that the children should be given information about their family with indirect contact to be initiated with their half sister and managed by CAFCASS. The father objected to this proposal on the basis that it would re-open potentially negative memories for the children of their maternal family. Initially the court decided that there was no real benefit to the children in knowing about their half sister and that the father should be allowed to determine what his children knew about their family. The half sister appealed. The judge, in allowing the appeal, decided that the original court had given insufficient weight to the right of the children to a wider family life, which would include their half sister, and had erred in placing the father's anxiety above the potential benefits for the children. He ordered that H be introduced to the children through indirect contact over a period of six months, managed by CAFCASS.

Relationships with children

Social workers need to cultivate the attitudes and attributes required to act as the responsible, committed, insightful, positive, passionate, energetic and tenacious individuals which all children in care deserve and which they require if they are to see the true value of relationships in achieving their full potential.

(Winter, 2009, p458)

What is needed is a corporate parenting framework that places emphasis on the positive experiences of being parented, cared about and nourished rather than on the bureau-cratisation of service delivery. Reviews should be regarded as part of a process that helps to build relationships and foster effective communication rather than an administrative necessity.

(Leeson, 2010)

Lord Laming (2003) emphasised the importance of relationships with children in the context of effective child protection and it is an essential aspect of most social work activities with children and families.

The *Common Assessment Framework* (DoH, 2000, para. 3.42) sets out five key components of direct work with children, most of which can only successfully be undertaken in the context of a mutually trusting and consistent relationship:

- seeing children;
- observing children;
- engaging children;
- talking to children;
- activities with children.

RESEARCH SUMMARY 3.1

Mantle et al. (2007) explored how family court social workers sought to reduce the effects of parental influence on children who were the subject of family court proceedings. They identified the importance of establishing trust and rapport so that points of reference, including the existence of attachments which might affect children's views, could be identified. Clear expectations, accurate appraisal of maturity and verbal skills such as reflecting, challenging and summarising were also significant.

An inspection by OFSTED (2012c) of local authority services for disabled children found that contact between the child and social worker was limited in some cases, with insufficient use made of information from professionals who had a good knowledge of the child and their circumstances and could advocate on their behalf. Where children could not communicate directly, or had profound and complex disabilities, careful and close observation by people who knew the children well was key to interpreting their behaviour and building up a picture of children's lives.

ACTIVITY 3.2

In relation to the case studies below, identify the factors that influence the development of productive relationships between the professionals, volunteer panel members and young people concerned. Does policy and guidance assist or hinder practice in this context? Would any changes in law or policy help minimise any barriers you have identified?

1. *James was 12 when he accepted responsibility for causing danger to road users by knocking over bollards and temporary road signs. Subsequently, he and his father attended a youth offending panel meeting at which the Chair was made aware of the fact that James had been found by the Youth Offending Team (YOT) worker to be difficult to engage and communicate with. Initially, in an attempt to put James at ease, the Chair did most of the talking. James was not encouraged to join in and he appeared uninterested and impassive. Later he was asked about his interests and spoke authoritatively and enthusiastically for several minutes about his enjoyment of rollerblading and trampolining. However, when discussion reverted to the offences, he became monosyllabic or silent altogether. As a result the panel learned nothing about what had triggered the offending or what James now thought about it. In an interview with a researcher after the meeting James continued to appear awkward and unsure, looking to his father for responses to the simple questions asked.*

2. *Sam was 11 when he admitted to causing harassment, alarm and distress. At the hour-long youth offending panel meeting he was unresponsive and withdrawn and towards the end he started to bite the raised letters on his sweatshirt, gradually tearing them off with his teeth. Panel members ignored this behaviour and at the conclusion of the meeting Sam was given a sheet of closely typed paper detailing what would be required of him as part of the referral order imposed. The YOT worker asked Sam if he could read and when he said 'no' she spent twenty minutes going through the list with*

ACTIVITY **3.2** *(CONT.)*

him, even though it was clear that his attention span had been exhausted and he wanted to leave.

(Newbury, 2011)

Comment

In relation to James you might consider factors such as the age of criminal responsibility, the principles underpinning the youth justice system, the process by which a youth offending panel operates, what preparation James might have had and how he was supported and treated at the meeting. Also relevant is knowledge of human growth and development, including James's level of maturity, his social, educational and behavioural needs and the attention span required to take a full part in such a meeting.

Sam, too, is very young to be expected to absorb so much at any one time. The panel seems uncertain as to how formal the proceedings should be and it is not clear whether the emphasis should rest primarily on Sam's welfare needs or on addressing his offending behaviour. The process assumes that participants can read and absorb important information in a short space of time and no thought seems to have been given to how any stress or anxiety experienced by Sam could be mitigated.

CASE STUDY **3.1**

In an effort to improve and nurture the relationships between looked-after children and their social workers, a summer activity day was organised for both groups at which the emphasis was on having fun, and all talk about 'official' matters was banned.

This example demonstrates recognition of the fact that the legal and policy framework of social work can impede the development of the kinds of relationship with social workers that are often sought by children and young people, particularly when in the role of 'corporate parent'.

Interviewing children in more formal contexts

An ability to communicate effectively is an essential skill for social workers. However, so varied are the circumstances in which such communication takes place that the range of skills required is wide. Official guidance in the context of interviewing children more formally, other than for assessment purposes, is primarily concerned with the need to obtain information that can be used as evidence in the course of a criminal investigation, and as such has limitations in terms of its usefulness to social workers. However, it does offer a framework based on psychological research which can contribute to your professional communication 'toolkit', particularly in relation to questioning techniques (MoJ, 2011a).

ACTIVITY *3.3*

Consider which specific communication and interviewing skills might be applicable to the situations given below. Do any official guidelines exist to help you? How might you seek to improve your practice so as to develop the range of options available to you in such circumstances and defend your actions against possible future challenge?

- *A 7-year-old child has been referred by a head teacher as being very distressed and refusing to go home.*

- *A looked-after child aged 8 is approaching their statutory review.*

- *A 16-year-old boy has arrived at reception, saying he has been turned out of his home and has nowhere to go.*

- *A child of 6 who is the subject of child protection procedures needs their wishes and feelings assessed.*

- *Prior to a 9-year-old child's planned adoption placement, you have been asked to undertake life story work.*

- *A young person of 14 with whom you are working has been a victim of a serious assault and needs to be supported as a witness in a criminal trial.*

The Home Office's original *Memorandum of Good Practice* (1992) on interviewing children for the purposes of criminal investigation followed the recommendations of the Cleveland Report and was based on the premise that professionals (primarily police and social workers) should work together to enable children to tell their story, taking account of their individual cognitive, linguistic and emotional needs. It recognised the need to consider children's needs separately from those of adults and promoted a process of building a rapport, followed by free narrative, questioning and closure, supported if necessary by prompts and open questions.

RESEARCH SUMMARY *3.2*

Evaluative research (Aldridge and Wood, 1998) showed police officers to be enthusiastic about the guidance while social workers expressed concern that the child's welfare needs were being overlooked in favour of producing data suitable for court. It was felt by both groups that the skills needed to interview young children were very different from those needed to interview teenagers and that specific guidance for children at different developmental stages would be useful.

The *Memorandum* was revised by *Achieving Best Evidence in Criminal Proceedings* (MoJ, 2011a) which promotes the practice of semi-structured interviews, supported by the use of free recall. Free recall requires the interviewer to invite the child to talk, without suggesting or directing them to a particular topic, for example, by saying 'What shall we talk about?' which helps to develop a situation in which the child does most of the talking and the interviewer does most of the listening.

Guidance on the questioning of children during the course of family court proceedings is also applicable to less formal settings in which information is sought from children or their views ascertained (FJC, 2011):

- go at the child's pace consistent with their understanding, which should be continually checked;
- use simple common words and phrases;
- repeat names and places frequently;
- ask one short question or focus on one idea at a time;
- let the child know the subject of the question;
- follow a structured approach, signposting the subject;
- avoid negatives;
- avoid repetition;
- avoid suggestion or leading, including 'tag', questions;
- avoid 'do you remember?' questions;
- avoid restricted choice questions;
- allow sufficient time to answer;
- be alert to literal interpretation;
- take care with times, numbers and frequency;
- avoid asking the child to demonstrate intimate touching on his or her own body (if such a question is essential, an alternative method, such as pointing to a body outline, should be agreed beforehand).

Formal interviews should be conducted with prior planning if possible. In the rapport stage, the interviewer seeks to establish a relationship with the child, the interview aims are explained through ground rules, and the child's social, cognitive and emotional development are assessed. During the free narrative stage the interviewer offers open-ended invitations to speak so that interviewer direction or influence is minimised. The questioning stage starts with open-ended questions which may be followed by closed and, if help with focusing is needed, leading questions although they are generally to be avoided if possible. The guidance contains detailed advice on questioning techniques, and specifically those that might be helpful when inter-viewing children. For example, invitations to 'imagine' or 'let's pretend' should not be used where factual information is sought as they suggest fantasy or play; drawings, pictures, photographs, symbols, dolls, figures and props should be used with caution and never combined with leading questions (MoJ, 2011a, p89). In the closure stage, after summarising, checking understanding and any necessary clarification, the child should be offered the opportunity to ask questions before the interviewer turns to more neutral topics with the aim of leaving the child in a reasonably relaxed state of mind.

General factors to be assessed and explored prior to interviewing a child in a formal context

- *preferred name/form of address;*
- *ability and willingness to talk within a formal interview setting;*
- *the reason for the interview;*
- *ground rules for the interview;*
- *an opportunity to practise answering open questions;*
- *level of the child's cognitive, social and emotional development;*
- *the child's use of language and understanding of relevant concepts such as truth and time;*
- *any special needs the child may have;*
- *the child's competency to give consent to interview and/or medical examination.*

(MoJ, 2011a, p27)

Relationships with adults

Within child and family social work, relationships with adults are as important as those with children. In a consultation exercise, service users stated that what mattered to them most in terms of social work intervention was the quality of their relationship with their social worker, which depended primarily on the social worker's availability and reliability rather than any particular knowledge or skills (Wilson *et al.*, 2008, p2). Although it is important to be aware of the provisions of the Equality Act 2010, particularly in relation to service users' experiences as members of society, accepted standards of anti-discriminatory practice in social work generally are significantly higher than the legal minimum. Your ability to work with professional integrity within the relevant legal framework in these circumstances depends to a considerable extent on being able to identify, engage with and critically reflect on the dilemmas it presents. However, inevitably work with children and families will sometimes be the source of tension, mistrust and even open hostility between adult service users, social workers and the agencies they represent.

LEGAL CASE STUDY 3.4

The judgement in Re D (A Child) *[2010] EWCA Civ 1000 provides an illustration of the approach expected by courts in such circumstances:*

Mother's hostility to social workers raises a problem which is all too familiar in the family courts. A parent whose capacity to care for his or her children is put in question is likely to resent it. Social services on the other hand have a duty to inquire and in some circumstances to take action. Often there will be an important question whether, with a measure of support, the parent or parents can achieve good enough parenting. If the

LEGAL CASE STUDY 3.4 *(CONT.)*

parent has become resentful of the social workers whether for good cause or for bad, it will for that reason be that much more difficult to provide support. This very often leads to the parent being criticised for lack of cooperation with the social workers, and, in turn, to the parent's resentment of the social workers' intrusion growing rather than diminishing. It becomes a vicious circle. It can sometimes then be easy for social workers to think that an uncooperative parent is for that reason also an inadequate parent, but the one does not follow from the other. A refusal to do the social workers' bidding or even to be polite to them, whilst it may be regrettable, is not by itself any justification for the making of the care order. It may of course contribute in some cases to the unhappy conclusion that there is no scenario in which the parent can be supported to the extent that he or she needs. In other cases it may contribute to the yet more unhappy conclusion that the anger displayed towards the social workers is simply an example of generalised angry violence to which the children are likely to be subject as well. But neither of those conclusions are necessary ones. It all depends on the facts of the case. It is not uncommon for hostility and lack of cooperation to be confined to those who are perceived, however unfairly, to be wrongly interfering in the family; and if that is the case it is quite often possible to find other agencies who can establish a working relationship with the parent and provide the necessary support. To try to do that is part of the job of the social worker.

(para. 15)

ACTIVITY 3.4

The importance of developing a cooperative working relationship is emphasised so that parents or caregivers feel respected and informed; they believe staff are being open and honest with them and in turn they are confident about providing vital information about their child, themselves and their circumstances. The consent of children or their parents/caregivers, where appropriate, should be obtained for sharing information unless to do so would place a child at risk of suffering significant harm. Similarly, decisions should also be made with their agreement, whenever possible, unless to do so would place the child at risk of suffering significant harm.

(DfE, 2010b, p135)

On first reading, this extract from Working Together to Safeguard Children *contains a clear expectation that children and families social workers will establish relationships with service users to facilitate participation and partnership. However, look carefully and you will see that not all is as it seems.*

- *How is it to be established that parents or caregivers 'feel respected and informed'?*

- *Believing that staff are being open and honest is not the same as 'staff actually being open and honest'.*

ACTIVITY 3.4 *(CONT.)*

- It is often not possible to decide whether information is 'vital' without the benefit of hindsight.

- What criteria are to be used to decide whether it is 'appropriate' to obtain the consent of children or their parents/caregivers?

- Who can decide that it is not possible to make decisions 'with their agreement'?

- Is there any means of redress for those who feel they have been poorly served in these circumstances?

This example, one of many occurring in official documents, shows that despite the existence of vast quantities of guidance and policy, much of it is worded too vaguely to be of much practical use.

Professional relationships

Workplace relationships

The relationships that you have with colleagues are influenced by legal, policy, organisational, managerial, resource and personal factors. In a legal context you have an obligation to do the job for which you are employed to a competent standard and to follow any reasonable instructions. Your employer has responsibilities towards you, in the context of the amount of work you are expected to undertake, the resources necessary to do this and any risks to which you may be exposed whilst carrying out your duties as an employee. You also have rights not to be discriminated against or harassed. However, this is a complex area in which you should seek specialist advice if necessary. What is made clear by studies and research is that productive and supportive personal workplace relationships are an essential element of effective social work with children and families.

RESEARCH SUMMARY 3.3

OFSTED (2012e) reported on the extent to which organisational culture impacted on child protection work in children's social care services. Local authorities which had created a relationship-based culture in which there was an emphasis on mutual respect, an 'open door' management style, shared responsibility for risk and recognition of the emotional impact of the work, achieved the most effective results in terms of measurable improvement in families. The crucial role of social work team colleagues in providing practical, emotional and intellectual support and in promoting continuity for service users was also highlighted. This was contrasted with what Munro (2011) described as blame cultures in which social workers feared criticism and became defensive in their practice. Managers played an important role in facilitating a strong supervision culture through clear standards and policies and in scrutinising and challenging plans and decisions which front-line staff stated made them feel less anxious, safer and more confident.

CASE STUDY **3.2**

A baby was made subject to a child protection plan following the making of a supervision order by the family proceedings court. Given the continuing uncertainty as to how the injury which led to the care proceedings had occurred, anxiety about the level of risk remained high. The social worker was honest with her manager about her worries about what would happen 'if anything went wrong' and effective supervision enabled her to feel confident as the lead professional that the plan was robust and realistic. Consequently she was able to 'keep the child at the centre of my thinking, rather than my fears' and work with colleagues from partner agencies who were anxious about their own roles and responsibilities.

Children's guardians

As we will explore in Chapter 10, much of the legal and policy framework within which you work requires or encourages the cultivation of collaborative and cooperative relationships with other professionals. However, as a social worker you possess discrete and specific knowledge and skills, derived from training and experience, which are not necessarily held by other professionals, although there is likely to be overlap which can, in itself, be a source of tension. As we saw in the previous chapter, this specialist knowledge is recognised in law as entitling you to be regarded as an expert in relation to children's welfare (*F v Suffolk County Council* [1981] 2 FLR 208), which means that on occasions you may find yourself in disagreement with other experts, such as a children's guardian. This, in itself, should not be a cause of anxiety, providing you are able to justify and defend your opinions, act fairly and transparently, remain open to alternative points of view and remember that your primary duty is to assist the court. However, it does mean that some of your professional relationships might not fall strictly within the definition of cooperation or collaboration, since a degree of assertiveness may be necessary on your part in order to fulfil your professional responsibilities as an expert.

PRACTITIONER REFLECTION **3.1**

CAFCASS manager:

Family courts can appear to have a club-like atmosphere, with much of the business conducted between the same small group of people. As members of that group, children's guardians usually are in good standing with judges, magistrates and lawyers, whereas social workers tend to be more fleeting visitors who have to prove themselves every time.

As children's guardians usually come from the same professional background as social workers and are working to the same goal (the best interests of the child), it might be expected that working relationships between them would be relatively straightforward. However, it is not surprising in view of the complexity of much of the work that this is not always the case and it is important to anticipate, and thus minimise, potential areas of difficulty, so that they do not detract from the shared aim of achieving the best, or occasionally least unsatisfactory, decision for the child or children concerned. In many situations, professional differences can contribute to more robust decision-making in that they can provide a framework for constructive debate and the opportunity seriously to consider alternative points of view.

RESEARCH SUMMARY 3.4

Beckett et al. *(2007) found that it was often perceived by social workers that courts gave more weight to guardians' views, even if based on more limited evidence:*

> It's almost like the proceedings is the start of involvement. They don't see involvement as being you've tried for years to make a difference with this family. You can give them a load of history . . . and it just seems to be wiped away.

> I've heard the judge say 'this is the expert on the child'. And you just sit there and your blood boils.

> It's nine times out of ten guaranteed that guardians have more status within the court proceedings than a social worker who has far more contact with the child and the family.

However, Stanley (2004) found that overt disagreement between professionals was rare, and differences of opinion as between children's guardians and local authority social workers tended to be explored and negotiated positively.

Legal advice and representation

As social work with children and families is so firmly based within a legal and policy framework, it is likely that receiving and acting upon legal advice, and being legally represented on occasions, will form part of your professional role. Although it is unlikely that you will seek legal advice directly yourself, at least initially, it is important that you are able to establish constructive professional relationships with people whose training, experience and personal attributes are different from your own. As shown in Table 3.1, your role and responsibilities contrast with those of lawyers in a number of significant respects. In addition, some of the people you encounter from the legal team may be legal executives or paralegals and therefore not bound by the tight professional codes of conduct which govern barristers and solicitors (Bar Council, 2004; SRA, 2011).

Table 3.1 Contrasting roles of expert witness and lawyer

Expert witness (social worker)	Lawyer
Independent	Partisan
Neutral	Puts client's case
Knows social work, not law	Knows law, not social work
Never argues	Argues if necessary
Assists court	Persuades court
Not a 'hired gun'	Paid by, or on behalf of, client
Can coach lawyer in understanding case	Cannot coach social worker as witness

(Bond *et al.*, 2007, p62)

RESEARCH SUMMARY **3.5**

Dickens (2005, 2006) explored how local authority social workers, their managers and lawyers worked together in family cases. Generally inter-professional relationships worked well, but tensions were never far from the surface and the strongest criticisms from social workers were directed at lawyers who appeared unwilling to listen to and respect the social workers' opinions. Less experienced social workers and those who felt they were getting insufficient guidance from their own managers looked to lawyers for practical and emotional support and most also wanted them to be strong advocates in court. Some lawyers, however, felt unhappy about being drawn into social work issues: 'It clearly got to the stage where I wasn't advising on legal issues at all . . . I was trying to prop up someone who wasn't receiving support from their own manager' (Dickens, 2006, p29).

A potential area of tension is the precise nature of the relationship between you and the lawyers representing you, or more accurately your employers, since it is they who pay the bill. In most lawyer/client relationships the client gives instructions, considers the advice offered and decides how they wish to proceed in the light of the advice, subject to any constraints such as cost. However it can sometimes be unclear who exactly is the client (you, your line manager, a service manager or your employer as a whole, who might also be the lawyer's employer) and it is sensible to clarify your position and the decision-making process in your agency at the outset. The rapid pace of organisational change in most social care departments means that anyone not directly employed by your agency will not be as up-to-date as you are in relation to matters such as management structure, resources, terminology, financial control, monitoring, eligibility criteria, recording systems and any partnerships that exist with other agencies (Seymour and Seymour, 2011).

PRACTITIONER REFLECTION **3.2**

Child protection team manager:

In care proceedings in which the mother of the child concerned was herself looked after, the cross-examination of the social worker on behalf of the mother and the children's guardian focused on the services, or lack of them, provided to the mother, even though this was not my team's responsibility. We also get questioned about other service areas such as mental health or adult learning disability teams.

LEGAL CASE STUDY **3.5**

DL & Anor v Newham LBC *[2011] EWHC 1127 (Admin)*

In this case, in which prospective adopters (the claimants) were challenging a local authority's decision to remove a child from their care, the judge referred to deficiencies in the local authority's evidence and emphasised the role of legal advisers in supporting social workers with the production of evidence:

LEGAL CASE STUDY 3.5 *(CONT.)*

Sadly, I have to record that the evidence put in by the local authority and its disclosure fell well below the standards that the court and the claimants are entitled to expect. I was told that part of the reason for the deficiencies was the electronic storage of records and the legal department's access to them. It is not fair on the social worker or appropriate to place on him the obligation of extracting all relevant material. He is not trained for this and the exercise should be carried out, or supervised and checked, by a lawyer or other suitably trained and experienced person.

(paras 40–42)

Understanding each professional's role, whatever their background, is essential if you are to maximise your own effectiveness. Brammer (2010) suggests that barriers to effective relationships between social workers and lawyers would be reduced by joint training, multi-disciplinary interest groups, dissemination of information such as legal fact sheets, and clarification of roles and responsibilities. It would be worth meeting with a children's guardian and a local authority lawyer outside any actual legal proceedings to gain an understanding of their responsibilities and explore potential areas of misunderstanding or tension. Also important is an appreciation of the need for far-reaching decisions to be tested by as many means as possible, although this can conflict with the principle of avoiding delay. Ultimately, in much child and family social work there is no *right* answer, or at least little possibility of a result that can be evaluated without the benefit of hindsight (Seymour and Seymour, 2011). Beckett *et al.* (2007) argue that the quality of decision-making, and also, we would add, the challenges arising from working with others, would benefit from (our italics):

- a less adversarial approach *on the part of everyone, both inside and outside formal decision-making arenas*;

- better support for participants (also highlighted by Dickens, 2006), *particularly service users*;

- information from the present being seen in the context of what has happened in the past, *particularly by courts and other professionals. High quality social work recording and reporting is essential in this context.*

In addition, Dickens concludes, and we agree, that the valuing of difference, rather than its avoidance or suppression, is at the heart of effective inter-professional relationships:

Differences of opinion and ways of working can be productive, sometimes supporting workers and sometimes challenging them, but always pushing them to reflect on, and account for, their beliefs and practices.

(2006, p30)

FURTHER READING

www.cfswp.org

The Centre for Social Work Practice aims to develop and sustain relationship-based practice in contemporary social work.

Chapter 4
Participation

CHAPTER OBJECTIVES

This chapter supports the PCF requirement for social workers to engage in ethical decision-making, which includes seeking to establish partnerships with people who use their services. It explores the ethical dilemmas presented by this concept and considers how it is reflected in policy and case law. Within this chapter we are primarily concerned with participation of service users at an individual level. Inter-professional communication and collaboration is considered in Chapter 10.

Introduction

Although the value base of social work has always embraced the concept of empowerment and self-determination, developments in law and policy incorporate a significant shift towards collaborative and partnership-based practice, together with a weakening of the traditional notion of the 'professional expert'. The growing commitment to the principle of service user involvement in recent years has led to a proliferation of policy and guidance documents aimed at increasing participation. However, participation is not an end in itself and in the context of social work with children and families, it needs to be meaningful and appealing to the people concerned, effective in bringing about improvement and sustained beyond formal decision-making arenas.

As we have seen, the United Nations Convention on the Rights of the Child and the European Convention on Human Rights both promote children's right to be heard and Articles 6 and 8 of the ECHR incorporate the rights of any individual, children included, to respect for family life and to a fair trial (or hearing). Although the Children Act 1975 included a requirement to ascertain, though not necessarily take account of, children's wishes and feelings when making decisions about them, events in Cleveland in the 1980s and the resulting departmental review of child care law laid the foundations for the CA 1989, which reflected the growing belief in minimal state intervention and commitment to the philosophy that children are best looked after within their own families. Nevertheless, despite the centrality of children's welfare needs, social work with children and families continues to concentrate resources on children at risk of significant harm, often at the expense of the much larger numbers of children who fall within the definition of being in need. Thus, the concept of meaningful participation and the achievement of consensual solutions remain problematic, since much effort is necessarily focused on information-gathering, assessment, intervention, monitoring and evaluation (DoH, 1995). A further difficulty in the context of promoting and achieving participation is the language adopted: cooperation, consultation, involvement and partnership, for example, are aspirational words which do not indicate what must be done to achieve the desired result, are difficult to evidence and mean little in a legal context.

Within children and families social work, the concept of participation, which is closely linked to partnership, has several dimensions. The most obvious is that of encouraging, facilitating and taking notice of the expression of the opinions, needs, fears and aspirations of service users, whether adults or children. These can occur informally in the course of day-to-day contact, more formally as in the sharing of records or involvement in decision-making meetings, or when required by statute and guidance, as in the processes set out within the guidance pertaining to public law proceedings (MoJ, 2010). At the next level, participation incorporates the enabling of formal or informal groups within society to express their views and contribute to decisions that affect them, as a sheltered housing project residents' association might do. However, the principle of participation is also important in the context of working effectively with other professionals, a theme that is increasingly prevalent within the legal and policy framework of social work as successive governments have recognised that social problems cannot be effectively addressed by any individual or organisation acting in isolation from others (Wilson *et al.*, 2008).

ACTIVITY 4.1

To demonstrate the relationship between participation and partnership

Scale of service user involvement in recording:

1. *Service user (SU) informed of right to see their records.*

2. *SU advised of how to achieve this.*

3. *SU informed of content of record, social worker (SW) offers to share it if SU wishes.*

4. *SW informs SU what they intend to write.*

5. *SW offers to show SU what has been written.*

6. *SW shows SU what has been written.*

7. *SW discusses with SU what should be written.*

8. *SW offers to show SU what is written following discussion.*

9. *SW shows SU what has been written following discussion.*

10. *SW writes record in SU's presence.*

11. *SW seeks SU's opinion on each point being recorded.*

12. *SW includes SU's contributions in record.*

ACTIVITY **4.1** *(CONT.)*

13. *SU writes own record to be placed alongside SW's record.*

14. *SU's sole record is placed on file.*

* *In relation to your work setting, consider which point of the scale matches your agency policy.*

* *Next, assess which point matches your actual practice.*

* *Does this meet legal requirements?*

* *Does it vary according to the circumstances?*

* *At what point could partnership be said to start?*

* *At what point could participation be said to start?*

Children's participation

All children are vulnerable to some extent by virtue of their age, immaturity and dependence on adults and the voices of adults are often heard over those of children. Children, unlike adults, cannot influence policy via the ballot box and although in most circumstances, their parents can be relied on to speak for them if necessary, this does not necessarily apply when the parents are the source of the child's problems.

(Munro, 2011, p22)

We can't do what we do unless we actively involve children and young people. If you're going to stand in the face of powerful social processes, you have to do that alongside your clients, and our clients are children . . . So in outreach you couldn't say to a child 'we understand from all the adults in your life that your problem is travelling to and from school because you've trashed seven taxis, so we will do X'. You have to say can we come in the taxi with you, can we see how it is and then can you help us to make it better? The children are central to working out where the 'problem' is and what needs to change.

(Disabled children's project worker quoted in Kirby *et al.*, 2003, p53)

Children should feel that they are active participants and engaged in the process when adults are trying to solve problems and make decisions about them.

(HMG, 2010, p4)

Statutory framework

Article 12 of the UNCRC states that: 'States parties shall assure to the child who is capable of forming his or her own views, the right to express those views freely in all matters affecting the child, the views of the child being given due weight in accordance with age and maturity of the child.'

The CA 1989 (as amended by the CA 2004) provides that when working with children in need, their wishes and feelings should be ascertained and used to inform decisions. Before making any decisions with respect to a child that the local authority is looking after or is proposing to look after, the authority must, so far as reasonably practicable, ascertain the wishes and feelings of the child and due consideration should be given to those wishes and feelings, having regard to their age and understanding. Section 1(3) requires a court, when considering whether to make an order in respect of a child, to have regard to the ascertainable wishes and feelings of the child concerned in the light of his age and understanding. However, wishes and feelings comprise only part of the welfare checklist and courts have discretion as to how much weight to give to each aspect of it and how the child's views are elicited and presented.

The Children Act 1989 Guidance and Regulations Volume 2 (HMG, 2010) states that the child's view as expressed should be discussed, recorded and given due consideration. When visiting a looked-after child, social workers must see and speak to the child alone (ibid., p75). The exceptions to this are: where the child refuses (and is of sufficient age and understanding to refuse); where the social worker considers it inappropriate to do so (having regard to the child's age and understanding); and where the social worker is unable to do so, for example because the child is out. If a child has particular communication difficulties, specialist resources must be sought in order to ensure that the child has the opportunity to express their wishes and feelings.

The Framework for the Assessment of Children in Need and Their Families (DoH, 2000), **the Common Assessment Framework** (CWDC, 2009) and the **Integrated Children's System** all require children's views to be included within assessment and planning processes.

The Independent Reviewing Officer Handbook sets out the statutory duty of IROs to 'ensure that any ascertained wishes and feelings of the child concerning the case are given due consideration by the appropriate authority' (DCSF, 2010a, para. 2.9).

Statutory Guidance on the Management of Children's Services (DCSF, 2009b) states that local authorities must enable the voices of children and young people to be heard, in particular those who are disabled or living in placements away from their home area.

The Adoption and Children Act 2002 places a duty on local authorities to provide advocacy services for looked-after children and those leaving care.

The CA 2004 established the role of the Children's Commissioner in England to promote awareness of the views and interests of children, particularly in relation to the five *Every Child Matters* outcomes (DfES, 2003). The Children's Commissioner for Wales has a more extensive remit, arising from the recommendations of the Waterhouse Report into child abuse in North Wales, to safeguard and promote the rights and welfare of children, including monitoring the complaints, whistleblowing and advocacy procedures of care providers, and the power to investigate and report on individual cases (Williams, 2008).

OFSTED includes the post of **Children's Rights Director** whose role is to monitor and report on the actions of local authorities in relation to safeguarding the rights and welfare of children and young people and the effectiveness of complaints procedures.

The Children (Leaving Care) Act 2000 requires local authorities to ensure that young people have access to independent advocacy services to support them through complaints procedures.

The **Mental Capacity Act 2005** and the **Mental Health Act 2007** introduced the roles of Independent Mental Capacity Advocates and Independent Mental Health Advocates.

Law and policy in this area is shaped by the belief that many children have an understanding of what underlies any difficulties that they or their family face, what their needs are and what intervention is most likely to be effective. In addition, involving children in decisions about their lives helps to develop their strengths and promote their resilience. However, the application of these concepts poses practical dilemmas that are not always anticipated within the statutory provision and guidance. For example, when using a generic term such as 'children's participation' we need to recognise that children are not a single homogeneous group and differ in their personal circumstances (age, sex, ethnicity, culture, disability, social and economic situation) and in their changing attributes, achievements and priorities as they develop and mature. What works for one child may not be suitable for another and listening to children's views is not necessarily the same as taking them into account or acting upon them. In addition, as is recognised within the National Minimum Standards for Fostering (DfE, 2011f), it might not always be possible or desirable to act in accordance with a child's wishes.

LEGAL CASE STUDY 4.1

Although the case law on the relative importance of a child's wishes and feelings is sometimes inconsistent, as the child's welfare remains paramount under CA 1989 s1(1) it has been established that a court can override the wishes of a child of any age if to follow them would seriously compromise his or her long-term welfare (Re W (A Minor) (Medical Treatment: Court's Jurisdiction) *[1993] Fam 64 and* Re R (A Minor) (Wardship: Medical Treatment) *[1992] Fam 11).*

Re A (Children) *[2010] EWCA Civ 208 involved a local authority which, as a result of the distress caused to a 12-year-old by his mother's behaviour, had applied for contact to be terminated. The child's guardian was largely supportive of the local authority but her opinion was not wholly reflective of the wishes of the child who, while expressing anxiety about his mother's behaviour, wanted contact to continue. Consequently, the child wished to instruct a solicitor to act for him separately from his guardian. The judge at the initial hearing said that the test to be applied was whether the child 'wishes to give instructions which conflict with those of the children's guardian, and is able, in the light of his understanding, to give such instructions'. He decided that this child was not mature enough to weigh up all the considerations that had to be taken into account, and that there was no conflict of interest as between the child and the guardian. The decision to refuse the application for separate representation was upheld in the Court of Appeal, which said:*

> There are cases involving children in post-pubertal adolescent rebellion for whom it is very difficult for a guardian to act. Their position, their wishes, their feelings, their opinions so conflict with an objective view of welfare that there has to be a parting of the ways, and our system generously provides for two distinct and equally constituted litigation teams thereafter. That is an extremely expensive solution, and in present days when the Family Justice system is obliged to seek economy wherever and whenever it can, orders granting separate representation under this rule should be issued very sparingly.

RESEARCH SUMMARY 4.1

Birnbaum and Saini (2012) undertook a review of research over 20 years across 11 countries into children's participation in court processes concerning family disputes. Generally, the research showed that children want to be involved in decision-making processes, even if they are not making the ultimate decisions themselves. Some studies found that the presence of domestic violence and high levels of family conflict caused children to be less likely to want to be engaged in decisions about residence and contact, although they still wanted to speak to the person responsible for making the final decision. They understood that having a voice is not the same as making a choice. The reviewers concluded that children's experiences are shaped by constraining adult factors that can facilitate or hinder the expression of their views.

As with most ethical principles, the need to take account of children's views poses dilemmas in practice. For example, it is necessary to balance the concept of children's rights with an appreciation of their vulnerability in terms of what they have experienced previously, possible conflicts of loyalty, their capacity for involvement and the potentially adverse effects of the process of participation itself. In addition to chronological age, assessment of capacity should incorporate maturity, competency, independence, character and personality. However, an overly protectionist approach can suppress children's views and what is offered as support and facilitation could potentially seem more like professional interrogation. Ultimately, representation of children's views is, at best, only hearsay, filtered through the beliefs and prejudices of the agent.

CASE STUDY 4.1

Amina, a 15-year-old girl who had experienced physical and verbal abuse by her parents, was accommodated under the CA 1989 s20. Amina expressed concern to her social worker about the risks that her parents posed to her sisters who remained in the family home. She also wished to have regular contact with them. The local authority took no action regarding contact between the sisters or the concerns raised. Amina consulted a children's legal centre which applied within private law proceedings for her to have contact with her sisters. As a consequence of this action the local authority initiated safeguarding procedures in relation to the sisters and set up regular contact between them. However, this should have happened earlier as a consequence of Amina's expressed views.

(Pona and Hounsell, 2012, p20)

CASE STUDY 4.2

Following an incident in which it was alleged that an 11-year-old boy had been physically assaulted by his stepfather, the stepfather was asked to leave the home, which was made a condition of his police bail although no criminal charges were ultimately brought. A child protection plan was agreed, which stipulated how contact between the boy and his stepfather was to be supervised pending the stepfather undertaking an alcohol dependency

---

CASE STUDY 4.2 (CONT.)

programme and counselling. Subsequently the boy wrote to the social worker and his stepfather's solicitors saying that he had lied about what had happened, his stepfather was a 'fantastic' dad and he wanted him home. When the social worker talked to him about the risks that had been identified and tried to explain how they were trying to help the family, he became angry and said that no one was listening to him.

(Pona and Hounsell, 2012, p20)

Assessing understanding

An important aspect of children's participation is the extent to which they are able, or can be expected, to contribute on account of their age. A very young child is usually able to express preferences in relation to the food they eat or the clothes they wear and an older teenager may be able to take a full part in decisions that affect them. However, in between there is considerable potential for the exercise of professional judgement. The following framework may help (DfE, 2011h):

Does the child:

1. Understand the issue and the reasons behind it?

2. Understand what the alternatives are?

3. Understand what will happen if they decide one way rather than the other?

4. Weigh up the relevant factors for themselves?

5. Say (or otherwise communicate) what they think, with or without help?

6. Maintain the same view consistently over time or change it according to the circumstances?

LEGAL CASE STUDY 4.2

In Re L (A Child) (Contact: Domestic Violence) *[2000] 2 FLR 334, the judge gave guidance on the question of the relevance of age when taking account of a child's wishes and feelings:*

The older the child the more seriously they should be viewed and the more insulting and discrediting to the child to have them ignored. As a rough rule we would see these as needing to be taken account of at any age; above 10 we see these as carrying considerable weight, with 6–10 as an intermediate stage and at under 6 as often indistinguishable in many ways from the wishes of the main carer (assuming normal development). In domestic violence, where the child has memories of that violence we would see their wishes as warranting much more weight than in situations where no real reason for the child's resistance appears to exist.

PRACTITIONER REFLECTION 4.1

Team manager for looked-after children:

> Children often don't want to attend their reviews. They may not understand the procedure and language or be particularly interested in having it explained. What child is going to want everyone to hear that they are wetting the bed three times a week?

Reviews for looked-after children should be child-centred and the social worker is expected to consult the child about who they would like to attend and where the meeting will be held. The involvement of the child is subject to their age, understanding and welfare which is, of course, open to professional judgement. The possibility of a child being supported by an advocate should be considered (DCSF, 2010a).

Although there are now more opportunities for young people who are looked after to express their views to those who represent their 'corporate parent' and contribute towards the planning and delivery of services, there is evidence that many young people feel that they were not consulted enough, or that their views were not taken sufficiently seriously.

RESEARCH SUMMARY 4.2

Mantle et al. (2007) explored how family court social workers sought to elicit children's views and identified the key issues as:

- *where the interview took place and who was present;*

- *how the nature and limits of confidentiality were explained to and understood by the child;*

- *the role of play and how 'free' or guided it should be;*

- *the way in which questions were formulated and what information was sought from children;*

- *the techniques or aids used for interviewing children of different ages and ability;*

- *how the interview was concluded;*

- *how the interview was recorded, analysed, evaluated and used.*

Leeson (2007) found that children's experience of participation whilst in care often amounted to little more than tokenism, and described the feelings of helplessness experienced as a consequence of not being involved in decision-making. She found that looked-after children tended to lack the necessary resilience to face social and emotional challenges later in life and, as a result of lack of practice, had little confidence in their own decision-making skills. With hindsight the experience of 'corporate parenting' was felt to be impersonal and systems-oriented, rather than child-centred.

An assessment by OFSTED (2009) of local authority services to young carers found that young carers' views were not routinely considered when assessing, or providing services to, disabled parents.

RESEARCH SUMMARY 4.2 *(CONT.)*

Hanley and Doyle (2010) investigated the practice of CAFCASS family court advisers (FCA) and local authority children's social workers (CSW) in the context of ascertaining children's wishes and feelings. They found that the ages of the youngest children considered able to express their wishes and feelings ranged from 3 to 7 for the FCAs and from 2 to 11 for the CSWs. The decision to seek children's wishes and feelings was determined, in descending order of importance, by their own skills in direct work with children, their knowledge of child development and their views about children's rights and responsibilities. Half of each group stated that they had had no specific training in ascertaining wishes and feelings.

A review by OFSTED (2010a) of the findings of serious case reviews highlights key messages in the context of children's participation:

- *the child was not seen frequently enough by the professionals involved, or was not asked about their views and feelings;*

- *agencies did not listen to adults who tried to speak on behalf of the child and who had important information to contribute;*

- *parents and carers often prevented professionals from seeing and listening to the child;*

- *practitioners focused too much on the needs of the parents, especially if they were regarded as vulnerable, and overlooked the implications for the child.*

The Children's Rights Director for England (OFSTED, 2011b, p20) reported that just over half of looked-after children felt that their opinions were always or usually sought, with a similar number believing that this had made a difference to their lives. Just over two-thirds of children said that they are usually, or always, told what is going on when major changes are going to happen, with younger children more likely to feel they were kept informed than those over 14. Around 14 per cent said that they were never, or rarely, consulted about things that mattered to them.

In a separate survey of looked-after children (CRDE, 2011a), fewer than a quarter (22 per cent) thought their wishes and feelings had made some difference or a lot of difference in the context of decisions made about their care, while 67 per cent thought their wishes and feelings had made not much difference or no difference at all. Eighteen per cent said that their social worker always talked to them on their own, and, almost as many, 15 per cent, that their social worker never saw them on their own. Almost a third said that they could not get in touch with their social worker when they needed to and 70 per cent said they wanted to see their social workers more often than they did. Over half the children (53 per cent) thought their wishes and feelings usually didn't make, or never made, a difference to the decisions made about them while just over a quarter (27 per cent) thought they always or nearly always made a difference.

ACTIVITY 4.2

The 'ladder' of participation below illustrates the potential range of approaches for involving children in decision-making and offers a framework against which practice can be measured. Which approaches most closely mirror those you use in your care planning and review processes? Next consider how you could move your practice up the ladder.

Levels of participation	When might you use this approach?
The child is given information, support and resources to make their own decisions.	
The child is given responsibility for most decisions while adults retain overall control.	
Adults explain possible options and consequences to the child, who can express preferences which are acted upon if possible.	
Adults make most decisions, incorporating the child's views as far as possible and explaining when this is not possible.	
Adults ask the child for their views, which may or may not be taken account of, depending on the type of decision to be made.	
Adults explain options to the child who may or may not express an opinion.	
The child is informed of decisions which have been made by others.	

CASE STUDY 4.3

A social work student on placement in a primary school introduced a 'Talk to Me' box which was decorated by a group of children and placed by the school entrance, together with a supply of cards and some pencils. She visited each class to explain that these were for children to raise any matters that were causing them worry or upset. She was surprised to find that each day there were several cards in the box, raising concerns about a wide range of difficulties arising both in and out of school, which she was able to address with each child individually. Without the medium of the box, it seems unlikely that these concerns would have come to light.

no longer a presumption, or even a starting point, against children giving evidence in such circumstances. In each case the court should carry out a balancing exercise between the possible advantages that the child will bring to the determination of truth, as against the risk of harm to the child from giving evidence. Factors such as their wishes, feelings, needs, abilities, age, maturity, vulnerability, understanding and the support available to them all form part of this exercise. The court should consider the possibility of questions being put to the child separate from the occasion of the substantive hearing and seek to ensure that the skills of the questioner match the child's communication needs. There must be advance judicial approval of any questions to be put and an opportunity for the child to visit the court beforehand. The child should be accompanied by a known neutral supporter and there should be no possibility of confrontation with anyone at court which might cause distress to the child. An unwilling child should rarely, if ever, be required to give evidence.

RESEARCH SUMMARY 4.5

Research undertaken by the Children's Rights Director for England (OFSTED, 2010b) found that children whose views had been sought in family law proceedings disliked having strangers discussing their lives and problems. They would have welcomed prior information about what was likely to happen, who would be present and how long each hearing would last. Comments made to researchers included:

- *'The court made me feel like an ant against a human'.*

- *'It seemed as if my life was in the hands of a random group of strangers'.*

- *'I thought my views and opinions would be taken with a grain of salt and barely heard, much less considered'.*

- *'I felt I had to say what they wanted to hear'.*

Children's participation in decisions to accommodate

Government guidance in relation to young people who are, or are at risk of being, homeless (CLG and DCSF, 2010) states that if a young person does not wish to be accommodated, a local authority should consider that the young person's wishes are decisive only as part of an overall judgement of their assessed welfare needs and a key aspect of the assessment involves understanding how the young person views their needs. Whoever conducts the assessment is expected to provide realistic and full information about the support that the young person can expect as a looked-after child and, subsequently, as a care leaver and what assistance may be available to them, including from housing services under Part 7 of the Housing Act 1996, if they do not become looked after. Young people should have access to independent advocacy and support to assist them in coming to a balanced decision. The fact that a young person might be reluctant to take part in the assessment process is not, in itself, a basis for assuming that they have rejected an offer to provide them with accommodation. Lack of cooperation is not a reason for the local authority to abandon its duties under the CA 1989. In these

Disabled children

RESEARCH SUMMARY 4.3

A review by OFSTED (2012c) of local authority services to disabled children found that the extent to which their views, wishes and feelings were obtained and recorded varied. In many cases professionals knew children well, and were skilled in communicating with them and in using observation to assess how they were feeling. However, children were not always spoken to directly about concerns for their welfare, even when they could communicate well. Advocacy was usually not considered and was rarely used.

There is evidence that participation is still only experienced by small numbers of disabled children, usually those who are most confident and able to communicate. Examples of poor practice include disabled children not being involved in life story work and of assessment forms being completed with 'not applicable' written in the section for 'child's view' (Baker, 2011). Children with disabilities or communication impairments are particularly likely to be excluded from child protection and legal processes: 'We were told about a court report by a children's guardian that diligently detailed how a disabled non-verbal child could communicate using an electronic communication board, but then stated that the child's view was not available' (Kirby et al., 2003, p110).

LEGAL CASE STUDY 4.3

B (A Local Authority) v AM *[2010] EWHC 3802 (Fam)*

This case raised the question of whether and, if so, on what basis, a court considering an application for a care order in respect of a young person aged over 16 with lifelong disabilities should transfer the case to the Court of Protection to be dealt with under the MCA 2005 rather than the CA 1989. The court stated that it was not possible to ascertain the wishes and feelings of AM because 'it is not possible for her to understand the implications of the position in which she finds herself' (para. 11).

AM was 17 and had multiple disabilities. She was not expected to be able to live independently and required a high level of support to ensure that her needs were met. Threshold in the care proceedings had been conceded and AM was living in temporary care, although a move would be necessary in the near future. AM's mother wished the local authority to accommodate her under the CA 1989 s20 but the local authority and children's guardian wanted a care order on the basis that the mother had never accepted the difficulties caused by AM's profound disabilities and, despite all the evidence, continued to believe that she could care for her at home which she saw as her family duty. The judge acknowledged the family's commitment to AM: 'I would have no difficulty in understanding a sense of rebuff and feelings of marginalisation were a care order to be made' (para. 23), and posed a number of questions.

LEGAL CASE STUDY **4.3** *(CONT.)*

- *Is the child over 16?*

- *Does the child manifestly lack capacity in respect of the principal decisions which are to be made under the CA?*

- *Are the disabilities giving rise to the lack of capacity lifelong or long-term?*

- *Can the decisions which arise in respect of the child's welfare all be taken and all issues resolved during the child's minority?*

- *Are the Court of Protection's powers or procedures more appropriate to resolve the outstanding issues?*

- *Can the child's welfare needs be fully met by those powers?*

It was decided that the Court of Protection would better serve AM's long-term welfare: 'This is a case in which AM's interests are not served by conflict. The local authority must proceed with reasonable expedition and the family with patience' (para. 34).

Child protection

> *All these people were looking at you and I'm like oh my God and it was hard because my mum was there . . . and it was like I was holding stuff back because I knew that once I go back to her who knows what I will be facing.*

> *Having social services involved and sticking their beaks in puts mother in a mood, which is going to make her more likely to do something stupid like what happened in April.*

> (Young people subject to safeguarding procedures, quoted by Cossar and Dunne, 2010)

Child protection is an area in which children are not always offered the opportunity to participate, despite the strong legal framework supporting the relevance of their contributions. It is not uncommon for social workers to focus on engaging parents and carers in situations of potential conflict, and for steps to be taken to minimise children's exposure to disagreement and confrontation. As the following research shows, children's involvement needs to be planned and executed with great care, particularly in relation to how children are prepared and the support available to them afterwards.

RESEARCH SUMMARY **4.4**

Cossar and Dunne (2010) asked young people what they thought about their participation in child protection conferences:

- *most had positive views of the people who chaired the conference and felt they were independent;*

RESEARCH SUMMARY **4.4** *(CONT.)*

- *they had differing opinions about when and how they wished to give their views – several had become frustrated and walked out of the meeting;*

- *some felt that they had not been asked about key issues;*

- *those who did not attend received very little information about what happened in the meeting; for those who did attend reading the minutes was often upsetting;*

- *young people had little knowledge of what was in their child protection plan;*

- *there was a stigma attached to being subject to a child protection plan;*

- *attendance does not equal participation; not attending should not mean not participating.*

Family court proceedings

The pre-proceedings process contained within the policy framework for public law care proceedings (MoJ, 2010) is notable for its failure to provide for the involvement or representation of the children who are likely to be the subject of such proceedings (Masson, 2010). This is all the more remarkable given that, at the point at which the pre-proceedings process begins, around 90 per cent of families have been known to the local authority for over a year and two-thirds of children are already subject to a child protection plan (Masson et al., 2008).

Once care proceedings have started, the representation of children's views is managed primarily by children's guardians and their legal representatives. When a care order is made, however, representation of the child by the children's guardian ceases so that if, for example, a placement order is made as a consequence of the care order, there are no longer any formal independent means by which a child's wishes and feelings can be considered by the court unless or until a further application is made to court.

The judiciary in England and Wales has acknowledged the need for family courts to be more proactive in seeking to facilitate the expression of children's views. In particular, they suggest that the obligations contained within the UNCRC need to be demonstrated by (Ryder, 2012, p15):

- an engagement with children to facilitate their understanding of the proceedings where that is consistent with their welfare;

- the ascertainment of a child's wishes and feelings and an opportunity to be heard, where the child wishes it; and

- an explanation of the court's decision.

At the same time they acknowledge the dilemmas that such actions pose in the context of preserving the confidentiality of a child's private and family information in both public and private law family court proceedings.

Practice guidance in relation to children giving evidence in family court proceedings (FJC, 2011) followed the Supreme Court judgement in *Re W* [2010] UKSC 12 which states that there was

circumstances, the local authority should carefully record how it has attempted to engage with the young person to assess their needs in order to determine and provide appropriate services. Ultimately, however, it is accepted that is not possible to force services on young people who persistently refuse them, so long as they are competent to make that decision.

Children's participation in youth justice

Current youth justice policy is founded on the need to balance the principles of *due process* and *rule of law* with the desire to maximise the effectiveness of responses to the social circumstances thought to underlie offending behaviour (Newbury, 2011). However, these contrasting approaches are both largely reactive in that they seek to address a situation that has already manifested itself. The policies adopted are largely process-orientated and increasingly based on the concept of restorative justice which involves conference-style meetings and discussions which are intended to be participative but which may be beyond the comprehension of many younger teenagers (see example in Chapter 1).

Advocacy

Advocacy incorporates representation, support, empowerment and the protection of rights on behalf of people who are less able to speak up for themselves. Although many professionals working with looked-after children see advocacy as an integral part of their role, there is a distinction between the role of a social worker and that of an independent advocate:

- The advocate's role is to ensure that the child's views and experiences are considered when decisions are made about their future, which might be different from representing their best interests.

- Research (Oliver and Dalrymple, 2008) indicates that the quality of the relationship between a young person and their advocate is the most significant factor in facilitating children's participation in decision-making and enabling them to discuss matters that they might be reluctant to raise with other professionals.

- Advocates play a role in securing young people's access to services.

Although the ACA 2002 established the right of looked-after children to an advocacy service, it does not have to be independent of the local authority, which has raised concerns as to whether in-house services can be truly participative.

RESEARCH SUMMARY 4.6

Lindley et al. (2001) reported that parents whose children were the subject of child protection plans, and who had received pre-proceedings advocacy support, found that it helped them work with the local authority and facilitated the building of bridges between them. The advocates had a key role in translating jargon, helping explain the nature of the welfare concerns and providing support at meetings, a particular source of stress.

The Children's Rights Director for England (OFSTED, 2008) found that just over half of looked-after children had heard of advocacy and knew about the types of help an advocate could offer. Almost all children who had been supported by an advocate rated their advocates very highly on how well they listened to them, put over their points of view and encouraged others to take account of their opinions.

A review of advocacy services for looked-after and disabled children run by the Children's Society across England and Wales (Pona and Hounsell, 2012) concluded that:

- *independent advocates enable looked-after children and young people to communicate their wishes and feelings and to play an active role in decision-making about key aspects of their lives;*

- *advocacy services support local authorities to meet their duties as corporate parents to children in care by improving both children's experience of the care system and their achievements, in addition to delivering financial savings;*

- *statutory obligations on local authorities and the National Advocacy Standards and guidance are inadequate, resulting in inconsistency in provision and opportunities for children and young people to access independent advocacy.*

An assessment of safeguarding services for disabled children (OFSTED, 2012c) found that advocacy is rarely used to ascertain the views and wishes of disabled children, even when there are concerns about their well-being.

Parental participation

Talking openly about my dirty washing.

You may be involved, but you have no control.

Humiliating, nerve-wracking, daunting, embarrassing, intimidating, frightening.

(Parents of children subject to child protection procedures,
quoted by Buckley *et al.*, 2011)

Organisations working with children, particularly younger children, highlight the importance of working with parents as a way of encouraging participation by children. Involving parents can help build their support for the agency's work and also enables them to observe the methods and potential benefits of working in a participatory way (Kirby *et al.*, 2003).

LEGAL CASE STUDY **4.4**

The case of Re G (Care: Challenge to Local Authority's Decisions) [2003] EWHC 551 (Fam) concerned meetings at which decisions were made to readmit to care four looked-after children who had previously been placed back with their birth family. The judge commented on 'a mindset and a culture seemingly oblivious to the imperative requirements of article 8 of the European Convention for the Protection of Human Rights and Fundamental Freedoms, and unwittingly careless of the need to treat parents with fairness' (para. 2). After stating that 'the fact that a local authority has parental responsibility for children pursuant to section 33(3)(a) of the CA 1989 does not entitle it to take decisions about those children without reference to, or over the heads of, the children's parents' (para. 43), he subsequently set out the nature of the local authority's duty to provide a full and frank disclosure to parents of documents, including notes, agendas and minutes of conversations and meetings and in particular its duty to:

- *inform parents promptly of its plans, together with the rationale;*

- *give parents the opportunity to attend and address any significant meetings and to make representations in respect of any allegations made against them.*

Importantly from a practice point of view the judge commented:

> the local authority takes a decision and then it 'shares' it with the parents. That, I'm afraid, is not good enough: what it should have been doing was to involve the parents much more centrally in, and throughout, the process which led up to the decision being taken.
>
> *(para. 57)*

LEGAL CASE STUDY **4.5**

In the case of Re X (Emergency Protection Order) [2006] EWHC 510 (Fam) the judge set out the basic requirements applicable in cases in which parents are not present at a child protection case conference:

(a) If the circumstances are sufficient to justify the exclusion of the parents from part of a case conference, or the parents are otherwise absent, a full minute should nevertheless be taken of everything that is said during the conference;

(b) If it is considered necessary to treat part of what is minuted as confidential from the parents, that part of the minutes should be disclosed for approval to the professionals who attended the conference, but should be maintained separately from the body of the minutes which are sent to the parents;

(c) The non-confidential section of the minutes should expressly record at the appropriate stage that confidential information was disclosed or discussed;

(d) The need for continued confidentiality with respect to confidential sections of the minutes should be kept under review by the conference chair, with confidentiality only maintained if it continues to be necessary.

(para. 29)

Although parents should normally be included in child protection conferences, *Working Together to Safeguard Children* (DfE, 2010b) acknowledges that this might not always be possible. In the context of child protection it is common for professionals to meet together, as a 'core' or 'legal planning' group, which invites the question as to whether the parents of those children, most of whom retain sole parental responsibility for them, have been fairly treated in the context of participation and partnership.

RESEARCH SUMMARY 4.7

A study of service users' views of child protection procedures (Buckley et al., 2011) found that most parents did not see themselves as partners in a process which they regarded as one in which professionals prescribed action requiring compliance on their part. Stress was reduced if the social worker spent time with parents before and after meetings which they were expected to attend, so that they were prepared for what was likely to happen and had the opportunity to ask questions afterwards. The factor most likely to influence parental attitudes was the quality of the relationship between the social worker and the family, with availability and punctuality particularly valued. Service users' perceptions of harm and risk often differed from the terms and definitions used by professionals, leading to misunderstanding, confusion and conflict.

Partnership: a slippery ideal?

Partnership with service users is a core value within the framework of social work with children and families. However, in a legal context many people would equate the concept of partnership with a business arrangement in which there are commitments, shared risks and potential benefits on both sides. Marriage and civil partnerships are legally recognised relationships which incorporate responsibilities and entitlements for both parties and reflect the principle of equality between its members. In social work, the concept of partnership is closely allied to participation, a principle promoted by both sides of the political spectrum in that it is regarded by the left to be the key to empowering those who are disadvantaged and by the right as a means of promoting individual responsibility, choice and independence. However, a common dilemma in social work is whether it is possible to achieve a meaningful partnership between two people who are not equal in terms of the power they hold, whether this stems from statutory definition or from differential levels of ability, knowledge or skills. We suggest that the political popularity of the concept of partnership may have resulted in it being paid lip-service within legislation, policy and guidance rather than providing the framework for a workable and enforceable means of influencing practice.

Aldgate (2001) defines the key aspects of partnership as:

- shared commitment to negotiations and actions concerning how best to safeguard and promote a child's welfare;

- mutual respect for the other's point of view;

- recognition of the inequality of power between parents and professionals;

- recognition that parents have their own needs;

- good communication on the part of professionals;

- trust between all parties;

- integrity and accountability;

- shared decision-making;

- recognition of the constraints of the service offered;

- recognition that partnership is not an end in itself.

Most of these aspects of partnership are supported by legislation and guidance, although often the language lacks the detail and rigour necessary for it to be of much assistance in situations of difficulty or dispute. Partnership is not specifically mentioned in the CA 1989, although its philosophy underpins many of its provisions. Statutory guidance, however, is increasingly including references to specific actions that are intended to promote the principle of partnership, both in relation to individual work with children and families and in the context of service delivery. For example, *Working Together to Safeguard Children* (DfE, 2010b) states that local authorities should carry out their duties to safeguard and promote the welfare of children in need in their area in partnership with parents, and since 2006 Local Safeguarding Children Boards have been required to publish an annual report on the effectiveness of safeguarding in their area and to appoint two representatives of the local community as members of each board.

The *Public Law Proceedings Guide to Case Management* (MoJ, 2010) is focused on the aspiration of cooperative partnerships between parents and professionals, even when the local authority is attempting to limit the exercise of parental responsibility by giving notice of its intention to commence legal proceedings. The defined pre-proceedings process, which includes planning meetings and setting out the local authority's concerns in writing to parents and carers, is intended both to narrow and focus the issues at stake and, if possible, to achieve solutions by agreement rather than having them imposed by a court after a potentially expensive and damaging trial. The requirement to submit evidence that the possibility of voluntary, non-legal solutions has already been investigated, and the responsibility placed on local authorities to ensure that parents are given notice of intended actions and helped to understand the courts processes, reflect the principles of partnership, albeit in rather non-specific terms. Thus, it was envisaged that parents may be given the incentive to address the factors that are causing concern, make arrangements for alternative care within their family or perhaps agree to CA 1989 s20 accommodation as an alternative to court action. However, such arrangements, if not truly cooperative, risk simply masking actual or potential conflicts between the local authority, parents, carers and children, and legally insecure arrangements could also expose children to an unacceptable level of risk (Masson, 2010).

The concept of partnership does not remove the overriding duty of the local authority to safeguard and promote the welfare of children so that, for example, making numerous unsuccessful attempts to bring about improvement in a family's circumstances could be considered as misapplying the law (Brayne and Carr, 2010). It can also be hard to reconcile official guidance with the fact that the failure of parents to cooperate with plans is often the precipitating factor in public law care proceedings (Brophy, 2006).

Broadhurst and Holt (2010) suggest that, as cooperative parents might find it harder to get a service than those who are more assertive and challenging, the principle of partnership is further undermined in practice. If, for example, accommodation is offered under the CA 1989 s20 to 'buy time' to negotiate the public law procedures in a situation in which the threshold criteria appear to have been met, as might be suggested by the principle of partnership with parents, those with parental responsibility have no automatic right to free legal representation and the placement and care plans are not subject to the same legal scrutiny. Family group conferences, put forward as a method for promoting partnership and participation, as yet have a scanty evidence base and have no clear lines of accountability in relation to their decisions. The practice of 'twin track' and 'parallel planning', promoted as a means by which permanency can be achieved more speedily in the course of public law proceedings, is also seen by some practitioners as somewhat dishonest in the context of genuine partnership with parents.

FURTHER READING

www.barnardos.org.uk

Barnardo's works with vulnerable children and young people in the UK and produces resources for professionals. The Committed to Rights section gives information and practical tools to help practitioners working in the criminal justice system. *Say it your own way: children's participation in assessment* comprises a printed guide and CD-ROM containing resources to support professionals in giving children a voice. *Meeting with respect* is a resource pack for social workers seeking to promote child-centred meetings.

www.childrenscommissioner.gov.uk

The Children's Commissioner provides an independent, national voice for children and young people, especially those who are vulnerable or disadvantaged.

www.childrenslegalcentre.com

Coram Children's Legal Centre provides free legal information, advice and representation to children, young people, their families, carers and professionals on child law and children's rights.

www.crae.org.uk

Children's Rights Alliance for England is a coalition of voluntary and statutory organisations committed to the full implementation of the UN Convention on the Rights of the Child.

www.thenayj.org.uk

National Association for Youth Justice promotes the rights of children within the criminal justice system.

www.nya.org.uk

The National Youth Agency supports those involved in young people's personal and social development. The Hear by Right section of the site contains a standards framework for organisations to assess and improve practice and policy in relation to the involvement of children and young people.

www.participationworks.org.uk

Participation Works disseminates policy and practice in the context of children and young people's participation across the UK.

www.rights4me.org.uk

The website of the Children's Rights Director for England includes a *Young Persons' Guide to the Care Planning, Placement and Case Review (England) Regulations 2010* and other resources aimed at encouraging children's participation.

www.ukyouthparliament.org.uk

UK Youth Parliament aims to give young people between the ages of 11 and 18 a voice to be heard by local and national government and providers of services for young people.

Chapter 5
Support

CHAPTER OBJECTIVES

This chapter evaluates the legal and policy basis for the rather imprecise, but widely used, social work term 'support'. It encourages critical thinking, augmented by creativity and curiosity, and highlights the key importance of clarity of language when working within legal and policy frameworks. Thus it encourages you to synthesise your own practice experience, service user and carer experience together with research-based, organisational, policy and legal knowledge as set out in the requirements of the PCF.

Introduction

It is not possible to separate the protection of children from the wider support to families. Indeed often the best protection for a child is achieved by the timely intervention of family support services.

(Laming, 2003, p6)

Thinking systematically about improving children's safety and well-being must involve an analysis of the political commitments of successive governments to 'welfare'.

(Featherstone et al., 2012, p619)

Family support finds little resonance with frameworks which are shaped by ideologically driven performance demands.

(Broadhurst and Holt, 2010, p101)

Notwithstanding the increasing recognition of the significance of children's rights in the context of child welfare, the philosophy of the United Nations Convention on the Rights of the Child is that these rights are primarily protected by the state giving proper support to families and it is not suggested that states should regard the interests and rights of children in isolation from those of their families (Henricson and Bainham, 2005). However, although prevention remains a key political priority, not least for economic reasons, family support services generally have not flourished under the Children Act 1989 and there remains a paucity of intervention options and resources available for the increasing number of families experiencing difficulties that do not meet the threshold for statutory intervention (Rowlands and Statham, 2009). Many local authorities separate services for children in need of protection from those for children in need of support, which disregards the obvious fact that children at risk are in need, and children in need are more likely to become children at risk than those who are not in need (Wilson *et al.*, 2008). Indeed, one of the key organisational factors which contributed to local authority failings in the case of Victoria Climbié was that at the point of referral she was categorised as a child in need rather than a child in need of protection, resulting in lower priority being given to her situation:

Q: Here we are at the beginning of June and you were still being asked to do an assessment. Did that surprise you, or is that normal?

A: I think at the time it was difficult. We usually assessed people via housing needs, rather than being child focused.

(Extract from social worker cross-examination, Victoria Climbié Inquiry, 4 October 2001, **www.nationalarchives.gov.uk/ERORecords/VC/2/2/Evidence/Archive/**)

Children Act 1989

The CA 1989 s17 imposes a general duty on the local authority to:

a. *safeguard and promote the welfare of children within their area who are in need; and*

b. *so far as is consistent with that duty, to promote the upbringing of such children by their families, in particular by providing a range and level of services appropriate to those children's needs.*

The definition of a child in need is broad. A child is taken to be in need if:

a. *he is unlikely to achieve or maintain, or to have the opportunity of achieving or maintaining, a reasonable standard of health without the provision for him of services by the local authority;*

b. *his health or development is likely to be significantly impaired, or further impaired, without the provision of services by the local authority, or*

c. *he is disabled.*

The CA 1989 s17(1) was the subject of consideration by the House of Lords in *R (G) v Barnet LBC* [2004] 2 AC 208 when it was decided that, while the legislation imposes a general duty to provide an appropriate range and level of services, it does not impose a mandatory duty on a local authority to take specific steps to satisfy the assessed needs of individual children in need, regardless of the local authority's resources. Children in need are *eligible* for the provision of services but have no absolute right to them. Such right as they have must be found elsewhere in the CA 1989 or in other legislation.

There were 382,400 children assessed as in need in England at 31 March 2011, a rate of 346 per 10,000 children, and 735,500 episodes of need were recorded by local authorities in the course of 2010/2011 (DfE, 2011g).

ACTIVITY 5.1

The CA 1989 (sch.2 and s17) states that local authorities 'shall provide, as it considers appropriate, for the following services to be available to children in need living with their families':

* advice, guidance and counselling;

* occupational, social, cultural or recreational activities (such as after school clubs and parenting groups);

* home help, including laundry facilities;

* travel costs to enable families to access services;

* holidays;

* family centres, which could offer any of the above services;

* accommodation, respite care and short breaks, including day care;

* assistance in kind or cash, which should take account of individual means.

In what respects do these provisions reflect social attitudes prevailing at the time the Act was passed? In your area are they primarily provided by the local authority, by voluntary agencies in partnership with the local authority, by voluntary and charitable organisations only or not at all? How easy is it for families to access them? Is any recourse available to service users who do not receive the services they need? What changes would you like to see in the provision of prevention and support services? What role, if any, should the law have in effecting such changes?

LEGAL CASE STUDY 5.1

MM v Lewisham LBC *[2009] EWHC 416 (Admin)*

This case concerned a local authority's system for receiving and assessing referrals for 'child in need' assessments. After a 17-year-old girl was referred by telephone by a refuge to the local authority for support due to being 'vulnerable and lacking life skills', the referral was marked 'CH CASE NOT CIN' followed by ' Duty worker to inform referrer that YP should seek help via family if appropriate or via victim support'. The social worker subsequently gave evidence that the referral was 'vague' to which the judge commented:

If she felt that the details being provided were vague at the time of the telephone conversation I can see no reason why she did not request further details nor why her manager did not instruct her to obtain more details.

(para. 9)

LEGAL CASE STUDY 5.1 (CONT.)

and

Rather than considering the issues to which the facts gave rise, which bore upon the question as to whether the claimant was a child in need, the social worker concentrated on the facts which she thought could be taken as pointing towards social services not accepting responsibility. The summary nature of her consideration, along with her manager, of the referral is borne out by the casual nature of the communication of the referral and fell far below the standard required by law.

(paras 13–14)

The judgement concluded that steps should be taken to ensure, inter alia, that:

(1) child in need assessments are not carried out in a summary manner as occurred in this case; and

(2) that the imminence of a child attaining 18 years is not taken as a basis for failing to take any action.

(para. 37)

LEGAL CASE STUDY 5.2

The Local Government Ombudsman (LGO) found that a local authority's 'inexcusable' failures to assess a 16-year-old boy as a 'child in need' and to accommodate him meant that he spent nine months living in a tent and suffered physical and mental ill-health. J became homeless when he was 16. As a younger teenager he had been taken into care and placed with foster parents. He returned to his mother but she told him to leave when he objected to her relationship with a drug user. A youth centre manager referred him to children's services by telephone but those contacts were not recorded and for six months no action was taken. A subsequent written referral resulted in the local authority giving J financial assistance, thus affirming that he met the criteria of a 'child in need', but he was not offered accommodation. Under pressure from other agencies the housing authority offered him a flat conditional upon him having an adult guarantor for the tenancy but it refused to accept a guarantee from children's services.

The LGO found maladministration because:

- *the local authority failed to fulfil its duties to J under the CA 1989; and*

- *the housing authority failed to fulfil its duties to J under the Housing Act 1996 and failed to follow its joint protocol with children's services.*

The local authority's failure to accommodate J under the CA 1989 s20 meant that he did not become entitled to advice and assistance under the Children (Leaving Care) Act and to remedy this injustice the LGO stated that J should be treated as if he was entitled to that support.

(LGO Reports 09017510 and 09017512)

Where a child who is not an eligible child ceases to be looked after because they return home, they become a 'child in need' and a plan should be drawn up to identify the services that will be needed by the child and family to ensure that the return home has the best chance of success (HMG, 2010, p99).

Every Child Matters and the Children Act 2004

The Green Paper *Every Child Matters* (DfES, 2003), which laid the foundations for the CA 2004, set out government plans for what it claimed were radical managerial reforms of child care systems, identified by Laming (2003) as necessary in order to improve the nature and effectiveness of multi-disciplinary working, promote integrated service delivery and increase accountability. A key constituent of *Every Child Matters* are the five outcomes against which children's welfare is to be measured and which can be seen displayed in almost every building that houses services for children.

ACTIVITY **5.2**

In relation to the Every Child Matters *outcomes and aims set out below (CWDC, 2009, with CA 2004 interpretation in brackets), assess the extent to which the words and phrases are objectively measurable (for example, what does 'healthy lifestyles' mean in a legal context? How do you assess whether a child is 'ready for school'? What constitutes 'positive behaviour'?). What implications does this have for practitioners working within this policy framework and for service users seeking access to services? What changes could you make to the language used so as to make it possible to assess or provide evidence of achievement of the framework's aims?*

- *Be healthy (physical and mental health and emotional well-being)*
  - o *physically healthy*
  - o *mentally and emotionally healthy*
  - o *sexually healthy*
  - o *healthy lifestyles*
  - o *choose not to take illegal drugs*
- *Stay safe (protection from harm and neglect)*
  - o *safe from maltreatment, neglect, violence and sexual exploitation*
  - o *safe from accidental injury and death*
  - o *safe from bullying and discrimination*
  - o *safe from crime and anti-social behaviour in and out of school*
  - o *have security, stability and are cared for*
- *Enjoy and achieve (education, training and recreation)*
  - o *ready for school*
  - o *attend and enjoy school*

---

    o *achieve stretching national educational standards at primary school*

    o *achieve personal and social development, and enjoy recreation*

    o *achieve stretching national educational standards at secondary school*

• *Make a positive contribution (the contribution made by them to society)*

    o *engage in decision-making and support the community and environment*

    o *engage in law-abiding and positive behaviour in and out of school*

    o *develop positive relationships and choose not to bully and discriminate*

    o *develop self-confidence and successfully deal with significant life changes and challenges*

    o *develop enterprising behaviour*

• *Achieve economic well-being (social and economic well-being)*

    o *engage in further education, employment or training on leaving school*

    o *ready for employment*

    o *live in decent homes and sustainable communities*

    o *access to transport and material goods*

    o *live in households free from low income*

The CA 2004 requires agencies actively to consider the need to safeguard and promote children's welfare while carrying out their normal functions, coordinated and monitored by Local Safeguarding Children Boards (see Chapters 6 and 10). 'Safeguarding' is not defined within legislation but in describing the processes by which children are offered services to promote their well-being it can be contrasted with the more interventionist term 'protection' which underpins the CA 1989 (Brayne and Carr, 2010).

Early intervention

A review by OFSTED (2011c) of early intervention services across 11 local authorities found that the young people and families concerned highly valued the support they had received and could clearly identify changes it had made to their lives. In many cases they regretted that this type of help had not been available to them at an earlier stage. As a result it was possible to identify the factors that were most likely to be successful in preventing children from becoming looked after, although it was not always possible to quantify success from the information contained within case records:

RESEARCH SUMMARY 5.1 *(CONT.)*

- *the quality, persistence and reliability of the key professional;*

- *the employment of explicit models and methods of intervention, supported by a repertoire of tools (although it was not found that one model was more successful than others);*

- *strong multi-agency working, both operationally and strategically;*

- *clear and consistent referral pathways;*

- *clear and consistent decision-making processes, based on thorough assessment of risks and strengths within the family network;*

- *a prompt and flexible approach, incorporating the views of the young person and the family, and utilising their strengths;*

- *a clear plan for intervention, based on thorough assessment and mutually agreed goals;*

- *regular reviews of progress and risk factors, with robust arrangements between agencies in respect of risk management;*

- *a clear plan for closure, including the means by which progress could be maintained when the service ceased.*

Munro (2011) has recommended that the government place a duty on local authorities and their statutory partners to secure the sufficient provision of local early help services for children, young people and families, with the expectation that this will lead to the early identification of need and the provision of appropriate help in cases in which assessed needs do not match the criteria for being offered statutory services.

Family Intervention Services

Family Intervention Services (FIS) form part of the government's commitment to provide support to families with a range of social, economic, health and behaviour difficulties. The services and projects, which worked with 5,400 families during 2010/11 (DfE, 2011e), offer intensive support for the whole family coordinated by a key worker. Statistical evaluation focused on family functioning and risk; crime and anti-social behaviour; health; education and employment. For each of these four domains, indicators were identified and a percentage reduction in risk calculated, based on reports from key workers. All areas were found to have shown significant statistical improvement although the report acknowledges that it was not possible to establish whether the results were directly attributed to the FIS, as change amongst families may occur naturally over time or because of other services received. In addition, risk may continue to exist (for example, that a family member may be convicted of a crime) after families have completed an intervention programme, even though the level of risk might appear statistically to have reduced. These factors highlight the difficulties inherent in objective monitoring and evaluation of social and community services.

Family and children's centres

The CA 1989 Schedule 2 states that every local authority shall provide such family centres 'as they consider appropriate in relation to children within their area'. Family centres may provide occupational, social, cultural or recreational activities and advice, guidance or counselling. In practice, they provide a range of services to support children and families and complement field social work, particularly in relation to assessment.

Sure Start Children's Centres (SSCCs) were introduced in 1998 and by 2010, 3,500 had been established. Children's centres are funded at different levels, depending on the measurement of area deprivation, and are required to offer the following services to families:

- integrated day care (not required in phase three centres) and early learning;
- drop-in sessions and activities;
- child and family health services (provided by the NHS and other partners);
- outreach and family support;
- links with Jobcentre Plus for training and employment advice;
- support for childminders;
- support for parents of children with special needs.

The universal basis of children's centres was considered to be an important foundation for their work with the neediest families in that it was hoped it would bring them into contact with the majority of local families, providing a vehicle for early identification and ensuring a good social mix. Although there have been concerns that assertive middle-class parents may displace those who are less confident in making use of children's centres, evaluation suggests that a social mix helps to improve the effectiveness of services for disadvantaged children and that it is possible to maximise take-up by particular groups by means of good planning and individually targeted approaches (Pinney, 2011). Despite severe economic pressures, the government has reiterated its commitment to Sure Start provision although it will be subject to closer scrutiny in terms of measuring achievement. Families considered to be 'at risk of poor outcomes', and therefore priority groups for SSCC services, are (DfES, 2006):

- teenage parents;
- lone parents;
- families in poverty and workless households;
- families in temporary accommodation;
- parents with mental health, drug or alcohol problems;
- families with a parent in prison or engaged in criminal activity;
- families from minority ethnic communities;
- families of asylum seekers;
- parents of children with disabilities; and
- parents with disabilities.

However, children's centres themselves (Pinney, 2011) have identified other groups that should be included within their target users, which illustrates how government guidance, usually based on political priorities, can prove restrictive or even discriminatory at times and needs to be continuously reviewed in the light of evidence gained from practice:

- fathers, particularly those who have experienced disadvantage and social exclusion;

- families affected by domestic abuse;

- isolated parents including those with depression, no family support or living in rural areas;

- travellers and other transient families, including recent immigrants.

Family group conferences

A family group conference (FGC) is a voluntary family-led process of planning and decision-making in respect of children whose safety or well-being may be at risk. FGCs originated in New Zealand in response to concerns expressed by the indigenous population about the impact of child welfare decisions on their traditional way of life. FGCs have been found to be an effective method of engaging and utilising potential support from wider family, friends and community resources (FRG, 2011) and they can provide evidence that the local authority has attempted to engage the wider family and encouraged the parties to use alternative dispute resolution prior to a court application as required by the Public Law Outline (MoJ, 2010). FGCs may also help to avoid sequential assessments of potential carers which can be a cause of delay

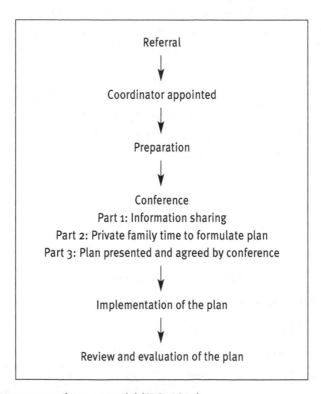

Figure 5.1 Family group conference model (FRG, 2011)

in care planning within public law proceedings. FGCs are based on the principles of the CA 1989 and the philosophy that families, if properly supported, will make safer and more effective plans for their children than those imposed on them by professionals. Local authorities are therefore encouraged to have a local policy framework within which they can offer FGCs to help families devise solutions to identified difficulties and risks. Three-quarters of local authorities in England and Wales run or commission FGCs or are planning to do so. However, there is no legal mandate for convening FGCs in England and Wales, they are not suitable for use in an emergency and should not replace or remove the need for child protection conferences (DfE, 2010b).

A fundamental principle of FGCs is that the coordinator is both independent and neutral (that is, they have no case-holding, statutory or decision-making responsibilities in relation to the child) and that they should be run independently of the team responsible for the child's safety and well-being.

Children with disabilities

As children with disabilities come within the statutory definition of children 'in need', any referral of a disabled child to children's services should result in an initial assessment, although they might also be entitled to services under alternative legislation. The general duty to provide support services under the CA 1989 s17 is dependent on the authority determining that the provision of services is appropriate, whereas the duty under the Chronically Sick and Disabled Persons Act 1970 s2 is triggered by the authority being satisfied that the services are necessary. As there is little, if any, difference between these tests (although consistency of language would have been sensible), a local authority can decide that a disabled child is not eligible for support services unless it is satisfied that they are necessary. However the authority must be able to explain the process by which eligibility is determined.

LEGAL CASE STUDY **5.3**

In R v Gloucestershire CC ex p Barry [1997] 2 WLR 459 the use of eligibility criteria was held to be lawful provided it is in keeping with the principles of the relevant legislation. However, whilst the use of such criteria is well argued in adult case law, the judgement in R (JL) v Islington LBC [2009] EWHC 458 (Admin) in which the local authority's criteria was found to be unlawful in seeking to impose a maximum limit on the amount of respite care provided for disabled children, regardless of the result of assessment, stressed the need for guidance on eligibility criteria for children's services. The judge explained the somewhat confusing situation as follows:

There are a number of statutory provisions under which a local authority may have a duty or a discretion to assess and/or provide for particular needs of a (disabled) child. The extent to which a local authority is entitled to rely upon eligibility criteria depends upon which type of statutory provision is in play. The claimants concede that where the local authority merely has a discretion to make provision, it is free to use eligibility criteria. Where a statutory duty arises, the precise nature of the duty must be identified. It may, for example, be an absolute duty to provide for a particular need of an individual child, in which case

---

LEGAL CASE STUDY **5.3** *(CONT.)*

there is no room for eligibility criteria. It may, on the other hand, be a duty which is qualified in some way, for instance a duty to 'take reasonable steps' to achieve a particular objective, in which case the local authority can take into account, amongst other things, its overall financial resources and can, if it wishes, introduce eligibility criteria. Much argument has accordingly been directed to establishing under which statutory provision the local authority are making provision for JL and what the attributes of the relevant statutory provision are.

(para. 46)

In another case, a mother and her two autistic children successfully settled judicial review proceedings that challenged the introduction by their local authority of thresholds to be met before children's services would accept referrals, conduct assessments or provide services. After the claimants' support had been withdrawn following the introduction of the eligibility criteria they challenged: (1) the lawfulness of the criteria; (2) the process by which it was introduced; and (3) the decision-making process in their own case. Under the settlement the family achieved the services they sought. The local authority was also required to withdraw its eligibility criteria and to undertake a 12-week public consultation if it intends to introduce criteria in the future.

(www.familylawweek.co.uk/site.aspx?i=ed98673)

If there exists a duty to meet an assessed need of a disabled child under the CSDPA 1970 s2, the duty should not be avoided by the local authority deciding to act under the more discretionary target provisions of the CA 1989 s17.

The CSDPA 1970 s2 details the services that councils must provide to disabled children (and adults):

• practical assistance in the home;

• respite care or short breaks;

• wireless, television, library, 'or similar recreational facilities' (an example of dated legislation);

• recreational and educational facilities;

• assistance with travel;

• home adaptations;

• holidays, meals and telephones.

RESEARCH SUMMARY 5.2

OFSTED (2012c), in a thematic inspection of local authority services for disabled children in need, found that work was not always well coordinated, some assessments were out of date, many plans lacked detail and cases were not reviewed regularly or sufficiently thoroughly, which contributed to a lack of robust monitoring and delays in identifying ongoing concerns. Assessments did not consistently identify and analyse key risk factors, including previous concerns, which led to delays in some children getting the right level of support and intervention. It was emphasised that lack of rigour in the management of child in need work increased the likelihood of child protection concerns not being identified early enough.

Local authorities have powers to make direct payment to anyone with parental responsibility for a disabled child and any assessment under the CA 1989 s17 should be complemented by assessments under the CSDPA 1970, Education Act 1996 and Disabled Persons (Services, Consultation and Representation) Act 1986. If a child receives a short break or is cared for by a sitter or overnight carer provided by the local authority under the CA 1989 s17, they do not become looked after within the meaning of the Act. However, children who have a substantial number of short breaks, or whose families may have difficulties providing support to their child while away from home or monitoring the quality of care received, might be protected more effectively by being accommodated under s20. In such circumstances the placement must be with local authority foster carers, in a registered children's home or other approved setting (HMG, 2010, p108).

Potential or actual homelessness

Young people who present themselves, or who are referred, as homeless pose particular challenges in practice as they often act, and expect to be treated, as if they were adults, resistant to anyone, whether the state, a parent or anyone else, exercising parental responsibility for them.

Government guidance to local authorities in the context of young people who are homeless, or who are at risk of homelessness (CLG and DSCF, 2010), is based on the principle that it is in the best interests of most young people to live in their family home or, where this is not safe or appropriate, with responsible adults in their wider family and friends network. Local authority children's services should be the lead agency in assessing and meeting the needs of 16 and 17 year olds who seek help because of homelessness and are expected to work with young people and their families to identify and resolve the factors that have led to the crisis. This could involve family support, such as family mediation or family group conference, or accommodation under the CA 1989 s20 while work is undertaken with a view to reunification. This preventive work should be undertaken alongside the statutory assessment processes and should not delay assessment or the delivery of statutory services. Assessment, support and accommodation services should take into account the existence of young people's relationships and any dependent children. Where a 16 or 17 year old moves from one local authority area to another, the duty to assess falls on the authority from which they actually seek assistance.

Most of the recent legal cases where local authority responsibilities in these situations have been at issue illustrate the gateway principle of children's services: that is, the CA 1989 provides certain points at which local authority assessments of children are mandatory and determine whether the child is offered services, referred elsewhere or advised that they do not meet the criteria for intervention. The gateway decision by the local authority in relation to whether a young person should become 'looked after' has important financial implications for the young person in terms of eligibility for post-care support and for anyone who might be caring for them.

The following cases involved young people who had been turned out of their family home and define the local children's authority's duty in such circumstances.

LEGAL CASE STUDY 5.4

R (M) v Hammersmith and Fulham LBC *[2008] UKHL 14*

In this case, a 16-year-old girl approached her local housing authority requesting accommodation after her mother asked her to leave. The House of Lords stated that she should have been referred to children's services for assessment: 'the Children Act duties supersede the Housing Act duties towards a 16- or 17-year-old young person' (para. 15). It was not contemplated that, had she been assessed as falling within the criteria contained within the CA 1989 s20(1), she might have been referred back to the housing department:

> The clear intention of the legislation is that these children need more than a roof over their heads and that children's services authorities cannot avoid their responsibilities towards this challenging age group by passing them over to local housing authorities. There is all the difference in the world between the services which an eligible, relevant or former relevant child can expect from her local children's services authority, to make up for the lack of proper parental support and guidance within the family, and the sort of help which a young homeless person, even if in priority need, can expect from her local housing authority.

> *(para. 24)*

LEGAL CASE STUDY 5.5

R (on the application of G) (FC) v Southwark LBC *[2009] UKHL 26*

This case concerned a 17-year-old boy who asked his local authority to accommodate him under the CA 1989 s20. The local authority provided bed and breakfast accommodation whilst they carried out an initial assessment after which they declined to accommodate him under s20 as he required only 'help with accommodation' under s17. Consequently he was referred to the local housing authority under homelessness provision which, since the enactment of the Homelessness (Priority Need for Accommodation) (England) Order 2002, includes children aged 16 and 17 among those with priority need, whilst excluding those to whom a local authority owes a duty under the CA 1989 s20. The House of Lords, however, stated that:

LEGAL CASE STUDY 5.5 *(CONT.)*

Parliament has decided the circumstances in which the duty to accommodate arises and then decided what that duty involves. It is not for the local authority to decide that, because they do not like what the duty to accommodate involves or do not think it appropriate, they do not have to accommodate at all.

The judgement went on to state that 'it cannot seriously be suggested that a child excluded from home who is "sofa surfing" in this way, more often sleeping in cars, snatching showers and washing his clothes when he can, is not in need' (para. 28). Although a children's authority can ask a housing authority for help in the exercise of their functions, 'this does not mean that they can avoid their responsibilities by "passing the buck" to another authority; rather that they can ask another authority to use its powers to help them discharge theirs' (para. 33). The court decided that A had been accommodated under the CA 1989 s20(1) and therefore became an 'eligible child' within the meaning of paragraph 19B(2) of Schedule 2, and subsequently a 'former relevant child' within the meaning of section 23C(1).

Government guidance arising from these legal decisions (CLG and DCSF, 2010) states that local authorities must accommodate homeless 16- and 17-year-old young people under the CA 1989 s20(1) if:

- they are a 'child in need'; and

- there is no one who has parental responsibility for the child, they have been abandoned, or the person who has been looking after them is unable to provide them with accommodation.

In addition, even if the above criteria do not apply, ss20(3) and 20(4) require that:

- every local authority shall provide accommodation for any child in need within their area who has reached the age of 16 and whose welfare the authority considers is likely to be seriously prejudiced if they do not provide him with accommodation; and

- a local authority may provide accommodation for any child within their area (even though a person who has parental responsibility for him is able to provide him with accommodation) if it considers that to do so would safeguard or promote the child's welfare.

This duty on children's services authorities takes precedence over housing authorities' duties towards homeless people contained within the Housing Act 1996, and the specific duty owed under the CA 1989 s20 takes precedence over the general duty owed to children in need and their families under s17. Housing authorities are expected to provide homeless 16 and 17 year olds with immediate, suitable interim accommodation and refer them, and any young person likely to become homeless within 28 days, to children's services for assessment. Bed and breakfast accommodation is specified in the guidance as unsuitable in this context, even in an emergency. If the assessment concludes that the young person should be accommodated under s20 they become eligible for leaving care support under the provisions of the CLCA 2000. Young people accommodated under s20 are not eligible for welfare benefits, including housing benefit, and children's services have a duty to maintain them, including meeting the cost of accommodation. Where young parents are provided with accommodation and become looked after, it does not follow that their child is also looked after; this is an issue for a separate assessment based on the needs of the child concerned. Determining who is in need and the extent of any needs requires professional judgement, based on careful assessment, ascertaining the wishes and feelings of the young person and their family, and consultation with other professionals.

Young carers

Under the Carers (Recognition and Services) Act 1995 any young person aged under 16 years who is caring for a disabled adult can request a carer's assessment, which must be undertaken whenever the person they care for is being assessed or reassessed for community care. However, there is evidence that many young carers are unaware of this entitlement and that professionals are unclear as to how a 'young carer' should be defined, particularly when the adult's difficulties stem from drug or alcohol misuse (OFSTED, 2009). Under the Community Care (Direct Payments) Act 1996 and the Carers and Disabled Children Act 2000 local authorities are empowered to make cash payments to people who have been assessed as needing services, in lieu of social service provisions. Direct payments can be made to disabled people aged 16 or over, to people with parental responsibility for disabled children, and to carers aged 16 or over in respect of carer services, and could therefore be used as a means of supporting disabled adults with the care of their children.

Age assessment

The duty of local authorities towards children under the CA 1989 depends on them being under the age of 18. For migrant young people who come to the United Kingdom unaccompanied by their families, their age is therefore, initially at least, the most important characteristic in determining whether they are owed a duty at all and, if found to be a 'child in need' under s17, the nature of the assistance provided. Age also determines how the young person is treated by the immigration authorities.

No statutory guidance exists on assessing age. The guidelines adopted by many local authorities since 2003 were approved in the case of *R (B) v Merton LBC* [2003] EWHC 1689 (Admin), and subsequently known as the *Merton guidelines*. Key constituents of the guidelines are:

- two qualified and properly trained social workers should conduct the age assessment;

- an appropriate adult should be present;

- the child should be informed of the purpose of the assessment;

- physical appearance and demeanour are not determinative of age;

- the assessment process must consider all aspects of the child's life and development;

- social workers must obtain as much information as they can about the chronological life-history and development of the young person;

- a young person may lie about aspects of their life unrelated to age (such as reasons for seeking asylum) and inconsistencies should not be counted against the young person automatically;

- as a matter of fairness, any inconsistencies should be put to the young person so that they have an opportunity to clarify matters before a conclusion is reached on their age;

- reasons must be given for decisions made;

- the local authority must make its own decision and cannot simply adopt the assessment of the UK Border Agency.

The Supreme Court judgement in the case of *R (A) v Croydon LBC* [2009] UKSC 8 further defined the process to be followed when age assessments are disputed.

- Decisions about a child's welfare needs are best left to the evaluation of the social worker. There is often no clear right or wrong answer but the court can supervise such decisions by ensuring that they are fair, rational and take account of all relevant material whilst disregarding irrelevant material.

- A person's age is, however, an objective fact.

- As local authorities' duties under the CA 1989 are dependent on knowing whether a person is a child, the fact of age needs to be established.

- Decisions on age cannot rest on the judgement of the social worker alone. The starting point is the Merton guidelines, but if the matter is disputed the court can assume the role of the decision-maker and determine the fact of age for itself, with the decision being binding on both the local authority and the UK Border Agency.

Since the 2009 Supreme Court judgement there have been 16 reported judgements of substantive age assessment cases:

- In five of 16 cases, a declaration was made in favour of upholding the young person's claimed age.

- In six cases, there was a finding in favour of the age assessed by the local authority.

- In the remaining five cases, the court arrived at a different date of birth, three of which were somewhere between the assessed and the claimed date of birth. In the other two, the court arrived at an entirely different date of birth, older even than that assessed by the local authority.

A report for the Office of the Children's Commissioner (Brownlees and Yazdani, 2012) found that although in a few cases the court was unimpressed by the evidence from the assessing social workers, generally their evidence was regarded as expert, balanced and measured. The authors found that local authorities' wariness of litigation was having a detrimental impact on age assessment decision-making in that some social workers were conceding to a young person's claimed age, rather than risk a protracted and expensive legal dispute. There was also concern as to whether judges had the knowledge and experience required to make age assessments any more accurately than social workers.

> *We do a holistic assessment, but it's not an exact science . . . and it's scary having to go to court and be asked to defend something you don't know with 100 per cent certainty.*
> (Social worker, quoted in Brownlees and Yazdani, 2012, p73)

A pregnant young woman from Cameroon, claiming that she was 15 years old, was assessed by her local authority as being an adult. Consequently, the local authority did not provide accommodation for her and she looked to the National Asylum Support Service for support. She was subsequently refused discretionary leave to remain in the UK until her eighteenth birthday, which would have happened if she had been adjudged a child. It later transpired, on the basis of genuine official documents, that the girl had been truthful about her age and she made a complaint to the Local Government Ombudsman (LGO). The LGO found maladministration because the age assessment had not been carried out in accordance with the Merton guidance. In particular:

1. *The assessment form did not record the questions asked of the girl and the answers given.*

2. *The girl's ethnicity, culture and customs were not explored as part of the judgement as to whether her account of how she arrived in the UK was correct.*

3. *No consideration was given to whether a medical examination would be of assistance.*

4. *The girl was not given the opportunity to comment on alleged inconsistencies in her story.*

5. *The girl was not provided with reasons for the council's decision.*

(Local Government Ombudsman decision 08 005 858)

Private fostering

Although private fostering is substitute care in that privately fostered children are living away from their own families, from a social work point of view it involves exercising legal duties in the context of monitoring, support and, occasionally, protection. Some local authorities automatically consider privately fostered children to be 'children in need' and there is increasing recognition of the needs of children living in these circumstances.

Which of the following situations come within the legal definition of private fostering? Answers are at the end of the chapter.

1. *A 14-year-old girl spends a couple of months with her best friend's family after a row with her parents.*

2. *A 17-year-old Italian boy is lodging with a local family whilst taking a three-month English language course.*

3. *A 15-year-old looked-after child is placed with foster carers via a private fostering agency.*

4. *A 10-year-old Nigerian boy has been living with an unrelated godparent for the last two years while his parents are at university.*

5. A nine-month-old baby is looked after by her grandparents for four months while her mother serves a prison sentence.

6. A 15-year-old boy recently arrived in the UK and seeking asylum is living in the same house as two adults from his home country.

7. Victoria Climbié at the time of her death.

Many children avoid entering the public care system because parents arrange for relatives, friends or neighbours to care for their children if they are unable to do so themselves. A privately fostered child is under 16, or 18 if disabled, and living with someone who is not a close relative or a person with parental responsibility for more than 28 days. Close relatives include step-parents, siblings, brothers or sisters of a parent, and grandparents. There is potential for confusion with what is known as kinship care but if a child is placed by a local authority with friends and family either by parental agreement under the CA 1989 s20, or under a care order, then the child becomes looked after and their carers should be approved as local authority foster carers. In exceptional circumstances, a local authority may make time-limited payments under the CA 1989 s17 to support a child's placement with relatives or friends as an alternative to accommodating them under the CA 1989.

Parents and carers have a legal duty to notify the local authority when entering into a private fostering arrangement; local authorities are then required to carry out an assessment, and to monitor the arrangement. Although not directly responsible for arranging or providing care to privately fostered children, local authority responsibilities, set out in the CA 1989 as amended by the CA 2004 s44, related regulations and the national minimum standards (DCSF, 2005) include the duty to:

- respond to notifications of private fostering arrangements, where possible before they start;

- determine what arrangements have been made for safeguarding the welfare of children and young people, and take relevant steps if they are not satisfied that children's welfare is being protected and promoted, which might include the disqualification of the private foster carer;

- visit the child or young person at least every six weeks during the first year of placement, and then three monthly, in order to:

  i. satisfy themselves that the child or young person is being properly cared for;

  ii. monitor the arrangements for the child or young person's care;

  iii. ascertain the child or young person's wishes and feelings, preferably by speaking to them alone; and

  iv. offer advice and support to children and young people who are privately fostered.

  Whilst recognising that these are 'minimum' standards, they are nevertheless notably unambitious with respect to enhancing children's quality of life or life chances more generally.
  (Shaw et al., 2010, p97)

It could be argued that a more detailed policy framework with specific outcome indicators for privately fostered children is needed, similar to those for looked-after children. However, it would be difficult to identify measurable indicators of relevance to the diversity of children and situations included within the definition of private fostering. For example, for children being looked after away from home for weeks rather than months, the duty to promote safety and welfare might be sufficient. However, for those in longer-term arrangements with little contact with those who have parental responsibility for them, health and education increase in significance and there is little, if any, accepted research-based understanding as to what constitutes effective practice in private fostering.

RESEARCH SUMMARY 5.3

Shaw et al. *(2010) found that despite the legal duty to notify local authorities in advance about private fostering arrangements, this rarely happens in practice and awareness of private fostering was low among practitioners working with children. Private fostering was situated in a range of different locations within local authority structures, resulting in inconsistency in assessment and the level of support provided. The concepts of attachment and permanence, together with the longevity of some cross-cultural arrangements and some birth parents' misunderstanding of the context for private fostering within the UK, resulted in some birth parents 'losing' their children to private foster carers after they were granted a residence order. The term 'private fostering' was thought confusing, although a tension was identified between a broad 'catch-all' definition and the multiplicity of different types of arrangement and requirements that needed to be addressed within it.*

LEGAL CASE STUDY 5.7

R (A) v Coventry City Council *[2009] EWHC 34 (Admin)*

A 15-year-old boy (T) went to live with a friend as a result of family conflict. Subsequently the friend's mother contacted the local authority to say she was finding it difficult to support him although she did not want him to be taken into care, which is what would happen if she did not receive financial assistance. This triggered an Initial Assessment, which took five months, instead of the seven days required by the Framework for the Assessment of Children in Need. *The foster carer believed that the result of the assessment was that she would be offered financial assistance, although the local authority subsequently maintained that as T was being privately fostered it had no duty to accommodate him under the CA 1989 s20 and she should look to his parents for payment. Although it was suggested that the foster carer had not understood the financial implications of the term 'private fostering' the judge stated that: 'this is not a sustainable assertion. If there was a private fostering arrangement, it was not one made as a result of anything done by the boy's father' (para. 20). The local authority agreed to make weekly payments under the CA 1989 s17 until T's 16th birthday when, they said, he could claim housing benefit. The court decided that the local authority's decision that it was a private fostering arrangement was unsupportable as, without certainty in relation to accommodation, T was a child in need requiring assistance. Therefore, T was a looked-after child and the local authority should pay the appropriate weekly allowance to the foster carer until his 18th birthday.*

FURTHER READING

www.frg.org.uk

Family Rights Group is a charity that advises families whose children are involved with or need children's services because of welfare needs or concerns.

www.lag.org.uk

The Legal Action Group is a national charity that aims to promote equal access to justice for members of society who are socially, economically or otherwise disadvantaged.

Answers to Activity 5.3:

Numbers 1, 4, 6 and 7 come within the definition of private fostering; numbers 2, 3 and 5 do not.

Chapter 6
Protection

This chapter aims to further encourage critical thinking by exploring the interface between social work practice, society's attitudes and the legal framework that determines how our child welfare systems operate, particularly in relation to the protection of children. By demonstrating how the law is subject to interpretation, it supports the requirements of PCF by encouraging you to develop sound judgement and be able to use authority to intervene with individuals, families and communities to prevent harm, neglect and abuse whilst exercising your legal powers and duties.

Introduction

The relationship between the Government's investment in supporting the family as a whole – early prevention and supporting the larger net of families in need – and its investment in targeting children at risk is a fraught one.

(Henricson and Bainham, 2005, p46)

Don't just think because nothing was proved that it's OK for the child to be at home.

(Looked-after child quoted in CRDE, 2011b, p20)

While awareness of neglect is increasing, we now face the stark reality that the majority of social workers feel powerless to help.

(Burgess et al., 2012, p4)

Social workers are in a very difficult place. If they take no action and something goes wrong, inevitable and heavy criticism will follow. If they take action which ultimately turns out to have been unnecessary, they will have caused distress to an already distressed parent. On the other hand they also have access to draconian powers and, if child protection is to command public respect and agreement, such powers must be exercised lawfully and proportionately and be the subject of public scrutiny. This litigation shows that child protection comes at a cost: to an innocent parent who is subject to it based on emergency assessment of risk, and to public authorities who have to account for their exercise of power. It is, however, a cost that has inevitably to be exacted if the most vulnerable members of our society, dependent children, are to be protected by the state.

(Judgement in *A v East Sussex County Council & Ors* [2010] EWCA Civ 743)

We had intended to entitle this chapter 'Safeguarding', which gradually replaced 'child protection' as the term used to describe the processes by which the safety of children at risk of significant harm should be secured. However, the concept of child protection is reappearing in policy and guidance, which again demonstrates the significance of language as an indication of prevailing cultural and political ideology. The term 'safeguarding' suggests the preservation of a satisfactory state, whereas 'child protection' is more reflective of a proactive, interventionist approach.

The Children's Rights Director for England (2010) reports that children themselves rank protection from abuse first among children's rights, and safeguarding of children has been at the heart of our family welfare services since their inception. Legislation and policy in this area are shaped by a range of influences including human rights, social attitudes, political priorities and economic necessity alongside messages from inquiries and research and, increasingly, target-driven performance evaluation. Inevitably, this complex mix results in a framework that can present ethical challenges, procedural overload, inconsistency and uncertainty rather than a solid foundation for sound and confident decision-making.

Alan Jones, author of the second serious case review (SCR) into events surrounding the death of Peter Connelly in 2007, stated that the main lesson to be learned from almost every SCR he had written or studied was the need for social workers to be more challenging and assertive. However, he also suggested that much government guidance, with its emphasis on supporting and keeping families together, prevents social workers from being as authoritative as they sometimes need to be (**www.communitycare.co.uk**, 10 November 2010), a theme further advanced within Munro's review of child protection (2011).

ACTIVITY 6.1

As part of society's attempts to use the law to protect those of its citizens who are regarded as vulnerable, one of the most common legal sanctions relates to age. At what age can you do the following?

1. *Buy a pet.*

2. *Open a bank account.*

3. *Drink alcohol at home.*

4. *Be convicted of a criminal offence.*

5. *Become a street trader.*

6. *Possess a shotgun, airgun, air rifle or ammunition.*

7. *Buy cigarettes or tobacco.*

8. *Be left alone at home.*

9. *Take paid employment.*

10. *Give consent to medical treatment.*

ACTIVITY 6.1 (CONT.)

11. Act as a babysitter.

12. Have a tattoo.

In relation to 3, 8 and 11 the law does not provide an answer, so the exercise of individual judgement is required.

- *What dilemmas arise from relying on the law to decide who needs to be protected and in what circumstances?*

- *What needs to be taken into account when making such decisions?*

- *What implications does this have for parents, carers, social workers and society in general?*

Historical context

During the late 1970s and 1980s, several recurring themes were found in reports of inquiries into circumstances in which children appeared to have been inadequately protected against abuse and neglect (Jasmine Beckford, 1985; Kimberley Carlisle and Tyra Henry, 1987). These included:

- failure of social workers to identify and perform their legal duties;

- poor inter-agency communication;

- inadequate social work recording;

- social workers uncomfortable and lacking confidence in an authoritarian role.

In response, social workers became more proactive in the field of child protection but events in Cleveland (1987), in which children were removed from home on the basis of the diagnosis of sexual abuse by a single consultant paediatrician, were used by parents, lawyers, pressure groups and MPs to press for legislative reform. In particular, there was a move to challenge professional power by involving courts more closely in decision-making throughout the process of assessment and care planning. These contradictory forces led to the development and implementation of the Children Act 1989, which initiated changes in the relationship between the state and the family and reflected increasing recognition of the concept of children's rights, although they are not specifically articulated as such (see Chapter 1).

The CA 1989:

- introduced a single route into care (previously children could be placed in care as a consequence of a criminal conviction or being in moral danger, in addition to welfare factors);

- established a threshold for care and supervision orders;

- provided for local authority services for children in need and others;

- affirmed that the best place to bring up children is usually within their own family;

- promoted the philosophy that services are most likely to be effective when provided in partnership with parents and other carers;

- included a statutory requirement to take account of children's wishes and feelings when making decisions about their welfare;

- incorporated the welfare, no order and no delay principles within the provisions relating to statutory intervention.

The CA 1989 also introduced a new language for dealing with the welfare of children:

- contact replaced access;

- residence replaced custody;

- parental rights and duties became parental responsibilities; and

- significant harm became the sole criterion for statutory intervention.

However, legislation is only the framework for change; actual change comes through the interpretation and implementation of the law over time, which is why it is helpful to take an interest in court decisions. Major areas of law relating to children remain outside the CA 1989, notably adoption, youth justice and services for children leaving care.

Every Child Matters and *Working Together to Safeguard Children*

Legislation, policy and guidance have developed with good intentions, but a distance has developed between common-sense empathy with the unhappiness of hungry, tired, unkempt and distressed children and an overly bureaucratic and anxiety-ridden system for reaching out to help them.

(Burgess *et al.*, 2012, p19)

The *Every Child Matters* Green Paper (DfES, 2003) includes 'being safe' as one of five key 'outcomes' for children. In this context, key provisions of the CA 2004 were:

- the creation of Children's Trusts, now on a statutory footing as Children's Trust Boards;

- the establishment of Local Safeguarding Children Boards (LSCBs); and

- the duty on all agencies to safeguard and promote children's welfare.

Lord Laming's (2009) progress report on child protection made recommendations relating to: leadership and accountability, support for children, inter-agency working, children's workforce, improvement and challenge, organisation and finance, and the legal framework. Many of these recommendations were addressed by statutory guidance *Working Together to Safeguard Children* (DfE, 2010b) which contains almost 400 pages. As its title suggests, cooperation between agencies and partnership with parents are key components of child protection law and policy, and carry considerable legal authority (Williams, 2008). As part of the government's expressed commitment to simplify the child protection system and reduce the bureaucracy identified by Munro (2011) as inhibiting the exercise of professional judgement and robust decision-making, this has been redrafted and condensed to 21 pages of guidance in checklist form, to be supplemented by two separate guides to assessing children in need and to SCRs, amounting to less than 10 per cent of the length of the current document. However, in view of the large quantity of government guidance issued in the past few years, it will be surprising if this bold aim is borne out in practice. The proposed new guidance confirms the government's intention to replace nationally prescribed timescales for assessment and its commitment to publishing every SCR in full. The consultation period in relation to the proposed changes ended in September 2012.

Local Safeguarding Children Boards

Local Safeguarding Children Boards (LSCBs) are the mechanisms for determining how the relevant statutory, independent and voluntary organisations in each local authority area cooperate to safeguard and promote the welfare of children, and for ensuring the effectiveness of what they do.

Their functions include (DfE, 2010b):

- developing policies and procedures, including those on:

  o actions to be taken where there are concerns about the safety and welfare of a child, including thresholds for intervention;

  o training of people who work with children or in services affecting the safety and welfare of children;

  o recruitment and supervision of people who work with children;

  o investigation of allegations concerning people who work with children;

  o safety and welfare of children who are privately fostered; and

  o cooperation with neighbouring children's services authorities and their LSCB partners.

- communicating and raising awareness;

- monitoring and evaluation, by means of peer review, self-evaluation, performance indicators and joint audit;

- participating in planning and commissioning;

- undertaking an SCR into the death of any child in their area, including deaths by suspected suicide, in custody or while detained under the Mental Health Act 2007 or where abuse or neglect are known or suspected to have been a factor.

ACTIVITY *6.2*

- In relation to the LSCB functions listed above, what kinds of performance indicators or other evidence would you like to see attached to them?

- How might the guidance be rewritten to make it possible realistically to assess and evaluate local performance?

- What can front-line professionals contribute to LSCBs?

- How might LSCBs make a difference to the work of social workers?

This activity should help you look beyond the language that is widely used in policy documents and consider whether it contributes to a comprehensive, transparent and accountable service likely to withstand challenge, meeting the needs of both the professionals involved and the people it seeks to support or protect.

Duty to investigate

The CA 1989 s47(1) contains the local authority's duty to 'make, or cause to be made, such enquiries as they consider to be necessary to enable them to decide whether they should take any action to safeguard or protect the child's welfare' if it has 'reasonable cause to suspect that a child who lives, or is found, in their area is suffering or is likely to suffer significant harm'. Use of the word 'suspect' signifies a lower threshold for investigation than that required for the making of any court order to protect a child (Brayne and Carr, 2010). The *Framework for the Assessment of Children in Need and Their Families* (DoH, 2000) provides the structure for the scope of s47 enquiries and *Working Together to Safeguard Children* (DfE, 2010b) currently specifies the timescales within which initial and core assessments should be completed.

In England in 2010–11, 111,700 children were subject to an s47 enquiry. Nearly half of these resulted in an initial child protection conference, 69.2 per cent of which were held within the specified 15 working days, and 49,000 children subsequently became the subject of a child protection plan (DfE, 2011g). Child protection conferences have been the primary tool for the coordination of child protection investigations since the inquiry into the death of Maria Colwell in 1974. However, they remain non-statutory in that neither their role nor their composition is set out in legislation, although there is detailed guidance as to their functions in *Working Together to Safeguard Children*.

> When and how to intervene in cases of child neglect poses a dilemma not only for social workers but also for the legal profession. To social workers, legal decision-making may appear to favour the carer over the child. To lawyers, social workers may appear to allow cases of neglect to drift from bad to worse for years, hoping that parents will change and improve the quality of their child care because they said so, or because the neglect is associated with situational circumstances beyond their control.
>
> (Iwaniec *et al.*, 2004, p423)

RESEARCH SUMMARY 6.1

A review of the implementation of the Framework for the Assessment of Children in Need and Their Families *showed that although it had brought about some improvements, practitioners often lacked confidence in their ability to analyse the data that they collected (Cleaver and Walker, 2004).*

Dorsey et al. (2008) identified the poor accuracy of much decision-making in the course of safeguarding processes, with some assessments deemed to be only slightly better than guesswork.

Neglect is the most common category identified for children subject to a child protection plan, representing 44 per cent of such children in England and Wales, 43 per cent in Scotland and 50 per cent in Northern Ireland. Over 50 per cent of social workers have felt powerless to intervene when they have suspected that a child is being neglected (up from just over a third in two years), primarily because they considered that the point at which they could intervene was too high. However, there are no statistics to show how many children experience neglect (www.actionforchildren.org.uk/media/4320832/evaluation_uk_neglect_project_2012.pdf).

Radford et al. (2011), in a comparative study, found little change in reported lack of care as between 1998 and 2011, and although 81 per cent of staff in universal services (teachers, nursery staff and health care professionals) had encountered children whom they suspected to have been neglected, many found it difficult to get a response to their concerns.

Masson et al. (2008) analysed public law care proceedings court documents.

- *42 per cent of applications were prompted by a crisis, with a further 22 per cent arising from planned action to protect a newborn baby;*

- *Almost three-quarters of applications related to actual harm; with 27 per cent based on likely harm, most of which involved newborn babies.*

- *Harm was most frequently attributed to parents. Harm was attributed to partners in 31 per cent of cases where the parent had a partner, and to others (former partners, relatives or family friends) in 13 per cent of cases. The source of harm was unknown or disputed in only 5 per cent of cases.*

- *Of the four categories of harm (neglect, physical, sexual and emotional abuse) neglect was most common, alleged in 75 per cent of cases; emotional abuse was alleged in 64 per cent, physical abuse in 45 per cent and sexual abuse in 17 per cent. At least two categories of harm were cited in two-thirds of cases, the most common combination being neglect and emotional abuse, with the latter most likely to be alleged in cases involving domestic violence.*

- *Almost three-quarters of children were separated from their parents when the proceedings started.*

- *Lack of cooperation with welfare agencies featured in a significant proportion of cases, with mental illness, substance misuse, learning difficulties, domestic violence or chaotic lifestyle described as precipitating factors in 85 per cent of cases.*

- *Allegations relating specifically to neglect, inconsistent parenting, emotional abuse, physical abuse and school attendance were recorded in almost 80 per cent of cases.*

- *Over half of the children were subject to a child protection plan at the date of the application.*

- *A third of mothers were stated to have no support from their own families, with four-fifths receiving no support from their children's father's families.*

- *Almost half of the families had been known to the local authority for more than five years prior to the care application being made.*

- *The most frequently offered service prior to the court application was s20 accommodation (38 per cent) which was accepted by 89 per cent of those who were offered it. Financial help had been offered to 12 per cent of families and accepted by almost all of them. The least acceptable services were treatment for substance misuse and therapeutic input for adult mental health difficulties, although often they were accepted initially but subsequently abandoned due to poor compliance.*

- *Over four-fifths of children had a change of placement during the course of the proceedings, with a mean number of 1.7 moves.*

A thematic inspection by OFSTED (2012c) of local authority practice in safeguarding children with disabilities found that where neglect was the key risk, many children had received extensive support as children in need. Despite the lack of improvement, there were delays in recognising that levels of neglect had met the child protection threshold. In the majority of cases where the children were subject to child protection plans good progress was made in improving the quality of parenting or reducing risk. Having their child on a child protection plan helped some parents to understand and accept the seriousness of what was happening. On occasions poor parenting was masked by large support packages in that when parents assumed sole responsibility for their children's care, its quality dropped to unacceptable levels. Many plans were considered to be insufficiently focused on outcomes, making it difficult to hold agencies and parents to account and to measure progress.

Brandon et al. (2012) analysed SCRs conducted between 2009 and 2011:

- *10 per cent of the children concerned had been subject to a child protection plan, a reduction since the previous two biennial reviews in a period when the number of children with child protection plans had risen;*

- *42 per cent of the children and families were receiving services from children's social care;*

- *23 per cent of cases had been closed, sometimes because of non-cooperation;*

- *in 14 per cent of cases a referral had been made but not accepted, suggesting that referral thresholds were set too high;*

- *21 per cent of the children had never been referred to children's social care.*

The threshold test and significant harm

A key principle of the CA 1989 is that legal proceedings should not be brought solely to provide access to services.

From a legal point of view there are two important issues: first, what has to be proved and second, what standard of evidence is required in order to satisfy a court that the threshold has been reached. Sometimes difficulties arise as a result of these separate issues being combined.

Before making an order the court must be satisfied on *the balance of probabilities*, the civil standard of proof (the criminal standard of proof is *beyond reasonable doubt*), that the child *is suffering, or likely to suffer significant harm which is attributable to a lack of adequate parental care or the child being beyond parental control* (s31(2)). As the Supreme Court explained in *Re S-B* [2009] UKSC 17: 'As to the test, it is not enough that the social workers, the experts or the court think that a child would be better off living with another family. That would be social engineering of a kind which is not permitted in a democratic society' (para. 7).

The term *harm* is defined as incorporating ill-treatment or the impairment of health (physical or mental) or the impairment of physical, emotional, social or behavioural development and, since an amendment included in the Adoption and Children Act 2002, includes that attributed to seeing or hearing the ill-treatment of another. Consequently, police forces usually notify local authority children's services of incidents of domestic violence in households that include children.

RESEARCH SUMMARY 6.2

Stanley et al. (2010) found that unless the family was already known to children's services, or included a child under a year old, the likelihood of any services being offered as a result of police notification of a domestic violence incident was low. Many local authorities sent a letter warning the family of possible consequences, but this was found to be no more effective than taking no action at all in that over half of the families in each group were subsequently re-referred following a further incident. Social workers expressed themselves uncomfortable about the practice of insisting that mothers protect their children by separating from their partners if necessary, which many regarded as discriminatory.

Where the question of whether the harm suffered is significant relates to the child's health and development, 'his health or development shall be compared with that which could reasonably be expected of a similar child' (CA 1989 s31(10)). However, this type of definition is insufficiently specific to be of much practical assistance when evaluating individual cases. It has been suggested that the existence of the threshold test has generated a forensic investigative system in which the emphasis is on identifying 'hard evidence' which might not be helpful in situations in which neglect or abuse is cumulative and unpredictable, and where its effects may take longer accurately to assess than is permitted by procedural requirements (Burgess *et al.*, 2012, p16). Accurate assessment in these circumstances often requires reflection and observation over time, which is not achievable within the timescales currently used as a means for measuring performance in child protection.

The threshold for state intervention is intentionally high so as to protect the autonomy of parents. That the words of the statute are very wide, but not intended to apply in their full width, was recognised by the Supreme Court in *Re S-B* [2009] UKSC 17: 'It cannot have been intended that a parent whose child has been harmed as a result of a lack of proper care in a hospital or at school should be at risk of losing her child' (para. 21). However, the fact that a care order may be made where significant harm is likely to occur, but has not yet done so, is indicative of the difficulties that arise when the law is trying to balance support for the family with protecting children from harm (Keating, 2011). In the case of *Re M and R* [1996] 4 All ER 239, the judge said that: 'the fact that there might have been harm in the past does not establish the risk of harm in the future. The very highest it can be put is that what might possibly have happened in the past means that there may possibly be a risk of the same thing happening in the future.' In addition, whilst 'harm' is defined in s31(9) the adjective 'significant', which is clearly intended to protect families from unwarranted intrusion, is not. In the case of *Re C (A Child)* [2011] EWCA Civ 918 the judge stated that

'significant' means what it says. The harm must be great enough to justify the interference by the local authority in the autonomous life of the family. To put it in another way, in order to reflect the need for respect to family life the interference must be a necessary and proportionate response to the concerns which impel the application for the care order being made.

(para. 2)

This is not, perhaps, the level of clarification that most social workers seek.

Government guidance itself acknowledges the lack of definition:

There are no absolute criteria on which to rely when judging what constitutes significant harm. Consideration of the severity of ill-treatment may include the degree and the extent of physical harm, the duration and frequency of abuse and neglect, the extent of premeditation, and the presence or degree of threat, coercion, sadism and bizarre or unusual elements. Each of these elements has been associated with more severe effects on the child, and/or relatively greater difficulty in helping the child overcome the adverse impact of the maltreatment. Sometimes, a single traumatic event may constitute significant harm, for example, a violent assault, suffocation or poisoning. More often, significant harm is a compilation of significant events, both acute and long-standing, which interrupt, change or damage the child's physical and psychological development. Some children live in family and social circumstances where their health and development are neglected. For them, it is the corrosiveness of long-term emotional, physical or sexual abuse that causes impairment to the extent of constituting significant harm. In each case, it is necessary to consider any maltreatment alongside the child's own assessment of his or her safety and welfare, the family's strengths and supports, as well as an assessment of the likelihood and capacity for change and improvements in parenting and the care of children and young people.

(DfE, 2010b, para. 1.28)

The guidance goes on to describe a range of factors that may constitute physical, emotional or sexual abuse or neglect (ibid., paras 1.32–1.36).

In the case of *Re M* [2009] EWCA Civ 853 the judge endorsed a previous judgement which stated that 'society must be willing to tolerate very diverse standards of parenting, including the eccentric, the barely adequate and the inconsistent' (para. 50) but as the original case concerned parents with learning difficulties who needed intensive assistance, the focus on parenting rather than the nature of the harm and its impact on the child could be regarded as controversial (Keating, 2011).

Harwin and Madge (2010) suggest that the lack of a clear operational definition for *significant harm*, whilst theoretically permitting the exercise of professional discretion in complex family situations, also encourages 'panic' reactions to alleged safeguarding failures, with consequent unpredictable variations in numbers of care applications placing additional demands on over-stretched public resources. They propose an alternative model of a problem-solving court in which the focus is on possible solutions (inquisitorial) rather than scrutiny of the nature of the harm which triggered the application (adversarial).

The complexity of the task of determining the nature of significant harm and the point at which the threshold criteria are engaged is illustrated by the fact that since 2004 the government has issued 10 separate guidance documents concerned with specific factors arising in the context of safeguarding children who are disabled, in whom illness is fabricated or induced, whose abuse may be linked to a belief in spiritual possession, or who may have been trafficked, subject to sexual exploitation, genital mutilation, gang activity, forced marriage, bullying or internet abuse. A further difficulty in practice is that the physical chastisement of children by parents is still lawful in England and Wales so long as it does not result in actual bodily harm (see Chapter 1).

Culture and religion

Balancing a respect for differing beliefs and styles of parenting with the need to protect children from harm is a key aspect of child protection. Social workers risk being criticised for over-reacting to the existence of alternative customs and traditions or for misattributing evidence of abuse, as in the case of Victoria Climbié (Laming, 2003). However, Brophy *et al.* (2003) suggest that cases in which allegations of harm to a child rest solely on behaviour defended as culturally acceptable by a parent, but unacceptable by a professional, are rare.

In response to situations in which it appeared that social workers had confused evidence of abuse and neglect with cultural variations in the treatment of children, guidance now states that while professionals should be sensitive to differing family patterns and lifestyles, child abuse cannot be condoned for religious or cultural reasons (DfE, 2010b). A judicial comment you might find surprising in this context was made in the case of *Re K: A Local Authority v N and Others* [2005] EWHC 2956 (Fam):

> *The court should be slow to find that parents only recently arrived from a foreign country, particularly one in which standards and expectations may be different, have fallen short of an acceptable standard of behaviour if they have done nothing wrong by the standards of their own country.*

> (para. 26)

Reducing the need for legal action

If it appears to a local authority that a child is suffering, or is likely to suffer, harm from someone living in the same household, there is a power to provide assistance (including cash) with obtaining alternative accommodation to the person suspected of being responsible for the ill-treatment (CA 1989, schedule 2), which supports the principle that children are best brought up within their own homes. If the person concerned is unwilling to move out, a court can be asked to make an exclusion order (CA 1989, ss38A and 44A as amended) as part of an application for an Emergency Protection Order or Interim Care Order. However, as this is subject to the consent of the person continuing to care for the child, who might have been expected to have taken action themselves if they recognised it as essential to the child's welfare, this provision is of limited practical use.

Legal action to protect children

The procedural framework for legal action by local authorities to protect children is provided by the *Public Law Proceedings Guide to Case Management*, commonly referred to as the *Public Law Outline* (MoJ, 2010). As its title suggests, its aim was to streamline and manage the process so as to reduce damage caused to children by lengthy and often confrontational court proceedings and, of course, contain costs. However, it has had little impact on the time it takes to conclude public law care applications and the Family Justice Review has established the basis for more radical change (see under future changes to family court proceedings below).

Emergency protection

An Emergency Protection Order (EPO) (CA 1989, ss44 and 45) can be made for up to eight days, extendable for a further seven days, if there is reasonable cause to believe that the child is likely to suffer significant harm if:

a. he is not removed to accommodation provided by or on behalf of the applicant; or

b. he does not remain in the place in which he is then being accommodated.

In the case of local authority applications, it is necessary to show that enquiries under the CA 1989 s47 are being frustrated by access to the child being unreasonably refused and that there is reasonable cause to believe that access is urgently required. Originally, application for the discharge of an EPO was not permitted within 72 hours of it being made, but a Northern Ireland court judgement, whilst not binding on courts in England and Wales, persuaded the government to include within the Children and Young Persons Act 2008 the removal of this restriction so as to ensure compatibility with Articles 6 and 8 of the European Convention on Human Rights.

Legal case guidance on Emergency Protection Orders

The judgements in the cases of X Council v B (Emergency Protection Orders) [2004] EWHC 2015 (Fam) and Re X: Emergency Protection Orders [2006] EWHC 510 (Fam) together set out the principles applicable to circumstances in which an EPO is being considered.

- *An EPO is a 'draconian' and 'extremely harsh' measure, requiring exceptional justification.*

- *Immediate removal of a child should only be contemplated if it is essential to secure the child's safety; 'imminent danger' must be actually established.*

- *Both the local authority and the court must pay 'scrupulous regard' to the ECHR rights of both the child and the parents.*

- *A delay in the appointment of a children's guardian is wholly unacceptable in the context of cases where emergency removal is contemplated.*

- *Cases of possible emotional abuse will rarely, if ever, warrant an EPO, let alone an application without notice.*

- *Cases of possible sexual abuse where the allegations are non-specific with no evidence of immediate risk, and cases of fabricated or induced illness with no medical evidence of immediate risk of physical harm to the child, will rarely warrant an EPO.*

- *If the purpose of the local authority's application is to facilitate assessment, a child assessment order (CAO) might be more appropriate (s43). Lack of knowledge or need for assessment do not of themselves justify the making of an EPO.*

- *The evidence to support an application for an EPO must be full, detailed, precise and compelling.*

- *Social work evidence should come from the social worker with direct knowledge of the case and case conference minutes should be produced to the court.*

- *Other than in wholly exceptional circumstances, parents must be given adequate prior notice of the application and of the evidence being relied upon.*

- *The local authority has a continuing duty under s44 to keep the case under daily review to ensure that parent and child are separated for no longer than is necessary to secure the child's safety.*

- *Contact arrangements must be driven by the needs of the family, not stunted by lack of resources.*

The police have powers to remove a child from a dangerous situation in an emergency (s46), often wrongly referred to as a Police Protection Order. These are the only circumstances in which compulsory measures can be taken to interfere with the exercise of parental responsibility without a court order. Children who are placed away from home under emergency protection become looked-after children.

Orders in care proceedings

- **Care Order** (ss31, 33) gives the local authority parental responsibility and the right to determine, usually in consultation with others holding parental responsibility, the child and significant others, the way in which the child is brought up. The local authority can restrict the exercise of parental responsibility by others where it is satisfied that it is necessary in order to safeguard the child's welfare. Therefore the concept of shared parental responsibility can more realistically be regarded as balanced in favour of the local authority. Care orders last until the child becomes 18, unless discharged earlier by a court. Interim care orders can be made for up to eight weeks initially, renewable for up to four weeks at a time (s38), if the court has reasonable grounds for believing that there are grounds for a care order, although they do not presuppose that a care order will be made.

- **Supervision Order** (ss31, 35) places a child under the supervision of the local authority, who is required to advise, assist and befriend the child. The supervisor has power to direct the child, the person caring for the child or a person with parental responsibility to take certain action, for example to engage with training or therapeutic services. Supervision orders last for 12 months, renewable for up to three years. Interim supervision orders can be made in the same way as interim care orders (s38).

- **Family Assistance Order** (s16) requires the supervisor, usually a CAFCASS officer or local authority social worker, to advise, assist and befriend any person named in the order, for example someone with whom the child is living. The maximum duration is 6 months and they are not much used.

- **Placement Order** (ACA 2002, s21) authorises a local authority to place a child with prospective adopters. It gives the local authority parental responsibility for the child and suspends existing contact orders. Placement orders are a key stage in plans for the adoption of any looked-after child.

- **Residence Order** (s8) determines where and with whom a child lives and confers parental responsibility on the person who is granted the order. Where a residence order is made in care proceedings the local authority has no continuing rights or duties in respect of the child, other than those it owes to children in general.

- **Special Guardianship Order** (ss14A–14G). See Chapter 8.

- **Contact order** (s34) regulates contact between a child and others, usually the parents and other family members. The order may specify the frequency, length and location of contact, impose conditions such as supervision, or permit the local authority to refuse it. Contact orders under s8 regulate contact in the context of private family law proceedings. There is a statutory presumption in favour of contact, although decisions must be proportionate and carefully balance the respective rights of those involved.

Welfare checklist

The judgement in the case of *C (A Child)* [2011] EWCA Civ 918 states that:

If the threshold is crossed, then whether the court is considering making an interim order just as much as when it is considering making a final order, the child's welfare is the paramount consideration and the checklist in section 1(3) of the Act is engaged. Among the factors to which regard must be had is the range of powers available to the court, and they include the making of no order, or (and this may sometimes be forgotten) making a supervision order. Once again, proportionality has to be borne in mind to give effect to Article 8.

(para. 3)

The welfare checklist (CA 1989 s1(3)) specifies the matters to be considered by a court in applying the principle that the child's welfare is paramount and was intended to promote more sound and consistent decision-making in courts hearing public law applications and contested private law cases (Brammer, 2010). For social workers accustomed to undertaking core assessments, however, it provides a barely minimum standard, although the prime position of the ascertainable wishes and feelings of the child is significant.

The court must have regard in particular to:

a. the ascertainable wishes and feelings of the child concerned (considered in the light of his age and understanding);

b. his physical, emotional and educational needs;

c. the likely effect on him of any change in his circumstances;

d. his age, sex, background and any characteristics of his which the court considers relevant;

e. any harm that he has suffered or is at risk of suffering;

f. how capable each of his parents, and any other person in relation to whom the court considers the question to be relevant, is of meeting his needs;

g. the range of powers available to the court under this Act in the proceedings in question.

ACTIVITY 6.3

In relation to the welfare checklist above, consider:

• What does 'ascertainable' mean?

• How would you show that the child's wishes had been 'considered in the light of his age and understanding'?

• Would different types of decision require a different standard of enquiry? (For example, a decision as to with whom a child lives as against a decision as to whether they should have their ears pierced)?

• In relation to (d), what other 'characteristics' would you consider potentially relevant?

• What do you think of the need to assess how 'capable' parents or others are?

• Can you think of a more suitable way of describing the sort of assessment that needs to be undertaken in this context?

• What else do you think should be included in a 'welfare checklist'?

RESEARCH SUMMARY 6.3

Research by CAFCASS (2012a), based on the views of children's guardians, contrasts the approaches adopted by local authorities in care proceedings as compared with three years earlier. There were a number of key findings.

• In 67 per cent of cases, guardians thought that the care application was timed appropriately, compared with 54 per cent in 2009. In 29 per cent of cases they felt that the application was late, a reduction from 44 per cent in 2009. Just 4 per cent of applications were considered premature.

RESEARCH SUMMARY **6.3** *(CONT.)*

- *In 85 per cent of cases guardians believed that the care application was the only viable action. Their suggested alternatives included a robust child protection plan, family group conferences and parenting education programmes.*

- *As compared to 2009, local authorities made applications at an earlier stage of their involvement. 20 per cent of children had not been known to children's services prior to the circumstances giving rise to the application, almost double the proportion identified in 2009. 47 per cent of children had had more than a year of continuous involvement, compared with 61 per cent recorded in the 2009 study. Only 9 per cent of children had been continuously involved with children's services for more than five years, a significant reduction from 2009.*

- *Applications where the child's involvement with the local authority had been brief prior to the application were more likely to be considered as appropriately timed than those with longer involvement.*

- *Guardians considered that in 40 per cent of cases the local authority had met the requirements of the Public Law Outline entirely, with 46 per cent having met them partially. 'Late' or 'premature' applications were viewed as being less well prepared. Applications from London boroughs tended to be regarded as better prepared than those from other local authority types.*

- *There was a greater prevalence of neglect than found in the 2009 study, with children subject to child protection plans under the category of neglect known to local authorities for a shorter time, suggesting that applications where neglect is a feature are being made at an earlier stage than in 2009.*

- *There is an inverse relationship between the appropriateness of the timing of the application and the age of the child, suggesting that guardians are supportive of early detection of serious safeguarding concerns and swift legal action to address them.*

LEGAL CASE STUDY **6.1**

FH v Greenwich LBC *[2010] EWCA Civ 344*

In the original hearing the judge concluded that the father had broken a baby's arm and that the mother had failed to protect her by waiting too long before seeking medical help. Accordingly, the court accepted that the 'significant harm' threshold was made out. Although the mother subsequently stated that she was separating from the father, the judge accepted evidence from the local authority that they remained in contact and, consequently, the mother could not be trusted to secure her children's safety. The mother appealed against the making of care and placement orders, when the court criticised the local authority for its negative attitude towards both parents which had 'pervaded' the case and for failing to help the mother separate from her violent partner:

LEGAL CASE STUDY 6.1 *(CONT.)*

I find it difficult to believe that in 2010, more than 18 years after the implementation of the Children Act, a local authority can behave in such a manner. Here was a mother who needed and was asking for help to break free from an abusive relationship. She was denied that help abruptly and without explanation. That, in my judgement is very poor social work practice. If we have learned anything in the past few years it is quite how difficult some women find it to break away from abusive relationships, however rational such a breach would appear to a disinterested outsider. Here, in my judgement, was a mother demonstrating that this is what she wanted to do. She both needed and sought help, and was quite improperly rebuffed by a local authority which had plainly pre-judged the issue.

(para. 106)

The court went on to state that the fact that a person has told a lie (in this case the mother, in relation to contact with the father) is not necessarily an indication of guilt. The lie might be explained by some other factor.

LEGAL CASE STUDY 6.2

Re M (A Child) *[2009] EWCA Civ 1486*

In this case the Court of Appeal reiterated that it is for a local authority to decide where a child in care is to live, whether under an interim or full care order. Ultimately, a court cannot impose its view of how a child should be cared for during the conduct of proceedings even if it considers that a different plan to that proposed by a local authority would be preferable.

LEGAL CASE STUDY 6.3

P v Nottingham City Council & the Official Solicitor *[2008] EWCA Civ 462*

In this case the judge gave guidance as to how local authorities should act when care proceedings are initiated in respect of children of parents with learning disabilities:

It is, I think, inevitable that in its pre-proceedings work with a child's family, the local authority will gain information about the capacity of the child's parents. The critical question is what it does with that information, particularly in a case where the social workers form the view that the parent in question may have learning difficulties. At this point, in many cases the local authority will be working with the child's parents in an attempt to keep the family together. In my judgement, the practical answer is likely to be that the parent in question should be referred to the local authority's adult learning disability team for help and advice. If that team thinks that further investigations are required, it can undertake them: it should, moreover, have the necessary contacts and

LEGAL CASE STUDY 6.3 *(CONT.)*

resources to commission a report so that as soon as the pre-proceedings letter is written, and proceedings are issued, the legal advisers for the parent can be in a position, with public funding, to address the question of a litigation friend. It is, I think, important that judgements on capacity are not made by social workers from the child protection team. A litigation friend, whether the Official Solicitor or otherwise, cannot become involved unless and until proceedings are issued. Once proceedings are issued, the question of the parent's representation becomes and remains a matter for the parent's legal advisers. Prior to the institution of proceedings, the issue is a different one, and the local authority should feel free to offer whatever advice is appropriate.

(paras 175–179)

LEGAL CASE STUDY 6.4

A County Council v K & Ors (by the child's guardian HT) *[2011] EWHC 1672 (Fam)*

This case arose from a dispute concerning the living arrangements for a two-year-old boy (T) during care proceedings. The local authority proposal that he be placed in foster care pending assessment of his parents' ability to care for him was opposed by his parents and the children's guardian (G), and the court decided that he could remain at home whilst subject to an interim care order. However, an agency worker in the social work team who had previously worked for CAFCASS overheard discussion about the case and sent an anonymous e-mail to CAFCASS suggesting that G had 'blocked' T's removal from home and that the interim care order was insufficient to protect him. CAFCASS subsequently informed the court that G's recommendation was unsafe, her appointment was terminated by the court and the local authority requested the court reconsider the decision to allow T to remain at home. The parents submitted that it was unfair to revisit the question of T's placement when the request to do so had not arisen out of concern for their parenting, but out of a series of events that had been far from transparent and in which G's independence had been undermined. The judgement stated that there was nothing unhealthy or wrong about a disagreement between professionals, but the process should be both transparent and fair. CAFCASS's monitoring of the quality of work undertaken by its staff had to be balanced against the guardian's independence and where there was irrevocable disagreement between them, it was for the court to determine.

In addition to clarifying the importance of the independence of children's guardians and the role of the court where there are disputes between professionals, this judgement also provided guidance about transparency of communication in care proceedings by stating that where discussions take place outside the court room, they should be (a) rare, (b) strictly necessary for the proper progress of the case, (c) minuted and (d) disclosed to all parties and made available to the court if required. Whilst noting that the conduct of the agency employee was plainly reprehensible, it was a matter between her and her employer.

Children's guardians

Children's guardians have a wide range of responsibilities arising from their duty to safeguard the interests of children in family court proceedings, both public and private, and have unrestricted access to local authority records. Their role is set out in Practice Direction 16A, which supplements the Family Procedure Rules 2010 (SI 2010 No. 2955). In 2011/12 CAFCASS acted in over 10,000 public law care applications, an increase of 11 per cent on the previous year, while the number of private law cases fell. There was also an increase in the number of cases involving placement and special guardianship orders, with a fall in numbers of family assistance orders and adoption applications dealt with (CAFCASS, 2012b).

RESEARCH SUMMARY 6.4

Broadhurst et al. (2012) have reported on a pilot research project, now to be extended, in which children's guardians or family court advisers were appointed to work with families at the pre-court proceedings stage. They identified particularly the advantages of their independence and potential ability to encourage previously hostile parents to engage with the local authority: 'The guardian can be the voice of calm when the parents are very upset with the local authority' (Lawyer, quoted in ibid., p25).

Independent social workers

The Family Justice Review (2011) has suggested that the use of independent social workers to provide expert reports in care proceedings is causing duplication and delay and should be curtailed. However, Brophy *et al.* (2012) found that most independent social work reports provide new evidence not previously available to the court, and are almost always delivered by the date specified in their letters of instruction. They suggest that not only would courts be hampered by lack of access to such expertise, particularly in the context of the case management required to meet the six-month timescale proposed for care proceedings, but also that independent social workers can often help where the relationship between the parents and the local authority has broken down.

Future changes to family court proceedings

The government has responded to the Family Justice Review (2011) by setting out its proposed Children and Families Bill, expected to be introduced during 2013 (HMG, 2012). The key public law provisions, primarily concerned with streamlining processes and reducing delay in the family courts, are:

- creation of a time limit of 26 weeks by which *non-exceptional* care proceedings must be completed, with provision for extension by periods of 8 weeks if it is necessary for the just resolution of the proceedings;

- case management decisions should be made only after impacts on the child, their needs and the timetable have been considered;

- focusing the court on those aspects of the care plan which are essential to deciding whether to make a care order;

- allowing the judge to set the length and renewal requirements of interim orders;

- requiring courts to consider the impact of delay on the child when commissioning expert evidence and whether the court can obtain information from parties already involved;

- requiring parents to consider mediation, rather than litigation, as a means of settling disputes by making attendance at a mediation information and assessment meeting a statutory prerequisite.

The judiciary has also been working on plans to support changes in culture and reduce delay in the family courts:

> *Care cases can be complex and each family is unique and deserving of the court's full attention. That is not to say that in every case every theoretical welfare option needs to be investigated by the court. In many cases, options will already have been tried or assessed before the proceedings were issued and it will neither be a necessary nor proportionate way of undertaking case management to re-assess all of those options. To do so may breach the overriding objective, which is the principle arising out of legal policy, that should determine case management in the individual case within the context of the management of the overall workload, to ensure a fair and timely hearing in every case.*

(Ryder, 2012, p8)

The plans include proposals to produce a virtual Family Court Guide containing information on the rules, practice directions and good practice which it is hoped will improve the quality of analysis and decision-making by the professionals involved (ibid., p10) including:

- local authority work to prepare for proceedings;

- the content of social work evidence;

- how to decide on the timetable for the child;

- what is key issue identification;

- what is the threshold;

- how and when to use experts;

- how to represent an incapacitated adult party and how to identify and ask for special measures to assist vulnerable parties and witnesses;

- what scrutiny is to be expected of placement proposals and care plans;

- how to use published and peer-reviewed research in court (see Further Reading below);

- a statement of evidential principles for use in children proceedings to assist everyone to understand that except in relation to adversarial fact-finding sufficient to make the ultimate decision before the court, the judge's function in a welfare determination is investigative.

In relation to private law proceedings it is proposed to replace residence and contact orders (CA 1989 s8) with a child arrangements order which sets out details of where a child will live and with whom they will have contact. It is intended to repeal the Matrimonial Causes Act 1973 s41 and the Civil Partnership Act 2004 s63 so as to remove the requirement that in proceedings for divorce, dissolution of a civil partnership, nullity or judicial separation where there are children of the family, the court should consider whether to exercise its powers under the CA 1989. Any dispute about the arrangements for a child resulting from divorce or dissolution will in future be dealt with by way of free-standing application to the court under the CA 1989. At the time of writing, these are only proposals. However, it is clear that the government is determined to strengthen the role of mediation so as to reduce the number, length and complexity of cases that come before family courts.

Other potential developments are contained in the Crime and Courts Bill 2012 which will, if enacted, create a single family court with one point of entry to replace the existing three tiers. All levels of the judiciary, including magistrates, would sit in the new court, with work allocated according to the assessed complexity of the case. This might not bring about significant change in practice in that the same people will be doing the same thing, mostly in the same place, and it is often only as court hearings progress that the level of complexity becomes apparent. However, it is envisaged that High Court judges will sit regularly in the new family court, providing stronger leadership in the interpretation and application of legislation, rules, practice directions and existing case law.

FURTHER READING

Brown, R and Ward, H (2012) *Decision-Making Within a Child's Timeframe*. London: Child Wellbeing Research Centre.

Provides an overview of current research evidence for family justice professionals concerning child development and the impact of maltreatment.

Walsh, E (2006) *Working in the Family Justice System: a Guide for Professionals* (2nd edition). Bristol: Jordan Publishing.

www.cafcass.gov.uk

Provides statistical and research resources in relation to the work of family court advisers.

www.judiciary.gov.uk

Provides access to resources of the Family Justice Council (FJC), which promotes better and quicker outcomes for those involved with the family justice system.

www.legislation.gov.uk

Legislation and statutory instruments can be found here.

Chapter 7
Substitute care

CHAPTER OBJECTIVES

This chapter builds on the previous one in that it explores the legal and policy framework which requires or permits social workers to make arrangements for children to be looked after, usually temporarily, away from their parents or primary carers. Thus it reflects the PCF requirement for you to be able to employ a range of interventions: promoting independence, providing support and protection, taking preventative action and ensuring safety, whilst balancing rights and risks.

Introduction

There were 67,050 looked-after children in England at 31 March 2012, an increase of 2 per cent from 2011 and 13 per cent since 2008. Sixty per cent were subject to court orders, with the remainder accommodated by agreement with those with parental responsibility. The majority (62 per cent) were being looked after as a consequence of abuse or neglect, with family stress or dysfunction accounting for a further 23 per cent. Sixty-seven per cent of looked-after children had been in the same placement throughout 2011/2012, 22 per cent had two placements and 11 per cent had three or more (DfE, 2012c).

Historically, the legal framework governing substitute care stems from two contrasting philosophical stances. One approach promotes care as a preventive service to support families and enable children to remain with, or return to, their birth parents as soon as practicable, while the contrasting view sees care as a means of protecting children from harm and, if necessary, providing them with permanence away from their birth family. Both of these philosophies, and consequently the legal framework, are based on the premise that public care should be avoided wherever possible, and therefore removing children from their family usually only occurs when all other options appear to have failed and harm may have already been incurred in the context of their health and well-being (Hannon et al., 2010).

> **RESEARCH SUMMARY 7.1**
>
> *Research by the Children's Rights Director for England found that 68 per cent of looked-after children thought that coming into care had been the right thing for them and 89 per cent rated the care they received as good or very good (OFSTED, 2011b). However, ChildLine (2011) reported an increase of a third over five years in the number of looked-after children calling its helpline, with 4 per cent of all looked-after children having been counselled by its service in 2009/10, many as a result of being unsettled by placement moves. Further research by OFSTED (2012a, pp6–9) identifies aspects of being in care that children valued at the point of leaving care:*
>
> * *feeling part of a family;*
>
> * *receiving support and having someone to talk to;*
>
> * *making or living with new friends;*
>
> * *having a better education;*
>
> * *getting involved in activities in and out of school;*
>
> * *having money and things they would not have had if they had not been in care.*
>
> *Factors that most concerned them included:*
>
> * *loss of contact with family and friends;*
>
> * *being treated differently from other children;*
>
> * *the number of changes of placement they experienced;*
>
> * *restrictions and rules;*
>
> * *social workers being difficult to get hold of, late for appointments, not keeping agreements, or failing to take account of their views.*

Children Act 1989 s20

Whilst the Children Act 1989 s17 describes local authority powers to provide services for children in need and is primarily concerned with reducing the likelihood that a child becomes looked after, s20 imposes a duty to provide accommodation for any child in need who appears to require it as a result of:

a. there being no person who has parental responsibility for him;

b. his being lost or having been abandoned; or

c. the person who has been caring for him being prevented (whether or not permanently and for whatever reason) from providing him with suitable accommodation and care.

Although a duty, s20 accommodation is part of the range of services intended to support parents in exercising their parental responsibility. Local authorities also have a power to provide accommodation, even in situations in which someone else is willing and able to do so, if it is necessary to promote the child's welfare. In relation to children under 16, this is subject to parental consent. If that is not forthcoming, or is withdrawn, the local authority can only accommodate, or continue to accommodate, a child by means of a court order, as illustrated by the legal case study below. A person with parental responsibility may remove a child from s20 accommodation at any time without notice, which raises questions as to its suitability for children where there are serious welfare concerns, and there have been signs of judicial disquiet at its use in situations in which the threshold criteria for care proceedings might have been met.

LEGAL CASE STUDY **7.1**

Re CA (A Baby) *[2012] EWHC 2190 (Fam)*

This judgement provides guidance as to social workers' duty to be satisfied that anyone consenting to CA 1989 s20 accommodation has capacity to do so, is fully informed and that there are reasonable grounds for removal, which must be proportionate.

A local authority applied for final care and placement orders in respect of a young child, CA, whose mother had significant learning difficulties described by the judge as follows: 'whilst she clearly loves her children and is committed to the concept of caring for them, and whilst she can often manage well in the context of supervised contact, she has no instinctive or intuitive feel for parenting nor any capacity for consistency' (para. 4). The assessments supported the permanent removal of CA, although suggesting that the mother be offered therapeutic treatment.

CA was removed at birth, apparently under an s20 agreement. The mother, who knew of the local authority's plan and had 'demonstrated submission but not consent to it' (para. 11), experienced considerable trauma during the birth and initially refused to consent to her baby being accommodated. However, when approached again after being medicated, she agreed.

The judge stated that social workers have a duty to be satisfied that the person giving consent has the capacity to do so. The social worker should consider the criteria contained within the Mental Capacity Act 2005 s3 and if there is any doubt there should be no further attempts to obtain consent at that time. If the social worker believes that the person has capacity, they must also be satisfied that they are fully informed of the consequences of refusal of consent, the range of choices available, and all of the facts and issues material to the giving of consent, which must be fairly obtained. The social worker must also be satisfied that removal of the child is both fair and proportionate.

An s20 agreement should not be 'compulsion in disguise' (para. 27) or obtained where a court order would not have been granted: 'It can never be permissible to seek agreement to do that which would not be authorised by order solely because it is known, believed or even suspected that no such authorisation would be given and in order to circumvent that position' (para. 35). The care and placement orders sought were made but the judge stated that 'willingness to consent cannot be inferred from silence, submission or even acquiescence. It is a positive stance' (para. 44).

In the case of S (by the Official Solicitor) v Rochdale MBC and another [2008] EWHC 3283 (Fam) the Official Solicitor, representing a girl accommodated under s20, made the following submission, although the judge did not definitively accept or reject it since agreement was reached between the parties on the matter in dispute. However, it raises important issues in the context of partnership with parents and the local authority's role when parental responsibility is not being exercised by those who hold it:

Children are 'accommodated' when parents accept or are persuaded (perfectly properly) that they can no longer meet the needs of their children at home. They may sometimes wish to avoid the instigation of care proceedings where they run the risk of adverse findings being made against them, sometimes with a potentially adverse impact upon other children within the family. The very fact that a parent is unable to care for a child at home ought perhaps to signal that they may not always be well placed to exercise their parental responsibility (PR) in a child's best interests at all points within his or her period of accommodation. When such parents do not regularly attend reviews that ought to be regarded as a 'trigger' to alert the Independent Reviewing Officer to consideration of the need to instigate proceedings. The absence of parental input in circumstances where PR is not shared with a local authority should be seen as powerful evidence pointing to the local authority's need to acquire PR. The alternative is that the 'accommodated' child whose parents have disengaged is left in a legal limbo.

CA 1989 s20 is a provision by which the state can assist rather than intervene in family life where there are identified problems. It can and ought to provide a structure in which the autonomy of family life is respected and preserved. The inappropriate use of it fails to respect or protect the autonomy and rights of the child. If it were to become a device to circumvent the scrutiny of the court and the CAFCASS appointed guardian that is likely to excite either judicial review and Human Rights Act applications or may well lead to pressure for legislative reform to curtail the local authority's exercise of its s20 jurisdiction (the undesirable consequence of which might in fact be an increase in the number of care proceedings issued). For this reason it is important that the scheme under which accommodated children are assisted should be clear and effective. They require the same access to professional expertise stimulated by independent scrutiny as those children who find themselves subject to proceedings.

(para. 100)

Research by OFSTED (2012b) into the causes of delay in achieving permanence for looked-after children found that some children experienced lengthy spells of CA 1989 s20 care prior to care proceedings being initiated. Although it was considered that this might be appropriate while social workers assessed whether it was necessary to secure the children's longer-term safety through care proceedings, researchers identified an uncertainty about how to balance the 'no delay' and 'no order' principles of the CA 1989 alongside human rights considerations. Some local authorities admitted to a culture of using s20 care whenever possible, even in cases where children were the subject of long-standing and continuing child protection concerns. A judge commented: 'voluntary care should be used to avoid care, not as a precursor to care' (ibid., p13).

The local authority as parent

The local authority gains parental responsibility (PR) for children who are subject to care or interim care orders under the CA 1989 s31. PR is not removed from those who already hold it and the expectation is that all those with PR will work in partnership in the interests of the child. However, it is not an equal partnership in that the local authority has powers to make certain decisions, such as where and with whom a child lives, without consent if necessary. The local authority has limited PR under an Emergency Protection Order, exercisable only as far as is reasonably required to safeguard and promote the child's welfare. During the course of a placement order (see Chapter 8), PR is shared between the adoption agency and the birth parents until an adoption order is made.

The powers and duties of local authorities in relation to the children they look after are set out in the CA 1989 as amended by the Children (Leaving Care) Act 2000, the Adoption and Children Act 2002, the Children and Young Persons Act 2008, (and amplified by) the Care Planning, Placement and Case Review Regulations (2010) and associated guidance (HMG, 2010). The latter contains considerable detail regarding the local authority's responsibilities in this context, some of which might appear unnecessarily prescriptive. For example, do social workers really need to be advised to check that bathing and toilet facilities are sufficient for the number of residents in accommodation being assessed? Or that visits provide an opportunity to talk to the child? The risk of including such basic detail is that professional autonomy is undermined and important and useful information becomes obscured.

Social work's knowledge and evidence base, together with policy statements, clearly support the importance of stable and settled placements for looked-after children. The CYPA 2008 s22 states that where children are cared for away from home, the responsible authority must ensure that, as far as reasonably practicable, the placement:

* allows the child to live near their home;

* does not disrupt their education, particularly at Key Stage 4;

* enables a child to live with their brothers and sisters if they are also looked after by the local authority;

* provides accommodation suitable to the child's needs; and

* is within the local authority's area.

Ideally all proposed placements will meet all of these criteria; however this is unlikely to be the reality and social workers, their managers, family placement workers and resource panels may find themselves faced with difficult choices and decisions.

(HMG, 2010, p40)

In fact nearly three-quarters of looked-after children with brothers or sisters also in care are separated from at least one of them (OFSTED, 2011b). Over a third are living in placements outside their home local authority area, with almost 8,000 over 20 miles away (DfE, 2012c). It is not clear how far a local authority should go in terms of obtaining suitable placements and unless such a decision is challenged, the local authority will not normally have to justify it. However, the Parliamentary Children, Schools and Families Committee (House of Commons, 2009) has indicated that placement breakdowns should be treated as seriously as the prospects of a child being removed from home in the first place.

The CYPA 2008 aims to improve the stability of placements and improve the educational experience and attainment of young people in care or those about to leave care. For this to be achieved it goes without saying that additional financial and human resources are needed.

The principal provisions of the CYPA 2008 are:

- local authorities may appoint Independent Reviewing Officers (IROs) independent of the local authority;

- a designated member of staff at maintained schools to hold responsibility for the promotion of the educational achievement of looked-after children;

- a duty on local authorities to provide assistance to young people who have left care to pursue education and training, up to the age of 25;

- the local authority's power to make cash payments to children in need and their families is extended to circumstances that are not exceptional;

- parents who are caring for disabled children can be given respite breaks;

- the rights of relatives who are entitled to apply for residence or special guardianship orders without leave of the court extended to include those with whom the child has lived for a continuous period of one year.

Cultural and religious needs

Local authorities are required to ensure that the children they look after are brought up in the religion of their birth parents, with full understanding of their cultural heritage (CA 1989 s33). If parents change their religion this must be taken account of, subject always to promoting the child's welfare. Government guidance (HMG, 2010) states that even where a child does not have a formal religion, they should be supported and encouraged to develop a spiritual dimension to their life. Where there are differences between carers and birth families in matters such as religious observance, dress code and diet, the aim should be to preserve and strengthen the child's links with their birth family, particularly when the plan is for the child to return home.

Dilemmas in practice include:

- To what extent should cultural or religious factors influence welfare decisions in relation to looked-after children?

- What should happen if the child is unable to appreciate their significance, or does not regard them as relevant?

- What account should be taken of the child's age and maturity?

Re: P (a child) (residence order: child's welfare) *[2000] Fam 15*

This case concerned a child with Down's Syndrome. When she was a year old, her parents, who were orthodox Jews, asked the local authority to accommodate her as they felt unable to meet her needs, and she was placed with foster carers who were non-practising Roman Catholics. Subsequently, the foster carers obtained a residence order, with reasonable contact with the parents. When she was eight, the parents requested the child's return, arguing that she had a right to be brought up by her birth parents in her own religion.

In her judgement, Butler-Sloss LJ, said:

At eight there have to be strong reasons to move any child who has inevitably put down strong roots from a family where she has lived for seven years. The sometimes over-emphasised status quo argument has real validity in this case. No one would wish to deprive a Jewish child of her right to a Jewish heritage. If she had remained with a Jewish family, it would have been almost unthinkable, other than in an emergency, to remove her from it . . . but in this case her parents were not able to accommodate her within her community. It was then, not now, that she was deprived of her opportunity to grow up within the Jewish community . . . her religious and cultural heritage cannot be the overwhelming factor, nor can it displace other weighty welfare matters. Her perception of the foster carers as her real parents, her inability to understand why she would lose them and the reasons for the move, the impossibility of a structured and gradual handover, the adjustment to the new home where she has not lived since a baby, the move from school as well as home (the two pillars of her security) are powerful reasons against a move and it is patently obvious that this child cannot move.

In agreeing, Ward LJ said:

In this case the psychological tie outweighs the blood tie.

Re: A & D *[2010] EWHC 2503 (Fam)*

This case concerned a child of Muslim parents who was placed under a care order with her maternal grandparents with parental contact four times a year. The grandparents were not Muslim but were willing to bring the child up in that religion. The father opposed the placement, preferring the child to be fostered, or even adopted, by a Muslim family. The mother subsequently reverted to Roman Catholicism and wished the child to be brought up as a Roman Catholic. The grandparents were raising the child with knowledge of both Catholicism and Islam. The father's application alleging breach of duty by the local authority failed and the care order remained in place, although the court said that the local authority should do more to support the teaching of the child's Islamic religion and culture.

Education

Local authorities have a duty under the CAs 1989 and 2004 to promote the educational achievement of children they look after, wherever they are living. Even taking into account the fact that nearly three-quarters of looked-after children have been assessed as having special educational needs, statistics suggest that they are struggling to perform this duty, particularly at GCSE stage. Of 44,400 children who on 31 March 2011 had been looked after for at least a year (DfE, 2011c):

- 58 per cent achieved the expected level in reading and 62 per cent achieved the expected level in maths at Key Stage 1;

- 13 per cent gained five or more GCSE passes at grades A*–C, including English and mathematics, compared to 58 per cent of children not looked after.

Local authorities' performance in promoting the educational achievement of looked after children is measured against the following (DCSF, 2010b, p7):

- looked-after children achieve educational outcomes comparable to their peers;

- the authority demonstrates robust procedures to monitor educational progress and a commitment to secure the highest educational achievement for looked-after children;

- looked-after children are encouraged to have high expectations of themselves and achieve their full potential;

- training, development and support for carers, schools and local authority staff ensure that they understand the needs of looked-after children;

- there are clear chains of accountability for discharging their duty which are monitored by a senior manager in the local authority.

Although there is a lack of clarity in the language used which makes it difficult for performance to be evaluated in any meaningful way, OFSTED includes the following indicators within its inspection criteria for local authority children's services (**www.ofsted.gov.uk**):

- the percentage of looked-after children achieving level 4 at Key Stage 2 in English and mathematics;

- the percentage of looked-after children achieving five A*–C GCSEs (or equivalent) at Key Stage 4, including English and mathematics.

We explore collaboration between children's social care and education services in Chapter 10.

Care planning

Assessing the needs of children and deciding how best to meet those needs is a fundamental part of social work with looked-after children which requires an effective conceptual and practice framework. The care plan is the means by which information from the assessment across the dimensions of the child's developmental needs and from any other assessments is brought together (DoH, 2000). If not prepared in advance or for a court hearing, a care plan must be completed within 10 working days of a child becoming looked after.

A care plan should include (HMG, 2010, pp18–23):

- the developmental needs of the child and the services required to meet those needs, including services to be provided to family members and arrangements for contact;

- why a particular placement has been chosen;

- specific, achievable, child-focused outcomes intended to safeguard and promote the welfare of the child and identify how progress will be measured;

- realistic strategies and specific actions to bring about the changes necessary to achieve the planned outcome;

- the roles and responsibilities of family members, the child's carers and practitioners (for example, GP and designated teacher), and the frequency of contact of those practitioners with the child, their carer and/or family members;

- the long-term plan for the child, including timescales:

- contingency arrangements if the proposed plan for the child is not achievable;

- the name of the child's IRO;

- details of the health and personal education plans; and

- the wishes and feelings of relevant people about the arrangements for the child.

Placement plans

Before a child is placed away from home, or within five working days in an emergency, the local authority must draw up a placement plan setting out how the placement will meet the child's needs as identified in the care plan (HMG, 2010). The placement plan is integral to the care plan and is concerned both with what needs to happen in the placement to achieve the permanence plan and with how a child's day-to-day needs are to be met. Again the guidance demonstrates little confidence in social workers' professional capability, stating, for example, that it is important for foster carers to have information about a child's health, diet and general routine.

Unless the care plan states otherwise, decisions about activities such as overnight stays and school trips can be taken by carers after undertaking the kinds of checks that any reasonable parent would make. The Children's Rights Director for England is monitoring the effects of this policy change; recently only 21 per cent of looked-after children said that their carers could give permission for everything that other children's parents can (OFSTED, 2011b, p38).

Pathway plans

Young people reaching the age of 16, who have been looked after for at least 13 weeks since the age of 14 and who are still looked after, must have their care plan reassessed in anticipation of it becoming their pathway plan (see Chapter 9).

Reviews

A review must take place within 20 days of a child becoming looked after, with the second review within three months of the first and the third and subsequent reviews at six-monthly intervals. This specified frequency is a minimum standard. Where there is a need for changes to the care plan, the date of the review should be brought forward. No significant change to the care plan can be made unless it has been considered at a review, unless this is not reasonably practicable (HMG, 2010, p88). There is no definition of 'not reasonably practicable'. Where a looked-after child is also the subject of a child protection plan, it should be reviewed as part of the overarching care plan (DfE, 2010b).

At a review the social worker should be prepared to report on:

* the progress made in implementing the plan;

* any changes required to the provision of services; and

* any change required to the legal status of the child.

A series of pre-planned short breaks for a child in the same placement can be treated as a single placement for the purposes of the Care Planning, Placement and Review Regulations 2010.

PRACTITIONER REFLECTION 7.1

Designated teacher for looked-after children:

Generally IROs are helpful but they must be able to see what's behind the words which tend to be shaped by templates and checklists. Often I'm not invited to reviews and don't know how my report is presented and received. Once I had a lot of concerns about a child and read in the review notes that 'he is progressing well at school'.

The ACA 2002 introduced a requirement for local authorities to appoint an IRO to review the care plans of looked-after children, monitor the local authority's performance and ensure that the views and wishes of the child concerned are included within the planning process. The CYPA 2008 includes provisions to further strengthen the role of the IRO, whose responsibilities include (DSCF, 2010a, p20):

* ensuring that care plans are based on a detailed and informed assessment, are up to date, effective and provide a real and genuine response to each child's needs;

* identifying any gaps in the assessment process or provision of service;

* offering a safeguard to prevent any 'drift' in care planning and the delivery of services;

* monitoring the activity of the local authority acting as a good corporate parent in taking all reasonable steps to ensure that care plans have given proper consideration and weight to the child's current views, wishes and feelings and that the child fully understands the implications of any changes to their care plan; and

* making sure that the child understands how an advocate could help and their entitlement to one.

ACTIVITY 7.1

- Critically assess the description of the IRO's responsibilities listed above.

- How far does it contribute to robust social work planning and decision-making in practice?

- How easy would it be to evaluate or challenge a local authority's actions on the basis of this description?

- What changes could you suggest to improve its clarity and authority?

Comment

Much of the language used is insufficiently precise to be of much practical use. For example, what constitutes an 'effective' care plan or a 'good corporate parent'? What is the difference between 'real' and 'genuine'? What is to follow if gaps in the assessment or provision of services are identified?' How exactly is the local authority's activity to be monitored?

It has been suggested (Ryder, 2012) that the role of IROs needs to be re-examined in the light of proposed changes to the management of public law care proceedings so as to consider whether their duties and responsibilities to oversee the implementation of care plans and refer cases back to court are sufficient in the context of plans to reduce the scrutiny of such matters by the court. NAGALRO (2012), which represents family court advisers, children's guardians and independent social workers, makes a strong plea for the IRO system to be independent of local authorities, as originally envisaged within the CYPA 2008.

RESEARCH SUMMARY 7.3

Recent research (OFSTED, 2011b, p40) found that only just over half of looked-after children knew that they have a reviewing officer while two-thirds knew what a care plan was, of whom 72 per cent knew what was in it and 60 per cent said they had had a say in what it contained. Only around 60 per cent of young people who should have a pathway plan were aware of its existence.

Foster care

More than 50,000 children (75 per cent of those who were looked after at 31 March 2012) are in a foster placement (DfE, 2012c). The National Minimum Standards for Fostering (DfE, 2011e) are underpinned by the Fostering Services (England) Regulations 2011 which set out requirements in relation to the operation of fostering agencies, assessment and approval of foster carers, their support and training, and the nature of written agreements and records to be kept. Statutory guidance for fostering services (HMG, 2011a) sets out the wider brief for local authorities as providers and commissioners of fostering services. Both regulations and guidance are modified in relation to short breaks in recognition of the fact that parents retain primary responsibility for their child in these circumstances. However laudable their intention to promote good practice, in practical terms these documents pose considerable difficulties, primarily as a result of their imprecise language, for example:

> *Children should be matched with an appropriate foster carer capable of meeting their needs. They should feel welcomed into the foster home, treated and valued as a member of the family, and included in the everyday life of the family. They should in due course leave a placement in a planned and sensitive manner which makes them feel valued.*

> (ibid., para. 3.1)

An important provision is that foster carers should be given full information about any child they are asked to look after, given legal significance by the case of *W and others v Essex County Council* [2000] 2 All ER 237 in which foster carers successfully sued the local authority which placed a child with them without informing them that he had previously sexually abused his sister. Foster carers may not administer corporal punishment to a child in their care (HMG, 2011a, Sch.5 2(c)).

Kinship care

PRACTITIONER REFLECTION 7.2

Looked-after children team manager:

Kinship care is often regarded as a default position but in the context of the large number of moves that many looked-after children have it should not be seen as second best.

Around 300,000 children in England and Wales are cared for full-time by a relative, friend, or other person previously connected with the child, of whom just over 7,000 are officially looked after by a local authority (DfE, 2011f).

Many children benefit from living with relatives or friends because they are likely to provide more continuity than a placement with previously unknown carers. Such arrangements can preserve a child's sense of belonging to a wider family network, a close attachment is more likely to exist or develop, and there is evidence that relatives are less likely to reject a child if difficulties arise (HMG, 2010). However, not all relatives are able to safeguard and promote a child's welfare and in some families, the tensions and difficulties that exist or arise between family members may outweigh any potential benefits for the child.

Statutory guidance on family and friends care (DfE, 2011b) requires local authorities to publish a policy setting out how they will promote the needs of children living with kinship carers. Services should be determined by the child's needs rather than by their legal status, and children should receive support necessary to safeguard and promote their welfare, whether or not they are looked after. Standard 30 of the National Minimum Standards for Fostering (DfE, 2011f) specifically relates to kinship care.

An amendment to the CA 1989 s17(6) removed the restriction on local authorities to provide financial assistance *only in exceptional circumstances* and payments can now be made to kinship carers of children who are not looked after. Core assessments should include exploration of the capacity and willingness of family members to provide care, in particular before any application for a care or supervision order.

ACTIVITY 7.2

Children and their families should receive good quality services which meet the needs of different organisations, and specialists need to work effectively together to ensure a comprehensive approach to early intervention. To enable family and friends to offer appropriate care for children and young people who cannot live with their parents, access to a range of high quality support services at universal, targeted and specialist levels will be needed.

(DfE, 2011b, para 2.11)

- *Consider how, as a service manager, you might devise a policy that responds to these statements contained within government guidance on kinship care.*

- *How could you evidence that the services you are providing are 'good quality' and that your staff are 'working effectively'?*

- *Are the essential components of 'appropriate care' universally recognised and agreed?*

- *Rewrite the statement above with the level of detail necessary to support the need to evaluate local authority performance.*

RESEARCH SUMMARY 7.4

A comparative study (Farmer and Moyers, 2008) found that although family and friends carers were more likely to face practical difficulties such as poverty, inadequate housing, ill-health and lack of social work support, the children they cared for were doing as well as, or better than, those placed with foster carers previously unknown to them, even though each group of children had had similar care needs prior to placement. The authors concluded that with more effective support, the contrast would have been even greater.

Hunt and Waterhouse (2012) found that many kinship carers lack essential support from their local authorities. There were a number of key findings.

- *Most children, irrespective of legal status, had been exposed to substantial adversities prior to placement and consequently presented significant challenges to carers.*

- *There was no correlation between the support provided by children's services, challenges presented by the child or the needs of the carers.*

- *There was evidence of unmet need across all types of legal status and 72 per cent of kinship carers rated the support they received as poor or very poor. Only half could think of anything helpful (other than financial assistance) resulting from their contact with the local authority.*

- *Local authorities appeared reluctant to confer foster carer status, even where they had been involved in making the arrangements.*

RESEARCH SUMMARY 7.4 *(CONT.)*

- *Carers were rarely in a position to make informed decisions about the legal status of care arrangements and were not usually signposted to independent sources of information and advice.*

Roth et al. (2012) examined the extent to which local authorities complied with statutory guidance and identified best practice in relation to family and friends care. They, too, made a number of key findings.

- *Three-quarters of local authority policies did not refer to local demographic and needs data or collaboration with local partner agencies as specified in the guidance.*

- *83 per cent of policies referred to the principle that children should be enabled to live within their families unless inconsistent with their welfare and 57 per cent stated that children's wishes and feelings should be taken into account. However, less than half referred to the principle that children should not be looked after longer than is necessary and 42 per cent made no reference to support being based on the child's needs rather than their legal status.*

- *The majority of policies made no reference to an evidence base or to consultation with children, carers and parents.*

- *Only two-thirds of policies included information on possible legal safeguards for family and friends carers.*

- *A third of policies explained eligibility for financial help under the CA 1989 s17. However, two-thirds failed to mention the need for a written agreement and half did not state that payments should be calculated as foster carer allowances.*

- *More than half of policies did not consider the rights of children and carers, nor include information on how they could influence decisions.*

LEGAL CASE STUDY 7.5

In a case concerning the role of the local authority in supporting the placement of children with relatives, the Court of Appeal in R (SA) v Kent County Council [2011] EWCA Civ 1303 decided that A was a looked-after child following placement with her grandmother who was therefore entitled to the full fostering allowance. The local authority had been paying a lesser 'kinship allowance' under the CA 1989 s17 on the basis that it was a private family arrangement. The court decision was based on the fact that the arrangements were made by the local authority arising from discussions with the social worker and not from discussions with A's mother. The local authority's continuing involvement with the placement was consistent with it being one in which they had taken the lead and it had not been suggested to the grandmother that she was expected to support A without financial assistance from the local authority.

Residential care

Permanently staffed establishments which accommodate more than three children come within the definition of residential care. Although the number of children cared for in residential homes has steadily decreased, they remain an important, if expensive, resource for looked-after children and young people with challenging needs. The Children's Homes Regulations 2001 and the Children's Homes (Amendment) Regulations 2011, complemented by guidance (HMG, 2011b) and the national minimum standards inspection framework, set out requirements relating to their staffing and management. The 2011 amendments, which are highlighted in the original document (**http://media.education.gov.uk/assets/files/pdf/t/the %20childrens%20homes%20regulations%202001%20amended.pdf**), are an interesting reflection of how law and policy respond to changes in society's expectations. For example, it is no longer thought necessary to state that children's homes are 'kept free from offensive odours' whereas the importance of participation in school activities and access to e-mail is emphasised. Children's homes are subject to inspection by OFSTED, which publishes its reports on its website (**www.ofsted.gov.uk**).

PRACTITIONER REFLECTION **7.3**

A magistrate:

Magistrates who sit in the Youth Court often see young people who live in children's homes. They sometimes attend court without an appropriate adult, many have not been in trouble before and frequently they are charged with offences that have occurred within the home. Often this behaviour is at the lower end of offending and in a reasonable family environment would never be dealt with by the police or courts. The welfare principle is fundamental to the work of the Youth Court and we are distressed when we find that the young person has been prosecuted purely for insurance purposes. Some cases we have seen recently include:

- a young person charged with criminal damage after throwing a phone against a wall;

- a young person charged with arson with intent to endanger life after waving a cigarette lighter in the face of a member of staff;

- a child charged with assault after hitting another child whilst arguing. I am sure that most parents have experienced their offspring fighting and would not call the police or have their children arrested for assault.

Magistrates understand that it is difficult to care for troubled young people, but we do not want to see them entering the criminal justice system for minor offences which, if they were living in a normal family situation, would not be considered criminal.

(InHouse Newsletter for the residential sector, March 2012, p17,
www.media.education.gov.uk)

Secure accommodation

Lock down! We didn't have enough members of staff to deal with all 11 of us – so breakfast in bed for us . . . Annie left today – she's been in secure for 18 months – I gave her a hug and she broke down in tears, I'm going to miss her.

(15-year-old young person in secure accommodation, quoted in OFSTED, 2011a, p22)

Very occasionally, a child's circumstances and behaviour are such that they cannot safely be cared for in ordinary residential or foster care. A child may not be placed in secure accommodation (CA1989 s25) unless:

- it appears that the child has a history of absconding;

- the child is likely to abscond from any other type of accommodation;

- if the child absconds, he is likely to suffer significant harm; or

- if the child is kept in any other type of accommodation, the child is likely to injure himself or other people.

A local authority may place a looked-after child in secure accommodation for up to 72 hours in any 21 days without a court order. If longer is thought necessary, an application must be made to court, with the child represented by a lawyer and children's guardian. Placing a child in secure accommodation potentially engages their right to liberty under the European Convention on Human Rights Article 5 (see Chapter 1) and the decision-making process which precedes it engages their right to a fair trial under Article 6 (*Re M (A Child) (Secure Accommodation)* [2001] EWCA Civ 458).

One hundred and eighty children were living in secure children's homes as at 31 March 2012, a number that has steadily decreased over the previous five years (DfE, 2012c).

LEGAL CASE STUDY *7.6*

A City Council v T, J & K *[2011] EWHC 1082 (Fam)*

The court was determining whether K should attend the hearing of an application by the local authority to keep her in secure accommodation. K was 13, had no wish to be in care and was difficult to manage. Her wish to attend court was supported by the children's guardian but opposed by the local authority on the basis that she was at risk of absconding, might refuse to return to the secure unit, and meet her parents outside agreed contact times. The court stated that a starting point for reaching a decision was an evaluation of the consequences of her attendance or non-attendance in terms of her welfare and the court's ability to manage the proceedings fairly. The following factors were relevant:

a. the child's age and level of understanding;

b. the nature and strength of the child's wishes;

c. the child's emotional and psychological state;

d. the effect of influence from others;

LEGAL CASE STUDY **7.6** *(CONT.)*

e. the matters to be discussed;

f. the evidence to be given;

g. the child's behaviour;

h. practical and logistical considerations; and

i. the integrity of the proceedings.

Looked-after children in custody

Just to keep in touch with me would be nice.

(Looked-after child in custody, quoted in HMIP, 2011, p40)

Social workers should continue to work with young people who retain their looked-after status in custody, in liaison with the Youth Offending Team case manager and the supervisor within the establishment. A visit should be made within one week of the young person entering custody in order to assess their needs and maintain an up-to-date care plan. Subsequent visits must occur at not more than six-week intervals for the first year and at least three monthly subsequently. The young person is entitled to advice, support and assistance from the local authority throughout their time in custody and there is a duty to conduct reviews within statutory timescales (DCSF, 2010d). However, in practice there is evidence of inconsistency in the service provided and the judgement in the case of *R (J) v Caerphilly CBC* [2005] EWHC 586 (Admin) described one local authority's plans for a looked-after child in custody as 'little more than useless'.

Children who are accommodated under the CA 1989 s20 currently lose their looked-after status if they are remanded into custody or receive a custodial sentence. However, where a child ceases to be looked after in these circumstances, the local authority previously responsible for their care must appoint a representative to visit them and assess their needs within 10 working days of their arrival in custody (DCSF, 2010d). The Legal Aid, Sentencing and Punishment of Offenders Act 2012 creates two new entry points to looked-after child status in that any child in youth detention accommodation will become looked after, and remands for 17 year olds will be either to local authority or to youth detention accommodation, both of which will give them looked-after status. These changes are likely to prove challenging for local authorities in that these young people may be more resistant to intervention than other children, and out-of-area placements are more expensive and logistically challenging for social workers and reviewing officers. There is also likely to be increased demand for leaving care services.

Children missing from care

It is estimated that looked-after children are three times more likely than other children to run away, representing over 10,000 children during the course of a year (UK Missing Persons' Bureau, 2012).

A report from the All-Party Parliamentary Group (APPG) responsible for runaway and missing children and adults, looked-after children and care leavers (2012) exposes the extent to which some looked-after children are being failed by systems intended to protect them.

> *Trafficked children from abroad particularly are being let down and their needs ignored because the authorities view child trafficking as an immigration control issue. Hundreds of them disappear from care every year, many within 48 hours. The majority of these children are never found again.*

(ibid., p10)

Placements can sometimes be made for economic reasons rather than based on what is in the best interests of the child, which is in breach of statutory requirements and likely to increase the chances that the child will not be able to settle: 'It not always the social worker who makes the placement decision, but commissioning colleagues in the local authority' (ibid., p16).

The report's 31 recommendations include:

- Children in care should have a statutory right to independent advocacy.

- Before placing a child in another area, the home local authority should, in collaboration with the receiving local authority, assess the area to determine whether it is safe for the child, based on what is known about the risks facing the child.

- The Care Planning, Placement and Case Review (England) Regulations 2010 should be amended to meet the needs of children who go missing. For example, they should require the placing authority to call a placement review meeting whenever a child for whom they are responsible is missing, to assess the level of risk and agree an action plan with the host authority and local police.

- A legal advocate with parental responsibility should be appointed for all unaccompanied migrant children.

- For the term 'out-of-area placements', which defines a process, to be abandoned in favour of 'cross-boundary children in care' to be recognised as an especially vulnerable sub-group within the looked-after children population.

This last recommendation is an interesting example of the tendency of those responsible for developing and enacting statutory frameworks to hope that a change in language, without necessarily being accompanied by the necessary resources, is all that is needed to bring about realistic improvements in practice.

Complaints

The CA 1989 s26 requires local authorities to have a complaints and representation procedure for looked-after children and the Children Act 1989 Representations Procedure (England) Regulations 2006 and supporting statutory guidance set out the framework. The Children's Commissioner, whose role was established by the CA 2004, works with the Children's Rights Director to research children's and young people's experiences and views on complaints procedures in health and local authority services and the juvenile justice system, as well as examining the accessibility of mechanisms available for them to complain. However, the Office of the Children's Commissioner is concerned with promoting the welfare of all children and does not have powers of independent investigation, except in Wales. The legal case studies in this book which include the reference (Admin) arise from judicial review proceedings, which is a key constitutional mechanism whereby the actions of public bodies can be scrutinised by the courts. Judicial review is concerned with the legality of the decision-making process itself, rather than the conclusion which resulted, so a local authority could make the same decision again even if it was decided that the process leading to the first decision was unlawful. There is an expectation that internal complaints procedures have been exhausted before an application is made for judicial review.

FURTHER READING

There is a large number of research and inspection reports relating to the legal and policy framework for looked-after children accessible via the Department for Education (**www.education.gov.uk**) and OFSTED (**www.ofsted.gov.uk**) websites.

British Agencies for Adoption and Fostering (**www.baaf.org.uk**) has a wide range of useful publications relating to substitute care.

Chapter 8
Permanence

CHAPTER OBJECTIVES

This chapter describes the legal framework which can provide for a child to be cared for permanently by someone other than their birth parent, and considers the policy and value bases that inform the present system. It supports the requirements of the PCF by encouraging you to identify, distinguish, evaluate and integrate multiple sources of knowledge and evidence, and to respond to the opportunities that arise from changing political priorities, social contexts and constructs.

Introduction

It is permanence that provides the gold standard of security, continuity and a sense of belonging for looked-after children who have experienced loss, disadvantage and distress.

(NAGALRO, 2012, p3)

The proportion of looked-after children who leave care and the length of time that elapses before permanent and legally secure placements are achieved for them attracts considerable political and media interest, closely linked as it is to the demands on the public purse. Consequently, social work practice in this sphere is subject to frequent and often confusing policy initiatives.

Permanence is defined in statutory guidance (DCSF, 2010a, p24) as 'the framework of emotional permanence (attachment), physical permanence (stability) and legal permanence (the carer has parental responsibility) that gives a child a sense of security, continuity, commitment and identity'. Achieving permanence for a child is expected to be a key consideration from the time they become looked after, and care planning regulations (HMG, 2010) require that each care plan incorporates plans for permanence by the time of the second review.

There exists a range of options by which permanence for looked-after children can be achieved:

- return to their birth family;
- kinship care, with or without legal safeguards;
- long-term foster care or, rarely, residential care;

- special guardianship;
- adoption.

Therefore, whenever a child starts being looked after away from home, there are a number of questions that need to be addressed.

1. Is the plan for them to return to their birth family?

2. If so, what needs to happen in order for them to do so?

3. Does their current legal status meet their needs now and is it likely to do so in the future?

4. If they do not return to their birth family, what legal status should they have and how should it be achieved?

5. What links should they maintain with their birth family?

Adoption

Adoption is a process by which the legal relationship between a child and their birth parents is terminated in favour of a new relationship between the child and adoptive parents. It is one of the few legal decisions that is permanent and irrevocable, even if the basis for the decision-making leading to the adoption, such as the grounds on which a care order was made, is subsequently found to have been flawed.

LEGAL CASE STUDY 8.1

Re W (Children) *[2009] EWCA Civ 59*

In this widely reported case, it was decided that adoption orders could not be overturned despite the fact that medical evidence that led to the care orders which preceded them subsequently had been found to be wrong. The judge said:

> The public policy considerations relating to adoption, and the authorities on the point – which are binding on this court – simply make it impossible for this court to set aside the adoption orders even if, as Mr and Mrs W argue, they have suffered a serious injustice.
>
> *(para. 148)*

During the year ending 31 March 2011, 3,050 children were adopted from care, a decrease of 5 per cent from 2010 and the lowest number since 2001. Over 6,000 children are waiting for a permanent placement at any one time and on average 2 years and 7 months elapses between children entering care and being adopted, with the average age at adoption being 3 years 10 months (DfE, 2011c).

Historically, more weight has been attached to parental wishes in relation to adoption than in most other areas of the law concerning children and there were circumstances in which the birth parent's objection to adoption was upheld despite a professional view favouring adoption on welfare grounds (Henricson and Bainham, 2005). Surprisingly, adoption was only included within the provisions of the Children Act 1989 in relation to the substitution of the concept of 'parental responsibility' for that of 'parental rights and duties' and the designation of adoption proceedings as family proceedings, giving courts hearing adoption applications the power to make any order permitted by the CA 1989 should the child's welfare require it. The enactment of the Adoption and Children Act 2002, however, made the welfare of the child the paramount consideration throughout adoption proceedings, and incorporates a welfare checklist similar, although not identical, to that contained within the CA 1989.

The main provisions of the ACA and the substantial quantity of regulations and guidance which supplement it are:

- local authorities must provide a comprehensive adoption service, including post adoption support;

- local authorities must produce an adoption plan incorporating the roles of health and education authorities and voluntary adoption agencies;

- a national register is to be maintained containing details of children suitable for adoption and of approved prospective adopters;

- local authorities must provide a children's guide to its adoption services;

- the question of permanence must be considered at the four-monthly review of looked-after children;

- adoption reports may only be prepared by social workers with 'necessary experience', defined as three years post-qualifying experience in child care social work;

- permission to place a looked-after child for adoption can only be given by a court; it may also be part of the care plan in care proceedings;

- national standards for adoption introduced (DfE, 2011i), incorporating the principles contained in the CA 1989 and used by OFSTED as the framework for inspection of adoption agencies;

- the regulation of inter-country adoptions.

Who can adopt?

- Adoptions by step-parents comprise around half the number of adoption orders made. Formerly, this had to be a joint application, so in effect a natural parent was adopting their own child. Now it can be a single application by a step-parent, who must have lived with the child for at least six months but does not need to be married to the birth parent.

- Single people aged over 21. Someone who is married may adopt as a single person if the court is satisfied that the person's spouse cannot be found, they are permanently separated or the spouse is incapable of making an adoption application.

- Couples, which can include two people of the same sex. One must be domiciled in the UK and both must have been habitually resident in the UK for one year. This provision resulted in the closure of a number of voluntary church adoption agencies which felt unable to accept applications from same-sex couples.

- Age and health requirements are subject to agency policy. However, both applicants must be over 21 unless one is a birth parent and is over 18, in which case the other must be over 21.

Placement conditions

To be adopted a child must be under 18 and have been living with the applicants for 10 weeks before application is made, or six months in the case of a step-parent application. For foster carers wishing to adopt, the child must have been living with them for a year. Either each person with parental responsibility must have consented to the child being adopted or a court has decided that conditions are met for consent to be dispensed with. A child can be placed by an adoption agency, either with parental consent alone, or under a placement order authorising the agency to place a child who is subject to a care order. The consent of those with parental responsibility is still required, unless dispensed with. Placement, therefore, can be with consent of those with parental responsibility or by court order. Placement with consent results in parental responsibility being shared between the agency, parents and prospective adopters until an adoption order is made. Once the adoption application has been made, a birth parent cannot request the child's return or oppose the adoption order without leave of court, which would only be considered if there has been a significant change in circumstances, and even then may be refused (see Legal Case Study 8.4 below). The care order is suspended and any CA 1989 s8 orders are revoked. A placement order ends when the child is adopted, becomes 18 or marries. Parental consent to adoption cannot be given before a child is six weeks old. It must be unconditional and with full understanding of what is involved. There are two grounds for dispensing with consent:

- the parent cannot be found or is incapable of giving consent; or

- the welfare of child requires consent to be dispensed with.

The consent of the child itself is not required, although their wishes and feelings must be considered by the court hearing the adoption application.

Adoption applications can be made to magistrates', county or High Courts, with the majority heard by county courts. Reports in adoption applications are provided by a reporting officer (if application is not contested, in which case they are responsible for obtaining necessary consents) or children's guardian.

Adoption panels monitor and ensure the quality of social work decisions and are concerned with three main issues:

- whether adoption is in the best interests of the child;

- the assessment of prospective adopters;

- matching the child with prospective adopters.

An important responsibility of the placing agency, and a key aspect of adoption 'matching', is to provide prospective adopters with background information about the child before placement.

LEGAL CASE STUDY *8.2*

The significance of this in a legal context is illustrated by the case of A and another v Essex County Council [2003] EWCA Civ 1848 in which adoptive parents sued the agency which placed their child with them, claiming that important information about the child's background was withheld. The court decided that once an adoption agency decides what information should be provided (which might not be all that it possesses), it has a duty to pass it on. In this case, therefore, because the agency did not provide the adopters with that information it was liable for any harm which had resulted from that failure, but only until the adoption order had been made: 'From that point on the adopters become as much like birth parents as it is possible for them to be'. The judge went on to state that: 'The long-term calculation of gains and losses involved in this delicate piece of social engineering cannot be done on the cold computer programme of the law'.

LEGAL CASE STUDY *8.3*

The case of R (W) v A Local Authority [2010] EWHC 175 (Admin) arose from a birth mother's wish to halt the adoption of her child. It was decided that the child had been placed for adoption on the day on which the adoption agency approved the 'match' and the child had met the prospective adopters, but before she physically took up residence in the prospective adopters' home. The judge said: 'The process of Introduction is the first step in the relationship between a child and prospective adopters'.

LEGAL CASE STUDY *8.4*

Re R (a Child) [2010] EWCA Civ 187 involved a mother who separated from a violent partner and undertook self-help and child care courses in an effort to show that she was able to resume care of her children, who were subject to placement orders although not yet living with a new family. She sought permission to apply for revocation of the placement orders and while the court accepted that there had been a change of circumstances, it noted that prospective adopters had already been identified. As it would take many months before the mother's application could be heard, the likely delay in settling the children's future, together with the fact that the mother still had more to do to prove that she could be a good parent, led the court to refuse her permission to apply for the placement orders to be revoked.

Where a child is 'authorised to be placed for adoption' (that is, they are either subject to a placement order or those holding parental responsibility have consented to their adoption) or has been placed for adoption, their reviews are subject to the Adoption Agencies Regulations 2005, as amended, until an adoption order is made. Where the child has not yet been placed in their prospective adoptive family, the first review must take place within three months of the agency obtaining authorisation to place, and thereafter at no longer than six-monthly intervals. After a child has been placed for adoption, the first review must be held within four weeks of placement, the second no later than three months after this, with subsequent reviews held at six-monthly intervals until an adoption order is made or the child is no longer living with the prospective adopters. One important factor is that, once a child has been placed with them, the prospective adopters have a key role and must be consulted about matters relating to the child's welfare, whereas the extent to which birth parents are involved is a matter for the agency's discretion. Birth parents would not normally attend review meetings after a child has been placed with prospective adopters and, as we see below, post adoption contact between a child and their birth family is largely a matter for individual judgement.

Support for birth relatives

PRACTITIONER REFLECTION 8.1

Looked-after children team manager:

The question of post adoption contact needs to be considered very carefully in a long-term context. Twice a year might seem realistic when the order is made but really it's a compromise which may not serve anyone's interests. What if the adopters move away? What if there are changes in their circumstances? They are the parents and should be able to make whatever decisions they feel are necessary for their child's welfare.

The ACA introduced the potential for practice development in the context of post adoption contact and support for birth relatives, reflecting the movement from secrecy to openness in the field of adoption over the past 50 years. However, the law still remains generally neutral in its provisions, neither actively promoting nor discouraging post adoption contact with birth relatives, although courts are obliged to consider the issue, which means that each case must be considered individually.

RESEARCH SUMMARY 8.1

Research into the experiences of the birth relatives of children who had been compulsorily adopted found that the adoption process was commonly described as 'an unfair, hostile and alienating experience in which they had little power to influence events' (Neil et al., 2010, p4). Researchers also uncovered significant levels of psychological distress and a low take-up of support services by a significant number of birth relatives. Those for whom post adoption contact was part of the plan had to wait for between six months and two years after the adoption order was made for contact to be established.

A subsequent review of research into post adoption contact support found that birth families were unlikely to receive a service that protected and promoted their interests and the role of the adoption social worker was primarily concerned with controlling and correcting their behaviour so as to minimise its effect on the placement. The most usual type of contact was via a 'letterbox' whereby letters and photos were exchanged through the adoption agency (Neil et al., 2012).

Re T (A Child) *[2010] EWCA Civ 1527*

When T, aged 2, was adopted there was an expectation on the part of the adopters, his birth grandmother, J, and the local authority that there would be limited direct contact between T and J. However, the adopters subsequently became apprehensive and contact was not facilitated. J applied for a contact order but after hearing evidence from the children's guardian that the proceedings were having an adverse effect on the adoptive parents and thus on T, the court rejected the application. In dismissing J's appeal the Appeal Court referred to the principle established in Re R (Adoption: Contact) *[2005] EWCA Civ 1128 that:*
'The imposition on prospective adopters of orders for contact with which they are not in agreement is extremely, and remains extremely, unusual' whilst acknowledging the development of greater flexibility in the attitude of courts in certain cases. However, the judge also observed that:

> the ground [in relation to post adoption contact] is fertile for misunderstanding and the placing local authority must take particular care to try to minimise the risk of it. . . . Where the ultimate stance of adopters in relation to future contact is neither a 'no' nor a 'yes' but a 'maybe', the precise terms in which that stance is articulated should, as a matter of good social work practice and of elementary fairness, be communicated to the family member whose contact is under address.

(paras 3 and 16)

Oxfordshire County Council v X, Y & J *[2010] EWCA Civ 581*

The birth parents of J, who had been adopted, wished to receive an annual photograph from the adoptive parents who, supported by the local authority and the children's guardian, wanted the photograph to be shown to them at the local authority's offices as they feared that if it was supplied directly there was a risk that the internet might be used to trace J. At the initial hearing the judge accepted that the adopters' concerns and perceptions were genuine but decided in favour of the birth parents. The adopters appealed successfully and the judge stated that:

> The question may seem a very narrow one but it has to be remembered that, in the very delicate and sensitive context of adoption, issues such as this are profoundly important in human terms. The case also raises again the equally delicate question as to how far the court can or should go in imposing on adoptive parents obligations which they may be reluctant to assume voluntarily.

(para. 3)

Because J had been adopted, the relevant welfare 'checklist' to be applied was that of the CA 1989 and not that of the ACA. The essential question was whether the adoptive parents' fears had no reasonable basis:

LEGAL CASE STUDY 8.6 (CONT.)

The adoptive parents are J's parents; the natural parents are not. The adoptive parents are the only people with parental responsibility for J. Why, unless the circumstances are extremely unusual – and here, in our judgement, they are not – should that responsibility be usurped by the court? We can see no good reason either on the facts or in law. On the contrary, there is much force in the point they make, that they wish their status as J's parents to be respected and seen to be inviolable – not for themselves but in order, as they see it, to give J the very best chance for the adoption to be successful.

(para. 36)

Future policy developments

Successive governments have, in recent years, taken a keen interest in the process of looked-after children being placed with adoptive families and although there is plenty of evidence that delay in achieving permanence is damaging to children, cynics might also note that the level of parliamentary interest has increased in proportion to the urgent need to reduce public expenditure. Prime Minister Tony Blair's adoption 'initiative' in 2000 achieved a temporary increase in the number of children adopted from care but it did not maintain momentum alongside the parallel policy emphasis on keeping families together, which meant that adoption began to be regarded by some as an anachronism (Farmer *et al.*, 2010) further evidenced by an increase in the number of special guardianship and residence orders made. In addition, adverse publicity from some media sources sought to portray social workers as more concerned with achieving adoption targets than meeting the long-term welfare needs of individual children. The government's current policy arises from a belief that delay in making adoption placements is avoidable and that many looked-after children under five could and should be in more permanent placements: 'For too long children in care have been let down by local authorities and the family justice system' (DfE, 2011a, p6).

The government's *Action Plan for Adoption* (DfE, 2011a) sets the scene for what is hoped will be a more robust policy framework for adoption. The plan seeks to impose performance indicators, or *scorecards*, incorporating the length of the child's journey in care, the proportion of looked-after children who are in a permanent placement and the effectiveness with which prospective adopters are recruited, assessed, trained and matched with a child. It hopes to ensure swifter and more widespread use of the national adoption register and to encourage local authorities to place children for adoption in anticipation of a court's placement order, an extension of the previous system of *concurrent* or *parallel* planning, although it is not clear how this will be achieved without pre-empting court decisions. The Children and Families Bill, expected to be introduced in 2013, is likely to include provision to prevent local authorities from delaying adoption placements to find the perfect match and so, in many cases, matching the ethnicity or religious background of a child with that of prospective adopters will have a lower priority than the speed with which a child can be placed in a permanent home.

RESEARCH SUMMARY 8.2

Selwyn et al. (2006) examined the chronologies of 130 looked-after children between the ages of one and ten years who were the subject of adoption 'best interests' decisions.

- *In 68 per cent of cases they identified delayed removal from home, evidenced by lack of planning or reassessment of the approach being adopted when there had been no sign of improvement or a worsening in family circumstances after 12 months of social work intervention.*

- *35 per cent of families had initially appeared to comply with agreed plans but were subsequently found to have been uncooperative or untruthful.*

- *14 per cent had moved or been difficult to locate at some stage, resulting in a new social worker having to initiate another assessment.*

- *41 per cent waited more than a year after becoming looked after before a permanence plan was made, with the average delay being 2.7 years.*

- *Legal hold-ups accounted for 34 per cent of delays.*

Research by OFSTED (2012b) in some respects reflects that of Selwyn et al. in suggesting that the primary cause of delay in making adoption placements is lengthy court proceedings involving multiple assessments which often go unchallenged due to lack of confidence and assertiveness on the part of social workers and children's guardians. Little evidence was found of delay caused by unrealistic searches for perfect ethnic matches. Most adopters reported that they had received a welcoming response from local authorities and that the time taken to complete their assessments was necessary: 'The first assessment was over a relatively long period and this was right – we needed the time to deal with the challenging emotional nature of what we were doing' (adoptive parent, quoted at ibid., p29).

The government is seeking to reduce court delays by imposing a six-month time limit on care proceedings and removing the requirement that local authority adoption panels consider the suitability for adoption of children whose cases are before the court. It is also promoting the practice of concurrent planning for looked-after children under two years old, for whom adoption is likely to be the best option, but where there still exists a possibility of a return to their birth family (DfE, 2012b). This would allow a child to be placed with carers who have been approved both as foster carers and as prospective adopters while efforts continue to support the birth family with a view to the child's return. However, if these efforts fail, the child could then be adopted by their existing carers without the lengthy procedures and consequent delay which would occur if an adoption plan had to be initiated from scratch. Concurrent planning is different from the more common practice of parallel or twin-track planning in that the child is placed with the potential adopters whilst decision-making proceeds, rather than in a temporary foster placement. Concurrent planning places significant demands on social workers and carers, not only in terms of time. They must continue to work with the birth family to give them the best chance of addressing the issues that led to the child coming into care and they must maintain contact between the child and their birth family as against the possibility that the child does return home. Carers must be properly trained and supported so that they can cope emotionally and practically with the fact that they may not ultimately adopt the child they are caring for.

PRACTITIONER REFLECTION 8.2

Looked-after children team social worker:

We just hate concurrent and parallel planning: it goes against all the principles of partnership with parents and seems so dishonest somehow, quite apart from all the time it takes.

NAGALRO, an organisation that represents family court advisers, children's guardians and independent social workers, has urged caution in respect of the policy commitment to increase the number of children adopted from care which, it states, risks directing resources away from the whole range of looked-after children, particularly those for whom other permanence options might be preferable. They suggest that in a significant proportion of cases delay is caused by poorly-focused work with families and lack of clarity, experience and confidence on the part of social workers in respect of thresholds and evidence for court (NAGALRO, 2012).

RESEARCH SUMMARY 8.3

Coram (Laws et al., 2012), which is working with a group of local authorities to achieve more timely adoption and permanent family placements for looked-after children via concurrent planning, reports that of the 57 children placed through the scheme between 2000 and 2011, 54 have been adopted by their Coram Concurrent Planning (CCP) carers and three returned to their birth families. At the time of reporting, there had been no post placement disruptions and no child had been returned to care. The average age of children adopted by CCP carers was 17 months, compared with the national average of 3 years and 11 months, while children placed for concurrent planning took on average 14 months from entry to care to being adopted as against the national average of 2 years and 7 months (DfE, 2011c).

ACTIVITY 8.1

Think of possible reasons for delay in achieving a permanent placement for a looked-after child. How many of these are likely to be reduced by enacting additional legal or policy requirements? What can social workers and their managers contribute towards minimising such delays? Are performance targets a help or a hindrance in practice?

Post adoption support

Under the ACA and Adoption Support Services Regulations 2005, local authorities have a duty to appoint an Adoption Support Services Adviser (ASSA) to give advice and information to people who are affected by adoption. They are also required to undertake an assessment when requested by an adoptive parent, adopted child, birth parent or former guardian and to maintain an adoption support service. However, the nature and extent of services provided are subject to powers rather than duties. The ACA defines adoption support services as incorporating:

* financial support;

* facilities to enable adoptive children, adoptive parents and natural parents or former guardians of an adopted child to discuss matters of common interest;

* assistance, including mediation services, in relation to contact between an adopted child and a natural parent, natural sibling, former guardian or a relative of the adopted child;

* therapeutic services for adopted children;

* assistance for the purpose of ensuring the continuance of the relationship between an adopted child and his adoptive parent, including training for adoptive parents to meet any special needs of the child, and respite care;

* assistance where post adoption disruption has occurred, or is at risk of occurring, making arrangements for the provision of mediation services and organising and running disruption meetings;

* counselling, advice and information.

RESEARCH SUMMARY *8.4*

Research undertaken on behalf of Adoption UK (Pennington, 2012) found a lack of understanding among adopters of their entitlement to support services, which were not consistently provided by local authorities.

* *64 per cent were not informed of their right to an assessment for support after adoption.*

* *30 per cent had requested an assessment, of whom 63 per cent had an assessment undertaken, of whom 81 per cent had support needs identified, of whom only 31 per cent received all of the services identified as needed.*

* *Of those who received support services, 63 per cent rated them as good or excellent. Only 14 per cent described them as poor.*

* *57 per cent described the working relationship between agencies, such as health, social services and education, as poor.*

  It is daft that adopters have a right to have their needs assessed, but then no right to have those needs fulfilled.

(Adoptive parent, ibid., p42)

Special guardianship

The concept of special guardianship was introduced by the ACA as an amendment to the CA 1989 s14. Its aim was to increase the options available for achieving permanence in situations where adoption is not possible or desirable, particularly those in which the child's link with their birth family needs to be preserved, and it introduced a means of ensuring stability, short of adoption, whilst removing the potentially negative consequences of remaining a looked-after child. Again, the influence of human rights can be seen in that special guardianship was seen as a possible alternative in situations where adoption by the foster carers might be seen to be a disproportionate interference with the ties existing between the child and his birth family. Special guardianship may also meet the needs of a child who is permanently placed with relatives, since it does not obscure the reality of family relationships in the same way that adoption does. However, other than the fact that a child subject to a special guardianship order retains their original birth certificate and name, the most significant distinction between adoption and special guardianship is that although the special guardian potentially can restrict the exercise of parental responsibility by those who hold it (usually the birth parents), it remains shared, which can result in unanticipated consequences which special guardians might have to face without support, financial or otherwise, from their local authority.

Who can apply?

A child's parents may not become their special guardian. Those who may apply for special guardianship are (CA 1989 s14A):

- a guardian of the child;

- a local authority foster carer with whom the child has lived for one year immediately preceding the application;

- anyone holding a residence order with respect to the child, or who has the consent of all those in whose favour a residence order is in force;

- anyone with whom the child has lived for three out of the last five years;

- where the child is in the care of a local authority, any person who has the consent of the local authority;

- anyone who has the consent of all those with parental responsibility for the child;

- any person who has been granted permission by a court.

Effects of a special guardianship order (SGO)

- *An SGO can be made in any family proceedings without anyone having applied for it, but not until a report that specifically addresses the question of special guardianship has been submitted to court by the local authority responsible for the child.*

- *It lasts until the child reaches 18 unless ended by a court.*

- *It does not sever the ties with the birth parent or result in any change to the child's birth certificate.*

- *It discharges any existing care order on the child.*

- *It gives parental responsibility to the special guardian who may restrict the exercise of parental responsibility by others, although, as special guardians are not subject to the*

---

public law that applies to a local authority, such restriction is not subject to the need to be satisfied that it is necessary to safeguard or promote the child's welfare (CA 1989 s33).

- Special guardians may not change a child's surname, take them abroad for more than three months or consent to their adoption without the agreement of those with parental responsibility, or of a court.

- Special guardians can appoint a testamentary guardian to look after their child in the event of their death.

- If a child was looked after immediately prior to the making of an SGO, the child, special guardian or parent has a right to an assessment by the local authority for support services, which may include financial support and leaving and after-care services. 'Financial issues should not be the sole reason for a special guardianship arrangement failing to survive' (Special Guardianship Regulations Reg. 6).

- Local authorities, adoption and fostering agencies and health authorities have powers to provide mediation, training and therapeutic services to families in which there exists an SGO. Where such services are provided they must be reviewed annually and if it is proposed to vary or terminate the service, an opportunity must be provided for representations to be made.

ACTIVITY *8.2*

Shamira and Ashok, aged 9 and 11, are subject to SGOs in favour of foster carers with whom they have lived for five years. The foster carers have regular holidays in Spain, where they have a second home and where they now wish to live permanently. Shamira and Ashok's birth parents, who are divorced, both hold parental responsibility and see the children approximately six times a year. Their father is happy for the move to take place, but their mother will not agree as she does not want them removed from the English culture and thinks that she will not be able to see her children as frequently as previously. It is open to the special guardians to apply to a court to determine the matter by means of a specific issue order (CA 1989 s8), but due to restrictions on the availability of civil legal aid they feel they cannot afford to initiate such action themselves.

The special guardians approach you as their previous social worker and ask if you can help. Your team manager advises that as this is essentially a private law matter, the local authority cannot assist. Is there anything else you would wish or ought to do?

RESEARCH SUMMARY *8.5*

Research by the government-funded Adoption Research Initiative (2010) reported on how the provision for SGOs was being implemented in practice. There were a number of key findings.

- The degree to which local authorities approached special guardianship was highly variable and where a dedicated social work team was involved at all stages, services were more coherent and comprehensive.

RESEARCH SUMMARY 8.5 (CONT.)

- Most take-up initially was from relatives (86 per cent), with grandparents in the majority. Over half the children involved were aged five or under. Most (74 per cent) had been living with their carer before the application, often for a lengthy period.

- Over two-thirds had been looked after by the local authority immediately before the application, just under half in kinship foster care and the remainder in unrelated foster care.

- Unrelated foster carers expressed concerns about financial uncertainty, the likely loss of social work support and the potential difficulties of managing birth family relationships.

- While there were signs of take-up within some minority ethnic communities, there was little evidence that unaccompanied asylum-seeking children had been considered for special guardianship as envisaged initially.

- Practitioners were concerned about the three-month timescale for completing assessments and court reports.

- Most special guardians felt that their assessment had been covered in sufficient depth. However, some were frustrated by delays and the duplication of information collected. Some also felt that the process was overly intrusive.

- Once the SGO had been made, the response of special guardians was overwhelmingly positive, although a minority felt that they had been subject to pressure from social workers or the courts to apply. Other orders were quite commonly attached, such as contact or supervision orders.

LEGAL CASE STUDY 8.7

In R (TT) v Merton LBC [2012] EWHC 2055 (Admin) it was decided that a local authority was wrong to have paid a kinship carer who had been granted an SGO an allowance which was one-third lower than that paid to foster carers. 'Compliance (with the guidance) is not achieved by ignoring the additional costs of caring for a child not born into the family or assessing them at nil' (para. 67).

Residence order

A residence order (CA 1989 s8), like adoption and special guardianship, determines with whom a child should live and gives parental responsibility to the person in whose favour it is made. It lasts until the child is 16, which may be extended to the age of 18. However, unlike adoption, it does not remove parental responsibility from those already holding it, such as a birth parent. It does, however, discharge any existing care order. Foster carers can apply for a residence order with the consent of the relevant local authority and have an automatic right to apply without consent if they have cared for a child for three years or are related (grandparent, brother, sister, uncle, aunt or step-parent) to the child. A residence order can incorporate supplementary provisions relating to contact or other aspects of a child's care. The Children and Young Persons Act 2008 attempted to reduce some of the barriers that might have discouraged relatives from applying for residence orders and it was hoped, as a consequence, that there would be fewer public law applications for care orders. However, this appears to have had little impact, with the cost of court applications and restrictions on civil legal aid a disincentive to private individuals who might otherwise be willing to apply. Unlike special guardianship, a birth parent or the child concerned does not require a court's permission to apply for the discharge or variation of a residence order.

Returning home from care

Existing legal provision and policy guidance in relation to looked-after children leaving care focuses almost exclusively on independence and the transition to adulthood, with little attention paid to children returning home as part of their plan for permanence. As a result, practice tends to vary between local authorities: for example, some place emphasis on early intervention and are less likely to consider reunification once a child has entered care, while others actively pursue the possibility of reunification from the point at which the child becomes looked after (NSPCC, 2012).

Returning to their family is the most common outcome for looked-after children. In 2010/11, 26,830 children left care in England and Wales, of whom 10,350 returned to their families.

RESEARCH SUMMARY 8.6

Almost half of the children who enter care as a result of abuse or neglect experience further abuse or neglect after returning home and 40 per cent of returns are unplanned (Farmer et al., 2008). An earlier study (Biehal, 2006) found that 50 per cent of children who return home from care become looked after again subsequently, often within six months, and a third of looked-after children suffer repeated failed attempts to reintegrate them with their family with no other options for permanence actively considered.

In a study supporting a recent report, 70 per cent of a sample of looked-after children who had returned home said that they had not felt ready to return to their families.

> When I return a child home, they are registered as a child in need. But I know the case will be closed within a couple of months.
>
> *(Social worker, quoted in NSPCC, 2012, p18)*

The NSPCC (ibid., p5) suggests that work is required in relation to the following:

- *the quality of assessment about whether, and when, a child should return home from care;*

- *the planning and preparation required prior to their return;*

- *the support available to children and their parents to tackle issues such as substance dependency and domestic violence, and to support children's and parents' mental health needs.*

A child who is accommodated under CA 1989 s20 ceases to be accommodated if they return home to live with a parent. The placement of a child who is subject to a care, or interim care, order with a parent, or other person with parental responsibility for a period of more than 24 hours, is subject to the Care Planning, Placement and Case Review Regulations (2010, SI No. 959) which requires that the decision has been part of the care plan incorporating the child's views and that an assessment of suitability has been undertaken for all members of the household who are aged 18 or over and any other people who might have contact with the child, such as grandparents (HMG, 2010, p53). The placement plan must include:

- details of the support and services to be provided to the parents;

- the parents' obligation to notify the local authority of any relevant change in circumstances and to keep any information provided confidential;

- circumstances for obtaining approval for the child to live in another household;

- arrangements for requesting a change to the agreement; and

- circumstances in which the placement will be terminated.

Social work visits and reviews must continue.

FURTHER READING

www.adoptionresearchinitiative.org.uk

The ARI is a group of major research projects that focuses on permanence planning, matching, support for adoptive placements and the costs of adoption.

www.adoptionuk.org.uk

Adoption UK supports prospective adopters before, during and after the adoption process.

www.baaf.org.uk

The British Association for Adoption and Fostering offers resources to professionals and those interested in adoption.

Chapter 9
Independence

Here we explore the interface between the law's role in protecting children and its increasing acceptance of the need to define the responsibilities of local authorities, whether acting as 'corporate parent' or in accordance with other powers and duties, to support young people towards secure and responsible adulthood and independence. This requires the use of critical thinking to inform professional judgement and the ability to evaluate legal case decisions, and the chapter particularly supports PCF requirements in relation to Intervention and Skills.

Introduction

Local authorities have a responsibility towards the children they look after to prepare them for independence as any other parent does. However, the need to plan for independence does not only arise at the point of leaving care, and situations in which there is conflict and dispute between parents and young people arising from the path to independence commonly can result in social care referrals. In addition, social workers often have to assess the capacity of children and young people to contribute to decisions that affect them, which is discussed in Chapter 4. In social work with children and families, tensions potentially can arise between service users' autonomy and rights to privacy and family life, risk and protection, assessed needs and available resources, and the expressed wishes of the child against those of the parent or the expectations of society, all of which require the exercise of professional judgement within the relevant legal and policy framework.

Children's autonomy and maturity

Whether a child is considered to be mature enough to make decisions that might otherwise be made by adults is not simply a question of age, despite the fact that this remains the criterion for most other circumstances in which children may need legal protection (see Chapter 6).

LEGAL CASE STUDY 9.1

The concept of 'Gillick competency' arose from the case of Gillick v West Norfolk & Wisbech Area Health Authority *[1986] AC 112. Mrs Gillick, who had five daughters under 16, was concerned that her children might be given contraceptive advice or treatment without her knowledge or consent, and sought assurance from her local health authority that this would not occur. When the authority responded that this was a decision for each individual doctor, Mrs Gillick brought proceedings against both the authority and the Department of Health and Social Security, arguing that the advice amounted to condoning the commission of offences by doctors and that giving contraceptive advice or treatment to girls under 16 without parental consent was inconsistent with parental rights. The House of Lords (now the Supreme Court) eventually decided against Mrs Gillick and the judgement set out the court's analysis of the issues:*

> Whether or not a child is capable of giving the necessary consent will depend on the child's maturity and understanding and the nature of the consent required. The child must be capable of making a reasonable assessment of the advantages and disadvantages of the treatment proposed, so the consent, if given, can be properly and fairly described as true consent . . . parental rights exist only for the benefit of the child and 'dwindle' with increasing age of the child. The parents' rights consequently yielded to the child's when she reached sufficient understanding and intelligence to be able to make up her own mind.

Lord Scarman's comments in the judgement are often referred to as the test of Gillick competency:

> It is not enough that she should understand the nature of the advice which is being given: she must also have a sufficient maturity to understand what is involved.

The Fraser guidelines refer to those set out by Lord Fraser, one of the judges in the Gillick case, and specifically relate to the giving of contraceptive advice and treatment. However, the principles are generally considered applicable to other situations in which professionals need to assess whether a young person is able to make important personal decisions.

LEGAL CASE STUDY 9.2

The judgement in the case of Mabon v Mabon *[2005] EWCA Civ 634 referred to the need for the law to 'reflect the extent to which, in the 21st century, there is a keener appreciation of the autonomy of the child' (para. 26).*

LEGAL CASE STUDY 9.3

In R (Axon) v Secretary of State for Health *[2006] EWHC 37 (Admin) the judge said: 'the right of young people to make decisions about their own lives by themselves at the expense of the views of their parents has now become an increasingly important and accepted feature of family life' (para. 79).*

Government guidance on information sharing (DCSF, 2008, p19) deals with the question of children's autonomy as follows, although you may find it too general to be of much practical assistance:

1. *In most cases, where a child cannot consent or where you have judged that they are not competent to consent, a person with parental responsibility should be asked to consent on behalf of the child. If a child or young person is judged not to have the capacity to make decisions, their views should still be sought as far as possible.*

2. *Where parental consent is required, the consent of one such person is sufficient. In situations where family members are in conflict you will need to consider carefully whose consent should be sought. If the parents are separated, the consent would usually be sought from the parent with whom the child resides. If a care order is in force, the local authority will share parental responsibility with parent(s) and practitioners should liaise with them about questions of consent.*

3. *If you judge a child or young person to be competent to give consent, then their consent or refusal to consent is the one to consider, even if a parent or carer disagrees. Where parental consent is not required, you should encourage the young person to discuss the issue with their parents. However, you should not withhold the service on the condition that they do so.*

ACTIVITY 9.1

Sasha, who is 16, revealed to the deputy head of her school that she had been seriously sexually assaulted by a former boyfriend. The deputy head had promised to keep it a secret but discussed the matter with the head teacher who informed children's social care and the police. Sasha felt let down by the school, which exacerbated her distress. She was adamant that her parents should not know and the police took the position that the parents did not have to be informed. However, the social worker was concerned that Sasha's distress was clouding her judgement, that she would need support if the case came to trial and that safeguarding procedures would be ineffective if Sasha's parents remained unaware of what had happened.

- *What is the relevance to this situation of the decision in the Gillick case?*

- *Do the guidelines referred to above help?*

- *What options are open to the social worker?*

- *What should the social worker take account of when recording their actions?*

In relation to children's autonomy in legal proceedings, there are signs that courts increasingly are inclined to attach weight to children's opinions although there tends to exist a sliding scale of capacity depending on the nature of the decision and the risk of harm associated with it (Gilmore and Herring, 2011). This means that there is likely to be an area of uncertainty requiring the exercise of professional judgement between the point at which it is clear that a child or young person is able to make an informed decision and the point at which they are obviously not mature enough to do so.

The powers of parents to agree to, or remove a child from, accommodation under the Children Act 1989 s20 do not apply to young people over 16, who are responsible for making their own decisions in this context.

Leaving care

The legislative and policy framework within which leaving care services are delivered should ensure that the approach to providing settled accommodation for care leavers is well thought out and strategic, not just a safety net for vulnerable young people.

(NCAS, 2009b, p3)

I had an interesting conversation with a work colleague today, she is same age as myself (20). She told me that she's never met someone who lived in the care of social services before and she expected young people in those circumstances to be out binge drinking and wearing tracksuits all day. I guess stereotyping is something no one can escape from.

(Former looked-after child, quoted in OFSTED, 2011a, p35)

We call it the Leaving and No Care Service.

(Designated teacher for looked-after children)

When the state assumes the responsibility for looking after children who cannot live safely with their birth family, it creates a unique relationship between the child and the state-as-parent that is not replicated elsewhere in the dealings that citizens have with their government (NCAS, 2012a). The CA 1989, amended and supplemented by the Children (Leaving Care) Act 2000, the Children and Young Persons Act 2008 and associated regulations and guidance provides the general legal framework for young people leaving care.

ACTIVITY 9.2

Ryan came into care when he was 12 and had several residential and foster care placements. As he approached his 16th birthday his social worker and personal adviser recognised that although he had practical skills, he had little prospect of gaining any educational qualifications and, with no contact with any birth relatives, his emotional resilience appeared fragile. After his 17th birthday Ryan moved into a supported housing project where he stayed for a year. It became clear that he was vulnerable to peer pressure and he began smoking cannabis and drinking alcohol to excess. He was uninterested in training or education programmes, and spent most of the day in bed or out with his friends, often missing appointments with professionals. When Ryan reached 18, his social worker left and he was allocated social housing by the local authority. Although support was offered, he was unwilling to accept a new social worker and within six months had accrued considerable debts. Ryan eventually abandoned his flat and gave the keys to a so-called friend who caused damage to the property. Ryan relied on friends to put him up but his continual failure to pay for his board resulted in him being asked to leave. His social worker found emergency hostel accommodation but again he had to leave when he damaged his room and did not pay his expenses. Ryan was then placed in bed and breakfast accommodation as no other housing provider would accept him due to his behaviour and the housing department had assessed him as being intentionally homeless. He was subsequently charged with theft, burglary and criminal damage and received a custodial sentence.

- In what respects is this situation assisted or exacerbated by existing law and policy?

- What changes would you suggest in order to address the difficulties Ryan experienced and to seek to avert the predictable outcome?

Every year, around 6,000 looked-after children leave care, of whom 21 per cent are 16, 17 per cent are 17, and 61 per cent are 18 (Hannon *et al.*, 2010). The average age at which young people leave home in the general population is around 24, which means that a significant proportion of young people are leaving care possibly ill-prepared for the realities of adult life. In addition, the preparation offered to young care leavers has been found to be inadequate in a number of significant respects, evidenced by the poor outcomes they achieve in terms of education, health, and economic and social stability (CRDE, 2012).

The CA 1989 reflected growing recognition of the patchy and haphazard nature of support available to care leavers by introducing a duty towards children aged 16–21 who were leaving care, or had previously been looked after, to advise, assist and befriend them (s24). However, as might have been anticipated from the general nature of the language used, services provided continued to make little impact in terms of addressing the social, educational, economic and personal disadvantages this group of young people faced.

There was, therefore, optimism that improvements would follow the enactment of the CLCA in 2000 which imposed additional duties on local authorities towards children leaving care. However, not everyone supported the concept of the local authority as *corporate parent* and the assumption that care leavers could benefit from an experience of the transition to adulthood similar to that enjoyed by non-care leavers (Stewart *et al.*, 2004). In addition, it is hard to understand how the terminology used in the CLCA ever came to be introduced, with its bureaucratic and institutional connotations and complex eligibility criteria. The Children's Rights Commissioner for England considers the legislation *complicated* and referred to a recent court judgement in which it was described as *impenetrable* (OFSTED, 2012a, p31).

> What is needed is a more consistent interest in the young person from Year 7 through to Year 11. At present all the attention seems to land on them at once in Year 11 when they have enough to think about. The transfer to the 'Leaving Care Team' has not yet been successful for us, it seriously frightens our youngsters and there seems to be a lack of empathy. The disruption is most damaging at the point of exams; the change has to happen sooner or later, but the timing is completely off at the moment.
>
> (Teacher, quoted in NCAS, 2009a, p3)

The White Paper *Care Matters: Time for Change* (DfES, 2007), which preceded the CA 2008, set out the government's expectations that young people leaving care should receive the same level of support that others would expect from a reasonable parent and that no young person should be made to feel that they must leave care before they are ready. Central to the legal provisions is pathway planning, which builds on care planning and is managed within the role of the personal adviser. By the age of 16 each young person must have a regularly reviewed pathway plan which sets out their progress towards independence in relation to accommodation, life skills, education and training, employment, financial support, specific support needs and contingency plans if independent living breaks down.

> *A pathway plan must clearly identify the child's needs, and what is to be done about them, by whom and by when. Or, if another aphorism would help, a pathway plan must spell who does what, where and when.*
> (R (J) v Caerphilly County Borough Council [2005] EWHC 586 (Admin), para. 45)

Local authorities have a duty to maintain contact with care leavers until they are 21. Care leavers up to the age of 25 who have returned, or wish to return, to education or training are entitled to an assessment and the support of a personal adviser while they pursue their training, provided it is included within their pathway plan.

An *eligible child* is a looked-after child aged 16 or 17, who has been looked after for a total of at least 13 weeks which began after they reached the age of 14, and ended after they reached the age of 16.

A *relevant child* is a young person aged 16 or 17 who was an eligible child but is no longer looked after. A child who has lived for a continuous period of six months or more, whether that period commenced before or after they ceased to be looked after, with a parent or other person holding parental responsibility is no longer a relevant child, unless the arrangements break down.

A *former relevant child* is a young person aged 18 or over (that is, legally adult) who was either an eligible or relevant child. The local authority has duties in relation to former relevant children until they reach 21, or 25 if they are still in education or training.

A *qualifying child* is a young person under 21, or 25 if in education or training, who ceases to be looked after or accommodated in a variety of other settings, including private foster care, after the age of 16.

Local authority duties and responsibilities towards children leaving care (CA 1989, ss23 and 24, as amended by CLCA):

- *For eligible children:*
  - *meet accommodation, personal and education-related expenses;*
  - *carry out a needs assessment;*
  - *prepare a pathway plan, building on the child's existing care plan;*
  - *regularly review the pathway plan;*
  - *appoint a personal adviser.*
- *For relevant children:*
  - *carry out a needs assessment;*
  - *prepare a pathway plan;*

o *regularly review the pathway plan;*

o *provide a personal adviser;*

o *arrange suitable accommodation and provide household equipment;*

o *provide an allowance, which must not be less than if they were receiving social security benefits. Relevant children cannot claim benefits unless they are disabled or a lone parent;*

o *pay for any additional costs set out in the pathway plan;*

o *keep in touch with the young person.*

• *For former relevant children:*

o *maintain the pathway plan;*

o *provide a personal adviser;*

o *contribute to the costs of support set out in the pathway plan, in so far as the young person's welfare requires this;*

o *contribute towards the costs of education and vacation accommodation;*

o *keep in touch with the young person.*

• *For qualifying children:*

o *give advice and support;*

o *keep in touch with the young person;*

o *may also help with paying expenses related to the young person's education.*

A description of the scope of assessment, the functions of the personal adviser and the content of the pathway plan is contained within the Care Leavers (England) Regulations 2010, SI 2010 No. 2571.

LEGAL CASE STUDY **9.4**

R (TG) v Lambeth LBC *[2011] EWCA Civ 526*

TG, who was 16 and known to the local authority's Youth Offending Team (YOT), sought assistance from the local authority's homeless persons unit following the breakdown of his relationship with his mother with whom he had lived. Although a social worker from the YOT provided a report stating that TG fulfilled the child in need criteria under s17(10) of the CA 1989, he was not referred to children's services but was provided with accommodation under the Housing Act 1996 s188 for seven months until he was 17. The local authority subsequently refused to provide him with services as a 'former relevant child' when he became 18. The court decided that as TG fulfilled the criteria of a child in need, the local authority owed him a general duty under the CA 1989 s17(1) and should have provided him with accommodation under s20. Consequently, from his 18th birthday TG had the status of a former relevant child for the purposes of the CA 1989 s23C.

R (O) v Barking & Dagenham LBC *[2010] EWHC 634 (Admin)*

This case concerned a young person from Eritrea who had been accommodated by his local authority under the CA 1989 s20. As a former looked-after child who had been accommodated for more than 13 weeks, he was entitled to leaving care services when he became 18. Although local authorities have a duty to provide former relevant children with 'other assistance, to the extent that his welfare requires it' (CA 1989 s24) the High Court agreed that this does not authorise the provision of accommodation unless it relates directly to work or educational needs, which did not exist in this case. As a result, the local authority had no power to accommodate the young man after the age of 18 under leaving care legislation and, as he was still pursuing an asylum claim, a responsibility to accommodate him lay with the UK Border Agency, which could choose simply to reimburse the local authority for the accommodation provided. Young people who are disabled may continue to be entitled to accommodation from a local authority after the age of 18 under community care legislation (National Assistance Act 1948 s21).

The Children's Rights Director for England (2012) sought the views of young people who had recently left care which produced the following key messages:

* *around half of those surveyed thought they had left care too early, with insufficient preparation;*

* *the majority (61 per cent) thought that being in care had made their lives better, while a quarter said it had made their lives worse;*

* *care leavers felt poorly prepared emotionally for living alone;*

* *young people need someone to call on readily for help and advice once they are living independently;*

* *young people leaving care need more help with handling money and everyday practical skills such as cooking;*

* *half of care leavers think there exists prejudice against people who have been in care and try to conceal the fact that they have been in care.*

Hannon et al. (2010) identified the factors that can significantly improve a young person's experience of leaving care and their future life chances:

* *the age at which they leave care;*

* *the speed of their transition;*

* *their access to preparation before leaving care and support after leaving care;*

* *stability and secure attachments after leaving care.*

RESEARCH SUMMARY 9.1 (CONT.)

A survey of local authority leaving care services to assess the impact of budget restrictions found that half were experiencing a reduction in provision. The main findings were (NCAS, 2012b):

- *while the number of young people in and leaving care has increased, in the majority of services budgets have remained static or reduced;*

- *a third of managers reported that workers were seeing young people less frequently and that intervention was more likely to occur in response to crises;*

- *services for older care leavers were most likely to be affected by financial constraints;*

- *three-quarters of managers reported that external services used to support young people were being cut;*

- *over half of services had cut some elements of education, training or employment support for young people, such as interview and work-related expenses, educational materials and equipment, further and higher education support, and incentives for employment and education, and a fifth reported reductions in funding for rent deposits.*

A particular recommendation was that services for care leavers should be prioritised in all sections of the local authority, not just within children's services.

Financial support for care leavers

CASE STUDY 9.1

A freedom of information request about the level of grants made to children leaving care to live independently received responses from 114 of the 152 local authorities in England. At the lower end of provision three councils offered maximum leaving care grants of £750, £784 and £850 respectively. The maximum leaving care grant was set at £1,000 by 17 councils and stood between £1,100 and £1,500 in 56. Only 24 councils offered a maximum setting up home grant of £2,000 or more. However, it was found that the actual amount young people received was often much less than the maximum amount set by policy, ranging from £145 in one local authority to £2,274 in the most generous. At the same time the cost of the minimum amount of equipment considered necessary to set up home independently was assessed as around £2,800.

(Care Leavers' Foundation, 2011)

The CLCA strengthened local authorities' financial responsibilities towards looked-after children approaching independence by removing 16- and 17-year-old care leavers from the benefits system and placing a duty on local authorities to provide for their accommodation and maintenance. Leaving care policy has continued to develop and more care leavers are being offered extended support by former foster carers and their local authority, in some cases into their mid-20s, as is common in the general population. However, they still experience financial disadvantage compared with other young people. The benefits system is a poor replacement for the support that most young people receive from their families (NCAS, 2010) and it has been argued that the powers held by local authorities for the discretionary interpretation of the circumstances of care leavers and the provision of services to them do not, for the most part, meet the needs of this group of young people (Stewart *et al.*, 2004). For example, young people leaving care might have to claim housing benefit from the age of 18, even if they remain living with their former foster carers, resulting in their carers effectively becoming their landlords, potentially altering the nature of their relationship.

Local authority support for care leavers is primarily dependent on young people's needs rather than their age, which is intended to ensure that they are not arbitrarily forced into independent living without account being taken of their ability to manage on their own. By contrast, the benefits system provides some types and levels of assistance for which eligibility is determined by age. Restricted budgets mean that local authorities must ensure that young people maximise the income they receive from the benefits system, although local authorities have powers to top up benefits or support young people financially in some circumstances. However, local authorities are not expected to be care leavers' primary source of funding after the age of 18 unless they remain in full-time education or training: the CYPA 2008 extended the role of the personal adviser and allows young people to return to their local authority for support with education and training until the age of 25.

An additional factor to be considered when determining policy in this area is that having been in care can be stigmatising, and targeted systems that provide support specifically for looked-after children and care leavers, which in doing so identify them as such to their peers, may be less acceptable, and therefore less effective, than more universal services. Support arrangements that are subject to local implementation and poorly understood, such as the pupil premium, 16–19 bursary and university student finance arrangements, also create significant barriers for young people leaving care (Who Cares? Trust, 2012).

CASE STUDY 9.2

Mr S became subject to a care order in 2000 aged 13. He was accommodated in foster placements until 2004 when he took up his own council tenancy. In 2009 he complained via the Local Government Ombudsman (LGO) that there were shortcomings in the services provided to him as a former relevant child and that he had not been supported as a vulnerable young person leaving care should have been. Mr S's personal adviser (PA) was unsuccessful in making contact with Mr S between September 2006 and March 2007 when a pathway plan was sent to him with a request for his telephone number. The PA again wrote to Mr S in April 2007 requesting his contact number and expressing concern about his rent arrears. Meanwhile Mr S was receiving therapeutic care and financial support from a charity which paid his rent arrears, so that he could retain his tenancy, fees for a college course and maintenance payments. Mr S's PA wrote to him again in June 2007 suggesting a final meeting in July 2007, just before his 21st birthday. Mr S told the LGO that he had difficulties remembering appointments but usually attended them if reminded beforehand. He did not attend the July meeting and the relevant council subsequently ceased assisting him. In August 2007 Mr S's solicitors wrote to the council's Leaving Care Team asking for support for their client beyond his 21st birthday. No reply was received. In 2008 Mr S submitted a formal complaint, claiming that the council had taken no proper account of his vulnerability when offering him services, that it had failed to appreciate that, due to his depression and mental health problems, he needed support over and above that provided for young people without

CASE STUDY **9.2** (CONT.)

such problems and that it should have made efforts to remind him of his appointment as a concerned parent would have done. The council accepted that his 2006 and 2007 pathway plans were flawed, that agreed actions were not completed or followed up and, in particular, that Mr S's financial needs were not assessed. It agreed to implement a range of remedial actions to provide Mr S with the help he needed. However, Mr S complained to the LGO on the grounds that the council had failed to undertake these within a reasonable timescale.

The LGO found that there had been maladministration causing injustice, partly due to the extended absence of Mr S's PA, and required the council to:

a. *complete the review of Mr S's pathway plan so that he had clarity with regard to financial matters and the support that the council would provide for him;*

b. *pay Mr S £5,000 in recognition of the injustice he had suffered as a result of the council's maladministration; and*

c. *pay the charity £2,000 in recognition of the role it had played in Mr S's life in the absence of effective support from the council.*

(LGO complaint number 08013283)

Children with disabilities

The period during which disabled children progress to adulthood is usually referred to as *transition* and is potentially a difficult time for them and their families. The National Service Framework (DoH, 2004, standard 8) described the main focus of transition planning as: 'The fulfilment of the hopes, dreams and potential of the disabled young person, in particular to maximise education, training and employment opportunities, to enjoy social relationships and to live independently.' However, frequently the services and support provided for them as children are not offered to the same standard by adult services, even though the fundamental duties owed to them under the Chronically Sick and Disabled Persons Act 1970 remain the same. It has been suggested (Broach *et al.*, 2010) that this has been exacerbated by the separation of children's and adult services which followed the CA 2004, despite the existence of statutory guidance requiring that local authorities make 'adequate arrangements to ensure continuity of care for young disabled people throughout their transition to becoming adults' (DoH, 2006). However, as in so many government documents, the use of the imprecise description *adequate* significantly weakens the authority of the statement and makes it difficult, if not impossible, to challenge any alleged shortfall in services. The LGO has repeatedly expressed concern about failures in transition planning, in particular emphasising the duty to continue to meet assessed needs and not to 'use available services as a starting point and just fit people into them' (LGO complaint 03/C/16371).

The Disabled Persons (Services, Consultation and Representation) Act 1986 ss5 and 6 endeavours to address the challenges of transition to adulthood in relation to disabled children for whom there is a statement of special educational needs (SEN). The DPSCRA s5 requires that when the child becomes 14 a social care assessment of their needs is undertaken so that services are in place when educational provision ceases. After assessment, a plan should be formulated to ensure that the assessed needs are met. The young person and their family should understand the purpose of the assessment, how it will be conducted and the nature of the decisions that rest on it. The statutory emphasis is on person-centred planning and providing disabled young people with opportunities to take decisions about their lives with the necessary support.

Despite these provisions, there is evidence that disabled young people experience unsatisfactory transitions from children's to adult services or to independence. Services for disabled care leavers are not always coordinated and planned with mainstream leaving care services (Baker, 2011). A particular example is the provision of residential accommodation, whether or not provided in the context of short breaks. While a young person is under 18, this service will be provided under the CA 1989 ss17 or 20. From their 18th birthday, however, it will generally be made under the National Assistance Act 1948 s21, although there is no reason for this change to make any practical difference so long as the service continues to meet the young person's assessed needs.

Children with mental health needs

A review of the services provided by Child and Adolescent Mental Health Services (CAMHS) recognised the risk that young people can fall through the net as they approach the age of 18. Specific recommendations included:

Young adults who are approaching 18 years of age and who are being supported by CAMHS should, along with their parents and carers:

- *know well in advance what the arrangements will be for transfer to adult services of any type, following a planning meeting at least six months before their 18th birthday;*

- *be able to access services that are based on best evidence of what works for young adults, and which have been informed by their views;*

- *have a lead person who makes sure that the transition between services goes smoothly;*

- *know what to do if things are not going according to plan;*

- *have confidence that services will focus on need, rather than age, and will be flexible.*

(DoH, 2008a)

However, as is depressingly familiar, much of this language is non-specific and non-measurable, giving young people little or no redress if things go wrong.

ACTIVITY **9.3**

- *In relation to the recommendations set out above, how would you define the precise meaning of 'well in advance'? One year? Six months? Three months?*

- *How could it be shown that the CAMHS service had been 'informed by their views'?*

- *Who is to decide whether the transition 'goes smoothly' and what are the consequences if it does not?*

- *Who is to decide whether 'things are not going to plan'?*

- *What exactly does 'flexible' mean in the context of service delivery?*

Young people in custody

The status of both eligible and relevant children remains unchanged while in custody and the local authority retains responsibility for providing the support to which care leavers are entitled. The local authority must allocate a personal adviser and work with the young person to prepare a pathway plan which focuses on the arrangements for support to be provided on release, including accommodation, personal support and financial maintenance until the age of 18. As with other care leavers, this support should continue until the young person is 21 or while they remain in an approved programme of education or training (DCSF, 2010d).

FURTHER READING

www.councilfordisabledchildren.org.uk

The Council for Disabled Children is the umbrella organisation for the disabled children's sector in England.

www.leavingcare.org

The National Care Advisory Service (NCAS) is a national advice, support and development service focusing on young people's transition from care.

Chapter 10
Cooperation

CHAPTER OBJECTIVES

In this chapter we explore the legal and policy framework and practical challenges that arise from the need to work collaboratively with other professionals and agencies in order to maximise the effectiveness of social work intervention. Again we encourage you to adopt a critical and enquiring approach so that you can use authority constructively and take account of cultural and organisational differences that exist between agencies. This supports the requirements of all the PCF domains, particularly that which relates to Professional Leadership.

Introduction

Multi- and inter-agency work to safeguard and promote children's welfare starts as soon as it has been identified that the child or the family members have additional needs requiring support or services beyond universal services, not just when there are questions about possible harm.

(DfE, 2010b, p135)

You need to adopt a 'Rottweiler attitude' in working with some agencies and persist until they cooperate.

(Children's centre manager, quoted in Pinney, 2011, p7)

The government as a whole and each department within it must consider how they, as care leavers' corporate 'uncles', 'aunts' and 'grandparents', can open doors of opportunity for them. They need to come together to offer support, whether this is to provide work experience or a job in the 'family business'; a 'home' to return to when it is needed or be a 'pushy' parent that advocates for their children across the system.

(NCAS, 2012a, p7)

In many situations referred to children's social care, no single agency can provide all the services required to safeguard and promote the welfare of the child and meet the needs of their family. Almost every statute, government guidance and policy document emphasises the importance of integrated working across services and yet almost every public inquiry and serious case review identifies situations in which it has not been achieved. The Laming Inquiry (2003) into the death

that poor inter-agency working was a contributory factor in the failure
emphasised that the ability to safeguard children depended on services
n, housing, police and social services working effectively together. Since
of local authorities towards the children they look after has become
parenting' in recognition of the fact that they cannot fulfil their
the cooperation and support of a range of other agencies (HMG, 2011a,
ublic Law Proceedings Guide to Case Management (MoJ, 2010) is intended
to reinf........ rtance of a coordinated, multi-agency approach to situations in which
statutory intervention is being considered. In a strategic context, however, although government
policy supports effective local partnerships, it is becoming less prescriptive as to how they are
organised so as to allow local innovation and solutions to emerge.

Information sharing

*Information sharing is key to the government's goal of delivering better, more efficient
public services that are coordinated around the needs of the individual. It is essential to
enable early intervention and preventative work, for safeguarding and promoting welfare
and for wider public protection. Information sharing is a vital element in improving
outcomes for all.*

(DCSF, 2008, p5)

*90 per cent of the time we work well with other agencies. Any problems usually stem from
practical matters, such as different geographic boundaries, or lack of understanding about
referral criteria.*

(Children's social worker)

The Laming Report (2003) noted that confusion over the legality or otherwise of sharing
information between agencies was a significant factor in the communication failures that
occurred between the professionals involved in Victoria Climbié's life. However, the sharing of
information can pose dilemmas in relation to the core professional principle of confidentiality
(see Chapter 2), and in the context of participation (see Chapter 4), in that children and families
who are taking part in planning and decision-making meetings in accordance with the
provisions of statute and guidance usually prefer the smallest possible number of professionals
to have access to the personal data likely to be shared in such circumstances (HMG, 2011a).
There also exist legal inhibitors to the sharing of personal information:

- the common law duty of confidentiality which provides that where there is a confidential relationship, as between a social worker and service user, a person receiving confidential
information has a duty not to pass it to a third party. However, the duty is not absolute
and information can be shared in certain circumstances without breaching the common law
duty (see below);

- the Human Rights Act 1998, incorporating the right to protection for private and family life
(Article 8 of the European Convention on Human Rights);

- the Data Protection Act 1998;

- the potential sanction of judicial review if disclosure is considered to have been beyond the
powers of the person who made it, or was irrational or unfair.

All of these potential inhibitors are, nevertheless, subject to the proviso that other relevant legislation containing express or implied powers to share information might exist and that disclosure may be justified in the interests of wider society. A public interest can arise, for example, in the context of protecting children from significant harm or the prevention of crime. The key factors in deciding whether or not to share information are whether it is likely to contribute to the prevention of risk and whether the public interest in sharing information overrides any individual interest in preserving confidentiality. Therefore, it is necessary to assess the consequences of information being shared against what might happen if it is not. The nature of the information to be shared is a relevant factor, particularly if the implications are likely to be especially significant for the individual or their relationship with the agency you represent.

LEGAL CASE STUDY 10.1

W. v Edgell *[1990] 1 All ER 835*

After shooting several people, W was detained in a secure psychiatric hospital. Subsequently he applied to a tribunal to be discharged, and while his responsible medical officer supported the application, it was opposed by the Secretary of State. W's solicitors asked Dr Edgell, a consultant psychiatrist, to prepare a report to support W's application for release. However, this concluded that W had a psychopathic disorder which, combined with an interest in firearms and explosives, made him a continuing risk to the public. After Dr Edgell's report was received by his solicitors, W withdrew his application and the report would not normally have been disclosed to anyone else. When Dr Edgell discovered this, he sent a copy to the hospital, which passed it to the Secretary of State, who sent it to the tribunal. W sued Dr Edgell for breach of confidence, but his claim failed on the ground that the public interest in disclosing Dr Edgell's opinion was greater than the public interest in maintaining W's confidentiality.

Government guidance (DCSF, 2008) anticipates the following circumstances in which information may need to be shared:

- as part of early intervention and preventative services;
- to support transitions;
- where there are concerns about possible significant harm to a child or young person;
- where there are concerns about possible harm to a third party;
- where there exists a statutory duty or court order;
- in an emergency.

> ### Seven golden rules of information sharing
>
> *1. The DPA 1998 is not a barrier to sharing information but provides a framework to ensure that personal information is shared appropriately.*

2. *Be open and honest from the outset about why, what, how and with whom information will, or could, be shared and seek the agreement of those concerned, unless it is unsafe or inappropriate to do so.*

3. *Seek advice if you are in any doubt, if possible without disclosing the identity of the person concerned.*

4. *Share with consent where appropriate and, where possible, respect the wishes of those who do not consent. You may still share information without consent if, in your judgement, lack of consent can be overridden in the public interest.*

5. *Base your information-sharing decisions on the safety and well-being of the person and others who could be affected by their actions.*

6. *Ensure that the information you share is necessary for the purpose for which you are sharing it, is shared only with those people who need to have it, is accurate and up-to-date, is shared securely and in a timely fashion.*

7. *Keep a record of your decision and the reasons for it. If you decide to share, record what you have shared, with whom and for what purpose.*

(DSCF, 2008, p11)

The Children Act 1989

Under the Children Act 1989 s47 local authorities have a duty to make enquiries where they have reasonable cause to suspect that a child in their area could be at risk of suffering significant harm. The CA 1989 s27 provides that a local authority can ask a range of other statutory authorities to assist them in the exercise of their duties and the relevant agencies must comply, providing the request is compatible with their own statutory duties and would not unduly prejudice the discharge of their own functions. The following authorities must assist if requested:

- other local authorities;
- education authorities;
- housing authorities;
- health authorities;
- any person authorised by the Secretary of State.

There is no requirement for information to be shared in breach of confidence, but an authority should not refuse a request without taking account of the relative risks of sharing information, if necessary without consent, against the potential risk to a child if information is not shared.

The Children Act 2004

Under the CA 2004 s10 each children's services authority has a duty to make arrangements to promote cooperation with relevant partner agencies to improve the well-being (determined by the five *Every Child Matters* outcomes) of children in their area. The CA 2004 s11 contains a duty to ensure that all staff in contact with children are aware of the most effective ways of

RESEARCH SUMMARY 10.1

Research into the factors that most influenced effective service delivery by Sure Start Children's Centres (Pinney, 2011) found that collaboration between local agencies was the single most important factor influencing the centres' ability to reach vulnerable and disadvantaged families. The key elements of successful collaboration identified were:

- *timely information sharing (for example, new births, children becoming ill or a parent being taken into custody);*

- *trusted practitioners such as midwives, health visitors and GPs encouraging families to use children's centre services;*

- *partnership working with health visitors, who have information on new births and knowledge of families with young children who are not coping well;*

- *taking services out to the homes of families who are reluctant to come to the children's centre.*

Children's centres that were well embedded in the network of local services were the most confident in their reach of vulnerable groups. By contrast, where local partners were reluctant to share information, often attributed to data protection concerns, the task of locating, and delivering services to, such families was more difficult.

Research into private fostering (Shaw et al., 2010) showed that numerous agencies were often involved in privately fostered children, most typically health, education, police, UK Border Agency and housing, although the extent of inter-agency cooperation varied. Different interpretations of rules and regulations were found to undermine effective collaboration across local authority boundaries.

A report by OFSTED (2012e) on the most significant elements of professional support for child protection social workers found that colleagues from partner agencies were considered most effective when they:

- *understood the social worker's role;*

- *prioritised the child's needs and shared the same goals;*

- *accepted their own accountability;*

- *contributed their knowledge, skills and experience;*

- *participated in conferences and meetings;*

- *carried out tasks assigned to them within the child protection plan.*

Local Safeguarding Children Boards had a central role in achieving effective partnership working, by organising multi-agency training and audits of practice, and by acting as mediator in situations where there was disagreement. Support from other agencies was of key significance when decisions were taken to discontinue child protection plans.

sharing information if it is necessary to promote their safety or welfare. There is also a power for partner agencies to pool budgets and resources.

Children's databases

Throughout the development of government plans to reform children's services, the importance of improving information sharing both within and between agencies has been a key theme, supported by the findings of public inquiries. Possibly the most ambitious, and controversial, development has been the introduction of a range of computer systems and assessment tools intended to promote information sharing about vulnerable children. The two main systems are:

- the Integrated Children's System; and
- the Common Assessment Framework.

The third element envisaged, the ContactPoint database, has since been abolished (see below).

The Integrated Children's System (ICS)

The ICS, an information management system which became operational in 2007 after seven years' development, formed part of the government's commitment to the aims and objectives of *Every Child Matters* (DfES, 2003). The ICS was intended to provide a standard set of procedures and record-keeping applicable throughout the country to facilitate communication between different agencies concerned with child welfare, ultimately replacing previous arrangements by which child protection registers were managed by individual local authorities. In addition, the ICS was intended to support practitioners and managers in undertaking key tasks of information-gathering, assessment, planning, intervention and review.

The ICS has been promoted by statutory provision (CA 2004 ss12 and 19), the allocation of grants and dissemination of government guidance. However, in response to the Social Work Task Force recommendations (SWTF, 2010) there was something of a retreat on the part of the government, which issued a circular (LA170609002) stating that, while it remained committed to the system in principle, local authorities could determine how information management systems can best be used to support effective practice, and they were not required to comply with the published ICS specifications as such. An 'expert panel' was set up by the Department for Education to support local authorities in making their systems more practical and relevant for those who use them whilst also meeting statutory requirements. Nevertheless claims that it is not fit for purpose continue to be made (Munro, 2011) and an interesting suggestion in the context of clarity of language is that there was a basic misunderstanding at the development stage in relation to subtle differences of meaning attributed to the terms 'database' and 'record' between those with information technology (IT) background and those without (Ince and Griffiths, 2011):

Is a database . . .

- *. . . a collection of unstructured documents stored in a number of files? (non-IT definition)*
- *. . . a collection of fixed-length IT records that are logically linked? (IT definition)*

Is a record . . .

- *. . . a collection of documents relating to a child? (non-IT)*
- *. . . a fixed-length collection of data and text held in the memory of a computer? (IT)*

In addition, the legality of some of the processes was questionable in that information about children was potentially accessible by people who did not have a legitimate interest in it without the consent of the subjects, contravening the principles of data protection. Equally significant in the context of the legally established principle that a decision to place a child on the child protection register can be subject to judicial review (*R v Norfolk County Council ex parte M* [1989] 2 All ER 359), is the functionality of the ICS in being able to demonstrate that recorded decisions were supported by valid evidence and reached in accordance with fair, transparent and established procedures, taking account of the interests of those concerned. Another potential problem is that an event has not officially occurred until it is recorded. Thus, for example, until a decision has been formally 'signed off' by the person responsible for sanctioning it, it may not become a statistical reality and a looked-after child could return home immediately after a review meeting, but not be recorded as having left care until the minutes of the meeting are signed by the IRO some time later.

Munro (2011) asserted that a system that places so much emphasis on procedures results in insufficient attention being given to developing and supporting the expertise to work effectively with children, young people and families:

> Practitioners and their managers told the review that statutory guidance, targets and local rules have become so extensive that they limit their ability to stay child centred. Services have become so standardised that they do not provide the required range of responses to the variety of need that is presented.

> (ibid., p7)

Common Assessment Framework

PRACTITIONER REFLECTION 10.1

Head of pastoral care in a secondary school:

We must have completed a couple of dozen CAFs over the past few years and I don't think we've had a response to any of them. I wish I knew what they are supposed to be for. In most cases we just have to get on with it ourselves.

The Common Assessment Framework (CAF) is a voluntary, collaborative assessment and planning system for use by any professional who considers that a child has additional needs requiring the involvement of more than one service. Introduced in 2006 with the aim of strengthening prevention and early intervention by promoting shared responsibility between agencies and a common language, it is complementary to, rather than a substitute for, other assessment requirements and consists of:

- pre-assessment checklist;
- standard form to record the assessment;
- delivery plan and review form.

The assessment covers three areas – development of the child or young person; parents and carers; family and environment – and aims to provide a generic and holistic picture of a child or young person's strengths and needs to enable decisions to be made about how best to meet those needs, both in terms of what the family can do and what services can be provided to support them (CWDC, 2009).

Anyone wishing to proceed with a CAF must obtain the informed consent of the child or young person and/or their parent/carer to undertake the assessment, record the information and share it with other named professionals and agencies, unless it is judged that there is sufficient public interest to share it without consent. Therefore, the subjects of the CAF must understand the process and its implications (CWDC, 2009). The completion of a CAF does not guarantee a service from a particular agency although 'it should considerably increase the likelihood that services will be engaged and consider your request in a positive way' (ibid., p54). It does not require much reading between the lines to see the rather hollow meaning of these words.

ACTIVITY *10.1*

Kyle is 15, lives with his mother and younger brother, and has a mild form of autism. He has no contact with his father, and his grandfather, to whom he was close, died a year ago. Kyle has recently been stealing from shops and damaging property, including cars. When he does attend school he is disruptive and resistant to rules and recently appeared to be under the influence of alcohol. After meeting with Kyle's mother, who said she was finding it difficult to cope with Kyle and that his brother was also showing signs of challenging behaviour, Kyle's head teacher referred the family to children's services via the CAF.

The following professional services and agencies exist in the area:

- *education welfare;*

- *youth offending team;*

- *council youth worker;*

- *neighbourhood police officer;*

- *children's services family support worker;*

- *school counsellor;*

- *youth drop-in and advocacy service;*

- *school nurse;*

- *special educational needs coordinator;*

- *family centre;*

- *young people's drug and alcohol service;*

- *child and adolescent mental health service.*

Consider the legal and policy framework within which each agency operates.

- *How might this influence the way in which they respond to referrals?*

ACTIVITY *10.1* *(CONT.)*

- If you are the designated 'lead professional' responsible for setting up and coordinating a plan to address Kyle's needs, how would you begin?

- What barriers to inter-professional collaboration do you anticipate and how could you make constructive use of law and policy in order to establish effective partnerships?

- What provisions, if any, exist for Kyle or his family to challenge any decisions made as a result of the CAF process?

RESEARCH SUMMARY *10.2*

It was hoped that the CAF would bring about improvement in the quality, consistency and evidence base of referrals but early indications were that factors precipitating CAF assessments were dominated by, and expressed in terms of, adult (usually school-based) concerns, particularly those relating to the behaviour of boys. Few children actually received a service as a result, fathers were thought to be insufficiently involved and the CAF had quickly become another rationed service (Gilligan and Manby, 2008).

ContactPoint

Every Child Matters (DfES, 2003) proposed that there should be local 'information hubs' with information on all children in the area and the professionals involved with them, and the CA 2004 provided for the database to include 'information as to the existence of any cause for concern'. It cost £224 million to set up but following widespread privacy concerns and a number of serious security breaches it was decommissioned in 2010 as part of the Coalition Government's stated aim to reverse the erosion of civil liberties and reduce state intrusion into people's lives. The government is continuing to consider the feasibility of a more proportionate approach to supporting professionals to protect vulnerable children from harm (**www.education.gov.uk**).

Adult social care

Adult mental health services – including those providing general adult and community, forensic, psychotherapy, alcohol and substance misuse and learning disability services – have a responsibility in safeguarding children when they become aware of, or identify, a child at risk of harm.

(DfE, 2010b)

In some families children's health and development are affected by difficulties being experienced by their parents, and serious case reviews (Brandon *et al.*, 2012) consistently emphasise the importance of understanding and acting on concerns about children's safety and welfare in households where parental problems exist. Supporting adults in their role as parents is highlighted in practice guidance, and the experience of professionals providing specialist services for adults can contribute to assessments of children in need living with parental mental illness, learning disability, substance misuse or domestic violence. However, collaboration between adults' and children's services in relation to assessment is rare (Cleaver *et al.*, 2011).

Whilst the same knowledge and values must be applied to safeguarding and promoting the welfare of children of disabled parents as to the children of non-disabled parents, such families have particular needs which require specific skills if they are to receive an equitable service. Under the Equality Act 2010 local authorities have a duty to promote equality of opportunity for disabled people by making 'reasonable adjustments' to enable them to receive services as close as it is reasonably possible to get to the standard offered to non-disabled people. The duty is 'anticipatory' in that it is necessary to consider in advance what disabled people might reasonably need in order to access services. The Act also provides for people not to be directly discriminated against because they have an association with a disabled person or are wrongly perceived as disabled.

Where a parent has a learning difficulty there is evidence of lack of communication, cooperation and joint-working across adult and children's services, and also between health and social services. In addition, it has been shown that children and families social workers sometimes believe that adult learning disability services do not pay sufficient attention to children's welfare, whilst some adult learning disability social workers feel that children and families social workers have insufficient understanding of the needs of learning disabled parents (Tarleton *et al.*, 2006). Children's services practitioners and adult learning disability social workers rarely have a good working knowledge of the policy and legislative framework applicable to their respective areas of work, and there is patchy evidence of social workers making use of professionals with specialist knowledge or taking advantage of relevant tool kits, questionnaires or scales designed for assessing the parenting abilities of adults with learning disabilities (Cleaver and Nicholson, 2008). Government guidance advocates an approach to parenting and learning disability which recognises that if the focus is on factors that can be changed, such as inadequate housing, and needs that can be met, such as equipment to measure baby feeds, rather than on impairment or personal limitation, there are many more possibilities for effecting improvement. Good coordination and communication between children's and adult services are promoted as essential prerequisites to effective interventions with children in these circumstances.

Five key features of good practice in working with parents with learning disabilities are identified as:

- accessible information and communication;
- clear and coordinated referral and assessment procedures and processes, eligibility criteria and care pathways;
- support designed to meet the needs of parents and children based on assessments of their needs and strengths;
- long-term support where necessary; and
- access to independent advocacy.

(DoH and DfES, 2007, p7)

It is particularly important to avoid the situation where poor standards of parental care which do not meet the threshold of significant harm to a child subsequently deteriorate because of a lack of support provided to the parent.

(ibid., p24)

RESEARCH SUMMARY *10.3*

A review by OFSTED (2009, p16) of services to young carers found that in most local authority areas, professionals did not consistently consider children's views when assessing disabled parents. Only one local authority stated that social workers made home visits at times that would enable them to include children's views in the assessment of their disabled parents. Generally, professionals did not see school-age children with their family at home and some assessments were undertaken outside the home, such as at outpatient clinics. Particular difficulties identified included a prevailing culture where adult services tend to focus on the needs of the adult rather than considering each family member, and a lack of inter-agency training. Young carers were described as a casualty of the organisational split between adult and children's local authority social services.

CASE STUDY *10.1*

*A Local Safeguarding Children's Board (**www.haringeylscb.org**) produced a joint protocol for children and young people's services and adult mental health services in relation to assessing and working with mentally ill parents and their children. In addition to setting out the relevant statutory frameworks and the overarching operating principles, the protocol includes resources to assist staff in each team to understand the needs of their service users in the context of the duties and responsibilities of the other service. Children's social work teams include a member with lead responsibility for adult mental health and adult mental health teams include a lead for children. The collaborative responsibilities of children and families social workers and mental health professionals are defined, together with the points at which consultation and liaison should occur as part of assessment, intervention and review: 'The review process should take account of the fact that the needs of people with mental health problems constantly change in both foreseen and unforeseen ways' (p9). Resources included a Child in Need and Risk form for adult mental health staff and an Adult Mental Health Screen for use by children and families social workers.*

CASE STUDY *10.2*

A mental health professional and child protection social worker visited together to deliver a jointly agreed response to a mother's threats of self-harm and the mental health worker arranged for the social worker to meet the mother's psychiatrist. As a result the social worker became more knowledgeable and confident in her safeguarding work with the child and the mother was reassured to know that the professionals were working together.

(OFSTED, 2012e)

Child and Adolescent Mental Health Service (CAMHS)

Multi-agency teams are the primary method for providing services to children and young people with severe and complex mental health needs. Inspection reports have noted that arrangements for monitoring the health and well-being of looked after children generally work well and that fast-tracking to CAMHS and therapeutic services have improved for those with acute needs, such as anorexia and risk of self-harm. However, children and young people with lower levels of need often have to wait long periods before receiving assessment (DoH, 2008a). A possible reason for this is that a 'stable' placement is often a prerequisite for specialist therapeutic input but delay in providing help can itself trigger placement breakdown and the transient circumstances of many looked-after children mean that they may lose contact with services while waiting to be seen.

A number of barriers to effective cooperation between CAMHS and other social care agencies have been identified (DoH, 2008a, p60):

- variations in administrative arrangements: for example, line management and information-recording systems;

- lack of clarity around lines of accountability;

- financial factors: services may be unwilling to fund posts that they see as being outside their 'core' business;

- differences in the professional cultures of health, education and social care;

- no single, universally agreed language exists to describe mental health and psychological well-being;

- multi-agency working can be time-consuming and consequently expensive.

Education

More training for social workers on education issues would be valuable – such as specialist provision for SEN children, exclusion rules, school support services and the range of learning needs such as dyslexia.

(Teacher quoted in NCAS, 2009a, p77)

ACTIVITY 10.2

Below is the entire published child protection policy applicable to a primary school (not an extract). Critically analyse it, paying particular attention to the language used:

There are three main elements to our child protection policy.

1. Prevention through the creation of a positive school atmosphere and the teaching and pastoral support offered to pupils.

ACTIVITY 10.2 *(CONT.)*

2. Protection by following agreed procedures, ensuring staff are trained and supported to respond appropriately and sensitively to child protection concerns.

3. Support to pupils who may have been abused.

Commitment

We recognise that for our pupils' self-esteem, confidence, supportive friends and clear lines of communication with a trusted adult helps prevent abuse. Our school will therefore:

a. establish and maintain an environment in which pupils feel safe and secure, are encouraged to talk and are listened to;

b. ensure that pupils know that there are adults within the school who they can approach if they are worried or in difficulty;

c. include in the curriculum activities and opportunities for personal, social and health education which equip pupils with the skills they need to stay safe from abuse;

d. include in the curriculum material which will help pupils develop realistic attitudes to the responsibilities of adult life, particularly with regard to child care and parenting skills;

e. ensure that wherever possible every effort will to made to establish effective working relationships with parents and colleagues from other agencies.

- *Does the policy clearly set out the school's legal responsibilities?*

- *Does it support collaborative working?*

- *Does it support partnership with parents?*

- *Does it provide clear guidance for all levels of school staff on how to respond to safeguarding or welfare concerns?*

- *If you received a referral from this school, what expectations would you have in the context of this policy?*

- *What changes, if any, would you make to the policy and why?*

This activity shows that cultural differences between professions, together with the pervasive influence of imprecise and jargon-inspired language and a lack of attention to detail, can result in policies which are of little practical use, and create barriers to effective collaborative working.

Under the Children and Young Persons Act 2008, supplemented by the Designated Teacher (Looked After Pupils etc.) (England) Regulations 2009, maintained schools must appoint a designated teacher to promote the educational achievement of looked-after children.

Their responsibilities include (DCSF, 2009b):

- promoting a culture of high expectations and aspirations for how looked-after children learn;

- ensuring that young people have a voice in setting learning targets;

- providing advice for staff about differentiated teaching strategies appropriate for individual children and in making full use of Assessment for Learning;

- ensuring that looked-after children are prioritised in one-to-one tuition arrangements and that carers understand the importance of supporting learning at home.

The designated teacher is responsible for the development and implementation of the personal education plan (PEP) which forms part of the individual care plan. It is expected that PEPs should 'set high quality expectations of rapid progress and put in place the additional support the child or young person needs in order to succeed' (DCSF, 2009b, p15). Specifically, they should:

- identify developmental and educational needs in relation to skills, knowledge, subject areas and experiences;

- set short- and long-term educational attainment targets agreed in partnership with the child and the carer where appropriate;

- be a record of planned actions, including the target dates, that the school and others will take to promote the educational achievement of the child based on an assessment of their educational needs;

- include information on how the child's progress is to be monitored;

- record details of specific interventions and targeted support that will ensure that personal education targets are met;

- set out how a child's aspiration, self-confidence and ambition are being nurtured, especially in relation to longer term goals towards further and higher education, work experience and career plans;

- be a record of the child's academic achievements and participation in extra-curricular activities in and out of school;

- provide information which helps those who are supporting the child's educational achievement;

- specify who is responsible for each aspect of the plan.

PRACTITIONER REFLECTION 10.2

Designated teacher for looked-after children:

I have never been told about the background of any looked-after child. I'm not interested in the story as such, but I am interested in how the child is dealing with it. I have to work with four different local authorities and much of my time is spent chasing information which should have come to me in the first place. Sometimes I pick up details at meetings, and sometimes the child tells me things; at best I have to work with that.

In addition, in every local authority a senior official, or 'virtual school head' (VSH), should track the schooling of every looked-after child with the aim of maximising their achievement and continuity of education (DCSF, 2009a). However, as with most policies, its effectiveness depends to a large extent on the personal commitment, skills and teamwork of the professionals involved.

RESEARCH SUMMARY *10.4*

OFSTED (2011b) found that 17 per cent of looked-after children feel that they are made to stand out from others at school or college because they are in care, half of whom regarded it as helpful:

> It depends on the individual child, which is why one size does not fit all. In year 9, some children want to tell the world that they are in care, but by year 11 I'm surprised if they want to see me. In the sixth form, often they don't want anyone to know and essentially lead two different lives as between school and home.
>
> *(Designated teacher for looked-after children, ibid., p50)*

An examination of how far the care system helps children progress into further and higher education (Who Cares? Trust, 2012) found evidence that while recent government policies – the Pupil Premium, 16–19 bursary and university tuition fee arrangements – have theoretically delivered more financial support for looked-after children and care leavers, many young people and those advising them do not understand how the schemes work. The research suggests that schools, colleges and universities were given inadequate guidance and are subject to minimal central scrutiny of how they spend the money, resulting in confusion and inconsistency.

A report by OFSTED (2012d) showed that virtual schools have promoted better communication between professionals, helped to improve school attendance and reduce exclusions, but there is little evidence that this has yet been translated into better educational achievements for looked-after children.

The potential for strengthening effective professional partnerships by the exchange of briefings between agencies is illustrated by research into private fostering (Shaw et al., 2010) which found that only 13 per cent of professionals working in schools thought that they were well-informed about private fostering. A quarter stated either that they had heard of it but did not know what it was, or that they had never heard of it at all. As schools are likely to be in the best position to identify private fostering situations, the implication is obvious.

Health services

> *Health care professionals have an important role to play in enabling looked-after children to overcome disadvantages and to reach their full potential.*
>
> (RCPCH *et al.*, 2012, p5)

A health plan should be included within care plans for looked-after children and statutory guidance states that these are not solely the responsibility of the health service but depend on the social worker, foster carer or residential worker and NHS staff working together. This should be facilitated by one person taking the lead for the NHS and acting as a central point of contact (DCSF and DoH, 2009).

The General Medical Council (2012) has identified the principles to be followed by doctors in the context of safeguarding and promoting the welfare of children and young people, the most relevant of which from a social work point of view are numbers six and seven:

- *children, young people and their families have a right to receive confidential medical care and advice – but this must not prevent doctors from sharing information if this is necessary to protect children and young people from abuse or neglect;*

- *decisions about child protection are best made with others – consulting with colleagues and other agencies that have appropriate expertise will protect and promote the best interests of children and young people.*

In addition, doctors are advised that 'when you care for an adult patient, that patient must be your first concern, but you must also consider whether your patient poses a risk to children or young people' (ibid., p11).

The requirements for doctors to work effectively with other professionals are described in strong terms (ibid., pp19–28).

- *You must work and communicate effectively with colleagues in your team and organisation and with other professionals and agencies. This includes health visitors, other nurses, social workers and the police.*

- *You should understand and respect the child protection roles, responsibilities, policies and practices of other agencies and professionals and cooperate with them. You must be clear about your own role and responsibilities in protecting children and young people, and be ready to explain this to colleagues and other professionals.*

- *If you are asked to take part in child protection procedures, you must cooperate fully. This includes going to child protection conferences, strategy meetings and case reviews to provide information and give your opinion. You may be able to make a contribution, even if you have no specific concerns.*

- *If meetings are called at short notice or at inconvenient times, you should still try to attend. If this is not possible, you must try to provide relevant information about the child or young person and their family to the meeting, either through a telephone or video conference, in a written report or by discussing the information with another professional, so they can give an oral report at the meeting.*

- *You should consider all requests for information for child protection purposes seriously and quickly, bearing in mind that refusing to give this information, or a delay in doing so, could increase the risk of harm to a child or young person or undermine efforts to protect them.*

In a review of private fostering (Shaw *et al.*, 2010) it was reported that some health practitioners regarded notifying the local authority of a private fostering arrangement as a breach of patient confidentiality if there were no child protection concerns. In addition, lack of awareness or a perception that private fostering was not their responsibility meant that sometimes simple questions about where a child was living and who had parental responsibility for them were not asked. It will be interesting to see whether the GMC policy statement results in more effective communication and collaboration between doctors and social workers in the future.

The needs of vulnerable children are addressed in guidance to doctors, hospital staff and mental health professionals when undertaking their duties under the Mental Health Act 1983 (DoH, 2008b) which advises that practitioners should ensure that:

- children and young people are provided with information about their parents' illness;

- appropriate arrangements are in place for the immediate care of dependent children;

- the best interests and safety of children are always considered in arrangements for children to visit patients in hospital; and

- the safety and welfare of dependent children are taken into account when clinicians consider granting leave of absence for parents with a mental disorder.

The Royal Colleges of Paediatrics and Child Health, General Practitioners and Nursing (2012) have produced a joint competency framework for health practitioners working with looked-after children.

Housing authorities

Many children and young people under the age of 18 who come to the attention of housing authorities because they are actually or potentially homeless are likely to have additional needs that would meet the criteria required to trigger a CAF referral and possibly result in them being assessed as a 'child in need'.

In addition to the provisions contained within the CA 1989 s27, a statutory requirement for local authorities and their 'relevant' partners to cooperate to improve children's well-being is set out in general terms in the CA 2004 s10.

Guidance on joint working between housing and children's services (CLG and DCSF, 2008, p29) defines the aims of joint working to prevent and tackle homelessness as:

- young people remaining in, or returning to, the family home unless it would be unsafe or inappropriate for them to do so;

- improved relationships with their families, whether or not they can live at home;

- clear and flexible accommodation and support pathways towards independent living for those who need them;

- a personalised support package for every young person, based on an assessment of their needs across all five *Every Child Matters* outcome areas, and involving all appropriate agencies, to help them achieve their aspirations and make a positive transition to adulthood.

The guidance identifies the groups at particular risk of the consequences of poor collaboration between housing and children's services as:

- 16 and 17 year olds who are homeless or at risk of homelessness;

- care leavers aged 18 to 21;

- children of families living in temporary accommodation;

- children of families who have been, or are at risk of being, found intentionally homeless by a housing authority.

Local authority housing and children's services are expected to have established the following key elements to prevent and mitigate the effects of homelessness on children and young people (ibid., p13):

- formal joint working protocols, including other relevant agencies such as youth offending teams, health, education and voluntary agencies which work with vulnerable young people;

- a shared ethos of prevention;

- effective use of joint resources to achieve shared aims;

- sharing of information;

- use of the CAF;

- involvement of children, young people and parents;

- joint working arrangements for promoting and planning care leavers' transition to adulthood;

- joint protocols to ensure a quick, safe and supportive response to care leavers who are homeless or at risk of homelessness.

In addition, where a young person under the age of 18 seeks help because of actual or likely homelessness, assessments should, where possible, be undertaken jointly by children's and housing services. Alternatively, assessment and referral processes should be underpinned by appropriate information sharing so that young people do not have to repeat their stories and navigate between geographically separate offices. The lead agency is children's services, given their responsibilities towards children in need (CLG and DCSF, 2010).

LEGAL CASE STUDY **10.2**

In R (TG) v Lambeth LBC [2011] EWCA Civ 526, discussed in Chapter 9, the court responded to the implication that vulnerable children were suffering as a result of failures of coordination between housing and children's services departments by stating that 'local authorities should take urgent steps to remedy any such failures'.

CASE STUDY **10.3**

There were increasing concerns that the development of a child with significant hearing and sight impairment was being avoidably impaired through the parents' reluctance to help their child to use hearing aids and spectacles. It was also thought that the child was not eating well. The parents were socially isolated and resistant to support and the child's health appointments were often missed. The peripatetic teacher for the deaf as the lead professional coordinated an action plan with the teacher for visual impairment, health visitor, nursery teacher and social worker for deaf children. Patient multi-agency work with the parents resulted in significant improvements for the child who now uses the aids, attends nursery regularly and is making good progress.

(OFSTED, 2012c, p12)

CASE STUDY **10.4**

A Young People's Support Service (YPSS) was established in a city centre with the aim of providing an integrated, partnership based service to young people in need or leaving care. YPSS, led by the local authority and including staff from youth, education and housing services, youth offending team and the primary care trust, provides the leaving care service and assessment, advice and support to any young person in need aged 13–21. Supporting People and local authority funds are used to commission supported accommodation for young people who are offered help with:

- *housing and homelessness;*

- *personal finance and welfare rights;*

- *education, training and employment;*

- *emotional and physical health, including counselling;*

- *substance misuse;*

- *asylum and refugee matters;*

- *sports and leisure opportunities.*

The YPSS uses the CAF's initial assessment tool, and all young people in need have their details recorded on the Children's and Young People's Services database. Young people are involved in the development and running of the service and only three care leavers were accepted as homeless during a year in the city in which around 50 young people leave care annually. It was estimated that 97 per cent of care leavers were living in suitable accommodation at the age of 19.

(CLG and DCSF, 2008)

Police

PRACTITIONER REFLECTION 10.3

Looked-after children team manager:

Recently we were told that a particular police officer couldn't attend a strategy meeting because there wasn't a car available and it's difficult to get hold of officers due to their shift patterns. It doesn't matter how good the protocols and processes are if there's no commitment to make them work.

When it appears that a child has suffered, or is likely to suffer, significant harm, a strategy meeting takes place involving the local authority, the police and other relevant professionals (DCSF, 2010d). If a criminal investigation needs to be carried out, the police take responsibility for it, including any investigative interviews, video-recorded or otherwise (MoJ, 2011a). However, provided both the police officer and social worker have been trained to interview child witnesses, either may lead the interview, dependent on who is better able to establish a rapport with the child. Where a police officer leads the interview, the local authority retains its duty under the CA 1989 s47 by ensuring that the interview is properly planned and that the social worker has an effective role in monitoring it (ibid., p 15).

The Family Procedure Rules 2010 (paras 12.73 and 14.14) permit the disclosure to police officers as 'professionals acting in furtherance of the protection of children' of information contained in documents filed with the court in private and public law family proceedings. Court documents remain under the control of the court, although in practice a court is likely to agree to copies being made available to the police if necessary. The judgement in the case of *Borough Council v A* [2006] EWHC 1465 (Fam) established that preparatory documents compiled by the local authority or CAFCASS are confidential and subject to public interest immunity. If social workers find it necessary to pass information to the police they should indicate the source of the information, or the document in which it is contained, unless it is confidential, and notify all parties to the proceedings, usually through their legal representatives, of the information that has been disclosed.

Working Together to Safeguard Children reinforces the role of the police in identifying and safeguarding children living with domestic violence: 'patrol officers attending domestic violence incidents should be aware of the effect of such violence on any children normally resident within the household' (DfE, 2010b, p71). However, improved cooperation has been slow to develop.

RESEARCH SUMMARY 10.5

Stanley et al. (2010) found that when police became involved with domestic violence in homes where there were children, there was limited communication between them and local authority children's services beyond the initial notification, and little evidence of collaboration between local authorities and specialist domestic violence agencies.

Youth justice

We don't speak the same language as social workers; we're unable to ask the right questions.

When a looked-after child comes into custody their care plan goes out of the window.
                    (Young Offender Institution (YOI) staff, quoted by HMIP, 2011, pp25 and 35)

The Crime and Disorder Act 1998 created the Youth Justice Board and defined the principal aim of the youth justice system as the prevention of offending (s37). Youth Offending Teams (YOTs) are locally organised, multi-agency teams that have moved away from primarily relationship-based interventions to focus on:

- reinforcing the unacceptability of offending;

- the victim perspective and restorative justice;

- risk assessment and management;

- structured, intensive, community-based alternatives to custody; and

- providing young people with the personal resources to avoid crime.

The inclusion of social workers in YOTs represents the continuing importance of the concept of welfare in youth justice but there remain tensions between society's expectations in respect of punishment and deterrence, and the holistic, needs-based, empowerment and solution-focused approaches which shape much of social work training.

The Criminal Justice and Immigration Act 2008 introduced the youth rehabilitation order which is a generic community sentence. Other orders applicable to the pre-court, first tier, community order and custody stages of disposal are also defined within this Act.

To meet the complex needs of looked-after children who are over-represented within the custodial system, it is expected that there is collaboration between the professionals involved. The social worker from the local authority responsible for the child should work with the YOT case manager to support the child whilst in custody, coordinate arrangements for release and ensure that their needs are met when they return to their community (DCSF, 2010d).

RESEARCH SUMMARY 10.6

A review of collaborative practice between custodial institutions and social workers responsible for looked-after children in custody (HMIP, 2011) found that the involvement of local authorities was often dependent on the commitment of individual social workers. A significant number of custodial staff felt that social workers sought to end their involvement while the young person was in custody and it was rare for them to make initial contact. Attendance by social workers at training planning meetings was said to be poor, despite their key role. Only half of young people had received a visit from their social worker, financial support or clothing. Adequate and early planning for release was a key concern of establishment staff and young people. Several establishments viewed it as the local authority's responsibility to make release arrangements and were unclear about their own

---

RESEARCH SUMMARY *10.6* (CONT.)

role. Accommodation was often not confirmed until close to the release date or even the day of release itself. One YOI staff member said they had worked hard to develop productive partnerships with external YOTs and suggested that the same effort needed to be invested in relationships with local authorities: 'Maybe we should do something similar with social workers. Don't know how receptive they'd be though' (ibid., p47).

*A Restorative Project Officer was appointed by a YOT to train and support local authority residential child care staff in restorative justice models with the aim of reducing the criminalisation of looked-after children in residential settings. This resulted in a substantial reduction in offences committed both inside and outside the homes and considerably fewer internal incidents requiring police presence (**www.justice.gov.uk/youth-justice**).*

Family justice system

The Family Justice Board, established in 2012, accountable to ministers and comprising representatives of organisations involved with the family justice system, is focusing on reducing delays, by means of the introduction of a statutory six-month time limit on public law care applications and less use of independent experts. The board is also working to build cross-agency coherence, tackle local variations in performance and ensure that family law disputes involving children are resolved out of court wherever possible.

FURTHER READING

www.caipe.org.uk

The Centre for the Advancement of Inter-professional Education is an independent think tank working with organisations in the UK and overseas to improve collaborative practice, and thereby the quality of care, by professions learning and working together.

www.education.gov.uk

The Department for Education has a number of publications which explain the legal and professional framework of information sharing and offer advice to practitioners.

Conclusion

This text does not provide a detailed account of the law relating to children in England and Wales, which is readily available from other sources and can prove rather indigestible on its own. We have enormous sympathy for social workers and managers who have been bombarded with vast quantities of official guidance in recent years, much of it bland, repetitive and jargon-ridden, such that frequently it can be difficult to see the wood for the trees. Instead we have sought to provide a framework, supported by case examples and research, to help you gain confidence in exercising your legal powers and duties and to support the development of your analytic skills which are such a vital component of promoting children's welfare. By demonstrating the value that can be gained by exploring how the law operates in practice, we also hope that we have sparked your interest in the law/social work interface, which involves so much more than simply trying to remember the provisions of the various statutes and filling in required templates. By engaging in debate with other professionals, looking at legal case decisions, considering messages from research and taking time to consider the experience of service users you will find that the law is no more of an exact science than most other disciplines, and that it has much in common with social work in that its interpretation and application depend heavily on prevailing values, ethical principles and, increasingly, political priorities:

> It is right that we seriously examine whether our principles and processes are fit for the social norms of our time and indeed for the foreseeable future.
>> (Mr Justice Ryder, judge in charge of modernisation of family justice in a speech to the Association of Lawyers for Children, 16 November 2012, **www.familylawweek.co.uk**)

Appendix

Domains within the Professional Capabilities Framework

The Professional Capabilities Framework has nine domains (or areas) within it. For each one, there is a main statement and an elaboration. Then at each level within the PCF, detailed capabilities have been developed explaining how social workers should expect to evidence that area in practice.

The nine capabilities should be seen as interdependent, not separate. As they interact in professional practice, so there are overlaps between the capabilities within the domains, and many issues will be relevant to more than one domain. Understanding of what a social worker does will only be complete by taking into account all nine capabilities.

Professionals and their practice will be assessed 'holistically', by which we mean that throughout their careers, social work students and practitioners need to demonstrate integration of all aspects of learning, and provide a sufficiency of evidence across all nine domains.

1 PROFESSIONALISM – Identify and behave as a professional social worker, committed to professional development
Social workers are members of an internationally recognised profession, a title protected in UK law. Social workers demonstrate professional commitment by taking responsibility for their conduct, practice and learning, with support through supervision. As representatives of the social work profession they safeguard its reputation and are accountable to the professional regulator.

2. VALUES AND ETHICS – Apply social work ethical principles and values to guide professional practice
Social workers have an obligation to conduct themselves ethically and to engage in ethical decision-making, including through partnership with people who use their services. Social workers are knowledgeable about the value base of their profession, its ethical standards and relevant law.

3. DIVERSITY – Recognise diversity and apply anti-discriminatory and anti-oppressive principles in practice
Social workers understand that diversity characterises and shapes human experience and is critical to the formation of identity. Diversity is multi-dimensional and includes race, disability, class, economic status, age, sexuality, gender and transgender, faith and belief. Social workers appreciate that, as a consequence of difference, a person's life experience may include oppression, marginalisation and alienation as well as privilege, power and acclaim, and are able to challenge appropriately.

4. RIGHTS, JUSTICE AND ECONOMIC WELLBEING – Advance human rights and promote social justice and economic wellbeing

Social workers recognise the fundamental principles of human rights and equality, and that these are protected in national and international law, conventions and policies. They ensure these principles underpin their practice. Social workers understand the importance of using and contributing to case law and applying these rights in their own practice. They understand the effects of oppression, discrimination and poverty.

5. KNOWLEDGE – Apply knowledge of social sciences, law and social work practice theory

Social workers understand psychological, social, cultural, spiritual and physical influences on people; human development throughout the life span and the legal framework for practice. They apply this knowledge in their work with individuals, families and communities. They know and use theories and methods of social work practice.

6. CRITICAL REFLECTION AND ANALYSIS – Apply critical reflection and analysis to inform and provide a rationale for professional decision-making

Social workers are knowledgeable about and apply the principles of critical thinking and reasoned discernment. They identify, distinguish, evaluate and integrate multiple sources of knowledge and evidence. These include practice evidence, their own practice experience, service user and carer experience together with research-based, organisational, policy and legal knowledge. They use critical thinking augmented by creativity and curiosity.

7. INTERVENTION AND SKILLS – Use judgement and authority to intervene with individuals, families and communities to promote independence, provide support and prevent harm, neglect and abuse

Social workers engage with individuals, families, groups and communities, working alongside people to assess and intervene. They enable effective relationships and are effective communicators, using appropriate skills. Using their professional judgement, they employ a range of interventions: promoting independence, providing support and protection, taking preventative action and ensuring safety whilst balancing rights and risks. They understand and take account of differentials in power, and are able to use authority appropriately. They evaluate their own practice and the outcomes for those they work with.

8. CONTEXTS AND ORGANISATIONS – Engage with, inform, and adapt to changing contexts that shape practice. Operate effectively within own organisational frameworks and contribute to the development of services and organisations. Operate effectively within multi-agency and inter-professional settings

Social workers are informed about and pro-actively responsive to the challenges and opportunities that come with changing social contexts and constructs. They fulfil this responsibility in accordance with their professional values and ethics, both as individual professionals and as members of the organisation in which they work. They collaborate, inform and are informed by their work with others, inter-professionally and with communities.

9. PROFESSIONAL LEADERSHIP – Take responsibility for the professional learning and development of others through supervision, mentoring, assessing, research, teaching, leadership and management

The social work profession evolves through the contribution of its members in activities such as practice research, supervision, assessment of practice, teaching and management. An individual's contribution will gain influence when undertaken as part of a learning, practice-focused organisation. Learning may be facilitated with a wide range of people including social work colleagues, service users and carers, volunteers, foster carers and other professionals.

(College of Social Work, 2012, **www.collegeofsocialwork.org/pcf.aspx**)

References

Adoption Research Initiative (2010) *Special guardianship in practice.* www.adoptionresearchinitiative.org.uk

Adoption Research Initiative (2011) *Belonging and permanence.* www.adoptionresearchinitiative.org.uk

Aldgate, J (2001) Safeguarding and promoting the welfare of children in need living with their families, in Cull, L-A and Roche, J (eds) *The law and social work: contemporary issues for practice.* Basingstoke: Palgrave.

Aldridge, M and Wood, J (1998) *Interviewing children: a guide for child care and forensic practitioners.* Chichester: John Wiley and Sons Ltd.

APPG for Runaway and Missing Children and Adults and APPG for Looked After Children and Care Leavers (2012) *Report from the joint inquiry into children who go missing from care.* www.childrenssociety.org.uk

Baker, C (2011) *Permanence and stability for disabled looked after children.* Glasgow: Institute for Research and Innovation in Social Services.

Bar Council (2004) *Code of conduct of the Bar of England and Wales* (8th edition). London: The Bar Council.

Barlow, J, Fisher, J and Jones, D (2012) *Systematic review of models of analysing significant harm.* London: Department for Education RR199.

Beckett, C (2001) Waiting for court decisions. *Adoption and Fostering*, 24: 55–62.

Beckett, C, McKeigue, B and Taylor, H (2007) Coming to conclusions: social workers' perceptions of the decision-making process in care proceedings. *Child and Family Social Work*, 12: 54–63.

Biehal, N (2006) *Reuniting looked-after children with their families: a review of the research.* London: National Children's Bureau.

Birnbaum, R and Saini, M (2012) A qualitative synthesis of children's participation in custody disputes. *Research on Social Work Practice*, 22(4): 400–410.

Bond, C, Solon, M, Harper, P and Davies, G (2007) *The expert witness: a practical guide* (3rd edition). Crayford: Shaw and Sons.

Brammer, A (2010) *Social work law* (3rd edition). Harlow: Pearson Education Ltd.

Brandon, M, Sidebotham, P, Bailey, S, Belderson, P, Hawley, C, Ellis, C and Megson, M (2012) *New learning from serious case reviews 2009–2011.* London: DfE Research Brief 226.

Brayne, H and Carr, H (2010) *Law for social workers* (11th edition). Oxford: Oxford University Press.

Broach, S, Clements, L and Read, J (2010) *Disabled children: a legal handbook.* London: Legal Action Group.

Broadhurst, K and Holt, K (2010) Partnership and the limits of procedure: prospects for relationships between parents and professionals under the new PLO. *Child and Family Social Work*, 15(1): 97–106.

Broadhurst, K, Doherty, P, Holt, K and Kelly, N (2012) *Coventry and Warwickshire pre-proceedings pilot: interim research project.* www.lancs.ac.uk/fass/groups/cwru/documents/CAFCASS

Brophy, J (2006) *Care proceedings under the Children Act 1989: a research review.* London: Department of Constitutional Affairs research series 5/06.

Brophy, J, Jhutti-Johal, J and McDonald, E (2005) *Minority ethnic parents and their solicitors and child protection litigation.* London: Department of Constitutional Affairs research series 5/05.

Brophy, J, Jhutti-Jhohal, J and Owen, C (2003) Assessing and documenting child ill-treatment in ethnic minority households. *Family Law*, 33: 756–764.

Brophy, J, Owen, C, Sidaway, J and Jhutti-Johal, J (2012) *The contribution of experts in care proceedings: evaluation of independent social work reports in care proceedings.* Oxford University.

Brownlees, L and Yazdani, Z (2012) *The fact of age: report into the age assessment of children seeking asylum.* London: Office of the Children's Commissioner.

Buckley, H, Carr, N and Whelan, S (2011) Like walking on eggshells: service users' views and expectations of the child protection system. *Child and Family Social Work*, 16: 101–110.

Burgess, C, Daniel, B, Scott, J, Mulley, K, Derbyshire, D and Downie, M (2012) *Child neglect in 2011.* Watford: Action for Children and University of Stirling.

CAFCASS (2012a) *Three weeks in November, three years on: CAFCASS care application study 2012.* London: CAFCASS.

CAFCASS (2012b) *Annual Report and Accounts 2011/12.* London: CAFCASS.

Care Leavers' Foundation (2011) *A bed or a cooker? Choice for care leavers.* www.leavingcare.org/publications_training_consultancy/resource_library

ChildLine (2011) *ChildLine casenotes: looked-after children talking to ChildLine.* London: NSPCC.

CRAE (Children's Rights Alliance for England) (2011) *State of children's rights in England.* London: CRAE.

CRDE (Children's Rights Director for England) (2008) *Children's views on advocacy.* Manchester: OFSTED.

CRDE (2010) *Children on rights and responsibilities.* Manchester: OFSTED.

CRDE (2011a) *Children on independent reviewing officers: a report of children's views.* Manchester: OFSTED.

CRDE (2011b) *Messages for Munro: a report of children's views.* Manchester: OFSTED.

CRDE (2012) *Learning independence: views of care leavers on moving on to adult independent life.* Manchester: OFSTED.

Children's Society (2011) *Make runaways safe.* London: Children's Society.

Cleaver, H and Nicholson, D (2008) *Parental learning disability and children's needs: family experiences and effective practice.* Report for the Department for School, Children and Families. TSO.

Cleaver, H and Walker, S (2004) *Assessing children's needs and circumstances: the impact of the Assessment Framework.* London: Jessica Kingsley Publishers.

Cleaver, H, Unell, I and Aldgate, J (2011) *Children's needs – parenting capacity* (2nd edition). Report for the Department for Education. TSO.

Cocker, C and Allain, L (eds) (2011) *Advanced social work with children and families.* Exeter: Learning Matters.

CLG and DCSF (Communities and Local Government and Department for Children, Schools and Families) (2008) *Joint working between housing and children's services: preventing homelessness and tackling its effects on children and young people.* London: TSO.

CLG and DCSF (2010) *Provision of accommodation for 16 and 17 year old young people who may be homeless and/or require accommodation.* London: TSO.

Cossar, J and Dunne, C (2010) *Young people's involvement in the child protection process.* CAFCASS Research Conference paper. www.cafcass.gov.uk

Council of Europe (2012) *Report concerning the implementation of the Council of Europe Convention on action against trafficking in human beings by the United Kingdom.* Strasbourg: Council for Europe.

CWDC (Children's Workforce Development Council) (2009) *The Common Assessment Framework: a guide for practitioners.* Leeds: CWDC.

DCSF (Department for Children, Schools and Families) (2005) *National minimum standards for private fostering.* London: TSO.

DCSF (2008) *Information sharing: guidance for practitioners and managers.* London: TSO.

DCSF (2009a) *The role and responsibilities of the designated teacher for looked after children.* London: TSO.

DCSF (2009b) *The roles and responsibilities of the lead member for children's services and the director of children's services.* London: TSO.

DCSF (2010a) *The IRO Handbook.* London: TSO.

DCSF (2010b) *Promoting the educational achievement of looked-after children: statutory guidance for local authorities.* London: TSO.

DCSF (2010c) *Think Family toolkit – improving support for families at risk.* London: TSO.

DCSF (2010d) *Responsibilities of the local authority to children who cease to be looked after children in custody: Statutory guidance to the Children Act 1989.* London: TSO.

DCSF and DoH (2009) *Statutory guidance on promoting the health and well-being of looked after children.* London: TSO.

DfE (Department for Education) (2009) *Building a safe, confident future: the final report of the social work task force.* London: TSO.

DfE (2010a) *Outcomes for children looked after by local authorities in England, 2010.* London: TSO.

DfE (2010b) *Working together to safeguard children: a guide to interagency working to safeguard and promote the welfare of children.* London: TSO.

DfE (2011a) *An action plan for adoption: tackling delay.* London: TSO.

DfE (2011b) *Family and friends care: statutory guidance for local authorities.* London: TSO.

DfE (2011c) *Children looked after by local authorities in England year ending 31 March 2011: statistical release 21/2011.* London: TSO.

DfE (2011d) *Outcomes for children looked after as at 31 March 2011: statistical release 30/2011.* London: TSO.

DfE (2011e) *Monitoring and evaluation of family intervention projects and services to March 2011: statistical release 14/2011*. London: TSO.

DfE (2011f) *Fostering services: national minimum standards*. London: TSO.

DfE (2011g) *Characteristics of children in need in England 2010/11: statistical release 26/2011*. London: TSO.

DfE (2011h) *Voice of the child: trainer guide*. London: TSO.

DfE (2011i) *Adoption: national minimum standards*. London: TSO.

DfE (2012a) *Children's homes in England: data pack*. London: TSO.

DfE (2012b) *Proposals for placing children with their potential adopters earlier*. London: TSO.

DfE (2012c) *Children looked after by local authorities in England year ending 31 March 2012: statistical first release 20/2012*. London: TSO.

DfES (Department for Education and Skills) (2003) *Every child matters*. London: TSO.

DfES (2004) *Safeguarding and promoting the welfare of children and young people in custody, LAC (2004)26*. London: TSO.

DfES (2005) *Special guardianship guidance*. London: TSO.

DfES (2006) *Sure Start practice guidance*. London: TSO.

DfES (2007) *Care matters: time for change*. London: TSO.

Dickens, J (2005) The 'epitome of reason': the challenges for lawyers and social workers in care proceedings. *International Journal of Law, Policy and the Family*, 19: 73–101.

Dickens, J (2006) Care, control and change in child care proceedings: dilemmas for social workers, managers and lawyers. *Child and Family Social Work*, 11(1): 23–32.

Dickens, J, Howell, D, Thoburn, J and Schofield, G (2007) Children starting to be looked after by local authorities in England: an analysis of inter-authority and case-centred decision-making. *British Journal of Social Work*, 37: 597–617.

DoH (Department of Health) (1995) *Child protection: messages from research*. London: TSO.

DoH (2000) *Framework for the assessment of children in need and their families*. London: TSO.

DoH (2001) *The Children Act Now – messages from research*. London: TSO.

DoH (2004) *National service framework for children, young people and maternity services*. London: TSO.

DoH (2006) *Guidance on the statutory Chief Officer Post of Director of Adult Social Services issued under s7(1) Local Authority Social Services Act 1970*. London: TSO.

DoH (2008a) *Children in mind: the final report of the national CAMHS review*. London: TSO.

DoH (2008b) *Code of practice: Mental Health Act 1983*. London: TSO.

DoH and DfES (2007) *Good practice guidance on working with parents with a learning disability*. London: TSO.

DoH and Home Office (2003) *The Victoria Climbié Inquiry: report of an inquiry by Lord Laming*. London: TSO.

Dorsey, S, Mustillo, S, Farmer, E and Elbogen, E (2008) Caseworker assessments of risk for recurrent maltreatment: association with case-specific risk factors and re-reports. *Child Abuse & Neglect*, 32(3): 377–391.

Farmer, E and Moyers, S (2008) *Kinship care: fostering effective family and friends placements*. London: Jessica Kingsley Publishers.

Farmer, E, Sturgess, W and O'Neill, T (2008) *The reunification of looked-after children with their parents: patterns, interventions and outcomes*. DCSF Briefing Paper RBX-14-08.

Farmer, E, Dance, C, Beecham, J, Bonin, E and Ouwejan, D (2010) *An investigation of family finding and matching in adoption*. Department for Education Briefing Paper RBX-10-05.

Farmer, E, Sturgess, W, O'Neill, T and Wijedasa, D (2011) *Achieving successful returns from care: what makes unification work?* London: BAAF.

Featherstone, B, Broadhurst, K and Holt, K (2012) Thinking systematically, thinking politically. *British Journal of Social Work*, 42: 618–633.

FJC (Family Justice Council) (2011) *Guidelines in relation to children giving evidence in family proceedings*. London: FJC.

Fortin, J (2009) *Children's rights and the developing law*. Cambridge: Cambridge University Press.

FRG (Family Rights Group) (2011) *Family group conferences in the court arena*. London: FRG.

General Medical Council (2012) *Protecting children and young people: the responsibilities of all doctors*. Manchester: GMC.

Gilligan, P and Manby, M (2008) The Common Assessment Framework: does the reality match the rhetoric? *Child and Family Social Work*, 13: 177–187.

Gilmore, S and Herring, J (2011) 'No' is the hardest word: consent and children's autonomy. *Child and Family Law Quarterly*, 23(1): 3–25.

Hale, B, Pearl, D, Cooke, E and Monk, D (2009) *The family, law and society: cases and materials* (6th edition). Oxford: Oxford University Press.

Hanley, G and Doyle, C (2010) *Communicating with young children in legal contexts*. CAFCASS Research Conference paper. www.cafcass.gov.uk

Hannon, C, Wood, C and Bazalgette, L (2010) *In loco parentis*. London: Demos.

Harwin, J and Madge, N (2010) The concept of significant harm in law and practice. *Journal of Children's Services*, 5(2): 73–83.

Health and Care Professions Council (2012) *Standards of proficiency for social workers in England*. London: HCPC.

Henricson, C and Bainham, A (2005) *The child and family policy divide: tensions, convergence and rights*. York: Joseph Rowntree Foundation.

HM Government (2010) *The Children Act 1989 guidance and regulations Vol 2: care planning, placement and case review*. London: TSO.

HM Government (2011a) *The Children Act 1989 guidance and regulations Vol 4: fostering services.* London: TSO.

HM Government (2011b) *The Children Act 1989 guidance and regulations Vol 5: children's homes.* London: TSO.

HM Government (2012) *Draft legislation on family justice.* London: TSO.

HMIP (HM Inspector of Prisons) (2011) *The care of looked after children in custody.* London: HMIP.

Hollis, F (1981) *Casework: a psychosocial therapy* (3rd edition). New York: Random House.

Home Office (1992) *Memorandum of good practice on video recorded interviews with child witnesses for criminal proceedings.* London: HMSO.

Home Office (2003) *Hidden harm: responding to the needs of children of problem drug users.* London: TSO.

Horwath, J (2011) See the practitioner, see the child: the framework for the assessment of children in need and their families 10 years on. *British Journal of Social Work*, 41: 1070–1087.

House of Commons, Children, Schools and Families Committee (2009) *Third report of session 2008–9. Vol 1.* London: TSO.

Hunt, J (2010) *Parental perspectives on the family justice system in England and Wales: a review of research.* London: Family Justice Council.

Hunt, J and Waterhouse, S (2012) *Understanding family and friends care: the relationship between need, support and legal status – carers' experiences.* London: Family Rights Group.

Hunt, J, Waterhouse, S and Lutman, E (2008) *Keeping them in the family: outcomes for children placed in kinship care through care proceedings.* London: BAAF.

ICO (Information Commissioner's Office) (2010) *Guide to the Data Protection Act.* London: ICO.

Ince, D and Griffiths, A (2011) A chronicling system for children's social work: learning from the ICS failure. *British Journal of Social Work*, 41: 1497–1513.

Iwaniec, D, Donaldson, T and Allweis, M (2004) The plight of neglected children: social work and judicial decision making and management of neglect cases. *Child and Family Law Quarterly*, 16(4): 423–436.

James, C (2009) *Ten years of family policy.* London: Family Parenting Institute.

Keating, H (2011) *Re MA:* the significance of harm. *Child and Family Law Quarterly*, 23(1): 115–127.

Kirby, P, Lanyon, C, Cronin, K and Sinclair, R (2003) *Building a culture of participation: involving children and young people in policy, service planning, delivery and evaluation.* London: DfES Research paper.

Kirton, D, Feast, J and Goddard, J (2011) The use of discretion in a 'cinderella' service: data protection and access to child care files for post-care adults. *British Journal of Social Work*, 41: 912–930.

Laming, Lord (2003) *The Victoria Climbié inquiry: report of an inquiry by Lord Laming.* London: TSO.

Laming, Lord (2009) *The protection of children in England: a progress report.* London: TSO.

Laws, S, Wilson, R and Rabindrakumar, S (2012) *Concurrent planning study: interim report.* London: Coram.

Leeson, C (2007) My life in care: experiences of non-participation in decision-making processes. *Child and Family Social Work*, 12: 268–277.

Leeson, C (2010) *The involvement of looked after children in making decisions about their present and future care needs.* CAFCASS Research Conference paper. www.cafcass.gov.uk

Lindley, B, Richard, M and Freeman, P (2001) Advice and advocacy for parents in child protection cases: what is happening in current practice? *Child and Family Law Quarterly*, 13: 167.

Mantle, G, Moules, T and Johnson, K (2007) Whose wishes and feelings? Children's autonomy and parental influence in family court enquiries. *British Journal of Social Work*, 37: 785–805.

Masson, J (2010) A new approach to care proceedings. *Child and Family Social Work*, 15: 369–379.

Masson, J, Pearce, J and Bader, K (2008) *Care profiling study.* London: Ministry of Justice research series 4/08.

Matthews, A (2012) *Landing in Dover: the immigration process undergone by unaccompanied children arriving in Kent.* London: Office of the Children's Commissioner.

MoJ (Ministry of Justice) (2010) *Public law proceedings guide to case management.* London: TSO.

MoJ (2011a) *Achieving best evidence in criminal proceedings: guidance on interviewing victims and witnesses, and guidance on special measures* (3rd edition). London: TSO.

MoJ (2011b) *Family Justice Review: final report.* London: TSO.

Munro, E (2010) *Review of child protection, interim report.* London: DfE.

Munro, E (2011) *Review of child protection, final report.* London: DfE.

Munro, E and Lushey, C (2012) *The impact of more flexible assessment practices in response to the Munro Review of Child Protection: emerging findings from the trials.* London: Childhood Wellbeing Research Centre.

Munro, E and Ward, H (2008) Balancing parents' and very young children's rights in care proceedings: decision-making in the context of the Human Rights Act 1998. *Child and Family Social Work*, 13: 227–234.

NAGALRO (2012) *Consultation response to House of Lords select committee on adoption legislation.* www.nagalro.com

NCAS (National Care Advisory Service) (2009a) *Evaluation of virtual school head pilots.* www.leavingcare. org.uk

NCAS (2009b) *Journeys to home: care leavers' successful transition to independent accommodation.* London: NCAS.

NCAS (2010) *What could make the difference? Care leavers and the welfare benefits system.* London: NCAS.

NCAS (2012a) *Access all areas.* London: NCAS.

NCAS (2012b) *Funding leaving care: making the cut one year on.* London: NCAS.

NOMS (National Offender Management Service) (2010) *Physical control in care training manual.* London: TSO.

National Children's Bureau (2008) *Delivering Every Child Matters in secure settings: a practical toolkit for improving the health and well-being of young people.* London: NCB.

Neil, E, Cossar, J, Logelly, P and Young, J (2010) *Helping birth families: a study of service provision, costs and outcomes.* Norwich: University of East Anglia Centre for Research on the Child and Family.

Neil, E, Beek, M, Thoburn, J, Schofield, G and Ward, E (2012) *Contact arrangements for adopted children: what can be learned from research?* Norwich: University of East Anglia Centre for Research on the Child and Family.

Newbury, A (2011) Very young offenders and the criminal justice system: are we asking the right questions? *Child and Family Law Quarterly,* 23(1): 94–114.

NSPCC (2012) *Returning home from care: what's best for children.* London: NSPCC.

OFSTED (2008) *Looked after children – good practice in schools.* London: TSO.

OFSTED (2009) *Supporting young carers.* London: TSO.

OFSTED (2010a) *Learning lessons from serious case reviews.* London: TSO.

OFSTED (2010b) *Children on family justice: a report of children's views for the Family Justice Review by the Children's Rights Director for England.* London: TSO.

OFSTED (2011a) *100 days of care: diary entries of children and young people in care, in residential education or receiving social care.* London: TSO.

OFSTED (2011b) *Children's care monitor 2011: children on the state of social care in England.* London. TSO.

OFSTED (2011c) *Edging away from care: how services successfully prevent young people entering care.* OFSTED report 110082.

OFSTED (2012a) *After care – young people's views on leaving care: report by the Children's Rights Director for England.* Manchester: OFSTED.

OFSTED (2012b) *Right on time: exploring delays in adoption.* Manchester: OFSTED.

OFSTED (2012c) *Protecting disabled children: thematic inspection.* Manchester: OFSTED.

OFSTED (2012d) *The impact of virtual schools on the educational progress of looked after children.* Manchester: OFSTED.

OFSTED (2012e) *High expectations, high support, high challenge.* Manchester: OFSTED.

Oliver, C and Dalrymple, J (eds) (2008) *Developing advocacy for children and young people: current issues in research, policy and practice.* London: Jessica Kingsley Publishers.

Parr, S (2009) Family intervention projects: a site of social work practice. *British Journal of Social Work,* 39: 1256–1273.

Partington, M (2010) *Introduction to the English legal system* (5th edition). Oxford: Oxford University Press.

Pennington, E (2012) *It takes a village to raise a child: survey on adoption support.* www.adoptionuk.org.uk

Pinney, A (2011) *Reaching families in need.* Ilford: Barnardo's.

Pona, I and Hounsell, D (2012) *The value of independent advocacy for looked after children and young people.* London: The Children's Society.

Preston-Shoot, M (2000) Making connections in the curriculum: law and professional practice, in Pierce, R and Weinstein, J (eds) *Innovative education and training for care professionals: a providers' guide*. London: Jessica Kingsley Publishers.

Radford, L, Corral, S, Bradley, C, Fisher, H, Bassett, C, Howat, N and Collishaw, S (2011) *Child abuse and neglect in the UK today*. London: NSPCC.

RCPCH (Royal College of Paediatrics and Child Health) (2012) *Looked after children: knowledge, skills and competence of health care staff*. London: RCPCH.

Read, J, Clements, L and Ruebain, D (2006) *Disabled children and the law: research and good practice* (2nd edition). London: Jessica Kingsley Publishers.

Roth, D, Aziz, R and Lindley, B (2012) *Understanding family and friends care: local authority policies – the good, the bad and the non-existent*. London: Family Rights Group.

Rowlands, J and Statham, J (2009) Numbers of children looked after in England: a historical analysis. *British Journal of Social Work*, 14: 79–89.

Ryder, Mr Justice (2012) *Judicial proposals for the modernisation of family justice*. London: Judiciary for England and Wales. www.judiciary.gov.uk

SCIE (Social Care Institute for Excellence) (2005) *Teaching, learning and assessment of law in social work education*. Bristol: Policy Press.

Selwyn, J, Frazer, L and Quinton, D (2006) Paved with good intentions: the pathway to adoption and the costs of delay. *British Journal of Social Work*, 36: 561–576.

Seymour, C and Seymour, R (2011) *Courtroom and report writing skills for social workers* (2nd edition). Exeter: Learning Matters.

Shaw, C, Brodie, I, Ellis, A, Graham, B, Mainey, A, de Sousa, S and Willmott, N (2010) *Research into private fostering*. London: DCSF Research Report 229.

Shaw, I, Bell, M, Sinclair, I, Sloper, P, Mitchell, W, Dyson, P, Clayden, J and Rafferty, J (2009) An exemplary scheme? An evaluation of the integrated children's system. *British Journal of Social Work*, 39(4): 613–626.

Smallridge, P and Williamson, A (2008) *Review of the use of restraint in juvenile secure settings*. London: Ministry of Justice.

Smeeton, J and Boxall, K (2010) *Birth parents' perception of professional practice in childcare and adoption proceedings*. CAFCASS Research Conference paper. www.cafcass.gov.uk

Social Exclusion Unit (2003) *A better education for children in care*. London: TSO.

Social Work Reform Board (2012) *Professional capabilities framework*. www.collegeofsocialwork.org.uk

SRA (Solicitors' Regulation Authority) (2011) *Solicitors' code of conduct*. London: SRA.

Stanley, L (2004) Children's guardians and the local authority: managing disagreement. *Family Court Journal*, 2(2).

Stanley, N, Miller, P, Richardson-Foster, H and Thomson, G (2010) *Children and families experiencing domestic violence: police and children's services responses*. London: NSPCC.

Stewart, J, Broadhurst, K and Grover, C (2004) Transitions to adulthood: some critical observations of the Children (Leaving Care) Act 2000. *Social Work and Social Sciences Review*, 11(1): 5–18.

SWTF (Social Work Task Force) (2010) *Building a safe, confident future – the final report of the Social Work Task Force*. London: DfE.

Tarleton, B, Ward, L and Howard, J (2006) *Finding the right support: a review of issues and positive practice in supporting parents with learning difficulties and their children*. Bristol: University of Bristol. www.baring foundation.org.uk

UK Missing Persons' Bureau (2012) *Children missing from care*. London: UKMPB.

Wade, J, Biehal, N, Farrelly, N and Sinclair, I (2011) *Caring for abused and neglected children: making the right decisions for reunification and long-term care*. London: Jessica Kingsley Publishers.

Who Cares? Trust (2012) *Open doors, open minds: is the care system helping looked-after children progress into further and higher education?* London: Who Cares? Trust.

Williams, J (2008) *Child law for social work*. London: Sage Publications Ltd.

Wilson, K, Ruch, G, Lymbery, M and Cooper, A (2008) *Social work: an introduction to contemporary practice*. Harlow: Pearson Education Limited.

Winter, K (2009) Relationships matter: the problems and prospects for social workers' relationships with young children in care. *Child and Family Social Work*, 14: 450–460.

YJB (Youth Justice Board) (2011) *Annual Report and Accounts*. London: Ministry of Justice.

YJB (2012) *Managing the behaviour of children in the secure estate*. London: YJB.

Index

Disabled children

RESEARCH SUMMARY 4.3

A review by OFSTED (2012c) of local authority services to disabled children found that the extent to which their views, wishes and feelings were obtained and recorded varied. In many cases professionals knew children well, and were skilled in communicating with them and in using observation to assess how they were feeling. However, children were not always spoken to directly about concerns for their welfare, even when they could communicate well. Advocacy was usually not considered and was rarely used.

There is evidence that participation is still only experienced by small numbers of disabled children, usually those who are most confident and able to communicate. Examples of poor practice include disabled children not being involved in life story work and of assessment forms being completed with 'not applicable' written in the section for 'child's view' (Baker, 2011). Children with disabilities or communication impairments are particularly likely to be excluded from child protection and legal processes: 'We were told about a court report by a children's guardian that diligently detailed how a disabled non-verbal child could communicate using an electronic communication board, but then stated that the child's view was not available' (Kirby *et al.*, 2003, p110).

LEGAL CASE STUDY 4.3

B (A Local Authority) v AM *[2010] EWHC 3802 (Fam)*

This case raised the question of whether and, if so, on what basis, a court considering an application for a care order in respect of a young person aged over 16 with lifelong disabilities should transfer the case to the Court of Protection to be dealt with under the MCA 2005 rather than the CA 1989. The court stated that it was not possible to ascertain the wishes and feelings of AM because 'it is not possible for her to understand the implications of the position in which she finds herself' (para. 11).

AM was 17 and had multiple disabilities. She was not expected to be able to live independently and required a high level of support to ensure that her needs were met. Threshold in the care proceedings had been conceded and AM was living in temporary care, although a move would be necessary in the near future. AM's mother wished the local authority to accommodate her under the CA 1989 s20 but the local authority and children's guardian wanted a care order on the basis that the mother had never accepted the difficulties caused by AM's profound disabilities and, despite all the evidence, continued to believe that she could care for her at home which she saw as her family duty. The judge acknowledged the family's commitment to AM: 'I would have no difficulty in understanding a sense of rebuff and feelings of marginalisation were a care order to be made' (para. 23), and posed a number of questions.

LEGAL CASE STUDY 4.3 (CONT.)

- *Is the child over 16?*

- *Does the child manifestly lack capacity in respect of the principal decisions which are to be made under the CA?*

- *Are the disabilities giving rise to the lack of capacity lifelong or long-term?*

- *Can the decisions which arise in respect of the child's welfare all be taken and all issues resolved during the child's minority?*

- *Are the Court of Protection's powers or procedures more appropriate to resolve the outstanding issues?*

- *Can the child's welfare needs be fully met by those powers?*

It was decided that the Court of Protection would better serve AM's long-term welfare: 'This is a case in which AM's interests are not served by conflict. The local authority must proceed with reasonable expedition and the family with patience' (para. 34).

Child protection

All these people were looking at you and I'm like oh my God and it was hard because my mum was there . . . and it was like I was holding stuff back because I knew that once I go back to her who knows what I will be facing.

Having social services involved and sticking their beaks in puts mother in a mood, which is going to make her more likely to do something stupid like what happened in April.
(Young people subject to safeguarding procedures, quoted by Cossar and Dunne, 2010)

Child protection is an area in which children are not always offered the opportunity to participate, despite the strong legal framework supporting the relevance of their contributions. It is not uncommon for social workers to focus on engaging parents and carers in situations of potential conflict, and for steps to be taken to minimise children's exposure to disagreement and confrontation. As the following research shows, children's involvement needs to be planned and executed with great care, particularly in relation to how children are prepared and the support available to them afterwards.

RESEARCH SUMMARY 4.4

Cossar and Dunne (2010) asked young people what they thought about their participation in child protection conferences:

- *most had positive views of the people who chaired the conference and felt they were independent;*